# Management Control in Nonprofit Organizations

**The Robert N. Anthony/Willard J. Graham Series in Accounting**

THIRD EDITION

# Management Control in Nonprofit Organizations

ROBERT N. ANTHONY, D.B.A.
Professor Emeritus
Graduate School of Business Administration
Harvard University

DAVID W. YOUNG, D.B.A.
Associate Professor of Management
School of Public Health
Harvard University

1984
RICHARD D. IRWIN, INC.
Homewood, Illinois 60430

Case material of the Harvard Graduate School of Business Administration and the Harvard School of Public Health is made possible by the cooperation of business firms and other organizations who may wish to remain anonymous by having names, quantities, and other identifying details disguised while basic relationships are maintained. Cases are prepared as the basis for class discussion rather than to illustrate either effective or ineffective handling of administrative situations.

ISBN 0-256-02960-1

Library of Congress Catalog Card No. 83–82135

*Printed in the United States of America*

3 4 5 6 7 8 9 0 MP 1 0 9 8 7 6 5

# Preface

Courses for which this text has been designed have existed for about 10 years in many universities. As the field of management control in nonprofit organizations has developed, so have our own ideas about the material in this book. In addition, in the four years that have passed since the Revised Edition, a great deal of literature has been published relating to both the management of nonprofit organizations, in general, and *management control* in those organizations, in particular. Finally, Regina Herzlinger, the second author for the first two editions, has become involved in a variety of new professional activities, many of which are in the nonprofit field, and has decided not to continue as an author; hence a new author's perspective has been introduced to this edition.

As a result of the above developments, several substantive changes have been made in both the organization and content of the book. Organizationally, the book has been structured into four parts: introduction, management control principles, management control systems, and implementation of management control systems. Part II has two new chapters: general purpose financial statements and cost accounting, which we hope will provide readers with some of the basic knowledge necessary for their subsequent analyses of management control systems. While some material from previous editions has been incorporated into these two chapters, by and large they contain completely new material.

Part III makes a clear distinction between the *structure* of a management control system (Chapter 6) and the *process* of management control (Chapters 7–13). In discussing the management control process, we now move systematically through the various stages of the control cycle described in Chapter 1. In making this distinction, we have both reorganized much of the material from the Revised Edition and prepared some new material.

Finally, we have introduced many new cases into this edition. Whereas the Revised Edition had 37 cases, this edition has 48. Thirty-six of them are new to the Third Edition. One advantage of this greater number of cases is the increased choice available to instructors, allowing them to use the book in courses for either beginning or advanced students, or to explore a particular subject in some depth, beginning on a relatively elementary level and moving to a more advanced one. Moreover, the larger number of cases also permits instructors to focus more attention on certain types of nonprofit organizations (e.g., health or education) than previously was the case.

## Use of the Book

This book is primarily intended for a course on management control problems in nonprofit organizations in general. It is not primarily a book on accounting. Such a course is often offered by an accounting department, but the book has also been used in courses offered by economics and finance departments and by management departments in schools of education, medicine, public health, theology, and public administration.

Although written to apply to all types of nonprofit organizations, including governmental entities, the book can easily be adapted for a course that focuses on a single type, such as government or health care, by selection of cases appropriate to that type. The book may also be used in short programs designed for managers of nonprofit organizations. The selection of chapters for such programs depends on the nature of the short program. In one type of program the principal topics of the whole book may be discussed; in another type, the focus might be on a specific area of management control, such as programming, budgeting, or the evaluation of performance. Finally, the book also may be used by individual managers as background reading. The first edition was selected by the American College of Hospital Administrators as the outstanding book for this purpose.

## Case Reproduction

The 48 cases included in this book are listed in the index in alphabetical order. The first page of each case indicates its authors' names and, for non-Harvard cases, the copyright holder. For cases prepared at the Harvard Business School and the Harvard School of Public Health, the copyright holder is Harvard University. No case herein may be reproduced in any form or by any means without the permission of the copyright holder.

Permission to reproduce Harvard School of Public Health cases should be sought from the Pew Curriculum Center for Health Policy and Management, Department of Health Policy and Management, Harvard School of Public Health, 677 Huntington Avenue, Boston, MA 02115. Permission to reproduce Harvard Business School cases should be sought from HBS Case Services, Harvard Business School, Boston, MA 02163. Permission to reproduce Osceola Institute cases should be sought from Professor Young at the Harvard School of Public Health.

Comments on the text or cases, or new ideas for teaching the cases, are welcomed, and should be sent to Professor Young at the Harvard School of Public Health.

## Acknowledgments

We are grateful to many individuals for assistance in the preparation of the text as well as the cases which we authored. These include Roy E. Baxter, Professor of Social Work, Our Lady of the Lake University, San Antonio, Texas; John Byrne, Executive Director, Visiting Nurse Association of Greater St. Louis; Dr. Eleanor Chelimsky, U.S., General Accounting Office; Ronald Contino, Deputy Commissioner, Department of Sanitation, City of New York; William E. Cotter, President, Colby College; Martin Ives, First Deputy Comptroller, City of New York; Bernadina Knipp, Assistant Executive Director, Visiting Nurse Association, Home Health Service of Greater Kansas City; Thomas W. Morris, General Manager, Boston Symphony Orchestra; Stanley A. Nicholson, Administrative Vice President, Colby College; John M. Richardson, National Research Council; Russy D. Sumariwalla, United Way of America; Susumu Uyeda, Executive Director, Joint Financial Management Improvement Programs.

We are also appreciative of the financial support which was received from Harvard University and from the following sources for the preparation of certain cases:

The Edwin Gould Foundation for Children (Bureau of Child Welfare);

The Ford Foundation (Morazan and Izaltenango);

Line Publications (River Area Home Health Services, Pleasantville Home Health Agency, Centerville Home Health Agency);

The Pew Memorial Trust (Aftrain, Cameroon, Arnica Mission, Competitive Barriers Commission, Mountainview PSRO, and Yoland Research Institute);

The U.S. Department of Health and Human Services, Public Health Service (Rural Health Associates);

Both Professor Donald R. Simons of Boston University and Professor Stanley Blostein of The Ohio State University provided us with reviews of the Revised Edition which were extremely useful in the preparation of this edition. We are most thankful for their ideas, many of which were incorporated into the text. Finally, we greatly appreciate the editorial and secretarial assistance provided by Audrey Barrett, Jane Barrett, Emily C. Hood, Deborah Katz, Susan Keane, and Pat Lougee.

We, of course, accept full responsibility for the final product.

*Robert N. Anthony*
*David W. Young*

# Contents

# part I

# Introduction

Management control in nonprofit organizations—as an academic subject—is relatively new. Until recently, many nonprofit organizations survived on the strength of their mission and their ability to attract increasing amounts of public and private support for their activities. Although there have been gradual changes in the prevailing attitude toward nonprofit management on the part of both professionals (physicians, educators, artists, etc.) and managers (who generally were "former" professionals themselves), it was not until recently that the need was recognized for strong management skills in these organizations.

In this introductory section we discuss both the scope of the material covered and the nature of the organizations to which we intend to apply it. Specifically, Chapter 1 outlines the territory of the field of management control, indicating both what it includes and, equally important, what it does not include. Chapter 2 discusses the nature, size, and service extent of nonprofit organizations.

# chapter 1

# Management Control in General

In all organizations, even the tiniest, there is an activity called management control. In relatively large organizations it generally is rather formal and routinized; in smaller ones it may be quite informal and sporadic. The activity has existed as long as organizations have been in existence, but it has not been the subject of much systematic study and analysis until fairly recently. A landmark book, Chester Barnard's *Functions of the Executive,* which dealt with this as well as other management activities, was originally published in 1938.[1] Not until recent years, however, have principles evolved that are helpful in designing management control systems and in carrying on management control activities.

As is the case with all principles of management, management control principles are tentative, incomplete, inconclusive, vague, sometimes contradictory, and inadequately supported by experimental or other evidence. Some of them will probably turn out to be wrong. Nevertheless, they seem to have sufficient validity so that it is better for managers to take them into account than to ignore them. Most importantly, they seem to work in a considerable number of actual organizations.

Most studies of the management control process have been done in profit-oriented organizations, and most control techniques were developed in these

[1] Chester I. Barnard, *Functions of the Executive,* 30th anniv. ed. (Cambridge, Mass.: Harvard University Press, 1968).

organizations. Consequently, most descriptions of the management control process tend to assume, usually implicitly but sometimes explicitly, that the process being described is taking place in a business enterprise in which the primary objective is earning profits. This book, by contrast, is a study of management control in nonprofit organizations. Its thesis is that the basic control concepts are the same in both profit-oriented and nonprofit organizations, but that because of the special characteristics of nonprofit organizations, the application of these concepts differs in some important respects.

## THE MANAGEMENT CONTROL FRAMEWORK

Before comparing the similarities and differences of management control techniques in nonprofit organizations with those in profit-oriented ones, we shall provide an overview of the general characteristics of management control activities. The purpose of this overview is to place management control in its broader organizational context.

### Planning and Control

Two of the important activities in which all managers engage are planning and control. *Planning* is deciding what should be done and how it should be done; *control* is assuring that the desired results are obtained. In most organizations, three different types of planning and control activities can be identified: (1) strategic planning, (2) task control, and (3) management control. Since our focus is on management control, we shall describe the other two types of activities only briefly.

***Strategic Planning.*** Any organization has one or more goals. Generally, senior management decides, or participates in deciding, the general nature of the activities that the organization should undertake in order to achieve these goals. *Strategic planning* is the process of deciding on the goals of the organization and on the broad strategies that are to be used in attaining them. These decisions are made only occasionally and at the highest levels in the organization.

***Task Control.*** At the other extreme are processes that are used in carrying out the day-to-day activities of the organization. These consist of rules, procedures, forms, and other devices that govern the performance of specific tasks. *Task control* is the process of assuring that these specific tasks are carried out effectively and efficiently.

***Management Control.*** Between these two types of planning and control activities is an activity called management control. In this activity the strategies arrived at in the strategic planning process are accepted as given; management control has to do with the *implementation* of these strategies. Management control does *not* involve the detailed operating decisions and activities that are the focus of task control; rather, it is the means by which management assures that the organization carries out its strategies effectively and efficiently.

### Source Disciplines

In part, the management control activity helps management decide on the optimum allocation of resources, and to this extent it is governed by the principles of *economics.* In part also, management control influences the behavior of people, and to this extent it is governed by the principles of *social psychology.* Both disciplines must be considered jointly in the management control effort.

### Management Control Systems

Part of the management control activity is carried out by means of a management control *system.* As is the case with any system, a management control system can be described in terms of both its structure and its process; that is, what it is and what it does. In studying the human body, for example, one needs to understand both anatomy and physiology; in studying management control one needs to consider these two aspects also. The description in this book is therefore organized according to these two main categories.

## THE MANAGEMENT CONTROL STRUCTURE

Any organization except the smallest is divided into units called *responsibility centers.* A responsibility center is a group of people working toward some organizational objective and headed by a manager who is responsible for its actions. In large organizations there is a complicated hierarchy of responsibility centers: units, sections, departments, branches, and divisions. Except for those at the bottom of the organization, each responsibility center consists of aggregations of smaller responsibility centers, and the entire organization is itself a responsibility center. One function of top management is to plan, coordinate, and control the work of all these responsibility centers.

> ***Example:*** A university consists of a number of responsibility centers, called schools and colleges, such as the Schools of Law and Medicine and the College of Arts and Sciences. Each of these schools and colleges is in turn composed of separate responsibility centers, such as the language department and the physics department. These departments may in turn be divided into separate responsibility centers; for example, the language department may be composed of sections for each language. The management control function is to plan, coordinate, and control the work of all these responsibility centers.

Exhibit 1–1 shows the essence of what any responsibility center does, using a steam-generating plant as an analogy. The plant exists for a purpose,

**Exhibit 1–1**
Nature of a Responsibility Center

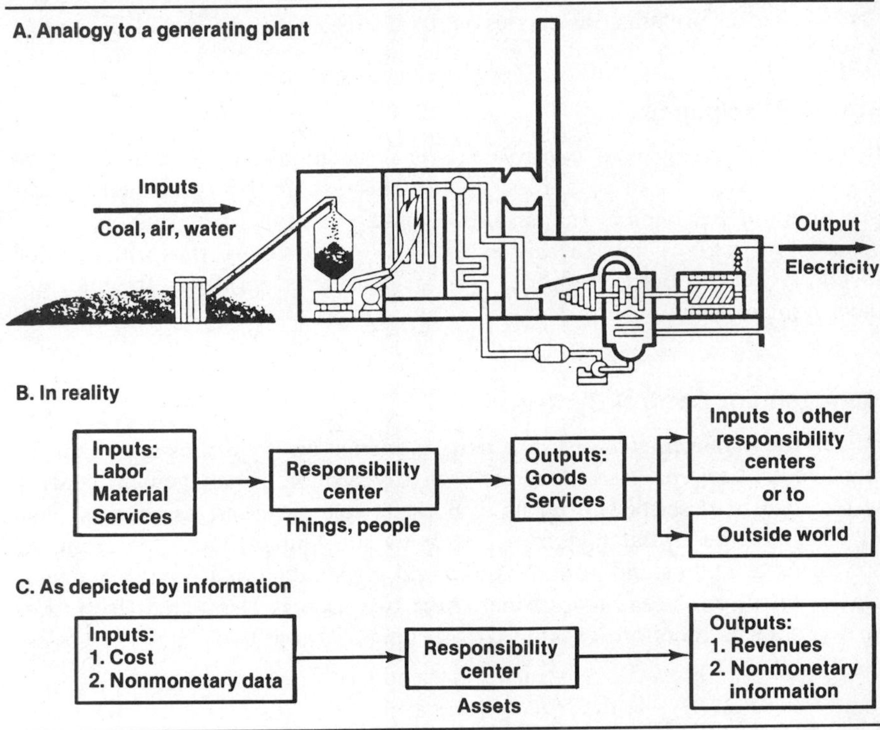


namely, to generate electrical energy. In order to accomplish this purpose, it has furnaces, turbines, smokestacks, and other physical resources. In operating, the generating plant uses fuel; this is its input. The energy that it produces is its output.

Any responsibility center exists to accomplish one or more purposes; these purposes are its *objectives.* Presumably, the objectives of an individual responsibility center are intended to help achieve the overall goals of the whole organization, which were decided in the strategic planning process.

A responsibility center has inputs of labor, material, and services. In the case of the language department in the above example, there are inputs of faculty, staff, educational materials, and maintenance services. The department uses these inputs to produce outputs of goods or services. If the responsibility center has been well designed its outputs will be closely related to its objectives. One output of the language department is the knowledge and skill in language acquired by the students; another might be instructional recordings for use outside the university. These outputs are related to the language department's objectives and presumably help satisfy one or more of the university's goals.

### Types of Responsibility Centers

There are four principal types of responsibility centers: (1) revenue centers, (2) expense centers, (3) profit centers, and (4) investment centers. The principal factor determining the selection of one type over another is that of *controllability*. The manager of a responsibility center should be held accountable for those inputs and outputs over which he or she can exercise a reasonable amount of control (not necessarily *total* control, however).

***Revenue Centers.*** If a responsibility center is charged only with attaining some predetermined monetary level of output, i.e., revenue, it is classified as a *revenue* center. Many marketing departments in profit-oriented organizations are revenue centers. The development office in a university might also be considered a revenue center.

***Expense Centers.*** If the management control system measures the expenses incurred by a responsibility center but does not measure the monetary value of the unit's output, the unit is an expense center. Although every responsibility center *has* outputs (i.e., it does something), in many cases it is neither feasible nor necessary to measure these outputs in monetary terms. It would be extremely difficult to measure the monetary value that the accounting department contributes to the whole organization, for example. Although it would be relatively easy to measure the monetary value of the outputs of an individual production department, there may be no good reason for doing so if the responsibility of the factory supervisor is simply to produce a stated *quantity* of output at the lowest feasible cost.

In a business enterprise most individual production departments and most staff units are expense centers. In many nonprofit organizations, *all* the responsibility centers are expense centers. For these, the accounting system records expenses incurred, but not revenue earned.

***Profit Centers.*** Revenue is a monetary measure of output, and expense is a monetary measure of input, or resources consumed.[2] Profit is the difference between revenue and expense. Thus, in a profit-oriented business, if performance in a responsibility center is measured in terms of both the revenue it earns and the expense it incurs, the unit is called a *profit center*. Many nonprofit organizations have responsibility centers which charge fees for their services and incur expenses in delivering those services. This is the case with many departments of a hospital; with the housing, food service, and other auxiliary services of a university; and with utilities, refuse collection, and

---

[2] The term "expense" is not synonymous with "cost." Cost is a measure of resources consumed for any specified purpose, whereas expense always refers to resources that are consumed in operations of a *specified time period*. Outlays to manufacture a product are costs in the period in which the product is manufactured, but they become expenses only in the period in which the product is sold and the related revenue is earned.

similar enterprises of a municipality. In these instances, the responsibility center can be thought of as a profit center, even though use of the term "profit center" in a nonprofit organization may seem to be a contradiction of terms.

***Investment Centers.*** In an investment center, the management control system measures not only profit but also the capital employed in generating that profit. Thus, an investment center adds more aspects to the manager's job than is the case with the profit center, just as the profit center involves more aspects than does the expense center. Although the investment center concept is rarely used in nonprofit organizations, it would seem quite appropriate for those situations in which a manager is responsible for a clearly identified set of assets.

### Mission Centers and Service Centers

Responsibility centers also can be classified as either mission centers or service centers. The output of a mission center contributes directly to the objectives of the organization. The output of a service center contributes to the work of other responsibility centers, which may be either mission centers or other service centers; its output is thus one of the inputs of these responsibility centers.

Normally, a service center is either an expense center or a profit center. If the latter, it "sells" its services to other units, and its output is measured by the revenue generated by such sales. Its objective usually is not to make a profit—that is, an excess of revenue over expenses—but rather to break even. The extension of the profit center idea to service centers is relatively new, especially in nonprofit organizations. When properly set up, however, it can provide a powerful instrument for management control.

### Responsibility Centers and Programs

Many organizations distinguish between responsibility centers and programs. These organizations have program structures in addition to responsibility center structures in their management control systems. The responsibility center structure contains information that is classified by responsibility centers, and that is used for (1) planning the activities of responsibility centers, (2) coordinating the work of the several responsibility centers in an organization, and (3) controlling the responsibility center managers. Information about the programs that the organization undertakes or plans to undertake is contained in the program structure. The program structure is designed for three principal purposes:

1. To make decisions about the programs that are to be undertaken and the amount and kind of resources that should be devoted to each program.

2. To permit comparisons to be made among programs carried on by several organizations. For example, hospitals typically have a food service program; thus, food service costs in one hospital can be compared with those in another hospital.
3. To provide a basis for setting fees charged to clients or for reimbursement of costs incurred.

When there is both a responsibility center structure and a program structure, the management control system must identify their interactions. In some instances, a responsibility center may work solely on one program, and it may be the only responsibility center working on that program. If so, the program structure corresponds to the responsibility center structure. This is the case, for example, in municipal governments when one organization unit is responsible for providing police protection, another for education, another for solid waste disposal, and so on. In some instances this one-to-one correspondence between programs and responsibility centers does not exist, however. For example, a regional office of the Department of Health and Human Services, which is a responsibility center, works on several DHHS programs. Exhibit 1–2 depicts the relationship among mission and service centers, responsibility centers, and programs, using the example of a hospital.

**Exhibit 1–2**
Relation between Responsibility Centers and Programs

| | *Programs* | | | |
|---|---|---|---|---|
| *Responsibility Centers* | *Sports Medicine* | *Alcohol Detoxification* | *Drug Rehabilitation* | *Open-Heart Surgery* |
| *Mission centers:* | | | | |
| Routine care | 3,800 days | 1,200 days | 300 days | 8,000 days |
| Surgery | 1,000 operations | — | — | 500 operations |
| Laboratory | 2,000 tests | 500 tests | 300 tests | 2,000 tests |
| Radiology | 8,000 procedures | — | — | 1,500 procedures |
| Outpatient care | 12,500 visits | 10,000 visits | 8,500 visits | — |
| *Service centers:* | | | | |
| Housekeeping<br>Dietary<br>Laundry<br>Administration<br>Social service | | Cost allocated to mission centers for purposes of determining full cost of mission centers and program-related costs | | |

## THE MANAGEMENT CONTROL PROCESS

The management control process takes place in the context of an organization that has goals and that has decided on broad strategies for achieving these goals. As noted above, decisions on these goals and strategies are made in the *strategic planning process,* which is largely unsystematic and informal. The management control system collects information that is useful in strategic planning, but since strategic decisions are made only occasionally, and since each strategic issue requires information that is tailor-made to the requirements of that issue, this information cannot ordinarily be collected in any routine, recurring fashion. Rather, it must be put together when the need arises and in the form required for the specific issue.

Much of the management control process is informal. It occurs by means of memoranda, meetings, conversations, and even by such signals as facial expressions, control devices which are not amenable to a systematic description. Many organizations also have a formal system, in which the information consists of planned (or estimated) and actual data on both outputs and inputs. Prior to actual operations, decisions and estimates are made as to what outputs and inputs are to be; during operations, records are maintained as to what outputs and inputs actually are; and subsequent to operations, reports are prepared that compare actual outputs and inputs to planned outputs and inputs. When necessary, corrective action is taken on the basis of these reports. There are thus four principal steps in a formal management control process:

1. Programming.
2. Budget formulation.

**Exhibit 1–3**
Phases of Management Control

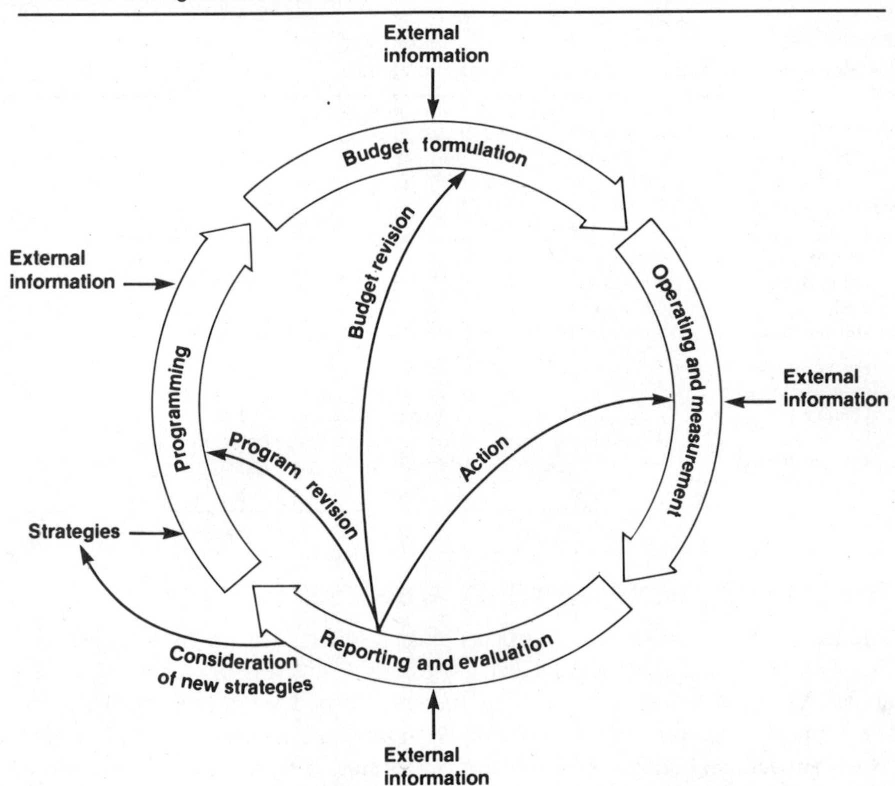

3. Operating (and measurement).
4. Reporting and evaluation.

The steps recur in a regular cycle, and together they constitute a "closed loop," as indicated in Exhibit 1–3.

## Programming

In the programming phase, decisions are made with respect to the major programs the organization plans to undertake during the coming period. These decisions either are made within the context of the strategies that have previously been decided upon, or they represent changes in strategy. If the latter, they are part of the strategic planning process, rather than the management control process; the two processes merge into one another in the programming phase.

Some organizations state their programs in the form of a "long-range plan" which shows planned outputs and inputs for a number of years ahead—usually 5 years, but possibly as few as 3 or (in the case of public utilities) as many as 20. Many organizations do not have such a formal mechanism for displaying their overall future programs; they rely instead on reports or understandings as to specific, important facets of the program, particularly the amounts to be invested in capital assets and the means of financing these assets.

In an industrial company the "programs" are usually products or product lines, plus activities (such as research) that are not relatable to specific products. The plans state the amount and character of resources (i.e., inputs) that are to be devoted to each program and the ways in which these resources are to be used.

To the extent feasible, program decisions are based on an economic analysis. In such an analysis, the revenues or other benefits estimated from the proposed program are compared with the estimated costs. For many programs in profit-oriented companies, and for most programs in nonprofit organizations, however, reliable estimates of benefits cannot be made. For these programs, decisions are based on judgment and are influenced by the persuasive abilities of program advocates and by political and other considerations.

## Budget Formulation

A budget is a plan expressed in quantitative, usually monetary, terms covering a specified period of time. The time period is usually one year, but in a few organizations it may be six months or three months. In the budget formulation process the program is translated into terms that correspond to the sphere of responsibility of those who are charged with executing it. Thus, although plans are originally made in program terms, in the budget formulation process they are converted into responsibility terms. The process of arriving at the budget is essentially one of negotiation between the managers of responsibility centers and their superiors. The end product of these negotiations is a statement of the outputs that are expected during the budget year and the resources that are to be used in achieving these outputs.

The agreed-upon budget is a *bilateral commitment.* Responsibility center managers commit themselves to produce the planned output with the agreed amount of resources, and their superiors commit themselves to agreeing that such performance is satisfactory. Both commitments are subject to the qualification "unless circumstances change significantly."

### Operating and Measurement

During the period of actual operations, records are kept of resources actually consumed and outputs actually achieved. The records of resources consumed (i.e., costs) are structured so that costs are collected both by programs and by responsibility centers. Costs in the former classification are used as a basis for future programming, and those in the latter are used to measure the performance of the heads of responsibility centers.

### Reporting and Evaluation

Accounting information, along with a variety of other information, is summarized, analyzed, and reported to those who are responsible for knowing what is happening in the organization and who are charged with attaining the agreed-upon level of performance. As indicated above, these reports essentially compare planned outputs and inputs with actual outputs and inputs. The information in these reports is used for three purposes.

First, the reports are a basis for coordinating and controlling the current activities of the organization. Using this information, together with information that is obtained from conversations or other informal sources, managers identify situations that may be "out of control," they investigate these situations, and they initiate corrective action if investigation shows such action to be necessary and feasible.

Second, the reports are used as a basis for evaluating operating performance. Such an evaluation leads to actions with respect to managers: praise for a job well done; constructive criticism if this seems to be warranted; and to promotion, reassignment, or, in extreme cases, termination of the managers of the responsibility centers. It may also lead to improved methods of operating.

Third, the reports are used as a basis for program evaluation. For any of a number of reasons, the plan under which the organization is working may turn out not to be optimum. If so, the budget or the program may need to be revised. This is why the management control system is a closed loop. Evaluation of actual performance can lead back to the first step, a revision of the program, or to the second step, a revision of the budget, or to the third step, a modification in operations. It can also lead to a reconsideration of the organization's strategies for achieving its goals.

## GENERAL SYSTEM CHARACTERISTICS

### A Total System

Ordinarily, a formal management control system is a *total* system in the sense that it embraces all aspects of the organization's operation. It needs to be a total system because an important management function is to assure that all parts of the operation are in balance with one another; and in order to examine balance, management needs information about each of the parts. By contrast, the information used in the strategic planning process is usually collected specifically for the plans under consideration, and these rarely embrace the whole organization. Also, information used in task control (e.g., production control, inventory control) is usually tailor-made for the requirements of each such activity.

### Goal Congruence

It is reasonable to expect that persons will act according to what they perceive to be their own best interests. A management control system should be designed so that the actions it leads managers to take in accordance with their perceived self-interest are also actions that are in the best interest of the organization. In the language of social psychology, the system should encourage *goal congruence:* it should be structured so that the goals of individual managers are, so far as feasible, consistent with the goals of the organization as a whole. Perfect congruence between individual goals and organizational goals does not exist, but as a minimum the system should not encourage the individual to act *against* the best interests of the organization. For example, a lack of goal congruence exists if the management control system signals that the emphasis should be on reducing costs but at the same time encourages managers to sacrifice quality, provide inadequate service, or engage in activities which reduce costs in one department but cause a more than offsetting increase in some other department.

### Financial Framework

With rare exceptions a management control system is *built around a financial structure;* that is, amounts are stated in monetary units. This does not mean that accounting information is the sole, or even the most important, part of the system; it means only that the accounting system provides a unifying core to which other types of information can be related. Although the financial structure is usually the central focus, nonmonetary measures such as minutes per operation, number of persons served, percent of applicants admitted, and reject and spoilage rates are also important parts of the system.

### Rhythm

The management control process tends to be rhythmic; it follows a definite pattern and timetable, month after month, and year and year. In budget formulation, certain steps are taken in a prescribed sequence and at certain dates each year: dissemination of guidelines, preparation of original estimates, transmission of these estimates up through the several echelons in the organization, review of these estimates, final approval by top management, and dissemination back through the organization. The procedure to be followed at each step in this process, the dates when the steps are to be completed, and the forms to be used can be, and often are, set forth in a manual.

### Integration

A management control system is, or should be, a *coordinated, integrated system;* that is, although data collected for one purpose may differ from those collected for another purpose, these data should be reconcilable with one another. In a sense, the management control system is a single system, but it is perhaps more useful to think of it as two interlocking subsystems, one focusing on programs and the other on responsibility centers. Furthermore, much of the data used in the management control system also are used in preparing a variety of other reports and analyses of use to both management and (occasionally) professional staff.

## THE ROLE OF INFORMATION

In any organization information can be viewed as a resource. As with all resources, it has both a cost and a use to which it can be put, and management must constantly assure that its value exceeds its cost. In many respects, a management control system is concerned with the kinds of information which flow to responsibility center managers in an organization, and the role of that information in facilitating decision making. However, since (*a*) different managers in an organization make different kinds of decisions, (*b*) any given manager will make a variety of decisions depending on the particular circumstances he or she faces at various times in the organization's life, and (*c*) organizations need information beyond that used in the management control system, the accounting system—as distinct from the management control system—must concern itself with a wide range of informational possibilities. At the heart of this set of possibilities is the structure and content of the organization's accounts.

## The Account Structure

An account is a device for collecting data about some phenomenon, as indicated by its title and as specified in the definition of what is to be collected therein. Accounts can collect data on either what has happened (historical data) or what is planned to happen (future data). As described previously, a management control system contains two principal account structures, namely, a program structure and a responsibility structure. In addition to the accounts needed for management control purposes, the accounting system must be able to collect the data needed for general-purpose financial reports prepared for outside parties. Principles governing the preparation of these financial reports are described in Chapter 3.

Beyond general-purpose financial reports, outside agencies may require reports prepared according to requirements that they specify. State and local government agencies that accept funds from the federal government, for example, must prepare reports on the uses made of these funds, and the content of these reports is specified by the agency that grants the funds. These reports may or may not be useful to the management of the organization that prepares them. Ideally, the information these special-purpose reports give should be summaries of the information contained in the management control system because outside agencies presumably do not need more, or different, information from that which is useful to management. This ideal is not always achieved, however. For example, the appropriation structure for agencies of the federal government that is specified by the Congress is not well adapted to the needs of management; it nevertheless governs the content of certain reports.

The accounting system also collects information needed for special purposes, such as in connection with litigation, and for any of a number of special studies.

The accounting system provides historical information; that is, information on what has happened, what the costs were. In addition, the management control system provides two types of information that are not found in the accounting system: (1) estimates of what *will* happen in the future and (2) estimates of what *should* happen. The former are called forecasts, and the latter are called standards or budgets.

## Account Content

Information that is collected in the account structure can be classified as either input or output, that is, information on resources used or on results achieved.

***Input Information.*** The amount of labor, material, and services used in a responsibility center are physical quantities: hours of labor, quarts of oil, reams of paper, kilowatt-hours of electricity, and so on. In a control system it is convenient to translate these amounts into monetary terms. Money provides a common denominator which permits the amounts of individual resources to be combined. The monetary amount is ordinarily obtained by multiplying the physical quantity by a unit price (e.g., hours of labor times a rate per hour). This amount is called cost. Thus the inputs of a responsibility center are ordinarily expressed as costs. As such, cost is a measure of resources used by a responsibility center.

Note that inputs are resources *used* by the responsibility center. The patients in a hospital or the students in a school are *not* inputs. Rather, the inputs are the resources used in accomplishing the objectives of *treating* the patients or *educating* the students.

Input information consists of essentially three basic types of cost construction: full costs, differential costs, and responsibility costs. Each is used for a different purpose, and considerable misunderstanding can arise when the cost construction that is used for one purpose is used inappropriately for another. Full costs and responsibility costs are ordinarily collected in the accounts; differential costs are not collected as such in the accounts.

*Full Cost.* Cost is a measure of the total amount of resources used for some purpose. The technical name for the purpose for which costs are accumulated is cost object, and full cost is the total amount of resources used for a cost object. Since cost objects often are programs, full costs often are called *program costs.* The full cost of a cost object is the sum of its direct costs plus a fair share of indirect costs.

Direct costs are costs than can be traced to a single cost object. For example, the salaries and fringe benefits of persons who work on a single program are direct costs of that program. Indirect costs are costs incurred jointly for two or more cost objects, and a fair share of these indirect costs must be allocated to each of the cost objects.

In recording full costs, items of direct cost are identified separately from items of indirect cost. In some management control systems, there is not enough need for full costs to warrant the expense of allocating indirect costs to programs. In these *direct cost systems,* no provision is made for such an allocation. Such systems are ordinarily found only in organizations in which the management control process is not highly developed.

*Differential Costs.* The costs that are different under one set of conditions from what they would be under another are differential costs. They are useful in many problems involving a choice among alternative courses of action, particularly short-run problems, because the analysis of such a problem involves an estimate of how the costs would be different if the proposed alternative were adopted. Since the costs that are relevant to a given problem depend on the nature of that problem, there is no general way of labeling a given item of cost as differential or not differential, and therefore no way of recording differential costs as such in the formal accounts. The analyst uses information from the program structure or the responsibility structure as raw material for estimating the differential costs for a particular proposed alternative.

In many alternative choice problems, an important classification of costs is whether they are variable or fixed. *Variable costs* are those that change proportionally with changes in volume, that is, the level of activity. Since twice as many workbooks are required to teach two first-grade students as one student, the cost of books used in education is a variable cost. By contrast, the amount of depreciation expense for teaching equipment does not change with the number of students, so the depreciation is a *fixed cost.* Other costs share features of both, changing as volume increases or decreases but not in direct proportion.

*Responsibility Costs.* Costs incurred by or on behalf of a responsibility center are responsibility costs. The focus is on the responsibility center as an organization unit, rather than on the program or programs with which the responsibility center is involved. When measured in monetary terms, the total resources consumed by a responsibility center for a period of time are the costs of that responsibility center. Total recorded costs are at best an approximation of the true inputs. Some inputs are not included as costs, either because the effort required to translate them into monetary terms is not worthwhile (e.g., minor supplies and services or small amounts of borrowed labor) or because measurement is not possible (e.g., certain types of executive or staff assistance; training).

Responsibility costs are classified as either controllable or noncontrollable. An item of cost is *controllable* if the amount of cost incurred in or assigned to a responsibility center is significantly influenced by the actions of the manager of that responsibility center. Note that "controllable" always refers to a specific responsibility center; as such, all items of cost are controllable by someone in the organization. Note also that the definition refers to a *significant* amount of influence, rather than a *complete* influence; few managers have complete influence over any item of cost.

***Output Information.*** Although inputs almost always can be measured in terms of cost, outputs are much more difficult to measure, and in many responsibility centers, outputs cannot be measured at all. In a profit-oriented organization, revenue is often an important measure of output, but such a measure is rarely a complete expression of outputs since it does not encompass everything that the organization does. In many nonprofit organizations, no good quantitative measure of output exists. A school can easily measure the number of students graduated, but it is more difficult to measure how much education each of them acquired. Although outputs may not be measured, or may not even be measurable, it is a fact that every organization unit *has* outputs; that is, it does something.

The degree to which outputs can be measured quantitatively varies greatly with circumstances. In a department making similar goods (e.g., cement), the *quantity* of output often can be measured precisely; but when the goods are heterogeneous (e.g., different types of health care services), problems arise in summarizing the separate outputs into a meaningful measure of the total. Converting the dissimilar physical goods to a monetary equivalent is one way of solving this problem. Such a monetary measure is called *revenue.* If fees are properly structured the total quantity of output of a hospital is reliably measured by the fees charged to patients, that is, by revenues—even though the services rendered consist of such dissimilar activities as use of beds, nursing care, use of operating rooms, and various laboratory, X-ray, and other technical procedures.

At best, revenue measures the *quantity* of output, however. Measurement of the *quality* of output is much more difficult, and often cannot be made at all. In many situations, quality is determined strictly on a judgmental basis. In some, there is a "go/no-go" measurement; either the output is of satisfactory quality or it is not. Moreover, it is always difficult, and often not feasible, to measure, even approximately, the outputs of such staff units as the legal department or the research department of a company, or the outputs of schools, government agencies, or churches.

In addition to the goods and services usually thought of as outputs, responsibility centers produce other intangible effects, some intentional and others unintentional. They may prepare employees for advancement; they may instill attitudes of loyalty and pride of accomplishment (or, alternatively, attitudes of disloyalty and indolence); and they may affect the image of the whole organization as perceived by the outside world. Some of these outputs, such as better trained employees, are created in order to benefit operations in future periods; that is, they will become inputs at some future time. Such outputs are therefore *investments,* since an investment is a commitment of current resources in the expectation of deriving future benefits; however, such investments in intangibles are rarely recorded in the formal system.

## Efficiency and Effectiveness

The concepts stated above can be used to explain the meaning of efficiency and effectiveness, which are the two criteria for judging the performance of a responsibility center. These criteria are almost always used in a comparative, rather than in an absolute, sense; that is, we do not ordinarily say that Organization Unit A is 80 percent efficient, but rather that it is more (or less) efficient than Organization Unit B, or that it is more (or less) efficient currently than it was in the past, or that it was more (or less) efficient than planned or budgeted.

***Efficiency.*** By calculating a ratio of outputs to inputs, or the amount of output per unit of input we can obtain a measure of efficiency. Unit A is more efficient than Unit B either (1) if it uses fewer resources than Unit B but has the same output, or (2) if it uses the same resources as Unit B and has more output than Unit B. Note that the first type of measure does not require that output be quantified; it is only necessary to judge that the outputs of the two units are approximately the same. If management is satisfied that Units A and B are both doing a satisfactory job and if it is a job of comparable magnitude, then the unit with the lower inputs, that is, the lower costs, is the more efficient. For example, if two elementary schools are judged to be furnishing adequate education, the one with the lower costs is the more efficient. The second type of measure does require some quantitative measure of output; it is therefore a more difficult type of measurement in many situations. If two elementary schools have the same costs, one can be said to be more efficient than the other only if it provides more education, and this is difficult to measure.

In many responsibility centers, a measure of efficiency can be developed that relates actual costs to some standard—that is, to a number that expresses what costs should be incurred for the amount of measured output. Such a measure can be a useful indication of efficiency, but it is never a perfect measure for at least two reasons: (1) recorded costs are not a precisely accurate measure of resources consumed; and (2) standards are, at best, only approximate measures of what resource consumption ideally should have been in the circumstances prevailing.

***Effectiveness.*** The relationship between a responsibility center's outputs and its objectives is an indication of its effectiveness. The more these outputs contribute to the objectives, the more effective the unit is. Since both objectives and outputs are often difficult to quantify, measures of effectiveness are difficult to come by. Effectiveness, therefore, is often expressed in nonquantitative, judgmental terms, such as "College A is doing a first-rate job"; "College B has slipped somewhat in recent years."

An organization unit should attempt to be *both* efficient and effective; it is not a matter of one or the other. Efficient managers are those who do whatever they do with the least consumption of resources; but if what they do (i.e., their output) is an inadequate contribution to the accomplishment of the organization's goals, they are ineffective. If, for example, in a welfare office the employees are invariably busy, and if they process claims and applications with little wasted motion, the office is efficient; but if the personnel have the attitude that their function is to ensure that every form is made out perfectly rather than that their function is to help clients get the services to which they are entitled, the office is ineffective.

***The Role of Profits.*** One important goal in a profit-oriented organization is to earn profits, and the amount of profits is therefore an important measure of effectiveness. Since profit is the difference between revenue, which is a measure of output, and expense, which is a measure of input, profit is also a measure of efficiency. Thus, profit measures both effectiveness and efficiency. Nevertheless, it is a less than perfect measure for several reasons: (1) monetary measures do not exactly measure all aspects of either output or input; (2) standards against which profits are judged frequently are not realistic; and (3) at best, profit is a measure of what has happened in the short run, whereas we are presumably also interested in the long-run consequences of management actions. In a nonprofit organization the difference between revenue and expense says nothing about effectiveness.

### Key Variables

Although the management control structure tends to be built around a formal set of accounts, one important aspect is often not part of this account structure. This is the concept of *key variables.* A key variable is one which can change unexpectedly and in which a change can have a significant effect on the success of the organization. For example, in many profit-oriented organizations the amount of orders booked is a key variable because the level of incoming orders usually cannot be predicted accurately, and a change in the level can have important consequences. Similarly, in a college the number of applicants is a key variable. In a health maintenance organization, a key variable is hospital days per 1,000 members.

A good management control system is designed to bring quickly to management's attention information about the behavior of key variables. Generally the number of such key variables is small, usually half a dozen or so, but they are extremely important.

## LINE AND STAFF RELATIONSHIPS

The person responsible for the design and operation of the management control system is here called the controller.[3] In practice, the person may have other titles, such as administrative officer or chief accountant.

The idea that the controller has a broader responsibility than merely "keeping the books" is a fairly recent one in profit-oriented organizations, but it is not yet well accepted in many nonprofit organizations. Not too long ago, controllers, who were then invariably called "chief accountants," were expected to confine their activities to collecting and reporting historical data. With the development of formal management control systems and the emphasis on information needed for planning and decision making, the controller's function has broadened.

Notwithstanding the broadened responsibilities, the controller remains a staff person. Decisions about management control should be made by the line managers, not by the staff. The job of the staff is to provide information that will facilitate making good decisions. In an organization whose chief executive officer is unwilling to assume overall responsibility, an operating manager with a problem of inadequate resources may be told, "Go see the controller." In making such a statement, the top manager gives up line responsibility, and the controller is put in the position of acting in a line capacity.

---

[3] In some organizations, the word is spelled "comptroller," but this is an erroneous spelling, with no basis in etymology, and is, in any event, pronounced as if it were spelled "controller." (Pronouncing it "*compt* . . ." is archaic.)

The controller then, de facto, becomes a manager, with a corresponding diminution in the responsibility of the person who nominally is charged with management. This usually leads to less than optimum management of the whole organization.

In some government agencies, this tendency for the controller to assume line responsibility became quite strong in the 1940s and 1950s. This was usually a consequence of top management's reluctance to accept overall responsibility. The controller, or more specifically the budget officer, was permitted to make many decisions regarding the allocation of resources. With the "power of the purse," the budget officer became one of the most powerful persons in the organization. It has been said that in some large military installations, the commanding officer was principally in charge of ceremonies, and the real boss was the budget officer. With the current tendency to select a good manager as the chief executive officer, the role of the budget officer has, fortunately, become more like the staff role that it should be.

When the controller or budget officer assumed the role of a line manager, the control system was usually designed to facilitate the controller's own work. Such a system slighted the needs of operating managers; that is, it did not provide them the information necessary to do their jobs. Consequently, operating managers created their own informal information systems—called a "desk drawer set of books" because the data were kept there rather than in the formal accounting records. Fortunately, this practice is dying out as operating managers increasingly recognize the importance of accurate and consistent information for decision-making purposes.

### Line Managers

It is important to emphasize that line managers are the focal points in management control. They are persons whose judgments are incorporated in the approved plans, and they are the persons who must influence others and whose performance is measured. Staff people collect, summarize, and present information that is useful in the process, and they make calculations that translate management judgments into the format of the system. Such a staff may be large in numbers; indeed, the control department is often the largest staff department in an organization. However, the significant decisions are made by the line managers, not by the staff.

## BOUNDARIES OF MANAGEMENT CONTROL

Management control is an important function of management, but it is by no means the whole of management. An even more important function is to make judgments about people: their integrity, their ability, their potential, their fitness for a given job, their compatibility with colleagues. Management is responsible for building an effective human organization and for motivating the people in that organization to work toward its goals.

Managers also have many functions that are not management as such. Kotter illustrates the external activities of a manager by describing the external agencies and persons on which the head of a large municipal, urban teaching hospital must depend: (1) the mayor's office—to approve the hospital's budget, to support the hospital publicly, and to avoid employing everyone to whom the mayor owes a favor; (2) other parts of the city bureaucracy for such services as construction; (3) a dozen unions or employee associations that could call a strike or work stoppage; (4) the civil service, which could make it easy or impossible to get adequate employees; (5) the city council, which could call hearings that could take up a hospital manager's time and be a source of embarrassment; (6) two accreditation agencies, which could put the hospital out of business; (7) the state government, which could constrain hospital activities in a number of ways; (8) the medical school with which it was affiliated, which supplies the hospital with physicians; (9) the local press, which could embarrass the hospital and upset the mayor; (10) the federal government, which supplies the hospital with some funds and regulates some activities; (11) other hospitals in the city whose major actions could have a positive or negative impact on this hospital; (12) the local community, which, if organized, could constrain the hospital's actions through the press, the mayor, or the city council; and so on.[4]

## BOUNDARIES OF THE BOOK

As already noted, management control is a process which occurs when the organization is engaged in work that is undertaken to reach its goal; it does not have anything to do directly with the formulation of these goals. This book therefore takes the goals as given.

There is also the assumption that the organization already exists. We are not concerned with whether or not there should be an organization, or with whether it should have the mission that it does have. Neither are we concerned with whether the goals are good or bad; the management control process occurs both in UNICEF and in the Mafia. Our focus thus prohibits us from criticizing the goals themselves, on moral or on any other grounds. We do not, for example, debate the question of the extent to which the government should be responsible for health care. We accept the fact that the Congress has assigned certain health care responsibilities to the Department of Health and Human Services and start our analysis with this as a given.

### Exclusion of Systems Approach

This focus on management control in an existing organization means that some exciting topics are not given the attention here that their importance

[4] John P. Kotter, "Power, Success and Organizational Effectiveness," *Organizational Dynamics,* Winter 1978, p. 12.

warrants. Of these, perhaps the most important is the systems approach. Health care, for example, should be viewed as a system, comprising all the individuals, organizations, and policies that are intended to provide an optimum level of health care. When viewed in this way, it is apparent that the health care system in the United States is deficient. Our morbidity rates, infant mortality rates, and other indicators of health, rank nowhere near the top of the list of developed countries, despite the fact that we spend more on health care per capita than do most other nations. Health care facilities are poorly distributed. Many ill people who could be treated inexpensively in a clinic are sent unnecessarily to expensive hospitals. Many people cannot afford adequate health care. All these facts are indications that the health care system needs a drastic overhaul, and that it should be possible to provide better health care at substantially lower cost by emphasizing new organizational arrangements, such as more ambulatory care facilities; a new mix of personnel, such as more nurse practioners and physician assistants; more emphasis on preventive medicine; and so on. In short, a focus on a study of health care as a system is fascinating, and an analysis of this system can lead to major improvements. Similarly, governmental organizations, higher educational facilities, and volunteer organizations are all best understood when viewed in a systemic perspective.

This book, however, takes a narrower focus, concerning itself with the activities of individual organizations. Within the health care system, our focus will be on a hospital, a clinic, or a nursing home, for example. Within the educational system, we focus on individual schools, colleges, or universities. The book accepts the role of an organization essentially as given, and concentrates on how improvements in the management control structure and process can help the organization to perform its function, whatever it may be, more efficiently and effectively.

Such a focus tends to be less than satisfying to many people because it rules out a discussion of certain glamorous, high payoff topics. These topics should of course be discussed, but they should be discussed in another context. It is important that there be a proper balance between an analysis of health care as a system and an analysis of the problems of one organization within that system. It is tempting to focus on the global systems problems and to neglect the problems of individual organizations, but that temptation is resisted here.

## Case 1–1

# HOAGLAND HOSPITAL*

In September 1976, Dr. Richard Wells, Chief of Surgery at Hoagland Hospital in Chicago, Illinois, announced that all full-time doctors in the Department of Surgery were required to join the Surgical Group Practice or leave the hospital premises. In his eight years as chief, Dr. Wells had initiated numerous changes in the department, but never one as controversial as the Group Practice. Looking back on it in 1978, he said:

> This has been one of the ugliest things I've ever done—all the personal abuse, just for following the damn rules the university sent down. It is the closest I've come to quitting my job . . .

Dr. Wells had established the Group Practice or "trust" in 1974 to serve two purposes. First, it was intended to regulate each surgeon's professional income to comply with the Kent Medical School Salary Regulation, and secondly, it would augment the department's income with funds not otherwise attainable. Additionally, Dr. Wells was convinced that as an academic department of Kent Medical School, the Department of Surgery needed guidelines to ensure a standard of excellence:

> I think this has to be done in any academic institution. Doctors here are supposed to provide ongoing patient care, carry on research, and teach. Now if you're at all good as a surgeon, your private practice will skyrocket, and your research and teaching will lose out. It's fun and lucrative to practice medicine, but in a teaching hospital you have other responsibilities, too.

## Background

The Department of Surgery was a clinical department of the 75 year-old-Hoagland Hospital in Chicago. A private, 450-bed hospital, Hoagland had been a teaching affiliate of Kent Medical School since 1925. In its 50 years as a teaching hospital, Hoagland had demonstrated a firm commitment to teaching and research as well as patient care. Insisting that the three were interdependent units which together enhanced the quality of medical care, Hoagland's medical staff had distinguished itself among hospital teaching staffs. In 1970, Hoagland was the most popular hospital among Kent medical students and attracted graduates of the top medical schools for its 175 intern and resident positions.

As part of the teaching hospital, Hoagland's clinical departments were subject to the guidelines of Kent Medical School. Prior to 1970, Kent's guidelines, which primarily stressed Kent's commitment to scholastic achieve-

---

* This case was prepared by Patricia O'Brien, under the direction of David W. Young, Harvard School of Public Health.

ment, had had little effect on the school's clinical departments. Dr. Wells explained:

> For years, we'd had what you'd call a "Gentleman's Agreement" with the medical school. They gave the department a modest budget and paid doctors something for their teaching and research. Other than that, doctors could work for the hospital and carry on a private practice making about as much money as they wanted. There was some innocuous stipulation in our agreement allowing doctors to make as much money as "didn't interfere with their scholarly activities."

By 1970, Kent Medical School was feeling the financial constraints besetting most academic institutions. Unable to continue supporting their clinical departments, they altered the agreement, asking that patient fees support hospital clinical departments. The school issued a Salary Statement Regulation, from which the following is excerpted.

> Total Compensation paid to full-time members of the Faculty of Medicine as of December 1, 1971, may not exceed the level set for each individual in the *Appointments and Compensation Requirements for the Faculty of Medicine at Kent University.* The member's total income is equal to the sum of his/her Academic Salary plus Additional Compensation plus Other Personal Professional Income and may not at any level exceed twice the member's Academic Salary.
>
> Each Clinical Department head shall be responsible for maintaining the records and reporting the income of all full-time members of the Department. . . . Fees earned that are in excess of an individual's compensation level must be reported and disposed of as directed by the institution responsible for setting the level of compensation in consultation with the Dean of the Medical School.
>
> Inasmuch as the System was adopted by the faculty and approved by the Kent Corporation, it is understood that no Faculty member may continue in the full-time system unless he/she is in full conformity with the system and the procedures designed to implement it.

According to Dr. Wells, this was a difficult confirmation for the chiefs to give:

> The new guidelines caused quite a commotion, as you can imagine. Doctors were critical of the policy because they now had to report their salaries—something they'd never had to do before.
>
> When I asked people in my department for income disclosures, some of them tried everything to get around the rules. They were giving me their salaries after taxes and expenses—and it was *unreal* what they were calling "expenses." They were, of course, making just what they had been before. And it was becoming clear to me that I couldn't enforce the regulation.

Meanwhile, the Department of Surgery's income, now derived from the hospital and grants, was not meeting the department's needs. Some surgeons joined Dr. Wells in his concern about their financial problems. Dr. Eleanor Robinson, Associate Director of the Department of Surgery, explained:

> We were finding the department had needs, mostly of an academic nature, that we didn't have the money to support. Occasionally, we'd want to send residents

to meetings or postgraduate educational programs but couldn't afford to. Or someone would need financial assistance for a small research project that wasn't covered by long-term NIH grants and the money just wasn't there.

## The Group Practice

Responding to these administrative and financial problems, in 1973 Dr. Wells decided to establish a group practice. He intended to structure the practice as a department fund that could pool surgeons' professional fees and pay them salaries, according to Kent's regulation. Any surplus of fees would be retained by the department for its use.

The Group Practice was organized as an educational and charitable trust fund with nonprofit, tax-exempt status. Although the hospital and medical school became the trust's beneficiaries, the trust maintained total responsibility for its policies and budget. Dr. Wells commented:

> I watched the Department of Anesthesia at Memorial Hospital form a group through their hospital about eight years ago. Everything goes into the hospital, and they give the group a yearly budget. The chief there is now having difficulty getting a run-down from the hospital on the department's contribution margin when he knows the department is making money. If he wants another anesthetist, he has to justify it to the hospital.
>
> I don't want to crawl to the hospital for what I need if I've got the space. Because of their problems, I chose not to do that.

Dr. Robinson, who aided in administering the trust, added:

> We generally agreed that patient income for the department's use should be administered outside of the hospital budget. Surgeons sometimes view themselves as more hardworking than the rest of the hospital and we didn't want our money used to subsidize other departments. We hadn't had problems with the hospital but it was a preventive measure.

The Surgical Trust offered members a salary in accordance with the medical school guidelines plus benefits and a conditional overage expense account. As an incentive, salaries were graded down from the guideline ceiling with increases based on yearly evaluation meetings between Dr. Wells and the doctor concerned. Dr. Wells explained:

> A doctor's salary is a function of his or her overall contribution to the department plus academic rank. What the medical school gave us is a maximum for each position. At the evaluation conferences, I decide, with the doctor, where he or she falls on that scale. In reality, we're all pretty close to our maximums but it's an incentive to get the work done.
>
> It is important to realize though, that salaries don't reflect the amount of patient fees generated by the doctor. If a surgeon has a steady practice and generates an average income in patient fees but is an invaluable teacher or researcher, he or she might be promoted academically and hence, be paid more than another surgeon whose best skills are in seeing patients.

Dr. Wells acknowledged that this could also be a disadvantage:

> There's a practical problem with tying salaries to academic rank. It isn't always possible for people to do all three things equally well. If they don't do the academics, their salaries suffer. For example, we have some super neurosurgeons—absolutely super—but they don't have time to write academic papers. Their salaries are stuck at their academic rank, whatever happens.
>
> But the fact is, this is an academic hospital and if doctors are interested in making money, they shouldn't be here. They can move up the street and make as much money as they want.

The trust's benefits were health, life, and malpractice insurance, long-term disability insurance, and a tax-deferred annuity program. The plan was designed to provide members with benefits that had previously been purchased with members' after-tax dollars. Thus, it sought both to maximize members' income potentials within the Kent ceiling and to offer tax advantages.

If doctors generated more income than their salaries reflected, they received an overage account for professional expenses. That is, 50 percent of a doctor's surplus income would be credited to the doctor to cover expenses such as subscriptions, books, and conference travel. According to the by-laws of the trust, however, overage money could not be converted into salary. The remaining surplus income was to be used for department expenses.

The department would collect supplemental income from "chief-service patients." Prior to the trust, those patients who did not have private physicians were the responsibility of the chief resident and received free professional services. Because chief-service patients were admitted to the hospital without private physicians, the surgical services they received did not qualify for Blue Shield reimbursement.

When the department established the trust, they employed the senior chief resident as the Group's "junior-staff surgeon" and admitted all junior-staff patients as patients of the professional group practice. The trust could then bill junior-staff patients through its provider status. As a result, the trust collected fees that were not available when each doctor maintained an independent practice.

The trust was to be governed by a board of trustees. the five-member board would be responsible for trust policies and approving loans and budgets. Board members were to be Dr. Wells, who held a permanent position, two trustees appointed by him, and two trustees elected by the department. In addition, Dr. Wells would hold periodic meetings for all trust members.

## Membership

By the winter of 1975, there were four members of the Surgical Group Practice: the junior-staff surgeon, Dr. Wells, and two other young surgeons. Critical of the trust's organization and planning methods, four or five doctors opposed joining. Dr. Melvin Jefferson, a general surgeon at Hoagland for 10 years, was the most vocal about his position:

> I was not going to join the trust until I knew exactly what was being proposed. A number of the important issues were left extremely vague. The reasons for establishing the trust were even vague, in my mind at least, and our meetings did little to clarify the specifics. Some of the important issues, especially reconciling salaries, faculty rank, and academic and financial contributions to the department, were unresolved. I don't think these things had been thoroughly thought out, yet we were being asked to join. So a few other doctors and I refused to join until we knew more about the details.

In the spring of 1976, Dr. Wells asked all surgeons to join the trust. A few doctors who had verbally committed themselves to the trust but had postponed joining became members. But because attitudes in the department continued to differ, Dr. Wells decided membership had to be mandatory for all full-time academic surgeons. He explained:

> Membership had to be a prerequisite for remaining in the department because I knew what was going to happen. I had a few nice guys, resigned to the idea of the trust, carrying the department. And there were these other fellows, you know, friends of everyone; they'd been here a long time and didn't want to join the group. Some of them were taking home $200,000 a year. Others, their friends, were towing the line.
>
> I knew that some people wouldn't go along with it, and maybe for good reasons. You have to be realistic about the specialty you're talking about; if cardiologists can make $300,000 a year, how can you keep them down on the farm? In another one of our subdepartments, everyone is leaving. They're moving down the street to private offices. They're good specialists and it's too bad we're losing them, but if they're interested in making money, that's where they should be.

At the announcement of mandatory participation, every surgeon was forced to make a decision. Dr. Ben Lewis, head of the urology subdepartment, explained his decision to join the trust:

> We were TOLD by Dr. Wells that the department was not in compliance with the medical school's financial guidelines. He TOLD us that we had to change our system to comply and that if we didn't want to, we'd have to leave.
>
> I said fine. I trusted Dr. Wells totally, I admired him greatly, and I liked my work. I was willing to change even though I knew the financial and emotional costs. I knew the financial cost because I subtracted their guideline figure from my salary and . . . that was my loss. The emotional cost, loss of independence, is harder to evaluate and still troubles me.
>
> It makes you wonder why people stay here. Why do they? I guess it's because they like Wells—I think that's the main reason everyone stays. He's created a good faculty and a relatively favorable environment.

Other surgeons, however, were still opposed to the Group Practice. Dr. Jefferson, the most reluctant to join, explained that his reticence stemmed from his impression of the trust's operational structure:

> In thinking about the Group Practice earlier, I'd had exalted goals in mind. I thought we could use the trust to make a more unified and cohesive Department

of Surgery. We could spread the operative experience to the younger surgeons and improve the department academically by removing some of the economic motivations. Somehow the trust got sidetracked into an instrument whose *sole* purpose was to collect chief-service fees for the department, which resulted in a lot of devisiveness in the department.

For example, look at the method of remuneration as initially spelled out: a salary based on faculty rank and an admittedly extremely modest fringe benefit package. That left the question of overages and benefits essentially unresolved. We were being asked to sign a document involving a significant financial decision that could theoretically and legally involve making considerably less money than before, without having the specifics spelled out. We were just told that "no one would be hurt."

I also thought it was absurd to erect a gigantic administrative superstructure on what is essentially a small department. If the purpose was simply to conform to the medical school guideline and earn a little extra money for the department, we didn't need this whole organization with a billing office and everything else. I think we should have started small and built up—the fact is, we just don't have any big earners who can support a trust of this size.

From Dr. Well's perspective, the trust had by then become

a tremendous can of worms. I had doctors philosophizing about everything, you should have heard them. All upset because of their "loss of control." It wasn't loss of control at all, it was loss of money. The absurd part of it was that a lot of those people weren't losing money. Believe me, surgeons can be a difficult bunch to work with.

Unfortunately, there's no uniformity in the way clinical departments interpreted the guidelines so doctors could point to other departments and claim that they weren't complying the way we were. They were right, particularly in this school, because the dean is afraid to interfere too much in the autonomy of the hospitals.

## Billing System

At the outset of the trust, Dr. Wells intended to have all members' billing managed by a central billing office. In the spring of 1973, he hired a business manager to administer billings, collections, and reports for members. He planned that each doctor would submit a daily "activity sheet" to the business office, detailing services rendered, patient names, and fees.

However, so many present and future trust members opposed the centralized billing plan that Dr. Wells postponed implementing it. Instead, upon joining the trust, each doctor had the choice of centralized billing through the business office or their previous system wherein secretaries billed for doctors' private practices. Given the choice, half the surgeons chose central billing and half chose to remain with the old system. Ann Miller, the business manager explained:

Doctors really hold a spectrum of opinions on billing; some don't care at all about their bills while others want to see and discuss every one. I think some doctors don't like the business aspect of medicine—they prefer not having to handle it. The others don't like not having control of it. They feel removed from their practice if they don't see the bills go out.

The doctors who remained with private billing were to submit duplicate bills and their monthly collections to the business office. But most doctors never forwarded their duplicate bills, leaving the office with incomplete billing information. Ms. Miller was forced to establish a bill-receipt record system, posting bills and receipts simultaneously and setting them equal to each other.

It was a crazy system and we knew it, but what could we do? Surgeons set their own fees, and we had no idea what they were. At the end of the month they would send us money with a record of patients' names and amounts paid. So we'd record that amount as billed and paid.

But it was no way to run a business office. For example, one day a doctor brought in $15,000 in checks, just like that. We hadn't expected it at all. we never had any idea of our accounts receivable or collection rates.

However, Ms. Miller added that centralized billing had developed its own complications:

Our main problem was that the information we received from doctors varied immensely from doctor to doctor. We didn't provide them with a formal activity sheet, so the doctors used their own systems of recording. As you can imagine, we were receiving dissimilar information from all of them.

From what they gave us, my three assistants would compile standard data sheets which was unbelievably time-consuming. On top of that, we were billing for 5 doctors, collecting and recording for 11 doctors, and attempting individual monthly reports for 11. It was taking us three weeks to do just the monthly reports.

It was also becoming obvious to Dr. Wells that the trust billing had to be uniform and managed by a central computer system:

Finally, I'd had it. The only efficient way to collect money for so many people was through one system. It had to be cheaper and more accurate plus it would keep everyone honest. I figured that if collections changed at all, they should increase because one office was handling all the data.

Many surgeons, however, disagreed with Dr. Wells on this issue. Among them was Dr. Lewis:

I felt all along that it was crucial that we do our billing independently. Very simply, no one is more interested in his collections than the person who worked for it: I can do it better because *I care*.

Secondly, there are complications in people's billings, which can only be settled by the doctor. A patient is on welfare and can't pay. After one bill, I'd know enough to drop it. A professional courtesy charge—I'm never sure what the billing office charged or if they understand my intention.

Sometimes people come in and say, "doctor, I've been in here three times and I haven't received a bill yet, why?" I have to say "I don't know," which makes me feel foolish. When my secretary did billing, I'd just step out, ask her and get the answer. Now with the business office all the way over in Talbot, geographically remote from the department, it is very difficult to know what the current situation is.

In January of 1977, the trust hired a computer company to manage all billings. The company was to receive billing and payment information from the business office and would process it by batches into claims and collections. They would apply claims and collections to physicians' balances and maintain a continual record of the trust's financial status. The computer company agreed to produce monthly printouts, by provider, so that doctors would have accurate records of their accounts.

Despite this contract, the computer company never produced the information. Ms. Miller explained:

> We had a terrible time with that company. The first problem was they never produced any reports according to doctor. We kept asking and they kept agreeing, but they never gave us anything useful.
>
> By the time we realized that we weren't going to get that out of them, we had a more serious problem: they had dropped $15,000 in payments from the records. They just hadn't applied it to any accounts, so although we had the money, we didn't know which accounts, i.e., doctors, it belonged to. That meant that the rates we had manually calculated were also meaningless. Well, we got rid of the company then, but I'm afraid it was too late.

Some doctors, affected by these errors, were already furious. With minimal billing information and startling fluctuations in collection rates, doctors blamed the centralized billing procedure. In an attempt to trace the problems, Dr. Robinson studied the collection data. After analyzing patient mix, payor class, and service mix, she reached no conclusion:

> I felt that centralized billing should, if anything, improve collections, but that wasn't our experience. Of course, with our other computer problems the issue became more complicated because our information was incomplete.
>
> Nevertheless, I think we have to separate questions of administrative efficiency from problems with the system itself. This is difficult to do, but we can't treat them as all one big problem with the billing system. Of course, we also have to consider that when surgeons turn their bills over to a collection office, they feel like they're losing control. That's the motive for doing the billing ourselves.

Dr. Wells considered the billing problem to be one of administrative oversights:

> Obviously, there were problems with that computer company but I don't see why this would be inherent to centralized billing systems. I've discussed the problem with other groups and our experience is atypical. It happened though, and we can't explain it.
>
> There's also the issue of overhead; doctors are seeing it now like never before. They can see costs that the hospital and department formerly picked up, like secretaries, coming directly out of the trust, and they're not pleased.

Other surgeons, including Dr. Lewis who had become an elected member of the board of trustees, maintained their opposition to the system. He commented:

> I've been against centralized billing from the start, and I think time has borne me out. For one year I've worked with no idea of what my collections have been. As a result, I don't know my overage, or if I even have one. If I submit receipts, I don't know if they'll be covered.
>
> I got some information for a few months last year and according to that, my collections had fallen by 33 percent. Yet, Dr. Wells calls this a more efficient system . . .
>
> This method must be costing us more. My secretary still prepares the background information on bills and sends that to the billing office to finish. She might as well do the whole thing. It's unnecessary and inefficient to involve that whole office.

Dr. Jefferson thought that, for himself, the system was less efficient than his previous one:

> Last year I tried to get some information about my collections and was appalled at how little they'd collected and how little they knew. They couldn't even give me records on patient payments. I did find out though that overhead was about 19 percent of my salary. We all agreed that this was excessive.

Dr. Lewis added that, in his opinion, the controversy over billing methods and other administrative matters was indicative of the trust's overall administrative policies:

> What happened with billing is typical of the way the trust is run. I like and respect Dr. Wells, but our finances are in shambles because he isn't interested in and doesn't have financial skills. For example, look at what happened with the computer company he and Ms. Miller engaged.
>
> What it comes down to is that the trust is really Dr. Wells's. It reflects his personality, plus he controls the majority of votes. Of the five board members, three are Dr. Wells and his two appointments, giving him 3/5 of any vote—it would be impossible to beat him. Not that there has been a showdown but the fact is, he's playing with a loaded deck. It's OK as long as you like and trust him, but it makes for an uncertain future.

## Evaluation

By the winter of 1978, all 14 full-time surgeons at Hoagland had joined the trust. Five doctors had left the department in the previous two years for reasons both related and unrelated to the trust. Some joined the staffs at other hospitals, others left to establish independent private practices. Dr. Wells gradually filled their positions with surgeons who joined the trust upon joining the department.

Although reactions in the department still differed on some aspects of the trust, there were also points of general agreement among members. One such area concerned the Trust's effect on the department's economic condition. Dr. Robinson commented on it:

> One of the most important results of the trust has been the increased revenue generated for the department. It remains to be seen whether any of this is from the changes in the billing system, but collecting chief-service patient fees has certainly helped us financially.
>
> Before the trust, the department was stretching to take care of the usual expenses. In the past few years we've not only covered our usual costs but we've been able to pay for postgraduate education and extend interest-free loans to residents. We even lent travel money to a resident so that his family could go to England with him when he was studying there.
>
> The problems in the trust were really administrative and business problems. People here are devoted to academic pursuits so they're not concerned about who is generating the most income—that's not the point of medicine. I think these problems are getting smoothed out and the trust will run much better in the future. I also think it will improve as more people join the department.

Although Dr. Jefferson agreed with Dr. Robinson that the trust had helped the department, he remained critical of the trust's operations:

> It's still difficult to get a handle on precisely what's going on. The process of forming the trust was not salutary on communication problems within the department, and these problems remain.
>
> In a way, the trust has had no real effect on me. I do exactly what I did before and am not significantly better or worse off because of it. The available funds have allowed the department to survive, which was important, but when the trust was formed, Dr. Wells was never as frank as he should have been about the economic problems of the department. He said "we'd make a little extra money" but we never knew that there was a significant economic problem. If we had, we might have all discussed it and come up with an agreeable solution. The emphasis was always on the Medical School guidelines.
>
> I think Dr. Wells is a much better chief of surgery than a businessman. There are many business issues and it was preposterous to go about them in an unbusinesslike way. I think Wells has the attitude that it isn't nice to talk about money. So because he can't talk about it we have a major communication problem. We still need frankness about this because we're getting new people into the trust and they have to know the details.

Dr. Lewis gave his opinion of the trust's shortcomings:

> It's a nice feature of the department to have supplemental funds. I've set up a library in my office for medical students and residents in urology. I've also used money for honoraria and visual aids, and residents have been reimbursed for expenses from urological meetings.
>
> I'd eventually like to see more money spent on teaching and conference equipment. We have considered a closed-circuit TV in the operating room.
>
> As for the other side, I would say that reduced personal income and loss of independence are disadvantages of the trust. And there have been mistakes. The whole concept of centralized billing is a big mistake. I've voted against it every

time it's come up, but it exists. Of course, the mistake was exacerbated by Wells's choice of computer companies.

I believe the real problem in organizing the trust was asking people to change. People were asked to go from a liberal, laissez-faire system to a structured one, and resisted. That's not unusual and could have been predicted.

Commenting on the trust four years after he'd organized it, Dr. Wells noted that some questions remained unanswered:

It's a difficult situation because there still is no uniformity in the medical school. I did what I thought had to be done to keep a Department of Surgery functioning academically, but some departments haven't done anything. And realistically, I know academic rank doesn't always reflect someone's contribution. But what could I do?

Then there's always been the budget problem. We never really know where we stand with any of our four budgets. We have budgets for the hospital, the medical school, the grants, and the trust; research funds for this department alone are $1 million. That's big business, and we're not trained for that.

You know, I sometimes wonder if the hospital could help us more than they have. I don't want them to run the trust, but I'd like to use them better than I have.

## Questions

1. Classify the activities of Dr. Wells into the categories of strategic planning, management control, and task control. How, if at all, does this assist you in understanding the problems faced by the trust?
2. How would you characterize the management control structure of the trust? The management control process?
3. What might Dr. Wells have done differently? Why?

# chapter 2

# Characteristics of Nonprofit Organizations

Although the precise line between profit-oriented and nonprofit organizations is fuzzy, the following definition is adequate for the purpose of this book: *A nonprofit organization is an organization whose goal is something other than earning a profit for its owners. Usually its goal is to provide services.* This definition corresponds approximately to that in most state statutes.[1]

The definition also emphasizes a basic distinction between the two types of organizations. This distinction is the cause of many management control problems that are peculiar to nonprofit organizations. In a profit-oriented company, decisions made by management are intended to increase (or at least maintain) profits, and success is measured, to a significant degree, by the amount of profits that these organizations earn. (This is not to say that profit is their only objective, or that their success can be measured entirely in terms of profitability; that would be, of course, an overly simplistic view of most businesses.) By contrast, in nonprofit organizations, decisions made by management are intended to result in providing the best possible service with the available resources; success is measured primarily by how much

[1] Some people prefer the term "not-for-profit" on the grounds that a business enterprise with a net loss is literally a "nonprofit" organization. *Black's Law Dictionary, Kohler's Dictionary for Accountants, Webster's Third New International Dictionary, Funk and Wagnalls Dictionary,* and *American Heritage Dictionary* do not list "not-for-profit," however. Practice varies widely among states and is not uniform for the statutes of a given state. In federal statutes, the usual term is "nonprofit."

service the organizations provide and by how well these services are rendered. More basically the success of a nonprofit organization should be measured by how much it contributes to the public well-being.

Since "service" is a more vague, less measurable concept than "profit," it is more difficult to measure performance in a nonprofit organization. It is also more difficult to make clear-cut choices among alternative courses of action in such an organization because in most nonprofit organizations the relationship between costs and benefits, and even the amount of benefits, are difficult to measure. Despite these difficulties, an organization must be controlled. Its management must do what it can to assure that resources are used efficiently and effectively. Thus, the central problem is to find out what management control policies and practices are useful, despite the limitations.

## Sharpening the Distinction

Our distinction is not black and white. A profit-oriented company must render services that its customers find adequate if it is to earn a profit, whereas a nonprofit organization must receive funds from operating revenues or other sources that are at least equal to its costs if it is to continue to render services. The distinction then is based not on the need for funds, per se, but on the predominant attitude toward the purposes for which these funds are used.

Some organizations that literally do not seek profits are nevertheless excluded from our class of nonprofit organizations. A mutual insurance company, for example, does not make a profit in the literal sense, but it returns an equivalent amount to its policyholders labeled "dividend." Its management control problems are similar to those of stock insurance companies, which do seek profits. Mutual investment funds, mutual savings banks, cooperative banks, and similar types of financial institutions are excluded on the same grounds. Conversely, some government organizations are in fact businesses even though they do not literally seek to earn a profit. Municipally owned power plants are an example.

Certain authorities and government corporations are borderline cases. These include port authorities, airport authorities, highway and bridge authorities, parking authorities, industrial development authorities, and the like at the municipal and state level; and Tennessee Valley Authority (TVA), Communications Satellite Corporation, Amtrak, and the U.S. Postal Service at the federal level. TVA, for example, operates a number of power generation and transmission facilities. Its decisions about these facilities are economic decisions, and its management control problems and practices with respect to them are essentially the same as those in an investor-owned utility. TVA also is involved, however, in the development and preservation of natural resources and in the economic development of the region. Its objectives with respect to these functions are service objectives, not profit-oriented ones. The management of these activities therefore comes within our purview. Moreover, authorities and government corporations tend to be responsible to political bodies, and this affects their management control problems as is the case with other public sector organizations.

Some hospitals, medical clinics, schools, even religious organizations are set up explicitly as profit-oriented organizations. These, too, are borderline situations, since many of the problems to be discussed here do arise in these organizations. In activities that are usually thought of as being "nonprofit," not all organizations are actually nonprofit. For example, the following table shows the distribution in three classes of hospitals and hospital beds in 1979 (as compiled by the American Hospital Association):

| | *Entities* | | *Beds* | |
|---|---|---|---|---|
| | *Number* | *Percent* | *Number* | *Percent* |
| Government | 2,644 | 37.3 | 594,300 | 42.8 |
| Nongovernment, nonprofit | 3,551 | 50.0 | 704,000 | 50.6 |
| Proprietary | 899 | 12.7 | 92,200 | 6.6 |
| Total | 7,094 | 100.0 | 1,390,500 | 100.0 |

In addition to the proprietary (i.e., profit-oriented) hospitals, an increasing number of nonprofit hospitals are being managed by profit-oriented companies.

## SIZE AND COMPOSITION OF THE NONPROFIT SECTOR

Exhibit 2–1 gives some idea of the magnitude of the class of organizations on which this book focuses. The figures are not exact because the census categories do not quite conform to the definition of "nonprofit" that is used here. They are, however, satisfactory as a basis of some general impressions. As can be seen, nonprofit organizations employ about 30 percent of the nation's workforce. Exhibit 2–1 shows the changes in the number of employees over the past 10 years, indicating that health services and education employ the largest number of individuals, (although the data for these two categories may be somewhat overstated, since there was no way of eliminating profit-oriented organizations). It also should be pointed out that many teachers and health professionals are actually paid by governments.

Only the federal government has seen a *decline* in the number of employees. Despite this decline, the federal government remains by far the largest single nonprofit organization. Its immensity is difficult to comprehend. In 1982 it had 24,500 separate installations in the United States, on which 405,200 buildings were located. It had more office space than the total office space of the nation's 10 largest cities. Just to clean and maintain these offices took 40,000 employees. It operated 450,000 nonmilitary vehicles, consumed 104 million pounds of paper, and administered 2,000 programs. More than 60 percent of its 2.9 million *civilian* employees are "white collar," and 705,000

**Exhibit 2–1**
Estimated Employees in Nonprofit Organizations

| | *Number of Employees (millions)* | | *1980 as Percent of* |
|---|---|---|---|
| | *1980* | *1970* | *1970* |
| State and local government | 4.9 | 2.6 | 188% |
| Federal government | 4.7 | 5.7 | 82 |
| Health services | 7.3 | 4.4 | 166 |
| Education | 7.7 | 6.1 | 126 |
| Welfare and religions | 1.6 | 0.8 | 200 |
| Other | 3.2 | 1.5 | 213 |
| Total nonprofit | 29.4 | 21.1 | 139 |
| Total employed | 101.4 | 81.8 | 124 |
| Nonprofit as a percent of total | 29% | 26% | |

Note: Government employees exclude government personnel in health services and education. Military personnel are included in federal government.

Sources: U.S. Bureaus of Labor Statistics, *Employment and Earnings,* and U.S. Bureau of the Census, *Public Employment,* as reproduced in *Statistical Abstract of the United States, 1982–83.*

of these are classified as strictly administrative or clerical. The largest department in terms of employees is the Department of Defense, which in 1983 spent $260 billion and had 3 million military and civilian employees. The Department of Health and Human Services spent more money ($268 billion), primarily because of the sizable amounts it disbursed for transfer payments, such as those for welfare, social security, and research grants, but it has far fewer employees (160,000). There are about 80,000 government units (e.g. states, municipalities, etc.) in the United States below the federal level.

## SUMMARY OF CHARACTERISTICS

In the remainder of this chapter we discuss certain characteristics of nonprofit organizations that affect the management control process in such organizations. These characteristics are arranged under the following headings:

1. The absence of a *profit* measure.
2. Their tendency to be *service organizations.*
3. *Constraints* on goals and strategies.
4. Less dependence on *clients* for financial support.
5. The dominance of *professionals.*
6. Differences in *governance.*
7. Differences in *top management.*
8. Importance of *political influences.*
9. A *tradition* of inadequate management controls.

Of these, the first characteristic is the most important, and since it affects all nonprofit organizations, it will be discussed at some length. Each of the others affects many, but not all, nonprofit organizations, and the effects vary. They therefore are tendencies, rather than pervasive characteristics. Furthermore, again with the exception of the first, these characteristics are not unique to nonprofit organizations.

## THE PROFIT MEASURE

All organizations use resources to produce goods and services, that is, they use inputs to produce outputs. An organization's *effectiveness* is measured by the extent to which its outputs accomplish its goals, and its *efficiency* is measured by the relationship between inputs and outputs. In a profit-oriented organization the amount of profit provides an overall measure of both effectiveness and efficiency. In many nonprofit organizations, however, outputs cannot be measured in quantitative terms. Furthermore, many nonprofit organizations have multiple objectives, and there is no feasible way of combining the measures of the several outputs, each of which is intended to accomplish one of these objectives, into a single number that measures the overall effectiveness of the organization.

The absence of a single, satisfactory, overall measure of performance that is comparable to the profit measure is the most serious problem inhibiting the development of effective management control systems in nonprofit organizations. In order to appreciate the significance of this statement, we need to consider the usefulness and the limitations of the profit measure in profit-oriented organizations.

### Usefulness of the Profit Measure

The profit measure has the following advantages: (1) it provides a single criterion that can be used in evaluating proposed courses of action; (2) it permits a quantitative analysis of those proposals in which benefits can be directly compared with costs; (3) it provides a single, broad measure of performance; (4) it permits decentralization; and (5) it facilitates comparisons of performance among entities that are performing dissimilar functions. Each of these points is discussed below.

***1. Single Criterion.*** In a profit-oriented business, profit provides a way of focusing the considerations involved in choosing among proposed alternative courses of action. The analyst and the decision maker can address such questions as: Is the proposal likely to produce a satisfactory level of profits, or is it not? Is Alternative A likely to add more to profits than Alternative B?

The decision maker's analysis is not so simple and straightforward as the above might imply. Objectives other than profit usually must be taken into account, and many proposals cannot be analyzed in terms of their effect on profits. However, these qualifications do not invalidate the general point: profit provides a focus for decision making.

***2. Quantitative Analysis.*** The easiest type of proposal to analyze is one in which the estimated cost can be compared directly with the estimated benefits. Such an analysis is possible when the objective is profitability: profit is the difference between expense and revenue, and revenue is equated to benefits. By contrast, when the "benefit" is something other than revenue, the analysis is necessarily much more subjective.

***3. Broad Performance Measure.*** Profitability provides a measure that incorporates within it a great many separate aspects of performance. The best manager is not the one who generates the most sales volume, considered by itself; or the one who uses labor most efficiently; or the one who uses material most efficiently; or the one who has the best control of overhead; or the one who makes the best use of capital. Rather, the best manager is the one who does best, on balance, on the combination of all these separate activities. Profitability incorporates these separate elements. The key consideration is not the details of the operating statement; rather it is the "bottom line." This measure is valuable both to the managers themselves and to those who judge their performance. It provides managers with a current, frequent, easily understood signal as to how well they are doing, and it provides others with an objective basis for judging the managers' performance.

***4. Decentralization.*** Because profit-oriented organizations have a well-understood goal and because the performance of many individual managers can be measured in terms of their contribution toward that goal, top management can safely delegate many decisions to lower levels in the organization. The principal management control device associated with such delegation is the profit center, which is a division or other operating unit whose manager is responsible for both revenues and expenses. In recent years, most large companies and many small companies have decentralized decision making by creating profit centers.

***5. Comparison of Unlike Units.*** The profit measure permits a comparison of the performance of heterogeneous operations that is not possible with any other measure. Assuming that the accounting rules used to calculate profits are similar, and that the amount of assets employed is properly taken into account, then the performance of a department store can be compared with the performance of a paper mill in terms of the single criterion, which was the more profitable? Profitability therefore not only provides a way of combining heterogeneous elements of performance within a company; it also provides a way of making valid comparisons among organizations that have the same goal, the goal of profitability, even though the size, technology, products, and markets of these companies are quite different from one another.

## Measurement of Performance in Nonprofit Organizations

By definition, the goal of a nonprofit organization is something other than earning profits. Rather than attempting to widen the difference between outputs and inputs, the goal is to render as much service as possible with a given amount of resources, or to use as few resources as possible to render a given amount of service. In most situations, the ideal *financial* performance in a nonprofit organization is a *break-even* one; that is, in general and over the long run, outputs should equal inputs.

Many growing organizations, and in an inflationary economy many organizations of all types—nonprofit or profit-oriented—must earn an excess of revenue over expenses if they are to provide for both working capital needs and the replacement of fixed assets. Under these circumstances, it is quite legitimate for a nonprofit organization to earn a "profit."[2] Beyond this, though, the relationship between revenues and expenses in a nonprofit organization must be viewed differently from that in a profit-oriented company. If a hospital's revenues exceed expenses by more than is necessary to provide for working capital and asset-replacement needs, this is a sign that its prices are too high or that it is not rendering enough service for what it charges. If revenues are less than expenses, and if the expenses are reasonable, the hospital's services are being produced at a cost that is more than the value which people assign to these services.

Revenue also should be viewed differently in a nonprofit organization. Revenue in a hospital assists in measuring performance only if one accepts the premise that patient charges are a good surrogate for output, and in general they are not. Similarly, the amount of tuition revenue in a college does not reflect the overall effectiveness of the college, at least in the short run.

The reason is that most nonprofit organizations cannot measure their outputs in monetary terms. At best, the amount of patient charges in a hospital may measure the quantity of care given, but it does not measure the quality of patient care any more than tuition measures the quality of education. (It can be argued that if the quality of care is inadequate, physicians will not send patients to that hospital, or if potential students perceive a college to be ineffective they will be unwilling to attend it. In both instances, these decisions will be reflected by a decrease in revenues.)

However serious these inadequacies may be, though, the amount of revenue earned by a hospital or university is a much better measure of output than that available in many other types of nonprofit organizations which do not even sell their services. The output of the State Department is "diplomacy," for example. The output of the Department of Defense is "readiness to defend the interest of the United States." These are terms that are difficult to define

---

[2] See David W. Young, "Nonprofits Need Surplus Too," *Harvard Business Review*, January–February 1982.

and impossible to quantify. The problems of measuring output are discussed at length in Chapter 11.

It should be noted that the measurement problem relates to outputs, not to inputs. With minor exceptions, inputs (i.e., costs or expenses) can be measured as readily in a nonprofit organization as in a profit-oriented one. The exceptions—such as the problem of measuring the value of volunteers in a hospital—do not arise in most situations and rarely have a significant impact on the management control problem.

### Consequences of Absence of the Profit Measure

The absence of a measure that corresponds to profit makes the management control problem difficult in a nonprofit organization. The difficulties can be described by contrasting the situation in a nonprofit organization with the five uses of the profit measure described above.

***1. No Single Criterion.*** Since a nonprofit organization has multiple objectives and since these objectives usually cannot be expressed in quantitative terms, there often is no clear-cut objective function that can be used in analyzing proposed alternative courses of action. The management team of a profit-oriented company may debate vigorously the merits of a certain proposal, but generally the debate is carried on within the context of how the proposal will affect profits. The management team of a nonprofit organization often will not agree on the relative importance of various objectives; members will view a proposal in terms of the relative importance that they personally attach to the several objectives of the organization. Thus, in a municipality, all members of the management team may agree that the addition of a new pumper will add to the effectiveness of the fire department, but there may be disagreement on the importance of an expenditure to increase the effectiveness of the fire department as compared to a comparable expenditure on parks, or streets, or welfare. This greatly complicates the problem of decision making.

***2. Difficulty of Relating Costs and Benefits.*** For most important decisions in a nonprofit organization, there is no accurate way of estimating the relationship between inputs and outputs; that is, there is no way of judging what effect the expenditure of $X$ dollars will have on achieving the goals of the organization. Would the addition of another professor increase the value of the education which a college provides by an amount that exceeds the cost of that individual? Would the addition of another social service worker benefit the community by an amount that exceeds the additional cost? How much should be spent on a program to retrain unemployed persons? Issues of this type are difficult to analyze in quantitative terms because there is no good way of estimating the benefits of a given increment of spending.

New analytical techniques have been developed in recent years that have greatly facilitated decision making in profit-oriented companies, but these techniques all assume the existence of some causal, measurable relationship between costs and benefits. In the absence of such a relationship, these techniques cannot be used. (This is not to say that analytical techniques are inappropriate in nonprofit organizations. They are valuable in many types of problems, as will be discussed in chapter 8.)

***3. Difficulty of Measuring Performance.*** Since the principal goal of a nonprofit organization should be to render service, and since the amount and quality of service rendered cannot be measured numerically, performance with respect to goals is difficult and sometimes impossible to measure. The success of an educational institution depends more on the ability and diligence of its faculty than on such measurable characteristics as the number of courses offered or the ratio of faculty to students, for example.

Although financial performance should be at most a secondary goal, its importance is sometimes overemphasized. This can happen when managers with experience in profit-oriented companies become involved in nonprofit organizations. Accustomed to the primacy of profits, they frequently find it difficult to adjust to their new environment.

***4. Centralization of Decisions.*** If an organization has multiple goals and no good way of measuring performance in attaining these goals, it cannot delegate important decisions to lower level managers to the same extent that is feasible in profit-oriented organizations. For this reason, in government organizations many problems must be resolved in Washington or in state capitals rather than in regional or local offices. The paperwork and related procedures involved in sending problems to top management and in transmitting the decisions on these problems back to the field can be quite elaborate, and give rise to part of the criticism that is levied against "bureaucracy." Such criticism is often unwarranted because, in the absence of something corresponding to the profit measure, there is no feasible way of decentralizing.

***5. Comparison among Units.*** In nonprofit organizations, organizational units can be compared with one another only if they have similar functions. One fire department can be compared with other fire departments and one general hospital with other general hospitals, but there is no way of comparing the effectiveness of a fire department with the effectiveness of a hospital. As already noted, dissimilar profit-oriented companies can be compared with one another in terms of the common measure of profitability.

## SERVICE ORGANIZATIONS

Most nonprofit organizations are service organizations. A company that manufactures and sells tangible goods has certain advantages, from a control standpoint, that a service organization does not have.

Goods can be stored in inventory, awaiting a customer order. Services cannot be stored. If the facilities and personnel that are available to provide a service today are not used today, the potential revenue from that capability is lost forever.

Service organizations tend to be labor-intensive, requiring relatively little capital per unit of output; it is more difficult to control the work of a labor-intensive organization than that of an operation whose work flow is paced or dominated by machinery. Although some service organizations are becoming capital-intensive, as computers replace clerks or as technological advances alter the capital/labor ratio, nonprofit organizations can be expected to remain relatively labor-intensive, and thus to have more difficult management control problems than, say, manufacturing companies.

It is easy to keep track of the quantity of tangible goods, both during the production process and when the goods are sold, but it is not so easy to measure the quantity of many services. We can measure the number of patients that a physician treats in a day, for example, and even classify these visits by type of complaint, but this is by no means equivalent to measuring the amount of service the physician provides to each of these patients. For many services, including most of those furnished by government organizations, the amount rendered by an organizational unit can be measured only in the crudest terms, if at all: number of welfare cases visited, but not what happened during the visits; number of customs inspections conducted, but not how thoroughly they were conducted; number of complaints investigated by the police, but not the actual services rendered during these investigations; and so on.

The quality of tangible goods can be inspected, and in most cases the inspection can be performed before goods are released to the customer. If the goods are defective, there is physical evidence of the nature of the defect. The quality of a service cannot be inspected in advance. At best, it can be inspected during the time that the service is being rendered to the client. Judgments as to the adequacy of the quality of most services are subjective, however, since for the most part, measuring instruments and objective quality standards do not exist.

## CONSTRAINTS ON GOALS AND STRATEGIES

Within wide limits, a profit-oriented organization can decide on the industry or industries within which it is going to do business, it can choose any of a number of different ways of competing in its industry, and it can change these strategies if management decides that a change is desirable. Most nonprofit organizations have much less freedom of choice, and they tend to change their strategies slowly, if at all. A university adds or closes a professional school less frequently than a large corporation adds or divests an operating division. A municipality is expected to provide certain services for its residents: education, public safety, welfare, and so on. It can make decisions about the amount of these services, but in general it cannot decide to discontinue them.

Furthermore, many nonprofit organizations must provide services as directed by an outside agency, rather than as decided by their own management or governing board. Private social service organizations must conform to state or municipal guidelines. Many hospitals must obtain a "certificate of need" in order to engage in large-scale capital projects. Organizations receiving support from the government must conform to the terms of the contract or grant. Moreover, the charter of many nonprofit organizations specifies in fairly explicit terms the types of services that can be provided.

## SOURCE OF FINANCIAL SUPPORT

A profit-oriented company obtains its financial resources from sales of its goods and services. If the flow of these revenues is inadequate, the company does not survive. Thus, the market dictates the limits within which the management of a profit-oriented company can operate. A company cannot (or, at least, should not) make a product that the market does not want, and it cannot sell its products unless their selling prices are in line with what the market is willing to pay.

Some nonprofit organizations also obtain all, or substantially all, their financial resources from sales revenues. This is the case with most community hospitals (as contrasted with teaching hospitals), with private schools and colleges that depend entirely on tuition from students, and with research organizations whose resources come from contracts for specific research projects. Such organizations may be called *client-supported* organizations. They are subject to the forces of the marketplace in much the same way as are profit-oriented organizations in the same industry: proprietary hospitals and colleges and profit-oriented research organizations.

Other nonprofit organizations receive a significant amount of financial support from sources other than revenues from services rendered. These may be called *public-supported organizations.* In these organizations there is no direct connection between the services received and the resources provided. Individuals receive essentially the same services from a governmental unit whether they pay high taxes or low taxes. Unrestricted grants by a government or by a foundation are not made because of services provided to the grantor. Appropriations made by a state legislature to a university, a hospital, or other organization are not related directly to the services received by the legislature from these organizations. Contributions provide financial resources for operating an organization, either directly or, in the case of endowment funds, through earnings on the endowment. In summary, sales revenues result from an exchange transaction; the organization furnishes goods or services in exchange for financial resources. In each of the above cases, there is no such direct relationship.

## Characteristics of Public-Supported Organizations

From a management control viewpoint, the most obvious difference between a client-supported organization and a public-supported organization is that in the former the amount of revenues in a period provide a good approximation of the quantity of output delivered, whereas in the latter there can be no corresponding measure of output. Other differences are also important.

In almost all instances, client-supported organizations want more customers, since more customers imply more revenues, and more revenues imply greater success. In public-supported organizations there is no such relationship between the number of clients and the success of the organization. If the amount of its available resources is fixed by appropriations (as in the case of government agencies) or by income from endowment or annual giving (as is the case with many educational, religious, and charitable organizations), additional clients may place a strain on resources. In a profit-oriented, or a client-supported nonprofit organization, therefore, the new client is an opportunity to be vigorously pursued. In some public-supported organizations, the new client may be only a burden, to be accepted with misgivings.

This negative attitude toward clients gives rise to complaints about the poor service and surly attitude of "bureaucrats." Clients of client-supported organizations tend to hear "please" and "thank you" more often than clients of public-supported organizations.

In some public-supported organizations, the contrast with the motivations associated with market forces is even stronger. A welfare organization should be motivated to decrease its clientele, rather than add to it; that is, it should seek ways of rehabilitating clients, thus removing them from the welfare roles. The Small Business Administration should work to change high-risk businesses into low-risk businesses which will no longer need the special services that the SBA provides. The idea that an organization should deliberately set out to reduce its clientele is foreign to the thinking of profit-oriented managers.

Competition provides a powerful incentive to use resources wisely. If a firm in a competitive industry permits its costs to get out of control, its product line to become obsolete, or its quality to decrease, its profits will decline. A public-supported organization has no such automatic danger signal.

Because the importance of what the organization does is not measured by demand in the marketplace, managers of public-supported organizations tend to be influenced by their personal convictions of what is important. As a substitute for the market mechanism for allocating resources, managers compete with one another for available resources. The physics department, the English department, and the library, all try to get as large a slice as possible of the college budget pie. In responding to these requests, senior management tries to judge what services clients should have, or what is best in the public interest, rather than what the market wants. In the public interest, Amtrak provides railroad service to areas where it is not economically warranted; similarly, the U.S. Postal Service maintains rural post offices.

Just as the success of a client-supported organization depends on its ability to satisfy clients, so the success of a public-supported organization depends on its ability to satisfy those who provide resources. Thus, a state university maintains close contact with the state legislature, and a private university may place somewhat more emphasis on athletics than the faculty thinks is warranted in order to satisfy contributors to the alumni fund. Furthermore, acceptance of support from the public carries with it a responsibility for accounting to the public, frequently to a greater degree than exists in a profit-oriented organization.

Nonprofit educational and health care institutions tend to look down on proprietary (i.e., profit-oriented) schools and hospitals, but the fact is that proprietary schools and hospitals must meet the needs of the market in order to survive. These institutions generally have no endowment and no income from alumni fund drives, yet they survive. Some nonprofit colleges in financial straits might learn from the practices that proprietary schools have developed. Similarly, many investor-owned hospitals have management control systems that could be highly instructive to nonprofit hospitals.

## PROFESSIONALS

In many nonprofit organizations, the important people are professionals (physicians, scientists, combat commanders, teachers, pilots, artists, ministers). Professionals often have motivations that are inconsistent with good resource utilization, and their success as perceived by their professional colleagues reflects these motivations. Some implications of this are given below.

Professionals are motivated by dual standards: those of their organizations and those of their professional colleagues. The former are related to organizational objectives; the latter may be inconsistent with organizational objectives. The rewards for achieving organizational objectives may be less potent than those for achieving professional objectives.

Professionals who are departmental managers tend to work only part time on management activities, spending a substantial part of their time doing the same work as their subordinates. The chief of surgery in a hospital does surgery. The chairman of the physics department in a university teaches and does research in physics. In organizations not dominated by professionals, management tends to be a full-time job, and managers do not do the same type of work that their subordinates do.

Many professionals, by nature, prefer to work independently. Examples are academicians, researchers, and physicians. Because the essence of management is getting things done through people, professionals with such a temperament are not naturally suited to the role of managers. For this and other reasons, managers in professional organizations are less likely to come up through the ranks than is the case in profit-oriented organizations.

Although the leadership job in a responsibility center of a nonprofit organization may require more management skills than professional skills, tradition often requires that the manager of such a unit be a professional. Many military support units are managed by military officers, even though a civilian might be a better qualified manager. Traditionally, the head of a research organization was a scientist; the president of a university, a professor; the head of a hospital, a physician. This tradition seems to be diminishing, however.

In a professional organization, the *professional quality* of the people is of primary importance and other considerations are secondary. Therefore, managers of professionals spend much of their time recruiting good people and then seeing to it that they are kept happy. The manager has correspondingly less time available for the aspects of the job that relate to efficiency. Also, in a professional organization, promotion is geared to the criteria established by the profession rather than those of the organization, per se, and thus may not place much emphasis on efficiency and effectiveness of the organization as a whole. These criteria do not always accurately reflect the individual's worth to the organization. Moreover, professionals tend to need a longer time to prove their worth than managers in profit-oriented organizations.

Professional education does not usually include education in management and quite naturally stresses the importance of the profession rather than of management. For this and other reasons, professionals tend to underestimate the importance of the management function. Bluntly, they tend to look down on managers.

> ***Example:*** At a university faculty meeting, the following motion was proposed, seriously debated, and almost adopted: "To effect economy and to bring back financial health to the University, be it resolved that the administration should be abolished and that a committee of faculty members should administer this University without an increase in salary."[3]

Financial incentives tend to be less effective with professional people either because they consider their current compensation to be adequate or because their primary satisfaction comes from their work. In Thoreau's words, the professional "hears a different drummer."

Professionals tend to give inadequate weight to the financial implication of their decisions. Many physicians, for example, feel that no limit should be placed on the amount spent to save a human life, although in a world of limited resources such an attitude is unrealistic.

## GOVERNANCE

Although the statement that shareholders control a corporation is an oversimplification, shareholders do have the ultimate authority. They may exercise this authority only in times of crisis, but it nevertheless is there. The movement of stock prices is an immediate and influential indication of what shareholders think of their management. In profit-oriented organizations, policy and man-

[3] Personal communication from John W. Field.

agement responsibilities are vested in the board of directors, which derives its power from the shareholders. In turn, the board delegates power to the president, who serves at the board's pleasure, acts as the board's agent in the administration of the organization, and who is replaced if there are serious differences of interest or opinion.

## Governing Boards in Nonprofit Organizations

In many nonprofit organizations the corresponding line of responsibility is often not clear. There are no shareholders, members of the governing body are seldom paid for their services, and they may be chosen for political reasons rather than for their ability to exercise sound judgment about the organization's activities. Although the governing body supposedly represents either the interest of the general public, or in some cases the interest of that part of the public that has provided major financial support, it frequently is insufficiently informed about major issues facing the organization, and its decisions therefore are not always optimal. Furthermore, what course of action best represents the public interest is much more difficult to decide than the course of action that is most likely to increase profits in a profit-oriented company. Thus, governing boards tend to be less influential in non-profit organizations than in profit-oriented companies.

The governing board of a nonprofit organization, as an absolute minimum, has the responsibility to act when the organization is in trouble. Since there is no profit measure to provide an obvious warning, the personal appraisal by board members of the health of the organization is much more important in a nonprofit organization than in a profit-oriented corporation. In order to have a sound basis for such an appraisal, board members need to spend a considerable amount of time learning what is going on in the organization, and they need to have enough expertise to understand the significance of what they learn.

Many governing boards do an inadequate job of this. There is not even a general recognition that this is the board's responsibility. In universities, for example, a widely-quoted maxim is that "The function of a Board is to hire a president and then back him, period."[4] In hospitals, boards frequently are dominated by physicians who are qualified to oversee the quality of care but who may neither have the expertise, nor are willing to devote the time, to check up on the effectiveness and efficiency of hospital management. In government organizations at all levels, auditors check on compliance with the statutory rules on spending, but there are few oversight agencies that

[4] Perhaps because the academic environment nourishes writing, more has been written about college and university trustees than about other types of governing boards. Publications of the Association of Governing Boards of Colleges and Universities, One Dupont Circle, Washington, D.C., contain much material about the governance of colleges and universities. The classic book is still Beardsley Ruml and Donald H. Morrison, *Memo to a College Trustee* (New York: McGraw-Hill, 1959).

pay attention to how well management performs its functions. Although legislative committees look for headline-making sins, many committees do not have the staff or the inclination to arrive at an informed judgment on management performance.

A detailed analysis of 7,000 board actions recorded in the minutes of over 100 meetings by 19 trustee boards of public colleges and universities showed that only 6 percent of the decisions were planning decisions. Most actions were routine decisions on administrative and operational matters, and about 25 percent of these were ratifications of decisions previously made by the administration.[5]

## Government Organizations

In government organizations, external influences tend to come from a number of sources, leading to a diffusion of power. Some of the reasons for this are given below.

In state and federal governments there is a division of authority among executive, legislative, and judicial branches. When there are coordinate branches of government, there are often conflicting judgments about objectives and the means of attaining them. In a profit-oriented company the board of directors and the chief executive officer usually have similar objectives.

There may also be a vertical division of authority among levels of government (federal, state, and local), each responsible for facets of the same problem. For example, the federal government finances major and many minor highways, and local governments construct and maintain other highways.

Agencies, or units within agencies, may have their own special-interest clienteles (e.g., Maritime Administration and shipping interests) with political power that is stronger than that of the chief executive of the agency.

Top management authority may be divided, particularly in those states where the expenditure authority is vested in committees of independently elected officials, and in local governments administered by commissions whose members each administer a particular segment of the organization (e.g., streets or health). Elected officials, such as the attorney general, the treasurer, the secretary of state, or the director of education may manage their organizations fairly independently. The mayor of Los Angeles has much narrower responsibility than does the mayor of New York because the county organization in California is responsible for many services that are performed by the city organization in New York.

The bureaucracy is often insulated from top management by virtue of job security and rules, and career civil servants may know that they will

[5] This study was conducted by the Center for Research and Development in Higher Education at the University of California, Berkeley, and summarized by the assistant director of that organization, James G. Partridge, in *AGB Reports* (Berkeley, Calif.: Association of Governing Boards of Universities and Colleges, March 1974), pp. 20–27.

outlast the term of office of the elected or appointed chief executive. If pet projects cannot be sold to the current boss, their sponsors may bide their time and hope to sell them to the next one. Conversely, if they dislike a new policy, they may be able to drag their heels long enough so that a new management will take over and possibly rescind the policy.

This fragmentation of authority complicates management control. A particularly significant consequence is that the public administrator comes to depend upon "political" power to influence those who cannot be directly controlled. Consequently, managers must manage their political credit as well as their financial credit; they must measure the political cost and benefit of alternative choices, as well as the financial cost and benefit. On the other hand, there are some strong compensating advantages to divided authority. Particularly in the coordinate government, each branch can serve as a check on the activities of the other branches.

In summary, in many nonprofit organizations there is no single outside group to which the management is clearly accountable. Even in those organizations in which such a group exists, there may not be a similarity between the objectives of the management and those of the outside group that is close to the similarity that exists when both groups are essentially interested in profits.

## TOP MANAGEMENT

Most organizations have a unitary boss, the chief executive officer, or CEO. In a very few organizations, authority is divided between two persons, or among a small top-management group, but these are exceptions to the rule and usually are not successful.[6] In most business organizations there is no doubt that the chief executive officer has responsibility for everything. On that person's desk, as was on President Truman's, there is at least figuratively the sign, "The Buck Stops Here."

In some nonprofit organizations the chief executive officer does not have such overall responsibility. The secretary of state typically has responsibility for foreign policy, but not for what is called the "administration" of the State Department. ("Administration," as used here, seems to mean the operation of the support functions of the State Department, rather than a term that is synonymous with management, which is the usual context.)

Presidents of universities may say that they are the leaders of a "community of scholars," and that they should not soil their hands by becoming involved in other aspects of university management, particularly the "business" aspects (although this attitude is much less prevalent today than it was a generation ago). The minister of a church may feel that it is inappropriate to become

[6] According to *Newsweek* (February 26, 1973), the Corcoran Gallery of Art in Washington, D.C., for four years was managed by two coequal persons, an "artistic director" and an "administrative director." This arrangement ended in 1972 when the two directors exchanged punches in public and then both resigned.

involved in temporal matters. Hospitals typically have two lines of authority: administrative and medical, and it generally is difficult for the CEO to become involved in management of the medical staff. That responsibility rests with the medical director.

In some organizations, top-management responsibility is divided between two persons. The Number One person is "Mr. (or Ms.) Outside," responsible for overall policy formulation and for relations with the outside world; the Number Two person is "Mr. (or Ms.) Inside," responsible for operations. This is the essential idea of the British parliamentary system; the Number One person is appointed by the party in power, and the Number Two person, the permanent undersecretary, is responsible for carrying out policies for whatever party is in power. Such a division of responsibility exists to a certain extent in U.S. government agencies, but in general it is not as well accepted or as widespread here as in the United Kingdom. A two-headed organization can be effective if, but only if, there is a close relationship between the two persons, and a clear understanding that Number One will not overrule Number Two in disputes relating to operations.

### Inadequate Compensation

A characteristic of many public-supported organizations is the relatively low compensation of top management. The reasons for this difference in management compensation are not entirely clear. It probably reflects a lack of understanding by the public and by those who control funds as to the importance of the management function and the importance of compensation as a motivating device. The problem of inadequate compensation is compounded by the widespread belief that nonprofit organizations should not use bonuses or other forms of incentive compensation.

## POLITICAL INFLUENCES

Many nonprofit organizations are political; that is, they are responsible to the electorate or to a legislative body that presumably represents the electorate. Some of the consequences of this status are discussed below.

### Necessity for Reelection

In government organizations, decisions result from multiple, often conflicting, pressures. In part, these political pressures are inevitable—and up to a point desirable—substitutes for the forces of the marketplace. Elected officials cannot function if they are not reelected. In order to be reelected, they must, at least up to a point, advocate the perceived needs of their constituents, even though satisfying these needs may not be in the best interests of the larger body that they are supposed to represent. Moreover, in order to gain support for programs that are important to them, elected officials may support certain of their colleagues' programs, even though they personally do not favor them. This "logrolling" phenomenon is also present in profit-oriented organizations, but to a lesser extent.

### Public Visibility

In a democratic society the press and public feel that they have a right to know everything there is to know about a government organization. In the federal government, this feeling is recognized by "freedom of information" statutes, but the channels for distributing this information are not always unbiased. Although some media stories that describe mismanagement are fully justified, others tend to be exaggerated, or to give inadequate recognition to the fact that mistakes are inevitable in any organization. By contrast, mismanagement in profit-oriented companies is publicized only when there is substantial fraud, a shareholders' suit, or other highly unusual occurrences. In order to reduce the opportunities for unfavorable media stories, government managers take steps to reduce the amount of sensitive, controversial information that flows through the formal management control system. This lessens the usefulness of the system. The number of problems to which formal analytical techniques are applied is thereby reduced because such techniques result in reports that may be open to public inspection.

### Multiple External Pressures

The electoral process, with institutionalized public review through news media and opposing political parties, results in a wider variety of pressures on managers of public organizations than on managers of private organizations, whether nonprofit or profit. There is more controversy about the decisions of elected public officials than those of business managers. In the absence of profit as a clear-cut measure of performance, these pressures may be erratic and illogical, or influenced by momentary fads. These pressures tend to induce an emphasis on short-term goals, and on program decisions that are not based on careful analysis.

### Inadequate External Pressures

Stockholders demand satisfactory earnings, whereas the public and governing bodies of nonprofit organizations tend to exert less pressure for good resource utilization. In part this is because of the difficulty of measuring performance, and in part it is because of the diffused responsibility and multiple pressures already mentioned.

### Legislative Restrictions

Government organizations must operate within statutes enacted by the legislative branch, which are much more restrictive than the charter and by-laws of corporations, and which often prescribe detailed practices. In many instances it is relatively difficult to change these statutes.

### Inadequate Management

When the Number One person in an organization is elected by the voters, the person is often chosen for reasons other than ability as a manager. A cabinet officer or other high-ranking appointed official is also likely to be selected for reasons other than managerial ability; the official may be more skilled in the process of formulating broad agency policies than in executing policies. The Number One person in an agency usually spends much time on political or politically related activities. In concept, these management inadequacies of the Number One person could be overcome by selecting a fully qualified manager as the Number Two person (e.g., the undersecretary) and giving that person full responsibility for the operation of the agency, but this is not always done.

### Management Turnover

In some public organizations top management tends to change rapidly because of administration changes, political shifts, military orders, and managers who only dabble in government jobs. Each change requires a "learning lead time," and many of them result in changes in priorities. This rapid turnover results in short-run plans and programs which produce quickly visible results, rather than substantive longer-range programs.

### Civil Service

Although there is a widespread belief that Civil Service regulations operate to inhibit good management control, it is by no means clear that Civil Service regulations are essentially different from personnel regulations in some large companies. The best case in support of this view of the inhibiting effects of Civil Service can be made in certain state and municipal governments. In many such organizations, Civil Service laws effectively inhibit the use of both the carrot and the stick. A Civil Service syndrome develops as a result of the tacit *caveat* signaled by the system structure: "You need not produce success; you merely need to avoid making major mistakes." This attitude is a major barrier to improving organizational effectiveness.

On the other hand, Civil Service regulations in many government organizations may be no more dysfunctional than are union regulations and norms in profit-oriented organizations. When one considers the restrictive and inefficient union rules regarding work assignments, such as the number of engineers and other personnel aboard trains, or the division between electricians and plumbers on a joint repair job, it appears that at least in some situations the Civil Service environment may be quite comparable. One difference is that union rules mostly affect those near the bottom of the organization, whereas Civil Service rules affect managers as well.

## TRADITION

In the 19th century, accounting was primarily *fiduciary* accounting; that is, its purpose was to keep track of the funds that were entrusted to an organization to ensure that they were spent honestly. In the 20th century, accounting in business organizations has assumed much broader functions. It furnishes useful information about the business both to interested outside parties and to management. Nonprofit organizations have been slow to adopt 20th century accounting and management control concepts and practices. This section contains a brief review of the development and status of management control in nonprofit organizations.

The principal concepts and techniques that distinguish modern management control from fiduciary accounting, arranged approximately in the chronological order in which they became generally accepted by business, are (1) the accrual concept, (2) cost accounting, (3) standard costs and variance analysis, (4) budgeting, and (5) responsibility accounting.

### The Accrual Concept

A simple but fundamental idea of modern accounting is the accrual concept, and particularly the emphasis on expense measurement. Other new techniques would not be possible without it. Essentially, the expense focus means that accounting should measure the cost of *resources consumed,* as contrasted with *resources purchased* (which is the "obligation" concept) or with *liabilities incurred* (which is the "expenditure" concept) or with *checks drawn* (which is the "cash" concept). Many federal government agencies and many state and local governments continue to emphasize the obligation concept, many other nonprofit organizations focus on the expenditure concept, and some still account on a cash basis. With the notable exception of hospitals, relatively few nonprofit organizations focus on the measurement of expenses.

In the federal government, the desirability of shifting to the accrual concept was suggested in the First Hoover Commission report in 1949[7] and was emphasized in the Second Hoover Commission report in 1955.[8] As a result of the 1955 report, legislation requiring that accrual accounting be adopted "as soon as feasible" was enacted (Public Law 84–863), but many agencies still have not done so. Full value cannot be obtained from any of the other new concepts and techniques until accrual accounting is adopted.

In state and local governments the inadequacies of accounting systems

[7] U.S. Commission on Organization of the Executive Branch of the Government (1947–1949), *Budgeting and Accounting* (Washington, D.C.: Government Printing Office, 1949).

[8] U.S. Commission on Organization of the Executive Branch of the Government (1953–1955), *Budgeting and Accounting* (Washington, D.C.: Government Printing Office, 1955).

came to widespread public attention when New York City almost went bankrupt in the early 1970s, and it was discovered that accounting records giving an accurate picture of the city's financial situation did not exist. Similar inadequacies were discovered in other cities.[9] In a 1973 report the controller of the state of New York pointed out that accrual accounting had been recommended by a legislative committee as long ago as 1937, but the recommendation had not been adopted.[10] He went on to say that the management control inadequacies that resulted from this are as bad currently as they were then. In this report, he once more strongly recommended the adoption of accrual accounting. Nevertheless, until 1983, the state of New York continued to account essentially on a cash basis.

### Cost Accounting

Early cost accounting systems were used principally for calculating selling prices. It therefore is not surprising that these systems were not adopted by most nonprofit organizations, since many do not set selling prices for the services that they render, and those that do set selling prices, until recently, did not base these prices on a careful analysis of costs. In recent years, businesses have found cost information useful for other purposes, but those nonprofit organizations that had not developed even rudimentary cost systems did not have the means of taking advantage of these new developments. Also, if an organization does not use accrual accounting, its cost accounting system is necessarily "statistical" in nature; that is, it is not tied to the basic debit-and-credit accounting records. Without the discipline that accrual accounting provides, cost information is likely to be so inaccurate as to be useless.

### Standard Costs and Variance Analysis

Standard costs are intended primarily as a control device, but they also permit simplifications in recordkeeping systems. They are widely used in business but are used scarcely at all in nonprofit organizations. Since standard cost systems are built on a foundation of conventional cost accounting, and since they were originally used in manufacturing organizations rather than in service organizations, this nonuse is not surprising. The analysis of variances between standard costs and actual costs according to the cause of the variance (e.g., volume, mix, price, efficiency) is a fairly recent development in business practice, although it has been described in textbooks for 30 years or more. Such

[9] See Coopers & Lybrand and the University of Michigan, *Financial Disclosure Practices of American Cities* (New York: Coopers & Lybrand, 1976); and Sidney Davidson et al., *Financial Reporting by State and Local Government Units* (Chicago: The Center for Management of Public and Nonprofit Enterprise, Graduate School of Business, University of Chicago, 1977).

[10] Arthur Levitt, "Discipline in the Fiscal Process," *New York State Comptroller's Studies on Issues in Public Finance,* Study no. 3 (September 1973).

an analysis provides a powerful control tool, which is not available to organizations that do not have standard costs.

The classification of cost elements between those that vary with volume and those that do not has facilitated the analysis of many business problems. Although fluctuations in volume are not as prevalent in nonprofit organizations as they are in business, there are many situations in which such a separation would be useful. In nonprofit organizations such a separation is rarely made, however.

### Budgeting

Budgeting in government has been around longer than budgeting in most businesses. It was started by the New York Bureau of Municipal Research in 1906, spread fairly rapidly to municipal and state governments, and was adopted by the federal government in 1921. In the early government budgets, the fiduciary attitude was dominant. The budget set forth how much an agency was permitted to obligate for personnel, supplies, travel, and similar "object classifications," rather than emphasizing the programs that should be undertaken and the amount that should be spent for each program. This "object class" or "line-item" approach still dominates many state and municipal budgets and many parts of the federal budget, although some agencies have successfully broken away from it. Moreover, many agencies continue to regard the budgetary process solely as a device for obtaining money (which is part of its function), rather than as a management tool to guide and control the work of the agency (which is an equally important part).

### Responsibility Accounting

Responsibility accounting has come into widespread use in business only within the last 30 years. As described more fully in Chapter 1, it focuses on the inputs and outputs of responsibility centers and provides a powerful tool for communicating with, motivating, and measuring the performance of the managers of such centers. Related developments of profit centers, investment centers, and transfer pricing are even more recent. Some nonprofit organizations have adopted these techniques in recent years, but adoption has not been as rapid as in business.

### Barriers to Progress

Since a nonprofit organization lacks the semiautomatic control that is provided by the profit mechanism, it needs a good management control system even more than a business does. Why have many such organizations, particularly government organizations, lagged behind? For government, there seem to be three principal explanations. First, for many years, there was a prevalent attitude to the effect that the differences between government and business were such that government could not use the management control techniques developed by business. Articles to this effect written by eminent authorities appeared as recently as the 1950s, and this attitude continues to be implicit in some texts on government accounting. Second, the Congress, and particularly the House Committee on Appropriations, having become thoroughly accustomed to a certain budget format, is reluctant to shift to a new format. Because of the importance of the budget, this affects the whole management control system. A similar problem exists in many states. In part the reluctance is based on simple inertia, but it also reflects a suspicion—a generally unwarranted suspicion—that the change is an attempt by the executive branch to "put something over" on the legislative branch. Third, many career officials appreciate the fact that a good management control system is two-edged: it provides new information for management, but it also provides new information for outside agencies—the Office of Management and Budget and the Congress. These officials are not anxious that outside agencies have access to the new and better information. In this regard, it is important to note that the second reason is based on the premise that the proposed formats provide poorer information, while the third reason is based on the premise that they provide better information; both cannot be correct.

## DIFFERENCES AMONG ORGANIZATIONS

The description in this chapter is intended to apply to nonprofit organizations in general; but, as emphasized at the beginning, the characteristics enumerated do not fit all such organizations equally well. In this section an attempt is made to relate the description to each of the principal nonprofit "industries." These are, of course, broad brush generalizations to which many exceptions can be found in individual organizations.

### Health Care Organizations

Hospitals, nursing homes, health maintenance organizations, clinics, and similar health care organizations closely resemble profit-oriented organizations. Indeed, were it not for the difference in objectives—service rather than profit—their management control problems would be similar to those of their profit-oriented counterparts. There are few differences between a voluntary hospital and a proprietary hospital. These organizations do have fewer competitive pressures than the typical business; most of their revenue is received from third parties (Blue Cross, insurance companies, and the government) rather than directly from clients; they are dominated by professionals; and they have no clear-cut line of responsibility to a defined group of owners. Spurred on by public concern about the rising cost of health care and by the necessity for justifying their fees on the basis of a plausible measurement of cost, and led by the American Hospital Association, the Hospital Financial Management Association, and the Congress of Hospital Administrators, many hospitals have made dramatic improvements in their cost accounting systems in recent years. Fewer, however, have improved their management control systems. Most clinics and health maintenance organizations have similarly underdeveloped management control systems.

## Educational Organizations

Private colleges and universities whose tuition approximates the cost of education also resemble their profit-oriented counterparts. To the extent that they are supported by contributions and endowment earnings, however, the relationship between tuition revenues and the cost of services is less close. As is the case with hospitals, they are dominated by professionals, and their governing boards tend to be relatively uninfluential. They are subject to strong competitive pressures, and these pressures will increase because of the decline in student population that is inevitable in the remainder of this century. In recent years, under the leadership of the National Association of College and University Business Officers, many of them have made substantial improvements in their management control systems.

State colleges and universities are supported primarily by appropriations from state legislatures. Although these appropriations may be based on a formula that takes into account the number of students or the number of credit hours, they are not the same as fees charged to clients because the individual student (or parent) does not make the decision that the education received is worth the amount charged. In other respects, they are similar to private colleges and universities. In recent years, the legislative oversight bodies of some states have paid much attention to the financial management of their colleges and universities, and this has led to great improvements in their management control systems.

Public elementary and secondary schools generally use an accounting system developed under the auspices of the U.S Office of Education, which is urged as a condition of federal support. Although revised in the late 1970s, it continues to be an inadequate system, and management control is hampered by its inadequacies. A few communities have developed excellent systems on their own initiative.

## Membership Organizations

Membership organizations are those whose purpose is to render service to their members. They include religious organizations, labor unions, trade associations, professional associations, fraternal organizations, social and country clubs, cemetery societies, and political organizations. To the extent that they are supported by dues from the membership, fluctuations in the amount of such dues is an indication of the perceived value of services rendered by the organization, even though there is not a direct connection between an individual's dues and the services received by that individual. Many are dominated by professionals and have weak governing boards. Certain membership organizations, such as religious organizations and certain labor organizations, face strong competitive pressures; others, such as professional associations, have no effective competition.

Until recently, many religious organizations have had notoriously weak management control systems. In recent years, however, several denominations have developed good systems and have encouraged their use at local levels. Religious organizations have a particularly difficult problem in deciding on the programs to be undertaken and in measuring the value of services rendered. ("Souls saved per pew hour preached" is not a feasible measurement.)

### Human Service and Arts Organizations

Human service organizations include family and child service agencies, the Red Cross, scouting and similar youth organizations, and various charitable organizations. Arts organizations include museums, public broadcasting stations, symphony orchestras, theaters, and ballet companies.

With some notable exceptions, these organizations rely heavily on public support, either from the government or from contributions by individuals, companies, and foundations. Their revenues therefore do not directly measure the value of services provided to clients. Some are dominated by professionals; others are not. Those who provide support tend to exercise an increasing amount of influence over the financial affairs of these organizations.

In recent years, considerable improvements have been made in the management control systems of these organizations, primarily because of the influence of such organizations as the United Way of America and professional associations of museums and broadcasting stations, but significant opportunities for further improvement remain.

### The Federal Government

Except for certain businesslike activities, such as the U.S. Postal Service, the federal government does not receive fees from clients. Its goals are multiple and fuzzy, and the value of its services is especially difficult to measure.

Governments are subject to external power influences and political influences more than is the case with other nonprofit organizations. These forces make its management control problem especially difficult. Furthermore, many federal agencies are unique (there is only one State Department), so there is no basis for comparing performance with other units. Some improvements have occurred in recent years, but, as illustrated by the fact that accrual accounting is still not fully implemented, much remains to be done.

### State and Local Governments

Collectively, state and local governments are by far the largest category of nonprofit organizations. They are subject to a variety of external power influences and to political influences, and therefore have a difficult management control problem.

Generally, their revenues are not directly related to services provided to clients. Although the person whose house is on fire is a "client" in one sense, the main function of the fire department is to protect the whole community. Proposals for specific programs are often political in nature and not subject to economic analysis. The objectives of these organizations are difficult to define in ways that permit measurement of their attainment. (What is adequate "fire protection" or "police protection"?)

Although management control in state and local government units is inherently difficult, good systems are likewise especially necessary. Such systems currently do not now exist in most governmental units, although there are a few notable exceptions. Development of adequate systems has been greatly hampered by the forces of tradition. Many government units keep their accounts solely on a cash receipts and disbursements basis, a practice that has been obsolete since the 19th century. Forces now at work, including public dissatisfaction because of recent revelations of poor management and pressures of the federal government in implementing the revenue-sharing program, seem likely to lead to improvements in the relatively near future.

## CONCLUSION

The characteristics of nonprofit organizations described in this chapter can be grouped into two classes, one technical and the other behavioral.

The first class consists of matters described under the heading the profit measure, that is, the difficulty of measuring outputs and the relationships between inputs and outputs. The important observation that can be made about this class is that the problems described therein are inherent in the fact that the organization is nonprofit. Great improvements in output measurement are indeed possible, and the problem is so important that a considerable effort to make such improvements is worthwhile; but it must be recognized at the outset that the resulting system will never provide as good a basis for planning or for measuring performance as exists in profit-oriented organizations.

The second class consists of all the other topics. The significance of these behavioral characteristics is twofold: (1) most of the behavioral factors that impede good management control can be overcome by proper understanding and education; and (2) unless these other problems *are* overcome, the improvements in the technical area are likely to have little real impact on the management control process.

## SUGGESTED ADDITIONAL READINGS

Anthony, Robert N. *Financial Accounting in Nonbusiness Organizations.* Stamford, Conn.: Financial Accounting Standards Board, 1978.

Clark, Robert C. "Does the Nonprofit Form Fit the Hospital Industry?" *Harvard Law Review,* May 1980, pp. 1417–89.

Ramanathan, Kavasseri V. *Management Control in Nonprofit Organizations.* New York: John Wiley & Sons, 1982.

Case 2–1

# BOSTON SYMPHONY ORCHESTRA, INC.*

For several years prior to 1982, Boston Symphony Orchestra, Inc. (BSO) operated at a deficit. For the four years 1978–81, the deficit totaled $4.5 million, an amount that had to be withdrawn from capital funds. Were it not for one special circumstance—a fund drive conducted in connection with BSO's 100th Anniversary in 1982—capital funds would have been exhausted within a decade if the deficit continued at the 1978–81 rate.

## Background

BSO owned two properties. One was Symphony Hall in Boston. The orchestra performed there, except in the summer and when it performed in other cities. When Symphony Hall was not needed for performances, rehearsals, or recording sessions, it often was rented to other organizations.

The other property was Tanglewood, a large complex in the Berkshire Hills, about 130 miles from Boston. The orchestra performed there for nine weeks in the summer. Several hundred students participated in training programs at Tanglewood each summer. (The principal buildings at Tanglewood were not winterized and could be used only in the summer.) In the summer of 1982, attendance at Tanglewood totaled 308,000.

In 1981–82, in addition to Tanglewood, the orchestra gave 107 concerts, of which 13 were in foreign countries and 14 in other American cities. The Boston Pops Orchestra, formed from symphony orchestra players, gave 63 concerts in Symphony Hall and 7 free concerts at an outdoor concert shell in Boston, known as the Esplanade. At the July 4 Esplanade concert, a Boston institution, attendance was estimated at 200,000. Nearly all orchestra and pops performances were sold out.

Management estimated that Symphony hall was used on 165 evenings a year, of which 130 were for BSO concerts and rehearsals, and 35 were for rentals to outside groups. In the afternoons there were 22 symphony orchestra concerts and approximately 25 rentals to outside groups. The orchestra used the hall on 125 to 150 afternoons annually for rehearsals, recording, or television sessions.

## Proposed Plan

The "BSO/100" fund drive raised about $20 million of capital funds (primarily endowment) over a five-year period. Management recognized, however, that the special stimulus of the 100th Anniversary could not be counted on to provide the funds needed to balance the budget in the future. Alternative ways of financing operations were discussed, and the trustees eventually agreed

* This case was prepared by Robert N. Anthony, Harvard Business School.

**Exhibit 1**

BOSTON SYMPHONY ORCHESTRA, INC.
Analysis of Revenue Contribution to Fixed Costs
For the Year Ended August 31,
($000)

| | *Actual* | | | | | *Projections* | | | | | | | |
|---|---|---|---|---|---|---|---|---|---|---|---|---|---|
| | 1978 | 1979 | 1980 | 1981 | 1982 | 1983 | 1984 | 1985 | 1986 | 1987 | 1988 | 1989 | 1990 |
| Fixed costs: | | | | | | | | | | | | | |
| Artistic | 3,902 | 4,243 | 4,514 | 5,176 | 5,608 | | | | | | | | |
| Facilities | 920 | 1,005 | 1,160 | 1,318 | 1,348 | | | | | | | | |
| Administration | 1,377 | 1,472 | 1,268 | 1,940 | 2,204 | | | | | | | | |
| Total fixed costs | 6,199 | 6,720 | 7,442 | 8,434 | 9,160 | 10,140 | 10,850 | 11,800 | 12,425 | 13,300 | 14,225 | 15,225 | 16,300 |
| Results from operations: | | | | | | | | | | | | | |
| Operations | | | | | | | | | | | | | |
| Concerts | 2,666 | 2,986 | 3,161 | 3,827 | 4,006 | | | | | | | | |
| Radio (BSTT) | 125 | 145 | 160 | 185 | 185 | | | | | | | | |
| Recording | 320 | 384 | 510 | 543 | 827 | | | | | | | | |
| Television | 139 | 225 | 289 | 223 | 246 | | | | | | | | |
| Occupancies | 101 | 91 | 186 | 252 | 244 | | | | | | | | |
| Education | (100) | (60) | (87) | (34) | (77) | | | | | | | | |
| Other Income | — | 12 | 32 | 35 | 278 | | | | | | | | |
| Marginal contribution | 3,251 | 3,783 | 4,251 | 5,031 | 5,709 | 6,160 | 6,675 | 7,325 | 7,775 | 8,375 | 9,025 | 9,750 | 10,500 |
| Percent fixed costs | 52.4 | 56.3 | 57.1 | 59.7 | 62.3 | 60.8 | 61.5 | 62.0 | 62.5 | 63.0 | 63.5 | 64.0 | 64.5 |
| Operating (deficit): | (2,948) | (2,937) | (3,191) | (3,403) | (3,451) | (3,980) | (4,175) | (4,475) | (4,650) | (4,925) | (5,200) | (5,475) | (5,800) |
| Percent fixed costs | 47.6 | 43.7 | 42.9 | 40.3 | 37.7 | 39.2 | 38.5 | 38.0 | 37.5 | 37.0 | 36.5 | 36.0 | 35.5 |
| Endowment Income: | 981 | 1,221 | 1,358 | 1,691 | 1,893 | | | | | | | | |
| Percent fixed costs | 15.8 | 18.2 | 18.3 | 20.0 | 20.7 | | | | | | | | |

| | | | | | | | | | | | | | |
|---|---|---|---|---|---|---|---|---|---|---|---|---|---|
| Annual fundraising: | | | | | | | | | | | | | |
| Total annual gifts | 1,133 | 1,121 | 1,211 | 1,334 | 1,786 | | | | | | | | |
| Special-purpose gifts transferred to operations | (162) | (302) | (268) | (299) | (355) | | | | | | | | |
| General-purpose gifts | 971 | 819 | 943 | 1,035 | 1,431 | | | | | | | | |
| Net project revenues | 176 | 209 | 229 | 264 | 723 | | | | | | | | |
| | 1,147 | 1,028 | 1,172 | 1,299 | 2,154 | | | | | | | | |
| Fundraising expenses | (549) | (441) | (414) | (553) | (442) | | | | | | | | |
| Total | 598 | 587 | 758 | 746 | 1,712 | | | | | | | | |
| Percent fixed costs | 9.7 | 8.7 | 10.2 | 8.8 | 18.7 | | | | | | | | |
| Total endowment | | | | | | | | | | | | | |
| Income and annual fundraising | 1,579 | 1,808 | 2,116 | 2,437 | 3,605 | 3,865 | 4,175 | 4,475 | 4,650 | 4,925 | 5,200 | 5,475 | 5,800 |
| Percent fixed costs | 25.5 | 26.9 | 28.5 | 28.8 | 39.4 | 38.1 | 38.5 | 38.0 | 37.5 | 37.0 | 36.5 | 36.0 | 35.5 |
| Surplus (deficit) | (1369) | (1129) | (1075) | (966) | 154 | (115) | -0- | -0- | -0- | -0- | -0- | -0- | -0- |
| Percent fixed costs | 22.1 | 16.8 | 14.4 | 11.5 | 1.7 | 1.1 | | | | | | | |
| Funding from (to) | | | | | | | | | | | | | |
| Unrestricted capital | 1,369 | 1,129 | 1,075 | 966 | (154) | 115 | | | | | | | |
| | -0- | -0- | -0- | -0- | -0- | -0- | -0- | -0- | -0- | -0- | -0- | -0- | -0- |
| Capital analysis: | | | | | | | | | | | | | |
| Added to endowment funds | 442 | 1,750 | 1,433 | 1,308 | 3,540 | 3,500 | 3,500 | 3,500 | 3,500 | 3,500 | 3,500 | 3,500 | 3,500 |
| Added (charged) to special reserve | | | | | 150 | (115) | | | | | | | |
| Funding of plant additions | 433 | 980 | 493 | 1,641 | 326 | 1,021 | 500 | 500 | 500 | 500 | 500 | 500 | 500 |
| Added to unexpended property fund balance | | | | | 241 | (241) | | | | | | | |
| Funding of deficit | 1,369 | 1,129 | 1,075 | 966 | | | | | | | | | |
| | 2,244 | 3,859 | 3,001 | 3,915 | 4,257 | 4,165 | 4,000 | 4,000 | 4,000 | 4,000 | 4,000 | 4,000 | 4,000 |
| Pooled investments: | | | | | | | | | | | | | |
| Cost | 10,343 | 12,018 | 13,850 | 15,822 | 19,465 | 23,000 | 26,500 | 30,000 | 33,500 | 37,000 | 40,500 | 44,000 | 47,500 |
| Market | 11,645 | 14,015 | 15,817 | 16,356 | 20,536 | | | | | | | | |
| Endowment share unit value | 12.54 | 13.20 | 13.67 | 13.78 | 14.19 | | | | | | | | |

on the plan given in Exhibit 1. In the BSO annual report for 1982 (i.e., for the fiscal year ended August 31, 1982), this plan was described as follows:

> As the orchestra embarks on the first decade of its second century, Trustees, Overseers, and Friends must make plans based upon the experience of the past and their best estimate of the economic climate in the years ahead. The single most important assumption in making such a projection is the rate at which "fixed costs" of maintaining the present organization and properties will increase due to inflation. Included in the Analysis of Revenue Contribution to Fixed Costs are projections based upon several assumptions:
>
> 1. That "fixed costs" will increase at a compound annual rate of approximately 7 percent through fiscal 1989–90.
> 2. That management will be able to increase the percentage of "fixed costs" financed by concert activities by ½ of 1 percent per year.
> 3. That the Investment Committee and the Resources Committee working together will be able to increase the percentage of "fixed costs" covered by endowment income by ½ of 1 percent per year.
> 4. That the Resources Committee will be able to raise on average about $6,000,000 per year, of which $2,000,000 per year will be available to balance the budget.
> 5. That the Buildings and Grounds Committee will be able to limit capital expenditures for depreciation, for necessary improvements, and for new facilities to $500,000 per year.
>
> Perhaps the most significant conclusions to draw from the projections (Exhibit 1) are:
>
> 1. That, in the absence of some new source of revenue, ticket prices will have to continue to increase so that the marginal contribution from concert activities can increase from $5,709,000 in 1981–82 to $10,500,000, or 64.5 percent of "fixed costs," in 1989–90.
> 2. That Endowment Income available for unrestricted use must increase from $1,893,000 in 1981–82 to $4,000,000, or 24.5 percent of "fixed costs," in 1989–90.
> 3. That the book value of Pooled Investments must be increased from $19,465,000 at August 31, 1982, to $47,500,000 in 1990 if the yield on endowment funds averages slightly over 8 percent over the period.
>
> During the past five years the orchestra raised a total of $20,000,000 for BSO/100 and $7,000,000 from Annual Fund Drives for a grand total of $27,000,000.
>
> The goal of $6,000,000 per year, or $30,000,000 over the next five years, is challenging, but the task is not much greater than the task already accomplished during the period of the BSO/100 campaign, and the organization is in place to do the job.
>
> The financial projections in the Analysis of Revenue Contribution to Fixed Costs and the above assumptions and conclusions will have to be reexamined annually in the light of economic conditions and the financial results of each year's operations, but the nature of the task facing management and volunteer fundraisers will probably not be materially changed by modest differences from the assumptions.

## Contribution to Fixed Costs

The concept of "contributions to fixed costs" referred to in the above description was explained in the Annual Report as follows:

> Each year the Trustees are faced with certain relatively fixed costs which are scheduled in the Analysis of Revenue Contribution to Fixed Costs report. These are primarily for the annual compensation of orchestra members, the general administration of the orchestra, and the basic costs of maintaining Symphony Hall and Tanglewood. Management earns a percentage of these "fixed costs" by presenting concert programs, through radio, television, and recordings, and through other projects which involve both direct expenses and related income from ticket sales, fees, and royalties.
>
> Each program or activity, of which there are over 40, is expected to make a "marginal contribution" to "fixed costs." The "marginal contribution" is the difference between direct income and direct costs of the particular program or activity. The orchestra continued to make progress toward its goal of increasing the percentage of "fixed costs" contributed from operation activities.
>
> The "marginal contribution" from all operations in 1981–82 covered 62.3 percent of "fixed costs" as compared to 59.7 percent last year and 43.0 percent in 1971–72.
>
> In fiscal 1981–82, the "fixed costs" amounted to $9,160,000, compared to $8,434,000 in 1980–81, an increase of 8.6 percent. Operations earned $5,709,000, compared to $5,031,000 last year, a 13.1 percent increase. This left an "operating deficit" to be funded from other sources, e.g., endowment income and unrestricted contributions, of $3,451,000 in 1981–82, compared to $3,403,000 last year.

## Other Information

The 1982 Annual Report contained the following explanation of endowment income:

> Investment Income reached an all-time high of $2,134,000 as compared to $1,838,000 in the prior year. Of this amount, $219,000 was used for restricted purposes, e.g. supporting the winter season programs ($35,000), providing fellowships for the Berkshire Music Center and other BMC activities ($101,000), supporting the Esplanade concerts ($47,000), underwriting the Prelude Series ($29,000), and other miscellaneous activities. An additional $22,000 went to nonoperational uses, leaving $1,893,000 for unrestricted use in support of operations. This compares to $1,690,000 in 1980–81, a 12 percent increase.

The Annual Report also explained how the budget for 1982 was balanced, as follows:

> The percentage of "fixed costs" that had to be provided by unrestricted gifts was reduced from 20.3 percent in 1980–81 to 17.0 percent in 1981–82, amounting to $1,558,000.
>
> The sources of the $1,558,000 required to balance revenues and expenses in 1981–82 were:

**Exhibit 2**

BOSTON SYMPHONY ORCHESTRA, INC.
Balance Sheets
August 31, 1982, and 1981

*Current Funds*

| *Assets* | *1982* | *1981* |
|---|---|---|
| Cash (including savings accounts of $49,835 in 1982 and $463,320 in 1981) | $ 119,888 | $ 501,962 |
| Short-term cash investments | 2,600,000 | 1,666,222 |
| Participation in pooled investments, at market | 1,979,960 | 1,681,781 |
| Accounts receivable—less allowance for doubtful accounts of $10,000 in 1982 and $32,000 in 1981 | 709,069 | 937,016 |
| Grants and other receivables | 285,900 | 291,071 |
| Prepaid salaries and wages | 343,962 | 345,195 |
| Deferred charges | 163,893 | 40,111 |
| Prepayments and other assets | 491,605 | 506,858 |
| | $ 6,694,277 | $ 5,970,216 |

| *Liabilities and Fund Balances* | *1982* | *1981* |
|---|---|---|
| Accounts payable | $ 564,677 | $ 591,559 |
| Accrued pension liability | 221,116 | 187,775 |
| Accrued expenses and other liabilities | 619,008 | 189,972 |
| Advance ticket sales and other receipts | 2,781,005 | 2,516,114 |
| Advance receipts—special events | 137,983 | 803,015 |
| Due to other funds | 240,528 | — |
| | 4,564,317 | 4,288,435 |
| Fund balances: | | |
| Unrestricted | 150,000 | — |
| Internally designated | 1,979,960 | 1,681,781 |
| | 2,129,960 | 1,681,781 |
| | $ 6,694,277 | $ 5,970,216 |

*Property Funds*

| *Assets* | *1982* | *1981* |
|---|---|---|
| Due from other funds | $ 240,528 | — |
| Properties and equipment at cost, less accumulated depreciation of $2,209,622 in 1982 and $1,956,005 in 1981 | 4,766,216 | $ 4,693,885 |
| | $ 5,006,744 | $ 4,693,885 |

| *Liabilities and Fund Balances* | *1982* | *1981* |
|---|---|---|
| Fund balance: | | |
| Unexpended balances | $ 240,528 | — |
| Investment in plant | 4,766,216 | $ 4,693,885 |
| | $ 5,006,744 | $ 4,693,885 |

*Endowment and Similar Funds*

| *Assets* | *1982* | *1981* |
|---|---|---|
| Cash management fund-annuities | $ 120,409 | $ 179,390 |
| Real estate and other property held for sale | 712,223 | 862,233 |
| Pooled investments at market | 20,536,010 | 16,356,225 |
| Less participation in pooled investments by other funds | (1,979,960) | (1,681,781) |
| | $19,388,682 | $15,716,057 |

| *Liabilities and Fund Balances* | *1982* | *1981* |
|---|---|---|
| Annuity payable | $ 67,778 | $ 103,662 |
| Fund balances: | | |
| Endowment principal and income restricted | 2,533,903 | 2,142,179 |
| Funds functioning as endowment—trustee designated | 16,787,001 | 13,470,216 |
| | 19,320,904 | 15,612,395 |
| | $19,388,682 | $15,716,057 |

1. Annual Fund (net): $989,000, up $250,000 or 34 percent over the previous year.
2. Projects (net): $723,000 up $459,000 or 174 percent over the previous year.

Since funds available from these two sources totaled $1,712,000, it was possible to transfer the excess gifts of $154,000 for other needs.

Exhibit 2 gives the balance sheet, taken from the Annual Report.

## Questions

1. Do the plans for 1983–90 seem reasonably attainable?
2. Speculate as to other possible ways that BSO should seek to balance its budget this period?

## Case 2–2

## AFTRAIN-CAMEROON*

Dr. Richard Matuvo, Director of Immunization Programs in Cameroon, reread the request which had reached his office last week. He had read it before—several times in fact—yet it still seemed unclear, as well as unusual: Dr. Sara Inambao, the Director of the Aftrain Training Center, was requesting a loan of F50,000,000[1] from the Ministry!

### Background

Aftrain was a United States-based private voluntary organization (PVO) dedicated to training preventive health workers in Africa. Its training activities were funded by private contributions and grants from international agencies, and in the 10 years since it began operations, Aftrain had developed an enviable record of training literally thousands of preventive health workers in 15 African countries.

Aftrain had initiated activities in Cameroon only a year ago, and was once again performing in a highly successful manner. Each training program lasted one month, with the number of trainees growing rapidly, at about 2 percent a month. Trainees completing the Aftrain program then worked in the Ministry of Health's immunization programs, and were doing so with remarkable success. The program was a laudable illustration of a symbiotic effort between a local PVO and a ministry of health.

---

* This case was prepared by David W. Young, Harvard School of Public Health.

[1] CFA francs. 50 CFA francs equal 1 French franc; $1 = 7.4 French francs in 1983.

Dr. Inambao's letter contained financial statements for Aftrain's first year of operations in Cameroon as well as projected statements for the next year (Exhibits 1 and 2). Additionally, Dr. Inambao had provided some estimates of the number of trainees for each month of the year, and the projected personnel requirements for the training programs (Exhibit 3).

## The Problem

The fundamental problem, according to Dr. Inambao, was that while Aftrain's U.S. headquarters reimbursed the Cameroon program on a per-trainee basis, actual cash payments took about two months to reach the Aftrain-Cameroon office. Dr. Inambao had explored the possibility of advance payments from Aftrain-U.S., but had been told that under the terms of Aftrain's contract for this project, payment could only be made after the completion of each training program. Delays with the mail system between the United States and Cameroon, and with currency conversions, meant that it was all but impossible to obtain cash payments any sooner than two months after submitting the monthly training reimbursement report.

The situation was beginning to reach crisis proportions since Aftrain was running very low on cash. Dr. Inambao had obtained a small loan from a local bank, but the interest rate was very high, and the interest payments were not reimbursable under the terms of the contract. The center already had been a week late in making one payroll payment, and both the trainers and the office staff were quite unhappy. While there seemed to be no immediate possibility that they would walk off the job, morale certainly had suffered, and the quality of the training programs was being affected by the staff's unhappiness.

**Exhibit 1**

AFTRAIN-CAMEROON
Income Statements
(in thousands of CFA francs)

| | | | *1983 (actual)* | | |
|---|---|---|---|---|---|
| | *1982* | *1983 (projected)* | *January* | *February* | *March* |
| Revenue | 372,168 | 468,000 | 36,400 | 39,200 | 44,800 |
| Expenses: | | | | | |
| Trainer wages | 195,718 | 250,000 | 23,015 | 24,602 | 28,747 |
| Clerical and administrative wages | 90,836 | 109,000 | 6,471 | 6,471 | 7,357 |
| Training Suppies, and materials | 28,615 | 36,000 | 2,925 | 3,150 | 3,600 |
| Rent and utilities | 36,000 | 48,000 | 4,000 | 4,000 | 4,000 |
| Other | 19,872 | 25,000 | 663 | 902 | 875 |
| Total expenses | 371,041 | 468,000 | 37,074 | 39,125 | 44,579 |
| Surplus (deficit) | 1,127 | -0- | (674) | 75 | 221 |
| Operating statistics: | | | | | |
| Total trainees | 662 | 850 | 65 | 70 | 80 |
| Cost per trainee | 560.5 | 550.6 | 570.4 | 554.8 | 541.9 |

**Exhibit 2**

AFTRAIN-CAMEROON
Balance Sheets
(in thousands of CFA francs)

| | 12-31-82 | 1-31-83 | 2-28-83 | 3-31-83 |
|---|---|---|---|---|
| *Assets* | | | | |
| Cash | 1,598 | -0- | -0- | -0- |
| Accounts receivable | 68,030 | 72,639 | 75,600 | 84,000 |
| Prepaid insurance | 6,905 | 8,707 | 9,124 | 8,724 |
| Total assets | 76,533 | 81,346 | 84,724 | 92,724 |
| *Liabilities and Fund Balance* | | | | |
| Liabilities: | | | | |
| Bank loan (overdraft) | -0- | 5,540 | 8,695 | 16,365 |
| Accounts payable | 406 | 353 | 501 | 610 |
| Total liabilities | 406 | 5,893 | 9,196 | 16,975 |
| Fund balance: | | | | |
| Start-up contribution | 75,000 | 75,000 | 75,000 | 75,000 |
| Retained surplus | 1,127 | 453 | 528 | 749 |
| Total fund balance | 76,127 | 75,453 | 75,528 | 75,749 |
| Total liabilities and fund balance | 76,533 | 81,346 | 84,724 | 92,724 |

**Exhibit 3**
Projected Trainees and Personnel Requirements

| | Clerical and Administrative Staff | Training Staff | Trainees |
|---|---|---|---|
| Actual first quarter | | | |
| January | 2 | 6 | 65 |
| February | 2 | 6.5 | 70 |
| March | 2.5 | 7.5 | 80 |
| Forecast for remainder of 1983: | | | |
| April | 3 | 10 | 100 |
| May | 3 | 10 | 105 |
| June | 3 | 11 | 110 |
| July | 4 | 11 | 115 |
| August | 4 | 11 | 115 |
| September | 4 | 11 | 115 |
| October | 5 | 12 | 120 |
| November | 5 | 12 | 125 |
| December | 5 | 13 | 130 |
| Total | | | 1,250 |

Dr. Inambao's letter to Dr. Matuvo went on to say that the local bank had indicated that it would not increase its loan above F20,000,000, so that in about a month another payroll would be in jeopardy. Since she knew that Aftrain's training programs were an important part of the Ministry of Health's immunization efforts, Dr. Inambao was now turning to Dr. Matuvo with a request for assistance.

As Dr. Matuvo reflected on Dr. Inambao's letter, he was perplexed. He knew how important the training programs were to the Ministry, and to his immunization program in particular, and he wanted to assure their continuation. A loan, though, was a highly unusual request. Furthermore, F50,000,000 was a sizable sum of money. He decided, however, that it was worth a try, and that his first step should be to set up a meeting with the Permanent Secretary, Mr. Frank Muigai. The Permanent Secretary had a well-deserved reputation for being tough; Dr. Matuvo already had had one very difficult set of meetings with him about the budget for the immunization programs. But Mr. Muigai also was a fair and reasonable person, and had good relations with both the Minister of Health and several key officials in the Ministry of Finance. He knew that if he could justify the need for a loan of F50,000,000 to Mr. Muigai that Mr. Muigai in turn would be able to make the necessary arrangements to secure the funds within a month. Aftrain would then be able to meet its payroll.

Dr. Matuvo realized that his first step should be to determine the accuracy of the F50,000,000 requested by Dr. Inambao. He then would need to project a repayment schedule for the loan. With this information in hand he knew he would at least have a chance of convincing Mr. Muigai of the importance of making an interest-free loan to Aftrain.

## Questions

1. How large a loan does Aftrain need?
2. When will they be able to repay it?
3. What should Dr. Matuvo recommend to Mr. Muigai?

## Case 2–3

## VISITING NURSE ASSOCIATION OF METROPOLIS*

Mr. James White, Executive Director of the Visiting Nurse Association of Metropolis, was reviewing the report of his organization's certified public accountants which he had received earlier in the week (Appendix). While he was pleased that the organization had generated a surplus during 1977, as contrasted with a deficit in the prior year, he nevertheless knew that he would have some explaining to do to his board.

At least two items would require explanation: in the first place, he would need to make clear to the board the reasons for the "Subject to" clause; secondly, there were several board members he knew to be quite concerned about the agency's surplus. Indeed, many board members had expressed their

* This case was prepared by David W. Young, Harvard School of Public Health.

concerns to him in the past, that, since the agency had been established as a nonprofit organization, it really was not legitimate to incur a surplus of any sizable magnitude. Thus, this too would need explanation. Finally, there were a number of "financial types" on his board who he knew would question anything unusual or out of line in the financial statements.

He thus went about preparing for his upcoming board meeting. As he began to gather his thoughts he realized that not only would he have to explain his financial statements, and particularly the surplus issue, to his board, but both the local United Way as well as Medicare also were concerned about the size of the agency's surplus. In fact, in the past, the United Way had reduced its contributions to many other organizations in the Metropolis area by the amount of their organization's surplus. Intuitively, he knew this was not right, but he was having some trouble demonstrating it. He decided that the best approach would be to undertake an analysis of the surplus required by his agency in order to sustain itself in the future.

## Questions

1. What is your assessment of the reasons for the "subject to" clause? What can be done about it?
2. Is there anything unusual or out of line in the financial statements? If so, how would you explain them to the board?
3. How do you explain the fact that the agency's cash declined from $153,318 in 1976 to $3,951 in 1977 despite the existence of a surplus of $53,190 in 1977?
4. What were the reasons for the $53,190 surplus as compared to the deficit of $26,953 in 1976? Is a surplus of this magnitude justifiable? Sufficient? Please be prepared to explain your reasoning with data from the exhibits.

# APPENDIX

The Visiting Nurse Association of Metropolis

FINANCIAL STATEMENTS
with
REPORT OF CERTIFIED PUBLIC ACCOUNTANTS
YEARS ENDED DECEMBER 31, 1977, AND 1976

REPORT OF CERTIFIED PUBLIC ACCOUNTANTS

The Board of Directors
The Visiting Nurse Association of
Metropolis
Metropolis, U.S.A.

We have examined the balance sheet of The Visiting Nurse Association of Metropolis (a U.S.A. not-for-profit corporation) as of December 31, 1977, and 1976, and the related statements of operations, changes in fund balance, and changes in financial position for the years then ended. Our examinations were made in accordance with generally accepted auditing standards and, accordingly, included such tests of the accounting records and such other auditing procedures as we considered necessary in the circumstances.

In our report dated March 18, 1977, our opinion on the 1976 financial statements was qaulified as being subject to the final determination of the Association's 1976 Medicare cost report. As explained in Note 2 of the financial statements, this matter was settled in 1977 and the cost incurred has been charged to operations in the current year as required by generally accepted accounting principles. Accordingly, our present opinion on the 1976 financial statements, as presented herein, is different from that expressed in our previous report.

As described in Note 2, the 1977 Medicare cost report is subject to audit and adjustment by the Medicare Program administrator.

In our opinion, subject to the effects on the 1977 financial statements of such adjustments, if any, as might have been required had the outcome of the uncertainty referred to in the preceding paragraph been known, the financial statements designated above present fairly the financial position of the Visiting Nurse Association of Metropolis at December 31, 1977, and 1976, and the results of its operations, changes in its fund balance, and changes in its financial position for the years then ended, in conformity with generally accepted accounting principles applied on a consistent basis.

U.S.A.
March 20, 1978

## THE VISITING NURSE ASSOCIATION OF METROPOLIS
Balance Sheet
December 31, 1977, and 1976

| *Assets* | *1977* | *1976* |
|---|---|---|
| Current assets: | | |
| Cash | $ 3,951 | $153,318 |
| Accounts receivable: | | |
| Medicare patients | 467,997 | 281,502 |
| Other, net of allowance for doubtful accounts of $45,000 in 1977 and $40,000 in 1976 | 177,480 | 177,128 |
| Inventory | 35,253 | — |
| Prepaid expenses | 30,069 | 12,854 |
| Total current assets | 714,750 | 624,802 |
| Investment, at cost | — | 25,000 |
| Property and equipment, at cost: | | |
| Furniture and fixtures | 314,362 | 241,438 |
| Leasehold improvements | 145,909 | 121,304 |
| | 460,271 | 362,742 |
| Less accumulated depreciation and amortization | 176,783 | 133,396 |
| | 283,488 | 229,346 |
| | $998,238 | $879,148 |

| *Liabilities and Fund Balance* | | |
|---|---|---|
| Current liabilities: | | |
| Accounts payable | $267,569 | $217,097 |
| Current portion of long-term debt | 27,021 | 16,310 |
| Accrued salaries and wages | 125,616 | 92,485 |
| Due pension plan | 56,675 | 56,900 |
| Payroll taxes payable | 11,049 | 8,921 |
| Payroll deductions payable | 14,351 | 9,866 |
| Total current liabilities | 502,281 | 401,579 |
| Long-term debt | 83,715 | 118,517 |
| Commitments and contingent liabilities | — | — |
| Fund balance | 412,242 | 359,052 |
| | $998,238 | $879,148 |

The accompanying notes are an integral part of the financial statements.

## THE VISITING NURSE ASSOCIATION OF METROPOLIS
Statement of Operations
For the Years Ended December 31, 1977, and 1976

| | *1977* | *1976* |
|---|---|---|
| Revenue from agency services: | | |
| Medicare | $3,972,294 | $2,899,283 |
| Other | 937,219 | 768,313 |
| | 4,909,513 | 3,667,596 |
| Indigent care and contractual allowances | (728,260) | (537,051) |
| | 4,181,253 | 3,130,545 |
| Operating expenses: | | |
| Salaries and wages | 2,790,456 | 2,139,376 |
| Payroll taxes | 153,294 | 117,280 |
| Employee benefits | 175,273 | 121,662 |
| Medical supplies | 483,607 | 353,004 |
| Office supplies and miscellaneous | 107,482 | 97,375 |
| Auto and transportation | 222,148 | 189,180 |
| Office rental, utilities and maintenance | 125,455 | 117,302 |
| Conferences, conventions and meetings | 83,008 | 61,920 |
| Telephone | 43,346 | 34,238 |
| Depreciation and amortization of furniture, fixtures and leaseholds improvements | 43,664 | 44,447 |
| Rental of data processing equipment | 50,262 | 36,026 |
| Professional fees and contract services | 40,753 | 46,294 |
| Public education | 11,185 | 21,005 |
| Insurance | 87,595 | 51,880 |
| Dues and subscriptions | 17,334 | 6,549 |
| Postage | 20,336 | 16,519 |
| | 4,455,198 | 3,454,057 |
| Deficiency of agency revenue over operating expenses | 273,945 | 323,512 |
| Public support and other revenue (expense): | | |
| United Way allocation | 335,000 | 297,879 |
| Contributions | 2,542 | 2,333 |
| Interest, net | (11,418) | (7,281) |
| Miscellaneous | 1,011 | 3,628 |
| | 327,135 | 296,559 |
| Excess (deficiency) of revenues and public support over expenses | $ 53,190 | $ (26,953) |

The accompanying notes are an integral part of the financial statements.

## THE VISITING NURSE ASSOCIATION OF METROPOLIS
Statement of Changes in Fund Balance
For the Years Ended December 31, 1977, and 1976

| | *1977* | *1976* |
|---|---|---|
| Fund balance at beginning of year | $359,052 | $386,005 |
| Excess (deficiency) of revenues and public support over expenses | 53,190 | (26,953) |
| Fund balance at end of year | $412,242 | $359,052 |

The accompanying notes are an integral part of the financial statements.

THE VISITING NURSE ASSOCIATION OF METROPOLIS
Statement of Changes in Financial Position
For the Years Ended December 31, 1977, and 1976

| | *1977* | *1976* |
|---|---|---|
| Source of cash funds: | | |
| Proceeds from loans | $ 124,000 | $ 245,000 |
| Proceeds from sale of investment | 25,000 | — |
| | 149,000 | 245,000 |
| Application of cash funds: | | |
| Operating expenses | 4,455,198 | 3,454,057 |
| Adjustments: | | |
| Depreciation and amortization | (43,664) | (44,447) |
| Increase in accounts payable and accrued expenses | (89,991) | (165,208) |
| Increase in inventory | 35,253 | — |
| | 4,356,796 | 3,244,402 |
| Revenue from agency services | 4,181,253 | 3,130,545 |
| Public support and other revenue (expense) | 327,135 | 296,559 |
| Total revenues | 4,508,388 | 3,427,104 |
| Adjustments: | | |
| Decrease (increase) in accounts receivable | (186,847) | 66,802 |
| | 4,321,541 | 3,493,906 |
| Cash funds applied to (provided by) operations | 35,255 | (249,504) |
| Repayment of loans | 148,091 | 205,173 |
| Purchase of property and equipment | 97,806 | 133,637 |
| Increase in investment | — | 2,000 |
| Increase in prepaid expenses | 17,215 | 3,268 |
| | 298,367 | 94,574 |
| Increase (decrease) in cash funds | (149,367) | 150,426 |
| Cash funds at beginning of year | 153,318 | 2,892 |
| Cash funds at end of year | $ 3,951 | $ 153,318 |

The accompanying notes are an integral part of the financial statements.

THE VISITING NURSE ASSOCIATION OF METROPOLIS
Notes to Financial Statements
December 31, 1977, and 1976

**1. Summary of accounting policies**

This summary of accounting policies is presented to assist in understanding the Association's financial statements. These accounting policies conform to generally accepted accounting principles and have been consistently applied in the preparation of the financial statements.

*Revenue recognition*

Revenue from services to patients is recorded at established billing rates during the period in which services are performed. Indigent care allowances, bad debts, and contractual allowances under cost reimbursement insurance programs are recorded separately as reductions to patient revenues.

*Depreciation and amortization*

Depreciation and amortization of property and equipment are provided on the straight-line method over the following estimated useful lives.

| | |
|---|---|
| Furniture and fixtures ....... | 7 and 10 years |
| Leasehold improvements ..... | Life of lease |

*Inventory*

In 1976 and prior years, the Association expensed all medical supplies at time of purchase. During 1977 the Association established the policy of recognizing inventory on hand. The inventory is stated at the lower of cost (specific identification method) or market at December 31, 1977.

**2. Medicare cost adjustment**

The Association is reimbursed during the year at interim rates based on estimates of cost for care rendered to medicare patients. Based on the 1977 Medicare Cost Report, $49,005 is expected to be received from the Medicare program as an adjustment to estimated cost. This amount has been included in Medicare accounts receivable at December 31, 1977.

The 1977 Medicare Cost Report is subject to audit and adjustment by the Medicare Program administrator.

In 1977 the Medicare Program administrator audited the Association's 1976 Cost Report. No significant adjustments to Medicare patient costs resulted.

**3. Pension plan**

The Association has a contributory pension plan in which, generally, all full-time employees may participate on a voluntary basis. It is the Association's policy to fund pension costs accrued. Past service costs are being amortized over approximately 10 years. The pension expense for the years 1977 and 1976, totaling $87,494 and $79,865, respectively, includes approximately $33,000 of amortized past service costs for each year. The actuarially computed value of vested benefits as of December 31, 1976, and 1975, exceeded the total of the pension fund and balance sheet accruals by approximately $50,800 and $33,600, respectively. The actuarial information for the plan year ended November 30, 1977, is not yet available.

**4. Leases**

The Association leases buildings and office equipment under noncancellable leases expiring through 1983. The building leases, one of which may be renewed for two three-year periods, require the Association to pay all maintenance costs and taxes on the property at 1000 Maple Avenue. A portion of one building was sublet through December 31, 1977. Data processing equipment is rented on a month-to-month basis and therefore its cost is not reflected in the future minimum rental payments reported.

Future minimum payments, by year and in the aggregate, under noncancellable operating leases with initial or remaining terms of one year or more consisted of the following at December 31, 1977:

| | |
|---|---:|
| 1978 .......... | $133,537 |
| 1979 .......... | 129,890 |
| 1980 .......... | 123,895 |
| 1981 .......... | 69,750 |
| 1982 .......... | 64,500 |
| Thereafter ...... | 63,450 |
| | $585,022 |

Rental expense for all operating leases consisted of:

| | Year Ended December 31 | |
|---|---|---|
| | 1977 | 1976 |
| Minimum rental | $131,497 | $ 13,339 |
| Sublease rental income | (6,000) | (6,000) |
| | $125,497 | $107,339 |

The Association presently accounts for leases entered into prior to January 1, 1977, in accordance with generally accepted accounting principles established prior to the issuance of FASB Statement No. 13, "Accounting for Leases." By 1981, the Association will have to restate its financial statements to reflect the accounting for these leases in accordance with the statement.

This change in accounting principles will result in the Maple Avenue property leases being capitalized with an increase in the amounts reflected in the Association's financial statements at December 31, 1977, as follows:

| | |
|---|---|
| Land and building | $412,000 |
| Capital lease obligations: | |
| Current | 43,958 |
| Noncurrent | 270,221 |
| Excess of revenues and public support over expenses | 27,955 |

**5. Resolution of prior contingencies**

During 1975, the United Way asked the Association to refund between $65,000 and $85,000 of its 1974 allocation. In 1976, this claim was settled for $37,121 and the amount of the settlement was charged against the United Way allocation in that period.

The Association had been a defendant in a lawsuit filed by a former employee in two counts: first, an alleged breach of an employment contract and second, a defamation claim. In 1976, both claims were settled for $6,000, which has been charged to operating expenses in that period.

**6. Long-term debt**

Long-term debt consists of the following:

| | December 31 | |
|---|---|---|
| | 1977 | 1976 |
| 8% unsecured note to the XYZ Foundation due April 17, 1980 | $ 43,517 | $ 59,827 |
| 5% installment note due February 10, 1982, with monthly payments of $1,364.68 including principal and interest and a final payment of $16,364.08. Secured by a chattel mortage on equipment | 67,219 | — |
| 6¾% unsecured note to Lindell Trust due January 22, 1977 | — | 75,000 |
| | 110,736 | 134,827 |
| Less current portion | 27,021 | 16,310 |
| | $ 83,715 | $118,517 |

# part II

# Management Control Principles

Before we can begin to discuss management control systems and their implementation, we must first outline some of the basic principles on which they are based. In Chapter 3, we describe general-purpose financial statements—the vehicles by which nonprofit organizations communicate their financial activities and results to "outsiders." In Chapter 4 we look at full and differential costs, discussing both the bases on which different types of costs are calculated, and the uses to which these various cost constructions might be put. Finally, in Chapter 5 we examine one of the more important principles of management control in nonprofit organizations—pricing decisions—discussing the bases on which such decisions should be made.

# chapter 3

# General-Purpose Financial Statements

This chapter describes concepts which underlie the statements that report the financial status and financial performance of an organization. We start with a description of the basic concepts of financial accounting, proceed to a description of the one important difference between profit-oriented and nonprofit organizations, and conclude with a discussion of some special characteristics of financial statements currently prepared by several types of nonprofit organizations.

## BASIC CONCEPTS: THE BALANCE SHEET

General-purpose financial statements are those prepared for the use of parties outside the organization. An organization's management uses these general-purpose statements, and it also uses special-purpose statements prepared for its own needs. Special-purpose statements can be prepared in any way that management finds useful. General-purpose statements, however, are prepared according to what are called Generally Accepted Accounting Principles (GAAP). These have evolved over a period of several hundred years, first as a matter of custom, and more recently as stated by authoritative bodies. Currently, GAAP are established by the Financial Accounting Standards Board (FASB), a private-sector body consisting of seven full-time members supported by a large staff with an annual budget of over $8 million.

Although the FASB establishes accounting principles for all nongovernment organizations, most of its pronouncements to date have related to profit-oriented companies. It accepted responsibility for "nonbusiness" organizations in 1979, but as of 1984 had published no accounting standards specifcally related to these organizations. Pending action by the FASB, accounting standards for nonprofit organizations are governed by five separate "Guides" issued by the American Institute of Certified Public Accountants (AICPA). They apply, respectively, to: colleges and universities, welfare organizations, hospitals, state and local governments, and "other" nonprofit organizations.

## Balance Sheet

The organization for which a set of accounts is kept is called the *accounting entity.* An entity can range in size and complexity from the corner drug store or an individual physician to a worldwide corporation consisting of hundreds of separate divisions.

In all entities, the basic accounting report is the *balance sheet.* Exhibit 3–1 shows the essence of a balance sheet. (As will be seen in a later section an actual balance sheet has much more detail than this.) Note first that the heading shows the entity to which the balance sheet refers and states that the report is "as of December 31, 19x1." (In these examples, we shall use 19x1 to refer to the first year of concern, 19x2 to the second year, and so on.) All balance sheets report the status of the entity *as of one moment of time,* in this case at the close of business on the last day of the calendar year, 19x1.

The balance sheet has two sides. The left-hand, or *Assets,* side shows the forms in which the entity's capital exists as of the balance sheet date. These are the resources that the entity can use to carry out its activities. Usually, capital is received first in the form of cash, i.e., money. Thereafter, the entity uses this cash to acquire other resources, such as equipment and buildings. Exhibit 3–1 shows that only $400,000 of the entity's capital is still in the form of cash, and the other $9,800,000 is in the form of other assets, not detailed here.

**Exhibit 3–1**

EXAMPLE ORGANIZATION
Balance Sheet
As of December 31, 19x1
($000)

| *Assets* | | *Liabilities and Equity* | |
|---|---|---|---|
| Cash | $ 400 | Liabilities | $ 9,000 |
| Other assets | 9,800 | Equity | 1,200 |
| Total assets | $10,200 | Total liabilities and equity | $10,200 |

The right-hand side, labeled *Liabilities and Equity,* can be described in either of two ways, both of which are correct. In one view, *the source of resources* view, this side shows the sources from which the entity has obtained the funds used to acquire its assets. *Liabilities* show the amount of funds obtained from those parties who are entitled to repayment of the amount they furnished plus, in many cases, interest. If a bank loans an entity $1,000, the $1,000 is an addition to its assets, and the entity is obligated to pay the bank the $1,000 (plus interest). The $1,000 owed to the bank is a liability.

*Equity* shows the amount of funds obtained from other sources. In a business, there are two types of such sources. Some funds are supplied by the owners (shareholders, if the entity is a corporation), and some are generated by the entity's own activities. The entity earns *income* by profitable operations, and this income is a source of its funds. Most nonprofit organizations do not have owners who supply capital to it, so their equity comes entirely from operating activities (plus certain types of contributions, to be described later.)

The other view of the right-hand side of the balance sheet, the *claims* view, is that it shows claims against the entity's assets. Liabilities are the claims of nonowners. In a business, equity is the claim of the owners. Although the entity does not have a legal obligation to pay its owners anything, they do have a *residual* claim against any assets that are left over after the claims of nonowners have been satisfied. Since most nonprofit organizations do not have owners, and in any event cannot legally distribute assets to their owners as such, the idea of "claim" is not particularly descriptive of the nature of equity in a nonprofit organization. Perhaps the most that can be said is that in a nonprofit organization, equity represents the entity's residual interest in the assets after the liability claims have been satisfied.

## The Accounting Equation

The two sides of the balance sheet add up to the same total, $10,200,000 in Exhibit 3–1. This equality of the left- and right-hand sides is a necessary characteristic of every balance sheet. It tells nothing about the financial condition of the entity. It merely reflects a truism, that can be stated in terms of either of the two views of the balance sheet. According to the "sources of funds" view the two sides are equal because all funds have been invested in assets of various types, and the total amount invested cannot be less or greater than the amount of funds supplied to the entity. According to the "claims against the assets" view, all the assets are claimed by someone, either the liabilities or (in a business) the owners, and the amount claimed by these parties cannot exceed the amount there is to be claimed.

Either view leads to the basic accounting equation:

$$\text{Assets} = \text{Liabilities} + \text{Equity}.$$

***Double Entry Accounting.*** The numbers on a balance sheet as of one moment of time are of course changed by accounting events that happen after that moment. Each such event is called a *transaction,* and the effect of a transaction is recorded in the accounts by an *entry.* From the basic accounting equation, there follows the concept that each transaction must affect at least two balance sheet items. If a transaction could change only one item, the equality of the accounting equation would be destroyed. Thus, if on January 2, 19x2, someone loaned $1,000 to the entity, the entity would have $1,000 more cash than the $400,000 shown in Exhibit 3–1; however, if only this increase in cash were recorded, total assets would become $10,201,000 which would exceed the total of $10,200,000 shown on the right-hand side and thus destroy the equality of the two sides. If, however, both the increase in cash of $1,000 and the corresponding increase of $1,000 in the liability to the lender are recorded, the equality is preserved. Both the asset side and the liabilities and equity side increase by $1,000. Similarly, if $2,000 of cash is used to buy supplies, cash decreases by $2,000, but the amount of supplies, which is another asset, increases by $2,000, so the total of the assets is unchanged.

Because every entry affects at least two items, accounting is referred to as *double-entry* accounting. There is no such thing as single-entry accounting.

## Measurement of Asset Amounts

Assets are resources that are owned or controlled by an entity. There are two main types of assets, monetary and nonmonetary. The amounts reported for each type are measured in quite different ways.

*Monetary assets* consist of cash and the entity's claims to specified amounts of cash. The amounts that hospitals have billed patients, tuition due from students in a university, or taxes levied on property owners by a municipality are monetary assets. They are called *receivables.* In each case, the entity is entitled to receive a specified amount of money. Cash is reported on the balance sheet as the actual amount on hand and in various bank accounts. Other monetary assets are reported as the amount of cash that is likely to be received. This may be less than the amount owed the entity because some patients (or payers on their behalf) may not pay their hospital bills, some students (or their parents) may not pay their tuition, and some property owners may not pay their taxes. If it is decided that not all debtors will pay what they owe, the amount reported on the balance sheet is adjusted downward by an estimate of the amount owed that will not be collected.

All other assets are *nonmonetary assets.* They are reported according to a fundamentally different concept, called the *cost concept.* The merchandise that a drug store has on its shelves is a nonmonetary asset. Its *value* is the amount that it can be sold for. Although the druggist expects to realize this value when the merchandise is sold, it is not reported at its selling price. Instead, it is reported at its *cost* to the entity. This is the case with almost all nonmonetary assets. When they are acquired, they are reported at their cost, that is, the amount paid to acquire them. Subsequently, as these assets are sold or used by the entity, accounting traces this cost in a way that will be described later on.

Failure to appreciate this point is probably the most common source of misunderstanding about accounting. Accounting does not, except for monetary items, report values; it reports costs. Land acquired many years ago at a cost of $10,000 is reported on the current balance sheet at $10,000, even though it currently could be sold for $100,000. The asset side of the balance sheet does not show what the entity is worth; it shows the amounts invested in various assets, measured at their cost. With one exception, to be discussed later on, a resource that did not cost the entity anything is not an asset. The most valuable resource of a university, for example, is its faculty, but no amount for this resource is reported on the balance sheet because, since the abolition of slavery, no one can legally "buy" another person. (The university buys the *services* of its faculty, but these are used up as soon as they are acquired, so there is no asset amount remaining to be listed on the balance sheet.)

Readers of a balance sheet would, of course, like to know what the assets are worth, i.e., what their value is. The reason why accounting does not attempt to measure values of nonmonetary assets is that such a focus would involve a great deal of estimating and judgment, and if the estimates were made by management, they would probably be biased. A system based on costs is much more objective; the amounts are much less affected by estimates.

## THE OPERATING STATEMENT

Although the balance sheet is the basic accounting report in the sense that it provides the details underlying the accounting equation, Assets = Liabilities + Equity, it is by no means the most important accounting report. (The federal government does not even prepare a balance sheet.) In most situations, the more important report is the operating statement, a report that describes financial performance of the entity *during a period of time.*

The usual period covered by an operating statement is one year. In some entities the accounting period is the 12 months ended December 31; in others, some other 12-month period is considered more useful. In most colleges and universities, for example, the accounting period is the 12 months ended June 30 because June 30 is a convenient dividing line between one academic year and the next.

Exhibit 3–2 relates the operating statement to the balance sheet. The balance sheet for 19x1 is given, with the same totals as in Exhibit 3–1, but in more detail. (For convenience in printing, liabilities and equity are shown beneath the assets, rather than to their right, but the two sections are nevertheless referred to as the "left-hand side" and "right-hand side," respectively.) Balance sheet figures for December 31, 19x2 are also shown. Since the amounts at the close of business on December 31 are the same as those at the beginning of business on the next day, January 1, these two balance sheets effectively

**Exhibit 3–2**

EXAMPLE ORGANIZATION
Balance Sheets
As of December 31
($000)

| | 19x2 | 19x1 |
|---|---|---|
| *Assets* | | |
| Cash | $ 450 | $ 400 |
| Accounts receivable | 900 | 500 |
| Inventory | 1,100 | 1,100 |
| Prepaid expenses | 500 | 300 |
| Land | 1,000 | 1,000 |
| Buildings and equipment | 6,600 | 7,000 |
| Total assets | $10,550 | $10,200 |
| *Liabilities and Equity* | | |
| Liabilities: | | |
| Accounts payable | $ 2,100 | $ 1,900 |
| Bank loan payable | 1,500 | 1,200 |
| Accrued liabilities | 500 | 600 |
| Precollected revenue | 0 | 300 |
| Mortgage payable | 5,000 | 5,000 |
| Total liabilities | 9,100 | 9,000 |
| Equity | 1,450 | 1,200 |
| Total liabilities and equity | $10,550 | $10,200 |

EXAMPLE ORGANIZATION
Operating Statement
For the year 19x2
($000)

| | |
|---|---|
| Revenues | $10,000 |
| Expenses | 9,750 |
| Net income | $ 250 |

show the entity's financial position at the beginning and the end of 19x2. Note that, during the year, equity increased from $1,200,000 to $1,450,000, an increase of $250,000. The sole purpose of the operating statement is to explain the causes of this change in equity during 19x2. More generally, *an operating statement explains the increases and decreases in equity arising from the entity's operating activities during a given accounting period.*

Transactions that result in an increase in equity are called *revenues.*[1] Transactions that result in a decrease in equity are called *expenses.* The difference between the revenues of the period and the expenses of the period is the *net income* of the period (or *net loss* if it is negative). Note that the net income in Exhibit 3–2 is $250,000, which is the same as the change in equity in the two balance sheets.

[1] The term "income" is sometimes used instead of "revenue," as in tuition income, interest income, and so on. This is incorrect and confusing. The term "income" should always refer to a difference. Net income is the difference between revenues and expenses.

## Significance of Net Income

The importance of the operating statement in a profit-oriented business is obvious. A primary goal of a business is to earn income, and the net income (referred to as the "bottom line") on the operating statement is an indication of how well the business has performed in attaining this goal. As a general rule, the larger the net income amount, the better the entity has performed.

Since the goal of a nonprofit organization is to provide service, rather than to earn income, the importance of its operating statement may be less obvious. Nevertheless, as described in Chapter 2, the operating statement does convey important information about financial performance in such an organization. If revenues do not at least equal expenses, that is, if the organization does not at least *break even,* there is a danger signal. If this situation persists, the organization will eventually go bankrupt. Conversely, if revenues exceed expenses by too wide a margin, there is an indication that the organization is not providing as much service as it should with the funds made available to it.

***Operating Capital Maintenance.*** If in a given year an entity's revenues at least equal its expenses, it is said to have maintained its operating capital. (A more precise statement is that it has maintained its operating *equity.*) Some entities try to maintain their operating capital each year; others do not. Some examples:

1. In many governmental units, the fiscal policy is to make spending equal to revenues, that is, to break even. Many states require such a policy, and rates of taxation are set so that this relationship will occur. In many other nonprofit organizations, the amount of revenues available in a given year is essentially fixed, and the policy is to limit expenses to the amount of these revenues. Again, the intention is to break even, "to live within one's income," "to have a balanced budget."

2. An organization may decide in a given year to have net income in order to recoup the loss of a prior year, to provide funds for expansion, to provide a reserve for contingencies, or for a variety of other reasons. An organization may also decide to operate at a deficit in a given year in order to use accumulated equity, to meet an unusual need, or for other reasons. The bottom line presumably reflects the results of these policies (it also may reflect the results of poor financial management, however).

3. Many membership organizations (e.g., clubs, professional associations, trade associations) have a governing board whose composition changes annually. In a given year, the membership may expect the governing board to conduct the affairs of the organization so that it uses all, but not more than, the revenues of that year. If the board does not use all the revenues, then it may not be providing the amount of services that the members have a right to expect. If the board spends more than the year's revenues, then there is a loss that must be made up out of accumulated equity, or from

revenues of future years. Similarly, if a governmental unit operates at a loss, those responsible for its management have, in effect, drawn on either past resources or future resources (supplied by future taxes or grants) to finance current operations.

## Accrual Concept

Only those transactions that change equity are reported on the operating statement. If the organization borrows $1,000 from a bank, its cash is increased by $1,000 but it has an additional liability, also of $1,000, so there is no effect on equity. (Interest on this loan does affect equity, but it is a separate transaction). Recall that accounting is a double-entry system in which every entry has at least two parts, each of which affects a balance sheet amount. Unless one of these parts effects equity, the transaction does not affect income and is not reported on the operating statement.

It follows that an entity's net income for the year is unlikely to be the same as the increase in its cash during the year. Consequently, an important activity for the entity's accountant is to examine transactions of all types and decide which of them change equity and which do not. In making these decisions, the accountant applies the *accrual concept,* a concept which is concerned with the measurement of changes in equity, regardless of their effect on cash. The accrual basis of accounting thus contrasts with the *cash basis* of accounting, which focuses only on changes in cash. Many small organizations do use the cash basis, but unless their only asset is cash, they cannot measure their net income. The reasons for this will become clearer once we have described the application of the accrual concept to the measurement of revenues and expenses.

## Revenues

*Revenues are the increases in equity associated with the operating activities of the year.* Revenues arise whenever an increase in an asset is not accompanied by an equal decrease in some other asset or an equal increase in a liability. If a municipality bills a property owner for $1,000 for 19x2 taxes and receives the $1,000 in 19x2, this is 1982 revenue. If the municipality bills another property owner $1,500 for 19x2 taxes, but the property owner does not pay the tax bill until 19x3, this $1,500 is nevertheless revenue for 19x2. Both the $1,000 and the $1,500 relate to 19x2 operating activities, that is, to the municipal services furnished in 19x2 and to the expenses of furnishing these services. As of December 31, 19x2, the municipality is owed $1,500, which is an asset, listed on the balance sheet as Accounts Receivable, or Taxes Receivable.

The collection of taxes receivable is *not* revenue. If in 19x3, the municipality receives $1,500 in cash from the second property owner, its cash increases by $1,500, but another asset, accounts receivable, decreases by $1,500, so equity in 19x3 is unchanged. The increase in equity occurred in 19x2, when the revenue was recorded.

***Sales Revenues.*** Amounts generated by the sales of goods and services in a period are revenues of that period. Patient charges in a hospital are revenues of the period in which the patient received hospital services, which is not necessarily the same as the period in which the patient (or a third-party payer) was billed, nor the period in which the cash was received.[2] The amount of revenue recognized is the amount that is highly likely to be received. If some patients are unlikely to pay their bills, revenues are the amount billed *less* an allowance for these possible bad debts.

***Membership Dues.*** Members of an organization pay dues in order to receive services for a specified period of time. These dues are revenues of that period, whether they are collected prior to the period (as is often the case), during the period, or after the period. If dues are not collected until after the period, the asset, dues receivable, at the end of the period must be adjusted downward to allow for the amount that probably never will be received. If the collection of dues is fairly uncertain (as is the case in organizations that have a high membership turnover), an exception to the general principle may be made, and dues may be recorded as revenues only when cash is received.

Life membership dues present a special problem. Conceptually, a part of the total should be recorded as revenue in each year of the member's expected life. As a practical matter, this calculation is complicated and requires considerable recordkeeping. Many membership organizations therefore take the simple solution of recording life memberships as revenues in the year received.

***Pledges.*** In accordance with the basic revenue concept, pledges of future financial support are revenues in the year to which the pledged contributions apply, even if the cash is not received in that year. Unpaid pledges are adjusted downward to allow for estimated uncollectible amounts, just as is done with other accounts receivable. Some people argue that the basic revenue concept should not apply to pledges because, unlike accounts receivable, they are not legally enforceable claims. Others maintain that the difficulty of estimating the amount of uncollectible pledges is so great that a revenue amount incorporating such an estimate is unreliable. Neither of these groups would count unpaid pledges as revenues.

***Tax Revenues.*** As described above, property taxes are revenues of the period for which they are levied, whether or not the cash is collected during that period. The National Council on Governmental Accounting

[2] For convenience in recordkeeping, some hospitals do recognize revenue in the period in which the patient is billed, which may be a few days later than the period in which the services were rendered.

recommends that property taxes be counted as revenues in the period in which they are "measurable and available." This is a slightly different test than that given above and is somewhat ambiguous, but as a practical matter it usually leads to the same result.

Amounts to be collected from income taxes, sales taxes, gross receipts taxes, parking meter revenues, fines, and similar sources often cannot be reliably estimated in advance of receipt. Such taxes are therefore usually counted as revenue when the cash is received. The National Council of Governmental Accounting describes this practice as a "modified" revenue concept. Actually, a business company faced with similar uncertainties would also record revenues on a cash basis, so this is not really a modification of business practices.

## Expenses

*Expenses are decreases in equity associated with operating activities of the year.* They represent resources consumed or used up by the entity in the course of its operations. If an employee earns $10,000 for services rendered in 19x2, there is an expense in 19x2 of $10,000, even though part of the earnings may not be paid in 19x2. The amount due the employee as of December 31, 19x2, is reported as a liability on the balance sheet called Accrued Liabilities or, more specifically, Accrued Salary Payable. Conversely, if the organization paid $1,000 in 19x1 for a fire insurance policy that provided protection in 19x2 and 19x3, $500 of the amount will be an expense in 19x2 and $500 an expense in 19x3. Therefore, on the December 31, 19x1, balance sheet the right to receive $1,000 insurance protection is reported as an asset, Prepaid Expense or, more specifically, Prepaid Insurance. Similarly, on the December 31, 19x2, balance sheet, the remaining right of $500 is reported as an asset. In summary, expenses can be *incurred* without cash payment, and a cash payment can be made without a corresponding expense.

## Difference among Expenses, Expenditures, and Disbursements

When an asset is acquired, either cash or some other asset is paid out or a liability is incurred. In either case, the entity makes an *expenditure.* The expenditure is equal to the asset's cost. Although "expenditure" is sometimes confused with the word "expense" they are not the same. The purchase of fuel oil in 19x1 is an expenditure in 19x1. If the fuel oil is still on hand on December 31, 19x1, it appears on the balance sheet as an asset, Inventory. If the fuel oil is consumed in 19x2, it is an expense in 19x2.

The payment of cash is a *disbursement.* If an asset is acquired for cash, the expenditure and the disbursement occur in the same period, but there is no necessary correspondence between an expenditure and the related disbursement. If fuel oil is received in 19x1, paid for in 19x2, and consumed in 19x3, there was an expenditure in 19x1, a disbursement in 19x2, and an expense in 19x3.

***Depreciation.*** Buildings and equipment (often called "fixed assets") are basically similar to the insurance policy mentioned above. When a truck is acquired, it is an asset. The truck provides service to the organization over several future years, and part of its cost is an expense of each of these years, just as part of the cost of the insurance policy is an expense of the years in which it provides protection. The difference is that the life of the insurance policy is known (two years in the example), whereas the life of buildings and equipment must be estimated because usually there is no way of knowing in advance how long these assets will be used.

The process of charging off a portion of the cost of buildings and equipment as an expense in each of the years in which these assets provide service is called *depreciation,* and the amount charged to a given year is the *depreciation expense* of that year. A truck costing $13,000 would be recorded as an asset at the time it was acquired. If it is estimated to have a useful life of five years and a trade-in value of $3,000 at the end of that time, $10,000 of its cost ($13,000 − $3,000) will be an expense of the five-year period.

The usual practice, called the *straight-line method,* is to charge an equal amount of depreciation expense each year. In this case the depreciation expense in each of the five years would be $2,000 (i.e. $10,000 ÷ 5).

***Fringe Benefits.*** When employees work for an entity, the entity's cost for their services includes not only their salaries but also the pension, leave pay, holiday pay, and various benefits to which they become entitled by virtue of having worked. The total cost of these services is an expense of the period in which the work was done. The same amount is an expenditure of the period. This is because the organization has incurred a liability to pay for the total cost, including benefits, at the time the services were acquired, even though in the case of pensions the actual cash disbursement may not be made until many years in the future. Nevertheless, many organizations, including some large cities and some states, interpret the term "expenditures" to include only items that will be paid for in the near future; they exclude payments that will be made at some more distant time. They therefore count pensions as expenditures and expenses only when the pension payments to retired employees are made.

Failure to record pension costs in the year in which they are incurred is one of the most serious weaknesses in state and local government accounting systems. Not only does this omission understate the costs of current operations, but it also puts the burden of providing for the pensions on future generations, rather than on the current one, even though the current generation received the benefit of the labor services. The latter point suggests the criterion of *generational equity:* the generation that receives the services should pay for them; the burden should not be passed on to future generations.

*Examples:* 1. According to the San Jose (California) *Mercury News* of November 24, 1977, one third of each 1977 tax dollar spent on pensions was paying for what California State Finance Director Roy Bell described as "the neglect, deliberate avoidance, or nonrecognition of costs of the last two generations."

2. In 1970 (according to *The Wall Street Journal,* November 24, 1975), Hamtramck, Michigan, paid twice as much in pensions to retired employees as its payroll for current services; it would have gone bankrupt had it not been rescued by the state.

3. In New York City, also according to the 1975 *Wall Street Journal* article, the amount of pension benefits that had been earned but not provided for had accumulated to approximately $6 billion (that's *billion*) in 1975.

The principles for measuring the current cost of personnel services are well worked out. For pensions, they are set forth in *Accounting Principles Board Opinion No. 8.* They apply both to nonprofit and profit-oriented organizations.

***Donated and Contributed Services.*** In many nonprofit organizations volunteers donate their services to the organization. Although these services are valuable, they are not ordinarily counted as revenues. In a few cases, if the organization can control the activities of their volunteers in the same way that they control the work of paid employees, the services are measured at the going wage rate and are counted as revenues. (This is sometimes referred to as the "rule of reprimand": if volunteers can be reprimanded in the same fashion as paid employees, the value of their services is recognized as revenue.) If these services are counted as revenues, an equal amount is reported as expenses, so there is no effect on net income.

In organizations operated by religious orders, the teachers, nurses, physicians, clergy, and other members of the order may be paid less than the going rate for their services. Such services are called *contributed services* (as distinguished from *donated services,* above). Usually, the religious order bills the organization in which these persons work at the going rate, and this amount is clearly an expense.

## Matching Concept

If a store sells an item in 19x2 for $100, it has revenue of $100. If the item cost $60, it also has an expense of $60 because the item is no longer an asset. The $100 is an increase in equity, and the $60 is a simultaneous decrease in equity, so the net effect on equity is an increase of $40. (Actually, it would be possible to record just the net increase of $40, called the *gross margin,* but it is more informative to record the revenue component and the expense component separately.)

The effect on equity of this transaction is not properly reported unless the revenue component and the expense component are recorded in the same period. If, for example, the merchandise had been purchased in 19x1 and sold in 19x2, and if the $60 had been recorded as in expense in 19x1 rather than 19x2, 19x1 income would be understated by $60 and 19x2 income would be overstated by $60. This illustrates the *matching concept,* which states that *when a given transaction affects both revenue and expense, the effect on each should be reported in the same period.*

For the sale of merchandise, the matching of revenue with the cost of the merchandise is easy to see because both amounts relate to the same item of merchandise. In other situations, the relationship is less obvious.

***Contributions and Grants.*** Suppose, for example, a foundation made a $30,000 contribution to a university in 19x1 on the condition that the university hold a conference in 19x2. The conference is held in 19x2, and $30,000 is spent on it. Clearly, there was an expense of $30,000 in 19x2, and the matching concept requires that the $30,000 contribution be reported as revenue in 19x2, *not* in 19x1 when it was received. The $30,000 cash received in 19x1 is a liability as of the end of 19x1, representing the university's obligation to incur expenses for the conference in 19x2, and is so reported on the balance sheet, with a title such as Precollected Revenue.

If the expenses of the conference were less than $30,000, and if the foundation did not require that the difference be returned, the university had income in 19x2. If the difference had to be returned, the revenue would be reduced by this amount, in which case the revenue would equal the expense. If the expense were more than $30,000, there would be a loss in 19x2.

## Reporting Expenses and Revenues

On the operating statement, expenses may be classified either by *elements* (e.g., salaries, fringe benefits, supplies, depreciation) or by *programs.* A program is a principal category of activity that the entity undertakes in order to achieve its objectives. For a college or university, for example, the National Association of College and University Business Officers recommends that expenses be reported in two main categories, (1) educational and general and (2) auxiliary enterprises (e.g., dormitories, food service, student union). In the educational and general category, the programs include, among others: instruction, research, academic support, student services, institutional support, and student aid.

Classification of expenses by programs is generally more informative than classifying them by elements. Some organizations report a main classification by programs, and report expenses by elements under each principal program. If some expenses are incurred for two or more programs, an equitable share of such *joint* or *common* expenses is allocated to each program. Techniques for doing this are described in Chapter 4.

If revenues can readily be identified with programs, they may be classified by programs. Another common basis for classifying revenues is by their source; for example, in a university, revenue sources include tuition, contributions from private parties, government grants, endowment revenue, and miscellaneous.

### Implications for the Balance Sheet

The examples given above illustrate a fundamental point about the balance sheet. Although the primary purpose of accounting is to measure the income of an accounting period, in assigning revenues and expenses to the proper period various balance sheet items are affected. Most nonmonetary assets—prepaid expenses, inventory, buildings and equipment—represent expenditures that will become expenses in future periods. The monetary asset, accounts receivable, arises from revenues of the current period that will be collected in a future period. Accrued liabilities arise from expenses of the current period that will not be paid for until a future period. Precollected revenues are liabilities that will become revenues in some future period. And so on. In essence, then, in order to measure income, the double-entry concept requires that some transactions consist, in part, of entries to various asset and liability accounts on the balance sheet. The purpose of a balance sheet is therefore, to a large extent, one of facilitating the proper measurement of income.

## CAPITAL CONTRIBUTIONS

### Nature of Capital Contributions

The preceding description applies to accounting in all types of organizations. Nonprofit organizations have one type of transaction that occurs only rarely, if at all, in profit-oriented businesses, and therefore is not dealt with in GAAP for businesses. This is the *capital contribution* (or *nonoperating contribution*), which is made for capital, as distinguished from operating, purposes.

Operating contributions are revenues. If the donor does not specify otherwise, they are revenues in the year in which they are received or pledged. If the donor specifies that they are to be used in a certain year, or for a certain purpose (such as the conference referred to earlier), they are revenues in the specified year or in the year in which expenses are incurred for the specified purpose. When recognized as revenue, they add to the resources available for use in operations and hence to the organization's equity.

Capital contributions are *not* revenues; they are direct additions to an organization's equity. There are two general types of capital contributions: contributions for endowment and contributions for plant. When a donor contributes to an organization's endowment, the amount of the contribution generally is held in trust indefinitely, and only the earnings on that amount are available for operating purposes. Similarly, when a donor contributes money to acquire a building or other item of plant, these funds must be used for the specified purpose and are not available to finance operating activities. Both types of contributions add to equity—they make the organization "better off"—but neither is associated with the operating activities of the period in which they are received, and therefore they are not revenues of that period. They are accounted for by establishing separate categories of equity, called "funds," accompanied by separate balance sheets showing the assets and, if relevant, the liabilities related to this equity.[3]

## Endowment

A donor may specify that the contribution is for the organization's endowment, that is, only the earnings are to be used for operating purposes. Alternatively, even if the donor does not make a legally binding restriction, the circumstances may clearly indicate that the contribution is for endowment purposes. If, for example, Morris University receives $1,000,000 from a bequest in which the donor states, "I bequeath $1,000,000 to Morris University," the size of the gift makes it obvious that it was not intended for use in the year in which the college received the money.

A legally binding contribution to endowment is called *true endowment;* the other type is called *quasi endowment.* The difference is that the principal amount of true endowment can never be used for operating purposes, whereas the governing board could vote to use a portion of quasi endowment for operating purposes. It normally would do so only in the event of a financial emergency, however.

The assets of the endowment consist principally of investments in stocks, bonds, and real estate. The assets are for the endowment fund as a whole, however, and are not separated according to individual donors, or even between those assets which relate to true endowment and those which represent quasi endowment.

A donor may specify that the income from his or her endowment may be spent only for a designated purpose, such as a scholarship aid, or even a scholarship to a student from the donor's home town. For internal management purposes, records of these restrictions must be maintained. These individual records do not appear in the general-purpose financial statements, however.

***Endowment Earnings.*** Until recently, the amount recognized as endowment revenue of a year was the amount of dividends, interest, rents, and other earnings of the endowment. This is still the practice of the majority of organizations. Beginning in the 1960s, however, some organizations calculated the amount of endowment revenue on a *spending rate* basis. They

[3] As an exception to the general rule that assets are recorded at cost, contributions of capital assets, such as works of art or museum pieces, are recorded at their "fair market value," even though they did not cost the entity anything.

applied a percentage, in most cases 5 percent or thereabouts, to the average market value of the endowment. There are two related reasons for this practice. First, dividends on common stock do not typically reflect the real "earnings" on that stock; in most instances, the investor expects that the stock will increase in value, and this increase is not reflected if the return is calculated on the basis of dividends alone. Second, if all of endowment earnings were used for operating purposes, the purchasing power of the endowment would decrease because of inflation. The use of a spending rate of 5 percent assumes that, if there were no inflation, invested funds would earn 5 percent. Earnings in excess of 5 percent are therefore expected to approximate the rate of inflation, and are retained in the principal of the endowment so as to maintain its purchasing power. (This topic is discussed in more depth in the Michael Morris University case, Case 3–2).

## Plant Contributions

Contributions for buildings, equipment, art or other museum objects, and similar purposes are reported in a separate classification of equity. Since art and other museum objects presumably have an indefinitely long life, there is no problem in reporting them on the balance sheet at their cost or fair market value at the time of acquisition. (An increase in the fair market value of art objects is not reflected in the accounts, consistent with the cost concept discussed earlier.)

Buildings and equipment, however, have a limited life, and for them there is a considerable difference of opinion as to how, if at all, this type of equity should affect net income. Should the cost of a building be charged as an expense to the periods in which the building provides service; that is, should the cost of a contributed building be depreciated? Some organizations do not depreciate contributed plant, but simply report the assets on the balance sheet at cost year after year, until they are retired. The argument for this practice is that since the buildings were contributed, they did not, and never will, require the use of revenues to finance them, and that inclusion of a depreciation component as an expense item on the operating statement would understate the amount of income associated with operating activities. Others maintain that the buildings are used for operating purposes and that omission of depreciation would understate the real expenses of operating the organization.

A recently proposed solution to this dilemma is to report depreciation on contributed plant as an expense, and to report an equal amount as revenue of the period. The revenue component represents the donor's contribution to the operations of the period, while the expense component reports the cost of using the facilities. Since the two amounts are equal, there is no net effect on income. Although recommended by an international accounting standards group, this practice has so far not been adopted in the United States.

## Financial Statement Presentation

In reporting balance sheet amounts, the assets in endowment and plant must be separated from operating assets. Cash in endowment, for example, is not available to pay current bills, and it would be misleading to combine endowment cash with operating cash and report the total as a single item. The practice therefore is to establish a separate *fund* for endowment. A fund is a self-balancing set of accounts, and *fund accounting* is a type of accounting that is found principally in nonprofit organizations. Thus, for a nonprofit organization, the balance sheet that was shown in Exhibit 3–2 would constitute the operating fund, often called the *general fund.* A separate balance sheet with assets, liabilities, and equity would be reported for the *endowment fund,* and there would be a third balance sheet with contributed buildings and equipment, for the *plant fund.*

An example of a balance sheet with three sections is given in Exhibit 3–3. As indicated, the first section is the same as that given in Exhibit 3–2. Note that each section is self-balancing, that is, total assets equal total liabilities and equity, and that each section contains its own cash account.

By definition, net income is the result of operating activities, so there is no operating statement as such for endowment or plant funds. In order to describe what has happened during the year, however, a *statement of changes in equity* is prepared for each fund. For the endowment fund, it shows contributions to endowment, and earnings from dividends, interest, rent, and the sale of assets as additions; the amount recognized as endowment revenue is

**Exhibit 3–3**

EXAMPLE ORGANIZATION
Balance Sheet
As of December 31, 19x1
($000)

| *Assets* | | *Liabilities and Equity* | |
|---|---|---|---|
| | *Operating Fund* | | |
| | (details as on Exhibit 3–2) | | |
| Total assets | $10,200 | Total liabilities and equity | $10,200 |
| | *Endowment Fund* | | |
| Cash | $ 10 | True endowment | $ 7,000 |
| Bonds | 9,100 | Quasi endowment | 13,010 |
| Stock | 10,900 | | |
| Total assets | $20,010 | Endowment equity | $20,010 |
| | *Plant Fund* | | |
| Cash | $ 20 | Accounts payable | $ 30 |
| Investments | 400 | | |
| Buildings and equipment | 11,200 | Plant equity | 11,590 |
| Total assets | $11,620 | Total liabilities and equity | $11,620 |

shown as a subtraction. (The statement may or may not report unrealized gains and losses, that is, changes in the market value of securities that remain in the endowment portfolio.) A similar statement describes additions to and subtractions from the plant fund equity.

## VARIATIONS IN PRACTICE

As described early in the chapter, there are five "Guides" applicable to accounting for various types of nonprofit organizations. These guides treat similar transactions differently, but they are simply "guides," that is, an organization is not required to adhere to the requirements of its particular guide. In due time the FASB will issue standards that will eliminate, or at least greatly reduce, the differences among accounting practices in these organizations, but until that time, readers of financial statements must understand and allow for the peculiarities that currently exist. We shall describe the more important of these, using the statements in the Guide for Colleges and Universities as an example. University accounting is about in the middle—between hospitals, whose accounting is basically similar to that described in the first section of this chapter, and state and municipal governments, whose accounting is fundamentally different.

Since the most important statement is the operating statement, we shall focus on it. Recall that the operating statement contains two, and only two, types of items: revenues, which are increases in equity associated with operating activities (or put another way, net inflows of resources), and expenses, which are decreases in equity associated with operating activities (or net outflows of resources).

### Terminology

Since we are interested in activities during the year, we look for a statement that reports such activities rather than the entity's status as of the end of the year.[4] It will be headed "for the year ended . . . ," rather than "as of (a stated date)." Such a statement from the College and University Guide is given in Exhibit 3–4. It contains the heading "Current Funds." In other organizations the heading might be "General Fund" or "Operating Fund." In some organizations, the corresponding statement has additional columns for plant funds, endowment funds, and other nonoperating funds. Since our focus is on operating activities, we should look principally at the columns relating to operations.

---

[4] A survey of the financial statements of 102 foundations uncovered 28 different titles for the operating statement or similar report. See Jack Traub, *Accounting and Reporting Practices of Private Foundations* (New York: Praeger Publishers, 1977), pp. 79–80.

## Restricted Operating Funds

Exhitit 3–4 has two columns for operating items. As is the practice with many nonprofit organizations, amounts for restricted operating contributions are shown separately from other amounts. This separation is relatively unimportant, because both restricted and unrestricted items are revenues of the period. Some organizations recognize restricted contributions as revenues in the period in which they are received, rather than in the period in which expenses are incurred for the restricted purpose; this is inconsistent with the matching principle.

## Expenditures versus Expense

Exhibit 3–4 uses the term "expenditures" rather than "expenses." This means that the amounts are for the goods and services *acquired* during the period, rather than for the goods and services *consumed* during the period. As explained earlier, the acquisition of inventory does not decrease equity; it merely increases one asset (inventory) and either decreases another asset (cash) or increases a liability (accounts payable) by the same amount; equity is unchanged. Thus, a report of expenditures does not correctly reflect the change in equity.

In the majority of situations, however, the error is not great. This is because most expenses are for services rendered, including such items as salaries and other costs of employees, telephone charges, and electricity. Services are consumed the instant they are acquired; they cannot be held in inventory. Thus, for these items the expense and the expenditure occur in the same period.

Expenditures differ from expenses for two principal types of items: inventory, and plant and equipment. For inventory, such as fuel oil or supplies, the expenditure occurs in the year in which the item was received, but the expense occurs when the item is consumed, which may be a later period. Even here, however, the difference may not be substantial. If new items flow into inventory at about the same rate as old items flow out for use in operations, the level of inventory remains unchanged, and expenses in a period are approximately equal to expenditures.

For items of plant and equipment, however, the difference between expense and expenditure is likely to be substantial. For such items the expenditure occurs when the item is acquired, but the related depreciation expense occurs in each year of the asset's life, which may be 5 years, 10 years, or 50 years. A possible offset to this error is the treatment of debt service, discussed below.

## Transfers

Below the educational and general expenditures listed on Exhibit 3–4 are three items labeled "Mandatory transfers"; two similar items appear below

**Exhibit 3–4**

SAMPLE EDUCATIONAL INSTITUTION
Statement of Current Funds Revenues, Expenditures, and Other Changes
Year Ended June 10, 19—

| | *Current Year* | | | |
|---|---|---|---|---|
| | *Unrestricted* | *Restricted* | *Total* | *Prior Year Total* |
| Revenues: | | | | |
| Tuition and fees | $2,600,000 | | 2,600,000 | 2,300,000 |
| Federal appropriations | 500,000 | | 500,000 | 500,000 |
| State appropriations | 700,000 | | 700,000 | 700,000 |
| Local appropriations | 100,000 | | 100,000 | 100,000 |
| Federal grants and contracts | 20,000 | 375,000 | 395,000 | 350,000 |
| State grants and contracts | 10,000 | 25,000 | 35,000 | 200,000 |
| Local grants and contracts | 5,000 | 25,000 | 30,000 | 45,000 |
| Private gifts, grants, and contracts | 850,000 | 380,000 | 1,230,000 | 1,190,000 |
| Endowment income | 325,000 | 209,000 | 534,000 | 500,000 |
| Sales and services of educational departments | 190,000 | | 190,000 | 195,000 |
| Sales and services of auxiliary enterprises | 2,200,000 | | 2,200,000 | 2,100,000 |
| Expired term endowment | 40,000 | | 40,000 | |
| Other sources (if any) | | | | |
| Total current revenues | 7,540,000 | 1,014,000 | 8,554,000 | 8,180,000 |
| Expenditures and mandatory transfers: | | | | |
| Educational and general: | | | | |
| Instruction | 2,960,000 | 489,000 | 3,449,000 | 3,300,000 |
| Research | 100,000 | 400,000 | 500,000 | 650,000 |
| Public service | 130,000 | 25,000 | 155,000 | 175,000 |
| Academic support | 250,000 | | 250,000 | 225,000 |
| Student services | 200,000 | | 200,000 | 195,000 |
| Institutional support | 450,000 | | 450,000 | 445,000 |
| Operation and maintenance of plant | 220,000 | | 220,000 | 200,000 |
| Scholarships and fellowships | 90,000 | 100,000 | 190,000 | 180,000 |
| Educational and general expenditures | 4,400,000 | 1,014,000 | 5,414,000 | 5,370,000 |

| | | | | |
|---|---|---|---|---|
| Mandatory transfers for: | | | | |
| Principal and interest | 90,000 | | 90,000 | 50,000 |
| Renewals and replacements | 100,000 | | 100,000 | 80,000 |
| Loan fund matching grant | 2,000 | | 2,000 | |
| Total educational and general | 4,592,000 | 1,014,000 | 5,606,000 | 5,500,000 |
| Auxiliary enterprises: | | | | |
| Expenditures | 1,830,000 | | 1,830,000 | 1,730,000 |
| Mandatory transfers for: | | | | |
| Principal and interest | 250,000 | | 250,000 | 250,000 |
| Renewals and replacements | 70,000 | | 70,000 | 70,000 |
| Total auxiliary enterprises | 2,150,000 | | 2,150,000 | 2,050,000 |
| Total expenditures and mandatory transfers | 6,742,000 | 1,014,000 | 7,756,000 | 7,550,000 |
| Other transfers and additions/(deductions): | | | | |
| Excess of restricted receipts over transfers to revenues | | 45,000 | 45,000 | 40,000 |
| Refunded to grantors | | (20,000) | (20,000) | |
| Unrestricted gifts allocated to other funds | (650,000) | | (650,000) | (510,000) |
| Portion of quasi-endowment gains appropriated | 40,000 | | 40,000 | |
| Net increase in fund balances | 188,000 | 25,000 | 213,000 | 160,000 |

Source: American Institute of CPAs, *Audits of Colleges and Universities,* (New York: AICPA, 1975) pp. 114, 115.

"Auxiliary enterprises" expenditures. In order to measure revenues and expenses, we must decide how, if at all, these items affect equity. If they increase or decrease equity from operating activities, they should be reclassified as revenues or expenses. If not, they should be excluded from the measurement of operating performance.

***Debt Service.*** The first item in each of these groups is labeled "Principal and interest." It represents the amount paid during the year to retire a debt, usually a mortgage loan entered into in order to finance the construction of a building or a major item of equipment, such as a large computer. (If the item were relatively inexpensive, it would be included in the expenditures listed above.) Interest on such a loan is an expense of the period. The part of the $340,000 ($90,000 + $250,000) which is the principal, however, is never an expense. It represents the decrease in an asset (cash) and a corresponding decrease in a liability (the loan) with no effect on equity.

Nevertheless, the principal portion may *approximate* an expense. In universities (and in many other nonprofit organizations) plant and equipment items are recorded at cost, and no depreciation is charged for them. If the loan is repaid over a period that approximates the life of the asset, the annual principal repayment may correspond to depreciation. Without further information, we do not know how close this approximation is, but probably the measurement of operating performance is closer to being right by including this amount as an expense than by omitting it. The principal portion of debt service is sometimes called a *surrogate* for depreciation.

***Renewals and Replacements.*** We do not know for sure what the $170,000 ($100,000 + $70,000) for "Renewals and replacements" represents. It does not represent expenditures for ordinary maintenance work because these are included as one of the operating expenditures. Nor is it the acquisition of new plant and equipment, because these expenditures are handled through the plant fund. Probably, the amount represents decisions to use some of the current year's net income to make major renovations of buildings or to replace obsolete equipment at some future time. If so, it is neither an expense nor an operating expenditure of the current period, and should be excluded from the report of performance entirely.

***Matching Grants.*** The $2,000 item for "Loan fund matching grant" reflects a requirement from a grantor that its contribution to the loan fund be matched by a contribution from the entity's operating equity. Other "transfers" of a similar nature may appear on the statements of colleges and universities. They represent decisions as to how the net income of the current period should be used in the future. They are *not* expenses. To the extent that net income is not transferred to another fund, it remains in the operating section of the balance sheet. Some transfers are labeled "mandatory," indicating that the organization is required by contract or by a policy decision of the governing board to make them. Others are "nonmandatory." They reflect a governing board decision in a given year. Both types should be excluded from the measurement of net income unless, as in the case of debt service, they are approximations of items that properly should be reported as expenses.

***Capital Contributions.*** As noted earlier, contributions for operating purposes are revenues, but capital contributions, for plant or endowment, are added directly to the organization's equity. In university accounting, only those capital contributions that are legally designated for plant or endowment go directly to these nonoperating funds. If not legally designated, they are recorded initially as unrestricted revenues of the current period. For major bequests, as explained above, this makes no sense because such amounts are not going to be used for operating purposes, certainly not in the current year.

University accounting corrects this error by subtracting as a transfer the amount that, as a practical matter, is intended for capital contributions. This is the $650,000 item labeled "Unrestricted gifts allocated to other funds" near the bottom of Exhibit 3–4. The nature of this transfer suggests that it should be subtracted from revenues, thus leaving in revenues only those amounts intended for operating purposes in the current year. By contrast, the $40,000 labeled "Portion of quasi-endowment gains appropriated" would appear to be a revenue item representing part of the earnings on endowment.

### Net Income

Exhibit 3–4 does not show an item labeled net income. As can be seen from the analysis of the above items, however, the total "Net increase in fund balances," $213,000, reduced by the $170,000 for renewals and replacements, is a rough approximation.

## STATE AND LOCAL GOVERNMENTS

The financial statements of state and local governments are more complicated and more difficult to understand than those of other nonprofit organizations. This is because, by tradition, government entities have carried the principles of fund accounting to extremes. For example, a municipality may create a separate fund to account for the installation of one half mile of sewer, and it may report this fund, along with each of dozens or hundreds of similar funds, separately in its financial statements. Each of these is a restricted fund as the term has been described above. No attempt is made here to describe the details of the accounting used for these funds; many of them are archaic. A few of the more important points are mentioned.

The general operating activities of a governmental unit are accounted for in a general fund, just as described above. Operating activities financed from special sources are accounted for in *special revenue funds,* such as highway maintenance, which is financed by a gasoline tax. For both the general fund and special revenue funds, operating statements are usually prepared on an expenditure basis rather than on an expense basis.

If the governmental unit operates an electric or gas utility, a water system, a subway, a toll bridge, or other activity for which fees are charged directly to users, these are accounted for in what are called *enterprise funds.* Accounting for enterprise funds usually is on an expense basis, including depreciation of capital assets.

Finally, when a governmental unit issues bonds to finance capital projects, there are special ways of accounting for the issuance of these bonds, including principal and interest payments which are unlike the accounting done by other organizations, both business and nonprofit.

### Encumbrance Accounting

Some governmental units elect to report encumbrances instead of, or in addition to, expenditures. An encumbrance occurs when an organization enters into a contract to acquire goods and services. It has no counterpart in business accounting; in business accounting, the first formal record of a transaction is made when goods are received or services rendered, not when the goods or services are ordered. A report of amounts encumbered during a period bears no relationship to the cost of services provided during that period. Additional details on encumbrance accounting are provided in Chapter 10.

### Other Variations

State and local governments are urged to follow principles set forth in *Statement 1, Governmental Accounting and Financial Reporting,* issued by the National Council on Governmental Accounting in 1979. Principles relating to income measurement are given in the City of New York case, Case 3–4. Only a small percentage of these organizations follow these principles, however.[5]

Thus, in order to ascertain the total picture of the operation of a governmental unit, one must take into account the three separate types of funds—the general fund, special revenue funds, and enterprise funds—and also the special

[5] A study of 43 cities by Coopers & Lybrand and the University of Michigan, *Financial Disclosure Practices of the American Cities: A Public Report,* 1976, showed that 16 cities made no disclosure about their obligations for retirement benefits; 7 of the 43 cities disclosed their total dollar obligations to employees for their vacations and sick-leave benefits; almost 30 percent of the cities did not maintain adequate records to account for land, buildings, and equipment; only 26 of the cities had their financial statements audited by independent certified public accountants, and of those, only 8 received an auditor's opinion that did not take exception to the cities' reporting of financial conditions and reports of operations.

As of 1981, only 12 states required municipalities and other bodies under their control to conform to the NCGA standard, *Governmental Accounting, Auditing and Financial Reporting.* Peter F. Rousmaniere and Nathaniel B. Guild, "The Second Wave of Municipal Accounting Reform," *Public Budgeting and Finance,* Spring 1981, p. 69.

accounting techniques used for bond issues, encumbrance accounting, and others.

## FEDERAL GOVERNMENT

The federal government does not publish a balance sheet or an operating statement for the government as a whole, although it does do so for business-like government agencies such as the U.S. Postal Service and the Tennessee Valley Authority. The financial viability of the federal government depends basically on its authority to print money, rather than on its assets as listed on a balance sheet, or on its operating activities that could be reported on an operating statement. Investors in government bonds know that because of this authority, the bonds will be repaid (short of a catastrophe that would destroy the whole fabric of government); they need not look to financial statements for an analysis of debt-paying ability; and they know that the federal government will not declare bankruptcy.

Managers in the federal government (and their representatives in the Congress) are interested primarily in financial reports that show how much government agencies spent compared with the amounts they were permitted to spend. Accounting principles governing the preparation of these reports are different in significant respects from those used in business accounting. Legislators and those interested in public finance need information on federal revenues, outlays, and the resulting deficit (or, occasionally, surplus). Special reports provide this information. Federal accounting is discussed in more detail in Chapter 10.

## SUMMARY

With one exception, revenues and expenses should be measured in the same way in all organizations, both profit-oriented and nonprofit. Revenues are increases in operating equity and expenses are decreases. Both should be reported in the accounting period to which they relate, in accordance with the accrual concept.

The exception is capital contributions, such as contributions of plant or endowment, which should be added directly to equity, and accounted for separately from operating transactions. Such a separation leads to individual funds for nonoperating items and the related practice of fund accounting, which has no counterpart in a business.

Despite the similarity of most transactions in all organizations, actual accounting practices vary greatly among various types of nonprofit organizations. These variations reflect primarily the different treatments suggested in the five Guides that apply to these organizations. The Financial Accounting Standards Board is now responsible for developing accounting standards for nonprofit organizations, and in due time it will eliminate, or at least greatly reduce, these variations.

## SUGGESTED ADDITIONAL READINGS


Financial Accounting Standards Board, Statement of Financial Concepts No. 4. *Objectives of Financial Reporting by Nonbusiness Organizations.* Stamford, Conn., 1980.

Gross, Malvern J., Jr., and William Warshauer, Jr., eds. *Financial and Accounting Guide for Nonprofit Organizations.* New York: John Wiley & Sons, 1983.

Hay, Leon B. *Government Accounting.* 6th ed. Homewood, Ill.: Richard D. Irwin, 1980.

Henke, Emerson O. *Accounting for Nonprofit Organizations,* 3d ed. Boston, Mass.: Kent Publishing, 1983.

Lynn, Edward S., and Joan W. Thompson. *Introduction to Fund Accounting,* Reston, Va.: Reston Publishing, 1974.

Lynn, Edward S., and Robert J. Freeman. *Fund Accounting Theory and Practice,* 2d ed. Englewood Cliffs, N.J.: Prentice-Hall, 1983.


### Education


American Institute of Certified Public Accountants. *Audits of Colleges and Universities.* New York, 1973.

National Association of Independent Schools. *Accounting for Independent Schools,* 2d ed. Boston, 1974.

National Association of College and University Business Officers. *College and University Business Administration.* 3d ed. Washington, D.C., 1974.

Ryan, L. V. *An Accounting Manual for Catholic Elementary and Secondary Schools.* Washington, D.C.: National Catholic Education Association, 1969.


### Federal Government


Comptroller General of the United States (General Accounting Office). *Manual for Guidance of Federal Agencies.* Washington, D.C.: Government Printing Office, 1969.

————. *Frequently Asked Questions about Accrual Accounting in the Federal government, 1970.*

————. *Accounting Principles and Standards for Federal Agencies, 1972.*

United Nations Organization. *A Manual of Government Accounting.*


### Health Care


American Hospital Association. *Chart of Accounts for Hospitals.* Chicago, 1976.

American Institute of Certified Public Accountants. *Hospital Audit Guide.* New York, 1972.

U.S. Department of Health Education and Welfare. *A Guide for Non-Profit Institutions. Cost Principles and Procedures for Establishing Indirect Cost Rates for Grants and Contracts with the Department of Health, Education and Welfare.* Washington, D.C.: Government Printing Office 1970. DHEW Publication No. (OS)72–28.

## State and Local Government

American Institute of Certified Public Accountants. *Audits of State and Local Governmental Units.* New York, 1974.

National Committee on Governmental Accounting. *Governmental Accounting, Auditing, and Financial Reporting.* Chicago: Municipal Finance Officers Association, 1968.

National Council on Governmental Accounting. *Statement 1, Governmental Accounting and Financial Reporting Principles.* Chicago: Municipal Finance Offices Association, 1979.

———. *Statement 2, Grant, Entitlement, and Shared Revenue Accounting by State and Local Governments.* Chicago: Municipal Finance Offices Association, 1979.

## Other

American Institute of Certified Public Accountants. *Audits of Voluntary Health and Welfare Organizations.* New York, 1974.

Association of Science—Technology Centers. *Museum Accounting Guidelines.* Washington, D.C.: Association of Science—Technology Centers, 1976.

Club Managers Association of America. *Uniform System of Accounts for Clubs.* 2d rev. ed. Washington, D.C.: Club Managers Association of America, 1967.

National Conference of Catholic Bishops. *Diocesan Accounting and Financial Reporting.* National Conference of Catholic Bishops, 1971.

United Way of America. *Accounting and Financial Reporting, A Guide for United Ways and Not-for-Profit Human Service Organizations.* Alexandria, Va.: United Way of America, Systems, Planning and Allocations Division, 1974.

## Case 3–1

# RIVER AREA HOME HEALTH SERVICES*

In November 1980, Ms. Carolyn Ringer, Treasurer of the River Area Home Health Services (RAHHS), was preparing a loan request to go to the Norten Municipal Bank. Less than eight months earlier, RAHHS had expanded their service and staff by 30 percent. At that time, the home health service had been in a secure financial position and Ms. Ringer, anticipating no financial problems, had spoken to the agency's board of directors in favor of the increase in services. However, in July, Ms. Ringer realized that although RAHHS had begun training and paying their new staff in June, the agency would not receive the additional revenue generated by the new staff until later in the year. With the staff totaling about 60 employees (full and part-time), Ms. Ringer realized that RAHHS could not always have on hand the cash they would require.

Faced with these unexpected expenses, Ms. Ringer had gone to the Norten Municipal Bank to apply for a short-term line of credit to cover the additional costs. Mr. Jansen, the bank officer, had granted RAHHS a line of credit which had reached almost $44,000 by September 1980. Although he had allowed the agency to continue using its line of credit into its next fiscal year,[1] he had raised some important considerations.

He explained that the bank was willing to continue a line of credit for the agency but he was concerned that Ms. Ringer had not adequately anticipated the agency's cash needs. He asked Ms. Ringer to present the bank at the outset with a detailed monthly statement of RAHHS's projected cash needs for fiscal year 1981. Consequently, Ms. Ringer began to review the agency's financial statements (contained in Exhibits 1 and 2) and collect data that would help her plan for RAHHS's future cash requirements.

## Background

River Area Home Health Services was a private, nonprofit home health agency founded in 1955 by four retired nurses. Each founder had between 10 and 35 years of experience working with elderly and disabled patients in Norten's hospitals. Realizing that a majority of their patients would not have needed hospitalization if Norten or the near vicinity had had a home health service, the nurses started their own agency. At first, RAHHS was small and operated out of one person's home. The agency then employed the four founders, a part-time social worker, and six home health aides, three of whom were volunteers.

---

* This case was prepared by Patricia O'Brien, under the direction of David W. Young, Harvard School of Public Health.

[1] RAHHS's fiscal year ran from October 1 to September 30. Fiscal year 1980 ran from October 1, 1979, to September 30, 1980.

**Exhibit 1**

RIVER AREA HOME HEALTH SERVICE
Balance Sheet
As of September 30, 1978–1980

| | *1978* | *1979* | *1980* |
|---|---|---|---|
| *Assets* | | | |
| Cash | $ 95,640 | $ 21,870 | $ 15,240 |
| Accounts receivable | 35,100 | 38,760 | 45,400 |
| Inventory | 17,748 | 20,520 | 26,640 |
| Prepaid expenses | 21,412 | 27,880 | 37,160 |
| Total current assets | 169,900 | 109,030 | 124,440 |
| Property and equipment (net) | 210,230 | 274,490 | 312,630 |
| Other assets | 9,060 | 10,650 | 11,100 |
| Total assets | $389,190 | $394,170 | $448,170 |
| *Liabilities and Fund Balances* | | | |
| Bank loan | -0- | -0- | 43,600 |
| Accounts payable | $ 1,830 | $ 2,361 | $ 1,950 |
| Salary and benefits payable | 20,700 | 21,600 | 23,400 |
| Due to third-party payor | 8,040 | 8,769 | 9,390 |
| Note payable, current | 14,160 | 17,490 | 19,380 |
| Mortgage, current | 7,500 | 7,500 | 7,500 |
| Total current liabilities | 52,230 | 57,720 | 105,220 |
| Mortgage payable | 112,500 | 105,000 | 97,500 |
| Other long-term debt | 180,000 | 180,000 | 180,000 |
| Total liabilities | 344,730 | 342,720 | 382,720 |
| Fund balance | 44,460 | 51,450 | 65,450 |
| Total liabilities and fund balance | $389,190 | $394,170 | $448,170 |

**Exhibit 2**

RIVER AREA HOME HEALTH SERVICES
Income Statements
Fiscal Years 1978–1980

| | *1978* | *1979* | *1980* |
|---|---|---|---|
| Gross patient revenue | $432,975 | $481,662 | $559,016 |
| Less: Contractual allowances and uncollectable accounts | 76,595 | 86,852 | 93,356 |
| Net patient revenue | $356,380 | $394,810 | $465,660 |
| Operating expenses: | | | |
| Salaries and benefits | $248,400 | $259,200 | $280,800 |
| Administration | 42,086 | 59,871 | 90,873 |
| Cost of medical supplies | 16,318 | 18,645 | 22,981 |
| Contract services | 5,415 | 5,760 | 6,820 |
| Equipment rental | 11,500 | 12,500 | 13,100 |
| Depreciation | 15,000 | 19,000 | 22,000 |
| Interest | 5,642 | 5,620 | 5,531 |
| Other expenses | 2,039 | 7,224 | 9,555 |
| Total operating expenses | $346,400 | $387,820 | $451,660 |
| Excess of revenue over expenses | 9,980 | 6,990 | 14,000 |
| Fund balance, September 30 | $44,460 | $51,450 | $65,450 |

By 1964, the organization had outgrown its "office space" as well as its organizational structure and objectives. Although two visiting nurse associations had sprung up in Norten in the early 60s, there was still a greater demand for RAHHS's services than the agency could provide. Demand had risen at an average rate of 10 percent per year, and forecasts at that time indicated a steady increase at the 10 percent level.

During the mid-60s, RAHHS underwent a gradual expansion. They purchased a small building in downtown Norten for management offices, employee training programs, and headquarters. They also bought some of the vehicles and equipment they had previously rented. In the subsequent 10 years, the staff grew from 10 to 30 people.

In early 1980, RAHHS was again faced with an increasing demand for home health services. A poll taken at Norten's three hospitals in March 1980 indicated that there would be a 20 percent increase for them in home health care patients. RAHHS management estimated that net patient revenue would reach $540,000 in FY 1981, an increase of 18 percent over the 1980 level. Further growth of between $50,000 and $70,000 a year was expected during the 1982–84 period.

Consequently, RAHHS was forced to decide whether to hold staff and services steady and hope that other health service organizations would fill in the gaps or to launch an expansion program aimed at providing more services to a greater number of patients in the Norten area. After examining RAHHS's financial position and talking to Norten's health care providers about the agency's services, the board voted overwhelmingly to expand.

## Data

Demand for RAHHS's services, like that for many other home health agencies, was seasonal. Over two thirds of the agency's annual home visits were made during the late fall and winter months. Exhibit 3 contains the forecasted monthly revenue for FY 80–81 based on the number of visits during FY 79–80. In making these projections, Ms. Ringer took into account the contractual adjustments and bad debts from RAHHS's third-party payors and indigent patients.

Although demand for the agency's services tended to be seasonal, RAHHS's employee salaries and benefits were expected to be relatively steady throughout the year. The agency had a firm policy of regular employment for both full and part-time employees which, according to management, enabled RAHHS to maintain a highly skilled and committed staff. RAHHS's management also believed that its employment policy contributed significantly to the agency's reputation for quality home health care. Employees were paid on the first of each month for earnings from the previous month. Starting in October, employee salary and benefit earnings were expected to be $27,500 a month except for June when many employees would be on vacation and

**Exhibit 3**
Estimated Monthly Revenue and
Month-End Accounts Receivable for FY 80–81

| | *Gross Patient Revenue* | *Net Revenue** | *Accounts Receivable, End-of-Month* |
|---|---|---|---|
| October | $ 45,000 | $ 37,200 | $ 78,300 |
| November | 64,000 | 52,500 | 98,700 |
| December | 90,400 | 74,100 | 141,900 |
| January | 93,300 | 76,500 | 171,600 |
| February | 104,300 | 85,500 | 185,400 |
| March | 58,900 | 48,300 | 157,200 |
| April | 49,000 | 40,200 | 95,400 |
| May | 40,900 | 33,600 | 78,300 |
| June | 35,600 | 29,200 | 51,000 |
| July | 21,900 | 18,000 | 39,700 |
| August | 23,000 | 18,900 | 40,000 |
| September | 31,700 | 26,000 | 59,800 |
| | $658,000 | $540,000 | |

* After adjustments for contractual allowances and bad debt.

some part-time wages would be eliminated; payments in July would thus decrease to about $20,000.

Disbursements related to overhead and administration were scheduled at $10,000 a month throughout FY 81. Included in that $10,000-a-month was Ms. Ringer's estimate of the monthly interest on the Norten Municipal Bank loan. The initial depreciation expense was forecasted to be $22,000. Medical and office supply purchases were projected at $2,280 per month. The agency's policy was to charge these items and pay for each month's purchases in the following month. Contract service expenses were forecast at $600 a month. Other miscellaneous expenses were projected to total about $1,000 per month.

The two new vans, ordered for the meals-on-wheels program, were due for delivery in December. The vans cost a total of $12,000 and would be paid for in four equal monthly installments, beginning on delivery. The vehicles had an economic life of four years, at the end of which their salvage value would be zero. Depreciation would begin in the month of delivery.

In FY 81, RAHHS would owe Dr. Wilson, one of the board members, $19,380 for a short-term, interest-free loan she had made to the agency. This amount was payable in equal installments in December and March. The agency was also the lessee on long-term leases of furniture, equipment, and automobiles, with terms ranging from three to five years, beginning at various dates. The payments owed on these operating leases totaled $15,000, payable in equal installments in December and June.

In October 1978 RAHHS had borrowed $120,000 from a life insurance company under a 16-year mortgage loan secured by the property and equipment. The current portion of the loan was repayable in equal installments in March and September of each year. Interest of 5 percent per annum on

**Exhibit 4**

RIVER AREA HOME HEALTH SERVICES
Cash Flow Worksheet

| | Oct. | Nov. | Dec. | Jan. | Feb. | Mar. | Apr. | May | June | July | Aug. | Sept. |
|---|---|---|---|---|---|---|---|---|---|---|---|---|
| CASH IN | | | | | | | | | | | | |
| CASH OUT: Salaries and benefits | | | | | | | | | | | | |
| Administration | | | | | | | | | | | | |
| Payment of A/P | | | | | | | | | | | | |
| Miscellaneous expense | | | | | | | | | | | | |
| Contract service | | | | | | | | | | | | |
| Payment of note/P | | | | | | | | | | | | |
| Vehicle expenditure | | | | | | | | | | | | |
| Equipment leases | | | | | | | | | | | | |
| Payment to third-party/P | | | | | | | | | | | | |
| Payment of mortgage/P | | | | | | | | | | | | |
| Mortgage interest | | | | | | | | | | | | |
| TOTAL OUT | | | | | | | | | | | | |
| Net inflow (+) or outflow (−) | | | | | | | | | | | | |
| Financing: (1) cash drawn down (+) or increase (−) | | | | | | | | | | | | |
| (2) Line-of-credit change | | | | | | | | | | | | |
| Beginning balance, bank loan | | | | | | | | | | | | |
| Ending balance, bank loan | | | | | | | | | | | | |

the unpaid balance was payable at the same time. In preparing her financial forecasts, Ms. Ringer planned to show separately the two principal payments, totaling $7,500, and the two interest payments, totaling $5,156, due in FY 1981.

The only other expenditure Ms. Ringer anticipated was $9,390 due to Medicare for payments received exceeding reimbursable costs for the period ending September 30, 1980. The sum payable is noninterest-bearing and due in equal installments in June and September. She did not expect to incur a liability of this sort during FY 1981. Inventory, prepaid expenses, other assets, and other long-term debt were expected to remain essentially unchanged during FY 1981.

Although Mr. Jansen had not hesitated to grant RAHHS a line of credit, he had stressed the importance of the bank's credit regulations. The bank required that for a loan of $150,000 or less, the agency maintain a compensating cash balance of $15,000 at all times. Secondly, the entire loan, including the $43,600 currently owed by RAHHS, was to be completely liquidated for at least one month during the year.

Using the worksheet in Exhibit 4, Ms. Ringer began to prepare a monthly cash flow forecast for FY 81 that, she hoped, would show how much money the agency would need on a monthly basis.

## Questions

1. Prepare the cash flow worksheet contained in Exhibit 4. What does this tell you about the operations of RAHHS?
2. Prepare *pro forma* financial statements for FY 80–81. What do these tell you about the operations of RAHHS? How can you reconcile the information in the cash flow worksheet with that in the financial statements?
3. What recommendations would you make to Ms. Ringer?

## Case 3–2

## MICHAEL MORRIS UNIVERSITY*

For about 15 years, the board of trustees of Michael Morris University had wrestled with the policy governing the amount of endowment earnings that should be recognized as operating revenue. Throughout the period 1980–82, the topic had been discussed at several meetings of the Finance Committee, and the committee hoped that the matter could be resolved once and for all at its May 1982 meeting.

---

* This case was prepared by Robert N. Anthony, Harvard Business School.

**Exhibit 1**
Michael Morris University
Basic Financial Data ($000)

| *Years Ending June 30* | *Market* | *Income* | *Additions* | *Cost* | *Book* | *Realized Gains* |
|---|---|---|---|---|---|---|
| 1953 ...... | $ 4,885 | $234 | $ 48 | $ 3,942 | $ 4,779 | $ 88 |
| 1954 ...... | 5,430 | 248 | 174 | 4,118 | 5,092 | 137 |
| 1955 ...... | 6,608 | 263 | 131 | 4,249 | 5,478 | 255 |
| 1956 ...... | 7,469 | 306 | 533 | 4,782 | 6,270 | 259 |
| 1957 ...... | 7,881 | 341 | 442 | 5,224 | 6,844 | 132 |
| 1958 ...... | 7,845 | 366 | 31 | 5,255 | 7,053 | 179 |
| 1959 ...... | 8,739 | 363 | 169 | 5,424 | 7,600 | 378 |
| 1960 ...... | 8,748 | 356 | 172 | 5,596 | 7,814 | 42 |
| 1961 ...... | 10,520 | 384 | 585 | 6,181 | 8,453 | 53 |
| 1962 ...... | 9,628 | 418 | 146 | 6,327 | 8,704 | 105 |
| 1963 ...... | 11,815 | 418 | 593 | 6,920 | 9,303 | 6 |
| 1964 ...... | 12,823 | 445 | 344 | 7,264 | 9,830 | 183 |
| 1965 ...... | 14,679 | 468 | 1,868 | 9,132 | 11,770 | 72 |
| 1966 ...... | 14,554 | 574 | 263 | 9,395 | 12,250 | 217 |
| 1967 ...... | 16,712 | 565 | 503 | 9,898 | 12,908 | 155 |
| 1968 ...... | 20,209 | 617 | 931 | 10,829 | 14,623 | 784 |
| 1969 ...... | 21,006 | 652 | 505 | 11,334 | 15,589 | 462 |
| 1970 ...... | 19,421 | 731 | 980 | 12,314 | 17,141 | 571 |

Arriving at a sound policy was important because the university adhered faithfully to a balanced budget each year. The amount of endowment revenue recognized had a significant effect on total revenue, and hence on the total amount of expenses that could be budgeted.

Michael Morris University was an old, relatively small, New England university. As shown in Exhibit 1, in June 1960 the market value of its endowment was $8.7 million, and its book value was $7.8 million. In June 1969 the market value reached a peak of $21.0 million, and the book value was $15.6 million. At that time, the policy was to recognize as endowment revenue interest income on bonds and dividends on stocks (plus some income from faculty mortgages and miscellaneous sources not relevant to the case). In the 1960s, the university invested fairly heavily, and successfully, in growth stocks. The investment objective was capital appreciation, and the dividends on these stocks were typically zero or low.

## Adoption of Total Return

In 1973 Michael Morris adopted a "total return" policy.[1] It recognized as endowment revenue 5 percent of the three-year average market value of the

[1] "Total return" means dividends, interest, and appreciation in market value, whether or not realized. Although the policy is usually referred to as a "total return" policy, actually it is a revenue recognition policy. As used here the term does *not* mean that the total return is recognized as revenue. Rather, it means that endowment revenue is based, not on interest and dividends, but rather on a "prudent portion" of the total return.

portfolio. Several other institutions shifted to a similar concept at about the same time, and the typical rate was approximately 5 percent. In his report to the board recommending the adoption of this policy, Mr. Clark, chairman of the Finance Committee, made the following comments:

> The Finance Committee has been trying to define endowment earnings for a considerable length of time. This sounds simple, but it is not. Heretofore, we have not included any increase in market values in endowment earnings. By not including increases in market value, we have been robbing the present generation to benefit future generations. Much of the endowment is made up of common stocks that pay very low or no dividends but have tremendous potential for appreciation. Today's investors give as much weight in their investment decisions to appreciation as they do to dividends. We are all aware of the "glamour" stocks such as Eastman Kodak, IBM, J&J, and Xerox that sell at fantastically high price/earnings multiples but return 1.0 percent or less in cash dividends. Obviously, they are selling at such high P/Es because the investor is paying for future growth. Therefore, when we talk about a total return, we mean the total of both dividends and appreciation during any set period of time.
>
> However, we cannot just take dividends plus appreciation because if this were done, inflation would reduce the purchasing power of the endowment. We also should use some sort of a multiyear moving average to even out peaks and valleys.
>
> After more than 20 computer printouts covering the effect of various formulas on the results of past years, we finally have come to the realization (along with a number of other people!) that a figure of 5 percent of the endowment market value fits our purpose. This means that if we have a 9 percent "total return" (dividends and interest plus appreciation) and allow 4 percent for inflation, our endowment earnings are 5 percent. That is basically it. We have built in a number of safeguards, such as using average market values of the endowment over the past three years and taking into account unused restricted income.

## The AICPA Audit Guide

In 1974, the American Institute of Certified Public Accountants issued an "Audit Guide" for colleges and universities. This contained a lengthy discussion of the total return concept, from which the following is excerpted:

> The law and the legal profession, while by no means in accord on the subject, appear to be heading in the direction of elimination of limitations on the governing board's right to appropriate gains for expenditure. The total return concept continues, however, to cause accountants difficulty in that the concept thus far has produced few, if any, practical applications which appear to be *objectively determinable.* No clear *redefinition* of traditional income yield has evolved. The exercise of prudence is subjective and not susceptible to measurement in an accounting sense. The practical applications of the total return concept utilized to date amount substantively to the selection of a "spending rate," usually relating the rate to the market value of the portfolio. They appear in some cases to involve an intolerable element of arbitrariness.
>
> Consequently, until a general practice evolves which is *objectively determinable,* the guide would do a disservice to higher education and the accounting profession

**Exhibit 2**
Basic Financial Data ($000)

| | *Beginning Market Value* | *Gifts and Other Additions* | *Appre-ciation* | *Interest and Dividends* | *Revenue Recognized* | *Ending Market Value* |
|---|---|---|---|---|---|---|
| 1972 ........ | $24,610 | $ 837 | $ 3,535 | $ 831 | $ (709)* | $29,104 |
| 1973 ........ | 29,104 | 609 | (4,997) | 918 | (778) | 24,856 |
| 1974 ........ | 24,856 | 532 | (3,209) | 1,047 | (942) | 22,284 |
| 1975 ........ | 22,284 | 736 | 1,169 | 914 | (852) | 24,251 |
| 1976 ........ | 24,251 | (647) | (962) | 1,003 | (937) | 22,708 |
| 1977 ........ | 22,708 | 192 | (1,091) | 965 | (930) | 21,844 |
| 1978 ........ | 21,844 | 506 | 214 | 955 | (930) | 22,603 |
| 1979 ........ | 22,603 | 258 | 579 | 1,141 | (1,116) | 23,465 |
| 1980 ........ | 23,465 | 1,314 | 1,523 | 1,322 | (1,262) | 26,362 |
| 1981 ........ | 26,362 | 706 | 2,128 | 1,529 | (1,358) | 29,367 |
| | | $5,043 | $(1,111) | $10,625 | $(9,800) | |

*Summary:*

| | |
|---|---|
| Market value, June 30, 1971 ....... | $24,610 |
| Gifts and other additions .......... | 5,043 |
| Interest and dividends ............. | 10,625 |
| Appreciation ...................... | (1,111) |
| Revenue recognized ................ | (9,800) |
| Market value, June 30, 1981 ....... | $29,367 |

* Revenue Recognized excludes income on some restricted funds that could not be used during the year. Revenue actually recognized was therefore roughly 5–10 percent less than it would have been if these funds could have been used.

to sanction as a permissible accounting treatment the inclusion in revenue of gains utilized under a total return approach.

Some members of the Finance Committee had been uneasy about the new policy, and this statement led to a reopening of the question. Moreover, as indicated in Exhibit 2, the market value of the portfolio had been declining during this period. After considerable discussion, the committee recommended a return to the former policy, and the board approved this in May 1975. Because the portfolio at that time consisted of a smaller proportion of low-dividend stocks than in 1973, this change did not make a substantial difference in the amount of income recognized.

## Return to Total Return

In 1980, the issue was reopened. One new factor was the high rate of inflation in recent years and the opinion of some committee members that the board had an obligation to protect the purchasing power of the endowment. In 1981, another factor arose in conjunction with the peculiar effect of a decision by the Investment Committee. The Investment Committee decided that too large a fraction of the endowment portfolio was invested in common stock, so it shifted several million dollars into bonds. Since the dividend yield on stocks was about 5 percent and the interest yield on bonds was about 14 percent, this change resulted in a reported increase in endowment income of about $300,000 a year. Some Finance Committee members doubted that the university's revenue actually was increased by this move.

A memorandum circulated to the Finance Committee at that time from Mr. Clark, its chairman, contained the following (references to other colleges and universities relate to a survey of their practices that the financial vice president had prepared for the committee):

> Our revenue recognition policy should not influence our investment policy. Investment decisions should not be influenced by a need to produce a specified amount of cash. If dividends and interest do not produce enough cash, securities can easily be sold to provide the balance.
>
> Our revenue recognition policy should be consistent with accounting standards. The bottom line on the published financial statements should be the same as the number we use for internal decision making. At present, the College and University Audit Guide recommends that endowment revenues consist only of dividends and interest; however, this is likely to be changed in the near future to accommodate the total return approach.
>
> Our revenue recognition policy should be rarely changed. It should not be subject to the Board's judgment each year. Such a policy leads to the practice of recognizing whatever amount of endowment revenue is needed to balance the budget. This results in a meaningless bottom line. The bottom line should show whether we actually operated at a surplus or a deficit. Yale tried this approach in the 1960s, with disastrous results. In the early 1970s Wesleyan used up a substantial fraction of its endowment with such a policy.
>
> Our policy should not be to increase the previous year's revenue by a stated percentage. Such a policy bears no relationship to the actual performance of the portfolio, and would not, I believe, be acceptable under the new accounting standards. (This seems to be the policy at Harvard, MIT, and Bowdoin.)
>
> Our policy should be to maintain the purchasing power of the endowment. Because universities have relatively low productivity increases, such a policy will not permit existing programs to be financed with the existing endowment, even when the purchasing power of the endowment is held constant. Endowment revenue finances only a fraction of existing programs. We must count on new contributions to endowment to finance the balance.
>
> A policy of recognizing dividends and interest as revenue will maintain the purchasing power of the endowment only by coincidence, that is, if the proportion of low-yield, high-growth stocks to high-yield stocks and bonds happens to work out so that purchasing power is maintained. (This is the traditional policy, and is apparently still used by Amherst, Colby, Columbia, Johns Hopkins, Notre Dame, and several others.)
>
> Our revenue recognition policy need not be influenced by, nor govern, the rate of return used in calculating payments to annuitants.
>
> Our policy should be to recognize as revenue approximately 5 percent of the average market value of the endowment over three to five years, adjusted for additions to endowment during that period. (This is the policy of Brown, Cal Tech, Chicago, Dartmouth, Smith, and a number of institutions not listed in the material furnished us.)
>
> Such a policy does not necessarily result in a more volatile revenue stream

> than a policy of recognizing dividends and interest as revenue. Although dividends or interest for a given security change less rapidly than does the market value of that security, a percentage of the market value of the whole portfolio is not necessarily more volatile than the total dividend and interest stream. In 1981 we saw how volatile this stream can be; a shift in the mix of debt and equity resulted in a great increase in interest income, even though this increase did not have much economic significance.

In meetings held to discuss the issue, some members supported the point of view of this memorandum. Others, however, pointed out that the college had been burned once by using the total return policy, and that the prudent course of action was to continue with the policy of recognizing only dividends and interest. Furthermore, they said, any departure from this policy probably would result in a qualified opinion by the university's auditors, and this might have an adverse effect on the attitude of creditors.

Mr. Henderson, the financial vice president, recommended a policy of recognizing 5 percent of the average market value of the endowment. He thought that the average should be lagged two years; that is, the amount recognized in 1983 should be the average for the five years ended in 1981. In preparing the 1983 budget (in April 1982), the latest available information was that for fiscal year 1981.

## Questions

1. Assuming a revenue recognition policy based on average market value, how should the amount of revenue recognized in a given year be calculated?
2. What policy would you recommend? (Be prepared to discuss each of the alternative policies mentioned in the chairman's memorandum.)

## Case 3–3

## NATIONAL HELONTOLOGICAL ASSOCIATION*

Each December the incoming members of the board of directors of the National Helontological Association (NHA) met in joint session with the outgoing board as a means of smoothing the transition from one administration to another. At the meeting in December 1978, questions were raised about whether the 1978 board had adhered to the general policy of the association. The ensuing discussion became quite heated.

* This case was prepared by Robert N. Anthony, Harvard Business School.

**Exhibit 1**

NATIONAL HELONTOLOGICAL ASSOCIATION
Estimated Income Statement
1978

| | |
|---|---|
| Revenues: | |
| Membership dues | $106,500 |
| Journal subscriptions | 12,040 |
| Publication sales | 4,400 |
| Foundation grant | 20,000 |
| Annual meeting, 1977, profit | 1,261 |
| Total revenues | $144,201 |
| Expenses: | |
| Printing and mailing publications | $ 34,220 |
| Committee meeting expenses | 18,220 |
| Annual meeting advance | 4,000 |
| Word processing machine | 18,000 |
| Administrative salaries and expenses | 56,840 |
| Miscellaneous | 9,280 |
| Total expenses | $140,560 |
| Excess of revenues over expenses | $ 3,641 |

NHA was a nonprofit professional association whose 3,000 members were experts in helontology,[1] a specialized branch of engineering. The association represented the interests of its members before congressional committees and various scientific bodies, published two professional journals, arranged an annual meeting and several regional meetings, and appointed committees that developed positions on various topics of interest to the membership.

The operating activities of the association were managed by George Tremble, its executive secretary. Mr. Tremble reported to the board of directors. The board consisted of four officers and seven other members. Six members of the 1979 board (i.e., the board that assumed responsibility on January 1, 1979) were also on the 1978 board; the other five members were newly elected. The president served a one-year term.

The financial policy of the association was that each year should "stand on its own feet"; that is, expenses of the year should approximately equal the revenues of the year. At the meeting in December 1978, Mr. Tremble presented an estimated income statement for 1978 (Exhibit 1). Although some of the December transactions were necessarily estimated, Mr. Tremble assured the board that the actual totals for the year would closely approximate the numbers shown.

Wilma Fosdick, one of the newly elected board members, raised a question about the foundation grant of $20,000. She questioned whether this item should be counted as revenue. If it were excluded, there was a deficit, and this showed that the 1978 board had, in effect, eaten into reserves and thus

[1] Disguised name.

made it more difficult to provide the level of service that the members had a right to expect in 1979. This led to detailed questions about items on the income statement, which brought forth the following information from Mr. Tremble:

1. In 1978, NHA received a $20,000 cash grant from the Workwood Foundation for the purpose of financing a symposium to be held in June 1979. During 1978 approximately $1,000 was spent in preliminary planning for this symposium and was included in the item, "Committee meeting expenses." When asked why the $20,000 had been recorded as revenue in 1978 rather than in 1979, Mr. Tremble said that the grant was obtained entirely by the initiative and persuasiveness of the 1978 president, so 1978 should be given credit for it. Further, although the grant was intended to finance the symposium, there was no legal requirement that the symposium be held; if for any reason it was not held, the money would be used for the general operations of the association.
2. In early December 1978 the association took delivery of, and paid for, a new word processing machine costing $18,000. This machine would greatly simplify the work of preparing membership lists, correspondence, and manuscripts submitted to the printer for publication. Except for this new machine, the typewriters, desks, and other equipment in the association office were quite old.
3. Ordinarily, members paid their dues during the first few months of the year. Because of the need to raise cash to finance the purchase of the word processing machine, in September 1978 the association announced that members who paid their 1979 dues before December 15, 1978, would receive a free copy of the book which contained papers presented at the special symposium to be held in June 1979. The approximate per-copy cost of publishing this book was expected to be $6, and it was expected to be sold for $10. Consequently, $12,000 of 1979 dues were received by December 15, 1978.
4. In July 1978 the association sent to members a membership directory. Its long-standing practice was to publish such a directory every two years. The cost of preparing and printing this directory was $8,000. Of the 4,000 copies printed, 3,000 were mailed to members in 1978. The remaining 1,000 were held to meet the needs of new members who would join before the next directory came out; they would receive a free copy of the directory when they joined.
5. Members received the association's journals at no extra cost, as a part of their membership privileges. Some libraries and other nonmembers also subscribed to the journals. The $12,040 reported as subscription revenue was the cash received in 1978. Of this amount about $3,000 was for journals that would be delivered in 1979. Offsetting this was $2,000 of subscription revenue received in 1977 for journals delivered in 1978; this $2,000 had been reported as 1977 revenue.

6. The association had advanced $4,000 to the committee responsible for planning the 1978 annual meeting held in late November. This amount was used for preliminary expenses. Registration fees at the annual meeting were set so as to cover all convention costs, so that it was expected that the $4,000, plus any profit, would be returned to the association after the committee had finished paying the convention bills. The 1977 convention had resulted in a $1,261 profit, but the results of the 1978 convention were not known, although the attendance was about as anticipated.

## Question

Did the association have an excess or a deficit in 1978?

## Case 3–4

## THE CITY OF NEW YORK*

In the 1970s the City of New York got into serious financial difficulty. The federal government came to its aid in 1975 by providing short-term financing, and again in 1978 by providing long-term loan guarantees. The federal loan guarantee legislation included several provisos, one of which was that in 1982 and thereafter the city would balance its budget, and that it would make "substantial progress" toward that goal in the immediately preceding years. The city reported a surplus of $128 million in fiscal year (FY) 1981, and no questions were raised about compliance with the proviso. In FY 1982, however, questions were raised.

Section 103 of the legislation (the New York City Loan Guarantee Act of 1978) required the city "to adopt and adhere to budgets covering all expenditures other than capital items, the results of which would not, for fiscal years of the city beginning after June 30, 1981, show a deficit when reported in accordance with generally accepted accounting principles. . . ."

Exhibit 1 is a balance sheet for the year ended June 30, 1982. Exhibit 2 is an operating statement relating to the general fund for FY 1982, and Exhibit 3 is an operating statement for enterprise funds.

---

* This case was prepared by Robert N. Anthony, Harvard Business School.

**Exhibit 1**

THE CITY OF NEW YORK
Combined Balance Sheet—All fund Types and Account Groups
June 30, 1982
($000)

| | *Governmental Fund Types* | | | *Proprietary Fund Type* | *Account Groups* | | *Total* |
|---|---|---|---|---|---|---|---|
| | *General* | *Capital Projects* | *Debt Service* | *(Enterprise)* | *General Fixed Assets* | *Long-term Obligations* | *(Memorandum Only)* |
| *Assets* | | | | | | | |
| Cash and cash equivalents | $ 827,869 | $342,183 | $ 145,228 | $ 75,039 | $ — | $ — | $ 1,390,319 |
| Investments, including accrued interest | 15,484 | | 2,593,595 | — | — | — | 2,609,079 |
| Accounts receivable: | | | | | | | |
| Real estate taxes (less allowance for uncollectible amounts of $165,724) | 86,964 | — | — | — | — | — | 86,964 |
| Federal, state, and other aid | 905,836 | 285,477 | — | — | — | — | 1,191,313 |
| Patient service, net | — | — | — | 316,850 | — | — | 316,850 |
| Other, net | 213,471 | — | — | 15,926 | — | — | 229,397 |
| Mortgage loans and interest receivable (less allowance for uncollectible amounts of $937,670) | — | — | 266,062 | — | — | — | 266,062 |
| Other assets | 14,000 | — | — | 20,997 | — | — | 34,997 |
| Due from other funds | 323,176 | — | 312,297 | — | — | — | 635,473 |
| Property, plant, and equipment | — | — | — | 1,113,657 | 12,134,881 | — | 13,248,538 |
| Accumulated depreciation | — | — | — | (508,003) | (3,975,434) | — | (4,483,437) |
| Amounts available in debt service funds | — | — | — | — | — | 3,271,586 | 3,271,586 |
| Amounts to be provided for long-term obligations | — | — | — | — | — | 15,866,335 | 15,866,335 |
| Total assets | $2,386,800 | $627,660 | $3,317,182 | $1,034,466 | $ 8,159,447 | $19,137,921 | $34,663,476 |

See accompanying notes to financial statement.

| | | | | | | | |
|---|---|---|---|---|---|---|---|
| *Liabilities* | | | | | | | |
| Accounts payable and accrued liabilities | $1,545,908 | $279,464 | $ 44,417 | $ 115,134 | $ — | $ — | $ 1,984,923 |
| Bonds payable | — | — | — | — | — | 13,114,639 | 13,114,639 |
| Lease purchase obligations | — | — | — | 1,221 | — | 871,172 | 872,393 |
| Capital lease obligations | — | — | — | — | — | 86,638 | 86,638 |
| Accrued real estate tax refunds | 1,191 | — | — | — | — | 220,000 | 221,191 |
| Accrued tax refunds—other | 99,693 | — | — | — | — | — | 99,693 |
| Accrued judgments and claims | 22,066 | 45,449 | — | — | — | 936,000 | 1,003,515 |
| Accrued vacation and sick leave | — | — | — | 62,600 | — | 720,000 | 782,600 |
| Deferred wages | — | — | — | 15,926 | — | 275,000 | 290,926 |
| Accrued pension liability | — | — | — | 125,090 | — | 2,914,472 | 3,039,562 |
| Deferred revenues | 124,631 | 40,295 | — | 2,391 | — | — | 167,317 |
| Due to other funds | 312,444 | 321,997 | 1,179 | (147) | — | — | 635,473 |
| Estimated disallowances of federal, state, and other aid | 313,434 | | | | | | 313,434 |
| Net revenues payable to the state and local governments | — | — | — | 3,587 | | | 3,587 |
| Total liabilities | 2,419,367 | 687,205 | 45,596 | 325,802 | | 19,137,921 | 22,615,891 |
| *Fund Equity* | | | | | | | |
| Investment in general fixed assets | — | — | — | — | 8,159,447 | — | 8,159,447 |
| Contributed capital | — | — | — | 604,590 | — | — | 604,590 |
| Fund balances (deficit), gross | (4,352,310) | (59,545) | 3,271,586 | 104,074 | — | — | (1,036,195) |
| Deficit financing | 4,319,743 | — | — | — | — | — | 4,319,743 |
| Total fund equity (deficit), net | (32,567) | (59,545) | 3,271,586 | 708,664 | 8,159,447 | — | 12,047,585 |
| Commitments and contingencies | | | | | | | |
| Total liabilities and fund equity | $2,386,800 | $627,660 | $3,317,182 | $1,034,466 | $ 8,159,447 | $19,137,921 | $34,663,476 |

See accompanying notes to financial statements.

**Exhibit 2**

THE CITY OF NEW YORK
General Fund Statement of Revenues and Expenditures
Financial Plan and Actual
For the Year Ended June 30, 1982
($000)

| | *1982* | | | |
|---|---|---|---|---|
| | *Initial Financial Plan* | *Modified Financial Plan* | *Actual* | *1981 Actual* |
| Revenues: | | | | |
| Real estate taxes | $ 3,588,000 | $ 3,595,000 | $ 3,602,818 | $ 3,298,090 |
| Sales and use taxes | 1,748,000 | 1,803,000 | 1,790,320 | 1,782,052 |
| Income taxes | 2,237,000 | 2,376,000 | 2,363,119 | 2,175,155 |
| Other taxes | 408,000 | 447,000 | 450,415 | 394,014 |
| Federal, state, and other categorical aid | 4,640,000 | 4,934,000 | 4,964,545 | 4,575,258 |
| Unrestricted federal and state aid | 896,000 | 844,000 | 804,376 | 811,680 |
| Charges for services | 576,000 | 605,000 | 607,714 | 592,079 |
| Other revenue | 479,000 | 477,000 | 479,331 | 411,447 |
| Total revenues | 14,572,000 | 15,081,000 | 15,062,638 | 14,039,775 |
| Other Financing Sources: | | | | |
| Transfer of OTB net revenues | 53,000 | 55,000 | 54,439 | 58,795 |
| Total revenues and other financing sources | 14,625,000 | 15,136,000 | 15,117,077 | 14,098,570 |
| Expenditures: | | | | |
| General government | 436,000 | 470,000 | 451,413 | 360,257 |
| Public safety and judicial | 1,527,000 | 1,566,000 | 1,558,167 | 1,374,985 |
| Board of Education | 2,963,000 | 2,987,000 | 2,982,793 | 2,712,635 |
| City University | 516,000 | 554,000 | 527,744 | 487,568 |
| Social services | 3,396,000 | 3,501,000 | 3,534,868 | 3,305,750 |
| Environmental protection | 535,000 | 524,000 | 517,946 | 473,494 |
| Transportation services | 404,000 | 458,000 | 456,373 | 383,509 |
| Parks, recreation and cultural activities | 145,000 | 148,000 | 147,744 | 121,838 |
| Housing | 328,000 | 343,000 | 347,225 | 319,376 |
| Health (including payments to HHC) | 617,000 | 626,000 | 626,689 | 578,522 |
| Libraries | 74,000 | 73,000 | 71,988 | 62,857 |
| Pensions | 1,424,000 | 1,421,000 | 1,418,060 | 1,303,300 |
| Judgments and claims—net of $161 million in 1982 ($185 million in 1981) transferred to long-term obligations | 80,000 | 120,000 | 122,904 | 92,580 |
| Other | 596,000 | 520,000 | 480,530 | 428,836 |
| Total expenditures | 13,041,000 | 13,311,000 | 13,244,444 | 12,005,507 |
| Transfers and Other Financing Uses: | | | | |
| For debt service | 1,440,000 | 1,433,000 | 1,439,454 | 1,451,298 |
| Sales taxes and per capita aid appropriated and paid by the state to MAC | 144,000 | 392,000 | 392,000 | 367,000 |
| For capital purposes | — | — | — | 147,000 |
| Total expenditures and other financing uses | 14,625,000 | 15,136,000 | 15,075,898 | 13,970,805 |
| Excess of revenues and other financing sources over expenditures and other uses | $ — | $ — | $ 41,179 | $ 127,765 |

See accompanying notes to financial statements.

**Exhibit 3**

THE CITY OF NEW YORK
Enterprise Funds
Combined Statement of Revenues, Expenses, and Changes in Fund Equity
For the Year Ended June 30, 1982
($000)

| | *Health and Hospitals Corporation* | *Off-Track Betting Corporation* | *Total* |
|---|---|---|---|
| Revenues: | | | |
| Patient service revenues, net | $1,044,092 | $ — | $1,044,092 |
| Operating revenues including payments from City | 365,251 | 209,576 | 574,827 |
| Other revenues | 30,705 | — | 30,705 |
| Total revenues | 1,440,048 | 209,576 | 1,649,624 |
| Expenses: | | | |
| Personal services | 910,625 | — | 910,625 |
| Affiliation | 225,685 | — | 225,685 |
| Racing industry compensation | — | 50,519 | 50,519 |
| Other operating | 306,150 | 69,163 | 375,313 |
| Administrative and selling | — | 14,620 | 14,620 |
| Depreciation and amortization | 61,529 | 1,891 | 63,420 |
| Interest expense (income), net | 63,015 | (3,324) | 59,691 |
| Total expenses | 1,567,004 | 132,869 | 1,699,873 |
| Allocation to the State and other local governments | — | 27,568 | 27,568 |
| | 1,567,004 | 160,437 | 1,727,441 |
| Excess (deficit) of revenues over expenses before other financing sources (uses) | (126,956) | 49,139 | (77,817) |
| Other Financing Sources | | | |
| Amounts from other OTB communities | — | 5,300 | 5,300 |
| Excess (deficit) of revenues and other financing sources over expenses | (126,956) | 54,439 | (72,517) |
| Other Financing Uses: | | | |
| Allocation of net revenues and other financing sources to the general fund | — | (54,439) | (54,439) |
| Excess of expenses and other financing uses over revenues and other financing sources | (126,956) | — | (126,956) |
| Fund equity at July 1, 1981 | 823,615 | — | 823,615 |
| Net increase to donor restricted funds | 256 | — | 256 |
| Contributed fixed assets | 11,749 | — | 11,749 |
| Fund equity at June 30, 1982 | $ 708,664 | $ | $ 708,664 |

See accompanying notes to financial statements.

# NOTE A: SUMMARY OF SIGNIFICANT ACCOUNTING POLICIES

## Reporting Entity

The accompanying financial statements present the accounts of the city, including the Board of Education and the City University of New York, and the financial statements of the New York City Health and Hospitals Corporation ("HHC"), and the New York City Off-Track Betting Corporation ("OTB"). Significant accounting policies and other matters concerning the financial status of HHC and OTB are described in Notes L and M, respectively. The city's operations also embrace those normally performed at the county level and, accordingly, transactions applicable to such functions of the five counties which comprise the city are included in these financial statements. The accounts of certain other public benefit corporations which provide governmental services to residents of the city are also included to the extent that they have incurred certain long-term obligations which are liquidated by the city through lease-purchase agreements, subsidies, or other contractual agreements. The revenues and assets of these public benefit corporations do not constitute revenues or assets of the City and are not generally available for payment of city obligations.

The National Council on Governmental Accounting (NCGA) has recently developed criteria to determine what constitutes state and local government entities for financial reporting purposes. The NCGA concluded in *Statement 3, Defining the Governmental Reporting Entity,* that the basic—but not the only—criterion for including a governmental agency, public authority, or other organization in a government unit's reporting entity for general-purpose financial reports is the exercise of oversight responsibility over such agencies by the governmental unit's elected officials. Oversight responsibility embraces such factors as financial interdependency, selection of governing authority, designation of management, ability to significantly influence operations, and accountability for fiscal matters. There may also be circumstances where factors other than oversight are so significant in the relationship between a particular agency and a reporting entity (e.g., special financing relationships) that exclusion of the agency from the reporting entity's financial statements would be misleading.

## Fund Accounting

The city records its transactions in the funds and account groups described below, each of which is considered to be a separate accounting entity. Operations of each fund are accounted for in a separate set of self-balancing accounts which comprise its assets, liabilities, fund equity, revenues, expenditures, or expenses and transfers.

## Governmental Fund Types

***General Fund.*** The general fund is the general operating fund of the city. Substantially all tax revenues, federal and state aid (except aid restricted for capital projects) and other operating revenues are accounted for in the general fund. This fund also accounts for expenditures and transfers as appropriated in the "Expense Budget" . . . , which provides for the city's day-to-day operations, including transfers to debt service funds for payment of long-term obligations.

***Capital Projects Fund.*** The capital projects fund accounts for resources used to construct or acquire fixed assets and capital improvements as appropriated for in the "capital budget" . . . Resources of the capital projects fund are derived principally from proceeds of bond issues and from federal, state and other aid. Capital projects fund expenditures are generally financed initially by the general fund; the cumulative deficit represents amounts expected to be financed from future bond issues which will be used to repay the general fund advances.

***Debt Service Funds.*** The debt service funds account for the accumulation of resources for, and payment of, interest and principal on long-term obligations. Separate funds are maintained to account for transactions relating to *(i)* the city's general debt service funds including its sinking funds and the debt service fund required by state legislation, *(ii)* MAC; and *(iii)* the indebtedness of, or the city's obligations to, certain public benefit corporations whose indebtedness has been guaranteed by the city, or with whom the city has entered into lease-purchase and similar agreements.

## Proprietary Fund Type

***Enterprise Funds.*** The enterprise funds account for the operations of HHC and OTB whose activities are considered to be part of the city entity for financial reporting purposes. These activities are accounted for in a manner similar to private business enterprises, where the focus is the periodic determination of revenues earned, expenses incurred, and net income generated.

## Account Groups[1]

***General Fixed Assets Account Group.*** The general fixed assets account group accounts for those fixed assets which are used for general governmental purposes and are not available for appropriation or expenditure. Such

[1] Note by case writer: The "account groups" are not funds. Essentially, they are single-entry listings of the items, not part of the double-entry system.

assets include substantially all land, buildings, and major equipment having a minimum useful life of five years and costing more than $15,000, except for certain elements of the City's infrastructure (including roads, bridges, curbs and gutters, streets and sidewalks, park land and improvements, subway tracks and tunnels) which are not required to be capitalized under generally accepted accounting principles. For management control purposes, however, the city has recorded its water distribution and sewage collection systems, which are also infrastructure.

### Long-term Obligations Account Group

The long-term obligations account group accounts for unmatured long-term notes and bonds payable which are paid through the debt service funds. In addition, the long-term obligations account group includes other long-term obligations for *(i)* lease-purchase obligations, *(ii)* capital leases, *(iii)* judgments and claims, *(iv)* real estate tax refunds; *(v)* unpaid vacation and sick leave, *(vi)* certain unpaid deferred wages, and *(vii)* certain unfunded pension liabilities, except that any estimated amounts currently due (i.e., to be liquidated with expendable available financial resources) are recorded in the general fund.

### Basis of Accounting

The measurement focus of the general, capital projects and debt service funds is on the determination of and changes in financial position. This concept emphasizes the acquisition, use, and balance of expendable available financial resources and related liabilities. These funds use the modified accrual basis of accounting. Under the modified accrual basis of accounting, revenues are recognized in the accounting period in which they become both measurable and available to finance expenditures of the fiscal period. Expenditures, other than interest on long-term obligations and certain estimated liabilities recorded in the long-term obligations account group, are recorded when the related liability is incurred. The accrual basis of accounting is followed by the enterprise funds, whereby revenues are recognized in the accounting period in which they are earned and expenses are recognized in the period incurred.

### Real Estate Tax

Real estate tax payments for the year ended June 30, 1982, were due in equal quarterly installments on the 15th day of July, and the 1st day of October, January, and April of that fiscal year. Recognized real estate tax revenue represents payments received during the year against the current year's levy and prior years' levies previously recorded as deferred revenue, and payments received within the first two months of the following fiscal year against the current and prior years' levies, reduced by tax refunds made in the same period.

Delinquent real estate taxes receivable which are estimated to be collectible but are not collected in the first two months of the next fiscal year are recorded as deferred revenues. An allowance for estimated uncollectible real estate taxes is provided against the receivable balance.

The city is permitted by the State Constitution to levy real estate taxes *(i)* in an amount up to 2.5 percent of the average full value of taxable real estate in the city for the last five years, for general operating purposes, and *(ii)* in unlimited amounts, for the payment of principal and interest on long-term city debt. Any collection in excess of the constitutional limit must be reserved for future years' debt service; for the years ended June 30, 1982 and 1981, excess collections of $298 million and $173 million, respectively, were so reserved by transfer to the debt service fund.

### Other Taxes and Revenues

Recognized sales, income, and other taxes represent payments received during the current fiscal year and material amounts collected by the state on behalf of the city in the current fiscal year and received by the city in the next fiscal year, net of estimated refunds.

Recognized water and sewer charges represent payments received during the current fiscal year not previously accrued, and payments of current year's charges received within the first two months of the next fiscal year.

Licenses, permits, franchises and privileges, fines, forfeitures and other revenues are generally not susceptible to accrual and are recorded when received in cash.

### Federal State and Other Aid

Categorical aid, net of a provision for estimated disallowances, is reported as revenue when the related reimbursable expenditures are incurred. Unrestricted aid is reported as revenue in the fiscal year of entitlement.

### Encumbrances

Encumbrance accounting, under which purchase orders, contracts, and other commitments for the expenditure of monies are recorded to reflect the use of the applicable spending appropriations, is employed by the general fund during the fiscal year to control expenditures. Pursuant to generally accepted accounting principles, however, encumbrance accounting is not used for recording expenditures for the period. Only the cost of those goods and services received or rendered on or before June 30 are recognized as expenditures. Encumbrances not converted to expenditures at year end are charged to the next year's appropriation without any reservation of the current year's fund balance.

## Transfers

Legally authorized payments or authorizations to make payment from a fund receiving revenue to a fund through which the resources are to be expended are reported as operating transfers. Such payments or authorizations include transfers for debt service and transfers of OTB net revenues.

## Materials and Supplies

Materials and supplies are recorded as expenditures at the time of purchase. Accordingly, the balances on hand at June 30, 1982 and 1981 (estimated at approximately $85 million and $64 million, respectively, based on average cost), have not been reported in the general fund. Had the city reported materials and supplies in the general fund balance sheets, such amounts would have been offset with a contra account, "Reserve for Inventories."

## Pensions

The provision for costs of pensions is recorded on the accrual basis. The provision includes normal costs, interest on pension costs previously accrued but not funded, and amortization of past service costs as determined by the city actuary.

## Accumulated Vacation and Sick Leave

Unpaid vacation and sick leave accruals representing estimated leave accumulated by employees which may be used in subsequent years or paid upon termination or retirement are recorded by the city in the long-term obligations account group. Current amounts, representing accumulated vacation and sick leave payable to those employees who have retired or otherwise left city employment, are included in accounts payable and accrued liabilities.

## Treasury Obligations

Notes and bonds payable included in the long-term obligations account group and the investments of the debt service funds are reported net of "treasury obligations." Treasury obligations represent city debt, MAC debt, and debt of certain public benefit corporations guaranteed by the city which are held as investments of the debt service funds and eliminated to report such obligations as if they had been redeemed.

## Judgments and Claims

The city is self-insured with respect to most risks including, but not limited to, property damage, personal injury, and workers' compensation. Expenditures for judgments and claims (other than workers' compensation and condemnation proceedings) are recorded on the basis of settlements reached or judgments entered within the current fiscal year, whether paid or unpaid. Expenditures for workers' compensation are recorded when paid, and estimated settlements relating to condemnation proceedings are reported in the capital projects fund during the year such claims are filed. The estimated liability for certain claims and proceedings which have not been adjudicated or settled at the end of a fiscal year is reported in the long-term obligations account group. The current liability for settlements reached or judgments entered but not yet paid is recorded in the general fund.

### General Fund Balance and Deficit Financing

In the late 1960s, the city began incurring substantial operating deficits each year and made extensive use of short- and long-term debt to meet current expenditures. The city lost access to the public credit market in 1975. During fiscal years 1975 through 1980, the city continued to incur substantial operating deficits, although in gradually smaller amounts. It was not until fiscal year 1981 that the city operated under a balanced budget.

The general fund cumulative deficit shows both the city's accumulated gross operating deficit and the extent to which such deficit was financed. The deficit was financed from proceeds of MAC bonds remitted to the city for payment of various expenditures, MAC acquisitions of city debt, and city bonds issued to finance operating expenditures.

The deficit financing credits resulting from the issuance of debt by the city and MAC are amortized over the life of the debt. As the debt giving rise to these credits is redeemed or otherwise reduced through transfers to the debt service fund, both the gross deficit and the deficit financing credits are reduced. Amortization of the deficit financing was $212.4 million and $184.5 million for the years ended June 30, 1982 and 1981, respectively.

### Financial Plans

As a consequence of the financial difficulties previously discussed and the resulting loss of access to the public credit markets, the city has been required by state and federal law to operate under a recurring Four-Year Financial Plan ("Plan"), approved by the Financial Control Board, a state oversight body. The plans are required to be balanced on a basis consistent with generally accepted accounting principles.

Operations under the expense budget must reflect the aggregate limitations contained in the approved plans and the expense budget is generally consistent with the first year of the plan. The city reviews its plan periodically during the year and, if necessary, makes modifications from time to time to incorporate actual results and revisions to assumptions. The Financial Control Board must approve all modifications to the plan before they become effective. The annual expense budget and the plan often do not agree, primarily because of timing differences in the adoption and modification of each.

* * * * *

## NOTE H: PENSION PLANS

The city sponsors or participates in pension plans covering substantially all full-time employees. Most plans require employee contributions. The plans provide pension benefits based on salary and length of service and also provide cost-of-living and other supplemental pensions to certain retirees. In the event of disability during employment, participants may receive retirement allowances based on satisfaction of certain service requirements and other plan provisions.

The total provisions for pension costs, exclusive of employee contributions, for the years ended June 30, 1982 and 1981, were approximately $1.5 billion and $1.3 billion, respectively. The amounts paid to the five major actuarial systems and to other systems and pension programs for the year ended June 30, 1982, were equal to the amounts recommended by the system's actuary and are as follows [details omitted].

The actuarial present values of credited projected benefits for active participants are based on current salaries with projected increases to retirement. The net assets available for benefits excludes the unamortized deferred realized gains and losses on bond sales and the accrued pension contribution of $2,914 million for amortization of the two-year payment lag reported in the long-term obligations account group. Prior to fiscal year 1981, pension contributions had been made on a statutory basis which reflected pension costs incurred two years earlier and phase-in of certain actuarial assumptions. As a result of legislation requiring amortization over 40 years of the liability resulting from the two-year lag the liability was transferred to the long-term obligations account group from the general fund as of June 30, 1981. At June 30, 1982, the five major systems had approximately 18.5 percent of their assets invested in city and MAC securities. As of June 30, 1982, the actuarial present value of vested benefits for the other systems and programs sponsored by the city is approximately $565 million.

* * * * *

## NOTE J: COMMITMENTS AND CONTINGENCIES

### Wage Deferral

Commencing in fiscal year 1976, certain employees deferred portions of negotiated wage increases and other items. In conjunction with a September 1982 collective bargaining settlement an agreement was reached whereby *(i)* certain wages deferred by eligible nonmembers of the retirement systems would be paid on July 1, 1984, and *(ii)* wages deferred by eligible members of the retirement systems would be paid as a one-time retirement system benefit available on July 1, 1984, with the city increasing contributions to the systems over the average working life of the members of each system (10 to 16 years). If for any reason this retirement system benefit is not implemented by legislation, is not approved by the Internal Revenue Service, or is otherwise ruled invalid on or before July 1, 1984, the parties will seek to negotiate an alternative payment plan whereby the deferred wages would be paid on or about July 1, 1984, and funded over a 10- to 16-year period. If such a plan cannot be effectuated, an alternative payment plan was agreed to whereby the same deferred wages would be repaid over a seven-year period commencing July 1, 1984, plus interest accruing on any unpaid balance from that date at a rate of 100 basis points higher than the annual rate then in effect for determining pension contributions. Assuming all labor unions enter into this agreement, approximately $275 million of wages previously deferred would be paid. Such amount is recorded in the Statement of Long-term Obligations.

### Capital Requirements

As a result of its financial difficulties and loss of access to the public credit market in fiscal year 1975, the city substantially curtailed its capital spending program and deferred routine maintenance on much of its infrastructure and capital equipment. Capital expenditures did not increase substantially until fiscal year 1981 during which time the city regained access to the long-term credit market. To address the documented need for significant infrastructure and public facility capital investments, the city has prepared a $34.7 billion 10-year capital spending program. The ability of the city to meet its capital spending plans or to obtain adequate capital financing cannot be assured.

* * * * *

## NOTE L: NEW YORK CITY HEALTH AND HOSPITALS CORPORATION

### General

The New York City Health and Hospitals Corporation (HHC), a public benefit corporation, assumed responsibility for operation of the city's municipal hospital system in 1970. HHC continues to receive funds from city appropriations through the general fund as support for patient care rendered to uninsured indigent and other patients, and for other costs, to the extent its cash needs exceed its cash receipts from all other sources. In addition, the city pays HHC's costs for claims for medical malpractice, negligence, and other miscellaneous torts and contracts, as well as certain other HHC costs such as interest on capital acquisitions through lease-purchase arrangements. HHC does not reimburse the city for such costs; accordingly HHC records a revenue in an amount equal to such expenditures.

### Revenues

Patient service accounts receivable and revenues are reported at estimated net collectible amounts. Substantially all direct patient service revenue is derived from third-party payors. Generally, revenues from these sources are based upon cost reimbursement principles and are subject to audit by applicable payors. HHC records retroactive rate adjustments resulting from settlement of subsequent routine cost determinations and appeals when the effect is reasonably determinable. Included in other revenue are certain payments made and other services rendered by the city on behalf of HHC of $125 million and $98 million for fiscal years 1982 and 1981 and transfers from donor restricted funds of $8 million and $21 million in fiscal years 1982 and 1981.

### Plant and Equipment

All facilities and equipment are leased from the city at $1 per year. In addition, HHC operates certain facilities which are financed by the New York State Housing Finance Agency and leased to the city on behalf of HHC. HHC records as an expense the interest portion of such lease-purchase obligations paid by the city. Since HHC is responsible for the control and maintenance of all plant and equipment, and depreciation is a significant cost of operations impacting on third-party reimbursement, HHC capitalizes such assets at cost or estimated cost based on appraisals. Depreciation is computed for financial statement purposes using the straight-line method, and for some third-party reimbursement purposes for certain movable equipment using the sum-of-the-years'-digits method based upon estimated useful lives averaging 10 years. As a result of modernization programs and changes in service requirements, HHC has closed certain facilities and portions of facilities during the past several years. It is the policy of HHC to reflect the financial effect of the closing of facilities or portions thereof in the financial statements when a decision has been made as to the disposition of such assets.

## NOTE M: NEW YORK CITY OFF-TRACK BETTING CORPORATION

The New York City Off-Track Betting Corporation was established in 1970 as a public benefit corporation to operate a system of off-track betting in the city. OTB earns revenues on its betting operations from *(i)* between 17 percent and 25 percent of wagers handled, depending on the type of wager, *(ii)* a 5 percent surcharge and surcharge breakage on pari-mutuel winnings, and *(iii)* breakage, the revenue resulting from the rounding down of winning payoffs. Pursuant to state law, OTB *(i)* distributes various portions of the surcharge and surcharge breakage to other localities in the state, *(ii)* allocates various percentages of wagers handled to the racing industry, and *(iii)* allocates various percentages of wagers handled and breakage together with all uncashed pari-mutuel tickets to the state. All remaining net revenue is distributable to the City. In addition, OTB acts as a collection agent for the City respecting surcharge and surcharge breakage due from other community off-track betting corporations.

## STATEMENT OF LONG-TERM OBLIGATIONS

The Statement of Long-Term Obligations (not reproduced here) reported the following amounts as of June 30:

| | *1982 ($000)* | *1981 ($000)* |
|---|---|---|
| Bonds payable | $13,114,639 | $12,315,869 |
| Lease-purchase obligations, less amounts to be provided by the state | 871,172 | 924,746 |
| Capital lease obligations | 86,638 | 99,893 |
| Accrued pension liability | 2,914,472 | 2,935,597 |
| Accrued real estate tax refunds | 220,000 | 330,000 |
| Accrued judgments and claims | 936,000 | 775,000 |
| Deferred wages | 275,000 | 0 |
| Accrued vacation and sick leave | 720,000 | 695,000 |
| Total | $19,137,921 | $18,076,105 |

### Question

Did the City of New York comply with the federal mandate in FY 1982? Consider among other things, these topics:

*a.* Whether the relevant accounting entity includes the two enterprise funds.
*b.* Deferred wages ($275 million).
*c.* Accrued vacation and sick leave ($720 million).
*d.* Depreciation.
*e.* Debt service.

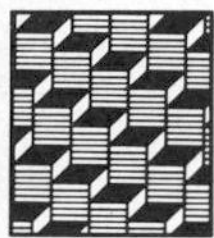

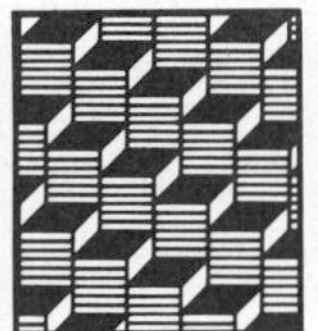

# chapter 4

# Cost Accounting

The measurement of costs in nonprofit organizations is important because cost information plays a central role in many management decisions (discussed in Chapter 1), in pricing the organization's services (discussed in Chapter 5), and in budget formulation and reporting systems (discussed in Part III). This chapter discusses some of the fundamental cost principles that are necessary for these purposes.

Any of three different types of costs are used for management decisions:

1. Full costs.
2. Responsibility costs.
3. Differential costs.

Full costs and responsibility costs should be incorporated into the accounts so that they can be collected on a regular basis. By contrast, differential costs change depending on the type of analysis being performed, and they therefore cannot be included in the accounts. This chapter discusses only full and differential costs. Responsibility costs are discussed in Part III.

## FULL COSTS

The question "What did it cost?" is one of the most slippery questions to answer in both profit-oriented and nonprofit organizations. Although the cost of *acquiring* resources, such as supplies and labor, is usually measured readily as the amounts paid for them, measuring the cost of using these resources for various purposes can be complicated. Even calculating a total cost per unit produced—be it a widget or 50 minutes of psychotherapy—is relatively easy so long as the organization produces a single type of product. Complications arise however, in organizations that produce different types of services because each type uses different amounts of resources and therefore has different costs.

### Decisions Required

Full cost means the total cost of the resources used for a specified purpose. In all organizations the measurement of the full cost of the goods or services delivered involves decisions about the definition of a cost object, the specification of cost centers, the distinction between direct and indirect costs, the choice of the bases for allocating service center costs to other cost centers, the determination of a "stepdown" sequence, the method of assigning cost center costs to cost objects, and a choice between process and job order accounting.

### The Cost Object

The cost object is the unit of good or service for which we wish to know the cost. Generally, as the cost object becomes more specific, the technique required to measure its costs becomes more complicated. In a university, for example, the cost object may be a student-year, i.e., the cost of educating a student for one academic year. Sometimes the student year applies to all students, regardless of level, and sometimes a distinction is made between graduate and undergraduate students. It is also possible to consider a different cost object, such as a classroom hour or a laboratory hour. As will be seen, the choice of cost objects can have a significant impact on the cost accounting methods used in a given organization.

### Cost Centers

Before being assigned to products, costs are first collected in cost centers. As a result, the choice of cost centers determines the manner in which cost data will be accumulated. In an organization that is producing a single product, the whole organization is one cost center. If the organization is divided into several cost centers, the cost of the end product is the sum of the costs attributed to it in each of the cost centers.[1]

There are two types of cost centers: service centers and mission centers. (These are sometimes called, respectively, intermediate centers and final cen-

---

[1] The distinction between a cost object and a cost center is occasionally quite subtle. On occasion, both can be viewed as "purposes" for which costs are collected; for this reason, cost centers are sometimes called "intermediate cost objects."

ters.) Mission centers are those that are directly related to the purposes of the organization. In a hospital, for example, housekeeping, plant maintenance, and the like are service centers, while inpatient care might constitute a single mission center. In a university, a cost accounting system might treat each individual school as a mission center.

## Direct and Indirect Costs

A third decision inherent in a cost accounting system is the distinction between direct and indirect costs. Direct costs are those costs which are associated with, or have been physically traced to, a specific cost object or cost center; indirect costs are those costs which apply to more than one cost object or cost center. If an organization produced only one product in one cost center, there would be no indirect costs. If, however, the organization has several cost centers, some costs become indirect, and these must be assigned to the cost centers to which they relate. This assignment can be carried out in either of two ways: (1) developing improved measurement techniques which convert indirect costs into direct costs, or (2) establishing assignment formulas which distribute indirect costs as fairly as possible to the appropriate cost centers.

> ***Example:*** A social worker in the Client Education program of a social service agency is supervised by a person who also supervises social workers in the Foster Home Care Cost Center. The salary of the supervisor is an indirect cost, since it applies to activities in both the Foster Home Care and Client Education cost centers. There are several possible ways of assigning the salary to the two centers. The supervisor might be asked to maintain careful records of the time spent in each cost center, which then could be used to distribute the salary. In this case the indirect cost would have been converted into a direct cost, since the cost (time) is now traceable to each cost center. Alternatively, an assignment formula might be established, using, say, relative hours of service or number of personnel in each cost center as the assignment mechanism.

## Allocation of Costs to Cost Centers

The fourth step in the cost accounting process is the allocation of service center costs to mission centers. Here, the principal choice concerns the *bases of allocation.* In general, the best basis of allocating the costs of each service center is the one that most accurately measures its use by the other cost centers. *Allocation* (or *apportionment*) is the process of distributing service center costs to mission centers in order to determine the full cost of each mission center. In deciding on allocation bases, it is important to note that generally increased precision adds to the expense of the cost accounting system. For example, in a hospital the basis of allocating housekeeping costs frequently is the number of square feet occupied by the cost centers that use housekeeping services. Alternatively, and more accurately, housekeeping costs could be allocated on the basis of hours of service rendered to each center by the housekeeping department. Although hours of service is a more accurate measure of the cause of the cost, its use requires that records of hours be maintained; this recordkeeping expense is not necessary in the simpler system.

The question of deciding on allocation bases depends in large part on the uses management will make of the information. If better information improves pricing decisions, or affects the organization's reimbursement from clients, or influences the behavior of people responsible for managing the cost centers, the extra expense may be worthwhile.

## The Stepdown Sequence

Although several methods are available for allocating service center costs to the mission centers, one called the "stepdown method" is the most commonly used. In general, its popularity is based on its relative ease of application, and the fact that it traditionally has been the method preferred by the government and by organizations such as the American Hospital Association.[2]

The stepdown procedure is basically a method of "trickling down" sequentially the costs of the service centers to other service centers and the mission centers. This process, illustrated in Exhibit 4–1, typically begins with those service centers that serve the greatest number of other centers in the organization. Then costs are spread over the remaining cost centers.

As Exhibit 4–1 indicates, the allocation process begins with the first service cost center, depreciation of buildings and fixtures in this case, and distributes its direct costs across all remaining cost centers; the column labeled "Depreciation Buildings and Fixtures" shows this distribution. The amount to be distributed from the next service center (housekeeping) will thus include not only its direct costs ($20) but also the amount allocated to it from previous steps ($25 of depreciation); the column labeled "Housekeeping" is therefore the sum of these amounts, or $45. The third step, Medical Records, includes its direct costs ($30), plus the amount of depreciation ($10) and housekeeping ($10) allocated to it, for a total of $50. Although the stepdowns, or cost reports, in most organizations typically contain many more cost centers, they generally follow this same approach.

Two important aspects of the stepdown are (1) that no reverse allocation takes place, i.e., once a service center's costs have been allocated, that service center receives no additional allocations from other service centers; and (2) service center costs are allocated both to other service centers and to mission

[2] Computer programs are available that make these allocations automatically. For example, the CADMS model of the National Center for Higher Education was developed for colleges and universities; it can be implemented in a few days. It provides for 26 steps to allocate costs to auxiliary enterprises and earnings operations. For an example of its use, see Michael E. Young and Ronald W. Geason, "Cost Analysis and Overhead Charges at a Major Research University," *Business Officer,* April 1983, pp. 17–20.

**Exhibit 4–1**
The Stepdown Procedure*

| | Cost Centers | Direct Costs | Depreciation Buildings and Fixtures | House-keeping | Medical Records | |
|---|---|---|---|---|---|---|
| Service Cost centers | Depreciation Buildings and Fixtures | 100 | | | | |
| | Housekeeping | 20 | 25 | | | |
| | Medical records | 30 | 10 | 10 | | |
| Mission Cost centers | Inpatient services | 1,000 | 40 | 20 | 30 | 1,090 |
| | OPD clinics | 500 | 25 | 15 | 20 | 560 |
| | | 1,650 | 100 | 45 | 50 | 1,650 |

* The three solid horizontal bars contain the direct overhead costs to be allocated plus, in the cases of housekeeping and medical records, those indirect amounts allocated from the previous cost centers. The three dotted vertical bars contain the individual amounts allocated to each cost center from the three nonrevenue producing cost centers. Note that, as the arrows indicate, the total amount in each horizontal bar has been redistributed within a vertical bar. This redistribution is done in accordance with the chosen allocation basis, e.g., by square feet for housekeeping.

centers, but mission center costs are not allocated to other mission centers. Because of the fact that no reverse allocation takes place, the sequence of the steps in the stepdown is an important cost accounting decision.

Although the effect of different stepdown sequences often is not great, in some circumstances the choice may have a significant influence on the costs allocated to the various mission centers.

In summary, in order to carry out the stepdown process, a "basis of allocation" is chosen for each service cost center which attempts to measure the usage of that cost center's services by the other cost centers. The total costs in the mission centers, then, are the sum of their direct costs, the indirect costs assigned to them, and the service center costs allocated to them.[3]

## Assignment of Costs to Cost Objects

In many cases, the mission cost centers are also cost objects; if so, the preceding step completes the cost accounting process. In some cases, however, the mission cost center works on several cost objects, and its costs must be assigned to each of these cost objects. For example, the research department

[3] Service center costs frequently are called "indirect costs." Additionally, a method similar to the stepdown, called reciprocal cost allocation, is being used increasingly in nonprofit organizations. With this method the cost allocation process, rather than being "stepped down," is performed by means of a set of simultaneous equations which measure and allocate each cost center's costs based on the use of its services by other cost centers. A computer easily solves the set of simultaneous equations.

of a university works on individual research projects, each of which is usually costed.

Direct costs of projects are charged directly to them. Indirect costs are allocated by means of an overhead rate. A frequently used overhead rate is the percentage of indirect costs to direct costs. This rate is often used both to estimate the costs of future work and as a basis for reimbursement for work already done. For example, when a university applies for a research grant or contract, it will normally estimate its direct costs and apply the overhead rate to estimate the associated indirect costs.

## Process versus Job Order

A final decision in a full cost accounting system concerns the way in which mission center costs are distributed to an organization's cost objects. Here, there are two principal choices within each of which are minor variations. One is the process method, which typically is used when all units of output are similar. The production of chairs, plastic cups, and so on—an activity often performed by a production line—usually calls for a process method of cost accounting. All mission center costs for a given accounting period are calculated and are divided by the total number of units produced to give an average cost per unit.

The other is the job order method, which typically is used when the units of output are quite different. An example is the research projects mentioned above, each of which probably requires different amounts of resources. In a job order system, the labor, material, and other direct costs of each job are collected on a job cost record, and indirect costs are assigned to the job on the basis of the overhead rate mentioned above.

Per diem reimbursement methods in hospitals and some other nonprofit organizations, particularly those which use an *all-inclusive* per diem, use a process costing method in which total inpatient (or client) care costs are divided by total inpatient (or client) days to give a cost per day. By contrast, if a hospital's billing department accumulates the cost of the various services received by each patient (medications, special dietary services, operating room usage, ancillary procedures, special nursing care, ICU usage, etc.) it is using a job order cost method. In choosing between these methods, one frequently is weighing the costs of the increased reporting and processing effort in the job order method with the managerial benefits (e.g., competitive pricing needs, management control potential) which such a system provides.

## Interactive Effects

As the above discussion indicates, the choices involved in developing a cost accounting system may be quite difficult. Moreover, they are interdependent. The choice of cost centers, as indicated, will influence the distinction between direct and indirect costs. The choice of a particular cost object frequently will require the use of certain kinds of cost centers. Allocation of service center costs to mission centers will be determined, in part, by the choice of the service centers themselves and the assignment process followed. And so on.

It is important to note that changes in the system that increase the cost of one cost object always are accompanied by corresponding decreases in the cost of other cost objects. This is because the total costs of operating the organization are unaffected; the cost accounting system merely divides this total among the cost objects. Nevertheless, changes in cost accounting definitions and techniques can have a significant effect upon the costs reported for a given cost center or cost object.

## Complicating Factors

Within the general framework described above, there are many detailed problems and complications. Most of them are appropriately dealt with in a cost accounting course. A few are discussed briefly below.

***Relevant Indirect Costs.*** Indirect costs are elements of cost that are incurred because of, or for the benefit of, both the service that is being costed and also other cost objects. Indirect costs exclude cost elements that are in no way associated with the service that is being costed; for example, the cost of athletic facilities may be an indirect cost for the several educational programs whose students use them, but this cost is not a cost of a university research project.

***Defining Direct Costs.*** There are significant differences in the way the line is drawn between direct costs and indirect costs. For example, in calculating the cost of university research projects, one university may count pension and other fringe benefits of researchers as direct costs, while another may count these items as indirect costs; one may charge secretarial assistance directly to projects, but another may charge all secretarial help to a common pool; if heat, light, and other utilities are metered, they are direct costs, and if not, they are indirect costs. These differences in accounting treatment may have no material effect on the *total* cost of a research project because approximately the same amount winds up as a cost, whether charged directly or indirectly. They do, however, affect the *relationship* between direct and indirect cost, so much so that comparisons of this relationship are of little use.

*Example:* A study of 1976 research costs in four universities showed that the reported percentages of indirect costs to direct salary and wages were as follows:

| *University* | *Overhead Percentage* |
|---|---|
| A | 85.77 |
| B | 79.95 |
| C | 57.00 |
| D | 54.23 |

Some people use data like these to infer that Universities A and B had much more overhead than C and D. Actually, the authors of the study concluded that the differences primarily reflected differences in the method of distinguishing between direct and indirect costs.[4]

***Capital Employed.*** In a profit-oriented company, the full cost of using a capital asset is greater than the depreciation charge for the asset. The use of the company's capital that is tied up in the asset also is an item of cost, even though a charge for the use of capital is not currently identified as a cost item in many accounting systems. If a nonprofit organization borrows money to finance the purchase of an asset, the interest on that money is correspondingly a cost. There are other situations in which a cost of using capital exists but is not so obvious.

Suppose a university uses $1 million of its endowment funds to finance the construction of a building. Some would argue that there is a capital cost associated with this transaction because, if the university had not used the $1 million to finance the building, it would have continued to invest it, earning perhaps $50,000 a year. It now forgoes that $50,000, and the $50,000 is therefore appropriately part of the annual cost of using the building.

Similarly, all organizations need working capital with which to operate. This working capital has a cost, just as the funds tied up in a building have a cost.

These cost elements are important in situations in which it is mutually agreed that the client will reimburse the organization for the full cost of the service rendered as, for example, in a research contract. Unless the reimbursement includes an allowance for items such as the above, the organization cannot maintain its capital from its revenues.

***Gifts and Endowment Earnings.*** If an organization has revenues from contributions and endowment income, should the amount of such revenue be deducted from the full cost calculation? This is an important question, and the answer depends largely on the intention of the donors. If donors intended that their gift be used to help finance general operations, then it is appropriately deducted from the cost of those operations; but if they intended that the gift be used to augment services rendered, or for some special purpose not of direct benefit to current clients, then no such deduction need be made. Among such special purposes are research and specialized equipment in universities and hospitals; financial aid, libraries, and athletic facilities in universities; and missionary activities in religious organizations.

If the intention of the donors is not clear, then it is desirable that management formulate a specific policy as to how such revenue is to be treated. In this connection, it is often useful to make a distinction between annual gifts, which are "soft money," and endowment earnings which are "hard

---

[4] Peat, Marwick, Mitchell & Co., *Study of Indirect Cost Rates of Organizations Performing Federally Sponsored Research.* Prepared for Stanford University, November 1977.

money." If annual gifts are used to finance educational operations of a university, for example, and if the tuition charge is lower than it otherwise would be because of these gifts, the university could easily have a crisis situation in a year in which annual giving declined. If, by contrast, the tuition charge was high enough to finance educational costs, and if the annual gifts were used to finance research, additions to the library, or other costs which could be temporarily reduced if the need arose, such a crisis might not occur.

**Opportunity Costs.** In most systems, costs are measured by monetary outlays. Conceptually, costs also can be measured by opportunity losses, but this is rarely practical.

> *Example:* The use of water is often controlled by public agencies, sometimes through public investment in public works, and sometimes (at least under western states' water law) because the agency is the legal holder of original water rights. As water becomes an increasingly scarce resource, the expense of some programs, such as waterfowl refuges, may come to be measured as the opportunity cost of water consumption rather than solely in terms of monetary outlays. Similar instances can be cited for public lands and public controls of private land.

**Imputed Costs.** In certain situations, *imputed costs,* which are a form of opportunity costs, need to be incorporated in the system. Control is facilitated if imputed costs are converted to actual monetary outlays.

> *Example:* In the United States the cost of polluting water is usually an imputed cost, that is, companies generally have not been charged for the social cost of the rivers that they pollute. In the Ruhr Valley in Germany, by contrast, polluters pay a charge which is based on the effect of the effluent on the river's need for dissolved oxygen, that is, its biochemical oxygen demand. The revenue derived from this charge is used to provide for water treatment. The effect is to convert an imputed cost into a monetary cost. In 1972, the amount involved was about $60 million per year.[5]

Conversely, consider a government-sponsored day care center that hires unemployed women at prevailing wage levels, even though these women undoubtedly could be induced to work at, say, the minimum wage. The cost to society of having the day-care center is overstated if the cost of these employees is measured by the amounts paid to them. Clients of the day care center should pay a price that reflects the market rate of employee services, which is less than the money cost; the difference should be made up by a direct subsidy to the center.

In situations in which the price charged by a tax-exempt organization is supposed to be a yardstick for profit-oriented organizations, as is the case

[5] From Barbara Ward and René Dubos, *Only One Earth,* an official report commissioned by the secretary general of the United Nations Conference on Human Environment (New York: W. W. Norton, 1972), chap. 7.

with Tennessee Valley Authority, the imputed cost of taxes are also properly recognized. In other situations, the case is not so strong. If a tax-exempt hospital includes an allowance for property taxes in its full cost calculation, what does it do with the funds that this fee generates? Should it then pay some form of property tax?[6]

## Use of Full Cost Information

Full costs are necessary if costs are to be used as a basis for pricing an organization's services, as in the TVA, the U.S. Postal Service, hospitals, and universities. They are also useful if judgments need to be made about the extent to which each of several programs should "pay for itself," which is conceptually almost the same problem. Full-cost information may also facilitate the comparison of the cost of performing certain services in nonprofit organizations with the costs of comparable services in profit-oriented organizations, although the innate difficulties of making such comparisons should not be minimized. However, because of the complications discussed above, some people believe that the techniques of full cost accounting cannot actually provide a reasonable approximation of full cost. This is particularly important when, as will be discussed more fully in Chapter 5, full costs are a significant factor in setting prices.

> ***Example:*** In an otherwise excellent article on pricing blood services, the statement is made, "Since there can be no precise measurement of cost, there can be no sure correspondence between cost and price. Therefore, administrative decisions about prices must be made on the basis of criteria other than cost."[7] This statement is used as an argument for basing prices on public policy considerations, and specifically for setting the price of whole blood well above the prices of blood components—red cells, plasma, platelets, and Factor VIII. The case made for such pricing differentials is strong, but it is a case that should rest on its own merit, and not on the premise that cost-based pricing is not feasible.

Some organizations base prices on cost, but they obtain cost data from a "statistical" system, that is, a system that is not tied directly to the accounts. Such cost data are likely to be of dubious validity. Furthermore, since they are not related to the actual costs incurred in responsibility centers, they are unlikely to be accepted as reliable measures by the managers of these centers. Once established, a "tied-in" cost system requires little, if any, more work to maintain than a statistical cost system. Although Chapter 5 is devoted exclusively to pricing issues in nonprofit organizations, some discussion here of the relevant full cost accounting considerations is appropriate.

---

[6] For additional thinking on this latter point see R. C. Clark, "Does the Nonprofit Form Fit the Hospital Industry?," *Harvard Law Review,* May 1980, pp. 1417–89.

[7] D. M. Surgenor et al., "Blood Services: Prices and Public Policy," *Science,* April 27, 1973, p. 387.

### Published Cost Principles

With the growth of full-cost pricing, many resource providers have published rules governing the way costs are to be measured for reimbursement purposes. The most broadly applicable set is that of the Cost Accounting Standards Board, a government organization, but there are many other sets for specific types of reimbursement. The Department of Health and Human Services prescribes rules for hospitals. The Office of Revenue Sharing of the Treasury Department prescribes principles for state and local governmental units. These principles are not in all respects consistent with one another, and an organization must be thoroughly familiar with the specific rules that are applicable to its pricing.

*Example:* Much university research is supported by the federal government. The support comes either in the form of a contract or a grant. If a contract, the university is reimbursed in accordance with principles set forth in Office of Management and Budget Circular A-21, *Cost Principles for Educational Institutions.* These principles provide for direct costs plus an equitable share of indirect costs, including a use allowance or depreciation of buildings and equipment, operations and maintenance of plant, general administration and general expenses, departmental administration, student administration and services, and library. They do not, however, permit reimbursement for interest on capital employed, a share of general research costs, or for time of professional staff not charged to any projects, all of which are allowable costs in nonuniversity research contracts.

With respect to grants, federal statutes require that the grant be for less than the full cost of the research project. The theory of this cost sharing is that research enhances the institution's reputation, attracts private contributions, and attracts topflight faculty and students, and that the university should pay for these benefits. Typically, a grant is from 85 percent to 95 percent of total project costs.

## DIFFERENTIAL COSTS

One of the most significant principles of cost accounting is the notion that "different costs are used for different purposes." The full cost accounting principles discussed in the previous section are valuable for activities such as pricing and reimbursement, but are inappropriate for certain other purposes. Specifically, they are not appropriate for alternative choice decisions which are made in nonprofit organizations, such as the decision to (1) add or drop a product or service, (2) contract out for services, (3) accept or reject a special request (e.g., by a Health Maintenance Organization to use a certain amount of a hospital's capacity), or (4) sell obsolete supplies or equipment. For these decisions, the appropriate information is *differential costs.*

The key question asked in an alternative choice problem is: "How will costs (and revenues) change under the proposed set of circumstances?" i.e., "What costs and revenues will be different?" In both the add/drop and contract-out decisions, for example, certain costs will be eliminated and other costs will be incurred. In the special request or obsolete asset situations, certain revenues will be received, but costs will not change. Using full cost information as a basis for deciding which costs will change or how costs will change under alternative sets of circumstances can be misleading and indeed can lead to decisions which will be more, rather than less, costly for the organization.

## The Nature of Costs

Fundamental to any discussion of differential cost analysis is the question of cost behavior. The section on full costs identified the distinction between direct and indirect costs. Many differential cost analyses use a different view of costs, dividing them between fixed and variable. Although the analysis of differential costs would be simplified if, as occasionally is assumed, all indirect costs were fixed and all direct costs were variable, this is by no means usually the case. Exhibit 4–2 contains an illustration of four different cost types and their fixed/variable, direct/indirect distinctions.

In analyzing costs, the fixed/variable distinction shows how a change in the volume of activity of a given cost center will affect cost behavior.

*Fixed costs* are those costs which remain at the same level regardless of the number of units of service delivered. While no costs are fixed if the time period is long enough, the "relevant range" for fixed costs, i.e., the span of units over which they remain unchanged, or the time period within which they are considered to be fixed, is generally quite large, so that graphically they can be viewed as follows:

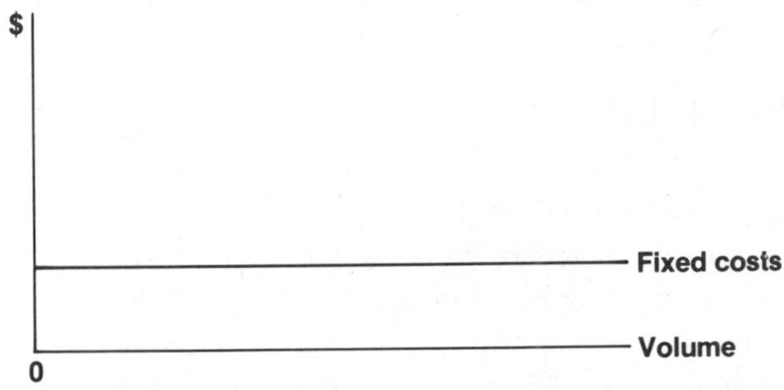


A good example of a fixed cost in most organizations is rent. Regardless of the level of activity which takes place, the amount of rent which the organization pays will remain the same.

*Variable costs* are those costs which behave in a roughly linear fashion in accordance with changes in volume. The principle is that as volume increases, total variable costs will increase in the same proportion. The result is a sloped line, the increase of which is determined by the amount of variable costs associated with each unit of output, as shown:

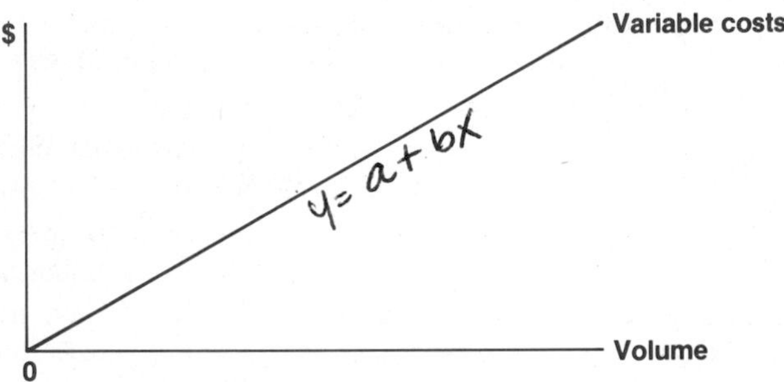


An example of variable costs is supplies, such as textbooks for students in a public school system. Some organizations will have relatively high variable costs per unit, resulting in a line which slopes upward quite steeply, while other organizations have variable costs which are relatively low for each unit of output such that the variable cost line slopes upward more slowly.

Total costs are then the sum of fixed and variable costs, as shown:

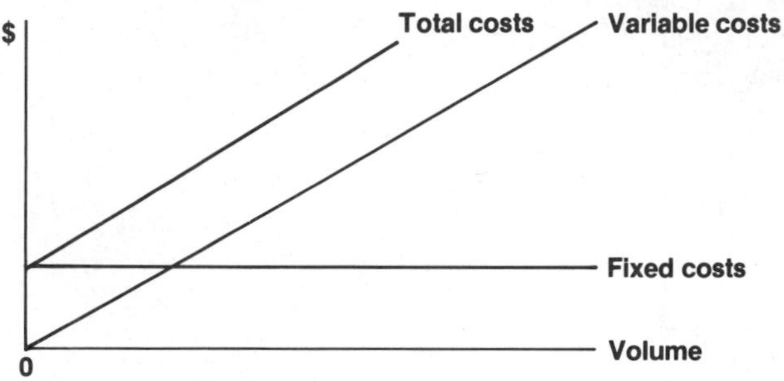


**Exhibit 4–2**
Cost Examples: Fixed/Variable versus Direct/Indirect in a Social Service Agency

| | *Fixed* | *Variable* |
|---|---|---|
| *Direct* | Supervisor's salary in the foster home care program. | Payment to foster parents for room and board. |
| *Indirect* | Portion of executive director's salary which is allocated to the foster home program. | Bank charges associated with checks to foster parents which are costs of administration, and allocated to the foster home program. |

Some other costs exhibit characteristics of both fixed and variable costs. Semi-variable costs, for example, have a fixed component but then increase in a linear fashion. A good example is electricity, which can have both a demand component (fixed) and a use component (variable). Step-function, or semi-fixed costs have a still different pattern, increasing in stepwise fashion with changes in volume. An example of a step-function cost is supervision. As the number of nurses, social workers, and the like in a hospital increases, supervisory personnel must be added. Since it is difficult for most organizations to add part-time supervisory help, the cost function for supervisors will behave in a steplike fashion.

## The Differential Cost Concept

Differential cost analysis attempts to identify the behavior of an organization's costs under different sets of assumptions, relating cost behavior to the type of differential decision. The following problem illustrates how this is done.

***Situation:*** Clearwater Ambulance Service operates a fleet of two ambulances. It charges 90¢ a mile for each "service mile" driven. Ambulance 1 drives 60,000 service miles a year; Ambulance 2 drives 30,000 service miles a year. The variable cost per mile for each ambulance is 20¢. The organization's revenues and costs are as follows:

| *Item* | *Ambulance 1* | *Ambulance 2* | *Total* |
|---|---|---|---|
| Revenue | .90 × 60,000<br>= $54,000 | .90 × 30,000<br>= $27,000 | $81,000 |
| Costs: | | | |
| Variable costs | .20 × 60,000<br>= $12,000 | .20 × 30,000<br>= $ 6,000 | $18,000 |
| Drivers | $15,000 | $15,000 | $30,000 |
| Indirect costs (rent and administration) | $20,000 | $10,000 | $30,000 |
| Total costs | $47,000 | $31,000 | $78,000 |
| Profit (Loss) | $ 7,000 | $ (4,000) | $ 3,000 |

***Question:*** Would the profitability of Clearwater Ambulance Service be improved if Ambulance 2, which is losing money, were discontinued?

***Analysis:*** The question is not whether Ambulance 2 is losing money on a *full cost* basic, but rather the nature of its differential costs and revenues, i.e., what revenues and costs would be eliminated if Ambulance 2 were discontinued, and what revenues and costs would remain. It appears that if we eliminate Ambulance 2, we discontinue its revenue, its variable costs, and the fixed cost of the driver. From all indications, however, the rent and administrative costs will continue, i.e., they are nondifferential. The result is a shift from a profit of $3,000 to a loss of $3,000, as the analysis on the next page indicates.

| *Item* | *Ambulance 1* |
|---|---|
| Revenue | .90 × 60,000<br>= $54,000 |
| Costs: | |
| Variable costs | .20 × 60,000<br>= $12,000 |
| Driver | $15,000 |
| Indirect costs (rent and administration) | $30,000 |
| Total costs | $57,000 |
| Profit (Loss) | $ (3,000) |

This example illustrates several important points. First, full cost information can produce misleading results if used for differential cost decisions—in this instance an add/drop decision. In the Clearwater case, the full cost data would seem to indicate that we could increase profits by dropping Ambulance 2, but this clearly was not the case.

Second, differential costs can include *both* fixed *and* variable costs. In the above example, the driver generally would be considered a fixed cost of Ambulance 2, and yet the elimination of Ambulance 2 eliminates this fixed cost. The key point here is that as long as we operate the ambulance, we have the fixed cost of the driver's salary; it does not fluctuate in accordance with the number of miles driven, within the relevant range. But when we eliminate the ambulance, we also eliminate this cost in its entirety; it is thus differential in terms of the decision we are analyzing.

A third point is that differential cost analysis invariably requires *assumptions.* Since we do not have perfect knowledge of the future, we must make some guesses about how costs will behave. In this example, there are three important assumptions: (1) the number of miles driven by Ambulance 1 will not increase with the elimination of Ambulance 2, (2) we will not be able to reduce or eliminate any indirect costs with the elimination of Ambulance 2, and (3) the unit costs and revenues will be the same in the future as in the example. Changes in these assumptions clearly would have an impact on the new profit (loss) figure, and might in fact actually make it profitable to eliminate Ambulance 2. It is therefore important in undertaking any form of differential cost analysis both to clarify the assumptions one is making and to explore how changes in these assumptions would affect the conclusions of the analysis. This latter activity generally is called "sensitivity analysis."

The final point illustrated by the example is that of the importance of structuring information for purposes of decision making. An important way of structuring differential cost information is in terms of *contribution.*

## The Concept of Contribution

As the above example indicated, a key question in many differential cost analyses is the behavior of indirect or overhead costs. In the example, a key assumption was that indirect costs (rent and administration) for the ambulance service would not be reduced if the second ambulance were eliminated. As indicated above, and as will be discussed in greater detail later, an assumption of this sort is not necessarily valid in a given situation. Nevertheless, in most instances an analysis of differential costs is most easily performed when the direct fixed and variable costs of the particular activity itself are analyzed separately from the indirect costs of the organization. Such an analysis can be structured in terms of the *contribution* of the particular service or program to the organization's indirect costs.

"Contribution" is the amount that each program in an organization contributes to the recovery of indirect costs. More specifically, a program (an ambulance in this case) provides some revenues and incurs some direct costs. The difference between the revenue provided and the direct costs (both fixed and variable) is the *contribution* of that program to the organization's indirect costs.

Returning to the example above, the cost data for the ambulance service could be structured in the following way:

| *Item* | *Ambulance 1* | *Ambulance 2* | *Total* |
|---|---|---|---|
| Revenue | $54,000 | $27,000 | $81,000 |
| Variable costs | $12,000 | $ 6,000 | $18,000 |
| Margin (for fixed and indirect costs) | $42,000 | $21,000 | $63,000 |
| Fixed costs (drivers) | $15,000 | $15,000 | $30,000 |
| Contribution (to indirect costs) | $27,000 | $ 6,000 | $33,000 |
| Indirect costs | $20,000 | $10,000 | $30,000 |
| Profit (Loss) | $ 7,000 | $ (4,000) | $ 3,000 |

What this example indicates is that both Ambulance 1 and Ambulance 2 are *contributing* to the coverage of indirect costs. Consequently, an elimination of either of these ambulances will reduce the total contribution to indirect costs, and thus either reduce the organization's profit or increase its loss. In fact, it was the $6,000 that Ambulance 2 was contributing that led to the change from a $3,000 profit to a $3,000 loss.

## Break-Even Analysis

One important technique used in differential cost situations is that of break-even analysis. The purpose of break-even analysis is to determine the volume of activity at which the total revenue for an organization will equal its total costs. A break-even analysis thus begins with the fundamental equation:

$$\text{Total Revenue } (TR) = \text{Total Costs } (TC)$$

Total revenue for many activities is quite easy to calculate. If we assume that an organization's charge or price per unit is represented by the letter $p$ and its volume by the letter $x$, then total revenue is unit price times volume, or:

$$TR = px$$

Total costs, as indicated previously, are the sum of fixed and variable costs. Thus, the breakeven formula is:

$$\text{Total Revenue} = \text{Fixed Costs} + \text{Variable Costs}$$

Fixed costs generally are represented by the letter $a$ and variable costs *per unit* by the letter $b$. Thus, total variable costs can be represented by the term $bx$ where, as before, $x$ represents volume. The resulting break-even formula can be shown as follows:

$$px = a + bx$$

Graphically we can represent the formula as follows:

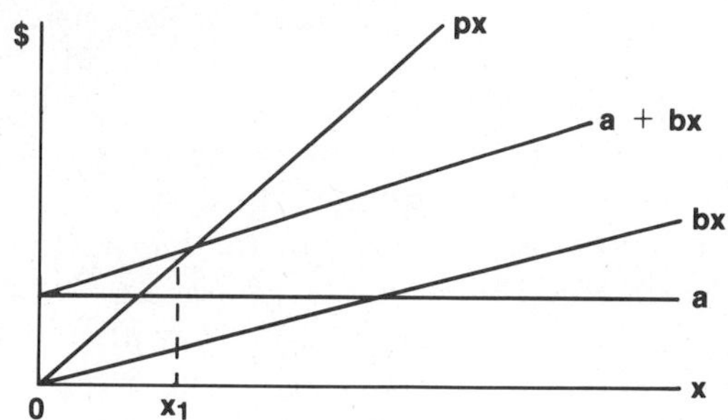


Point $x_1$ where $px = a + bx$ is therefore the break-even volume, i.e., it is the point at which total revenue *(px)* equals total costs *(a + bx)*. Thus, if we know unit price, fixed costs, and variable costs per unit, we can solve the formula algebraically for $x$ which would be our break-even volume.

***Example:*** The Littleton Home Health Agency has fixed costs of $10,000, variable costs per visit of $18, and charges $38 per visit. What is its break-even volume (number of visits)?

***Analysis:***

$$\begin{aligned} px &= a + bx \\ 38x &= 10{,}000 + 18x \\ 20x &= 10{,}000 \\ x &= 500 \end{aligned}$$

Break-even would thus be 500 visits. To confirm:

| | | |
|---|---|---|
| Revenue ....... | $38(500) = | $19,000 |
| Costs: | | |
| Variable ..... | $18(500) = | 9,000 |
| Fixed ....... | | 10,000 |
| Total .... | | $19,000 |

## Complicating Factors

***Nonquantifiable Aspects.*** Recognizing that differential costs are the proper costs to use for add/drop, contract-out, special request, or obsolete asset decisions is sufficient to provide a focus for the analytical efforts involved in such decisions, but it by no means makes either the decisions themselves, or the analytical efforts which underly them, easy. Indeed, as suggested above, there are a variety of strategic and other nonquantifiable aspects to these decisions which go beyond the financial analysis and which create highly complex situations. An adequate differential analysis must incorporate these factors.

***Problems with Allocated Costs.*** Complexities are introduced into the differential cost analysis when indirect costs are associated with a particular effort for which the differential analysis is to be made. This complexity can be viewed along three important dimensions. First, the bases of allocation used in the full cost accounting effort do not necessarily reflect actual use by mission or service cost centers. Thus, if the costs of a particular mission center are reduced, one result may be that the indirect costs *allocated* to that center will be reduced, but it is quite likely that these costs will be allocated to other cost centers and not necessarily eliminated for the institution as a whole. Second, while some indirect costs actually may be reduced as a result of reduced activity in a given mission center, the reduction may not accrue to that mission center, since the allocation basis may not change.

A good example of the first dimension is administration and general (A&G). A reduction of staff in a given mission center will lead to a reduction in total salaries in the center. If A&G costs are allocated to cost centers on the basis of salary dollars, there will be a reduction in the amount of A&G costs allocated to the center. It is unlikely, however, that there will be any reduction in the staff or other costs associated with the A&G service cost center. Thus, total indirect costs will not be reduced, but only redistributed to other cost centers.

An example of the second dimension is housekeeping. While a reduction in effort in a given mission center may reduce the need for housekeeping services, if housekeeping costs are allocated on a square footage basis, the system will not show a cost reduction unless the space utilized by the revenue center is also reduced. While costs allocated to the mission center will fall as a result of the lower amount of housekeeping costs overall, the *indicated* reduction on the full cost report will be much less than the *real* reduction which took place.

The third dimension arises because of the nature of the stepdown procedure. Since each service cost center is allocated to all remaining cost centers as one moves down the steps in the stepdown, those service centers farthest down in the report will have portions of the cost centers above them included in their totals. Thus, the total to be allocated from each service center includes both its direct costs and the costs which have been allocated to it from previous "steps" in the stepdown. For example, if social service is far down on the list, the total social service costs allocated to a particular mission center will carry a significant allocated component with it, e.g., administration, housekeeping, laundry and linen, etc. While it may be possible to reduce the use of social workers in a mission center by reducing the number of patients treated, the full impact of that reduction on the costs in the social service cost center will be overstated if one uses the fully allocated social services totals (including both direct and previously allocated costs). That is, the allocated component contains costs from a variety of other cost centers which may not be affected at all by the reduction in patient volume.

Recognizing these complexities and incorporating them into analytic efforts is one of the most challenging aspects of cost accounting in nonprofit organizations. Determining which costs are indeed differential and the extent of their differential nature is extremely difficult, particularly when a cost report (stepdown) is the principal source of information.

## SUGGESTED ADDITIONAL READINGS


Anthony, R. N., and James S. Reece. *Accounting Principles,* 5th Edition, Homewood, Ill.: Richard D. Irwin, 1983.

Dearden, J. *Essentials of Cost Accounting.* Reading, Mass.: Addison-Wesley Publishing, 1969.

Demone, H., and Gibelman (eds.). *Purchasing Human Services: Policies, Programs and Procedures.* New York: Human Sciences Press (forthcoming).

Lohmann, R. A. *Breaking Even: Financial Management in Human Service Organizations.* Philadelphia: Temple University Press, 1980.

Stein, H. *Organization and the Human Services: Cross Disciplinary Reflections,* Philadelphia: Temple University Press, 1981.

Suver, J. D., and B. R. Neumann. *Management Accounting for Health Care Organizations.* Oak Brook, Ill.: Hospital Financial Management Association, 1981.

Young, D. W.. "Contracting Out for Services: A Researcher's Perspective." in *Human Services Management: Priorities for Research,* ed. M. J. Murphy and T. Glynn. Washington, D.C.: International City Management Association, 1978.

Young, D. W., E. Socholitzky, and E. Locke. "Ambulatory Care Cost and the Medicare Cost Report: Managerial and Public Policy Implications." *Journal of Ambulatory Care Management,* February, 1982.

Young, D. W.. *Financial Control in Health Care: A Managerial Perspective,* Homewood, Ill.: Dow Jones–Irwin, (1983).

# Case 4–1

## PLEASANTVILLE HOME HEALTH AGENCY*

William Ellis, treasurer of the Pleasantville Home Health Agency, stared at a paragraph from the Reasonable Cost Guideline Proposal on his desk:

> Our intention is not to establish prospective limits on direct or indirect overall incurred costs or incurred costs for specific items or services as provided for in Section 405.460 of the Regulations and Section 223 of P.L. 92–603, but rather to develop an acceptable approach to applying the reasonable cost concept in those cases where specific limitations have not been developed. We have selected three areas of concentration. The areas are (1) physical therapy and home health aide, (2) skilled nursing facility inpatient routine service costs, and (3) hospital ancillary per diem costs.

Just that morning, Mr. Ellis had met with Eric Jackson, executive director of the Pleasantville Home Health Agency (PHHA), to discuss the Guideline Proposal set forth by the Division of Direct Reimbursement (DDR). They had concluded that the major objective of the guideline was to control Medicare costs by applying a "reasonable cost" ceiling to each type of service or commodity. The prospective cost limit would be applied to an institution whose costs are higher than those of another institution in the same area of comparable size, scope of service, and utilization.

Mr. Ellis and Mr. Jackson examined the proposal in an attempt to anticipate how the new guidelines would affect their agency. They were concerned because, in the past, PHHA's cost accounting method had been derived from Medicare reimbursement rates which had allowed them to use an average cost per visit for all the agency's services with the exception of home health aide visits. With the DDR guidelines, the cost for each type of visit would be considered independent of the agency's other visit costs and Mr. Ellis thought that their average figure might not be acceptable for some types of visits. He was also concerned because PHHA's costs would now be compared to those of other agencies, and he was afraid that PHHA's costs would appear high when compared to an agency's unaveraged costs.

For example, one type of visit the agency provided regularly was nursing. A typical nursing visit consisted of a home visit by a RN or LPN to check on a patient's condition, administer medication, and provide health education to the patient or patient's family. For nursing visits, PHHA charged its average cost per visit fee of $42. Mr. Ellis, however, was afraid that with the new guidelines, $42 might exceed the reasonable cost ceiling for a nursing visit.

After discussing the issue with PHHA's accountants, Mr. Ellis and Mr. Jackson decided to investigate a new cost system. Because the DDR guidelines

---

* This case was prepared by Patricia O'Brien under the direction of David W. Young, Harvard School of Public Health.

were designed to consider the cost of each type of visit separately, Mr. Ellis felt that their cost accounting method also must distinguish among the types of visits. Additionally, Mr. Ellis thought that if they separated their costs by services, they might obtain a measure by which they could judge performance.

## Data

Mr. Ellis had established PHHA's cost system according to Medicare's NLN I reimbursement method. The Medicare reimbursement rate for nursing visits, physical therapy visits, and medical social service visits was devised from combining the costs of the three types of visits and calculating an average cost per visit. To the total of all direct costs associated with these services, Mr. Ellis would add a percentage of overhead for administration, rent, and utilities and then divide that total visit cost by the total number of visits to arrive at an average cost per visit. Medicare then reimbursed the average cost per visit for all nursing care, physical therapy, and medical social service visits. For 1978, PHHA's average cost per visit was $42, as shown in Exhibit 1. (According to Medicare regulations, home health aide visits were charged for separately.)

The new cost system discussed by Mr. Ellis and Mr. Jackson would separate the total visit costs into three per-visit costs: (1) nursing, (2) physical therapy, and (3) medical social service. To derive these costs, Mr. Ellis reviewed the agency's 1978 figures and estimated the personnel and supply costs attributable to each type of visit, as shown in the right-hand columns of Exhibit 1. Because his records did not indicate the specific visit types to which the contract services pertained, Mr. Ellis decided to distribute the $69,216 according to the number of visits in each service group. To calculate the number of home visits for each type of service, Mr. Ellis reviewed the agency's employee visit records for 1978 and summarized the number of services that had been provided. Finally, Mr. Ellis decided to allocate overhead expenses to each visit type based on the total salary expense for each category.

**Exhibit 1**
Cost and Number of Visits, 1978

| *Costs* | *Total* | *Nursing* | *Physical Therapy* | *Medical Social Service* |
|---|---|---|---|---|
| Personnel | $422,934 | $113,388 | $221,310 | $ 88,236 |
| Medical and nursing supplies | 32,671 | 11,473 | 4,917 | 16,281 |
| Total direct | $455,605 | $124,861 | $226,227 | $104,517 |
| Contract services* | 69,216 | | | |
| Overhead | 131,131 | | | |
| Total cost | $655,952 | | | |
| Number of visits | 15,616 | 5,778 | 6,871 | 2,967 |
| Cost per visit | $ 42 | | | |

* Includes transportation.

## Response to the New System

While gathering the cost data, Mr. Ellis mentioned to Mr. Jackson that although he thought the new cost system would be more accurate, he perceived problems in the method. He explained:

> I think that, in general, we can get a more precise cost figure by breaking our expenses down into types of visits. The problem is that some of our expenses are not easily defined as belonging to one type of visit. Nursing salaries, for example. We have one RN who spends 50 percent of her time on supervisory work and 50 percent of her time on nursing visits. Her salary can be allocated to administration or to nursing services or be split between the two, but the process becomes very complicated.

Joyce Farrell, PHHA's nursing administrator, thought the new system could affect the quality of patient care provided:

> If you start tampering with the cost of each visit, you're going to make people very cost conscious and our patient care will suffer in the long run. I mean, you could actually start to value some visits more than others because of the cost factor.
>
> In my opinion, we should maintain a flat fee for all types of visits because it allows nurses to provide whatever the patient needs without thinking about costs.

Mr. Jackson withheld his opinion until after he could see some results from the new system. He agreed that the system might cause some additional complications for the agency's staff, but he also thought it posed some potential benefits for the agency.

## Questions

1. Calculate the cost per visit for the three types of visits.
2. Do you recommend that this method of calculating costs per visit be used instead of the present method?

## Case 4–2

## ROSEMONT HILL CHILDREN'S CENTER*

In March 1983, Mr. Frank Mitchell, Administrator of the Rosemont Hill Children's Center, expressed concern about the center's cost accounting system. The extensive funding Rosemont Hill had received during its early years

---

* This case was prepared by Patricia O'Brien under the direction of David W. Young, Harvard School of Public Health.

was decreasing, and Mr. Mitchell wanted to prepare the center to be self-sufficient, yet he lacked critical cost information.

At a meeting with Mr. Robert Simi, Rosemont Hill's new accountant, Mr. Mitchell outlined the principal issues:

> Our deficit is increasing, and we obviously have to reverse this trend if we're going to become solvent. But, for that, we have to know where our costs are, in particular the cost of each of the services we offer.

## Background

Rosemont Hill Children's Center was established in 1968 by a consortium of community groups. Situated in Roxbury, an inner-city residential neighborhood of Boston, Massachusetts, the center was intended to provide counseling and related services to residents of Roxbury and neighboring communities. Fifteen years after its inception, the center maintained strong ties with the community groups responsible for its development and subsequent acceptance in Roxbury.

Funding for Rosemont Hill was initially provided by the federal government as part of the Department of Health, Education and Welfare's attempt to provide social services to inner-city poverty areas in the United States. When these operating funds were depleted in 1981, the city of Boston supplemented Rosemont Hill's income with a small three-year grant. Because Mr. Mitchell realized that government support could not continue indefinitely, he intended to make the center self-sufficient as soon as possible. Rosemont Hill's income statement is contained in Exhibit 1.

**Exhibit 1**

ROSEMONT HILL CHILDREN'S CENTER
Income Statement
For the Year Ended December 31, 1982

| | |
|---|---|
| Revenue from patient fees | $690,900 |
| Other revenue | 10,000 |
| Total revenue | $700,900 |
| Expenses: | |
| Program services | $470,000 |
| Record keeping | 20,000 |
| Training and education | 50,000 |
| General and administrative | 184,000 |
| Total expenses | $724,000 |
| Surplus (Deficit) | (23,100) |

The center was composed of eight client-service departments: Homemaker Service, Family Planning, Counseling, Parents' Advocacy, Mental Health, Alcohol Rehabilitation, Community Outreach, Referral and Placement. In addition, the center has a Training and Education Department, which saw no clients, and a Client Records Department. The center had 22 paid employees and a volunteer staff of 6–10 students acquiring clinical and managerial experience.

Community Outreach, which had been designed by Rosemont Hill's consumers, was a multidisciplinary department providing a link between the health and social services at Rosemont Hill and the schools and city services of the community. The department was staffed by a part-time speech pathologist, a part-time learning specialist, and a full-time nutritionist.

The Referral and Placement Service was for clients whom Rosemont Hill felt, at the time it received a referral, it could not serve. The center attempted to locate another agency that could serve a client. Parents' Advocacy did not serve clients directly but rather worked on behalf of clients who were having difficulty with housing, schools, and so forth.

## The Existing Information System

Rosemont Hill's previous accountant had established a system to determine the cost per client visit (or related activity such as advocacy). According to this method, shown in Exhibit 2, the cost was a yearly average for all client visits. The accountant would first determine the direct cost of each department. He would then add overhead costs, such as administration, rent, and utilities, to the total cost of all the departments to determine the center's

**Exhibit 2**
Costs and Client Visits* for 1982, by Department

| *Department* | *Number Client Visits* | *Expenses* | | |
|---|---|---|---|---|
| | | *Salaries†* | *Other‡* | *Total* |
| Homemaker Service | 5,000 | $ 40,000 | $ 16,000 | $ 56,000 |
| Family Planning | 10,000 | 10,000 | 30,000 | 40,000 |
| Counseling | 2,100 | 60,000 | 32,000 | 92,000 |
| Parents' Advocacy | 4,000 | 54,000 | 12,000 | 66,000 |
| Mental Health | 1,400 | 30,000 | 16,000 | 46,000 |
| Alcohol Rehabilitation | 1,500 | 64,000 | 16,000 | 80,000 |
| Community Outreach | 2,500 | 10,000 | 20,000 | 30,000 |
| Referral and Placement | 6,400 | 40,000 | 20,000 | 60,000 |
| Subtotal | 32,900 | 308,000 | 162,000 | 470,000 |
| Administration | | 76,000 | 4,000 | 80,000 |
| Rent | | | 72,000 | 72,000 |
| Utilities | | | 20,000 | 20,000 |
| Training and Education | | 32,000 | 18,000 | 50,000 |
| Cleaning | | | 12,000 | 12,000 |
| Recordkeeping | | 14,000 | 6,000 | 20,000 |
| Total | | $430,000 | $294,000 | $724,000 |
| Number of patient visits | | | | 32,900 |
| Average cost per visit | | | | $22.00 |

* Client visits rounded to nearest 100; expenses rounded to nearest $1,000.

† Includes fringe benefits.

‡ Materials, supplies, contracted services, depreciation, and other nonpersonnel expenses.

total costs. Finally, he would divide that total by the number of visits. Increased by an anticipated inflation figure for the following year (approximately 8 to 10 percent), this number became the projected cost per client visit for the subsequent year.

In reviewing this method with Mr. Simi, Mr. Mitchell explained the problems he perceived. He said that although he realized this was not a precise method of determining costs for clients, the center's cost per visit had to be held at a reasonable level to keep the services accessible to as many community residents as possible. Additionally, he anticipated complications in determining the cost per visit for each of Rosemont Hill's departments:

> You have to consider that our overhead costs, like administration and rent, have to be included in the cost per visit. That's easy to do when we have a single cost, but I'm not certain how to go about it when determining costs on a departmental basis. Furthermore, it's important to point out that some of our departments provide services to others. Parents' Advocacy, for example. There are three social workers in that department, all earning the same salary. But one works exclusively for Counseling, another divides her time evenly between Family Planning and Homemaker Service. Only the third spends his entire time in the Advocacy Department seeing clients who don't need other social services, although he occasionally refers clients to other social workers. In the Alcohol Rehabilitation Department, the situation is more complicated. We have two MSW's, each earning $24,000 a year, and one bachelor degree social worker earning $16,000. The two MSW's yearly see about 1,500 clients who need counseling, but they also spend about 50 percent of their time in other departments. The BA social worker cuts pretty evenly across all departments except referral and placement, of course.

Mr. Simi added further dimensions to the problems:

> I've spent most of my time so far trying to get a handle on allocating these overhead costs to the departments. It's not an easy job, you know. Administration, for example, seems to help everyone about equally, yet I suppose we might say more administrative time is spent in the departments where we pay more salaries. Rent, on the other hand, is pretty easy: that can be done on a square-foot basis. We could classify utilities according to usage if we had meters to measure electricity, phone usage and so forth, but because we don't we have to do that on a square-foot basis as well. This applies to cleaning too, I guess. It seems to me that record keeping can be allocated on the basis of the number of records, and each department generates one record per patient visit.
>
> Training and Education (T&E) is the most confusing. Some departments don't use it at all, while others use it regularly. I guess the fairest would be to charge for T&E on an hourly basis. Since there are two people in the department, each working about 2,000 hours a year, the charge per hour would be about $8.00. But this is a bit unfair since the T&E Department also uses supplies, space, and administrative time. So we should include those other costs in its hourly rate. Thus, the process is confusing and I haven't really decided how to sort it out. However, I have prepared totals for floor space and T&E usage (Exhibit 3).

**Exhibit 3**
Rosemont Hill Children's Center Floor Space and T&E Usage, by Department

| *Department* | *Floor Space** | *T&E Usage†* |
|---|---|---|
| Homemaker Service | 1,000 | 1,000 |
| Family Planning | 1,300 | 200 |
| Counseling | 1,800 | 2,400 |
| Parents' Advocacy | 300 | 100 |
| Mental Health | 1,000 | — |
| Alcohol Rehabilitation | 500 | — |
| Community Outreach | 1,100 | 100 |
| Referral and Placement | 1,000 | 200 |
| Administration | 500 | — |
| Recordkeeping | 300 | — |
| Training and Education (T&E) | 1,200 | — |
| Total | 10,000 | 4,000 |

* In square feet, rounded to nearest 100.
† In hours per year, rounded to nearest 100.

## The Future

As Mr. Mitchell looked toward the remainder of 1983, he decided to calculate a precise cost figure for each department. The Center was growing, and he estimated that total client volume would increase by about 10 percent during 1983, spread evenly over each department. He anticipated that costs would also increase by about 10 percent. He asked Mr. Simi to prepare a stepdown analysis for 1982 so that they would know Rosemont Hill's costs for each department. He planned to use this information to assist him in projecting costs for 1983.

## Questions

1. What is the cost per visit for each department?
2. How might this information be used by Mr. Mitchell?

## Case 4–3

## GRINDEL COLLEGE*

At its meeting in January 1981 the board of trustees of Grindel College adopted a new policy governing charges made to off-campus students. This policy resulted in student dissatisfaction, culminating in a boycott of the annual drawing for dormitory rooms. At its meeting in April 1981 the board discussed whether this policy should be changed.

* This case was prepared by Robert N. Anthony, Harvard Business School.

## Background

Grindel College was a private, four-year, coeducational college with 1,800 students. It had dormitory accommodations for 1,650 students, including fraternity houses owned by the fraternities but located on college property. Fraternity houses had no dining facilities. The other 150 students lived in the community.

All residential students paid the same amount for room rent and meal charges, regardless of the age or location of the dormitory in which they lived. The amount of room rent collected from each resident in a fraternity house (200 students) was held by the college and used for fraternity house upkeep. All freshmen were required to live in dormitories.

The policy was to fill dormitories to their design capacity. (In practice, withdrawals, unexpectly large enrollments, and other considerations resulted in minor variations between actual occupancy and design capacity.) Since more than 150 students wanted to live off campus, a lottery was held each April to determine those who would be permitted to do so. Preference was given to students living with their parents (usually about 12), married students, and students age 24 or older. The remaining off-campus permissions were decided by lot.

## Financial Policies

Each January the board adopted a schedule of tuition, fees, room rent, and meal charges for the following academic year. The budget was prepared according to the principal financial policies summarized below (certain policies not relevant to this case have been omitted):

1. Tuition and fees are to be competitive with other colleges.
2. Tuition and fees, plus estimated revenue from annual gifts, endowment, and miscellaneous sources gives the total amount available for academic and general operations. Academic and general expenses are budgeted to equal this amount, approximately.
3. Auxiliary enterprises are to operate on a break-even basis.
4. Budgeted student resident expenses are divided by the number of dormitory residents (excluding fraternity residents) to give the room rent.
5. Budgeted food service costs (reduced by the estimated amount of revenue from casual meals and miscellaneous sources) are divided by 1,650 to give the meal charge.

Student resident and food service expenses included both direct cost and an equitable portion of common maintenance and operating costs (but not college-wide administration expenses). Student resident costs also included debt service, in lieu of depreciation, on funds borrowed to construct dormitories. For several years prior to 1979–80, the amount of debt service had been nominal.

In 1980–81, (i.e., the year ended August 31, 1981) tuition and fees were

$6,120, room rent was $1,070, and board was $1,310. As shown in Exhibit 1, these charges were not quite consistent with the financial policies, in that the student residences were budgeted to operate at a loss. The reason for this was that a new dormitory was completed in 1979, and in accordance with long-standing practice its cost was financed by a 25-year bond issue. Inclusion of the full amount of its debt service in the calculation of room rents would have increased room rents by an amount that was believed to be too great for one year. Thus, it was decided to increase room rents in 1979–80, and in the next three or four years also, by a smaller amount than the increase in estimated costs.

**Exhibit 1**

GRINDEL COLLEGE
Condensed Financial Data on Operations
($000 except per-student charges)

| | *Budget 1980–81* | *Current Estimate 1980–81* | *Proposed Budget 1981–82* |
|---|---|---|---|
| Education and general: | | | |
| Tuition and fees | $11,010 | $11,375 | $12,870 |
| Other revenue | 3,145 | 3,495 | 3,606 |
| Total revenue | 14,155 | 14,870 | 16,476 |
| Educational and general expenses | 13,782 | 13,964 | 16,245 |
| Educational and general income | $ 373 | $ 906 | $ 231 |
| Auxiliary Enterprises | | | |
| Student residences:* | | | |
| Revenue | $ 1,547 | $ 1,555 | $ 1,842† |
| Expenses | 1,811 | 1,865 | 2,020 |
| Net | (264) | (310) | (168) |
| Food service: | | | |
| Revenue | 2,177 | 2,244 | 2,352 |
| Expenses | 2,175 | 2,167 | 2,337 |
| Net | 2 | 77 | 15 |
| All other:‡ | | | |
| Revenue | 1,215 | 1,208 | 1,346 |
| Expenses | 1,301 | 1,248 | 1,404 |
| Net | (86) | (40) | (58) |
| Auxiliary net | $ (348) | $ (273) | (211) |
| Net income | $ 25 | $ 633 | $ 20 |
| Charges per student | | | |
| Tuition and fees (1,800 students) | $ 6,120 | | $ 7,150 |
| Room (1,450 students) | 1,070 | | 1,250 |
| Board (1,650 students) | 1,310 | | 1,410 |

* "Student residences" excludes fraternity expenses.

† Includes revenue from off-campus students.

‡ Includes student union, bookstore, conferences using campus facilities, and a few minor items.

## Meeting of January 1981

In January 1981, the administration recommended charges for 1981–82 to the Budget and Finance Committee of the board. Exhibit 1 is a condensed version of material used at that meeting (details of revenues and expenses have been omitted). It showed that although the budget for 1980–81 was essentially a break-even budget, the current estimate of revenues and expenses for 1980–81 indicated a surplus of $633,000. This was primarily because more students than budgeted were enrolled and because endowment earnings were highter than anticipated.

At this meeting John Bard, the president, and Russell Strong, financial vice president, recommended tuition and fees of $7,150, room rent of $1,250, and board charges of $1,410. These were consistent with the financial policies except that, as was the case in 1979–80, student residences were budgeted at a loss because of the decision not to recover the full amount of debt service.

The administration also proposed a change in the charges made to off-campus students. Until that time, they had not paid room or board charges. (They could eat meals on the campus at rates set on a per-meal basis.) The administration proposed that in 1981–82 and thereafter off-campus students be given a credit of 85 percent of the room rent and board charges. Students living with their parents would be given a credit of 100 percent of these charges.

Reasons given for, in effect, charging off-campus students 15 percent of the room rent and board charges were as follows:

1. Grindel was a residential college, and its facilities are available to all students whether they choose to use them or not. Off-campus students could, and did, visit friends in the dormitories and attend functions held in the dormitories. If some students choose not to live and eat on campus, this does not free them of an obligation to pay at least a portion of the residential costs.

2. Most dormitory costs were fixed. If a student moved off campus, dormitory costs were reduced only by an insignificant amount. Therefore, off-campus students were in effect being subsidized by dormitory residents because they did not pay anything toward the fixed costs of the dormitories. This was unfair to dormitory residents.

3. Off-campus students used a "commuter room" in the student union, and they often traveled to the campus in a college bus; they should bear the cost of these special facilities. (No student paid a separate charge for use of the student union.)

Mr. Strong reported that the Financial Priorities Committee, an advisory body of students and faculty, had voted approval of the new policy in principle, but had not felt competent to judge whether the 85 percent credit was the appropriate amount. After considerable discussion, the Budget and Finance Committee voted unanimously to recommend the policy to the board. At its meeting the following day, the board unanimously approved the proposed tuition, room, and board charges and the new policy for off-campus students.

## Developments after the January Meeting

Shortly after the January meeting, Mr. Bard, the president, notified parents of the charges for 1981–82. (Through an oversight, the letter went only to parents, and some students did not hear of the charges until some weeks thereafter.)

A number of students thought that the new policy for off-campus students was unfair. These included most students who wanted to live off campus, and some on-campus students. About 75 students met for more than two hours with the financial vice president, Mr. Strong. The points made at that meeting are summarized below, as excerpted from a lengthy, well-written letter sent subsequently to each member of the board of trustees:

> Grindel cannot house all its students, so off-campus living is an integral part of its activities . . . occasional use of the dormitories by off-campus students does not incur costs that come close to the claimed 15 percent surcharge . . . off-campus students promote closer town/gown relations . . . the surcharge would discriminate in favor of well-to-do students . . . the 15 percent surcharge should be applied to all students benefiting from the residential aspects but who also are not housed in dormitories, namely fraternity members . . . under the proposed policy, women have no opportunity to seek alternatives to dormitory life without paying extra, while men do (because only men can live in fraternity houses) . . . immediate implementation of an extra charge is grossly unfair to students who are currently enrolled and who planned to live off campus before knowing of the surcharge . . . students have not been told the rationale for the surcharge, and in particular for the amount of 15 percent.

Students requested that in 1981–82 the new charge be applied only to students not now enrolled, and that during that time the merits of the policy be restudied. This would in effect be a two-year delay because all freshmen were required to live in dormitories.

A number of letters expressing similar views were printed in the Grindel student newspaper. No letters supported the administration position.

As it happened, the deadline for signing up for the off-campus lottery was the day after the April board meeting. As an indication of the depth of their feeling, only one student had signed up as of the day before the meeting.

## Meetings of April 1981

At the Budget and Finance Committee meeting held on the day before the board meeting in April 1981, the president summarized the discussions, and reported that the financial vice president had proposed a compromise solution in his meeting with students: for the year 1981–82 off-campus students would be credited for $2,380, the amount of board and room charges for 1980–81, that is, this amount would be subtracted from the proposed board and room charges. The new policy would go into full effect in 1982–83. The president recommended adoption of this policy by the committee.

Mr. Bard also pointed out that if few students signed up for off-campus housing, all of them could be housed in the dormitories by putting in additional beds. In some prior years, the number of beds had been increased temporarily by similar measures, when enrollments had turned out to be higher than expected.

Most committee members continued to believe that the new policy was sound. Some, however, sought to defuse the issue by postponing implementation of the policy entirely until 1982–83. The president indicated that this was agreeable with him. Others pointed out that the financial vice president had already gone on record with a compromise solution and that to postpone implementation entirely would both undercut the administration and give the signal that students were free to question financial charges; this might open the door to controversy on other financial questions in future years.

Because a large "kick-off" dinner for a major capital funds drive took place that evening, the committee meeting had to adjourn before all views had been aired. By a small majority, the Budget and Finance Committee voted to recommend the compromise position to the full board, and this was done.

## Questions

1. As a member of the Budget and Finance Committee, what position would you have taken at the January meeting?
2. As member of the board, not on the Budget and Finance Committee, what position will you take at the meeting in April 1981?

## Case 4–4

## CENTERVILLE HOME HEALTH AGENCY*

In December, Mr. Joseph Blanchard became the controller of the Centerville Home Health Agency (CHHA). After 10 years in the accounting department of a consumer products firm, Mr. Blanchard decided to move into the not-for-profit field where he felt his expertise would be needed. CHHA, a small social service agency in East Hampshire, Kentucky, offered him that opportunity.

Before Mr. Blanchard accepted the position of controller, Ms. Louise Tucker, the director of the agency, briefed him on the agency's financial

* This case was prepared by Patricia O'Brien under the direction of David W. Young, Harvard School of Public Health.

position. Like other home health agencies, CHHA was reimbursed for all its patient visits by Medicare on an average-cost-per-visit basis. At the end of each fiscal year, the agency would total their operating costs, adjusting them according to Medicare regulations. They then divided the total costs by the number of visits to derive an average cost per visit which became the Medicare reimbursement rate. CHHA's average cost per visit calculation for 1978 is contained in Exhibit 1.

In September of 1978, CHHA was notified by Medicare that the agency's average cost per visit exceeded the "reasonable cost guideline" established by the Division of Direct Reimbursement for that Standard Metropolitan Statistical Area (SMSA). The letter reads as follows:

> We have reviewed your current interim rate of Medicare reimbursement in accordance with applicable Medicare regulations, and have found in accordance with Regulation No. 5, Subpart D, 405.451(C)(2), that your agency is being reimbursed at a rate which is substantially out of line with other home health agencies.

**Exhibit 1**
Expense Record—1978

| | *Detail* | *Total* |
|---|---|---|
| 1. Salaries | | $158,724 |
| Director, assistant director, controller | $54,000 | |
| Nurses (2) | 24,525 | |
| Psychologist (1) | 16,000 | |
| Social workers (2) | 21,346 | |
| Physical therapists (2) | 22,853 | |
| Support staff (3) | 20,000 | |
| 2. Transportation costs | | 21,000 |
| Automobile operation and insurance | 6,000 | |
| Automobile allowance for staff | 15,000 | |
| 3. Services purchased | | 1,750 |
| 4. Medical and nursing supplies | | 5,500 |
| 5. Space occupancy costs | | 12,530 |
| Rent | 12,300 | |
| Maintenance and repairs | 100 | |
| Taxes | 130 | |
| 6. Office costs | | 9,420 |
| Stationery and printing | 4,496 | |
| Telephone | 4,050 | |
| Postage and express | 874 | |
| 7. Other general costs | | 13,300 |
| Depreciation on furniture and equipment | 1,000 | |
| Legal and accounting fees | 3,900 | |
| Insurance (other than auto) | 4,100 | |
| Other | 2,700 | |
| Interest | 1,600 | |
| Total cost | | $222,224 |
| Number of visits | | 5,452 |
| Average cost per visit | | $40.76 |

The program recognizes that the cost of provider services may vary from one institution to another and the variations generally reflect differences in the scope of services, intensity of care, geographical location, and utilization. Regulation No. 5, Subpart D, 405.451(C)(2) states:

> "The provision in title XVIII of the Act for payment of reasonable cost of services is intended to meet the actual costs, however widely they may vary from one institution to another. This is subject to a limitation where a particular institution's costs are found to be substantially out of line with other institutions in the same area which are similar in size, scope of services, utilization and other relevant factors."

Our records indicate that your agency is currently being reimbursed at an average cost per visit of *$40.76* for Part A billings. In order to adjust your interim rate of reimbursement to a level of reimbursement that will not exceed the reasonable cost of services incurred by similar institutions, it will be necessary to reduce your interim rate to *$38* per visit.

We will institute the revised rate of interim reimbursement 90 days from the date of this letter, unless you are able to provide acceptable written documentation which would clearly provide evidence that the high costs incurred by your agency are unavoidable. The rate will be applied against services rendered as of December 1, 1978.

If you have any questions, or if we can be of any further assistance, please feel free to contact us.

Ms. Tucker was concerned because the 1978 charge had been $40.76 per visit and, according to her, at $38 per visit the agency could not meet its expenses. Ms. Tucker hired Mr. Blanchard with the hope that he could resolve this problem.

## Background

The Centerville Home Health Agency opened in 1970 to provide nursing visits to elderly and disabled residents of East Hampshire and neighboring towns. In 1973 the agency expanded to offer physical therapy and medical social service visits. Because another organization in town, The Hampshire Home Service, provided home health aide care, CHHA did not offer aide services.

In 1978, CHHA had a staff of 13. Two registered nurses, two physical therapists, two social workers, and one psychologist were responsible for the home health visits. The administration consisted of a director, an assistant director, the newly appointed controller, and a support staff of three. The skilled nursing care visits were handled by the two registered nurses. The two physical therapists worked exclusively on patient visits, and the social workers, with the help of the psychologist, provided all the social service visits.

The two registered nurses who handled all nursing visits could provide as many as seven visits a day each. However, because the case visits varied significantly in time, effort, and location for 1978, the nurses averaged only 4.54 visits per day. The physical therapists averaged three visits per day, although Ms. Tucker thought their capacity could be increased by at least 33 percent if they had the demand. CHHA's medical and social service visits were the most complicated. With the help of the psychologist, the social workers averaged 3.82 visits a day for 1978. Ms. Tucker thought these visits could be increased to about 4.6 a day, however. The CHHA staff worked an average of 240 days a year.

## Data

In his first few weeks, Mr. Blanchard reviewed CHHA's financial statements, employee service sheets and other working papers to become familiar with the agency's financial status and planning needs. He realized the agency had been operating without any cost objectives before Medicare imposed a guideline. After a cursory review of past records, Mr. Blanchard decided his first priority was to ensure that their current revenue met their costs. According to him, the agency needed to know the capacity at which their revenue would balance their costs.

Examining CHHA's Expense Record, shown in Exhibit 1, Mr. Blanchard determined that the agency had two types of costs: those that changed according to the number of visits provided and those that were unchanged, regardless of volume. Mr. Blanchard reasoned that at their break-even point, CHHA's revenue of $38 per visit would equal the total cost of the expenses generated by each visit plus the fixed expenses.

Mr. Blanchard reviewed each item on the Expense Record to determine which type of cost it was. He thought the medically related salaries and the medical and nursing supplies were items that varied directly with the number of visits. When he discussed his analysis with Ms. Tucker, she suggested that staff automobile allowance varied with the number of visits because it referred to mileage incurred by the medical staff in making home visits.

"Terrific," thought Mr. Blanchard. "Now I can calculate a variable cost per visit and in no time I'll know the break-even point. I can make them a graph showing their costs and revenue and where we'll have to operate to keep this agency in business."

## Questions

1. Identify the fixed and variable costs.
2. What is the break-even point?
3. What assumptions were necessary in answering questions 1 and 2?

## Case 4–5

## TOWN OF BELMONT*

It was 10 A.M., January 4th. Mr. James Castanino, the newly promoted head of the Highway Department, sat at his desk looking out across the sloping park toward the town's busy main shopping district. Opposite him was a member of his staff who had recently begun a project to determine the appropriate mix of town-owned and subcontract snow removal equipment.

The study came at an opportune time. The town's aging six Walther Snow Fighters were rapidly reaching the point of replacement, and it was Mr. Castanino's intention to replace them at a rate of one per year. Belmont, like most town governments, was finding it ever more difficult to increase its revenues rapidly enough to maintain previous levels of service. All of the town's departments were undertaking sustained cost cutting measures. The highway department had been a leader in such cost savings, doing volume purchasing and repairing all its vehicles. However, further cost cutting was necessary. With snow removal being the largest component of the department's budget, a reexamination of its snow removal subcontracting policies might yield significant savings.

In simplified terms, the decision Mr. Castanino faced contained two options. The first option was to replace his six Walther Snow Fighters on a one-to-one basis. The second was to not replace the Walthers and subcontract six more vehicles. Before making his decision he felt a number of important variables needed to be considered.

Belmont (triple A bond rating) was a suburb of Boston. Its population was predominantly middle class, with a high proportion of professional people. The town had a well-deserved reputation for providing its citizens with high-quality services, and the maintenance of this reputation was important. Indeed, during the two large blizzards of 1978 the Highway Department had managed to keep all roads passable and was one of the first in the state to have restored road conditions to normal.

The department heads reported to a part-time Board of Selectmen. This provided them with considerable autonomy in their day-to-day decision making. Capital expenditures greater than $5,000 required approval by the selectmen, the warrant committee, and the town meeting. As a result, Mr. Castanino was aware that any capital expenditure would face searching scrutiny before approval. The town also desired to maintain good relations with its employees. Thus, any cost-saving measure which improved working conditions would be highly attractive.

The town had 90 miles of roads, of which 40 were considered main thoroughfares. When salting or sanding was required, the main thoroughfares were covered each hour by four trucks equipped with spreaders.

* This case was prepared by Roy D. Shapiro, Harvard Business School.

The use of spreaders varied according to conditions. If only a trace of snow was expected, road conditions were watched closely. If road conditions seemed likely to worsen, one truck would be dispatched to cover the steeper gradients. If more than a trace but less than an inch was expected, four trucks with spreaders would be dispatched to cover the main thoroughfares. They would generally have to make two sweeps (at 10 miles an hour). If greater than an inch but less than three inches fell, seven trucks with spreaders would be dispatched to cover all roads. They would generally spend an hour per inch with an hour for mopping-up operations. If greater than three inches were expected, snowplowing procedures were initiated. Exhibit 1 contains relevant snowfall data, averaged for 30 years.

The department's resources consisted of its own vehicles and subcontractors. Belmont had 15 vehicles which could be used for snowplowing. They consisted of the 6 Walther Snow Fighters and 9 other vehicles that were

**Exhibit 1**
Snowfall data, 1950–1979

*November*

11 percent of November days had snow, sleet, or hail; of these days, measured snowfall was as follows:

| *Snowfall (inches)* | *Proportion of Days Having that Amount* |
|---|---|
| Trace | 72% |
| Under 1 | 18 |
| Over 1 | 10 |

*December*

34 percent of December days had snow, sleet, or hail; of these days, measured snowfall was as follows:

| *Snowfall (inches)* | *Proportion of Days Having that Amount* |
|---|---|
| Trace | 54% |
| Under 1 | 27 |
| 1–3 | 9 |
| 3–5 | 5 |
| 5–10 | 1 |
| 10–15 | 1 |
| Over 15 | 0.5 |

*January*

41 percent of January days had snow, sleet, or hail; of these days, measured snowfall was as follows:

| *Snowfall (inches)* | *Proportion of Days Having that Amount* |
|---|---|
| Trace | 47% |
| Under 1 | 29 |
| 1–3 | 11 |
| 3–5 | 7 |
| 5–10 | 4 |
| 10–15 | 1 |
| Over 15 | 0.2 |

**Exhibit 1 *(continued)***

*February*

39 percent of February days had snow, sleet, or hail; of these days, measured snowfall was as follows:

| *Snowfall (inches)* | *Proportion of Days Having that Amount* |
|---|---|
| Trace | 47% |
| Under 1 | 30 |
| 1–3 | 11 |
| 3–5 | 5 |
| 5–10 | 4 |
| 10–15 | 1 |
| Over 15 | 1 |

*March*

28 percent of March days had snow, sleet, or hail; of these days, measured snowfall was as follows:

| *Snowfall (inches)* | *Proportion of Days Having that Amount* |
|---|---|
| Trace | 50% |
| Under 1 | 27 |
| 1–3 | 12 |
| 3–5 | 6 |
| 5–10 | 4 |
| 10–15 | 1 |
| Over 15 | 0.4 |

*Source:* Local Climatological Data Monthly Survey (for Boston Logan International Airport) compiled by the National Oceanic and Atmospheric Administration Environmental Data Service.

used for other purposes in addition to snowplowing. On the average, 13 were available during a storm. Also on call were 15 subcontracted vehicles. Typically, 90 percent of those called in any storm would turn out. To ensure good relations with the subcontractors, Castanino's policy was to divide them into two groups—one group of seven and one of eight. If the expected snowfall was greater than three inches but less than five inches, he would call in only one group. The two groups would be chosen on an alternating basis. If greater than five inches was expected, all 15 subcontractor vehicles would be called. Subcontractors only performed plowing services, not the salting and sanding of roads. Like town employees, subcontractors would work until the snow was cleared, but they did not receive overtime pay. While the size and rental cost of subcontracted vehicles varied, an appropriate average was $34 per hour. Cost data for a town vehicle is contained in Exhibit 2.

Normal procedures called for the employees and/or subcontractors to work until the storm was cleared up. This would take roughly an hour for each inch of snow, plus an additional three hours for a three-inch storm. An eight-inch snowfall would take an additional four hours, and for a snowfall greater than 16 inches an additional eight-hour shift of all vehicles would be required to mop up. For any storm which dumped more than 12 inches, the usual policy required working 16-hour shifts. This meant that only two thirds of the vehicles would be on the road at any time. For snowfall in excess of two feet, all crews would be sent home for eight hours rest before clean-up operations were resumed. It was not a surprising demonstration of the innate perversity of weather conditions that, historically, 70 percent of all town employees' time spent on snow removal had been at overtime rates.

**Exhibit 2**
Cost of Operating a Town Vehicle, Salting and Sanding

| | |
|---|---|
| Labor | 2 persons per vehicle* |
| Salt | $27 per ton at 3 tons per hour† |
| or | |
| Sand | $3 per ton at 3 tons per hour† |
| Fuel | $6/hour |
| Repairs and maintenance | $10/hr |
| *Snow Removal with New Vehicles* | |
| Labor | 1 person per vehicle* |
| Fuel | $6/hour |
| Repairs and maintenance | $10/hr |
| Cost of new 18 GVW vehicle | $30,000 |

* Labor costs were $6 per hour, time-and-a-half for overtime.
† Normally half of the material spread was salt and half was sand.

It also had come to Mr. Castanino's attention that if the Walthers were retired but not replaced, it would be possible to redeploy their drivers as replacements for other drivers, reducing the expected time any individual driver would spend on the road in a 12-inch storm by 6.5 hours without increasing labor costs. The total labor cost per town vehicle would, however, remain the same.

Having discussed operating procedures, Mr. Castanino and his assistant began to discuss ways of determining the costs of these two options.

## Question

What action would you recommend?

## Case 4–6

## LAKESIDE HOSPITAL*

"A hospital just can't afford to operate a department at 50 percent capacity," said Dr. Peter Lawrence, Director of Specialty Services at Lakeside Hospital. "If we average 20 dialysis patients, it costs us $257 per treatment, and we are only reimbursed for $138. If a department like this can't cover its costs, including a fair share of overhead, it isn't self-sufficient and I don't think we should carry it."

Dr. Lawrence was meeting with Dr. James Newell, Chief Nephrologist of Lakeside Hospital's Renal Division, about the recent change in the Medicare reimbursement policy regarding hemo-dialysis treatments. A few years ago, Medicare had begun reimbursing independent dialysis clinics for standard dialysis treatments. Consequently, they had modified their hospital reimbursement policy to cover only treatments for start-up or overflow patients, inpatients, emergencies, and treatments with complications.

The change in policy had caused the dialysis unit's patient volume to decrease to 50 percent of capacity and produce a corresponding increase in per treatment costs. By February of the current fiscal year,[1] Dr. Lawrence and Lakeside's Medical Director were considering phasing down or closing the dialysis unit. At the end of February, Dr. Lawrence met with Dr. Newell to discuss the future of the dialysis unit.

Dr. Newell, who had been Chief Nephrologist since he'd helped establish the unit, was opposed to cutting down renal disease services and even more opposed to closing the unit. Although he was impressed by the quality of care that independent centers offered, he was convinced that Lakeside's unit was necessary for providing back-up and emergency services for the outpatient centers. Furthermore, although the unit could not operate at the low costs of the independent centers, Dr. Newell disagreed with Dr. Lawrence's cost figure of $257 per treatment. He resolved to prepare his own cost analysis for their next meeting.

### Background

At Dr. Newell's initiative, Lakeside had opened the dialysis unit in 1972 in response to the growing number of patients with chronic kidney disease. The Hospital's renal division had long provided acute renal failure care and kidney transplants, but by the 1970s, the most common treatment for end-stage renal disease was hemo-dialysis. During dialysis, a portion of a patient's blood circulates through an artificial kidney machine and is cleansed of waste

---

* This case was prepared by Patricia O'Brien, under the direction of David W. Young, Harvard School of Public Health.

[1] Lakeside's fiscal year (FY) ran from October 1 to September 30.

products. Used three times a week for 4 to 5 hours, the kidney machine allows people with chronic kidney disease to lead almost normal lives.

Lakeside's dialysis unit had 14 artifical kidney machines, but they were limited by their certificate of need to using 10 per hour and reserving 4 for break-downs and emergencies. Open six days a week with two shifts of patients daily, the unit could provide 120 treatments a week or accommodate 40 regular patients. From 1973, the year that Medicare began reimbursing for dialysis, all of Lakeside's dialysis patients were covered by Medicare. By 1975, the unit was operating close to or above 100 percent capacity, extending its hours and staff to accept emergency cases and avoid turning away patients.

Although Medicare initially had been hesitant about setting a precedent for reimbursing nonhospital facilities, in 1978 it began reimbursing independent centers for dialysis treatments because of the significant cost savings. Beginning in October of 1977, patients spent their first three months of dialysis in a hospital facility; if there were no complications when this "start-up" period had passed, patients were then required to transfer to independent centers. Currently, Medicare paid Lakeside $138 per dialysis treatment.

The independent dialysis centers were developed in the mid-1970s throughout the United States. Centrally owned and operated, they were organized in satellite groups of 8 or 10 spread throughout metropolitan and suburban areas. The centers' facilities were modern and attractively designed and, because they were separate from hospitals' institutional environments, they offered psychological advantages to patients dependent on dialysis. Centrally managed with low overhead, the independent centers could achieve economies unobtainable by similar hospital units. Supplies and equipment were purchased in bulk, and administrators watched staff scheduling and cost efficiency closely. As a result, the cost per treatment in outpatient centers was significantly lower than comparable treatments in a hospital facility. For example, treatments in a center operating at 100 percent capacity with 40 patients could cost the center as little as $80. Center charges varied from $113 to $150, depending on the volume and location.

## Lakeside Data

Lakeside's direct and allocated costs for the Renal Dialysis Unit in the previous fiscal year are detailed in Exhibit 1. Dr. Newell also obtained the unit's cost center report for the same fiscal year (Exhibit 2), which provided a breakdown of the unit's direct costs.

He intended to use the prior year's costs to calculate the per treatment cost at various volume levels for the current year. More importantly, he wanted to find the point at which the unit's revenue would meet its costs. He planned, however, to use only those costs that could be traced directly to dialysis treatments, omitting all overhead expenses. According to Dr. Newell, if the unit's revenue met those costs, the unit was self-sufficient. Dr. Newell considered Dr. Lawrence's treatment cost of $257 misleading

**Exhibit 1**
Cost Allocation for Dialysis Unit for the Prior Fiscal Year

| *Cost Center* | *Basis for Allocation* | *Costs Allocated to Dialysis Unit* |
|---|---|---|
| Depreciation | Square footage | $ 4,779 |
| Administration and general | Payroll dollars | 69,550 |
| Employee health and welfare | Payroll dollars | 44,266 |
| Operation of plant | Square footage | 4,281 |
| Laundry and linen | Pounds processed (dry) | 1,782 |
| Housekeeping | Square footage | 3,411 |
| Dietary | Number of meals | 9,471 |
| Maintenance of personnel | Salary dollars | 10,842 |
| Nursing service | Hours of service | 0 |
| Physician salaries | Hours of service | 65,477 |
| Medical supplies | Direct supply dollars | 279 |
| Pharmacy | Pharmacy revenue dollars | 1,827 |
| Medical records | Number of records | — |
| Social service | Hours of service | 50,878 |
| Intern and resident services | Hours of service | 10,425 |
| Total allocated costs | | 277,267 |
| Direct costs of dialysis unit | | 525,196 |
| Total costs of unit | | $802,463 |

**Exhibit 2**
Cost Center Report—Dialysis Unit,
Actual Expenses, Prior Fiscal Year

| *Expense* | *Oct.–Nov.* | *Dec.–Jan.* | *Feb.–Mar.* | *Apr.–May* | *June–July* | *Aug.–Sept.* |
|---|---|---|---|---|---|---|
| Medical Supply: | | | | | | |
| Dialyzers | 1,792 | 1,750 | 1,728 | 1,720 | 1,750 | 1,759 |
| C-Dak coils | 5,772 | 5,631 | 5,560 | 5,537 | 5,629 | 5,654 |
| Needles and syringes | 6,370 | 6,290 | 6,136 | 6,108 | 6,213 | 6,250 |
| General supplies | 12,446 | 12,070 | 11,981 | 11,938 | 12,142 | 12,190 |
| Concentrate | 2,058 | 2,008 | 1,982 | 1,974 | 2,014 | 2,018 |
| Saline | 4,390 | 4,283 | 4,229 | 4,211 | 4,283 | 4,301 |
| Blood tubing | 5,743 | 5,602 | 5,532 | 5,468 | 5,564 | 5,633 |
| Miscellaneous | 3,381 | 3,258 | 3,257 | 3,243 | 3,298 | 3,312 |
| Total | 41,952 | 40,892 | 40,405 | 40,199 | 40,893 | 41,117 |
| Purchased lab services | 2,116 | 2,026 | 2,000 | 1,994 | 2,042 | 2,060 |
| Salaries and wages: | | | | | | |
| Nursing | 17,500 | 17,500 | 17,500 | 17,500 | 17,500 | 17,500 |
| Technicians | 15,340 | 15,340 | 15,340 | 15,340 | 15,340 | 15,340 |
| Administration | 3,560 | 3,560 | 3,560 | 3,560 | 3,560 | 3,560 |
| Total | 36,400 | 36,400 | 36,400 | 36,400 | 36,400 | 36,400 |
| Employee expense | 2,350 | 2,350 | 2,350 | 2,350 | 2,350 | 2,350 |
| Water usage | 1,764 | 1,740 | 1,728 | 1,720 | 1,748 | 1,748 |
| Minor equipment | 1,904 | 1,904 | 1,904 | 1,904 | 1,904 | 1,904 |
| Major equipment depreciation | 2,188 | 2,188 | 2,188 | 2,188 | 2,188 | 2,188 |
| Number of treatments | 980 | 956 | 944 | 940 | 956 | 960 |

because it included substantial overhead. He argued that this year's overhead would differ from last year's because of the dialysis unit's changes in volume. However, Dr. Newell knew that this years overhead could not be calculated until the end of the fiscal year. Dr. Newell felt that an accurate cost analysis would first calculate the "real" cost of a treatment and, from there, define a "fair share of overhead."

In reviewing the cost center report, Dr. Newell realized that the nature of the costs varied. He defined three types of costs for his analysis: those that varied in proportion to volume, those that varied with significant changes in volume, and those that remained the same regardless of the unit's volume.

He first separated the costs of medical supplies, purchased laboratory services, and water usage because they changed according to the number of treatments provided. He then examined the salary and wages and employee expense costs; although these costs had not changed during the last year, the unit's number of treatments had also remained fairly steady. Dr. Newell thought that the significant reduction in volume this year might cause a corresponding reduction in salary and employee expenses. In the prior year, the unit had employed eight hemo-dialysis technicians, seven nurses, and two administrative people (their eight consultant nephrologists were on the hospitals' physicians' payroll). However, anticipating that the unit's volume would fall, Dr. Newell had not replaced the nurse or two technicians who'd left in January of the current year. Consequently, by February, the unit's monthly salaries and employee expenses had decreased by $3,000. Dr. Newell determined that the remaining costs on the cost center report would stay essentially the same regardless of the number of treatments.

As a final step in preparing for his meeting with Dr. Lawrence, Dr. Newell called a hospital equipment supply manufacturer to discuss the resale value of Lakeside's 14 artificial kidney machines. The company informed him that machines used for four years or more could not be sold, even for scrap. Lakeside had purchased the 14 machines five years ago for $105,000.

## Questions

1. What is the breakeven volume for the dialysis unit?
2. What assumptions are necessary for calculating the breakeven volume?
3. What are the non-quantitative considerations?
4. What should Dr. Newell do?

# chapter 5

# Pricing Decisions

In a profit-oriented company, pricing policies and practices are usually the responsibility of the marketing organization; apart from the provision of relevant cost information from the accounts, the topic is rarely mentioned in a description of management control practices. In a nonprofit organization, however, the prices charged for services rendered are an important consideration in management control. Many nonprofit organizations have not given enough thought to their pricing policies; they tend to regard all activities that come under the general heading of marketing as something that they need not worry about. This chapter discusses pricing principles primarily in terms of the relevant cost constructions and the impact on management control.

## GENERAL PRINCIPLES

This chapter is organized around five principles of pricing. All of these principles have exceptions, and none is universally accepted as being valid. These exceptions and disagreements are included in the discussion. The five principles are that *as a general rule:*

1. Services should be sold, rather than be given away.
2. The price should affect the consumer's actions.
3. The price should ordinarily be equal to full cost.

4. The unit of service that is priced should be narrowly defined.
5. Prospective pricing is preferable to cost reimbursement.

## WHEN SERVICES SHOULD BE SOLD

### Advantages of Selling Services

If services are sold, rather than being furnished at no charge, there are these advantages:

1. The resulting amount of revenues can approximate the value of the organization's output.
2. Clients are motivated to consider whether the services are worth their cost.
3. Managers within the organization are motivated to consider the value of the services they receive and furnish.
4. The measurement of management performance is improved.
5. The financial nature of reciprocal relationships among different organizations is clarified.

These advantages are realized most fully when the services are sold at a price that approximates their full cost.

***Output Measurement.*** If each service furnished by an organization is priced at its cost, the total amount of services furnished during the period is approximated by the total revenues recorded. For various reasons, revenue may not measure the real value of these services to individual clients or to society. Nevertheless, the amount of revenue may be a sufficiently good approximation to be a useful measure of the organization's output. If an organization's revenues in one year, adjusted for inflation, are lower than those in the preceding year, there is a clear indication that its outputs have decreased.

Measurement of output in nonmonetary terms, such as number of visits for a community health center or number of classroom hours, is likely to be cruder than a monetary measure. The unit prices charged for various types of services reflect the relative magnitude of each type, and the aggregate of these prices is thus a weighted total that takes into account differences in the types of services rendered. Consequently, if each type of service is priced appropriately, the amount of revenue measures the amount of services rendered.

***Motivate the Client.*** In some situations, charging clients for services rendered makes them more aware of the value of the service and encourages them to consider whether the services are actually worth as much to them as the price they must pay. In other instances, society has decided that a particular client-related service is sufficiently important that clients should not be deterred from receiving it by being charged a price which reflects its full cost. Examples are health and education. In these situations, clients may be asked to pay some portion of full cost (e.g., a copayment for Medicaid services or a reduced clinic fee) although the pricing policy must be carefully structured so as not to motivate the client inappropriately (e.g., to avoid seeking necessary medical care, or to postpone or eliminate necessary education). We return to these issues later in the chapter.

***Motivate Managers.*** If services are sold, the responsibility center that sells them becomes a "profit center," that is, a unit whose outputs and inputs are both measured in monetary terms. The manager of the profit center becomes responsible for operating the unit in such a way that the budgeted difference between revenues and expenses is achieved.

When this happens, the manager is motivated to think of ways of rendering additional service that will increase revenue, to think of ways of cutting costs, to become more vigilant in controlling overhead costs, and in general to behave like a manager in a profit-oriented company.

> *Example:* In many organizations there is a central computer center. If computer services are furnished without charge, users have no inhibition about asking for all the special runs, sophisticated analyses, and other services that they can get. They may even use an expensive computer for work that could be done as well on a typewriter. Assignment of computer time is the responsibility of the manager of the computer center, and such assignments are made according to the manager's perception of needs (or according to friendship with users). The manager has no financial incentive to provide high-quality computer services in a cost-effective manner.
>
> If the computer center is set up as a profit center, all these conditions change. Users now are motivated to think about whether possible uses of the computer are worth their cost, and they weigh the value of computer services against other possible uses of the funds made available to them. The manager of the computer center must now offer quality services at competitive prices, or users will be motivated to seek computer services elsewhere.

***Performance Measurement.*** Management performance in a profit center can be measured by an operating statement that resembles the operating statement of a profit-oriented company. Since a profit-oriented company's objective is to earn profits while a nonprofit organization's monetary objective is to break even, the meaning of the "bottom line" is different in a nonprofit organization. The bottom line does have a meaning, however. It shows whether a manager has been able to earn revenues and incur expenses as budgeted, and therefore perform financially in accordance with agreed-upon expectations.

***Reciprocity.*** When one organization agrees to exchange services with another, the services are sometimes furnished without charge. Several fire departments, for example, may agree to help one another out, but make no charge on the grounds that this mutual aid is for the common good. This practice has at least two disadvantages. First, it provides no record of the value of the services rendered. Second, it motivates each fire department to call on others without inhibition. (Of course, a responsible fire chief would not hesitate to call for mutual aid when there is a real need for it, regardless of the price.) Except in trivial matters, the information provided by pricing the services rendered is usually worthwhile.

### Services that Should Not Be Sold

Notwithstanding these advantages of charging for services rendered, there are many qualifications and *caveats* to the general principle stated above.

***Public Goods.*** The most important class of services that normally is furnished without charge to the client is that of *public goods.* Public goods are services which are for the benefit of the public in general, rather than for an individual client. Examples are police protection, as contrasted with a police officer who is hired by the manager of a sporting event, and foreign policy and its implementation, as contrasted with services rendered to an individual firm doing business overseas. Public goods are well described in the following passage:

> These are goods and services that simply cannot be provided through the market. They have two related qualities. First, they inevitably have to be supplied to a group of people rather than on an individual basis. Second, they cannot be withheld from individuals who refuse to pay for them.
>
> Take national defense, for example. The national security provided by our military forces is extended to all persons in the country. They all receive the same protection, whether they are willing to pay for it or not. There is no way of withholding the service, of creating a market which separates those who pay from the freeloaders. In fact, in this type of situation, rational consumers who are interested only in economics will never pay since they will get the benefit in any event.
>
> In the case of ordinary private goods, this difficulty does not occur. If one person likes some item of food or clothing or a service, and another does not, one will pay for it and receive it, and the other will not. If someone should refuse to pay yet wishes to obtain the product, the sellers would simply refuse to give the item or service.[1]

The classic example of a public good is a lighthouse. It is said that one ship's "consumption" of the warning light does not mean that there is less warning light for other ships to "consume" and there is no practical way that the lighthouse keeper can prohibit ships from consuming. On the other hand, a ship cannot refuse to consume the light; it is there.

***Quasi-Public Goods.*** Many services that superficially seem to meet the definition of "public goods" turn out upon analysis to be services for

---

[1] Otto Eckstein, *Public Finance,* 2d ed. (Englewood Cliffs, N.J.: Prentice-Hall, 1967), p. 8.

which prices can be charged. Even in the classic lighthouse example, it can be argued that shipowners, as a class, should pay for lighthouses, and that this will lead to at least some of the benefits listed in the preceding section. For example, if lighthouse costs become too high, the objections of shipowners may help to bring them back into line.[2] The point is closely related to the practice of charging users of highways for the cost of these highways via a tax on gasoline and diesel fuel, and of charging airlines and owners of private aircraft for the cost of operating the air traffic control system. In many countries, users of air waves are charged through a tax on television sets; in the United States, the air waves are regarded as a public good.

***Education Vouchers.*** A useful way of thinking about whether a given service should be sold or given away is to separate the question of whether a price should be charged from the question of who ultimately should pay this price. Thus, it is generally agreed that all children are entitled to an education and that the community as a whole is responsible for providing this education whether or not the child's parents are able to pay for it. Education is therefore a public good—not because it is impossible to withhold the service but because it is against public policy to do so. Nevertheless, it may be possible to accept this principle and still gain the advantages of "selling the service."

This is the idea behind the "education voucher" plan. Every child is provided with a voucher that provides the right to obtain an education without charge. On the voucher is a dollar amount, which generally is the average cost per pupil in the public school system. Within certain limits, the voucher can be used at any school that the parents elect, including private schools (but perhaps not parochial schools because of constitutional prohibitons). The purpose of such a price mechanism is not to affect clients' decisions as to *whether* to obtain the services, but rather to permit a consumer choice as to *what school* will provide the service. By using the tuition vouchers at the school of their choice, parents can express their pleasure or displeasure with individual schools and thus introduce an element of competition among schools. There is much controversy about whether the education voucher idea is sound public policy and much disagreement among researchers whether or not it has improved education in the places where it has been tried. Nevertheless, from a management control viewpoint, the idea has much to commend it.[3] A key management control question, however, is whether the long-run outcome of more cost-effective education for all will be achieved.

---

[2] In a fascinating article, Coase describes the history of British lighthouses, showing that they in fact successfully charged fees from the 17th century until the present. R. E. Coase, "The Lighthouse in Economics," *Journal of Law and Economics* 17 (October 1974), pp. 357–76.

[3] Much of the literature discusses the first experiment, which was started in Alum Rock, California, in 1972. For an analysis and a bibliography, see Paul M. Wortman and Robert G. St. Pierre, "The Educational Voucher Demonstration: A Secondary Analysis," *Education and Urban Society,* August 1977, p. 471.

***Charges within Public Organizations.*** Even when the principal service of an organization is a public good that is given away, there may be opportunities to charge for certain peripheral services rendered by the organization. For example, the Congress charges a fee for the copying of certain documents in its files,[4] federal agencies charge fees for copying documents made available under the Freedom of Information Act, municipal governments charge for dog licenses.

***Other Free Services.*** In addition to the general class of public goods, there are other situations in which prices should not normally be charged for services. These include the following situations:

1. Services are provided as a public policy, but clients cannot afford to pay for them (e.g., welfare investigations and legal aid services).
2. It is public policy not to ration the services on the basis of ability to pay. (*Example:* Legislators do not charge fees for assisting constituents, even though legislators' time is a valuable resource.)
3. The cost of collecting the revenue exceeds the benefits. This is an argument used against levying toll charges on automobiles under many circumstances.
4. A charge is politically untenable (e.g., public tours of the White House and the Capitol). The public clamor over such charges could be so harmful to overall organizational objectives that the services are provided without charge, even though a charge would be equitable and would promote good management control. A similar situation exists with respect to taxation. Even though an indirect tax may be relatively less equitable than a direct tax, the indirect tax may have a better chance of passage by the legislature and of acceptance by taxpayers because it is less visible.
5. Client motivation is unimportant. A nominal charge to a public park or bathing beach will not measure actual output, nor will it influence clients' decisions to use the facilities. A charge equal to full cost, by motivating less wealthy individuals to *avoid* using these facilities, may be inconsistent with public policy.

## Transfer Prices

When one responsibility center receives goods or services from another responsibility center and is charged for them, the amount of the charge is called the *transfer price.* A transfer price is therefore used for transactions within an organization, as contrasted with the *external* price which is used for transactions between the organization and its clients. The example earlier concerning the central computer center was an illustration of the use of a transfer price.

---

[4] In this particular case the price was deliberately set higher than cost in order to discourage copying of these documents, which is an unconscionable abridgement of the public's right of access to information. The principle nevertheless is economically sound.

In all organizations, the primary purposes of a transfer pricing mechanism are (1) to encourage the optimum use of the resources subject to transfer and (2) to facilitate decisions on setting prices charged to external clients. In general, the transfer price that is used to charge the cost of goods or services rendered to benefiting responsibility centers should be the market price. If a market price is not available, the transfer price usually should be based on the standard full cost of the service center. In some situations the transfer price should be based on the standard *direct* costs of the service center.

*Example:* The audiovisual center of the University of Puerto Rico charged users on the basis of full costs, including depreciation. These prices stimulated some departments to acquire their own audiovisual equipment. Consequently, the audiovisual resources of the center were only partially utilized. In such a situation, transfer prices based on direct cost would probably stimulate optimum use of the audiovisual equipment.

In other situations, the transfer price might be higher than full cost in order to discourage certain undesirable practices, such as excessive use of the facilities or services subject to transfer.

When a competitive market exists for the service, the transfer price should be no more than the market-based price in order not to discourage use of services furnished by the service center. If the service center were to charge a price that was higher than the market price, those needing the service would be motivated to seek it from an outside source. If the service center cannot provide the service at a cost that is not greater than the price charged by an outside organization, there is a serious question whether the service center should even exist. The transfer price for outsiders, if they are allowed to buy the services of a service center, should normally be a competitive price.

In some circumstances, in order to encourage organization units to make the proper use of the service centers, and at the same time absorb the total costs, a standard direct cost should be used as the primary transfer price, and the balance of the service center costs should be apportioned to the users as a fixed amount per period.

## IMPACT OF PRICES ON CONSUMERS

In some situations, although prices are charged for services rendered, the price is below full cost, and hence does not actually affect clients as strongly as would a price based on full cost. A similar motivation exists when the charges are paid by a third party (such as an insurance company), which has become the predominant way of paying for health care costs. In this instance, some observers have claimed that third-party insurance, by insulating patients from the full cost of health care, has contributed to escalating health costs. Others claim that such insulation is appropriate, since asking patients to pay full cost in this case is an abridgement of public policy. It must also be recognized that hospital patients cannot, as a practical matter, decide what services they need; they must rely in large part on the expertise of their physicians.

In other situations, the price is a mere bookkeeping charge with no direct effect on the client's decisions. Some universities, for example, allocate computer resources by providing students and faculty members with monetary "allowances" which entitle them to a certain amount of computer time. The allowances may be set so high or may be so easily supplemented that they do not motivate at all, although they nevertheless may be a useful way of keeping track of computer usage. Even if the allowances were set low enough to have an impact on computer usage decisions, the motivating force would be much stronger if computer users had the opportunity of trading off "dollars" of computer time for other resources, or if there was a reward of some sort for time not used. (Some universities intentionally provide liberal allowances or provide computer service at no cost in order to encourage computer usage.)

The National Commission on the Financing of Post-Secondary Education supported the position that "funds to reduce tuition would accomplish less in improving people's access to education than would the same amount spent on student grants awarded on the basis of financial need."[5] Its reasons were that direct grants provide students with a better means of making choices about higher education, and also that a given amount of aid would be used more efficiently in this way than by grants to institutions.

The influence of pricing as a motivating force is further illustrated by the situation that has arisen in certain state universities in which the legislature provides funds based on the number of student credit hours. In these universities, some administrators manipulated the number of credit hours by authorizing extra credit hours for dissertation work, informal seminars, and the like, and thus obtained additional funds from the legislature.

> ***Example:*** Shortly after introduction of a credit-hour funding plan, one state university campus reported a drop in the number of graduate students by head-count but an *increase* in the number of credit hours. All of the increase came in nonclassroom courses, such as "supervised teaching," "supervised research," and "directed dissertation."

In those universities in which tuition is based on the number of credit hours taken, there is a much greater reluctance for students to sign up for marginal credit hours, even though the tuition charge may be quite low, since every additional credit hour affects their pocketbooks. Again, however, in considering such a pricing policy, one must be certain that the organization's objectives are not compromised.

---

[5] *Report of the National Commission on the Financing of Post-Secondary Education,* submitted to the President and Congress, January 1974.

## FULL COST AS THE BASIS FOR PRICING

In general, a useful principle is that prices in nonprofit organizations should be equal to full costs. In this section, we discuss situations in which this principle is applicable, but also situations in which other pricing practices are more appropriate.

### Full-Cost Pricing

In recent years, there has been a substantial increase in the types of services that are priced at full cost. Many hospital costs are now reimbursed by Medicare and other third parties, and reimbursement is based on full costs. Government contracts with universities, nonprofit research organizations, and a wide variety of social service and welfare organizations provide for payment of full costs. The general policy of the federal government for interagency transactions is to base reimbursement on full costs. The profits of unrelated business activities of nonprofit organizations are subject to tax, so there is a tendency to calculate the full cost of these activities in order to minimize the tax. These situations and other similar ones have led to increased understanding of the meaning of full costs in many nonprofit organizations.

The rationale for full-cost pricing is as follows: A nonprofit organization often has a monopoly position. It should not set prices that exceed its cost, for to do so would be to take unjustifiable advantage of its monopoly status. Furthermore, the organization does not need to price above cost. If it does so, it generates a profit, and by definition no person can benefit from such a profit. Except for those situations discussed below, a nonprofit organization should not price below full cost because that would be providing services at less than they presumably are worth and this can lead to a misallocation of resources in the economy.[6]

***Peripheral Activities.*** A full-cost pricing policy should normally apply to services that are directly related to the organization's principal objectives, and to services that are closely associated with these objectives; but it does not necessarily apply to peripheral activities. Prices for these activities should ordinarily correspond to market prices for similar services.

*Example:* In a university, board and room charges should be based on full cost because students live in dormitories and eat in dining rooms as a necessary part of the educational process. Textbooks, laboratory supplies, and the like, should be priced at full cost for the same reason. But rental of space to outside groups, the price of special programs furnished at the request of outside groups, prices at soda fountains, and so forth, are not closely related to the main objective of the university. The university does not have a monopoly with respect to these services, and their prices should be market-based. Similarly, price for research

[6] Here the term "full cost" includes a return on the organization's equity. In some instances the price must also provide for the replacement of fixed assets.

projects conducted to accomplish the university's objectives should be based on full cost, as contrasted with the price of research for the benefit of a commercial client, which should be market-based.

***Mix of Prices.*** Although the pricing strategy normally should be to recover full cost for the organization as a whole, certain specific services may be priced above or below full cost. The relevant considerations are essentially the same as those that profit-oriented companies consider when they depart from full-cost pricing. For example, electric utilities charge a lower than average rate for energy used during nonpeak hours; this shifts demand away from peak hours and allows the utility to meet its total demand with a smaller capital investment than otherwise would be required. Off-hour prices on subways and buses are useful for similar reasons.

*Example:* The Port Authority of New York and New Jersey charges $1.25 for a trans-Hudson River tunnel crossing. The same charge is made for the George Washington Bridge as for the Holland Tunnel. Full costs per vehicle are lower for the bridge than for the tunnel because the bridge has twice the traffic of the Holland Tunnel, and its maintenance and repair costs are different. Tunnel users in effect receive a subsidy from bridge users, but the Port Authority, for sound transportation reasons, has decided to charge the same price for each service.

Similarly, some public bathing beaches or other nonprofit recreation areas charge a lower price for week days than for busier time so as to encourage off-peak use of the facilities. Clearly, if peaks in demand can be leveled off with a mix of prices, the total demand can be satisfied with a smaller investment in facilities and lower fixed operating costs.

In general, nonprofit organizations could give greater attention to the impact of price mix on utilization of services. In direct contrast to the recreation area pricing policy above, for example, the government of Mexico adopted a policy of eliminating many recreational charges on Sundays, presumably to encourage the use of these facilities by working-class families; this had the effect of adding to the crowding of these facilities on the busiest days.

***Tuition.*** The price charged for higher education is perhaps the outstanding example of a price that intentionally, but unnecessarily, is set below full cost. The difference between price and cost is especially wide in state universities.

The principal argument against full-cost tuition is that it would deprive worthy students of an opportunity for education. The counterargument is that students who are unable to pay full costs can be financed by loans or grants, which are provided from endowment or current gifts. Unless constrained by competition, a university will have a net increase in income if it increases tuition to an amount that is equal to full cost. This is so because additional revenue will be generated from those students who can afford to pay. Even though students who cannot afford to pay the higher tuition receive commensurately higher financial aid, and although this may be only a bookkeeping transaction, the revenue generated from these students certainly will be at least as much as it was before.

> ***Example:*** Assume that a college of 1,000 students charged $6,000 tuition, and therefore had gross tuition revenue of $6,000,000. Assume that of this amount endowment income provided $600,000 in the form of financial aid, and $5,400,000 came from cash received from students. If the college increased tuition to $7,000, its gross revenue would increase to $7,000,000. Even if as much as $400,000 of this $1,000,000 additional revenue was offset by additional financial aid to students who could not afford the additional tuition, the college would still receive an additional $600,000 in cash. In short, students who are able to pay, pay; other students can continue to attend because of the increased financial aid.

The argument is made that government should subsidize higher education because it provides benefits to society (by making the gross national product higher than it otherwise would be, by making the electorate better informed, etc.), as well as to the person who is being educated. It seems unlikely, however, that any reasonable basis for calculating such a subsidy can be devised.

The argument is also made that when tuition is less than full cost, the subsidy will be recouped later on from alumni contributions. This assumes a causal relationship between current subsidies and future gifts, which is at best a tenuous assumption. It also tends to neglect the low present value of future contributions.

*Implementation of Full-Cost Tuition.* Two important problems must be solved before a full-cost tuition policy could be adopted. First, competitive prices must be raised; and second, a method of making a gradual transition must be worked out.

The most important obstacle to solving the first problem is the low tuition charged by state universities and other public institutions. The arguments for this practice are weak in the case of residents because the tuition of needy residents can be provided by financial aid; the argument is not relevant at all for nonresidents. Nevertheless, the practice of low tuition is firmly established, and legislators perceive that voters would not like to see it changed. Because of the tuition gap between public and private schools, private colleges and universities have an increasingly difficult problem attracting students.

The problem of transition is easier to solve. Having decided that a full-cost price is appropriate and feasible, a university can devise a plan to make a gradual transition to that price over a period of years.

## Pricing at Other than Full Cost

Services for which a full-cost price is not appropriate can be grouped under three headings: (1) services whose price should be market-based, (2) services whose price should be set to encourage or to discourage the use of the service, and (3) services whose use should not be governed by ability to pay (these prices may be called distributional prices). In all these instances, managers must bear in mind that price is only one element of an organization's "marketing mix." Thus, the pricing analysis generally involves considerations which go beyond those discussed below.

## Market-Based Prices

A market-based price is a price set in accordance with the same factors that would be considered if the organization were profit-oriented. These factors include competitive prices, the elasticity of demand, and incremental costs. A market-based price may be higher or lower than full costs. If a nonprofit organization operates in a competitive environment, it usually should use competitive pricing practices, unless it is the "price leader" in a market. The price leader should set prices so as to recover its full costs.

*Example:* A university with an outstanding reputation for the quality of its education is, in the sense intended here, the price leader in its community. It should set its tuition equal to cost, even though its reputation would permit it to charge more. If this tuition is lower than tuition rates charged by comparable competing universities, there is an indication that the other universities are inefficient and that society's resources are being misdirected. An awareness of this fact may lead to a redirection of those resources; at least it should alert the managers of competing universities to the fact that a problem exists. If the leading university priced above its full costs, as a profit-oriented organization might do in similar circumstances, the effect would be to give it an unnecessary surplus and to mask the inefficiencies of the other universities.

***Peripheral Services.*** As indicated above, a market-based price is also appropriate for services that are not closely associated with the principal objectives of the organization. In a university, for example, educational programs designed for clients other than those for which the university primarily exists should be market-based. However, it frequently is difficult to draw the line between programs that are closely related to the organization's objectives—such as adult education programs in a municipal school system, or university extension courses—and programs where a market-based price is clearly appropriate—such as executive development programs.

## Subsidy and Penalty Prices

In certain situations an organization may depart from both the cost-based and the market-based concepts of pricing in order to facilitate the achievement of its objectives. It may deliberately price below full cost in order to encourage the use of certain services, or it may deliberately price above full cost in order to discourage the use of other services. The former is called a "subsidy price," and the latter a "penalty price."

***Subsidy Prices.*** An organization may use a subsidy price to encourage the use of its services by certain clients who are unable or unwilling to pay a price based on full cost, or when as a matter of policy the organization wishes to allocate its service on a basis other than ability to pay (e.g., public education, low-cost housing, health care). Unless the service is a public good, a price that is less than cost generally is preferable to providing the services free, since even a nominal price motivates clients to give some thought to the value of the service they receive. Such a subsidy price should preferably be a fraction of the cost of the services rendered, rather than a flat per-client amount, in order to increase the clients' motivation to be concerned about the quantity of services that they consume.

This idea is supported in a policy statement of the Healthcare Financial Management Association, which states that "Patient financial participation is essential in order to influence demand and choice of service, improve understanding, and contribute to accuracy and provide financial resources. Discretion and flexibility should be permitted." However, it recognizes that if patient participation is optional, few providers would elect the option.[7]

On the other hand, an organization should not attempt to use even nominal prices to encourage clients to defer *needed* services, particularly if there can be adverse social and financial consequences in the medium or long run.

*Example:* Milton Roemer reported that when Medicaid patients in California were charged $1 a visit for primary care, there was a sharp decline in patient visits, followed some months later by an associated increase in hospitalizations. Many of the hospitalizations could have been avoided if the patients had received timely primary care. Overall, the cost to Medicaid was higher as a result of this pricing policy.[8]

It should be recognized, however, that when clients are charged less than full cost, this is equivalent to stating that it is public policy to provide the service at less than its value. In these circumstances, the danger of a misallocation of resources exists. As each of the following examples illustrate, the issues are not simple, and important public policy questions are raised regarding the desirability of continued subsidy of operations.

*Examples:* 1. A university discovered that the cost of operating its nuclear reactor was $50,000 per student using the reactor. The reactor probably should be closed unless other uses can be found, unless increased utilization is expected to develop, or it has research value which can bring in supplemental revenues.

2. The pediatric department of a hospital operated at a loss when a price equal to that of other hospitals in nearby communities was charged. It was nevertheless decided to continue the department because no other pediatric facility existed in the community. The deficit was made up by the municipality.

[7] Healthcare Financial Management Association, *General Guidance,* May 28, 1982, section V.

[8] M. Roemer et. al, "Copayments for Ambulatory Care: Penny-Wise and Pound-Foolish," *Medical Care* 13, no. 6 (June 1975) pp. 457–66.

3. The U.S. Postal Service subsidizes rural post offices because it is public policy to provide convenient mail service to everyone. Should the Postal Service subsidize its money order service, however, in view of the fact that the private sector provides adequate facilities for transferring money?

Even if clients are unable or unwilling to pay a price based on full costs, there are advantages in stating a *gross* price at full cost, and providing the subsidy separately to those who need it, or to those whose use of the service should be encouraged. This policy focuses attention on the true cost of providing the services and thus (1) motivates clients to ask questions if they judge the services received to be worth less than their cost, which facilitates management control; and (2) motivates managers to consider whether available resources are properly allocated.

***Penalty Prices.*** An organization may charge more than full costs in order to discourage clients from using a certain type of service. This may be because the organization is required to provide this service and finds it disadvantageous for some reason, because it is ill-equipped to provide the service, or because providing the service has certain corollary adverse effects on the organization or its other services.

*Examples:* 1. A nonprofit regional stock exchange and clearing corporation charged proportionately more for small transactions because it wanted to encourage another type of business indirectly and because the small transactions were a nuisance to its members.

2. A hospital charged appreciably more for providing outpatient services to nonemergency patients than other hospitals in the area because its staff and facilities were fully utilized providing for its inpatients' requirements.

3. The civil aviation department of the government of India charged one rupee for every person coming to the major airports in Bombay, Calcutta, and other cities to see friends and relatives off, even though zero cost was incurred for these persons. The reason given was to discourage the crowds of people around the airport.

Some organizations deliberately set normal prices above full cost so as to generate a surplus that can be used for what are considered to be worthwhile purposes, even though they do not directly benefit the client. For example, a hospital's fees may provide a surplus that can be used for charity patients or for research. This raises the question of whether and to what extent a hospital should require its wealthy or fully insured patients to make an involuntary contribution to charity or research. Arguments can be advanced for and against this position.

Prices may also be set high in order to discourage certain socially undesirable activities. Thus, fees could be levied against polluters of rivers. The price could be either high enough to totally stop the practice, or it could be high enough to cover the cost of providing water treatment plants to repair the damage done. In the latter case it is essentially a price based on full cost.

When it is public policy to include, in effect, a tax in the price, the price may be regarded as being higher than full cost (e.g., prices in state liquor stores). Alternatively, this practice may be regarded as full-cost pricing, with the "tax" as an element of cost.

### Distributional Pricing

Some services are priced so as to ensure their equitable distribution among users who differ in their ability to pay. There may be a direct discount in the price to certain classes of users, such as to the elderly or handicapped, or the same result may be achieved by indirect means such as scholarships to students. In many cases, the impact of these special prices is not calculated, nor is careful consideration given to whether the distributional price is necessary to accomplish the desired social goal. Some would argue, for example, that when the elderly are given discounts for bus and subway transportation, parking, meals, theater tickets, and other services, the benefits are received by those elderly persons who are fully able to pay as well as by those who otherwise would be unable to afford the services.

## THE PRICING UNIT

The fourth principle of pricing is that, *in general, the smaller and more specific the unit of service that is priced, the better the basis for decisions about the allocation of resources and the more accurate the measure of output for management control purposes.* An overall price is not a good measure of output because it masks the actual mix of services rendered. An annual flat charge for the use of water, for example, is not as effective as a charge that reflects the quantity used. With an annual charge, the consumer is not motivated to be careful in using water.

### Qualifications

There is considerable disagreement about this principle, and there are some who reject it entirely. They argue that price should reflect an average mix of services and the needs of more detailed information for management control purposes can be met by other devices. Even those who support the validity of the basic principle accept two important qualifications.

The first is the obvious one that beyond a certain point, the paperwork and other costs associated with pricing tiny units of service outweigh the benefits. The precise location of this point is of course uncertain.

The second qualification is that the pricing policy should be consistent with the organization's overall policy. It is a fact that undergraduate English instruction costs less than undergraduate physics instruction, and these differences could feasibly be reflected by charging different prices for each course that a student takes. Nevertheless, a separate price for each course may cause students to select courses in a way that the university administration does not consider educationally sound. Since the total cost of a course is essentially fixed, such a pricing policy would lead students to shun courses with low enrollment, such as Greek and Latin, which have a high cost per student, and it would increase the enrollment in popular, but perhaps less valuable, courses that have a low cost per student.

By contrast, there are good reasons for charging higher tuitions to graduate students than to undergraduate students, so as to reflect the differences in the overall cost of graduate and undergraduate programs. Presumably these differences do not motivate individual students to make unwise choices.

## Hospital Pricing as an Example

Exhibit 5–1, which shows some of the approaches that could be used in pricing the various services furnished by a hospital, illustrates some of the considerations involved in selecting the unit of pricing. As one moves from *A* to *D* in Exhibit 5–1, the practices involve (1) an increase in recordkeeping, (2) a corresponding increase in the amount of output information for use in management control, and (3) charges to clients that more accurately reflect services rendered.

At one extreme, the hospital could charge an all-inclusive rate, say $450

**Exhibit 5–1**
Pricing Alternatives in a Hospital

| *(A)* *All-Inclusive Rate* | *(B)* *Daily Charge plus Special Services* | | *(C)* *Type of Service* | |
|---|---|---|---|---|
| $450/day | Patient care | $250/day | Medical/surgical: | |
| | Operating room | xx | 1st day | $280 |
| | Pharmacy | xx | Other days | 240 |
| | Radiology | xx | Maternity: | |
| | Special nurses | xx | 1st day | 240 |
| | | | Other days | 200 |
| | | | (plus special services as in *B*) | |

| *(D)* *Detailed* | |
|---|---|
| Admittance | $ 80 |
| Workup, per hour | 25 |
| Medical/surgical bed, per day | 180 |
| Maternity bed, per day | 160 |
| Bassinet, per day | 150 |
| Nursery care, per hour | 15 |
| Meals, per day | 25 |
| Discharge | 30 |
| (plus special services as in *B*) | |

per day. This practice is advocated by some people, both on the grounds that patients then know in advance what their bill will be (assuming that the length of stay can be estimated) and on the grounds of simplicity in recordkeeping. Its advocates point out that the more detailed information required for management purposes can be collected in the management control system, even though it is not reflected in prices charged. The weakness of the latter argument is that if detailed information is going to be collected for management purposes anyway, the all-inclusive price does not in fact result in significant savings in recordkeeping unless shortcuts and estimates are substituted for sound data collection methods. The only savings would be in the billing process, which is a small part of the total accounting function.

Another, and common, pricing practice is to charge separately for the cost of each easily identifiable special service and make a blanket daily charge for everything else. Radiology prices, for example, are customarily calculated according to a rather detailed point system that takes into account the size of the radiology plate and the complexity of the procedure. There is some incongruity in calculating prices for radiology in terms of points which are worth a few cents each and lumping everything else into an overall rate of, say, $250 per day. Nevertheless, certain services, such as radiology, laboratory, the operating room, and so on could be costed out and priced separately.

Column *C* indicates one approach to breaking the daily charge into smaller units. Different charges could be made for each department, and it would also be possible to charge more for the first day than for subsequent days, so as to take account of admitting and workup costs.

Column *D* indicates the job-cost approach that many profit-oriented businesses would use in situations of this type. In an automobile repair shop, for example, each repair job is costed separately. It is charged with the services of mechanics according to the number of hours they work on the job, and it is charged with each part and significant item of supplies that is used on the job. The sum of these separate charges is the basis for the price the customers pay, and customers would not tolerate any other approach. They would not, for example, tolerate paying a flat daily rate for repairs, regardless of what services were provided.

Many hospitals use a system like that in Column *B* for billing both their charge-paying payors and some cost-paying payors, such as Blue Cross or Medicare. In some states, Medicaid uses a system such as that in Column *A*. Few if any hospitals have a system as detailed as that shown in Column *D*. The Massachusetts Eye and Ear Infirmary in Boston has developed a particularly interesting procedure-based system for its patient care services; this system is somewhat more detailed than that in Column *C* but not as detailed as in Column *D*.[9]

---

[9] See Charles T. Wood, "Relate Hospital Charges to Use of Services," *Harvard Business Review*, March–April 1982.

## PROSPECTIVE PRICING

As a general rule, management control is facilitated when the price is set prior to the performance of the service, as contrasted with the alternative of reimbursing the service provider for the actual amount of costs incurred. When prices are set in advance, they provide an incentive for the organization to keep costs down, whereas no such incentive exists when the organization knows that costs will be recouped no matter how high they are.

This principle can be applied, of course, only when it is possible to make a reasonable advance estimate of what the services should cost. For many research or development projects, for example, there is no good basis for estimating how much money needs to be spent in order to achieve the desired result. Even so, it may be possible to establish overhead rates based on budgeted overhead costs and to require adherence to these rates.

The question of prospective pricing is a controversial one in health care organizations. Currently, in many states, Blue Cross reimburses hospitals essentially for actual costs incurred. Although the payment plan usually specifies that tentative reimbursement will be made on the basis of a schedule of prices, at the end of each year or shorter period an adjustment is made that in effect equates the total amount of reimbursement to actual costs incurred. Such a system provides little incentive to keep costs under control.

Experiments with a quite different approach to pricing are being conducted in several states. In this approach, which is called prospective reimbursement, the third party and the hospital agree in advance to a budget of costs for the forthcoming year, and prices are determined on the basis of this budget. The hospital is paid on the basis of these prices, adjusted in some cases for unforeseen changes in labor rates, material prices, and volume. If the hospital can keep its costs below the budgeted amount, it retains part or all of the saving. If its costs exceed budget, it must absorb some or all of the excess. In one state, New Jersey, a per-discharge price is established on the basis of the patient's diagnosis, classified into one of several categories of diagnoses, called diagnosis-related groups, or DRGs. With the DRG approach, the payment a hospital receives is based on the expected utilization of resources for the individual patient's illness. While the total amount of reimbursement a hospital receives is not determined prospectively, the amount per diagnosis is. In accordance with federal legislation in 1983, Medicare will use a DRG-based reimbursement plan beginning in 1984.[10]

A prospective reimbursement approach potentially can provide an incentive for cost control. An argument against it is the difficulty of making reliable budgets, and especially of forecasting a reliable volume figure, which is neces-

---

[10] For an argument in support of DRGs see Richard T. Fox, "DRGs: A Management Control Tool in Hospitals and Multi-Institutional Systems," *Hospital Progress,* January 1981. For an argument criticizing DRGs see David W. Young and R. B. Saltman, "Medical Practice, Case Mix and Cost Containment: A New Role for the Attending Physician," *Journal of the American Medical Association,* February 12, 1982.

sary in order to arrive at sound unit prices. Some opponents also assert that prospective pricing may lead to too much emphasis on cost control, with a consequent lowering of the quality of patient care.[11]

An organization that knows that it is going to recover its costs, whatever they are, is not likely to do much worrying about cost control. When reliable methods of setting prices in advance can be worked out, the incentive is much stronger. For example, it has been well established that hospital price control regulations in 1971–74 had the effect of stimulating hospital managers to give much more emphasis to the preparation of sound budgets, and had the indirect effect of lessening the opposition to prospective pricing. A well-designed, managerially appropriate prospective reimbursement system could have a similar effect.[12]

## SUGGESTED ADDITIONAL READINGS

Aleamoni, Lawrence M. "Proposed System for Rewarding and Improving Instructional Effectiveness," *College and University Business,* Spring 1976, pp. 330–38.

Arrow, Kenneth J. *Social Choice and Individual Values,* 2d ed. New York: John Wiley & Sons, 1963.

Bledsoe, Ralph C., et al. "Productivity Management in the California Social Services Program," *Public Administration Review,* November–December 1972, pp. 799–803.

Campbell, Donald E. "Democratic Preference Functions," *Journal of Economic Theory,* April 1976, pp. 259–72.

Conrad, Clifton. "University Goals—An Operative Approach," *Journal of Higher Education,* October 1974, pp. 504–16.

Hochman, Harold M. "Individual Preferences and Distributional Adjustments," *The American Economic Review,* May 1972, pp. 353–60.

Klein, David C. "Plan Accounting Systems for Special Needs," *Management Focus,* March–April 1979, pp. 22–25.

Lovrich, Nicholas P., Jr., and G. Thomas Taylor, Jr. "Neighborhood Evaluation of Local Government Services: A Citizen Survey Approach," *Urban Affairs Quarterly,* December 1976, pp. 197–222.

Mikesell, John L. "Government Decisions in Budgeting and Taxing: The Economic Logic," *Public Administration Review,* November–December 1978, pp. 511–13.

Musgrave, R. A. *The Theory of Public Finance,* chap. 6. New York: McGraw-Hill, 1959.

---

[11] For a more general discussion of prospective reimbursement see Robert F. Allison, "Administrative Responses to Prospective Reimbursement," *Topics in Health Care Financing,* Winter 1976.

[12] For a discussion of some important design considerations see David W. Young and R. B. Saltman, "Prospective Reimbursement and the Hospital Power Equilibrium: A Matrix-Based Management Control System," *Inquiry,* Spring 1983. For an argument in favor of a more market-based rather than regulatory approach see Alain C. Enthoven, *Health Plan* (Reading, Mass.: Addison-Wesley Publishing, 1981).

Newhouse, Joseph P. "Toward a Theory of Nonprofit Institutions: An Economic Model of a Hospital," *The American Economic Review,* March 1970, pp. 64–74.

Newman, Edward, and Jerry Turem. "The Crisis of Accountability," *Social Work,* January 1974, pp. 5–16.

Page, Alfred N. "Economics and Social Work: A Neglected Relationship," *Social Work,* January 1977, pp. 48–53.

Ramanathan, Kavasseri V. "Social Responsibility of Human Service Agencies," *Journal of Contemporary Business,* Winter 1977, pp. 31–41.

Schultze, Charles L. *The Politics and Economics of Public Spending,* Washington, D.C.: Brookings Institution, 1968.

Sen, Amartya. "Social Choice Theory: A Re-examination." *Econometrica,* January 1977, pp. 53–89.

Sen, Amartya. "The Welfare Basis of Real Income Comparisons: A Survey," *Journal of Economic Literature,* March 1979, pp. 1–45.

Shapiro, Benson P. "Marketing for Nonprofit Organizations," *Harvard Business Review,* September–October 1973, pp. 123–32.

Shirley, Robert E. "Measuring Performance of a University Accounting Department," *Management Accounting,* December 1978, pp. 51–53.

Wittrup, Richard D. "Economic Theory of Behavior of Social Institutions," *Hospital Administration,* Winter 1975, pp. 8–16.

## Case 5–1

## PLAYLAND*

Ms. Jo Ann Larson managed Playland, a nonprofit day care center in Market, North Dakota. In 1975 she asked Dr. S. Sam Sedki, a business professor at a nearby university, for advice. The university encouraged community service of this type, and Dr. Sedki agreed.

Playland was owned by a local nonprofit corporation that had been established by a church 11 years previously. It was licensed by the City Department of Child Services. The corporation's policy was that Playland should operate on approximately a break-even basis; that is, the church did not intend to use its own funds to finance the operation. Playland was one of seven day care centers in Market that had its own building. Many smaller centers were located in church basements or private homes.

Most Playland children were in families whose income was near the poverty level. In most cases both parents were employed. It charged $18 per week, the lowest rate of any of the seven centers. Rates in other day care centers were as high as $25 per week. Centers at the top of the scale attracted children from higher-income families. Most centers, including Playland, operated at capacity.

In 1975 the center had an average enrollment of about 45 children. About 40 attended during the day and received a lunch. The other five were students in a school across the street; they stayed at the day care center after school until parents picked them up on their way home from work. Each child was charged $18 per week.

Playland operated in a two-story wooden building located on a large lot owned by the corporation. It was old and needed repair. According to a recent inspection by the city fire marshal, it was in violation of the fire code because, among other things, the second floor did not have two outside exits, not all exit doors opened outward, smoke detection devices and emergency lighting were missing, stairwells were not enclosed, and materials used in ceiling and walls were substandard. A contractor, who was a member of the church, estimated that necessary repairs to the building would cost roughly $150,000. Furthermore, the Department of Child Care had indicated that it probably would no longer license centers in two-story buildings after the next few years. Several of the other centers were housed in one-story brick buildings.

The contractor also made a rough estimate of the cost of constructing a new one-story 30 x 30 building on the same lot. It came to $80,000, assuming that volunteer labor would do much of the interior finishing. After construction of the new building, the old building would be demolished.

---

 This case was prepared by Professor S. Sam Sedki.

The church was not willing to finance either the renovation of the old building or the construction of a new one. The United Fund, the leading welfare organization in Market, helped support one day care center in Market, and might support Playland to the extent of guaranteeing a bank loan. However, Ms. Larson had not approached the United Fund for help.

Playland had no formal accounting system. Ms. Larson had prepared an income statement for 1973. From bank deposits and checks, Professsor Sedki was able to prepare an approximate income statement for 1974. Both are shown in Exhibit 1.

Based on discussions with Ms. Larson, he prepared a budget for 1976, assuming the new building was in use at that time. This also is shown in Exhibit 1.

In preparing the budget, Professor Sedki made the following assumptions:

1. Seventy children would enroll at a fee of $25 each per week.
2. There would be six hourly employees at $2.10 per hour, one hourly employee at $2.50 per hour, an accountant, and a business manager. This was four more personnel than currently employed. The current staff was judged to be too small, even for 45 children.
3. Food costs would be $0.60 per child per day.
4. Miscellaneous costs, including repairs and supplies, would be $4,000 per year.

**Exhibit 1**

PLAYLAND
Financial Data

| | *Actual 1973* | *Actual 1974* | *Budget 1976* |
|---|---|---|---|
| Receipts* | $22,627 | $26,507 | $59,500 |
| Expenses: | | | |
| Manager salary | 4,000 | 4,000 | 5,000 |
| Other salaries and wages | 7,843 | 7,648 | 26,700 |
| Food | 4,198 | 5,082 | 7,100 |
| Utilities | 1,954 | 1,670 | 2,100 |
| Interest, current borrowings† | 413 | 1,054 | 600 |
| Supplies‡ | 457 | 914 | ‖ |
| Legal fees | 35 | 25 | — |
| Repairs | 124 | 544 | ‖ |
| Insurance | 504 | 651 | 800 |
| Miscellaneous§ | 1,362 | 3,730 | 4,000 |
| Depreciation† | 1,108 | 826 | — |
| Loan payment | | | 13,783 |
| Total expenses | $17,898 | $26,144 | $60,083 |
| Income (Loss) | $ 732 | $ (363) | $ (583) |

* Excludes bad debts of about $1,000 in both 1973 and 1974.

† Depreciation and interest were for an automobile purchased on an installment basis. The automobile was fully paid for by 1975.

‡ Several parents donated supplies; not counted as an expense.

§ 1974 amount probably included some nonrecurring items.

‖ Included in miscellaneous.

Professor Sedki judged that Ms. Larson was a conscientious person who worked well with children but who lacked management skills. If Playland closed, Ms. Larson planned to open a day care center in her home for 15 children.

## Questions

1. What is your assessment of the 1976 budget? How sensitive is this budget to changes in the assumptions?
2. How much should Playland charge?
3. What should Ms. Larson do?

## Case 5–2

## HASTINGS PUBLIC SCHOOLS*

In March of 1970 the Urban Action League proposed to the Hastings City Council that all of the city's elementary schools be funded through a voucher system. If the plan were adopted, Hastings would become eligible to be a test site for a government-funded voucher program.

### Background

At the end of the 1960s, teachers' unions across the country discovered the power of a threatened strike. As taxes rose to meet their demands for higher pay, many parents and taxpayers began to question whether a compulsorily funded public education system offered the most effective and efficient means of educating their children.

While economies of scale were once a compelling argument for a centralized school system, the population in many cities and suburbs had now become large enough to make diversity efficient. Furthermore, few publicly funded enterprises seemed inclined in recent years to achieve economies of any sort, since the amount of money forthcoming appeared unlimited.

In addition, more and more people felt that "bigness," rather than guaranteeing a better education, often worked against it by alienating students, frustrating teachers, and creating a cumbersome and overgrown bureaucracy. Others pointed out that the dream of equal opportunity that lay behind

---

* This case was prepared by Robert N. Anthony and Gerard Johnson, Harvard Business School.

public education still remained largely unfulfilled. A study[1] commissioned by the Office of Economic Opportunity (OEO) in the late 1960s concluded that—

1. Most public schools were still racially imbalanced, and federal and state busing programs were relatively ineffective.
2. The quality of education varied tremendously from one public school to another. Typically the schools in "better" (i.e., wealthier) neighborhoods were better schools.
3. The "education gap" was widening. Parents who could afford to do so still sent their children to private schools with restricted enrollments. As the public school system got worse, private schools were growing in enrollment and were thereby able to further upgrade their curriculum.

As parents took their concerns to administrators and politicians, they found the system slow to respond. Some of the large school systems were decentralized and some schools voluntarily opened up to greater parent involvement, but by and large, control remained vested in legislators, school boards, and educators. The difficulty of devising an objective measure for a school's output made it nearly impossible to exercise that control effectively from a distance.

The OEO study summarized what seemed to be the growing sentiment among many parents, conservative and liberal alike:

> If parents are to take responsibility for their children's education, they cannot rely exclusively on political processes to let them do so. They must also be able to take individual action in behalf of their own children.

The solution that the study proposed was a competitive education market in which all parents would be able to "shop around," using government-issued vouchers. A public agency would provide a voucher for one year's schooling to the parents of each eligible child. This voucher would be turned over to any school that had agreed to abide by the rules of the voucher system, and the schools would then turn in their vouchers for cash. Such a system, it was hoped, would create an incentive for *all* schools to provide quality education efficiently.

OEO planners supported the idea of a voucher system, and further decided that any plan adopted would have to meet the following objectives:

1. To improve the education of all children, but particularly of disadvantaged children.
2. To give all parents, but particularly disadvantaged parents, more control

---

[1] "Education Vouchers, A Preliminary Report on Financing Education by Payments to Parents" (Cambridge, Mass.: Center for the Study of Public Policy, 1970). This report, prepared under Grant CG8542 for the U.S. Office of Economic Opportunity, is the basis for many of the ideas presented in this case.

than they then enjoyed over the kind of education that their children would receive.

3. To prevent an increase in segregation by race, income, ability, or "desirable" behavior patterns.

In mid-1970, a few months after the study was completed, OEO began to look for sites to run a pilot voucher program.

## Hastings

Hastings was a medium-sized New England city with a population of about 70,000. Like many other such cities, Hastings had in the early 20th century been a very profitable mill town, dominated by a single major employer. But over the years, the mill had curtailed or closed many of its operations, leaving the economic future of Hastings uncertain.

The Hastings Urban Action League was founded in 1952 by a number of the city's leading citizens who wanted to secure that future by "broadening the economic underpinnings of the community." The League commissioned studies by outside consultants and drew up a master plan for the economic redevelopment of Hastings, with the financial support of private citizens as well as the business community. Partly as a result of the League's promotion effort, several new industries moved into Hastings.

In 1969 the Hastings City Council established the Hastings Redevelopment Authority (HRA) to carry on the work begun by the League. One of the last independent projects undertaken by the League had been the partial planning, funding, and building of a new elementary school system in the city. Through their work, individual members of the League became interested in the economics of public school systems, and particularly in the voucher system currently receiving national attention. They proposed to the City Council that Hastings endorse an experimental voucher program for their elementary school system and notify OEO of their interest in becoming one of the test sites that it was about to designate.

## Hastings' Public School System

In 1969, 6,661 elementary students and 2,106 secondary students were enrolled in Hastings's 17 public schools (see Exhibit 1). The schools were divided into five districts, each roughly corresponding to a neighborhood within the city. Of these five, the wealthiest, the Palmer Grove district, was generally considered to have the best schools; the Blue Hill district, the least wealthy, and the one containing most of Hastings's relatively small black population, was reputed to have the worst.

The schools were administered by the city's department of education under an appointed superintendent of schools. The superintendent, other key administrators, and all the principals were appointed by an elected board of education, whose five members served for staggered three-year terms. The teachers'

**Exhibit 1**
Municipal Statistics

### A. HASTINGS'S PROPERTY TAXES, FISCAL YEARS 1964–1969

| *Year* | *Population** | *Total Assessed Valuation†* | *Tax Rate per $1,000* | *Total Tax Levy* | *Tax Levy per Capita‡* | *Total Debt§* | *Debt per Capita‡* |
|---|---|---|---|---|---|---|---|
| 1964 | 69,070 | $ 96,885,500 | $ 88.80 | $ 8,603,424 | $143.60 | n.a. | n.a. |
| 1965 | 69,070 | 98,726,400 | 97.80 | 9,655,442 | 139.79 | n.a. | n.a. |
| 1966 | 69,070 | 99,885,500 | 99.30 | 9,918,630 | 143.60 | $6,249,000 | $ 90.47 |
| 1967 | 69,070 | 99,700,000 | 100.80 | 10,016,240 | 145.00 | 7,483,090 | 108.44 |
| 1968 | 69,070 | 99,653,000 | 102.20 | 10,185,000 | 147.45 | 8,887,000 | 128.66 |
| 1969 | 69,070 | 101,680,000 | 110.21 | 11,206,169 | 162.24 | 9,426,190 | 136.47 |

* Based on 1965 census.

† Estimated by Taxpayers Foundation to be 41 percent of full market value.

‡ Average tax levy per capita for the 19 municipalities in the state with populations of 50,000 to 99,999 was $186.59 in 1969; average debt per capita was $152.93.

§ About 28 percent of this debt is for school-related expenditures.

n.a.—not available.

### B. HASTINGS'S PUBLIC SCHOOL FINANCIAL DATA, FISCAL YEAR 1969

| *Revenues* | | *Expenditures* | |
|---|---|---|---|
| Local property tax | $4,739,729 | Instruction and administration | $3,787,684 |
| State contribution | 1,337,348 | Other operating* | 732,350 |
| Federal, all sources | 332,218 | Municipal services | 887,079 |
| Less adjustments | (3,843) | Total operating expenditures | $5,407,113 |
| | | Fixed assets | 61,381 |
| | | Regional assessment | 565,731 |
| | | Federal contracts | 259,856 |
| | | Other | 101,371 |
| Total revenues | $6,405,452 | Total expenditures | $6,395,452 |

* Includes attendance, health services, food, local transportation, student body activities, and so forth.

## C. LOCAL SCHOOL DATA

| | 1966 | 1967 | 1968 | 1969 | |
|---|---|---|---|---|---|
| Number of pupils to Grade 12 attending: | | | | | |
| Public schools | 8,179 | 8,806 | 8,840 | 8,767 | |
| Elementary grades | | | | 6,661 | |
| Secondary grades | | | | 2,106 | |
| Private schools | 3,989 | 4,323 | 4,203 | 4,912 | |
| Elementary grades | | | | 3,106 | (Catholic = 2,735) |
| Secondary grades | | | | 1,806 | (Catholic = 1,309) |
| Total | 12,168 | 13,129 | 13,043 | 13,679 | |
| Public schools: | | | | | |
| Number of teachers | | | | 326 | |
| Pupil-teacher ratio | | | | 26.9 | |
| Median teacher salary | | | | $8,505 | |
| Average per-pupil operating expenditure | | | | $616.75 | |
| —Elementary | | | | $531.70 | |
| —Secondary | | | | $885.78 | |
| Percent of local tax levy used | | | | 41.9% | |

## D. PRIVATE SCHOOLS

| *Location* | *Name* | *Grades* | *Boys* | *Girls* | *Evaluation** |
|---|---|---|---|---|---|
| Hastings proper | Sacred Heart | 1– 8 | 67 | 78 | M O O M |
| Hastings proper | City Catholic High | 9–12 | 791 | 0 | M O M X |
| Hastings proper | Nickerson Country Day | 4–10 | 48 | 0 | X X X O |
| Hastings proper | St. John | 1– 8 | 240 | 213 | X M M M |
| Hastings proper | St. Luke | K– 9 | 102 | 114 | M M M M |
| Hastings proper | Holy Family Elementary | 1– 8 | 258 | 264 | X M O M |
| Hastings proper | Holy Family High | 9–12 | 0 | 106 | M M M X |
| Hastings proper | St. Margaret | 1– 8 | 208 | 213 | O M O O |
| Hastings proper | St. Mary High | 9–12 | 0 | 173 | M M O M |
| 20-minute drive | William Anderson Elementary | 1– 8 | 169 | 158 | M X X M |
| Hastings proper | St. Paul | K– 8 | 127 | 108 | X M M M |
| Hastings proper | St. Anastasia | 1– 8 | 128 | 137 | M M M M |
| 30-minute drive | Barrett College | 9–12 | 0 | 483 | X M X X |
| Hastings proper | St. Erasmus | 1–12 | 288 | 429 | M M M M |
| | Total | | 2,426 | 2,486 | |
| | Total private in Hastings proper | | 2,257 | 1,845 | |

* Evaluation based on a study conducted by an independent consultant on the following four dimensions, respectively: (1) teacher qualifications, (2) administrative competence, (3) condition of physical plant, and (4) standard student test scores. The following key applies: X = above average, M = average, and O = below average.

salaries were set annually by the board with the advice of the local teachers' union.

Hastings's public schools received funds from three sources: local property tax revenues and state and federal funds. The local tax revenues were allocated to the schools each year by the mayor and the city council, based on the budget submitted to them by the school board.

State funds for education were calculated each year by a complicated formula based on the city's ability to meet its projected costs. In the past, the state had generally provided 22 percent funding to Hastings's 78 percent.

Funds from the federal government, although increasing each year in absolute amount, represented a gradually diminishing share of the cost of education in Hastings.

## Private Schools

In 1969 there were also 3,106 elementary pupils and 1,806 secondary pupils in Hastings's 14 private schools. Of the 14, all but 3 were Catholic schools. In Hastings, as in the rest of the country, Catholic schools were in financial trouble because of the diminishing number of religious personnel available to provide low-cost teaching services. Three of the 11 schools in Hastings were scheduled to close in 1970, requiring the public school system to absorb about 1,780 additional students.

A spokesman for the Urban Action League predicted that the trend would continue, putting an increasing burden on the public school system. An exploratory study commissioned by the League estimated that in the 10-year period from 1969 to 1979, the incremental operating costs required to absorb the enrollment from closing Catholic schools would add between $21.80 and $24.30 to the yearly tax rate. If full costs (including debt service) were considered, the average yearly increase was expected to range from $32.73 to $35.26. During this same 10-year period, the study estimated that the city's debts outstanding would more than double.

## The Voucher Proposal

The plan presented by the League was described as a "Regulated Compensation Model." (See Exhibit 2 for alternate models.) It established an initial fixed value for each voucher, equal to the average per-pupil expenditure in the public elementary school system. These vouchers would be backed by a public agency separate from the school board and city council, to which all tax receipts earmarked for elementary education were entrusted. The agency would establish standards for schools to qualify for the plan, manage the funds entrusted to it, and redeem vouchers presented by qualifying schools. It was anticipated that the voucher agency would also maintain a small surplus of funds to cover lags in tax-rate adjustments and to secure low-cost loans for schools that required expansion or modernization.

**Exhibit 2**
Seven Alternative Education Voucher Plans

1. *Unregulated market model:* The value of the voucher is the same for each child. Schools are permitted to charge whatever additional tuition the traffic will bear.
2. *Unregulated compensatory model:* The value of the voucher is higher for poor children. Schools are permitted to charge whatever additional tuition they wish.
3. *Compulsory private scholarship model:* Schools may charge as much tuition as they like, provided that they give scholarships to those children unable to pay full tuition. Eligibility and size of scholarships are determined by the Education Voucher Agency, which establishes a formula showing how much families with certain incomes can be charged.
4. *The effort voucher:* This model established several different possible levels of per-pupil expenditure and allows a school to choose its own level. Parents who choose high-expenditure schools are then charged more tuition (or tax) than parents who choose low-expenditure schools. Tuition (or tax) is also related to income; in theory the "effort" demanded of a low-income family attending a high-expenditure school is the same as the "effort" demanded of a high-income family in the same school.
5. *"Egalitarian" model:* The value of the voucher is the same for each child. No school is permitted to charge any additional tuition.
6. *Achievement model:* The value of the voucher is based on the progress made by the child during the year.
7. *Regulated compensatory model:* Schools may not charge tuition beyond the value of the voucher. They may "earn" extra funds by accepting children from poor families or educationally disadvantaged children. (A variant of this model permits privately managed voucher schools to charge affluent families according to their ability to pay.)

Under the plan, public schools would be permitted to charge whatever tuition they desired up to the value of the tuition voucher. Private schools would have no limit set on them at all. Parents who could afford to supplement the voucher with their own money to meet tuition at higher priced schools were free to do so; those who could not would be issued supplemental vouchers at their request to cover the additional tuition cost. The maximum amount of the supplemental voucher would be determined by the agency based on the parents' ability to pay. In this manner, all educational facilities would, at least in theory, be available to all children, and the market forces of supply and demand would be set free to increase the effectiveness and efficiency of the entire local elementary school system.

Any school participating in the plan would have to abide by the following regulations:

1. It must accept any applicant as long as it had vacancies.
2. If applications exceed vacancies, it must fill half the places in a truly random, nondiscriminatory manner.
3. It must adopt uniform standards of expulsion and suspension.
4. It must make a full public disclosure of financial and operating data, and widely disseminate information on its educational programs.
5. It must meet minimum state requirements for curriculum, staffing, and so forth.

Once the plan was in operation, the value of the voucher (and the corresponding tax rate) would be adjusted annually. There was some disagreement within the League about how the adjustment should be made. One group argued that the voucher value should be fixed permanently so that as costs and incomes continued to rise, the relative public burden for education would diminish. Parents who could afford to do so would contribute an increasing share of the costs of educating their own children. All others would continue to receive supplemental vouchers in an amount sufficient to cover the tuition at the school.

Another group argued that the voucher should be set at the budgeted cost per student in the public (city-operated) elementary schools. This would make clear the distinction between "private" and "public" education and make those choosing "private" education fully aware of the real marginal costs involved.

A third group argued that the value should be controlled directly by the city council, the only body fully able to analyze the impact of any increase in taxes needed to support the voucher.

The final plan presented to the city council advocated a value based upon the annual budgeted per-pupil expenditure of the "public" school system.

## Questions

1. Assume the role of the superintendent of schools for Hastings and outline your reaction to the League's proposal. Specifically, evaluate the proposal in terms of—
   *a.* Its probable impact on aggregate elementary school expenditures, both public and private.
   *b.* Its impact on the allocation of educational resources among different classes of students, well-to-do versus poor, white versus minority, and so forth.
   *c.* The ability of parents to determine what education is best for their children.
   *d.* Its impact on the quality of education offered by the "public" schools under your superintendency.
   *e.* The probable reaction of various political and special-interest groups.
2. Assuming that the city council and the school board had approved a voucher system in principle and has asked you to work out a specific plan, prepare such a plan, including answers to the following:
   *a.* Who should be eligible for vouchers?
   *b.* How should the value of each voucher be determined?
   *c.* Should parents be permitted to supplement vouchers with their own funds?
   *d.* What requirement should participating schools meet?
   *e.* What mechanism would you establish to ensure the education of children no school wanted?
   *f.* What procedure would you establish for providing transportation subsidies:
      (1) Cost to the nearest school only?
      (2) Cost to the school actually attended?
      (3) Flat grants to all?
      (4) Subsidy proportional to income?

g. How should the general eligibility of participating schools be determined? Would church-affiliated schools be eligible? Under what circumstances could a new school be established under the plan?

## Case 5–3

## MASSACHUSETTS EYE AND EAR INFIRMARY (A)*

Mr. Charles Wood, Executive Director of the Massachusetts Eye and Ear Infirmary, was reviewing the results of a new cost-accounting system that the hospital had installed in 1976. The new system contained several innovative features, and the past year had been a trial period for it. Central to Mr. Wood's thinking were three issues: (1) whether the system actually represented a more accurate picture of hospital costs, as its proponents claimed; (2) what impact the system was having on cost containment in the hospital; and (3) the transferability of the system, since some individuals had questioned whether the system was applicable to a general hospital.

### Background

In 1974 the Massachusetts Eye and Ear infirmary celebrated its 150th anniversary. During the century and a half from its inception in 1824 as a free clinic located on the second floor of Scollay's Building in downtown Boston, it had undertaken a wide variety of innovative and farsighted activities. Its founders, Drs. Edward Reynolds and John Jefferies, were both pioneers in the field of ophthalmology, a medical specialty that was not fully incorporated into general medicine until the early 1800s.

Demand for the hospital's services continually grew. Its most significant expansion, completed in the mid-1970s, allowed the hospital staff and patients to move into a new $34 million building on Charles Street in downtown Boston. Thus, as the nation celebrated its 200th anniversary, MEEI settled into its new hospital, research, and teaching complex.

By 1977, the independent, nonprofit hospital was admitting 11,273 patients and accommodating 80,000 outpatient visits per year. More striking was the increased demand on the hospital's emergency care: in a decade, emergency visits had surged from 10,000 per year to nearly 36,000. In addition, the hospital coordinated numerous community outreach programs, including screening clinics to detect chronic disorders, civic group lectures, and the preparation of health care education booklets.

---

* This case was prepared by Patricia O'Brien under the direction of David W. Young, Harvard School of Public Health. 

In 1977, a total of 1,000 employees staffed the hospital's three daily shifts. There were 136 eye specialists and 67 ear, nose, and throat specialists on the hospital's staff; 40 residents and 50 clinical and research fellows received specialty training each year. The hospital's condensed income statements are summarized in Exhibit 1.

**Exhibit 1**

MASSACHUSETTS EYE AND EAR INFIRMARY (A)
Condensed Income Statement—Operations

| | *1977* | *1976* | *1975* | *1974* |
|---|---|---|---|---|
| Patient service revenue | $20,901,732 | $19,646,627 | $16,666,801 | $13,786,026 |
| Adjustments to patient revenue for uncollectible accounts, free care, and contractual allowances | 1,582,873 | 1,780,733 | 1,344,750 | 305,072 |
| Net revenue, service to patients | 19,318,859 | 17,865,894 | 15,322,051 | 13,480,954 |
| Other operating revenue | 5,866,547 | 4,542,813 | 4,211,134 | 2,766,156 |
| Total operating revenue | 25,185,406 | 22,408,707 | 19,533,185 | 16,247,110 |
| Operating expenses: | | | | |
| Patient Service (inc. dep.) | 20,887,510 | 18,425,252 | 16,480,572 | 14,290,154 |
| Research and other specific-purpose direct expenses | 4,586,730 | 3,680,178 | 3,196,582 | 2,350,159 |
| Hospital operating income (loss) | (288,834) | 303,277 | (143,969) | (393,203) |
| Income from donations | — | — | — | 27,595 |
| Hospital net income (loss) from operations | $ (288,834) | $ 303,277 | $ (143,969) | $ (365,608) |

Dissatisfied with the usual per diem cost accounting methods used in hospitals across the country, Mr. Wood became convinced of the need for an accounting system that would allow hospitals to measure the cost of health care more accurately. He expained:

> For years I've been trying to improve the conceptual basis for identifying the cost of hospital care. Back in the 50s, I noticed that hospitals' costs were defined differently from state to state, depending on what qualified for reimbursement. Meanwhile, hospitals would try to make up for deficits by tacking on additional patient fees for services like admissions. These experiments were short-lived because the figures were arbitrary and not rooted in fact, but they stimulated me to think about hospital costs as units of service. We developed our present cost accounting system gradually; first, we developed a two-part rate composed of a per diem charge, including nursing, and a hospitalization charge. Then, as we improved our data systems, we expanded into our present three-part cost accounting method, which takes nursing out of the per diem portion and costs it out for separate charging.

By breaking down the lump sum per diem hospital rate into units which reflected the actual services each patient received, Mr. Wood hoped to develop a more equitable cost system. In addition, he thought the extensive information produced by such a system could provide tools for improving the management of the hospital.

Although he designed the system for MEEI's specification, Mr. Wood believed it had widespread potential for the hospital industry. In the hospital's 1976 annual report, he wrote:

> We have just completed the first full year of using our new cost accounting system, and I am happy to report that by any measure it is working successfully. Our program continues to be watched very closely by other hospitals around the country and by various local, state, and federal government agencies.
>
> Our first-year pilot program with Blue Cross of Massachusetts, Inc., exceeded even our expectations, and I am quite confident, despite the fact that we are a specialty hospital, that the system has widespread potential. We have worked with such a variety of conditions and amassed such a broad collection of data that we are certain of successful use in general hospitals.

## The Split Cost Accounting System

The split cost accounting system in use at MEEI was built around two basic concepts: (1) that not all days' care in a hospital were equivalent, and (2) that for any given patient, the cost of routine services was a function of three categories of costs that related to three elements of a hospital stay—hospitalization, routine daily costs, and intensity of service (or "clinical care") costs.

The hospitalization cost element is the effort of entering and discharging a patient. It includes scheduling for admission, the admission process, and other one-time operations such as maintaining medical records, preparing a bill, and various discharge-related activities. It also includes a per-patient apportionment of plant and administrative overhead—in effect, the cost of the hospital's availability and readiness. Hospitalization is a one-time cost, regardless of a patient's length of stay, and recognizes that one's entry and presence in the hospital engender costs that are measurable.

The cost per patient-day element encompasses the costs related to the patient's length of stay; i.e., the daily costs for room, meals, dietary needs, laundry, routine pharmaceuticals, medical and surgical supplies, and incidentals.

The clinical care element is the cost of direct patient care in accordance with diagnosis, surgical procedures, and the patient's point in progress toward recovery. This component is measured by clinical care units. A clinical care unit (CCU) is the numerical value given to a direct service or treatment which is provided to a patient. CCUs are measures of the amount of time necessary to perform various activities in relation to a patient's care in the hospital.

Mr. Wood emphasized that the system measured only the services that traditionally had been included in a per diem rate:

> It's important to recognize that our new cost accounting system is not a medical measurement system. It's a cost measurement system for productivity. By means of the data base which we created, we were able to develop what might best be

called a relative-value scale. This tells us how many clinical care units are needed for the entire range of procedures here at the Infirmary. The data base is updated periodically by sampling various procedures to see how they correspond to the existing data base, and making adjustments accordingly. Services such as the operating rooms, drug units, lab tests, and other ancillaries are billed separately so that the system focuses only on the ongoing care component of a patient's stay.

MEEI had calculated the amount of effort, or clinical care units, required by each procedure, and came up with a method of specifying the amount of care needed by each patient. Time values for clinical care units are shown in Exhibit 2, and the number of clinical care units necessary for various nursing activities is enumerated in Exhibit 3.

## Use of the Split Cost Accounting System

With the split cost accounting system, the expenses traditionally included in per diem cost for a patient's stay were distributed by categories as shown in Exhibit 4. From the CCU data base, MEEI could predict by diagnosis and surgical procedure how many clinical care units a given patient would be likely to require on each hospital day, from the day of admission to the day of discharge.

Mr. Wood commented on the system:

We know, for example, that a child with strabismus (squint) will require 15 clinical care units on the day he is admitted. The far more seriously ill laryngectomy patient, who is largely able to care for himself pre-operatively, will require only five clinical care units on the day of admission. By means of our data base, we have been able to develop a workload curve by diagnosis and surgical procedure on a day-to-day basis that can be used to predict clinical care requirements of patients in-house and those to be admitted. (See Exhibit 5.)

We recognize, of course, that every service provided as part of general clinical care is not a direct patient care service. We know that a portion of the time of every member of a nursing shift is spent in activities other than direct care, activities such as conferences with other members of the medical team, consoling the patient, and so forth. So, in determining the cost of a clinical care unit, we developed a

**Exhibit 2**
Time Values for Clincal Care Units

| | | | |
|---|---|---|---|
| 1 Unit | = | 7½ minutes | ± 2 minutes |
| 2 Units | = | 15 minutes | ± 5 minutes |
| 4 Units | = | 30 minutes | ± 5 minutes |
| 8 Units | = | 60 minutes | ± 5 minutes |
| 12 Units | = | 90 minutes | ± 5 minutes |

Source: M. Poland et al, "PETO—A System for Assisting and Meeting Patient Care Needs," *American Journal of Nursing* 70 (July 1970), p. 1479.

**Exhibit 3**
Classification of Patient Needs

| *Category* | *Description* | *Clinical Care Unit Value* |
|---|---|---|
| Diet | Feeds self without supervision, or family or parent feeds patient. | 1 |
| | Feeds self with supervision of staff; I&O. | 2 |
| | Tube feeding every 3 hours by patient. | 4 |
| | Total feeding by personnel, or instructing the patient or continuous IV, or blood transfusion. Tube feeding by personnel every 3 hours. | 8 |
| | Tube feedings every 1 to 2 hours. | 12 |
| Toileting | Toilets independently. | 0 |
| | Toilets with minimal assistance. | 1 |
| | Toilets with supervision, or specimen collection, or uses bedpan. Hemovac output. | 2 |
| | Up to toilet with standby supervision, or output measurement every hour. Initial hemovac setup. | 4 |
| Vital signs | Routine daily temperature, pulse, and respiration. | 1 |
| | Vital signs every 4 hours. | 2 |
| | Vital signs monitored, or vital signs every 2 hours. | 4 |
| | Vital signs and observation every hour, or vital signs monitored, plus neuro check. | 8 |
| | Blood pressure, pulse, respiration, and neuro check every 30 minutes. | 12 |
| Respiratory needs | Bedside humidifier, or blow bottle. | 1 |
| | Mist or humidified air when sleeping, or cough and deep breathe every 2 hours. | 2 |
| | Continuous oxygen, trach mist, or cough and deep breathe every hour. | 4 |
| | IPPB with supervision every 4 hours. | 8 |
| Suction | Routine post-operative standby. | 1 |
| | Nasopharyngeal or oral suction prn. | 2 |
| | Tracheostomy suction every 1 to 2 hours. | 4 |
| | Tracheostomy suction every ½ hour. | 8 |
| Bath | Bathes self, bed straightened. | 1 |
| | Bathes self with help, or supervision, daily change of bed. | 2 |
| | Bathed and dressed by personnel or partial bath given, daily change of linen. | 4 |
| | Bathed and dressed by personnel, special skin care, occupied bed. | 8 |
| Activity | Up with assistance once in 8 hours (or exercise). | 1 |
| | Up in chair with assistance twice in 8 hours or walking with assistance. | 2 |
| | Bedrest with assistance in turning every 2 hours or up walking with assistance of two persons twice in 8 hours. | 4 |
| | Bedrest with turning every hour. | 12 |
| Treatments | Once in 8 hours. | 1 |
| | Twice in 8 hours | 2 |
| | Three times in 8 hours. | 4 |
| | Four times in 8 hours. | 8 |
| | More than every two hours. | 12 |

Source: M. Poland, et al, "PETO—A System for Assisting and Meeting Patient Care Needs," *American Journal of Nursing*, 70 (July 1970), p. 1479.

**Exhibit 4**

MASSACHUSETTS EYE AND EAR INFIRMARY (A)
Classification of Expenses
Fiscal Year 1977

| | *Budgeted* |
|---|---|
| Cost per patient: | |
| Admitting and scheduling | $ 36,341 |
| Accounts receivable and cashier | 65,023 |
| Patient services | 17,532 |
| Property insurance | 23,875 |
| Legal Expenses | 2,193 |
| Social service | 163,253 |
| Medical records and library | 185,234 |
| Repairs and maintenance | 317,080 |
| Operation of plant | 251,208 |
| Housekeeping | 511,455 |
| Interest and depreciation | 677,481 |
| Free care and bad debts | 10,977 |
| Total cost | $2,261,652 |
| Number of admissions | 11,200 |
| Cost per patient | $201.93 |
| Charge per patient | 202.69 |
| Cost per patient day: | |
| House officers | 184,123 |
| M & S supplies | 407,916 |
| Dietary | 837,382 |
| Laundry / Linen | 257,730 |
| Pharmacy | 168,524 |
| Free care and bad debts | 9,053 |
| Total cost | $1,864,728 |
| Number of patient days | 53,984 |
| Cost per patient day | $34.54 |
| Charge per patient day | 41.25 |
| Cost per CCU: | |
| Nursing service—direct cost | 1,852,073 |
| Nursing education—direct cost | 215,145 |
| Nursing administration and supervision | 1,133,537 |
| Nursing maintenance of plant | 11,849 |
| Nursing operation of plant | 9,386 |
| Nursing housekeeping | 9,194 |
| Nursing laundry & linen | 1,251 |
| Nursing cafe | 91,843 |
| Nursing depreciation and interest | 25,698 |
| Free care and bad debts | 16,342 |
| Total cost | $3,366,318 |
| Number of CCUs | 753,373 |
| Cost per CCU | $4.47 |
| Charge per CCU | $4.54 |

**Exhibit 5**
Sample Distribution of Clinical Care Units

| Procedure | Day of | | Post-Operative Days | | | | | | | | | | | Day of Discharge | Total |
|---|---|---|---|---|---|---|---|---|---|---|---|---|---|---|---|
| | Admission | Surgery | 1st | 2d | 3d | 4th | 5th | 6th | 7th | 8th | 9th | 10th | Etc. | | |
| T & A | 3 | 24 | | | | | | | | | | | | 5 | 32 |
| Cataract extraction | 15 | 18 | 14 | 10 | 6 | | | | | | | | | 6 | 69 |
| Laryngectomy and radical neck dissection | 5 | 6 | 50 | 36 | 34 | 28 | 17 | 17 | 14 | 12 | 8 | 6 | 6* | 6 | 245 |
| Mastoid tympanoplasty | 4 | 17 | 21 | 13 | 7 | | | | | | | | | 6 | 68 |
| Scleral buckle, primary | 15 | 18 | 13 | 8 | 8 | 8 | 8 | 6 | | | | | | 6 | 90 |
| Vitrectomy pars plana | 15 | 17 | 21 | 13 | 13 | 13 | 13 | 11 | | | | | | 9 | 125 |
| Strabismus surgery | 15 | 9 | | | | | | | | | | | | 6 | 30 |
| Sybmucous resection | 3 | 17 | | | | | | | | | | | | 5 | 25 |
| Laryngoscopy and vocal cord strip | 8.5 | 10.4 | | | | | | | | | | | | 9.5 | 28.4 |
| Corneal transplant | 15 | 21 | 19 | 16 | 12 | 12 | 12 | | | | | | | 6 | 113 |

* Through 15th day.

ratio of direct patient care time to indirect patient care time, and then included indirect care and nursing department overhead along with direct patient care costs in the cost per clinical care unit.

As you might expect, we have found that the costs for various procedures under the new system are radically different from those under the traditional system when we simply used a per diem rate. Effectively, the split cost accounting system we are using closely aligns charges with diagnosis, surgical procedure, and identified required care.

## Evaluation of the Split Cost Accounting System

In reviewing the effects of the new accounting system, Mr. Wood first mentioned the advantages of the hospitalization charge:

> One of the big differences with our new system is the hospitalization charge. Compared with the present per diem system in use in most institutions, it has a greater impact on the short-stay patient. But it is nevertheless more equitable, since under the per diem system the long-stay patient (mostly the older and sicker patient likely to be less economically endowed) pays a proportionately larger share of the one-time costs and is, in fact, subsidizing the hospitalization of the short-stay patient.

Mr. Wood imagined that, used widely, the system would provide a common denominator to compare rates among several hospitals:

> The long-argued question of why day rates have varied so markedly from one institution to another over the years is a result of the day rate being a catchall category for many other cost factors. If the true elements of hospitalization are identified, the cost of providing a hospital room should be markedly closer everywhere, in that the same elements are assessed.

Mr. Wood added a long-range benefit for the health care industry:

> By costing out the elements of care and charging patients only for the care they receive, it will no longer be necessary to operate separate institutions or facilities for patients who require different levels of care. These facilities were created because traditional cost accounting systems are inadequate to measure and cost out the work output for each level of care. Currently, patients recovering from long or serious illnesses are moved from acute care facilities to skilled nursing care wings or to nursing homes because each facility charges different basic rates depending on the amount of care they offer. It makes sense that as patients need less nursing care, they no longer want to pay the same per diem rate they paid during their critical illness. With the split cost accounting system, a patient would pay different rates within the *same facility* as his or her needs became less. In addition to the obvious advantages of convenience to patients and saving administrative duplications, the system allows hospitals to effectively compete with skilled nursing facilities.

Mr. Anthony Reis, Manager of Fiscal Affairs at MEEI, discussed the impact of the system on cost containment:

When you have a flat room rate that covers all routine services, such as most hospitals do, if patient days go down you might make a decision that you need fewer nurses, which might not be the case at all. Now we can see more clearly how the costs break down. Let's assume, for example, that patient days decrease, but we also see that admissions are the same. This tells us that those services which relate to admissions can't be cut back, but perhaps services such as dietary can be. Next we would look at the CCUs. Just because patient days are going down doesn't mean that CCUs are decreasing also, so we see what's happening; then we decide if we want to cut back on nursing staff. That to me is the most important part, but for the general public, of course, the more important part is fairer billing.

As far as the costs and benefits of this system to the hospital are concerned, they are very difficult to measure. However, historically, our costs increased at the rate of the rest of the industry, but now they are increasing by only about 6 to 7 percent a year compared to 12 to 15 percent a year for the rest of the industry. Even though we are a specialized hospital, we essentially do everything the same as every other hospital, except, of course, we now group our cost centers into three categories.

## Blue Cross Reimbursement

In 1976–77, Blue Cross was the only third-party payor that reimbursed MEEI according to the split cost accounting system. At the end of the year, Mr. Paul Bushnell, Manager of the Blue Cross Office of Health Care Planning, reported favorably on the new system and added his intention to renew MEEI's contract using the split cost accounting method. According to Mr. Bushnell, Blue Cross was supporting the system for two major reasons:

First, I would agree with Charley Wood that the new system provided him with better management information to run his hospital. I think this was proven out. This year, his costs and efficiency were far better than the national average. His system did help him hold on to costs; I'd say his argument has merit.

Secondly, the system will in the long run, save money for Blue Cross, Medicare, and Medicaid. Rather than support a health system with 3,000–5,000 empty beds and a proliferation of nursing homes, all of us would benefit by using these beds and ending the duplication of facilities. Currently, the empty beds are probably costing us 70 percent of the full beds. If we can now provide skilled nursing facility care at reasonable rates in unutilized facilities, we will greatly improve hospital efficiency and save ourselves wasted dollars.

Mr. Bushnell added one advantage which, he noted, was still highly conjectural. He thought that accommodating patients in one facility for both their acute and skilled nursing care needs could possibly hasten some patients' recovery periods. This would represent a savings for the payor, the hospital, and the patient.

Like Mr. Wood, Mr. Bushnell has tried to interest Medicare and Medicaid in the split cost accounting method of reimbursement.

> The state's reluctance may derive from the fact that their payments would increase, at least initially, under the new system. Because the state sets payment rates from historic cost, they are traditionally less than a hospital's current costs. Using the Massachusetts Eye and Ear's cost accounting system, charges are based on current cost figures. This year, Blue Cross paid an additional $100,000 to MEEI, because of our patient mix. We consider this an investment in a more equitable health system and long-range savings. On the other hand, Medicare, because of the types of procedures for which Medicare patients are admitted to the Eye and Ear Infirmary, would pay less to the hospital than under a per diem rate.

Average length of stay and volume distributions are classified by payor in Exhibit 6.

**Exhibit 6**
Length of Stay and Volume Distribution by Financial Class (fiscal year 1977)

| | *Average Stay (Days)* | *Admissions* | *Patient Days* | *Clinical Care Units* |
|---|---|---|---|---|
| Self pay | 6.19 | 6.24% | 7.81% | 7.99% |
| Blue Cross of Massachusetts | 4.01 | 28.44 | 23.09 | 23.23 |
| Out-of-State Blue Cross | 6.26 | 7.36 | 9.32 | 9.00 |
| Commercial insurance | 4.34 | 18.47 | 16.23 | 16.44 |
| Workers' compensation | 6.25 | 1.12 | 1.41 | 1.51 |
| Welfare (Medicaid) | 4.31 | 6.25 | 5.45 | 5.41 |
| Medicare | 5.64 | 32.12 | 36.68 | 36.40 |
| Total | | 100.00 | 100.00 | 100.00 |
| Income per category | | $2,282,899 | $2,389,692 | $3,565,770 |

Mr. Bushnell had tried to persuade several community hospitals to develop split cost accounting systems. He believed that medical and diagnostic data can be standardized, as surgical data had been at MEEI. He commented on transferring the system to other hospitals.

> I am talking to several community hospitals because I definitely think they can use an accounting system like MEEI's. It should have been done long ago but the catch is the work involved in compiling the standard CCU data from historic records. What we really need is someone to put together one cookbook of clinical care units for the various diagnoses done at community hospitals. Besides, if every hospital devises its own clinical care unit structure, there will be no comparability between hospitals.

During the first year, Blue Cross paid MEEI the full amount they were billed. Mr. Bushnell explained that because MEEI was unique in their costing method, Blue Cross lacked any comparative information for the hospital's CCU estimates. Mr. Bushnell added that Blue Cross trusted the hospital and thought their utilization and review process kept their costs at a minimum.

## Questions

1. What is the difference between the budgeted 1977 routine care cost of a cataract operation under the old accounting method and under the new split cost accounting system? A T&A? A laryngectomy and radical neck dissection?
2. What accounts for the differences? Are they significant? Why does the short-stay patient have a greater cost impact than the long-stay patient?
3. What is your assessment of the rationale underlying the classification of costs into the three categories shown in Exhibit 4? How, if at all, would you change this classification scheme?
4. How would you respond to the three issues raised by Mr. Wood in the first paragraph of the case? What modifications, if any, would you make to the new system?

## Case 5–4

## TOWN OF WATERVILLE VALLEY*

At the 1980 town meeting, residents of Waterville Valley, New Hampshire, would be asked to authorize a major expansion of the town's water system. Some residents believed that the supply was adequate for the foreseeable future. Others, including the area's developer, thought that the supply was inadequate and would inhibit growth in the town.

The method of paying for an expanded water system was also at issue. The capital expenditure would be financed by a municipal bond issue. Alternatives for payment of the principal and interest on this issue were: (1) a lump sum to be charged to each new housing unit, to be paid by the developer and included in the price of the unit, (2) higher water rates for all users, or (3) an annual charge made to all new water users, that is, those whose service began after the expanded system went into operation.

Finally, there was the question of how water was to be charged to users. At present, residential users were charged a flat monthly amount, and some people thought that the charge should be based on usage.

### Background

The Town of Waterville Valley is in a valley surrounded on all sides by the White Mountain National Forest. The area of the town is about 700

* This case was prepared by Robert N. Anthony, Harvard Business School.

acres, and it is unlikely that its area can grow because the U.S. Forest Service probably would not sell additional land to private parties. One well-paved road, 11 miles long, provides access to the valley from an interstate highway. Waterville Valley is 130 miles from Boston and 60 miles from the state capital, Concord, which is the nearest city.

The town was incorporated in 1829. In 1965 the permanent structures consisted of an inn, accommodating 60 guests, 16 homes of residents, most of whom lived in the valley year round, and a small town hall.

In 1965 the inn and 506 acres of land were purchased by The Waterville Company, a privately owned corporation. Thomas Corcoran, president, moved to Waterville Valley. He planned to develop the area as a year-round resort and to sell land to developers and individuals.

By 1979 the area had become a major ski facility, with 10 lifts, 35 miles of downhill trails, many with snowmaking facilities, and many miles of cross-country trails. About 4,000 skiers used the facilities on peak days. The ski area was leased from the Forest Service by the Waterville Company. In addition, there was a nine-hole golf course, a pond for bathing and sailing, and 15 tennis courts. There were five inns with a capacity of about 200, a bunk house, 65 single-family houses, 6 condominium developments totaling approximately 300 units, a conference center with a capacity of 500, and a number of restaurants and stores. There were sleeping accommodations for about 2,000 persons. The ultimate capacity was estimated to be 7,000 persons. The official population, however, was 199.

## Water Supply

Until 1967, property owners provided their own water. The original inn was served by a spring, and individual homeowners used artesian wells. One consequence was that whenever a fire started, the property burned to the ground, as had happened to the inn twice before, and again in 1967.

In 1967, the Waterville Company, at its expense, drilled new wells and constructed a pumping station, a reservoir, a distribution system with an 8-inch main, and fire hydrants. In the 1968 town meeting, the voters unanimously agreed to buy this system from the Waterville Company, and voted a bond issue of $135,000 for this purpose and to finance further exploration for water.

In 1970 a bond issue of $105,000 was authorized to expand the water system, and in 1972 a third bond issue of $235,000 was authorized for this purpose. After this construction, the town had a half-million gallon storage capacity and water distribution lines throughout the town. However, by 1979, according to the town manager, existing wells were being used to 85 percent of capacity, and "a new source is necessary." Two pumps were used, and if one of them broke, water pressure would be seriously affected.

## Sewer System

The initial sewer system consisted of collection mains and a series of lagoons for filtering wastes. These were built, owned, and maintained by the Waterville Company. By 1972 these facilities had become inadequate. The Waterville Company, however, wanted to get out of the sewer business, and it proposed the following:

1. The company would give the existing system, preliminary engineering for an expanded system, and land for a sewage treatment facility to the Town, without consideration.

2. The town would set up a municipal services department to operate the water and sewer systems.

3. If in any year the operations of this system resulted in a cash loss, the town's maximum obligation from the general tax levy would be $2 per $1,000 of assessed valuation, assuming that the town would continue to assess property at full fair market value. Any additional loss would be made up by the Waterville Company. Payments made by the Waterville Company would be repaid in future years if operations (including the $2 tax levy) produced a profit in those years.

4. Water and sewerage fees would be at an agreed-upon schedule and would increase at stated percentages thereafter (details of these fees are described subsequently).

5. The Town would build a municipal sewer system, with the most modern sewage treatment facilities, to be financed with a bond issue of $1.8 million. This system would be adequate for the ultimate development of Waterville Valley to a 7,000-bed capacity.

6. The agreement would last until January 1, 1983, or until three years beyond the date of an additional bond issue to expand the water system, whichever was longer.

This proposal was approved at the 1973 town meeting, the bonds were issued, and the facilities were built. As shown in Exhibit 1, losses were experienced in 1975, 1976, and 1977; the Waterville Company reimbursed the town for these losses. In 1978, a profit was earned.

## Water and Sewer Rates

Users were charged a one-time, fixed, "tap" fee which entitled them to tap into the town water and sewer system. The fee was determined by a point and unit system. Points were determined by the number of bedrooms, bathrooms, and other water use outlets, such as kitchens, outdoor spigots, and sinks, that were part of a unit.

Ten points comprised one water or sewer unit. For example, a half-bath was assessed at ¼ point, a sauna at ¼ point, and a full bath at 3 points. Kitchens were assessed at 2½ points; bedrooms, living rooms, hallways, and

**Exhibit 1**

TOWN OF WATERVILLE VALLEY
Water and Sewer Calculations
($000)

| | *1974* | *1975* | *1976* | *1977* | *1978* |
|---|---|---|---|---|---|
| Revenues: | | | | | |
| Operations: | | | | | |
| Usage charges | $ 59.6 | $ 85.3 | $ 106.1 | $ 121.9 | $ 139.0 |
| Tap fees | 45.2 | 30.7 | 9.3 | 19.5 | 46.7 |
| Other | 5.6 | 3.7 | 1.3 | 2.1 | 2.3 |
| Subtotal | 110.4 | 119.7 | 116.7 | 143.5 | 188.0 |
| State contribution (40% of debt service) | — | 59.0 | 57.7 | 56.5 | 55.3 |
| Town tax revenues ($2/$1,000) | 32.5 | 36.3 | 36.5 | 45.5 | 50.6 |
| Other revenues | 40.4 | 55.6 | — | — | — |
| Total revenues | 183.3 | 270.6 | 210.9 | 245.5 | 293.9 |
| Expenditures: | | | | | |
| Operating expenses | 44.8 | 68.3 | 54.4 | 58.4 | 67.9 |
| Debt service: | | | | | |
| Principal | 27.6 | 100.8 | 100.9 | 100.9 | 102.1 |
| Interest | 89.0 | 110.5 | 106.1 | 100.6 | 95.5 |
| Total expenditures | 161.4 | 279.6 | 261.4 | 259.9 | 265.5 |
| Excess of revenues over expenditures | $ 21.9 | $( 9.0) | $( 50.5) | $( 14.4) | $ 28.4 |
| Tax base: Assessed valuations | $16,243.0 | $18,165.0 | $18,261.0 | $22,763.0 | $25,321.0 |
| Tax rate/$1,000 | $12.7 | $13.0 | $16.8 | $13.4 | $14.0 |
| Water consumption (millions of gallons) | | 19.4 | 22.9 | 25.2 | 27.0 |
| Sewage treated (millions of gallons) | | 10.5 | 16.3 | 21.0 | 22.0 |

Source: Town records.

lofts at 1 point. Water coolers, ice machines, and extra sinks were assessed at ¼ point each. There was a minimum of one sewer unit and one water unit per dwelling unit. The point system was also used to establish usage rates. See Exhibit 2 for recent rates.

Meters were used only for commercial establishments. The fee for installing a meter was $10, paid by the building's owner. It had been suggested that meters be installed in residential units as well as commercial ones. The town

**Exhibit 2**
Water and Sewer Department Rate Schedule

| | *1977* | *1978* | *1979* |
|---|---|---|---|
| Tap fee—per water unit | $315.00 | $330.00 | $345.00 |
| Tap fee—per sewer unit | 525.00 | 550.00 | 575.00 |
| Water usage—per water unit per month | 9.45 | 10.00 | 10.50 |
| Water usage—commercial metered per 1,000 gallons | 1.90 | 2.00 | 2.10 |
| Sewer usage—per sewer unit per month | 12.39 | 13.00 | 13.65 |
| Sewer usage—commercial rate | | (130% of water bill) | |
| Turn on–turn off charge—water | 20.00 | | |

Source: Town records.

treasurer favored this plan because it would probably provide more revenue for the system. In addition, he felt that it would be a more equitable way of determining charges and thus sharing expenses, and it would encourage conservation of water. This would become more important as it became more and more difficult to find new sources of water.

He noted that the only conservation measures now being applied were mandatory installation of water saver toilets and showers in new condominium and residential units. He felt that in the near future, there could conceivably be an outright ban on saunas and pools because of their prodigious consumption of water. He cited expense as the main reason the town had not seriously considered requiring installation of meters on residential units. Residential water meters cost $60 installed.

A large consumer of water was the snowmaking operations of the Waterville Company. The equipment, when operating, consumed 1,000 gallons per minute. The company had its own water supply for this purpose, which came partially from the Mad River and partially from one of the town's original wells. The company considered this "free" water and charged only the capital cost of the equipment, and the electricity and manpower to operate it, as expenses.

Many experts believe that the era of an inexpensive potable water supply is over.[1] As demands mount, nearby sources become inadequate. In addition, capital costs of developing new and large surface supplies of water are increasing. The possibility of using the pricing mechanism to control demand has become a widely considered alternative to increasing supplies.

In the past, consumption/pricing decisions made by public utility managers have caused inefficient supply and demand relationships. Peak users of water who create high short-term demands requiring expensive investment in equipment are not required to pay for the added capacity. Block prices are offered to major users, thus encouraging the inefficient use of water. States and communities have subsidized local utilities by developing reservoirs at public expense and by charging less than the cost of the water.

In a recent study for the National Water Commission undertaken by Resources for the Future, it was found that little incentive exists for homeowners to install water-saving devices. Currently available technologies could reduce residential water use (frequently considered to be inelastic) by more than 30 percent. Even greater reductions could be achieved for swimming pools and lawn sprinklers, with a more effective pricing mechanism.

This same study indicated that a change in price from 40¢ per 1,000 gallons (an average price) to $1 per 1,000 gallons would reduce the projected increase in residential demand for the Northeast, in this decade, by almost 20 percent.

---

[1] Based on Michael Greenberg and Robert W. Hordon, *Water Supply Planning: A Case Study and Systems Analysis* (New Brunswick, N.J.: Rutgers—The State University of New Jersey, 1976).

## Present Operations

The new sewer treatment plant was completed and operational in 1974. At that time water and sewer were combined into a Municipal Services Department with a separate budget and financial statement. All receivables and payables for the department were handled by the town bookkeeper. She estimated that she spent about five days per quarter billing and paying bills for this department. No part of her $9,095 annual salary was allocated to the department, nor were other town costs.

Similarly, the Public Safety Department was not charged for its use of water in firefighting. Although hydrants used in firefighting belonged to the town, they were paid for by the developer. The town manager estimated that each new hydrant cost $800.

The municipal services budget did not include an allowance for depreciation. The town treasurer said that the town budgets were based on a system

**Exhibit 3**

TOWN OF WATERVILLE VALLEY
Municipal Services Department
1978 Summary

| | *Sewer* | *Water* | *Solid Waste* | *Total Department* |
|---|---|---|---|---|
| Revenues: | | | | |
| Tap fees | $ 29,029.01 | $17,622.31 | | $ 46,651.32 |
| Usage | 73,903.78 | 65,069.33 | $ 11,556.00 | 150,529.11 |
| Other | 638.32 | 1,651.36 | | 2,289.68 |
| Revenues from operations | 103,571.11 | 84,343.00 | 11,556.00 | 199,470.11 |
| Additional revenues: | | | | |
| State grant | 55,274.00 | | | 55,274.00 |
| Total revenues | 158,845.11 | 84,343.00 | 11,556.00 | 254,744.11 |
| Operating expenses: | | | | |
| Wages | 15,961.30 | 9,442.40 | 6,820.76 | 32,224.46 |
| Vehicle operations | 1,128.02 | 1,390.81 | 3,896.97 | 6,415.80 |
| Telephone | 618.05 | 126.00 | | 744.05 |
| Electricity | 8,912.11 | 2,805.71 | 113.60 | 11,831.42 |
| Heating fuel | 6,743.88 | 501.51 | | 7,245.39 |
| System/plant maintenance | 3,919.91 | 12,494.91 | 310.76 | 16,725.58 |
| Chemicals | 3,394.41 | | | 3,394.41 |
| Disposal costs | | | 7,991.09 | 7,991.09 |
| Training and seminars | 90.83 | | | 90.83 |
| Retirement | | 336.04 | 336.02 | 672.06 |
| Total operating expenses | 40,768.51 | 27,097.38 | 19,469.20 | 87,335.09 |
| Income (loss) before debt service | 118,076.60 | 57,245.62 | (7,913.20) | 167,409.02 |
| Debt service: | | | | |
| Principal | 66,080.00 | 35,999.45 | 5,101.97 | 107,181.42 |
| Interest | 82,040.00 | 13,503.11 | 1,054.50 | 96,597.61 |
| Total debt service | 148,120.00 | 49,502.56 | 6,156.47 | 203,779.03 |
| Net profit (loss) of departments | $ (30,043.40) | $ 7,743.06 | $(14,069.67) | $ (36,370.01) |

Source: Annual Report.

of direct costs and that it would be confusing and arbitrary to try to allocate indirect costs. He also felt that since the town did not pay taxes, depreciation wasn't a necessary component of the budget.

Many water districts do not depreciate their capital plant and equipment for the following reasons: plants usually take a number of years to reach their full income potential although, from year one, their facilities must be adequate to serve the entire district; if depreciation were charged, the accumulating losses would have a disastrous effect on the sale of bonds; if rates were set high enough to allow for depreciation, they might not be affordable by users.

Details of the Municipal Services Department revenues and expenditures for 1978 are given in Exhibit 3. (The collection of solid waste was also a function of that department.) By comparison, total expenditures in 1970 were $22,500, of which $18,500 was for debt service.

Total revenues and expenditures for the town, as presented to the 1979 town meeting, are given in Exhibit 4.

**Exhibit 4**

TOWN OF WATERVILLE VALLEY
Income and Expenditures—1978

| | *1978 Estimated* | *1978 Actual* | *1979 Projected* |
|---|---|---|---|
| Revenues: | | | |
| State sources: | | | |
| Interest and dividends tax | $ 27,000.00 | $ 25,489.40 | $ 25,500.00 |
| Savings bank tax | 600.00 | 558.36 | 600.00 |
| Meals and rooms tax | 900.00 | 998.96 | 1,000.00 |
| Highway subsidy | 1,284.54 | 1,270.51 | 1,552.37 |
| Town road aid | 1,676.48 | | 2,111.49 |
| Forest Service lands reimbursement | 21,500.00 | 13,851.90 | 14,000.00 |
| Business profits tax | 350.00 | 372.52 | 400.00 |
| Sewage treatment grant | 55,274.00 | 55,274.00 | 54,062.00 |
| Antirecession funds | 00.00 | 224.00 | 00.00 |
| Local sources: | | | |
| Dog licenses | 60.00 | 90.30 | 100.00 |
| Motor vehicle permits | 6,500.00 | 7,250.50 | 7,250.00 |
| Permits and filing fees | 300.00 | 297.00 | 300.00 |
| Interest on taxes and deposits | 2,250.00 | 2,207.47 | 1,500.00 |
| Cemetery | 1,000.00 | 500.00 | 00.00 |
| Public Safety Department | 13,700.00 | 16,412.25 | 14,300.00 |
| Municipal Services Department | 180,000.00 | 199,470.11 | 215,000.00 |
| Highway Department | 00.00 | 1,010.62 | 00.00 |
| Recreation Department | 00.00 | 00.00 | 7,000.00 |
| Resident taxes | 1,200.00 | 1,540.00 | 1,500.00 |
| Timber yield taxes | 1,500.00 | 2,686.75 | 2,800.00 |
| Town Office | 25.00 | 24.92 | 25.00 |
| Revenue sharing | 3,000.00 | 3,811.00 | 4,500.00 |
| Short-term loans | 39,250.00 | 31,200.00 | 46,575.00 |
| Fire truck | 72,000.00 | 72,000.00 | 00.00 |
| Police cruiser sale | 800.00 | 00.00 | 00.00 |
| Proceeds—insurance claim | | 2,400.00 | |
| Total revenues | $430,170.02 | $438,940.57 | $400,075.86 |

**Exhibit 4 (concluded)**

| | 1978 Appropriation | 1978 Expenses | 1979 Requests |
|---|---|---|---|
| Expenditures: | | | |
| Town officers salaries | $ 4,075.00 | $ 4,147.52 | $ 3,400.00 |
| Town Office expense | 31,725.00 | 30,908.43 | 33,473.40 |
| Town Office—Public Safety Building maintenance | 5,900.00 | 6,543.34 | 6,650.00 |
| Property appraisal | 1,000.00 | 1,411.63 | 1,500.00 |
| Surveying and drafting | 4,500.00 | 3,720.00 | 2,000.00 |
| Osceola Library | 800.00 | 1,246.73 | 1,100.00 |
| Employees benefits | 11,241.97 | 9,680.09 | 15,226.64 |
| Public Safety Department | 97,516.30 | 103,161.36 | 114,006.12 |
| Municipal Services Department | 97,894.25 | 87,335.09 | 113,360.47 |
| Highway Department | 20,850.00 | 22,266.39 | 24,315.25 |
| Legal services | 5,944.65 | 4,303.61 | 5,000.00 |
| Planning and zoning | 500.00 | 4.00 | 1,200.00 |
| Advertising and regional | 4,275.00 | 4,275.00 | 2,025.00 |
| Hospitals and health | 887.25 | 877.25 | 873.25 |
| Conservation Commission | 800.00 | 800.00 | 1,000.00 |
| Municipal recreation | 2,000.00 | 3,691.86 | 20,250.00 |
| Post Office | 3,000.00 | 3,000.00 | 4,000.00 |
| Street lights | 1,200.00 | 1,230.94 | 1,570.00 |
| Cemetery | 600.00 | 00.00 | 250.00 |
| Insect control | 4,200.00 | 3,170.00 | 1,000.00 |
| Insurance | 19,000.00 | 20,998.00 | 25,000.00 |
| Capital equipment | 88,200.00 | 89,060.95 | 24,575.00 |
| Capital construction | 23,050.00 | 27,808.38 | 22,000.00 |
| Debt service | 228,072.61 | 232,488.07 | 246,136.07 |
| Contingency | 5,200.00 | | 6,000.00 |
| Total expenditures | $662,432.03 | $662,128.64 | $675,911.20 |
| Insurance proceeds—applied to principal | | 2,400.00 | |
| | | $664,528.64 | |

The total estimated revenues from all sources except property taxes deducted from total appropriations in the ensuing fiscal year gives estimated amount to be raised by property taxes.

## Current Issues

At the 1980 town meeting, the selectmen planned to present a proposal for additional water capacity. They would hire engineers to bore holes in a search for additional water. (A $17,000 survey in 1977 had found one additional well with an estimated flow of 80 to 100 gallons per minute. this well had not yet been developed.) The capacity of the system at that time was 400 gallons per minute.

Based on the findings of engineers, a plan for expansion of the water system would be submitted at a subsequent meeting. The cost of this plan would depend on the engineers' findings and on several alternatives for expansion. Each new well would cost from $30,000 to $40,000; and an additional storage facility would cost from $200,000 to $300,000. Engineers already had recommended some expansion of the 8-inch main distribution system, at a cost of roughly $200,000. In total, expansion of the system to accommodate the town's ultimate capacity might cost from $400,000 to $600,000, but this was a rough estimate because of the uncertainty of the exploration efforts and debate as to when ultimate capacity should be installed.

There was concern over the additional debt burden. Exhibit 5 shows the payments required by the bonds issued to date. It was customary to issue bonds with a 30-year maturity, with equal amount of principal payments each year and interest on the outstanding balance. The life of the bonds could be shorter than 30 years. The principal payment was not necessarily the same each year, although changing this practice might make the bonds less attractive.

The State of New Hampshire agreed to pay 40 percent of the debt service on the sewer bond issue of 1973. It was hoped that the State would similarly pay part of the cost of water expansion, but this was not certain.

Because of recent improvements in the water system, the town experienced a 12 percent reduction in insurance on private homes and a 10 percent reduction on commercial establishments. The State Insurance Commission indicated that additional water would likely result in another rate reduction.

One long-time resident of Waterville Valley, who considered himself a spokesman for the group who opposed further expansion of the system, expressed the concern that more water and another bond issue could not help but increase the tax rate beyond the promised $2 per thousand. He felt that the future residents, if there were to be any, should bear the entire cost of any improvements that they required. He stated the concerns of a number of retired residents, living on fixed incomes, who were alarmed at the present 5 percent yearly increase in their taxes. He felt that the past 12 years of development were already taking their toll on the community in terms of the impact on ecology, increased traffic, and the need for additional municipal services.

The president of The Waterville Company, who was also a selectman and a resident of the town, was convinced that the town was committed to expansion of its facilities to the limits imposed by its geography and should also be committed to expansion of its water supply. He felt that past records

**Exhibit 5**
Debt Payments (shown at five-year intervals)

| | *Water* | | *Sewer* | | |
|---|---|---|---|---|---|
| *Year* | *Principal* | *Interest* | *Principal* | *Interest* | *Total Payments* |
| 1970 | $10,000 | $ 8,504 | | | $ 18,505 |
| 1975 | 26,520 | 16,780 | $65,000 | $91,000 | 200,300 |
| 1980 | 26,520 | 9,433 | 65,000 | 75,010 | 175,963 |
| 1985 | 10,000 | 4,420 | 65,000 | 58,110 | 137,530 |
| 1990 | 10,000 | 1,820 | 60,000 | 42,120 | 113,940 |
| 1995 | | | 60,000 | 26,520 | 86,520 |
| 2000 | | | 60,000 | 10,920 | 70,920 |

Notes: Approximate amounts for the years not shown can be found by interpolation, except that in 1974 the total payments were $44,878. The final bond issue matures in 2003.

showed that municipal services could pay their own way from the revenues they generated. He believed that his company could work compatibly with the town. He acknowledged that his company benefited from the town's ability to borrow at favorable rates, but he also believed that the town had benefited from the company's expenditures for early water and sewer development and its help in underwriting the initial losses of the sewer system. He agreed that current residents should not have to shoulder all expenses for future improvements, and felt that through municipal borrowing, future residents would be sharing in the cost of improvements by helping to repay the debt.

## Questions

1. As a matter of general policy (but without attempting to arrive at specific numbers), how should the cost of an additional water system be divided between those who are now on the system, those who may subsequently become customers, and the general taxpayers (i.e., included in the tax rate)?
2. As a matter of general policy, how should the "tap charge" (i.e., the amount to amortize capital costs) and the "usage charge" be determined?
3. What is your estimate of the cost of the Municipal Service Department in 1978?
4. In calculating the cost that should be used in arriving at charges, should the capital cost be the amount of debt service (i.e., principal and interest) actually paid in the year, or is some other approach better?
5. Can you suggest tentative rates for each item on Exhibit 2 for a year in which expenditures are like those in 1978, with an additional capital charge of $500,000 financed by a 30-year bond issue?
6. Should meters be used to record usage by residential customers so that charges can be based on usage?

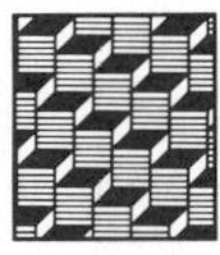

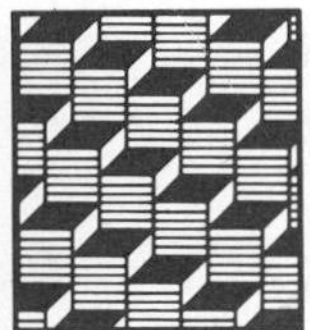

# part III

# Management Control Systems

As we indicated in Chapter 1, management control systems consist of both a structure and a process: structure is what the system *is,* and process is what it *does,* analogous to anatomy and physiology in the human body. Chapter 6 focuses on structure, and Chapters 7–13 describe the control process. Since process is a dynamic and complex set of activities, involving a wide variety of interactions among individuals in an organization, it requires more attention than does structure. Each step in the management control cycle—programming, budget formulation, measurement of output, and reporting on performance—is the subject of one chapter. Additionally, Chapter 10 looks at the question of control of operations—an aspect of the "measurement and operations" phase of the cycle. Finally, Chapter 13 is devoted to an aspect of the management control process that is particularly important for nonprofit organizations: evaluation. In a profit-oriented organization the amount of profit is a primary means of evaluation. This is not the case for nonprofit organizations.

# chapter 6

# The Control Structure

The structure of a management control system is sometimes given less consideration than it deserves. The control structure frequently is assumed to be identical to the organizational structure, and therefore no additional thinking needs to be done. Also structure can be a rather complex problem, involving several dimensions. This chapter addresses each of these concerns. We begin by defining structure, then move into a discussion of a program structure and the uses of program information. Finally we address the question of the account structure.

## DEFINITION OF STRUCTURE

As indicated in Chapter 1, the control structure consists, by and large, of a definition of the relationships between controllability and responsibility, or more precisely a specification of which managers are responsible for which resources in the organization. Although controllability may be difficult to pinpoint, it is a fact that someone in an organization has control over each resource-related decision. Sometimes this control is infrequent and has long-term implications, such as the acquisition of a fixed asset or the commitment to a long-term lease; sometimes, it is of shorter duration, such as the decision to sign a one-year supply contract; sometimes it is very short-run, such as the decision to ask employees to work overtime.

The key question which is asked in defining the control structure is "Who controls which resources?" The control structure then attempts to align each manager's responsibility with the resources over which he or she exerts reasonable, although not necessarily total, control. This is done through the mechanism of responsibility centers, which were discussed in Chapter 1.

It would be relatively easy to define the control structure if each program were a responsibility center and each program's resources were controllable in the same way. If, for example, (1) each program sold its services, (2) each program were staffed by personnel who worked in no other programs, and (3) each program manager had reasonable control over the hiring of program personnel, of other personnel decisions, and of all program-related supply purchase decisions, the design of the control structure would be quite easy—each program would be a profit center. These individual profit centers could then be grouped, according to the type of services they delivered, and each group would also be a profit center, headed by a higher level manager.

In most cases, however, entities are not organized in a fashion that lends itself to such tidy and well-defined control structures. Many organizations operate over large geographic areas, and must take this fact into consideration when defining their structures. Does a multihospital system, for example, have one director of alcoholic rehabilitation services with broad geographic responsibilities, or area directors who have responsibility for several programs in their area, including one on alcoholic rehabilitation? Does the director of the summer festival program for a symphony orchestra have control over either the number of personnel taking part in the festival or their salaries? Does the director of a master's degree program in a large university control the number of applications received, the tuition charged, or the salaries of the faculty who work in the program? Moreover, while performers in the orchestra or faculty in the university may take part in a particular program, their reporting relationships within the organization generally are not to the director of one program only.

In short, the process of aligning responsibility with controllability and developing a control structure within an organization's broader organizational structure is by no means a simple endeavor. For this reason, the selection of a program structure is one of the most critical tasks facing senior-level managers of nonprofit organizations.

## THE PROGRAM STRUCTURE

Every organization exists to carry out programs. Not every organization needs a separate program account structure, however. If a single responsibility center is responsible for a given program, then the responsibility account structure will provide the information needed for program purposes. A separate program structure is needed only when the responsibility for the execution of programs involves more than one responsibility center. A municipality that is organized so that each responsibility center performs a defined type of service (public safety, maintenance of highways, education, etc.) does not need a separate program structure; a federal government agency that executes many separate programs through its several regional offices does. So does a research organization that draws on the resources of several departments to carry out its research projects.

## Difficulty of Designing Program Structures

The closer the match of the responsibility structure to the program structure, the easier the implementation of a good management control system. When the match is reasonably close, the person who heads a responsibility center can be held accountable for a defined program or some part thereof.

> ***Example:*** When the U.S. Navy shifted to a responsibility accounting system, it changed its organizational responsibility so that it more nearly matched programs. Previously, the Chief of Naval Operations had little authority over the budgets and financial management of the fleets for which he was responsible; the principal authority was vested in bureaus and other staff agencies that were not under his direct control. Under the new system, the Chief of Naval Operations was given this authority. This led to better decision making because the new system permitted the Chief of Naval Operations to decide on resource allocations which were necessary to implement his judgments on fleet activities.

## Criteria for Selecting Programs

In a large organization, the program structure consists of several "layers." At the top are a relatively few major programs; at the bottom are a great many *program elements;* these are the smallest units in which information is collected in program terms. In between are summaries of related program elements, which are here called *program categories.* In a simple system, there may be no need for program categories; program elements are aggregated directly into programs. In a complex organization, by contrast, there may be several levels of program categories.

If the primary purpose of the classification of programs is to facilitate top-management judgment on the allocation of resources, the program structure should correspond to the principal objectives of the organization. It should be arranged so as to facilitate making decisions having to do with the relative importance of these objectives. Stated another way, it should focus on the organization's outputs—what it achieves or intends to achieve—rather than on its inputs—what types of resources it uses, or on the *sources of its funds.* A structure that is arranged by types of resources (e.g., personnel, material, services) or by sources of support (e.g., in a university, support sources can be tuition, legislative appropriations, and gifts) is not a program structure.

The optimum number of programs in an organization is approximately 10. The rationale for this number is that top management cannot weigh the relative importance of a large number of disparate items, and the programs should be limited to the number that management can so weigh. There are many exceptions to this generalization, however. The number of program categories varies widely in different situations.

The designation of major programs helps to communicate the objectives of the organization. The development of the management control structure may also clarify organizational purpose, and thus suggest improvements in the structure of the organization. Therefore, the program structure should not necessarily correspond to the *existing* categories on which decisions are based; rather, it should correspond to those categories which can reasonably be expected to be useful for decision making in the future.

The criterion that programs should be related to decision making is, of course, a general one. The following questions may suggest ways of making it more specific:

1. Is the structure output-oriented? Specifically, does it focus on what the agency does and/or the target groups that it exists to serve?
2. Does the structure permit management to decide to enlarge or decrease a program? Are the programs for which this can be done the programs that management actually wants to think about enlarging or decreasing?
3. Within a program, are there opportunities for trade-offs, that is, for different ways of achieving the objectives? Benefit/cost analysis, for example, is often feasible within a program but rarely between programs.
4. Can management actually influence the scope and nature of the activities that are conducted for a designated program?
5. Is there an identifiable outside pressure group interested in a part of the organization's activities? If so, is there a program category that corresponds to the interests of this group?
6. When there are criticisms that not enough effort, or too much effort, is being devoted to a certain activity, can information on the validity of these criticisms be obtained from the program structure?
7. Does the structure identify all important activities so that none are hidden from management's view? (For example, in a research organization if there is not a separate program for basic research, the pressures to devote resources to more attractive development projects will be strong and basic research may be slighted.)
8. Does the structure require a relatively small amount of cost allocation? If a large fraction of the program cost is an allocated cost, the structure is suspect.
9. Is the structure of some help to operating managers? As a minimum, it should never impede the work of operating managers.
10. Can program elements be associated with a *quantitative* measure of performance? (At the broad level of programs, however, no reliable measure of performance can be found in many situations.)

***Relation to Responsibility.*** Although there are advantages in relating program categories to organizational responsibility, this criterion is less important than that of facilitating top-management judgment. Sometimes the systems designer tries to change the organization so that it fits the program structure. In general, this should not be done. The system exists to serve the organization, not vice versa. Changes in organizational responsibility should be made if, but only if, such changes help the organization improve its performance. Sometimes the system designer does uncover a situation that would be improved by a reorganization. If the system designer can convince management, fine; otherwise, the system should be designed to fit the organization as it exists.

***Program Managers.*** Although the program structure need not match the organization structure, there should be some person who has identifiable responsibility for each program category and program element. This results in the *matrix type of organization*, the matrix consisting of program managers in one dimension and functionally organized responsibility centers in the other dimension. Program managers may have other responsibilities, and they may call on other parts of the organization for much of the work that is to be done on their program. The program managers are advocates of their programs and are held accountable for the performance of their programs. In some agencies, although there are managers for program categories, there is no overall manager for the program. This is the case in the Department of Defense, for example; no one is the manager of strategic forces, but there is a manager for the Army category, the Navy category, and the Air Force category. (In the Soviet Union, by contrast, there is a single manager for strategic forces.)

## Types of Programs

***Direct and Support Programs.*** Programs and program elements can be classified as either *(a)* direct or *(b)* support. (The terms "independent" and "dependent" are also used.) *Direct programs* are those directly related to the organization's objectives (in a college, these would be the instruction and research programs). *Support programs* are those that service more than one other program (in a college, the maintenance of grounds is an example). In making decisions about the allocation of resources, management attention will be focused primarily on the direct programs. Within limits, the amount of resources required for the support programs is roughly dependent on the size and character of the direct programs. This does not mean that no attention should be given to support programs, for there is often considerable room for innovation and increased efficiency within support programs.

***Administration.*** Ordinarily, there should be a program for administration. This support program might well include certain miscellaneous program elements which, although not strictly administrative in character, do not belong logically in other programs and are not important enough to set up as separate program categories. Alternatively, these miscellaneous program elements might be grouped in a separate program category.

The rationale for a separate program for administration is that top management usually wants to give special attention to administrative activities. As a general rule, as large a fraction as possible of the total resources of the organization should be devoted to direct programs and as small a fraction as possible to administration. In the absence of special attention, administrative activities tend to grow along the lines laid down in Parkinson's first law.

***Fund Raising.*** In organizations that obtain financial resources from contributors, there should be a separate program element for the costs associated with fund raising. Contributors and others are interested in how much of the amounts donated was used for the direct programs of the activity and how much was spent in raising the funds. This element corresponds closely to the marketing programs in a business company. There are practical difficulties in drawing an exact line between fund raising costs and direct program costs, however.

*Example:* Major contributors to a symphony orchestra or other arts organization may be given special preferences, such as use of a patrons' lounge. Although conceptually these are fund-raising costs, the amounts are rarely segregated as such.

*Example:* The American Cancer Society conducts advertising campaigns that are in part aimed at early detection of cancer, which is a direct program, and in part aimed at fund raising. It may not be feasible to divide the advertising costs between these two purposes.

***Transfer Payments.*** Some organizations, primarily governments and philanthropic foundations, carry out some or all of their programs by making grants to other organizations who actually perform the programmed activities. These transfer payments should be reported separately from the expenses actually incurred in operating the organization. They are, nevertheless, a part of the program costs.

## Conflict among Program Structures

The development of a sound program structure is an important task. Once it has been implemented, changes in the structure are difficult to make, so much effort is warranted in deciding at the outset on what the most useful structure is. This task can be frustrating, however, because two or more alternative structures may have almost equal merit, and each may have strong advocates in the organization. In these circumstances, it may not be possible to satisfy the needs of each group, although it may be possible to mitigate the differences by structuring major programs according to one concept, program categories according to an alternative concept, and using program elements or the responsibility structure for other alternatives:

*Example:* In designing the program structure for a state division of special education, several possibilities were considered. One was by type of disability or target group (e.g., visually handicapped, deaf, speech handicap, emotionally disturbed, mentally disturbed). Another was by geographic region within the state. Another was by objectives (e.g., improvement of curriculum, improvement of teacher training, improvement of foster homes, improvement of medical services). The solution decided upon was to use a target group as the basis for programs and to have categories for objectives within each of these programs. Information on regions could be obtained either by program elements or by responsibility centers, depending on whether there were identifiable organization units in each geographic region.[1]

## Program Elements

A program element represents some definable activity or related group of activities that the organization carries on, either directly in order to accomplish the organization's objective or indirectly in support of other program elements. As indicated above, program elements generally are aggregated into programs; in some instances they are grouped into program categories, which are then aggregated into programs.

If feasible, a program element should be the responsibility of a single manager. In any event, it is essential that program elements be related to the responsibility of a relatively small number of persons, and that the respective sphere of responsibility of each be specified. Items for which responsibility is widely diffused, such as "long-distance telephone calls," are not satisfactory program elements. Such items should appear not as program elements but as functional categories or expense elements in the responsibility structure. Management decisions about program elements cannot be enforced unless they are related to personal responsibility. A congruence of individual responsibility and program elements also leads to an increased sense of personal identification with programs which should result in a greater degree of commitment on the part of responsibility center managers. Management of an organization is difficult when the program structure is at "right angles" with the responsibility structure. The existence of such a situation is a symptom either that the program structure is incorrect or that the organization structure needs to be changed.

Exhibit 6–1 shows a program structure which, at least in elementary

---

[1] From Division of Special Education (A), a case distributed by Intercollegiate Case Clearing House, ICH 14C4.

**Exhibit 6–1**
A Dubious Program Structure

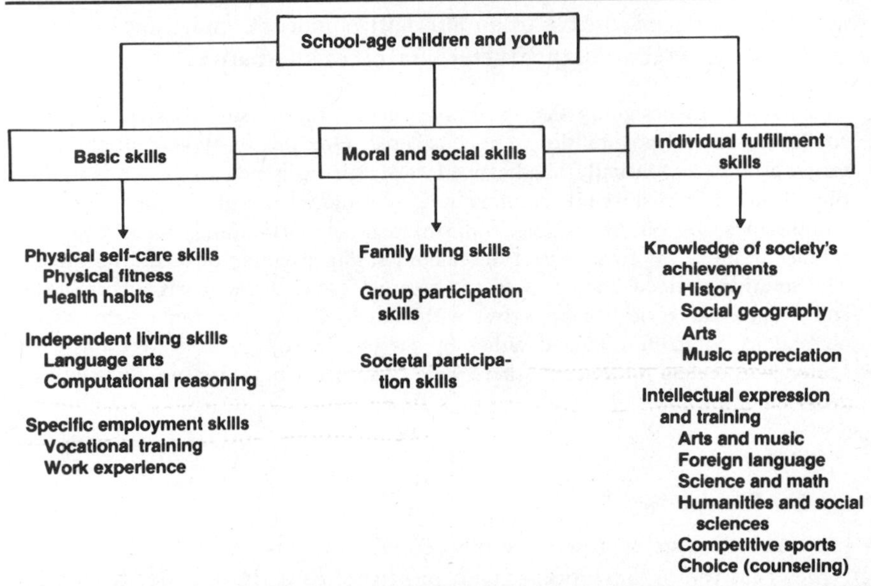


Source: Presented in Selma J. Mushkin and James R. Cleveland, *Planning for Educational Development in a Planning, Programming, and Budgeting System* (Washington, D.C.: National Education Association, 1968).

schools, probably does not correspond at all to the organization structure and therefore is of doubtful utility. Teachers may spend identifiable amounts of time on the subjects listed in the first and the third columns, but the activities listed in the middle column are unlikely to be planned separately or to be identifiable with significant amounts of resources.

As is the case with programs, program elements can be classified as either direct or support. There can be direct program elements within support programs; these are direct with respect to the program, even though the program is itself a support program with respect to the organization as a whole. In many programs, there also will be a separate program element for administration. It includes administrative activities associated with the program (as contrasted with the administration of the organization as a whole), and it may also include miscellaneous "catchall" activities. Catchall program elements can be used to eliminate the necessity of allocating costs.

***Program Element Classification.*** In large organizations, each major program typically is the sum of its program categories, and each program category is the sum of its program elements. If an element relates to more than one program category, there should be a separately numbered program element for each relevant program category. An example of a program structure is given in the Appendix.

## USES OF PROGRAM INFORMATION

Information from the program structure is used for one or more of the following purposes: (1) to facilitate decision making about programs, (2) to provide a basis of comparison of the costs and outputs of similar programs, or (3) to collect financial information for reporting purposes, as a basis for setting prices, or for reimbursement of costs. The program structure should be designed to meet these needs.

The information needed for one of these three purposes may differ from that needed by others. In that case, compromises in designing the structure may be required. In most situations, one of these purposes is clearly dominant, however, and the structure can be designed primarily to provide information needed for that purpose. In government organizations, the use of information as a basis for making decisions on programs tends to be by far the dominant purpose; whereas in many client-oriented organizations, pricing considerations tend to be dominant. If information is to be collected in a way that makes it comparable with information in other organizations, and if such a structure is inconsistent with the best structure for decision making or pricing purposes, then comparable data can be collected by other devices, such as a cost accounting system.

### Program Structures for Decision Making

Devising a program structure for decision-making is a problem in organizations in which programs cut across lines of responsibility. This problem first became serious in the 1960s when, following the lead of the Department of Defense, many organizations attempted to set up formal program structures.

In the Department of Defense, the need for a program structure was obvious. The lines of organizational responsibility ran to the Secretary of the Army, the Secretary of the Navy, and the Secretary of the Air Force; whereas defense programs cut across these lines. For example, the Department of Defense had a strategic program which was essentially related to a possible nuclear exchange with the Soviets, but part of this strategic mission was the responsibility of the Army (antiballistic missiles), part was the responsibility of the Navy (Polaris submarines), and part was the responsibility of the Air Force (strategic missiles and bombers). A mechanism that facilitated decision making about the strategic mission as a whole was necessary. The Defense Program Structure, in which Program 1 was Strategic Forces, provided such a mechanism.

When other organizations attempted to set up a program structure, however, they found that the selection of the right structure was a difficult task. In fact, several efforts to establish programming systems failed because the program structure was not arranged in a way that facilitated management decision making. Consequently, managers did not find the new information useful and paid no attention to it.

In other organizations the program structure consisted simply of new labels for existing account structures. This was particularly the case when the responsibility structures already provided an adequate basis for decision making. The effort was simply window dressing.

## Program Structures for Comparisons

If the same program structure is to be used by a number of similar organizations (e.g., schools, colleges, hospitals), then great care needs to be taken to assure that the structure will provide comparable data so that averages and other measures can be compiled and individual organizations can compare their own data with these averages. In such a structure, compromises are necessary because all of the participating organizations will not view their programs in the same way. As a general rule, the program structure that is used for comparisons should be quite broad, specifying only the data that actually will be used for this purpose. Each participating organization can then modify this structure (usually by subdividing program elements) so as to collect the more detailed information that is needed by its own management.

Although the primary criterion in designing a program structure may be its usefulness in decision making, if alternative structures are deemed to be of approximately equal usefulness in decision making, then the structure that is most likely to provide good data for comparisons with other organizations should be selected. For example, all municipalities must report spending under the revenue sharing program according to prescribed categories. Widespread use is made of these categories, and they therefore should be considered as the basis for a municipality's program structure. The categories are the following:

1. Public safety.
2. Environmental protection.
3. Public transportation.
4. Health.
5. Recreation.
6. Libraries.
7. Social services for aged or poor.
8. Financial administration.
9. Multipurpose and general government.
10. Education.
11. Social development.
12. Housing and community development.
13. Economic development.
14. Other.

Unfortunately, however, only a few structures that provide comparable data of even approximate validity currently exist. Good structures exist for hospitals, for colleges and universities, for social service organizations, and for certain municipal services. In some states there are good systems for primary and secondary education, higher education, municipal activities, and certain other functions. Some religious organizations have systems for their local units, and so do other membership organizations such as college fraternities, professional associations, chambers of commerce, and civic organizations. References of publications that describe structures for some of these organizations are given in the list of Suggested Readings for Chapter 3.

If the structure that has been developed for purposes of comparison does not fit into the program structure that is useful for decision making, then a separate cost accounting system is usually required to develop the comparative data.

## Program Structures to Collect Financial Information

If an organization receives funds whose use is restricted to a specified purpose, then the accounting system must be set up in such a way that the amounts spent for this purpose are separately identified. Such a separation is made in the program structure. Mechanically, many nonprofit organizations control the use of these resources by the device called "fund accounting."

Fund accounting is not used in a profit-oriented organization. In business accounting, all the available resources are, in effect, in one "pot"; that is, the balance sheet lists the assets for the whole entity. In a nonprofit organization, by contrast, the resources may be accounted for in several separate pots, each of which is called a fund. As described in Chapter 3, each fund has its own set of accounts, they are self-balancing, and each fund is therefore a separate entity, almost as if it were a separate business. The purpose of this device is to ensure that the organization uses the resources made available to each fund only for the purposes designated for that fund.

Some years ago, this segregation by funds was carried to extremes. It is said, for example, that the Post Office had one fund for first-class postage, another for third-class postage, another for money orders, and so on, and that each post office had to maintain a separate bank account for each fund. In recent years, there has been general recognition of the fact that the necessary control over spending can be obtained without an elaborate fund mechanism, and the number of separate funds has been greatly reduced. In general, those funds that remain do serve a useful purpose, although in many cases it is quite possible that the same objective could be accomplished without the fund mechanism.

***Relation between Funds and Programs.*** When accounts are set up for restricted funds, care must be taken to ensure that they do not obscure the amount spent for programs. For example, all states collect a gasoline tax which is used for maintenance of highways. In some states the amount of this tax is adequate to provide for all maintenance expenses; in other states, part of the amount needed comes from general tax revenues. In the latter states, highway maintenance costs will be recorded in two separate funds. The system should be designed so that these separate amounts can be aggregated to show the total cost of the highway maintenance program.

## THE ACCOUNT STRUCTURE

### Nature of an Account

In accounting, the device used for classifying information is called an account. The number and types of accounts determine the character of the information that is available from the system. Thus, if an organization needs an accounting record of the amount of cash it has in total, it uses a single account, "Cash"; whereas if it needs a record of the amount of cash in each of two different banks, it sets up one account for "Cash Bank A" and another for "Cash Bank B." Accounts are the smallest units of information. The amounts recorded in each account can be summarized in various ways by combining them with other accounts, but the system cannot provide information in more detail than that contained in the most detailed account. For example, if a company has accounts for Cash Bank A and Cash Bank B, it can obtain a summary of the total amount of cash simply by adding the amounts in these two accounts, but if another company has a single account for Cash, it cannot obtain from its accounts information about the cash in Bank A and the cash in Bank B. Thus, the selection of the proper account structure is important.

In this description, we shall use the word "account" in a somewhat broader sense than it is used in accounting. An accounting system is generally restricted to *(a)* historical information and *(b)* monetary information; whereas we are interested also in *(c)* estimates of future amounts and *(d)* nonmonetary information.

### Information Needs

A total system provides information for many purposes. By far the largest quantity of information is associated with certain necessary operating activities, such as the preparation of payrolls, keeping track of inventory, and paying bills. These activities are not part of the management control system as such, however, so we are not directly concerned with them here.

In designing a management control system, the needs of the following parties must be considered:

1. *Senior managers and governing bodies* who need information as a basis for making policy decisions, particularly decisions regarding the balance among programs and the relation of programs to objectives. These parties also need information on how the organization is performing.
2. *Planners and analysts* who need information that will assist in estimating the benefits and costs of proposed programs.
3. *Operating managers* who need information classified by responsibility centers because control is exercised through responsibility centers.
4. *Resource providers,* including contributors, legislative bodies, grantors, members, taxpayers, third-party payors, oversight bodies, and regulatory

agencies acting in their behalf, who need and are entitled to information about what the organization did with the resources provided to it. The needs of some resource providers can be met by general-purpose financial reports which were discussed in Chapter 3. Other resource providers, particularly legislatures and grantors, require reports prepared according to their specifications, and the system must be designed to meet these requirements, whether or not the organization finds such information useful for its own purposes.

### Conflicts among Needs

The needs of these parties may conflict with one another, and the system must strike a balance among the conflicting needs. The system must also represent a balance between the users' needs for information and the cost of collecting and processing the information.

The two principal parts of the account structure are the program structure and the responsibility structure. The former is designed principally to meet the needs of planners and analysts, and the latter to meet the needs of operating managers. The program structure emphasizes the full costs of carrying out programs, while the responsibility structure emphasizes the controllable costs of operating responsibility centers. Top management is interested in summaries drawn from both structures.

It follows that in designing a program structure, the needs of the planners should be given more weight than the needs of the operating managers. For example, a program structure may cut across lines of responsibility, even though such a structure is not as useful to operating managers as one that is consistent with lines of responsibility. Nevertheless, the system should reconcile both types of needs to the extent that this is feasible. Some information needed by planners that is inconsistent with that needed by operating managers (e.g., cost estimates that include prorated costs) may possibly be obtained outside the formal account structure.

In designing a responsibility structure, the needs of operating managers are paramount. Such a structure must be consistent with lines of responsibility, and this principle cannot be compromised to meet the needs of the planners.

In order to ensure that these conflicts are resolved in the most equitable way, the system design team should not be dominated by people who represent the point of view of either the planners or the operating managers. Ideally, systems designers should be independent of both types of users and should weigh equally the arguments of each, but the optimum balance is difficult to achieve in practice.

### Accounts for Management and Planning

In summary, most organizations need accounts for both responsibility centers and programs. Within these accounts there also should be accounts for functions and expense elements.

***Functional Categories.*** In order to facilitate the collection of data on the cost of performing functions that are common to several responsibility centers, a set of functional accounts may be prescribed within the responsibility centers. One of these accounts should be designated as a *mission* account, in which the costs of performing the mission are collected. For example, in the various regional and local offices of a job training program, there may be one functional category for the job training mission and others for public relations, training of agency personnel, building operation and maintenance, and administration.

***Expense Elements.*** In order to facilitate analysis, and under certain circumstances to control spending for discretionary elements of expense, several expense elements are set up for each responsibility center that spends a significant amount for the specified element. These elements are called *object classes* in some organizations. An example is given in the Appendix.

## Other Types of Accounts

In the preceding sections the emphasis has been on classifying costs and expenses. Similar considerations govern the classification of revenues. The complete accounting system includes, in addition, accounts for assets and liabilities, although these are not usually as important in the management control process as are the revenue and expense accounts. It also includes detailed operating accounts to keep track of such things as payroll and related taxes and withholdings. Two additional types of accounts that are necessary in some organizations are cost accounts and accounts for outside agencies.

***Cost Accounts.*** Every organization needs information about the cost of performing various functions or carrying on various activities. The process of cost accounting was discussed in Chapter 4. To the extent that the cost accounting functions or activities are set up as program elements, or to the extent they are represented by functional categories in the responsibility structure, this information can be obtained directly from the accounts described above. In some situations, however, such information is too detailed to be of interest to management, other than the manager of the responsibility center directly involved, and hence it is not worthwhile to clutter up the main structure (i.e., the program and responsibility accounts) with this detail. In these situations, the information can be collected through a cost accounting system. For example, the highway departments of municipal governments use a great deal of detailed information on the cost of constructing, repairing, resurfacing, and maintaining roads of various types. They collect this information in a cost system.

The mechanism that accountants use to relate a specialized set of accounts to the general account structure is called a "control account—subsidiary account" relationship. In the general accounts, one account is designated as the control account, and procedures are set up so that the total of all detailed items charged to the subsidiary accounts equals the total charged to the control account. A system in which such a relationship does *not* exist is called a "statistical cost system."[2] Such a system is of dubious utility because there is no way of verifying the validity of the charges made to the cost accounts. In particular, there is a temptation to "forget" to record costs if to do so would make the amount seem unduly high. In a tied-in system such lapses of memory are not possible because of the basic rule of accounting that debits must equal credits; that is, if a cost in incurred, it must appear in some cost account or the books will not balance.

Usually, statistical cost systems exist because those involved believe that the work entailed in installing a tied-in system is not worthwhile. In most cases, however, the incremental work of tieing a specialized cost system to the general system is less than imagined.

***Accounts for Outside Agencies.*** The accounts described above are those that management needs to plan and control the activities of the organization. Many organizations also must provide information to outside parties. Agencies of the federal government, for example, must report to the Congress and to the public. The U.S. Department of Education, which makes grants to public schools, is naturally interested in knowing what the schools do with those funds, and it consequently requires reports on how they were used. State agencies are interested in information about the hospitals that they regulate.

As a general proposition, it seems clear that no outside agency needs more information than that which local management needs for its own purposes; indeed, the outside agency should need much *less* information than internal management needs. Furthermore, the nature of the information that should interest an outside agency corresponds to the information that management finds useful for its own purposes. Rationally, therefore, information furnished to outside agencies should be a summary of the information collected for internal use.

Unfortunately, the real world is not this rational. A great many organizations must collect and report information which they consider useless, simply because an outside party requires it. When the outside party can enforce its request—because it provides funds, licenses the organization, or for similar reasons—the organization has no choice but to furnish the information. It can do so in one of two ways.

The safe, but expensive, way is to create a special account structure to collect the required information. This is the way that federal government agencies solve the problem of furnishing information to the Congress accord-

[2] The word "statistical" may suggest a sample, as contrasted with a complete set of costs. As used here, however, a statistical system means simply a system that is not tied in. It is not a sample.

ing to an "appropriation structure" that the agency does not need for its own purposes. In addition to being expensive, such a solution has the great disadvantage of requiring the maintenance of two sets of accounts to collect information about essentially the same phenomena. At a minimum, this can cause confusion within the organization since managers may be uncertain as to which type of information should be used for decision making. A more serious possibility is that operating managers may pay too much attention to the outsider's structure and give inadequate attention to the structure which actually best fits the needs of management.

An alternative to creating a special set of accounts, which is used by some organizations, is to prepare reports for outside agencies without relying on accounting information. A skilled and imaginative accountant can construct a plausible list of costs classified in any way that an outside agency specifies. Such a report does not, of course, reveal what the actual spending has been, except by coincidence, but it often satisfies the outside agency. This method is used when the requests from the outside agency seem obviously worthless, particularly when they require an undue amount of detail.

*Examples:* 1. The U.S. Department of Education requires that each school system which receives grants submit an elaborate cost report. Few, if any, school systems have an account structure that collects the information in the fashion required by this report; the report is therefore made out by an accountant who estimates what the costs probably were.

2. The reports required of hospitals by some states for rate-making purposes are archaic and require information of no conceivable use to management; the reports, while using accurate cost information, structure the information in such a way as to maximize a hospital's reimbursement from third-party insurers. Such reports are unreliable for any other purpose.

## Number of Accounts

The fact that several categories of accounts are listed above may give the impression that the control structure in a nonprofit organization is unduly complicated. Actually, the complications are not as great as they may appear. The effort required to record information in a system is not primarily a function of the number of accounts that the system contains; rather, it is a function of the number of transactions that must be recorded. The unit of recording is the individual transaction: the salary cost of one employee, the issuance of the material on one requisition, and so on. It makes little difference whether an individual transaction is recorded in 1 out of 100 accounts or in 1 out of 10,000 accounts; it must in any event be recorded in one account. With the advent of computers, the mechanical task of classifying transactions becomes relatively unimportant. Control systems may indeed be unnecessarily complex, but the complexity is likely to arise for reasons other than the sheer number of accounts.

## The Need for Articulation

All the accounts described above should make up a single, coordinated system. Technically, such a system is called an *articulated* system; each account is related to other accounts. The difficulties that arise when a cost system is not tied to the basic accounts have been mentioned above. Even more serious problems arise if the program accounts are not tied with the responsibility accounts and if the historical costs in each set of accounts are not related to the budgeted costs.

In some systems, a good program structure is used for planning purposes, but after the program has been completed and approved, it is not rearranged according to the responsibility centers that must execute the program. Instead, a separate budget is prepared for responsibility centers, often without relationship to the program budget. Actual spending is recorded by responsibility centers but not by programs. Some systems even do not collect actual costs according to the same structure in which the responsibility center budgets are stated.

There are two serious defects in such systems. First, since the system does not collect historical costs by programs, it denies the program planners information that is important as a basis for estimating the future costs of programs. Second, management has no adequate way of ascertaining whether its program decisions are actually being implemented. If top management decides that $1 million should be spent on a certain program, it needs to know whether the organization is in fact carrying out this program at the level of effort that $1 million represents. It cannot find this out unless the records classify actual spending in terms of programs.

One may ask why a system with these defects is permitted to exist. The explanation is that the idea of a program structure is relatively new in nonprofit organizations. Many organizations have not yet had the time to make the changes that are necessary to permit the recording of historical costs by program elements. Such changes are complicated and time-consuming and involve the training of a great many people, both accountants and managers. In the Department of Defense, for example, a formal program structure was used for planning purposes beginning in 1962, but the conversion of the accounting system to one which collected costs by program categories did not take place until 1968, six years later.

Although the program structure of the Canadian government is an excellent structure, for several years, the accounts were not articulated with that structure. Consequently, according to a 1976 report of the Auditor General of Canada:

> The state of financial management and control sytems of departments and agencies of the Government of Canada is significantly below acceptable standards of quality and effectiveness. . . . Departmental budgetary control and reporting systems lack:
> —Properly defined cost components and cost information so managers can be held accountable for performance.

—Detailed budgets by time period in accordance with the assignment of managerial responsibility.
—Consistency between budgeting and accounting.
—Timely periodic financial reports.
—Analysis of variances between planned and actual results.[3]

# APPENDIX

# A PROGRAM AND EXPENSE ELEMENT STRUCTURE

United Way of America has published a 319-page manual for use by the organizations whose activities it supports.[4] This appendix gives an abridged version of the program structure and the expense elements in this manual.

## PROGRAM STRUCTURE

### Goals

The structure has eight "goals" (corresponding to "programs" as the term is used in the text).

1. Optimal income security and economic opportunity.
2. Optimal health.
3. Optimal provision of basic material needs.
4. Optimal opportunity for the acquisition of knowledge and skills.
5. Optimal environmental quality.
6. Optimal individual and collective safety.
7. Optimal social functioning.
8. Optimal assurance of the support and effectiveness of services through organized action.

### Programs and Program Categories

The Manual lists and carefully defines 587 programs, corresponding to "program elements" as used in the text. These are grouped into 231 "services," which in turn are grouped into 33 "service systems"; these correspond to "program subcategories" and "program categories" as used in the text. In addition, the numbering system provides for additional programs, as desired by the individual agency.

[3] Quoted in R. J. Lord, "Canada Needs a Comptroller General," *The Business Quarterly,* 1977, p. 79.

[4] United Way of America, *UWASIS II: A Taxonomy of Social Goals & Human Service Programs* (Alexandria Va.: United Way of America, 1976). Used by permission.

The programs are classified as either (1) substantive or direct, or (2) supportive or indirect. The supportive programs are:

Comprehensive Planning and Development
Policy Planning
Research and Information Dissemination
Programs Development
Programs Evaluation
Programs Coordination
Consultation and Technical Assistance
Standards Setting, Accreditation and Monitoring
Public Education and Awareness
Personal Development and Training
Equal Access and Opportunity
Material Resources Provision
Ombudsman
Advocacy

As an example, a partial list of service systems, services, and programs for Goal 4, "Optimal opportunity for the acquisition of knowledge and skills," is given below:

- 100. Formal Educational Services System
  - 101. Pre-Elementary School Service
  - 102. Elementary and Secondary School Service
    - 01. Kindergarten
    - 02. Primary or Elementary School Education
    - 03. Secondary or High School Education
    - 04. Vocational and/or Trade High School
  - 103. Post-Secondary School Education Service
  - 104. Special Education Service for Exceptional Persons
- 200. Informal and Supplementary Educational Services System
- 300. Supportive Services System for the Acquisition of Knowledge and Skills
  - 301. Comprehensive Planning and Development Service
  - 302. Education Policy Determination Service
  - 303. Education Research and Information Service
  - 304. Educational Programs and Curriculum Development Service
  - 305. Educational Program Evaluation Service
  - 306. Education Program Coordination Service
  - 307. Education Program Consultation and Technical Assistance Service.

## EXPENSE ELEMENTS

Following is a partial list of the expense elements recommended by the United Way:

**Employee Compensation & related expenses**

Salaries
Employee health & retirement benefits
Payroll taxes, etc.

**Other expenses**

Professional fees
Supplies
Telephone
Postage and shipping
Occupancy
Rental and maintenance of equipment
Printing and publications
Travel
Conferences, conventions, meetings
Specific assistance to individuals
Membership dues
Awards and grants
Depreciation or amortization
Miscellaneous

## SUGGESTED ADDITIONAL READINGS

Abell, D. F. *Defining the Business: The Starting Point of Strategic Planning,* Englewood Cliffs, N.J.: Prentice Hall (1980), Chapter 10.

Davis, S. M., and P. L. Lawrence. *Matrix,* Reading, MA: Addison-Wesley Publishing Company (1977).

McLeod, R. K. "Program Budgeting Works in Nonprofit Organizations," *Harvard Business Review,* September–October 1971.

Also see the readings listed at the end of Chapter 3.

## Case 6–1

# POST OFFICE DEPARTMENT*

"The Mail Must Go Through." This had been the simple and traditional cry of the Post Office since 1789, the date of its establishment by Congress. The slogan was more likely to convey a picture of a pony express rider fighting off Indians or robbers than a system of people and equipment capable of carrying 72 billion pieces (12 billion pounds) of mail in 1965. In 1965 the Post Office was authorized and instructed by Congress to conduct 23 services for the public and the government. A complete list of these services, with the revenue and expense allocated to each service for fiscal year 1965, is attached as Exhibit 1.

**Exhibit 1**

POST OFFICE DEPARTMENT
*Apportioned Revenues and Expenses, Fiscal Year 1965*
($ millions)

| *Postal Services* | *Apportioned Revenue* | *Apportioned Costs* | *Public Service Loss* | *Revenue (under) over Costs* |
|---|---|---|---|---|
| First class | $2,193 | $1,965 | — | $ 228 |
| Domestic airmail | | | | |
| Letters and cards | 168 | 153 | | 15 |
| Parcel post | 75 | 45 | | 30 |
| Second class | 134 | 524 | $165 | (225) |
| Third class | 650 | 999 | 87 | (262) |
| Fourth class | 701 | 846 | 64 | (81) |
| International mail | | | | |
| Surface | 64 | 85 | — | (21) |
| Airmail | 76 | 62 | — | 14 |
| Air parcel post | 12 | 11 | — | 1 |
| Penalty | 117 | 97 | — | 20 |
| Franked | 7 | 7 | — | — |
| Free, for the blind | — | 3 | 3 | — |
| Registry | 33 | 47 | 14 | — |
| Certified | 11 | 15 | 4 | — |
| Insurance | 29 | 35 | 6 | — |
| Collect on delivery | 13 | 26 | 13 | — |
| Special delivery | 34 | 59 | 25 | — |
| Stamped envelopes | 15 | 20 | 5 | — |
| Money order | 59 | 72 | 13 | — |
| Postal savings | 3 | 3 | — | — |
| Box rents | 34 | 30 | (4) | — |
| Nonpostal services | 45 | 66 | 21 | — |
| Unassignable | 8 | 8 | — | — |
| Public service costs | — | 99 | 99 | — |
| Grand totals | $4,481 | $5,277 | $515 | $(281) |

Source: Cost Ascertainment Report, FY 1965.

* This case was prepared by Richard F. Vancil, Harvard Business School.

First, second, third, and fourth class mail were the most important postal services, representing 82 percent of both total revenue and total costs. First class mail alone accounted for 50 percent of total revenue and 37 percent of total cost. These four services were defined by Congress as follows:

First class mail—Written communications (including typewritten) in the form of envelopes, flats, or rolls.

Second class mail—Newspapers, magazines, or other periodicals approved by the Post Office as time-valued material.

Third class mail—Advertising, circulars, packages less than one pound and other material not included under first, second, or fourth class mail.

Fourth class mail—Parcel post and books, packages over one pound.

Congress alone sets rates for first, second, and third class mail. In the Postal Policy Act of 1958, however, Congress had left the rate setting authority for parcel post and other special services with the Postmaster General, who traditionally exercised this responsibility. The act also provided that a portion of the losses incurred by the Post Office in processing certain categories of second, third, and fourth class mail and all special services were in the public interest and automatically approved by Congress as "Public Service Losses." The magnitude and distribution of "Public Service Losses" is shown in Exhibit 1. After deducting these losses the Post Office incurred a deficit of $281 million out of a total operating budget of $5,277 million in fiscal year 1965.

## Organization and Management

In order to provide Congress and the Postmaster General with information on the revenues and costs attributable to each class of mail the Department produced the Cost Ascertainment Report, one of several information systems maintained by the Department. The Cost Ascertainment Division in the Bureau of Finance and Administration was in charge of preparing the report which was usually completed six months after the close of a fiscal year. During one week in each quarter the Cost Ascertainment Division performed statistical tests of revenue, expense, and volume at approximately 500 post offices. These tests were utilized to allocate the revenue received, and the full costs of operating the system to the 23 postal service categories. The system was oriented toward obtaining reliable statistical measures upon which to apportion costs and revenues, rather than toward determining the nature of expenses (fixed versus variable) incurred by the Post Office.

Although Congress received, reviewed, and acted upon financial information by service category, appropriations were made to the Department on a different basis. The primary postal appropriation categories and amounts for fiscal 1965 were (in thousands):

| | |
|---|---|
| Administration and regional operation | $ 85,941 |
| Research, development, and engineering | 17,956 |
| Operations | 4,241,059 |
| Transportation | 588,524 |
| Facilities | 199,476 |
| Plant and equipment | 75,000 |
| Grand total | $5,207,956 |

The relationship between funds budgeted and funds spent was the subject of a second information system. This study, called the Operating and Financial Report, was produced for each of 13 accounting periods during the fiscal year by the Assistant Comptroller for Accounting within the Bureau of Finance and Administration. The report also contained information about volume of mail, aggregate revenue received, productivity, and postal employment. Organization of the report, however, centered around the appropriation categories of the Department, shown above.

Organization of the Department was also closely aligned with appropriation categories. An organization chart is presented as Exhibit 2. The Department was organized on a parallel basis from the headquarters to regional offices to the local post offices. Headquarters contained 10 bureaus and offices, the largest one being the Bureau of Operations (FY 1965 appropriation—$4.2 billion). Administrative authority for field operations was transferred from the Postmaster General to 15 Regional Directors (under the Office of Regional Administration). Each regional office contained divisions paralleling the headquarters organization which received functional guidance from its headquarters counterpart and administrative guidance from the Regional Director. The larger post offices contained the same organizational divisions and maintained a similar functional-administrative relationship with the regional organization.

Because the Bureau of Operations received just over 81 percent of the Department's appropriation in fiscal year 1965, the Bureau's organization, and measurement system, were extremely important. The bulk of this appropriation was for mail handlers and clerks ($1,881 million) and collection and delivery carriers ($1,617 million). In total these accounted for over 80 percent of the Bureau of Operations budget. These two types of personnel handled a majority of the Post Office functions of collecting mail, receiving mail, providing mail window and special service, sorting mail, transferring mail, and delivering mail.

## Introduction of PPB

Planning, Programming, and Budgeting was introduced to the Post Office Department in a memorandum dated October 19, 1965, from the Deputy

**Exhibit 2**

Post Office Organization Chart (Relationships between Headquarters and Field)

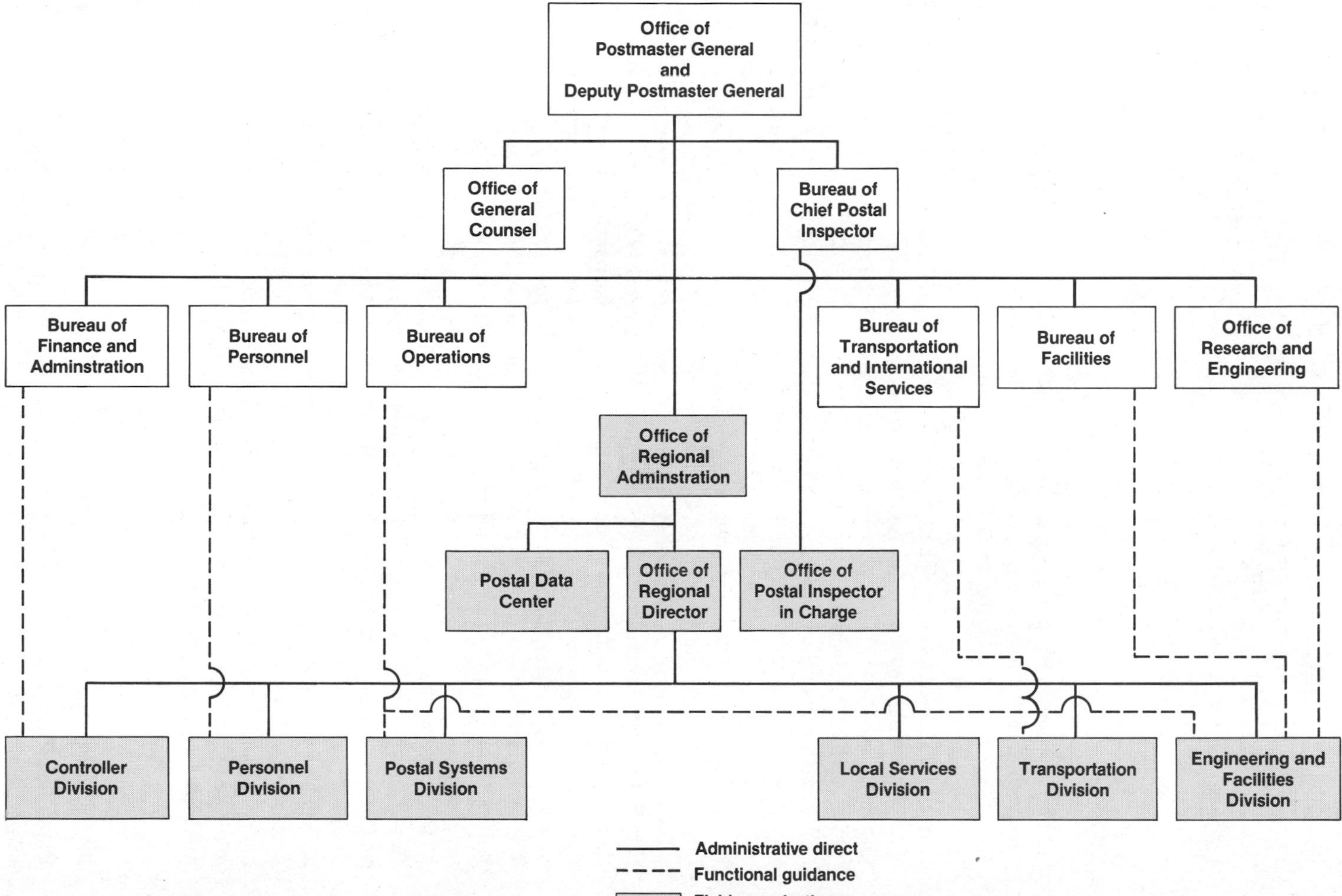

Postmaster General (DPMG). The main points made in this memorandum are:

1. The President announced on August 25 that he has asked all Departments and Agencies of the Federal Government to install a planning-programming-budgeting system. On October 12 the Bureau of the Budget issued a bulletin implementing the President's directive. While we are now en-

**Exhibit 3**
Preliminary Program Categories (October 19, 1965)

A possible program structure (based on Bureau- and Office-submitted objectives and goals) might be:

- Collection and delivery of mail
- Collection and safeguarding of postal revenue
- Sale and payment of money orders
- Operation of the Postal Savings System
- Enforcing postal laws and regulations
- Providing services to other government agencies

Let's look at this system in more detail—

Collection and delivery might be further subdivided into:

- Collection
- Processing and distribution
- Transportation between cities in the United States
- Transportation between the United States and other countries
- Delivery
- Providing special mail services, i.e.,
  - Parcel post
  - Special delivery
  - Registered mail
  - COD
  - Self-service postal units, etc.

Looking at "processing and distribution" we might have certain inputs with their supporting programs such as:

- Providing space programs:
  - Post offices
  - Air mail facilities
  - Truck terminals and transfer offices
  - Highway post offices
  - Railroad post offices
- Providing personnel programs:
  - Pay for clerks
  - Pay for contract services in terminals
  - New employment to reduce overtime
  - Overtime compensation for substitutes.

gaged in preparing a draft of the instructions for establishing the programming portion of this system in the Post Office Department, which will be circulated for comment when ready, we must take immediate action to meet the first major deadline of the Bureau on November 1.

2. Attached (Exhibit 3) is a preliminary version of the Post Office Department program objectives (or program categories) derived from the submissions of Bureaus and Offices last July.
3. Each addressee should review the attached summary of program objectives with particular attention to the first three pages. The Department must decide on its major program categories and submit them to the Bureau of the Budget by November 1. I expect we will have to live with these categories for some time so careful attention of the top staff to their formulation is extremely important. Please make your comments with respect to program categories to me, by close of business October 26.

Analysis of the responses to the memorandum was assigned by the DPMG to the Bureau of Finance and Administration. It was this bureau's responsibility to summarize the comments received from other bureaus and offices and to make final recommendations to the Program Review Task Force, headed by the DPMG, regarding the final Post Office program categories.

In response to the DPMG's memorandum the Special Assistant to the Postmaster General for Policy and Projects took exception to the preliminary version of program categories and proposed that the Post Office program categories should be constructed in line with the missions of the Department, rather than the activities conducted to achieve the missions. Excerpts from this memorandum are in Exhibit 4.

On November 19, 1965, the Bureau of Finance and Administration issued its summary of the alternatives submitted by the various bureaus and offices and also its recommended structure for Post Office categories and subcategories. The Bureau did not support the suggestion made by the Special Assistant for Policy and Projects that the program categories should reflect the "prod-

**Exhibit 4**

From: Special Assistant to the Postmaster General for Policy and Projects

October 26, 1965

(EXCERPTS)

We view the new system less as an improved budgeting technique than as a structure through which top management sets the direction of the Post Office, directs its operations, obtains the "real" costs of programs, and observes program successes and shortcomings.

Bulletin 66–3 describes the program structure as a series of output categories which, taken together, cover the total work of the agency. These will serve as a

**Exhibit 4** ***(continued)***

basic framework for the planning, programming, and budgeting processes (including work on systems analysis, reporting, evaluation of accomplishments, and other aspects of management), and for relating the processes to each other.

The program structure should show the principal missions of the Post Office, the resources devoted to each, and provide for each a physical measure of performance to indicate the extent to which each program is achieving its goals. It should be established, we suggest, not by compiling a list of what each Bureau reports as its Bureau's goals, but by an analysis of postal missions and activities to determine the objectives of the Post Office as a government agency. An attempt at such an analysis follows.

The mission of the Post Office is to deliver the nation's mail. This broad objective is accomplished through a number of activities directly related to moving the mail (acceptance, distribution, transfer, transportation, and delivery); a series of supporting activities needed to maintain the postal establishment (training, maintenance, inspection, recordkeeping, administration, etc.); and several investment programs intended to improve future-year effectiveness or efficiency (construction, research, and development). To a minor extent our resources are used on certain nonpostal activities (money orders and postal savings) and in certain convenience tasks for other government agencies (sale of migratory bird stamps, alien registration, etc.). Since all of these last activities add up to approximately 2 percent of our costs, they should be introduced into the basic program format as a miscellaneous category.

The basic tasks of the postal establishment are thus seen to be those primary functions involved in moving the mail. But are these tasks the missions of the Post Office? Is the Post Office in business to collect mail, to distribute it, and so on, or does it have a further end-purpose, a *mission* which may be more properly used as the output category?

Congress has entrusted to the Post Office four major responsibilities:

A. The delivery of private correspondence.
B. The delivery of periodical publications.
C. The delivery of direct mail advertising material.
D. The delivery of merchandise.

Each of these can be considered a distinct program coinciding almost exactly with the existing classes of mail. The classes of mail have differing service requirements, different rate structures, different unit costs of handling. In sum these four "products" constitute a statement of the missions of the Post Office.

The "physical measure of performance" which is an important element to each program under planning-programming-budgeting is readily defined: it is the service provided each class of mail. For example, for first class mail there are at present these standards of service we expect to provide:

1. ABCD local mail—same-day delivery.
2. Other local, metropolitan area, and short-range surface mail—next-day delivery.

**Exhibit 4** ***(concluded)***

3. Air mail—next-day delivery.
4. Other surface mail—2 to 5 days, depending upon distance.

(After 1967, Groups 3 and 4 will merge with a next-day service goal.)

For each group the service actually being provided can be readily determined by service test sampling, and inexpensive measurement independent of the process being tested. The measure of performance (after 1967) thus becomes the percentage of mail receiving next-day delivery.

This method constitutes a "system check" of the entire postal process and is far more meaningful than a series of separate measurements by function. It is also the same measure by which the public evaluates our effectiveness. Measurement of objectives by function (e.g., distribution efficiency) remains as an effective internal technique for management control, but our performance measurement cannot stop there.

Recommended Program Structure

We suggest that the following program structure be considered for the Post Office Department:

Principal Program #1—First Class Mail
Principal Program #2—Second Class Mail
Principal Program #3—Third Class Mail
Principal Program #4—Fourth Class Mail

Miscellaneous:
Support Program #1—Postal Administration
Support Program #2—Inspection
Support Program #3—Training
Support Program #4—Recordkeeping
Support Program #5—Maintenance
Support Program #6—Customer Services
Support Program #7—Occupancy

Investment Program #1—Construction of Facilities
Investment Program #2—Research and Development

In addition to program costs, the costs of mail-processing functions (acceptance, distribution, etc.) should be reported through the information system since certain of these (e.g., delivery) are managed along functional rather than program lines.

The costs of support and investment programs should be collected and examined separately from direct costs since these programs have their own objectives, performance measurements, and management control channels. Furthermore, their costs do not vary with mail volume, but rather with management objectives. For control purposes, investment decisions, or program evaluation, management will want to examine direct and indirect costs separately. On the other hand, for rate-making, or for determining fully allocated program costs, all support and investment expenses must be apportioned to a specific class of mail. Some support costs relate inherently to a single mail service (e.g., maintenance of parcel-sorting machines) while others are in the general overhead categories (e.g., postmaster salaries).

ucts" of the post office—classes of mail. The reasons given for not adopting the class of mail approach were:

1. The prime product of the Post Office was collection and delivery of mail which was independent of class of mail.
2. A primary breakdown by class of mail would tend to fractionate programs which should be considered on a broader basis.
3. Obtaining information by class of mail would be expensive and difficult. The cost ascertainment system does provide information by class of mail sufficient for rate purposes.

On November 27, 1965, the program categories recommended (Exhibit 5) by the Bureau of Finance and Administration were forwarded to the Bureau of the Budget by the Postmaster General for their comments. In addition, suggestions of output measures for the program subcategories were attached to the recommended categories and subcategories.

At the same time as the initial program categories were submitted, the Postmaster General indicated to the Bureau of the Budget Director that he was very interested in finding a highly qualified and experienced individual

**Exhibit 5**
*Revised Program Category Structure (*as submitted to the Bureau of the Budget, November 27, 1965)

**Program Category I—Collection and Delivery of Mail**

Program subcategories:
- Collection
- Processing
- Transportation
- Delivery
- Special services

**Program Category II—Nonmail Service**

Program subcategories:
- Assist monetary exchanges
- Operate a savings system
- Collect and safeguard postal revenues
- Enforce postal laws and regulations
- Support other government programs

**Program Category III—Supporting Activities**

Program subcategories:
- Management and direction
- Provide and maintain a work force
- Budgeting and accounting
- Provide space, equipment, and supplies
- Conduct research and development
- Management information systems

to direct the new Office of Planning. The Director pledged the support of the Budget Bureau in finding such an individual and also indicated that the new man, when selected, could continue the development of the final program categories for the Post Office.

Communications regarding the Post Office Department's program categories continued on December 1, 1965, with the issuance of another memorandum from the Policy and Projects Special Assistant to the Bureau of Finance and Administration. This memorandum is excerpted in Exhibit 6. Two subjects were raised in this new memorandum. First, it was suggested that the categories recommended by the Bureau would be more meaningful if the subcategories "Collection" and "Processing" were replaced with the three subcategories of "Acceptance," "Distribution," and "Transfer." Detailed reasons for this suggestion were presented in the memorandum. The second subject of the memorandum concerned "the value of, and the cost of," reporting functional (i.e., subcategory) data by class of mail.

**Exhibit 6**

December 1, 1965

Subject: Program Budgeting
From: Special Assistant to the Postmaster General for Policy and Projects
To: Bureau of Finance and Administration

(EXCERPTS)

The Bureau of Finance proposal for a program format appears to us to be an excellent document, the product of careful research and analysis. The suggestions we will make in this paper are an attempt to make even more useful a programming system which already promises to be a significant improvement over the present management information system. The grouping of postal work centers into functional categories, as the Bureau of Finance suggests, should transform the accounting system into a valuable management tool even without further refinement.

**Class-of-Mail Reporting**

As you know, the chief divergence of opinion between the Bureau of Finance and our staff centers about the value of, and the cost of, reporting functional (i.e., subcategory) data by class of mail.

We remain convinced that it would be highly valuable to have current information on the costs incurred in handling each class of mail.

Much of the attention of top postal management is directed to problems relating to a specific class of mail: the Priority Mail Program, ABCD, and airlift, for example, have to do with first class mail. Scheduled Service, damage prevention, detached mail unit policy, and certification affect only fourth class mail. The examination of policy alternatives would be easier and more accurate if financial information by the four classes of mail were available on a current basis.

**Exhibit 6** ***(continued)***

Furthermore, the effect of mechanizing or changing our practices in other ways could be observed quantitatively if system-wide costs were collected by class of mail.

Beyond its value as a planning and control device, we urge a class-of-mail approach because our service to the public must, in the final analysis, be considered by class of mail. The ultimate measure of our effectiveness, as a Department, is how long it takes us to deliver letters, and magazines, and circulars, and parcels. The peripheral activities we perform pale to insignificance beside the question of how well we perform our primary role. Since service analysis is a class-of-mail measure, we are led to suggest that it would be valuable to collect costs on the same basis, to determine how trends in service could relate to trends in costs, and to institute a service-oriented basis for our planning and programming system.

The difficulty of relying on the Cost Ascertainment Report for this data is twofold: the annual Cost Ascertainment Report apportions, as it must, to each class of mail the full cost of all supporting activities. This is indispensable for rate-making. For planning purposes, however, it is necessary to know the marginal costs of each class of mail. These can be determined only by examining our direct costs separately from our indirect costs.

The care with which the apportionment of indirect costs must be made and the highly refined techniques which must be used result in a long interval between the time costs are incurred and the time they are presented in a form useful to management. This time lag is a serious impediment to the use of Cost Ascertainment as a management tool.

By reporting direct costs for each class of mail on a current basis, the new information system could permit management to analyze postal programs in the same manner that businesses analyze their operations—on a current basis, by product line.

**The Cost of Class-of-Mail Reporting**

The principal issue over collecting costs by class of mail, however, concerns not the value of the data but the cost of getting it.

Some of our work centers are devoted exclusively to one class of mail—parcel post distribution, for example, or letter distribution at certain times of the day. There is little difficulty in preserving these costs by class of mail. Many postal costs, however, are joint costs. Since a high level of precision is *not* needed for planning purposes, statistical samples of mail mix at work centers can be used to determine the ratios to apply to total work center costs.

In its proposal, the Bureau of Finance considers "Collection" to be a subcategory separate from "Delivery" even though the same truck and driver are often used for both functions. The apportionment of cost between two separate functions is a well-established cost accounting practice. The possibility of a 2 percent error in that apportionment need not concern us: for planning purposes it is close enough. The driver's paycheck is based on a ledger account and will be exact. It is important, we suggest, to distinguish among our audit and payroll accounts which must be

**Exhibit 6** ***(concluded)***

exact, our functional subcategories which can be more approximate, and our totals for planning purposes which need not be nearly as precise.

There is obviously much work to be done before a comprehensive postal accounting system is perfected. Apportionments will be relied upon heavily, especially at first. For smaller offices, class-of-mail reporting may never be practical—instead, their total direct costs would be apportioned based on tests made in typical offices in a class.

The routine problems in any cost accounting system should not prevent us, however, from providing for a class-of-mail tag on costs coming up through the new accounting system. Many of these costs are readily identifiable now by mail class; others will be apportioned grossly at first but with greater precision as time goes on.

A system such as we suggest would eliminate the need for the many one-shot studies which now must be made for special purposes. Special studies add to the paperwork burden of supervisors and postmasters, and lack the validity of a continuously operating system. In a special cost study where there is no need to balance total costs, we find the recurring problem of "paper" savings which frequently never materialize in the account books.

We recognize that this approach raises many questions which have not yet been answered to everyone's satisfaction.

I am sure you agree, however, that despite the pressure of external deadlines the importance of the program format warrants an exhaustive review before a final decision is made. We would welcome the opportunity to present our views to the Program Advisory Committee.

---

On December 10, 1965, the Bureau of Finance and Administration again summarized program category suggestions received after their November 19th memorandum. This memorandum repeated the Bureau's objections to "class of mail" categories, attached recommendations received from other bureaus and offices, and recommended a new, slightly revised, program structure. This memorandum from the Bureau of Finance and Administration to the Deputy Postmaster General is excerpted in Exhibit 7.

At the end of December 1965 the Bureau of the Budget notified the Postmaster General that they had found someone to act as temporary Director of the Office of Planning until a permanent person was located. They suggested that a prominent economist, then a consultant to the bureau (BOB), be appointed as Acting Director. The Postmaster General agreed that such an arrangement would be very satisfactory and asked the economist to start immediately, even though formal announcement of his position would take some time.

## The Meeting on January 15, 1966

After reviewing the historical development of Post Office program categories, one of the Planning Director's first actions was to request that members of

**Exhibit 7**

---

December 10, 1965

Subject: Program Categories and Subcategories
From: Bureau of Finance and Administration
To: Deputy Postmaster General

Attached is a newly revised structure for program categories and subcategories for consideration by the Program Advisory Committee. This is the same structure forwarded to the Bureau of the Budget on November 27, and the structure we asked the Bureaus and Offices to comment on by December 1. However, there have been some changes in titles suggested by Bureaus and Offices which we have incorporated. Several changes have been recommended by Bureaus and Offices which you may wish the Program Advisory Committee to consider.

The Special Assistant to the Postmaster General for Policy and Projects has recommended that we consider a structure based upon class of mail, and has asked for an opportunity to present his proposal. He bases the proposal on the following considerations:

*A.* Many of the Department's problems are best looked at in terms of class of mail.
*B.* Service is best considered in terms of class of mail.
*C.* Statistical information techniques coupled with minor sacrifices in precision will enable us to produce the desired information at a reasonable cost.

As we indicated in our memorandum of November 19, on this subject, we do not believe the Department should adopt this proposal at this time because:

*A.* Our prime product should be viewed as a "collection and delivery service" which is not dependent on class of mail.
*B.* We believe that most program elements which the Program Advisory Committee will wish to review or compare will cut across classes of mail, and a primary breakdown by class of mail would tend to fractionate program elements which should be considered on a broader basis.
*C.* The changes in present information systems will be expensive and will be very difficult to make in the time required.

It should also be noted that class of mail is both an arbitrary and an unstable grouping.

---

the Policy and Projects (Policy) staff and Bureau of Finance and Administration (Finance) staff meet with him in the near future. This meeting was held on January 15, 1966. He opened the meeting with the following statement:

> I've called this meeting primarily for my own benefit. As you know, Post Office operations are brand new to me and I'm trying to gain an understanding of the nature of the Department.
>
> At the same time, I think that time pressure dictates that we all work to reach a final agreement on the composition of program categories in the Department. Our program memoranda are due at BOB on May 1st. That doesn't leave

much time for their preparation, much less for any further theoretical discussions concerning the categories.

Although I haven't gone as far as locking the doors and keeping you here until an agreement is reached, I am going to ask that you come up with a compromise structure by the end of January.

## Assignment

Summarize and evaluate the arguments presented in the memoranda.

## Case 6–2

## LOMITA HOSPITAL*

Dr. Charles Russell, Chief of Pathology at Lomita Hospital, was in the process of formulating his budget for fiscal year 1977. He had just received statistics from the Fiscal Affairs Department detailing the number of patient days and ancillary services used in the past two years and estimating the figures for FY 1977 (see Exhibit 1). One of Dr. Russell's responsibilities was to review the FY 1977 estimates and make whatever revisions he deemed appropriate. Once he and the other department heads had completed this process, the Fiscal Affairs Department could aggregate the totals and make overall hospital volume projections. The volume projections then were used to estimate hospital revenue which, in turn, determined the costs which the Fiscal Affairs Departments allowed each department within the hospital. Since the beginning of intensified third-party control by the state in 1975, a tight rein had been put on departmental costs. Therefore these statistics became highly meaningful to the Chief of Pathology as well as other service chiefs in the hospital. Each service chief had his or her own set of statistics which had to be analyzed in light of the hospital as a whole.

Dr. Russell's primary objection to the accounting statistics was that they were aggregated figures and, therefore, did not show the distribution of procedures undertaken by the various sections within his department. As a result, fluctuations within these sections were concealed. Since he felt that realistic projections of future volume could only be made on the basis of statistics for each section, the department kept its own records of numbers of procedures broken down according to section and specific laboratory process (Exhibit 2).

---

* This case was prepared by Pamela A. Sytkowski under the direction of David W. Young, Harvard School of Public Health.

**Exhibit 1**

Projected Hospital Statistics—Pathology and Laboratories

| Revenue Code | Department/Lab. | Inpatient Fiscal 1975 | Inpatient Projected 1976 | Inpatient Estimated 1977 | Inpatient Percent +(−) | Outpatient (OPD) Fiscal 1975 | Outpatient (OPD) Projected 1976 | Outpatient (OPD) Estimated 1977 | Outpatient (OPD) Percent +(−) | Totals Fiscal 1975 | Totals Projected 1976 | Totals Estimated 1977 | Totals Percent +(−) |
|---|---|---|---|---|---|---|---|---|---|---|---|---|---|
| Patient days | | 110,579 | 111,000 | 110,500 | | | | | | | | | |
| Patient visits | | | | | | 134,119 | 130,000 | 126,000 | | | | | |
| 212 | Cystoscopy lab. | 602 | 612 | 600 | (2.0) | 800 | 726 | 725 | — | 1,402 | 1,338 | 1,325 | (1.0) |
| 213 | Blood gas lab. | 20,465 | 23,296 | 25,000 | 7.3 | 998 | 1,378 | 1,600 | 16.1 | 21,463 | 24,674 | 26,600 | 7.8 |
| 220 | Chemistry lab. | 214,824 | 205,888 | 206,000 | 0.1 | 104,593 | 70,327 | 70,000 | (0.5) | 319,417 | 276,215 | 276,000 | — |
| 221 | Bacteriology lab. | 69,769 | 70,250 | 72,000 | 2.5 | 31,893 | 32,987 | 33,000 | 0.2 | 101,662 | 103,187 | 105,000 | 1.8 |
| 222 | Hematology lab. | 154,312 | 162,234 | 162,000 | (0.1) | 86,655 | 84,049 | 85,000 | 1.1 | 240,967 | 246,283 | 247,000 | 0.3 |
| 228 | Coagulation lab. | 433 | 894 | 900 | 0.7 | 899 | 857 | 970 | 13.2 | 1,332 | 1,751 | 1,870 | 6.8 |
| 229 | Outside lab. | 14,673 | 16,028 | 17,000 | 6.1 | 10,239 | 9,323 | 9,300 | (0.2) | 24,912 | 25,351 | 26,000 | 3.7 |
| 230 | Blood tests | 93,004 | 98,894 | 108,600 | 9.3 | 21,875 | 22,305 | 24,200 | 8.5 | 114,879 | 121,199 | 132,800 | 9.6 |
| 233 | Tissue typing | 100 | 76 | 90 | 18.4 | 975 | 720 | 990 | 37.5 | 1,075 | 796 | 1,080 | 35.7 |
| 235 | EKG lab. | 18,552 | 18,472 | 18,400 | (0.4) | 7,493 | 7,376 | 7,575 | 2.7 | 26,045 | 25,848 | 25,975 | 0.5 |
| 236 | Cardiac cath lab. | 2,187 | 2,974 | 3,900 | 31.1 | 952 | 1,278 | 2,190 | 71.4 | 3,139 | 4,252 | 6,090 | 43.2 |
| 240 | EEG lab. | 2,140 | 1,292 | 1,450 | 12.2 | 2,585 | 1,096 | 1,200 | 9.5 | 4,725 | 2,388 | 2,650 | 10.8 |
| 242 | Tissue typing—IHOB | 110 | 94 | 90 | (5.3) | 1,339 | 826 | 1,340 | 62.2 | 1,499 | 920 | 1,430 | 55.4 |
| 245 | Pathology | 4,618 | 4,524 | 4,700 | 3.9 | 3,705 | 3,513 | 3,820 | 8.7 | 8,323 | 8,037 | 8,520 | 6.0 |
| 246 | Cytology lab. | 1,907 | 1,830 | 1,860 | 1.6 | 7,752 | 6,290 | 6,506 | 3.4 | 9,659 | 8,120 | 8,366 | 3.0 |
| 247 | Frozen sections | 638 | 654 | 770 | 17.7 | 337 | 511 | 605 | 18.4 | 975 | 1,165 | 1,375 | 18.0 |
| 257 | Vascular lab. | — | 130 | 750 | 576.9 | — | 35 | 500 | 1428.6 | — | 165 | 1,250 | 757.6 |
| 264 | Blood preservation lab. | 50 | 44 | 50 | 13.6 | 22 | 10 | 10 | — | 72 | 54 | 60 | 11.1 |

**Exhibit 2**
Review of Test Statistics

| | 1976–1969 Differences | | | | | | | | | | |
|---|---|---|---|---|---|---|---|---|---|---|---|
| | Percent | Total over (under) | Est. 1976 | 1975 | 1974 | 1973 | 1972 | 1971 | 1970 | 1969 |
| Surgicals | 68.5 | 3,820 | 9,396 | 8,546 | 8,490 | 7,791 | 7,461 | 6,810 | 6,109 | 5,576 |
| Autopsies | 13.77 | 46 | 380 | 327 | 324 | 363 | 358 | 340 | 339 | 334 |
| Cytology | (20.29) | (1,935) | 7,600 | 9,358 | 10,579 | 10,457 | 13,676 | 12,426 | 12,097 | 9,535 |
| Specials: | | | | | | | | | | |
| | (1976–1970) | | | | | | | | | |
| Electron microscopy | 94.33 | 77 | 130 | 117 | 119 | 110 | 82 | 85 | 53 | — |
| Fluorescence microscopy | 594.44 | 107 | 125 | 118 | 97 | 84 | 31 | 62 | 18 | — |

Comparison of Fiscal Years, by Quarters

| | Q1 | Q2 | Q3 | Subtotal | Q4 | Q5 |
|---|---|---|---|---|---|---|
| Surgical Pathology 1974–75 | 2,141 | 2,126 | 2,173 | 6,440 | 2,025 | 8,465 |
| 1975–76 | 2,156 | 2,188 | 2,385 | 6,729 | 2,085 | 8,814 |
| Difference/% increase | 15 | 62 | 212 | 289 | 60 | 349 |
| Autopsies 1974–75 | 87 | 89 | 67 | 243 | 79 | 322 |
| 1975–76 | 92 | 95 | 98 | 285 | 101 (est.) | 386 |
| Difference/% increase | 5 | 6 | 31 | 42 | 22 | 64 |
| Cytology 1974–75 | 2,501 | 2,401 | 2,361 | 7,263 | 2,361 | 9,624 |
| 1975–76 | 2,239 | 1,910 | 2,014 | 6,163 | 2,201 (est.) | 8,364 |
| Difference/% increase | (262) | (491) | (347) | (1,100) | (160) | (1,260) |
| Electron microscopy 1974–75 | 30 | 37 | 33 | 100 | 21 | 121 |
| 1975–76 | 27 | 21 | 25 | 73 | 25 (est.) | 98 |
| Difference/% increase | (3) | (16) | (8) | (27) | 4 | (23) |
| Fluorescence microscopy 1974–75 | 17 | 26 | 23 | 66 | 15 | 81 |
| 1975–76 | 15 | 20 | 24 | 59 | 22 (est.) | 81 |
| Difference/% increase | (2) | (6) | 1 | (7) | 7 | — |

Dr. Russell was especially concerned with the projections of revenue and expenses insofar as they related to the cytology section of his department. There was a quite reliable rumor that the staff of the Gynecology Department would be leaving Lomita to set up their own clinic. If this should happen, it was by no means clear that the new, perhaps lesser known, staff would have the same volume of patients so as to generate the cytology work which the present staff gave to the Pathology Department.

Besides contemplating these issues and their effects on his budget proposal for the coming year, Dr. Russell was concerned about the request of one of his section heads, Dr. Pamela Gordon. She and Dr. Cornell Johnson were responsible for the major portion of the surgical service pathology done in the department, and Dr. Gordon was directly responsible for the administration of the histology lab (see Exhibit 3). Over the past few years Dr. Gordon had indicated that her lab was understaffed, and once again this year she had requested that a new technician be hired. She felt that the pressure put on the technicians as well as that put on herself was creating an unbearable situation in which both the quantity and quality of work in her lab were suffering. A new technician had not entered into Dr. Russell's initial calculation of expenses, and although the projected volume seemed to warrant the addition, these projections had not been available to him in January when he had made an emergency appeal for extra help. At that time, his request for an additional technician had been approved by Mr. Malcolm Gunderson, the Laboratory Administrator of the hospital, only after a detailed analysis of the pathology logs had been prepared. Dr. Russell knew that the histology lab technicians were still overworked—he *personally* was taking their overtime pay directly out of his Pathologist-in-Chief funds—yet administration had not been convinced in the past by overall hospital

**Exhibit 3**
Pathology Organization Chart

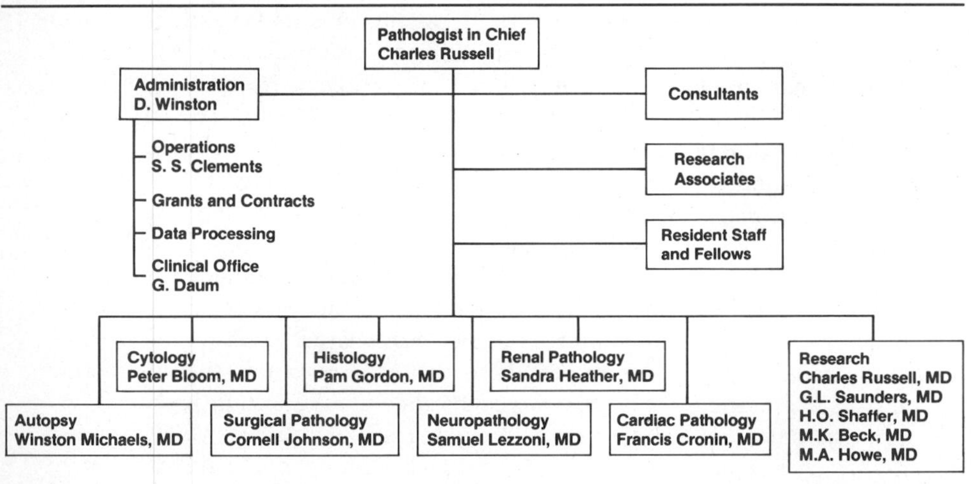

statistics, and it was now necessary to attempt again to justify this need. Dr. Russell, therefore, had asked Dr. Gordon and Dr. Johnson to prepare a detailed quantitative justification. Dr. Russell explained his problems in this regard:

> I ask my people to prepare a justification for all requests since I do not feel a hospital is any different from industry in this respect. In industry, expenses and budgets must routinely be justified either to the board of trustees or to the stockholders. A service chief must learn to do the same thing within the hospital setting. The problem is that my staff most often gives me emotionally charged justifications. There is never a justification in terms of numbers. Professionals must become aware of the necessity of using quantitative data in budgetary justifications. Very often I will get four or five justifications before one is finally written in terms of numbers which I can then relate to the administration. If the request cannot be put in terms of generating income or increasing productivity, the justification must be even more convincing. These statements can be in terms of loss of time, ease in handling, or better service. *But* none of these justifications can be emotional.

## Background

Lomita Hospital was a teaching hospital located in the heart of a large metropolitan area and affiliated with a local medical school. It employed some 2,000 persons and delivered well over 100,000 patient days of service a year. It admitted over 10,000 patients a year, had an average daily census of approximately 300, and an average occupancy rate of 92 percent. Its outpatient department handled over 100,000 patient visits a year. Exhibit 4 contains an organizational chart for Lomita Hospital.

## The Budgetary Process

Budgeting at Lomita depended on a justification procedure which took place at various levels in the line of management. Although projected revenue was based on the projected number of patient days and ancillary services as determined by the accounting unit, using historical data as well as trend analysis and simulation modeling, these projections were open to revision by each of the service departments if they were able to show that their numbers were more realistic. Each department chief, his or her administrator, and the Laboratory Administrator weighed the accounting unit projections against each department's own projections. When the department and the accounting unit agreed upon a projected volume, the accounting unit calculated a projected revenue figure. At this time, the department and the Laboratory Administrator could contest the numbers on the basis of previous years' experience in regard to the differential between charges and revenue credited to the department. In this respect, both past experience and the distribution of specific procedure projections were relevant since the accounting unit based its projected revenue figure on a "weighted average price" which was not always consistent with the department's evaluation of the distribution of

**Exhibit 4**
Administrative Organization Chart

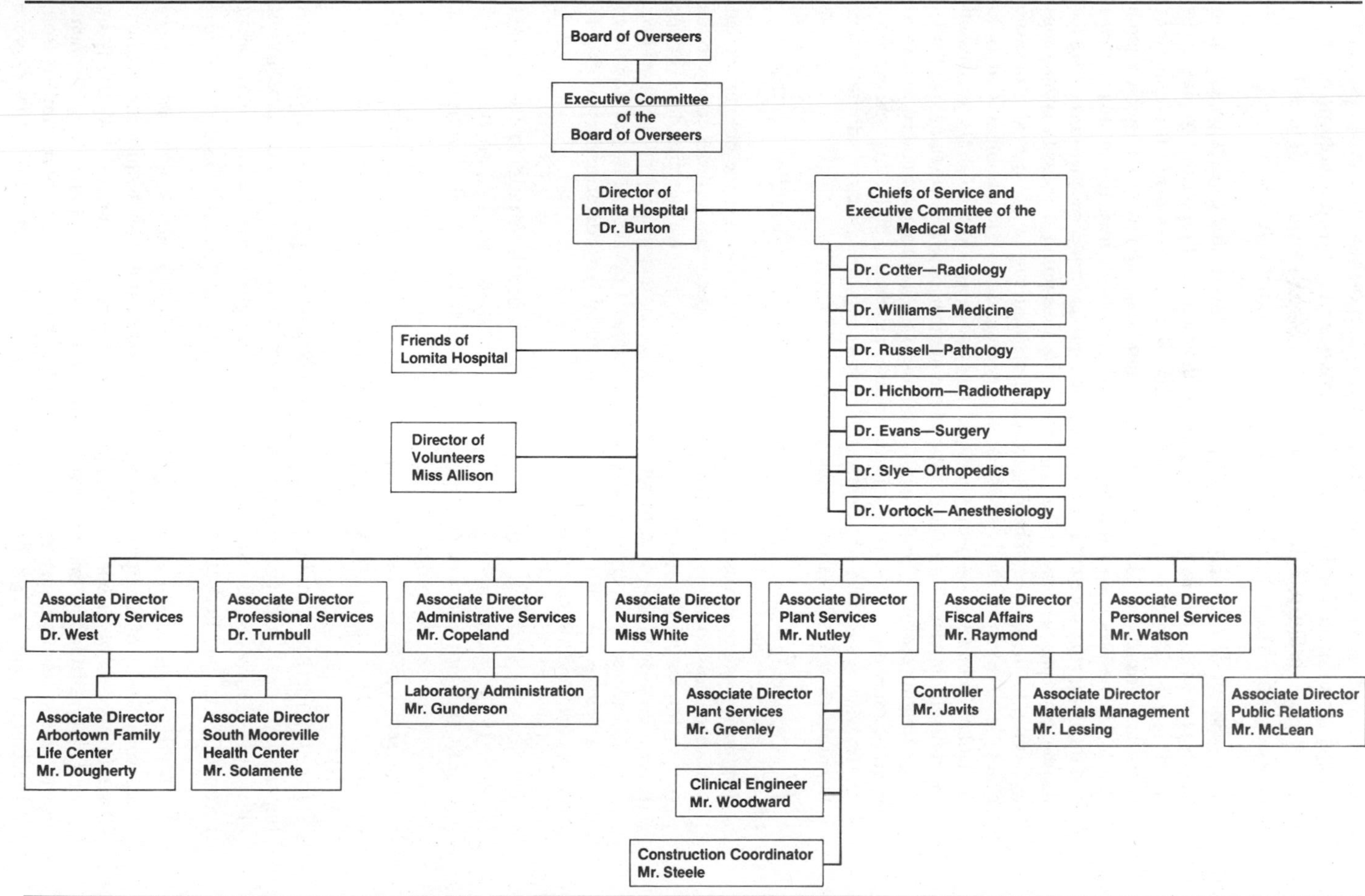

procedures. These projections were extremely important since the department was held responsible for both projected costs and projected volume.

Dr. Russell indicated that the projected cost and revenue figures for FY 1977 were more than simply a matter of estimating volume:

> The problem of cost accounting becomes especially acute when an increase in cost is seen as not merely due to an increase in volume but rather due to differences in efficiencies. The only increase the hospital will accept as a justifiable increase is one in terms of workload. The workload must be counterbalanced by the income which can be produced from that work. The problem here is that many items and many functions are not income-producing. For example, because of the advance in science, it has become easier but more time-consuming to classify lymphomas according to their types. There are many tests that can be performed before the exact classification of the lymphoma is agreed upon. To the administration or to Malcolm Gunderson, a lymph node is a lymph node. We must try to explain the difficulty in classification in terms of the number of slides which are necessary to thoroughly classify it. But when the number of slides hasn't changed, the argument becomes more and more difficult. Another problem in budgeting new expenses results when a situation has existed for such a long time that the administration feels that there is no reason to change it.

Dr. Cornell Johnson, Chief of Surgical Pathology, amplified on this:

> Arguments based on cost can cut both ways. For example, if the pressure to cut costs becomes too strong, one may undersample specimens in order to lower the cost of processing the specimens. This may result in extra hospital days for the patient because of the need to return and take another sample of the specimen, or even because of an error in diagnosis. Although I do not see this as a problem now, I believe one must bear in mind the potential hazards of undersampling as efforts are made to cut costs.

Dr. Russell also realized that any modifications he made to the budget for FY 1977 or any additional staff he wished to hire had to be justified not only through the Fiscal Affairs Department but to Mr. Gunderson as well. Mr. Gunderson, reported directly to the Associate Director for Administrative Services of the hospital, and as such was required to approve every change in status and every requisition for each clinical laboratory in the hospital.

Mr. Gunderson's main concern in the budgetary process was that each department head had the resources necessary to run his or her department efficiently. However, he also had an obligation to see that any increase in resources was justified appropriately. He commented:

> I feel that I am working with the departments, helping them to obtain budgetary approval for all of the personnel, supplies, services, and capital equipment demonstrably necessary to operate the clinical laboratory. The interest and ability in, or time available for, budget preparation varies from department to department. My role is to make sure that no major need or expense has been omitted from the budget. The budget workpapers are based on seven months actual expense

extrapolated to twelve months. It is, therefore, imperative to identify any continuing expense commitments made part way through the fiscal year or to be made subsequent to the preparation of the budget projection. I also work with the departments to identify anticipated new needs for the coming fiscal year and to develop justifications for the requests. For proposed new clinical tests I assist in the development of need analysis, a revenue and expense projection, and a cost/price analysis. These are required by the Cost Manager for his review prior to submitting a new test request to the state's Rate Setting Commission for approval.

I try to remain unbiased and truly evaluate the necessity of new projects and equipment requested in the budget. Then I call it as I see it. If the analysis supports the request, I will recommend approval; if not, I will recommend disapproval.

With respect to personnel, the Budget Worksheet provided by the Fiscal Affairs Department is not always complete (due to the time interval between the data processing run and actual budget preparation). Any positions vacant on the date the worksheet is run are automatically deleted and justification for continuing the availability of any such position, along with an indication of the length of time the position has been vacant, must be provided. The rationale for this is that if a department has been able to get along for a number of weeks without a position being filled it may be that the position is not essential and should be carefully scrutinized.

One of the functions of the Laboratory Administrator in the budgetary process is to carefully review each department's personnel worksheet to be sure that: (1) all of the hours for which they had received prior authorization, and which are demonstrably necessary, are reentered on the worksheet and the required justification submitted; and (2) that all anticipated position upgradings and new position requests have been included, also along with the required justification. Assistance is provided in developing the justifications.

If, by reviewing the laboratory test volume statistics, annual trends, and technical staff productivity—when possible employing the College of American Pathologists' (CAP) "Laboratory Workload Recording Method"—I conclude that a position should not be filled, I will so advise the laboratory director and the Associate Director for Administrative Services. He will either act on the recommendation or, in some circumstances, review it with the Director of the Hospital. In some instances a recommendation will be made for a complete study by the Management Engineering Department.

I did not approve a request for a new technician in the Pathology Department when it was initially requested in January of 1976. This was between budgetary periods. Our fiscal year runs from October 1 to September 30. Since the position had been vacant for a long time, there was a question as to whether it was necessary. Moreover, an examination of the Fiscal Affairs Department's Income Distribution Report revealed that the overall test volume in Pathology had declined 6 percent between calendar year 1974 and calendar year 1975. Excluding Cytology, chargeable test volume was nearly stable over the two years, having only a 1 percent increase. Useful as these data were as a very broad measure or indicator, I felt that a detailed count of the historical workload taken from the laboratory logs for at least the period covering the preceding two years (perhaps on a sampling basis) was needed to make a valid evaluation. The logs indicate the number of blocks, slides, routine and special stains prepared for each accession number. CAP workload units could then have been applied so as to approximate total workload.

I asked the Pathology Administrator to provide this summary, offering to supply clerical assistance if it was necessary.

Although this detailed summary from the logs, necessary for a workload computation, was not compiled, summary data were provided by Pathology comparing the total number of surgicals and autopsy slides prepared in 1975 with 1965 and providing a calculation of the average number of slides per "surgical" and per autopsy case. However, lacking the detailed summary, the position was disapproved again when it was requested in the budget in May. Later, in the summer of 1976, Pathology again requested approval for this position. Data taken from lab records were submitted indicating that the number of surgicals and autopsies in total had increased about 9 percent over the two-year period despite the fact that accounting data revealed almost no increase. A small part of this increase was represented by autopsies. However, a surgical represents a workload of 5.27 slides while an autopsy represents a workload of 28.6 slides. Therefore, to produce a meaningful basis of comparison I converted both surgical and autopsies to "slides prepared" and compared the total slides prepared for fiscal 74 with fiscal 75. This showed an increase of only 3 percent which did not appear to represent a significant increase in workload.

This analysis was presented to the Pathologist-in-Chief, who then directed his senior staff physician in charge of histology to carry out a tally of the pathology logs, summarizing the total number of slides stained, categorized by the type of stain. This showed an actual annual increase of 10,032 H&E[1] stained slides over the most recent two-year period, while the number of special stains rose by 2,614 slides. Since the CAP workload allocation for these two staining procedures is six and 23 man-minutes per slide, respectively, there apparently had been an increase in histology workload of 120,314 man-minutes which represents an increase in workload in excess of one full-time equivalent. On the basis of this analysis, approval of the position was granted and a budget addendum obtained.

I also try to distinguish the uses for which money is budgeted. If I determine that the operating budget is being inflated with research-related supplies or services, research employees, or other expenses, they will be deleted from the lab budget. I look at every increase and expenditure which is above the allowable inflationary increase and make sure there is a justification, in quantitative terms whenever possible, which Fiscal Affairs and the Director will require. If an additional employee is requested in the budget, I will assist the department, to the extent necessary, in preparing a justification which should include an explanation of the medical or other necessity of the work to be performed—including quantification of demand by diagnosis for proposed new tests, a workload analysis, a revenue and expense analysis showing (when possible) that the expense will be recovered through additional revenue generated, and also, for proposed new tests, a cost-price analysis. Similar justification is often required for capital requests. However, there may be other justifications for a capital purchase; for example, the age of an instrument, poor instrument repair record and high repair expense, equipment obsolescence, unsafe equipment, improved method, all of which cannot or need not be justified with a revenue and expense analysis. Here documentation of the problem with records and other factual material greatly facilitates obtaining approval. Although

[1] Hematoxylin and Eosin.

> quality of care is an important argument in any justification, it must be factually supported. Frequently a cost-benefit analysis is required to properly evaluate such a request. A request based on "quality of care" need without supporting justification will not hold.

Dr. Johnson, who was also an adviser to Dr. Russell on capital budget items for the Pathology Department, indicated that responding to the administration's needs was no simple matter:

> The hospital doesn't increase costs without justification, and the review process is necessary. Administration will always ask the question whether the needed item will generate revenue or increase quality of care. Therefore, a cost-benefit analysis always colors our perception of needs. This analysis takes into consideration the requirements of quality service, efficiency, and quality of care. For example, the department wished to purchase an ultraviolet microscope costing $10,000; it knew that it would need a highly trained technician. The estimated cost of the technician was $10,000/year plus the cost of training. Before going to administration and requesting the microscope, the department estimated the amount of revenue that would be generated through the use of the U-V microscope. It was decided that this use justified the purchase of such a large item. It could be seen that the microscope would be used by many people both within and outside the department.

Others in the hospital pointed out the difficulties inherent in the interrelationship among the three activities of patient care, teaching, and research. Frequently, equipment as well as personnel cut across all three areas and the costs incurred for various items could not easily be separated. Third-party payors had indicated they would not reimburse hospitals for the research and teaching portions of a particular item, thereby posing a difficult dilemma for a chief attempting to cost-justify a request or obtain adequate third-party reimbursement for a given expenditure.

An additional concern of Dr. Russell's was the need to defend his budget not only to the Laboratory Administrator, but to several other levels in the hospital's hierarchy. He commented:

> At each level, attempts will be made to cut the budget. Whether the cut is successful or not depends on the strength of your justification and the availability of funds. The checks and balances within the Lomita system are very good. Everyone operates under the impression that people under them inflate their needs—I know I do. Sometimes needs *are* inflated; sometimes not. The problem is that at times administration can be very capricious about matters.

## The Fiscal Affairs Department

The Fiscal Affairs Department of Lomita had the role of coordinating the budget preparation process. Once the data on income and expenses had been submitted by each department, the Fiscal Affairs Department prepared a pro forma budget. This pro forma budget had both revenue and expenses which were determined in accordance with the state's Rate Setting Commission regulations. Mr. Kenneth Javits, the hospital Controller, pointed out the value of the pro forma:

> This is termed our "Expense Budget before Adjustment." From this, we are able to deduce what the net income will be before the need for a rate increase or expense reduction. We must fit all costs into the 20 categories for calculation of allowed inflationary increases. Then we are able to determine how far cost is over the ceiling, and in which categories. The next problem is where to look when a cut is necessary. We usually do this in terms of measuring increases in productivity. We generally can judge where the budget looks spongy and where it looks quite hard. We look for excessive increases to be tied to the volume of business. We then look at new programs and determine whether a commitment has been made, whether the program appears necessary for the standing of the hospital, or if an impact is questionable in terms of any goal or policy of the hospital. This part of the budget is somewhat subjective and is the initial stage of the budget reduction process.

If Fiscal Affairs determined that the budget contained any "soft areas," it would request the Chief of Service to cut expenses. After as many cuts as possible had been negotiated, the budget was turned over to the hospital's Director, Dr. Henry Burton. According to Mr. Javits, the Fiscal Affairs Department played a coordinating role in this process but did not impose decisions on the various departments:

> Fiscal Affairs "proposes" expenses and "requests" cuts. We do not "cut." The Chiefs and Dr. Burton do that. After the budget has been negotiated as far as possible, we provide data and recommendations for the budget *we* propose to Dr. Burton. He must decide which items among the departments should be pushed and which should not. He must make an indirect evaluation of the contribution of each item on the budget to the hospital's final goal. At times, there is need for clinical judgment. In these instances, the Associate Directors, or "Administrative Physicians," as they are termed, will be called in to give judgment of clinical value. Dr. Burton will notify the Chief of Service that he has received specific budget recommendations from the budget unit which are contrary to the Chief's. The Chief is then allowed to decide whether he will push or not push for his decision over that of Fiscal Affairs. Ultimately, Henry Burton is able to negotiate through this process very well. If the Chief of Service does not feel that he is heard, he may request that the Board of Overseers intervene and make a judgment, but normally this does not occur.

The budget, as recommended by the budgeting unit and revised by Dr. Burton, then went to the Budget Finance Committee (a Board of Overseers Committee) which was composed of Dr. Burton, Mr. Colin Raymond (the Associate Director for Fiscal Affairs), and various Board members. The Chief of each service could address this group also if he specifically felt that his program needs were not being met. Again, according to Mr. Javits:

> The "relevancy" which is the criterion of our decision on each item is not what is relevant in terms of the Budget Committee but in terms of what the regulators—the Rate Setting Commission—will accept. The controlling aspect of our new

RSC regulations is enormous. The hospital retains the right to exercise considerable management prerogative, but only within the dollar limits allowed via these regulations. In essence, in a nongrowth environment, any new cost (above normal inflation) in an ongoing program must be matched by a like reduction elsewhere. This is the true budget "crunch."

According to one observer:

Uppermost in the minds of both Mr. Raymond and Dr. Burton is the hospital "Statement of Changes in Fund Balances" which reflects last year's costs and is the basis for the projection of the expected costs for the following year. This statement governs the budget from the beginning to the end, since administration is very concerned with the impact of the budget on the image of Lomita Hospital. Therefore, they are interested in working from the *bottom line* and fitting their costs and income in order to meet *this* objective.

The question now facing Dr. Russell was whether it would be possible for him to build an additional technician into his new budget. He did not feel, however, that this decision could be considered independently of the other decisions confronting him, namely (1) the department's projected volume and costs, (2) the needs of the primary care clinic, and (3) the volume projections for the cytology section, considering the change in the staffing of the Gynecology group. He knew that whatever changes and projections he made would have to be justified in a highly convincing manner.

## Questions

1. What are the key aspects of the management control structure at Lomita? What changes, if any, would you recommend?
2. What are the key aspects of the management control structure of the Department of Pathology? What changes, if any, would you recommend to Dr. Russell?
3. Trace through the budgetary process at Lomita. What is the role of a chief of service in this process? What should the chief's role be?

## Case 6–3

## NEW YORK CITY SANITATION DEPARTMENT*

The Bureau of Motor Equipment of the New York City Sanitation Department had about 1,200 employees and an operating budget of about $38 million. It was responsible for maintaining the Department's 5,000 vehicles. It operated

* This case was prepared by Robert N. Anthony, Harvard Business School.

75 repair garages located throughout the city and one major central repair facility.

According to a report of the New York State Financial Control Board, conditions in the Bureau of Motor Equipment in 1978 were chaotic. Over half the vehicles it was responsible for servicing were out of service on the average day, resulting in huge amounts of overtime pay for the personnel assigned to the remaining vehicles. Mr. Ronald Contino was placed in charge of the Bureau in late 1978. Within two years, the Bureau was supplying 100 percent of the primary vehicles needed every day. Mr. Contino estimated that $16.5 million of costs had been avoided during that period.

Mr. Contino attributed the change to two main factors: (1) a change in labor/management relations, and (2) the creation of "profit centers" as a substitute for work standards in the central repair facility.

Mr. Contino set up labor/management committees, each consisting of shop supervisors, trades people, and a shop steward. Their mandate was to investigate ways to solve problems, to improve the quality of work life, and to increase productivity. A committee was formed in each of the eight principal departments, called shops, in the central repair facility. (This case focuses only on the central repair facility.) The committees met monthly with the manager of the central repair facility.

In 1978 the central repair facility operated under negotiated work standards that covered practically every job, from rebuilding an engine to fixing a generator. Committee members were concerned that if suggestions for improving productivity were made and implemented, management would subsequently adjust the work standards upward.

After a number of discussions, the following plan was adopted: Management would no longer be interested in work standards as applied to specific jobs and individuals; individual records of time spent on jobs would no longer be required. Instead, management would be interested only in whether the shop as a whole was producing at an acceptable level. The "value" of output would be measured by what it would cost to purchase the same items or services from outside vendors, and the total value of output for a period would be compared with the total cost of operating the shop.

The output values were determined by checking outside price lists or by obtaining price quotes for specific jobs. If the electric shop repaired an alternator, for example, the shop would receive a credit equal to what it would cost to buy a rebuilt alternator from a private supplier. The costs included labor costs (salary, fringe benefits, sick pay, vacations, and jury duty), material costs, depreciation of machinery, and other overhead costs. The difference between output values and cost was called "profit," and the eight shops were therefore called profit centers.

According to Mr. Contino, the "profit center" work measurement system had a significant impact on production:

> This system provides a mechanism which measures productivity without threatening the individual worker . . . and labor has responded enthusiastically to this

concept. . . . In addition, employees in individual shops can now see how well they are doing compared to the private sector (each shop has a large chart in a visible location) and a degree of competitiveness has developed, further spurring their desire to increase efficiency. The combination of the "profit motive" and the elimination of threats has worked like magic.

As evidence of progress, Mr. Contino referred to the table in Exhibit 1. He also had data showing that productivity and profits had improved with the passage of time.

As shown in Exhibit 1, all profit centers except the Motor Room reported a profit in 1981. The situation in the motor room illustrated the difficulty of measuring output. Initially, the shop's credit for rebuilt engines was the same as the cost to buy new motors because reliable data on the price of rebuilt motors was not available. The first reports showed that productivity was less than 1.0, meaning that the City could have purchased new engines for less than it spent rebuilding engines. As a result of decisions made by the shop's labor/management committee, the motor room subsequently doubled its productivity and appeared to be producing at a substantial "profit." However, once a data base of the outside price of rebuilt engines had been developed, all the shop's past reports were converted to the rebuilt values, the reports then showed that the shop was operating at a "loss." This led the labor/management committee to take further steps to increase productivity, including the discontinuation of unprofitable products and the transfer of personnel from support functions to line functions. By March 1982, the motor room's productivity factor hit 1.19.

The relatively low productivity in the passenger car shop had a different cause. The problem was that shop employees were required to list the actual time it took to do each job on a "job sheet," and they feared that if they consistently beat readily available industry-wide standards, sooner or later management would either require more work from individuals or would track

**Exhibit 1**
Profit Center Status for 1981

| | | *Annualized ($000)* | | | |
|---|---|---|---|---|---|
| *Profit Center* | *Number of Weeks in Operation from Inception to End of 1981* | *Input* | *Output* | *Profit* | *Productivity Factor** |
| Transmission . . . . . . . | 37 | $ 350 | $ 716 | $ 366 | 2.05 |
| Unit repair . . . . . . . . | 40 | 1,280 | 2,146 | 866 | 1.68 |
| Upholstery . . . . . . . . | 35 | 126 | 183 | 57 | 1.45 |
| Radiator . . . . . . . . . . | 36 | 263 | 438 | 175 | 1.67 |
| Machine . . . . . . . . . . | 23 | 643 | 1,562 | 919 | 2.43 |
| Passenger cars . . . . . . | 30 | 494 | 534 | 40 | 1.08 |
| Electric . . . . . . . . . . . | 37 | 603 | 717 | 114 | 1.19 |
| Motor room . . . . . . . | 43 | 1,272 | 822 | (451) | .65 |
| Total | | $5,031 | $7,117 | $2,086 | 1.41 |

* Output ÷ Input

each individual's daily performance. Thus, they tended to omit certain jobs done from their daily work sheet.

After the low productivity became apparent, meetings between the labor/management committee and the entire shop's work force were held, and it was agreed that it would no longer be necessary for employees to list the actual time it took to do a job. The February 1982 report for the shop showed the results: productivity moved from 1.05 to 1.30.

Mr. Contino summarized his impressions of the results of the program as follows:

> I have found that the process of getting labor involved in the running of an operation is not only exciting and rewarding, but also extremely worthwhile in terms of improving productivity and service quality. BME's experience belies the common notions that the government worker cannot be productive or that the output of a government operation cannot be measured. There is no simple formula for succeeding in the change from a traditional approach to the labor/management approach, and there should be no doubt that management's commitment to the process is a critical factor. But given the effort and the true desire to see it succeed, it does work. The simple proof is what has been achieved by BME in operating in this fashion.

## Questions

1. What are the strengths and weaknesses of the profit measure developed for the central repair facility? Should its use be continued? Can you suggest possibilities for improving it?
2. Records on performance by individuals or on costs for individual jobs were discontinued. Do you agree with this policy?
3. Under what circumstances, if any, should work be contracted out to the vendors whose price lists were used in measuring output?
4. The 73 garages operated by the Bureau did minor repairs and maintenance. Because of the specialized nature of the Department's vehicles (e.g., street cleaning trucks, solid waste collection trucks), it was estimated that output values were available for only 20 to 30 percent of their work. Could some variation of the profit center idea nevertheless be applied to these garages?
5. Assume that adequate measures of value eventually can be developed for the 73 garages. Thereafter, should the work they do be charged to the departments that own the vehicles? If so, should the charge be the output value of this work, or should it be the cost?

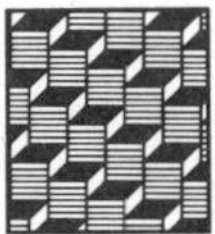

# The Programming Process

In Chapter 6 we described the structure of management control; that is, the nature of the information that is used for planning and controlling programs and responsibility centers. We turn now to a description of the management control process. The first step in this process, called programming, is described in this chapter and the next. In Chapters 9 through 13 we describe the other steps: budgeting, operating, and the evaluation of performance.

Programming is the process of deciding on the nature and size of the programs that are to be undertaken in order to achieve an organization's goals. Decisions about programs are of two general types. First, there are decisions on proposed new programs, and, second, there are decisions about the continuation of ongoing programs. This chapter is limited to a discussion of proposed new programs. The evaluation of ongoing programs is discussed in Chapter 13.

The programming process involves two related but separable activities. The first involves the preparation and analysis of individual program proposals and making decisions on these proposals. The second is the system for facilitating the flow and coordination of the separate proposals. Each is discussed in this chapter.

## NATURE OF PROGRAMMING

A program is a planned course of action that is intended to help the organization achieve its goals. It usually requires the commitment of a relatively large amount of resources, large enough to warrant the attention of senior management. Presumably, adoption of a program will have a significant effect on the activities of the organization. Also, execution of a program usually requires several years, and the program's impact often is not apparent until some time after it has been initiated.

## Programming and Budgeting

In many organizations, the programming process is combined with the process of budgeting. Both programming and budgeting involve planning, but the types of planning activities are different. The budgeting process focuses on a single year, whereas programming focuses on activities that extend over a period of several years. A budget is, in a sense, a one-year slice of the organization's programs, although, for reasons discussed in Chapter 9 this is not a complete description of a budget; the budgeting process involves more than simply carving out such a slice.

Many organizations do not make an explicit, formal distinction between the programming process and the budgeting process. Since the two processes are conceptually different, however, it is useful to think about these differences even if no formal distinction is made.

## Programming and Strategic Planning

In Chapter 1, we drew a line between two management activities: strategic planning and management control. Programming, although part of management control, is close to the line dividing these two processes, and it is therefore of some importance to distinguish between them. The distinction is not crucial, however, and as is the case in most matters relating to organizations, the line is not a sharp one. In fact, some authors use the term "long-range planning" to encompass both strategic planning and programming.

In the strategic planning process, management decides on the goals of the organization and the main strategies for achieving these goals. Conceptually, the programming process takes these goals and strategies as given and seeks to identify programs that will implement them. In practice, there is a considerable amount of overlap. For example, studies made during the programming process may indicate the desirability of changing goals or strategies. Conversely, strategic planning often includes some consideration of the programs that will be adopted to achieve goals.

An important reason for making a separation in practice between programming and strategic planning is that the programming process tends to become institutionalized, and this tends to put a damper on purely creative activities. Since strategic planning is an activity in which creative, innovative thinking is strongly encouraged, a separate strategic planning activity can provide an offset to this tendency.

Although the following comment makes no distinction between strategy formulation and programming, it provides a good rationale for the necessity of giving adequate management attention to the process:

> Nonprofit institutions need strategy far more than profit-making organizations. Their goals are more complex, their sources of support are more complex, and the interaction between their support and performance is more complex. Consequently, the problem of identifying optimal policies and potential strategies must be inherently more complex. In fact, most institutions would find their planning and policy formulation much easier if they were profit-making organizations. Then at least they would have a common denominator for their objectives and strategies.
>
> Strategy has many definitions but all definitions imply a goal, a set of constraints, and a firm plan for allocating resources. All of these factors interact and affect each other. Therefore, they must be considered simultaneously. Change one, and you may change them all.
>
> The goal of most nonprofit institutions is clear enough. Be it a hospital, a school or a governmental unit, the intuitive goal is this: "Get as much as possible in the way of resources; do as much as possible with these resources."
>
> But if the resources available are not enough to do everything, the definition of goals becomes more complicated. Which objective should be given priority? Should a school or hospital provide service to those who are willing to pay for its full cost; or should it be provided to those who can benefit most?
>
> Any strategy requires a compromise between the choice of goals and the resources available. To this extent every institution or organization is profit-making. It must attract resources at least equal to the requirements of its goals. . . .
>
> Whether the organization is a nonprofit institution or a profit-making business, the strategy problem is the same: "How do you produce an economic equilibrium between costs and incomes that is stable at a sufficiently high level?" Stable means that any reduction in services will cut cost more than it will reduce resources, . . .
>
> In a society of competitive institutions and philosophies, an explicit statement of strategy is one of the prerequisites for a productive and honored future.[1]

## Goals

A goal is a statement of intended programmatic output in the broadest terms. It is normally not related to a specific time period. Goals normally are not quantified, and hence cannot be used directly as a basis for a measurement system. The purpose of a statement of goals is to communicate senior management's decisions about the aims and relative priorities of the organization, and to provide general guidance as to the strategy that the organization is expected to follow.

***Constraints as Goals.*** Goals alternatively, but less desirably, may be expressed as constraints, as indicated in the following comment:

---

[1] *Strategy for Institutions* (The Boston Consulting Group, 1970). Used by permission.

The operational goals of an organization are seldom revealed by formal mandates. Rather, each organization's operational goals emerge as a set of constraints defining acceptable performance. Central among these constraints is organizational health, defined usually in terms of bodies assigned and dollars appropriated. The set of constraints emerges from a mix of the expectations and demands of other organizations in the government, statutory authority, demands from citizens and special interest groups, and bargaining within the organization. These constraints represent a quasi-resolution of conflict—the constraints are relatively stable, so there is some degree of resolution; but the constraints are not compatible, hence it is only a quasi-resolution. Typically, the constraints are formulated as imperatives to avoid roughly specified discomforts and disasters.

For example, the behavior of each of the U.S. military services (Army, Navy, and Air Force) seems to be characterized by effective imperatives to avoid: (1) a decrease in dollars budgeted, (2) a decrease in personnel, (3) a decrease in the number of key specialists (e.g., for the Air Force, pilots), (4) reduction in the percentage of the military budget allocated to that service, (5) encroachment of other services on that service's roles and missions, and (6) inferiority to an enemy weapon of any class.[2]

***Statement of Goals.*** Although every organization has one or more goals, many organizations give little attention to articulating these goals. Managements in most organizations will find it worthwhile to devote significant effort to thinking about what the organization's goals actually should be and to expressing them as concretely as it can. Such an exercise will greatly facilitate later steps in the management control process. This is not to say that management should try to state *all* the goals of the organization; rather, it should focus on the principal ones. The intention is to delineate the predominant goals, not to make an exhaustive list of them. Also, every organization carries on some activities that are not directly or obviously related to its stated goals.

*Example from Department of Defense:* 1. To determine what forces are required to support the political objectives of the United States.

2. To procure and support these forces as economically as possible.

*Example from the Visiting Nurse Association Home Health Services of Greater Kansas City:*

To offer community-based home health care and related services to the people of Greater Kansas City and neighboring areas; within the financial capability of the agency, care will be provided to any person regardless of ability to pay.

To provide high quality home health care and related services in a cost-effective manner.

[2] Graham T. Allison, *Essences of Decision: Explaining the Cuban Missile Crisis* (Boston: Little, Brown, 1971), p. 82.

To provide services which are preventive, treatment-oriented, educational, and rehabilitative in nature.

To utilize available resources in its approach to patient care and direct services appropriate to the needs of the individual.

To meet community needs for home health care and related services through utilization and coordination of regional and local planning efforts, other health care providers, and the medical community as resources in determining and serving those needs.

To evaluate its service areas and the scope of services offered to the end that these services meet a need and can be provided with quality and cost-effectiveness to the patient.

To take a position of leadership in educating health care professionals and the public in home health care.

To set a standard of excellence for home health care and related services in the areas it serves.

***Example:*** The dietary goals of the United States, as recommended by the McGovern Committee are as follows:

To avoid overweight, consume only as much energy (calories) as is expended; if overweight, decrease energy intake and increase energy expenditure.

Increase the consumption of complex carbohydrates and "naturally occurring" sugars from about 28 percent of energy intake to about 48 percent of energy intake.

Reduce the consumption of refined and processed sugars by about 45 percent to account for about 10 percent of total energy intake.

Reduce overall fat consumption from approximately 40 percent to about 30 percent of energy intake.

Reduce saturated fat consumption to account for about 10% of total energy intake; and balance that with polyunsaturated and mono-unsaturated fats, which should account for about 10 percent of energy intake each.

Reduce cholesterol consumption to about 300 mg a day.

Limit the intake of sodium by reducing the intake of salt to about 5 g a day.[3]

Although thinking about goals and attempting to express them in words is often a useful exercise, beyond a certain point the exercise can become frustrating and not worth additional effort. If a hospital has decided that it wants to be a general hospital, there may be no need to reduce to words an exact statement of the goals of a general-purpose hospital. Similarly, although many faculty committees have spent long hours attempting to find words that state the goals of a liberal arts college, the results sometimes are so vague that they have little operational impact. Nevertheless, particularly in large organizations, unless goals are clearly articulated, more detailed program planning can be inhibited.

[3] Select Committee on Nutrition and Human Needs, *Dietary Goals for the United States* (Washington, D.C.: Government Printing Office, 1977).

## Objectives

An objective is a specific result to be achieved within a specified time, usually one year or a few years.[4] A statement of objectives is a key element in a management control system because an organization's effectiveness can be measured only if actual outputs are related to objectives. As Lawrence Olewine has said, "It's tough to know when you're there if you don't know where *there* is before you start."

If feasible, an objective should be stated in measurable terms. Since measurement is always quantitative, if an objective is not stated in quantitative terms, performance toward achieving the objective cannot be measured; it can only be judged, evaluated, appraised, or weighed. If a statement of a particular objective in measurable terms is not feasible, the objective should be restated with sufficient clarity so that there is some way of judging whether or not it has been achieved. Exhibit 7–1 is an example.

**Exhibit 7–1**
Programs and Objectives, Fairfield Baptist Church, Chicago, Illinois (excerpts)

*Programs*

1. To Proclaim the Gospel to All People
   Objectives:
   *a.* To establish a church evangelism committee by April 15.
   *b.* To contact every person within the city limits (for whom we can find record) who ever attended a church function, but no longer does, with a personal visit from this church by May 1.
   *c.* To contact every home in our immediate census tracts by May 1.
   *d.* To adopt a comprehensive church-wide missionary education program by September 1.
2. To Promote Worship
   Objectives:
   *a.* To establish a church worship committee by April 15.
   *b.* To implement systematic membership participation in the church worship services by May 8.
   *c.* To involve all institutionalized (elderly and otherwise) members in regular church worship by June 1.

* * * * *

6. Community Service
   Objectives:
   *a.* To establish a church community service by April 15.
   *b.* To define the meaning of "service" and the extent of "community" by May 8.
   *c.* To establish communication with all community service agencies by May 1.

Source: Contributed by Dennis W. Bakke.

---

[4] Some writers use "goal" for the idea that is here described as "objective," and vice versa. Care must be taken to deduce the intended meaning from the context.

An objective should be consistent with the goals of the organization. Usually, the ordinary, ongoing activities that require little management judgment as to the amount of emphasis that is to be given to them are not included in a statement of objectives; that is, objectives are nonroutine.

> ***Example from the National Institutes of Health:*** To increase the output of schools of medicine and osteopathy by awarding grants to augment the present commitments for first-year enrollments by 400 in fall 1970 and by an additional 600 in fall 1971, and by awarding construction grants to increase capacity for 1973–75 first-year enrollments by 300.

> ***Example:*** An unsatisfactory statement of objectives from City of Long Beach Department of Community Development (these are *not* properly worded objectives because they are not stated in measurable terms and there is no way of judging whether or not they have been achieved):
>
> Completion of the City's Community Analysis Program and development of a schedule of programs to prevent and correct blighted areas as well as predisposing and precipitating factors.
>
> Expansion of the federally approved low-income housing program for additional housing units.

With some effort, it is often feasible to state objectives in a measurable way. For example, the following is a vague objective for third-grade instruction in geography:

> To learn to use the vocabulary, tools, skills, and insights of the geographer in interpreting and understanding the earth and our relation to it.

This objective becomes more useful if it is recast as follows:

> That 90 percent of the third-grade students attending the Booth Elementary School, by June 30, 1979, will score between 90 and 100 percent and the remaining 10 percent will score between 80 and 90 percent on a wide evaluative instrument and/or process which measures their ability:
>
> *a.* To understand why we have maps and why they are important.
>
> *b.* To understand the importance of the globe being marked with horizontal and vertical lines which represent degrees of longitude and latitude and that the earth consists of hemispheres, continents, and oceans.[5]

## OVERVIEW OF THE PROCESS

### Participants

The principal participants in the programming process are: the *advocate,* the person who wants a proposed program adopted; the *analyst,* the person who analyzes the merits of the proposal; *senior management* who decides

---

[5] From Larry Pauline, Education Systems Consultants.

on the adoption of the proposal; *resource providers* who must be sold on the merits of the proposal so that they will provide funds for its execution; and the *controller* who operates the programming system. Of these, we shall focus primarily on the program analyst.[6]

## Planning Staff

An organization that must make many decisions about programs usually has a staff unit to facilitate this process. This unit is here called the planning staff, but it also can be called the program office or the systems analysis office. The planning staff should be close to the top of the organization hierarchy, that is, it should report directly either to top management or to the controller. If the planning staff reports to the controller, however, there is a danger that it will become involved too much in the budget process, which is also a function of the controller. The budget process has a short-range focus and is carried out under considerable time pressure. If the planning staff gets too much involved in this process, or if the "budgeteers" in the controller organization are permitted to have too much influence on the programming process, the long-range view that is essential to good programming is likely to suffer. Thus, if the planning staff is a part of the controller organization, it probably should be kept separate from the part of that organization that is involved in the budget process.

If an appropriate separation between programming and budgeting activities can be achieved, there are good reasons for having the planning staff in the controller organization. This arrangement reduces the number of staff units reporting to top management, increases the likelihood that planners will have easy access to available data, and tends to even out the workload in the controller organization.

In organizations where the idea of a formal programming effort is relatively new, there tends to be friction between the planning staff and the operating organization. The planning staff may consist of young, technically oriented, bright, but inexperienced persons who tend to be unaware of, or to minimize the importance of, the rules of the "bureaucratic game." Such a staff may underestimate the value of experience and the importance of the pressures of day-to-day operations, and it tends to use a jargon that is unfamiliar to operating managers. To the operating organization, the planning staff may represent a threat, a challenge to the established way of doing things.

In order to minimize such conflicts, it is desirable to build up a planning staff gradually, starting with a small group and increasing its size only as it develops credibility and as resistance from operating managers subsides.

---

[6] For an excellent description of the work of program analysts in the federal government and their relationships with the other participants, see Arnold J. Meltsner, *Policy Analysts in the Bureaucracy* (Berkeley: University of California Press, 1976).

If feasible, at least some members of the initial staff should come from the existing organization. Moreover, the planning staff should never forget that it *is* a staff; it does not make decisions itself. It should spend considerable time—much more time than it usually prefers to spend—communicating with the operating organization, explaining its approaches to analysis, and attempting to establish good working relationships. Finally, the planning staff must gain and maintain the firm support of senior management. The operating organization must perceive that the programming effort is not a "trial" or a "fad" but a permanent part of the management process.

Whether or not the planning staff is part of the controller organization, the controller's office, as the office responsible for all information flows, should be responsible for the flow of programming information. If there is a formal programming system, the controller's office should oversee the operation of this system; that is, it should set up procedures governing the flow of information through the system, and it should assure that these procedures are adhered to. In some agencies, the planning staff operates the programming system, but this leads to unnecessary duplication of data and to a lack of coordination and consistency between programming data and other data.

## Steps in the Process

The steps involved in an individual program proposal are (1) initiation, (2) screening, (3) analysis, (4) decision, and (5) selling.

*Initiation.* The idea for a new program may come from anywhere: from any level within the organization or from people outside the organization. In order to encourage the internal generation of ideas, senior management must emphasize that they are welcome and must provide a clear mechanism for bringing them to the attention of the planning staff.

Generally, wherever an idea originates, it becomes a part of the programming process only after it has attracted the favorable attention of an influential person within the organization. That person thereafter can be considered the program advocate. The program advocate may personally do considerable work in developing the idea, or he or she may submit it in rough form to the planning staff for development. Planning staffs and senior managements also may be program advocates.

*Screening.* From the many ideas that come to its attention, the planning staff selects the relative few that seem to be worth detailed analysis. Ideas proposed by senior management are obviously in this category, unless it can be demonstrated clearly that they are unsound. Ideas proposed by resource providers generally are also worth detailed analysis.

An important criterion in this initial screening is whether the proposal is consistent with the goals of the organization. In their natural desire to grow or to obtain funding for their overhead costs, some organizations pursue ideas that are unrelated to their goals. A notable example of this behavior is the Port Authority of New York and New Jersey. Although that organization's goal is to facilitate the movement of people and goods in metropolitan New York, it sponsored the construction of two huge office buildings in the most crowded section of Manhattan. Movement of people to and from these buildings exacerbated the transportation problem, rather than helped solve it. Similarly, a university that attempts to cover its overhead costs by developing research proposals for projects that are outside its area of competence or marginally related to its goals, is making a screening mistake. Such projects are quite likely to be unsuccessful and thereby not only waste scarce resources but potentially damage the institution's ability to raise funds in the future.

The goals of the organization may need to be made fairly specific if the screening process is to be effective. The goal of the United Nation's International Children's Emergency Fund (UNICEF) is to help children in the developing nations, but there are 100 such nations and 800 million children in them, with a wide variety of needs. A narrower focus is essential.

*Analysis.* Proposals that survive the initial screening process are analyzed by the planning staff. Essentially, there are two types of analysis: technical and political. A technical analysis involves estimating the costs of a proposed program, attempting to quantify its benefits, and, if feasible, assessing alternative ways of carrying it out. A political analysis involves consideration of how the proposal is likely to be viewed by parties who are affected by it, particularly resource providers. Both types of analysis are discussed in Chapter 8.

*Decision and Selling.* Following analysis, the proposal is submitted to senior management for decision, or, more frequently, tentative proposals are discussed with senior management and then sent back for further work. This process may be repeated several times and usually involves the program advocate as well as the planning staff. The staff analysis may emphasize the technical aspects of the proposal, but the decision maker places considerable emphasis on the political aspects as well.

Usually, the proposal is not submitted as a "take-it-or-leave-it" proposition. Rather several alternative ways of accomplishing the objective are described, together with the merits of each. Although the planning staff may not state formally a preference for one alternative, its views usually become clear in the discussion. The program advocate invariably has a strong preference for one of the alternatives.

Since program proposals are important and normally involve substantial amounts of resources, they usually must be sold to resource providers before they can be implemented. In government organizations, resource providers are the Congress or corresponding legislative bodies at state and local levels. In other nonprofit organizations, resource providers are the governing boards of the organization, or outside organizations and individuals who may provide funds for it. This sales effort is carried out by senior management, assisted by the planning staff and often also by the program advocate.

## FORMAL PROGRAMMING SYSTEMS

Most organizations must, at some time, consider individual program proposals. Relatively few, however, have a formal programming system. A formal system is needed primarily in large organizations whose programs are subject to considerable change, such as most government organizations. Organizations with stable programs, such as hospitals, colleges, and membership organizations, normally do not need formal systems, although from time to time their managements find it useful to construct a long-range plan, which is an essential part of such a system. In general, a formal programming system is worthwhile if—

Several program decisions need to be made each year.

Interrelationships among the several parts of the organization are complicated.

Implementation of program decisions requires a fairly long lead time.

Complex scheduling of program elements is required to bring activities and capital investments into a particular sequence.

Resources are particularly scarce and the number of desirable programs is quite large.

Essentially, a formal system consists of (1) procedures prescribing the preparation and analysis of individual proposals and their flow through the organization up to the decision maker; and (2) a document that summarizes the costs, and, if feasible, the benefits of all approved programs for a series of future years. The latter document is usually referred to as "the program" or "the five-year program," or "the program summary." The program summary differs from the budget in that the former *(a)* often is not related to responsibility centers, *(b)* is less detailed than a budget, and *(c)* covers several years.

When such an overall program is prepared, senior management's ability to make judgments about the overall balance and relative priorities among the separate programs is increased. Furthermore, if the programming process is adequately understood by operating managers, it can lead them to think in a different and better way about their problems; that is, to take a longer-run point of view, to relate activities more closely to objectives, and to consider the impact of their activities on other responsibility centers.

***Time Period.*** Customarily, the time period covered by a formal programming system is five future years. The first year is the "budget year," and the other years are "out years." Separate numerical estimates are not necessarily prepared for each year. Many programs include only the budget year, the following year, and the fifth year. The fifth year shows the impact on operations on capital projects that are approved for the budget year and prior years. By contrast, in organizations with large programs for capital spending, such as highways, dams, or reclamation projects, the program may be projected, in summary form, for as many as 20 years.

*Example:* The Forest Service in the Department of Agriculture has a $2.2 billion annual budget. By law, the Service is required to develop a 50-year plan. Every 10 years, an assessment is made of outputs produced (e.g., board feet of timber) and expected demand based on population projections and demand data. During the assessment process, a supply/demand model is developed for the next 50 years. From this, a plan is developed for producing the outputs to meet projected demand. This assessment plan is updated every five years, and a management program is developed based on the long-range plan.[7]

## Steps in a Formal System

The process involves the following principal steps:

1. Preparation and dissemination of guidelines.
2. Preparation of program memoranda.
3. Staff analysis of program memoranda.
4. Discussion of proposed program with line managers.
5. Discussion with higher authority and approval.

In a complicated organization, such as the federal government, the formal programming process starts shortly after the budget for the coming year has been approved. Specifically, if the budget is completed by the end of December, the next programming cycle would start in January or February. It ordinarily would be completed in the summer, as a basis for the budgeting process which begins in the fall. In less complicated organizations, the cycle is of course shorter.

***Guidelines.*** The process starts with the preparation and dissemination of guidelines or "protocols." These are prepared by the programming staff, discussed with and approved by senior management, and disseminated to the managers who are responsible for programs. As a minimum, the guidelines contain *(a)* an indication of the constraints, principally resource limitations, within which the program should be prepared; *(b)* a discussion of what constitutes a program; and *(c)* instructions for the format and content of the program memoranda.

In deciding on the overall resource constraints, management and its staff take into account the probable needs of the organization, based on informal discussions and on proposals for major new programs that already may have come to their attention, and the probable amount of funds that will be available. It is essential that resource constraints be stated. If this is not done,

[7] From presentation by Jerome Miles at Joint Financial Management Improvement Program Symposium, Washington, D.C., 1981.

the initial program submissions are likely to be "wish lists" rather than realistic statements of what is feasible. In particular, managers will be reluctant to come to grips with the difficult problem of priorities; they will tend to recommend *all* worthwhile programs rather than deciding which are the more important. The initial constraint is of course subject to change in the course of preparing the program.

In some organizations, the resource constraint is stated as a range; that is, managers are asked to prepare programs for three funding levels: *(a)* the most probable level, *(b)* 5 percent (or 10 percent) above this level, and *(c)* 5 percent (or 10 percent) below this level. The purpose of this practice is to identify additional program opportunities and low-priority programs, but the experience generally has not been satisfactory. Managers have a difficult enough time preparing the "most probable" program, and give little thought to the other alternatives.

In the first attempt at a programming effort, programs are likely to be defined in a way that makes them correspond to organization units. Thus each responsibility center manager is also a program manager, and the "program" consists of a description of what that unit does. As the system becomes more refined, programs tend increasingly to cut across organization units.

***Program Memoranda.*** After receipt of these guidelines, each program manager prepares a document describing the proposed program. This document is called by various names, but "program memorandum" is fairly common. The program memorandum describes the objectives that are relevant to the program; the specific activities that are proposed for accomplishing these objectives; the resources that are estimated to be required in carrying on these activities, including both resources used by the organization itself and services that are required from other responsibility centers; and the anticipated outputs. Exhibit 7–2 shows how one such memorandum is organized.

To the extent that a major shift in activities is proposed, a program proposal, as described in the preceding section, should be prepared. If feasible, the proposal should be in the form of a benefit/cost analysis. In some organizations, these program proposals are submitted as part of the program memorandum; in others, they are submitted separately.

***Staff Analysis.*** When a program memorandum reaches headquarters, the planning staff makes a preliminary examination of it to ensure that it conforms to the guidelines. If it does not, a staff member sits down with the program manager and they rework the document so that it does conform. Next, the separate memoranda are combined into an overall picture of the program for the whole organization. This may be called a "program summary."

This "first cut" at the total program will probably reveal either or both of the following problems: (1) the total of individual program proposals exceeds the resources available; or (2) there is a lack of balance, such as mission

**Exhibit 7–2**
Excerpts from Narcotics Program

Program goals:

1.0 Reduce the abuse of narcotics and dangerous drugs in the United States.

1.1 Reduce the supply of illicit drugs.

- 1.1.1 Reduce the amount of legally manufactured drugs available for abuse.
- 1.1.2 Reduce domestic supply of illicit drugs.
- 1.1.3 Reduce foreign supply of illicit drugs introduced into the United States.

1.2 Reduce demand for illegal use of drugs.

1.3 Expand understanding of the problem.

1.4 Improve program management and administrative support.

Operating program objectives (for Goal 1.1.3):

- 1.1.3.1 Reduce smuggling into United States at ports and borders.
- 1.1.3.2 Reduce foreign cultivation, production, and trafficking.

Operating program activities (for Objective 1.1.3.1)

- 1.1.3.1.1 Conduct investigations of smuggling.
- 1.1.3.1.2 Arrest smugglers and conspirators and seize smuggled drugs.
- 1.1.3.1.3 Support prosecutions.
- 1.1.3.1.4 Identify international border points vulnerable to smuggling and strengthen them.
- 1.1.3.1.5 Inspect carriers, cargo, persons, baggage, and mail.
- 1.1.3.1.6 Develop and operate a program of mutual exchange of intelligence.

units planning to use more resources from service units than the service units can provide, or two managers planning overlapping programs on the same target group. The staff discusses these inconsistencies with program managers, attempting to resolve as many of them as a staff agency can, but remembering that senior management, not the staff, must make the actual decisions. If individual program proposals accompany the program memoranda, they also are analyzed at this time.

***Discussion with Line Managers.*** The purpose of the preceding step is to assemble information in a way that facilitates the discussion of proposed programs between senior management and the program managers, which is the most important part of the whole process. This discussion is conducted in various ways. One common method is to have a preliminary general meeting of all program managers, at which overall problems are discussed, and to follow this meeting with a discussion with each manager individually. This discussion must take place between line managers.

***Approval by Senior Management.*** Although staff people can provide clarification, data, and other assistance, the end product of the discussion is approval of the program, and such approval can only be given by senior management. This takes place at each level in the organization. When it has been completed at one level, it is repeated at the next higher level, with the process concluding at the level of the person or group that has the final say on the allocation of funds.

### The Program Summary

There are basically two different ways of constructing a program summary: (1) the summary is prepared anew each year, as one step in the programming process; or (2) the summary is continuously updated—that is, whenever a program decision is approved, the costs and outputs associated with that decision are incorporated into the program summary.

Few organizations use a continuously updated summary. The creation of the computer program that is required to maintain such a summary is a complicated job, although once this program has been developed, the maintenance of the summary is fairly simple. What is required is that the document that records each program decision set forth the costs and, if feasible, the outputs for each program element affected by the decision. If this is carefully done, the job of updating the program summary is purely a mechanical one.

*Taking Account of Inflation.* The money amounts in a program summary can be based either on the assumption that prices will not change or on the assumption that a specified amount of inflation is to be expected. Either basis will work; the important thing is that all parties must understand which basis is used and act consistently. If the program summary assumes no inflation, the calculations are easier to make, and the program is easier for users to understand since changes reflect purely physical magnitudes. If estimates of inflation are incorporated, the user may have difficulty in separating the physical changes from the changes in purchasing power. Furthermore, no one can make reliable estimates on the general rate of inflation over the next five years, and even less so of inflation rates of wages, various types of material, and other cost components.

On the other hand, inflation is a fact, and it may be unrealistic to disregard it. A program that does incorporate assumed rates of inflation is particularly useful if there is good reason to believe that different cost elements have different rates of inflation. As high rates of inflation persist, incorporation of an inflation assumption in programs becomes more common.

***Nature of the Program Summary.*** The program summary is fundamentally different from an approved budget. A budget is a bilateral commitment between a budgetee and his or her supervisor—the former committing to carry on activities with the resources stated in the budget, and the latter agreeing that such action constitutes good performance. A program summary does not represent a commitment; it is an estimate or best guess as to what will happen over the period covered. Also, actual spending usually will be quite close to the budgeted amounts, whereas actual spending in the later years of a program will probably vary considerably from the amounts set forth in the program summary. Both of these differences stem from the fact that the budget relates to the next year whereas the program covers several years in the future; the longer the time period, the greater the uncertainty.

A program summary therefore does not state what *will* happen; rather, it shows what is *likely* to happen if presently approved policies are continued unchanged.

Robert Bartnik highlights the purposes of the program summary in this statement about the "Working Memorandum" used at the Franklin Institute (which corresponds to the program summary as used here):[8]

> The Working Memorandum breaks the shackles of one-year planning and budgeting by emphasizing the horizon five years from now. It permits unit aspirations to be expressed creatively, with a minimum of budgeting and a maximum of activity in thinking through the future, selecting from alternatives through informed management estimates rather than precise pencil pushing. To promote realism, the Working Memorandum includes provision for thinking through funding sources.
>
> A focus on a single year tends to keep the manager's thinking fettered by the shortness of each year and by an acute awareness of things that have had to be postponed before. Long-range planning is *not* planning each year at a time; it *is* developing a five-year program during which realistic objectives can be attained *and then planning appropriate checkpoint and milestones during intervening years.* The manager is then able to do free, unfettered, yet realistic thinking, not frozen by existing organizational structures.

## Gap-Closing Program

In some entities, the formal program focuses on the projected "gap" between revenues and expenditures. The City of New York, for example, has a five-year program that shows revenues according to currently approved estimates and expenditures estimated from currently approved programs. If expenditures are estimated to exceed revenues in any year, there is a "gap" because the budget must be balanced each year. The program document describes "gap-closing measures," that is, plans currently being considered to increase revenues or decrease expenditures. This program is revised quarterly.

## The PPB System

The most widely known acronym in the programming literature is PPBS, which stands for Planning—Programming—Budgeting System. PPBS has three central ideas: first, it is a formal programming system, essentially like that described in the preceding two sections; second, it uses a program budget,

---

[8] Excerpted from "The Franklin Institute: Where we are going and how we plan to get there," May 22, 1974.

as contrasted with a line-item budget;[9] and third, it emphasizes benefit/cost analysis. The concept of a program budget will be discussed in Chapter 9. The "P" for Planning suggests that there is another central idea, but this is not so. Programming and budgeting are both forms of planning, and no third type of planning is involved in the PPB system; the inclusion of the first "P" in the acronym has led to some unnecessary misconceptions.

PPBS was first discussed in the 1950s, first applied in practice in the Department of Defense in 1962, spread to other government agencies in 1966, and by 1971 had been officially abandoned by the federal government. Because of its short life in the federal government, PPBS has become a dirty term. Its basic ideas, however, live on. They live, under other labels, in some federal agencies, in a number of state and municipal governments, and in other types of nonprofit organizations. A 1972 study of 1,873 public and private institutions of higher education found that 30 percent had implemented PPB systems.[10] The system continues essentially unchanged in the Department of Defense.[11]

The poor initial acceptance of PPBS was the result of faulty implementation. In August 1965, President Johnson directed wide use of PPBS. Instructions for implementation were issued on October 12, 1965, and these required that work on the new system begin immediately with implementation within 18 months. Charles Schultze, Director of the Bureau of the Budget, recognized that this was a dangerously short time period, but President Johnson decided that it was preferable to get something started and then improve it, rather than to go through a long period of preparation during which nothing happened.

PPBS received little support. Few Bureau of the Budget analysts were convinced that the new system was an improvement, and they paid little attention to it. In the Congress, the Appropriations Committees refused to examine a budget that was cast in program terms, and extensive hearings which had a generally critical tone were held by the Government Operations Committee. Members of Congress felt comfortable with the old budget format, and were suspicious of a new arrangement of the data, especially since its principal advocates were regarded as impractical "whiz kids." In retrospect, it was unreasonable to expect Congress to accept this new approach, without a thorough educational program, even though it gave a demonstrably better basis for making decisions. Some educational efforts were made, but they were inadequate.

---

[9] The idea of a program budget is much older than PPBS; PPBS gave the idea publicity. See, for example, Frederick C. Mosher, *Program Budgeting: Theory and Practice* (Chicago: Public Administration Service, 1954).

[10] Lawrence Bogard, "Management in Institutions of Higher Education," in *Papers on Efficiency in the Management of Higher Education* (Carnegie Commission on Higher Education, 1972), p. 11.

[11] See, for example, Burton B. Moyer, Jr., "Evolution of PPB in DOD," *Armed Forces Comptroller,* 18, (Spring 1973), pp. 21–26.

There was also inadequate time to educate agency heads as to the advantages of PPBS, let alone the techniques involved in it. Agency heads therefore gave little personal attention to PPBS, did not attempt to build up adequate programming staffs (without which the system could not function), and permitted the traditional budget process to continue essentially unchanged.

The PPBS effort was divorced from the traditional planning apparatus, and, what is just as important, it was divorced from the systems for collecting information on actual spending and actual outputs. (Unfortunately PPBS did not emphasize the necessity for a close tie between programming, budgeting, and accounting; it would have been preferable if an "A" for accounting had been included in the acronym.)

A 1974 survey of 17 federal agencies concluded that "PPB appears to be viewed by experienced officials as structurally and conceptually sound." This same survey identified 10 important pitfalls in using a PPB system that are important to keep in mind. These are, in order of their perceived importance by managers: (1) failing to select meaningful criteria of program effectiveness; (2) failing to ensure sufficient interaction between decision maker and analyst; (3) becoming so engrossed in current problems that insufficient time is spent on long-range planning, and the process thus becomes discredited; (4) failing to apply sufficient resources to the effort; (5) failing to assume necessary involvement of major operating personnel in the PPB process; (6) permitting concern over techniques to submerge the actual purposes of PPB; (7) misplacing the planning and program analysis functions organizationally relative to the budget function; (8) attempting too comprehensive an initial implementation effort; (9) failing to develop analytical capabilities in major operating units; and (10) injecting so much formality into planning that it lacks flexibility, looseness, and simplicity, and restrains creativity.[12]

***Current Status.*** This experience with PPBS does not demonstrate that the basic concepts of the system are unsound. It does tell us much about the necessity for a proper program of implementation, a topic discussed in Chapter 14. Allen Schick sums it up succinctly, as follows:

> PPBS is an idea whose time has not quite come. It was introduced government-wide before the requisite concepts, organizational capability, political conditions, informational resources, and techniques were adequately developed. A decade ago, PPB was beyond reach; a decade or two hence, it, or some updated version, might be one of the conventions of budgeting. For the present, PPB must make do in a world it did not create and has not yet mastered.[13]

---

[12] B. H. DeWoolfson, "Federal PPB: A Ten-Year Perspective," *The Federal Accountant,* September 1975, p. 55.

[13] Allen Schick, "Systems Politics and Systems Budgeting," *Public Administration Review, 29* (March/April 1969), p. 150.

Case 7–1

# COOK COUNTY HOSPITAL (A)*

On February 2, 1972, Dr. James G. Haughton, Executive Director of the Health and Hospital Governing Commission of Cook County, in testimony before the Illinois Legislative Investigating Commission said, "If I had been an executive who took over a business on the verge of bankruptcy and brought it back to solvency in one year and even paid a small dividend to our shareholders, I would probably have received a bonus from my firm and accolades from the shareholders. No one would have been overly concerned about the toes which were bruised in the process of recovery." He went on to add that "a leader should lead. One who does not have the courage to make decisions, and to take unpopular and sometimes controversial positions should not accept a position of leadership." The Investigating Committee agreed. In concluding their report they said "He is also an extremely farsighted individual with superb qualifications in comprehensive health care planning in large urban areas." Exhibit 1 presents key summary statistics for the period 1969–72 and illustrates the "extent of change" at Cook County Hospital under Dr. Haughton's leadership.

**xhibit 1**
ummary Statistics—1969–1973

| | *1969* | *1970** | *1971* | *1972* | *1973†* |
|---|---|---|---|---|---|
| er diem (public aid) | $73.02 | $91.05 | $126.69 | $172.47 | $170.00 |
| otal budget | $51,885,791 | $53,613,882 | $81,301,628 | $86,975,249 | $85,518,251 |
| ctual expenditures | n.a. | n.a. | 73,143,675 | 83,605,897 | — |
| udgeted employees | 5,783 | 5,795 | 6,883 | 7,479 | 6,266 |
| verage daily census | 1,824 | 1,597 | 1,413 | 1,180 | 1,197 |
| dmissions | 73,580 | 62,176 | 57,049 | 51,554 | 49,542 |
| otal inpatient days | 665,776 | 582,802 | 517,577 | 430,695 | 436,905 |
| verage length of stay (days) | 9.3 | 9.3 | 8.9 | 8.0 | 8.4 |
| utpatients seen | 337,391 | 287,701 | 297,238 | 306,451 | 319,746 |

a. = Not available.
Dr. James G. Haughton became the Executive Director of the Commission in the last week of November 1970.
Projected for the year 1973.

## Background

Cook County was one of the largest and most famous hospitals in the world. It had a bed capacity of 1,800 and a daily census of about 1,500 in 1970–71. The hospital opened its doors to patients in 1876 in the heart of Chicago's west side, and had expanded to comprise 21 buildings. In addition to inpatient services, it operated a large clinic for outpatients. CCH provided a wide

* This case was prepared by C. K. Prahalad and J. B. Silvers, Harvard Business School.

range of medical services and was particularly known for its Koch Burn Unit, trauma center, and pain clinic. The research wing of CCH was the Hektoen Institute, incorporated in 1943 as a nonprofit research organization.

CCH was the primary health care institution for the county's indigent sick. Emergency cases were admitted without regard to any eligibility requirement. However, according to a 1976 article in *The Wall Street Journal,*

> by the late 1960s, the institution had become too old, too big, and too enmeshed in the county's political patronage system to care for the poor effectively. Large, overcrowded wards were dirty and lacked sufficient nurses, privacy, or supplies. Surgeons sometimes had to swat flies while operating. . . .
>
> Politicians and the press clamored to close the "medical snakepit," and in 1970 the hospital seemed about to lose its accreditation.

When Dr. Haughton came to Cook County, he refused an employment contract, but insisted that the Commission give him full operating authority and support. He then, according to *The Wall Street Journal:*

> recruited a top caliber medical staff, streamlined the administrative structure, and collected $25 million in unpaid Medicare and Medicaid bills. In spending $12 million to clean up and modernize the facilities, he bought new beds rather than used ones, for the first time in memory. He ordered installation of patient call buttons and bed curtains and doubled the amount of nursing care. His improvements helped slash the hospital's death rate in half.

These changes did not come about without some difficulty, though; there was a threat of a walkout by hospital physicians in 1971, a nurses strike in 1972, a strike by interns and residents in 1975, the firing of several key physicians, and a series of threats on Dr. Haughton's life. Many of these difficulties resulted from Dr. Haughton's controversial style and unilateral approach to decision making. According to *The Wall Street Journal,* Dr. Haughton

> thinks the broader issue is whether he or physicians should run the hospital. "The Commission hired me to make decisions," he says flatly. "If I can wait for consensus, fine. Otherwise, I will make decisions myself."

## Organization

Until 1969, CCH was governed by the County Board. In 1969, the general assembly created the Health and Hospitals Governing Commission to remove the hospital from the political arena. The Commission had general responsibility for organizing, supervising, and managing Cook County Hospital, the Cook County School of Nursing, and Oak Forest Hospital.

According to Dr. Haughton, the Commission as constituted in July 1, 1969, was ineffective as an institution. "It was given all the responsibility for running the three institutions but none of the authority. It did not control its budget or its hiring practices, it could not set salaries, and it could not purchase. It was not until the spring of 1970 that amendments were passed giving the Commission all of these very necessary authorities."

An organization chart showing the relationships between the County Board, the Commission, and the hospitals is in Exhibit 1. The Commission, in its meeting of August 18, 1971, adopted a statement of the policies and goals for the Commission, which govern the growth and role of its constituents including CCH. The policy statement is shown in Exhibit 2. Estimated sources of revenue for FY 1973 are shown in Exhibit 3.

## The Budget

Dr. Haughton considered the budgeting system as an important element in the recovery of CCH, and in stabilizing the role of the Commission. He commented: "I believe that the budget is the best lever to change the character of an organization. I used to commute between New York and Chicago during October–November 1970, before I formally accepted the position here. My motivation was to participate in the preparation of the budget for FY 1971 and influence its direction."

**Exhibit 2**
Organization Chart

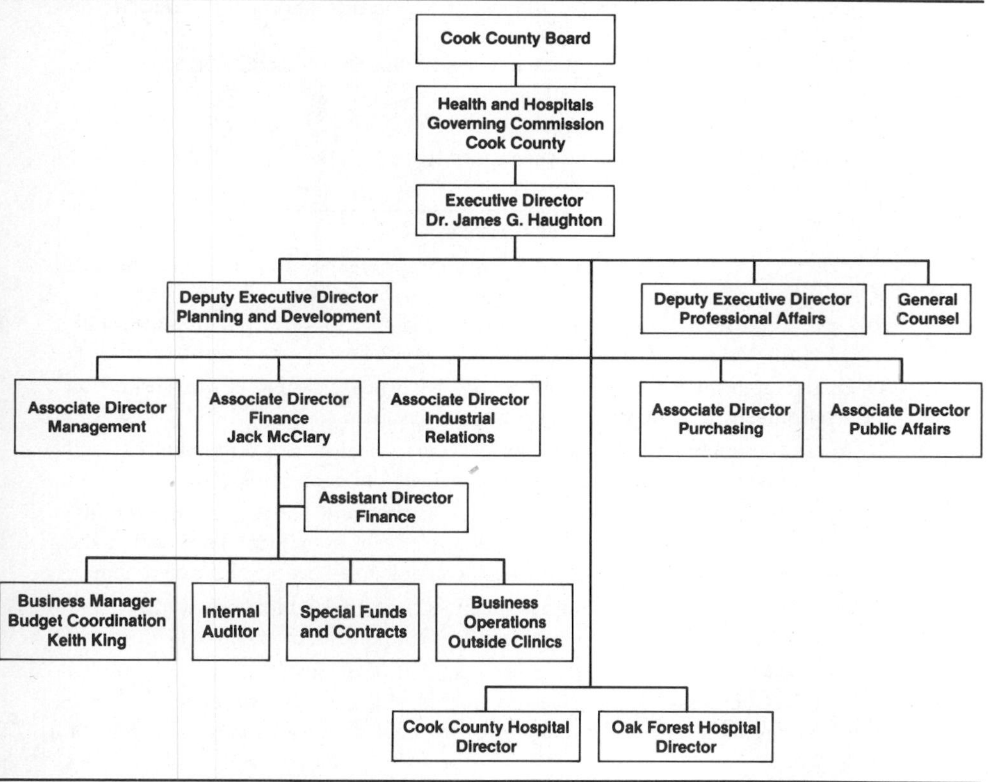

Some excerpts from an interview with Dr. Haughton are given below:

*Q:* You describe the budget as a lever. How did you use it, in fact, during the period October–November 1970?

*A:* I see the budget as more than mere dollar figures. It is a philosophy of managing. I asked each divisional head to develop objectives for his division and to put a dollar value on them. I was attempting to provide direction to the hospital by outlining within the budgeting framework both fiscal and technical guidelines. I was not interested in their telling me what equipment was needed. I wanted them to define programs—to tell me what they planned to do, what they needed, what was vital, what capability could be reasonably delivered, and used by the community. I was not interested in their "laundry lists" or "pies in the sky." I was interested in workable programs.

*Q:* What is new in this approach as contrasted to the budgeting system that was in use?

*A:* Quite a lot. It is a new ball game altogether. Earlier budgets were concerned with line items—pieces of equipment, hiring of a resident, or adding a fixture. The concern was primarily with dollars and with items of expenditure. I refused to look at both until I was satisfied with the programs. The division heads had to develop viable programs; for example, frozen blood, oncology—and I insisted that programs came first, dollars next. I also believe that a budget should not be rigid, should not kill the initiative of the division heads. I allow them the flexibility to change the budget, by either adding programs or by deleting them, as conditions change.

Approval of the budget does not mean that the division heads have the

**Exhibit 3**
Policies and Goals for the Health and Hospitals Governing Commission of Cook County

*POLICIES*

1. To deliver patient care that is based on appropriateness and timeliness instead of mere cost effectiveness. For example, it might be impossible to justify the cost of the enormous expenditures involved in cancer therapy, but these expenditures are a necessary adjunct to delivering adequate health care to the community.
2. To encourage teaching and research in our health care system in order to create the environment to support excellence in patient care.
3. To foster community participation in identifying health care programs that will be truly responsive to the needs of the people of the community.
4. To create an atmosphere in which voluntary institutions, the Governing Commission and community groups working cooperatively at a local level will make acceptable health and medical care readily available to all people of the community.
5. To encourage programs for improvement of housing, education, welfare, and transportation insofar as these are necessary components of effective health care.
6. To encourage opportunities for the participation of members of minority groups in all of the Commission's programs and relationships; and, to associate or affiliate only with organizations which adhere to this philosophy. (As amended October 2, 1971.)

**Exhibit 3** ***(concluded)***

*GOALS*

1. To promote primary neighborhood family care in areas of greatest need throughout the county.
2. To establish a system of backup facilities for this primary care in order to provide specialty and inpatient care for patients.
3. To establish a decentralized system for chronic care and to coordinate it with backup facilities.
4. To develop outreach programs that place less reliance on physical facilities.
5. To develop educational programs that foster health maintenance within our communities.
6. To stress the benefits of ambulatory care over inpatient care to third-party payors and providers as well as to consumers.
7. To train paramedical personnel to such a level of competence that they may be relied upon for many basic medical procedures.
8. To examine and redefine the functions of Fantus Clinic and other services at Cook County Hospital as well as Oak Forest Hospital.
9. To promote the development of a countywide system of rapid registry and retrieval of medical records.
10. To examine and recommend participation in such regional programs as are appropriate for health care in the community.

In order to accomplish the above goals, it will be necessary for the Governing Commission to coordinate its role with the activities of voluntary and proprietary institutions as well as other governmental agencies.

Adopted: September 21 , 1971

---

right to go ahead and implement their programs. We work here on a cash accounting basis, and we have to find the cash to go ahead. We allocate funds every quarter based on cash flow projections. At that time the division heads get yet another opportunity to review their programs.

*Q:* You said you look at programs and objectives first, dollars next. Who develops these objectives?

*A:* I provide the overall direction, and within that broad framework division heads develop programs and objectives for their divisions. I would not approve, at this stage, someone suggesting a kidney transplant at CCH. Not because I dislike transplants, but because I dislike duplication of facilities. There is an excellent transplant group across the street. What we need is a dialysis unit to keep the patients alive until a transplant can be attempted. We need a facility to harvest kidneys. Care of the alcoholics is yet another "bottomless pit." No one knows how to cure alcoholics effectively. I would at this stage encourage division heads to improve the process of care, using known techniques. Patients and the community come first.

The statement of objectives of the diagnostic radiology unit is provided in Exhibit 4 as a representative sample of the objective statements that all departments and divisions in the hospital had to prepare.

**Exhibit 4**

Departmental Objective Statements

Department: Main Department, Radiology

*Overall Objective Statement for Forthcoming Year*

**A. Reason for Existence of Budget Unit**

*1. Specific Activities Performed:* Upgrading the Division of Diagnostic Radiology to give acceptable consultation by this specialty, and to improve qualitative and quantitative, the aspect of the overall department operations.

To improve the efficiency and effectiveness in performing various subfunctions within the department, such as patient scheduling, film filing, storage and retrieval, quality of X-ray procedures, diagnostic reporting and the Radiological Technical School.

To perform radiological services for the patients of Cook County Hospital and the citizens of the County of Cook.

*2. Problem Areas:* Severe space shortage. No employee lounge area, inadequate locker space and inadequate office space.

Need for additional radiographic rooms, especially in the Main Department and the Outpatient, Fantus Clinic Radiology Department.

Future plans must comprehend the radiologic growth problem and not be confined by thinking of architectural designs and equipment designs.

*3. Budget:* Monthly financial statements concerning expenditures and revenues of the department were to have been made available. To date, however, this information has not been received. Therefore, it is virtually impossible to make a completely accurate estimate of capital, operational and impersonal needs.

*Medical "A"*

*1. Problem Areas:* Severe space shortage. No employee lounge area, inadquate locker and office spaces. Future plans must comprehend the radiologic growth problem and not be confined by thinking of architectural designs and equipment designs.

*2. Budget:* Monthly statements concerning expenditures and revenues have not been made available to the department to this date. Therefore, it is virtually impossible to make a completely accurate estimate of capital, operational and impersonal needs.

*Pediatrics*

*1. Problem Areas:* New construction is presently being completed.

*2. Space:* Waiting area for patients is of utmost importance.

**Exhibit 4 *(continued)***

*Fantus Clinic for Outpatients*

*1. Problem Areas:* Severe space shortage. Additional space is urgently needed for additional radiographic rooms. This need is acute if we are to provide adequate radiological service for the Outpatient Department. Future plans must comprehend the radiologic growth problem and not be confined by thinking of architectural designs and equipment designs. A hospital this size must have complete radiological facilities for proper outpatient radiological services.

Monthly financial statements are not available, therefore making it impossible to accurately project our future estimate of operational cost.

**B. New Objectives for Forthcoming Year**

*List of New Objectives Planned*

*1. Quality of Personnel:* Needs vast improvement. More work-study programs, procedural check, formal and informal teaching programs.

*2. Scheduling System:* Each section has to be reassessed with new efficiency and effectiveness applied, especially as it relates to transportation of patients to and from the radiology department.

*3. Quality Level of Diagnostic Interpretation:* The present level is not high enough. This should include a senior staff member with an equivalent of five years' training to receive this kind of personnel.

*4. Quality Level of Diagnostic Procedures:* All technical personnel must attend quality control conferences and will be evaluated according to their technical abilities. This level of quality must also improve.

*5. Film Viewing Area:* To install alternators for each surgical and orthopedic chief for viewing of radiological films and reports with the staff radiologist.

*6. Time Span between Writing of the Requisition to the Delivery of the Final Report Back to the Unit:* The scheduling system has improved this procedure. However, the proper flow still remains a problem.

*7. Patient Master & Teaching Cards:* The Master Card is of utmost importance to any proper filing system and patient examination control. The Teaching Card System is a requirement of the American College of Radiology for accreditation.

*8. Projected Volume by Section:* Check daily average procedure and volume chart. Nationwide, the average increase is usually 10 percent. We expect at least a 12 percent increase over last year (1972).

*9. Film File Libraries:* The file areas need new equipment, personnel changes, as well as additions. They also need a filing program.

*10. Lounge and Locker Areas:* Must continue to push for additional space for an employee lounge and locker space.

**Exhibit 4 *(concluded)***

*Why Activity Should Be Pursued*

To continue to improve radiological services for better patient care. It should also be realized that this division is presently functioning on an above average of what is expected of a Radiology Department in this Medical Center and Community.

*How You Intend to Reach Goal*

Hopefully by getting the cooperation and assistance from the Hospital Administration and the Health and Hospitals Governing Commission for additional space, equipment, and personnel.

*When You Should Realize Objective*

With the cooperation and assistance, hopefully within the next year.

**C. Activity to Be Eliminated or Curtailed in Forthcoming Year**

1. *Why Reduction:*
   Deletion of Radiology Medical Specialist "12"

2. Additional staff residents.

3. Utilization of registered X-ray technologists who have been trained by medical staff for injection of IVP. Approved by the AMA and ACR.

---

## Program Objects

Mr. McClary, the Associate Director of Finance, described his role as that of a "controller of a conglomerate" and an "integrator," translating the constituents' needs into a format understandable to the county and vice versa. Commenting on the budgeting system, he said:

> We, the Commission, are a unique animal. The amendment to the act in 1970 provided us a corporate identity. We can sue and be sued. We are dependent on the county tax—it provides us a third of our income, but they cannot tell us, if resources are short, what programs to eliminate or defer. It is our decision. We decide on our programs to eliminate or defer. We decide on our programs as well as priorities. We are allowed to make short-term borrowings, but all long-term commitments have to be approved by the County Board. We are in many ways like a college student. The county cannot tell us "how long the hair should be" or "how we should live"—that is up to us. They give us the funds—one third of them, and finance our college education, as it were. To put it in a nutshell, we are a dependent part with independent ways. The overall budget provides the boundaries within which we operate. This consists of several programs and each program is divided into four objects—personnel; impersonal services which consists of supplies, etc.; equipment; and construction. Each object can be further broken down into items and detailed accounting categories.
>
> We at the Commission do not worry about changes within an object, like

reducing two typists and hiring a stenographer. That is the responsibility of the management group at the hospital. I do not monitor the changes and shifts among objects, from equipment to personnel, closely. I keep track of trends. I can intervene and question the hospital if I want to. Changes in programs have to come up to the Commission. The entire budget is presented in such a way that we can identify changes in allocation at the level of an individual object in a program, or at the level of programs.

The budget format at the level of the hospital is shown in Exhibits 5 and 6. A similar format was used at the level of the Commission.

**Exhibit 5**

COOK COUNTY HOSPITAL
Inpatient and Outpatient Revenue Sources
1973 Budget Proposal (in $000)

| | *Inpatient* | | *Outpatient* | | *Total* | |
|---|---|---|---|---|---|---|
| *Source* | *Revenue* | *Percent* | *Revenue* | *Percent* | *Revenue* | *Percent* |
| Private sources | $ 6,322 | 8.3 | — | — | $ 6,322 | 7.2 |
| Public aid | 43,505 | 56.7 | $ 7,508 | 64.6 | 51,013 | 57.8 |
| Medicare | 10,749 | 14.0 | 153 | 1.4 | 10,902 | 12.4 |
| Miscellaneous | 1,115 | 1.5 | — | — | 1,115 | 1.2 |
| County | 14,938 | 19.5 | 3,962 | 34.0 | 18,900 | 21.4 |
| Total | $76,629 | 100.0 | $11,623 | 100.0 | $88,252 | 100.0 |

**Exhibit 6**
Program Expenditures by Object, 1973 Budget Proposal ($000)

| | *Personals* | *Impersonals* | *Equipment* | *Construction* | *Total* |
|---|---|---|---|---|---|
| Overhead | $21,178 | $ 6,244 | $ 585 | $2,424 | $30,432 |
| Inpatient services | 42,338 | 7,319 | 1,900 | 0 | 51,557 |
| Outpatient services | 1,957 | 982 | 162 | 0 | 3,101 |
| Special funds | 220 | 16 | 0 | 0 | 236 |
| Emergency services | 2,211 | 640 | 76 | 0 | 2,927 |
| Totals | $67,904 | $15,201 | $2,723 | $2,424 | $88,252 |

Mr. McClary commented on some of the other forms of control which were used:

We work on a cash accounting basis. This provides us a lever for control on the performance of the hospital management. For example, the fact that the budget is approved does not mean that it can be implemented. We have to worry about cash availability. The critical function, call it the key function, if you will, is the management of cash, here from my office. We make cash flow projections and determine cash availability. Allocations among programs are made quarterly. In case of restricted cash resources, trade-offs among programs have to be made within the budget frame. These trade-off decisions are normally made by the line departments. This provides us, via the cash allocation decisions, every quarter, yet another opportunity to review programs. Further, several functions, purchasing and cash management in particular, are centralized. I can replenish the revolving fund at the hospital level. I can, theoretically, cut off funds if they misbehave and they know it.

I see my job as the manager of the cash reservoir, adjusting the sluice gates and making sure that enough cash flows through to the constituents. We have so far had no problem and no major program has been stopped or postponed due to the nonavailability of resources. The managerial capabilities of the divisions have been the limiting factor—getting people, training them, installing equipment, and such technical problems.

Mr. McClary was assisted by Mr. King, the Budget Coordinator. He had the primary responsibility for cash flow management. He described his job as follows:

I see my job as having two important aspects—projecting cash flows and coordinating the preparation of the budget for presentation to the Commission. This involves the transformation of the individual institutional budgets into the Commission's budget and presenting it in the approved format.

We have been quite successful with our budgeting system. We have brought in the concept of programs, objectives, and set directions for growth. The weakness, at present, is how to measure performance against budgets. The budget frame changes—due to the inclusion of new programs. Changes in cash flows may alter priorities or lead us to drop some programs. You see, the achievements at the end of a year are in the general direction set by the budget frame but need not correspond to the budget frame on a one-to-one basis. Our system provides us tremendous flexibility but does not allow precise measurement, like in traditional budgeting systems.

Cash management is a key task here. Our cash flows can limit or expand the scope of our activity. The cash flow is based on "informed judgments." I talk to as many people involved and informed about it as possible before I develop it. It is still an art, and calls for a lot of gut level understanding of the system. It is hard for anyone outside the system to understand. I cannot refer you to a formal procedures manual.

## The Budget Process

The budget process consisted of several steps, as follows:

1. **Departmental Preparation and Submission.** The departments review their performance for the period June of the previous year to May of the current year. In preparing the budget for FY 1973, they would review performance for the period June 1971–May 1972 and project it for the period June 1972–November 1972. The budget for FY 1973 is for the period December 1972–November 1973. The departments then develop programs and objectives (Exhibit 4) and submit them for discussion. Three weeks were allowed for this activity.
2. **Institutional Review.** The institutional review is made by the executive director, director of the hospital, and the finance group. The emphasis at this stage is on the programs and objectives, per se, not necessarily the dollar implications. Once approved, it is incorporated in the budget frame for determining the dollar implications. Four weeks are allowed.

3. **Governing Commission Review.** The Commission reviews the programs as well as the financial implications and suggests changes/additions/modifications. Changes are necessitated by either program changes or cash flow restrictions. The budget is reworked on the basis of the Commission's recommendations. The Commission has eight days for this activity.
4. **Semifinal Rework.** The financial implications of the programs are worked out in detail and aggregated into the approved budget format. Three weeks.
5. **Public Hearings.** Public hearings are held by the Commission, and the budget is approved by the Commission. Ten days.
6. **Submission to the County Board.** The Budget Coordinator acts as the facilitator in this process.

Mr. King talked about his role as facilitator:

> I help coordinate the pieces. I have to work closely with the various constituents—CCH, Oak Forest Hospital, and so on. In general, the relationships between my office and the finance staff at the hospitals are quite cordial. We meet together and discuss the problems. I believe they see me as a source of help.

## The Future

The future of the CCH and the Health and Hospitals Commission, according to an insider, "looks very bright indeed. We seem to be on the go, no more plagued by lack of direction or dissensions. We seem to be poised for the golden era." The enthusiasm was widely shared. Dr. Haughton remarked:

> Our first objective was to upgrade the quality of medical care. We had to put in a massive effort and to commit resources. We have done that. The organization has stabilized, morale is high. We have recruited some excellent staff. Our next phase involves the implementation of our community-oriented family clinics and comprehensive health planning for the County of Cook. I saw my role as recapturing Cook County Hospital from the fiefdoms that was CCH—for the people of the county. We now have to create the health system that will take medicine to where it belongs—to the communities.

## Question

Evaluate the programming process at Cook County. What changes, if any, would you recommend?

## Case 7–2

## SUARD COLLEGE*

In October 1983 the management and the Trustee Budget Committee of Suard College would meet to discuss the question of whether the College should prepare a five-year program. There was disagreement as to whether

* This case was prepared by Robert N. Anthony, Harvard Business School.

such an effort was desirable, and if so, whether the results would be worth the cost.

## Background

Suard College was a coeducational residential, four-year liberal arts college of 2,000 students, of whom 1,900 lived in dormitories on the campus. Established in 1836, the original campus was small and located near the commercial center of a city. As the city grew, the environment became increasingly unattractive. Accordingly, in 1950 a new campus was started on 120 acres of land.

By 1982, the new campus was essentially completed. There were classrooms, laboratories, a library, a chapel, a museum, dormitories and cafeterias, a student center, indoor and outdoor athletic facilities, and administrative and faculty offices. The newest dormitory, accommodating 100 students, was completed in 1981; it was financed by a 30-year $4 million bond issue. Currently, a renovation of the library was under way, at a cost of $8 million. Most of the new plant had been financed from capital fund campaigns. The college had an endowment of $40 million.

Suard was invariably included in lists of "selective" liberal arts colleges, usually defined as the top 100 or so of the 3,000 colleges and universities in the United States. As was the case with other selective colleges, its tuition was relatively high.

Generally, Suard operated with a balanced budget. Revenues had equaled or exceeded expenses in most of the past 25 years. Faculty salaries were in the top quartile of all four-year colleges, according to the survey made annually by the American Association of University Professors. The student/faculty ratio was similar to the average of competing colleges. Approximately 55 percent of the faculty had tenure, a percentage that had been fairly stable for some years. Operating statements are given in Exhibit 1.

## Outlook

In the 1960s and 1970s, the total college population expanded dramatically, in part because a higher percentage of the college age population attended college, but primarily because the "baby boom" after World War II resulted in a higher college age population. By 1979, total college population reached a plateau, and forecasts were that by 1983 or 1984 it would start to decrease, reaching a low in 1995 at about 75 percent of the 1983 level. In Suard's region of the United States, the percentage decline was forecast to be even greater because of the shift in population from this region to the "sun belt" of the Southwest. Although Suard's total applications had declined slightly in the past few years, the admissions office currently had no difficulty in admitting a class that was equal to those of recent years in all measurable aspects of quality.

The majority of Board members and members of the administration be-

**Exhibit 1**

SUARD COLLEGE
Operating Statements
($000)

| | *1981–82 Actual* | *1982–83 Actual* | *1982–83 Budget* |
|---|---|---|---|
| Educational and general: | | | |
| Revenues: | | | |
| Student charges | | | |
| Tuition | $12,782 | $14,956 | $14,596 |
| Fees | 1,204 | 1,418 | 1,233 |
| Endowment | 1,562 | 1,677 | 1,687 |
| Gifts | 784 | 1,252 | 1,230 |
| Government grants | 473 | 699 | 565 |
| Other (principally interest) | 1,079 | 774 | 952 |
| Total | $17,884 | $20,776 | $20,263 |
| Expenditures: | | | |
| Instruction | $ 6,142 | $ 6,993 | $ 6,953 |
| Research | 194 | 225 | 225 |
| Academic support | 1,361 | 1,628 | 1,594 |
| Student services | 2,447 | 2,986 | 2,795 |
| Institutional support | 2,440 | 2,658 | 2,569 |
| Educational plant | 2,164 | 2,211 | 2,225 |
| Financial aid | 2,528 | 3,271 | 3,296 |
| Major renovations | — | 307 | 307 |
| Total | $17,276 | $20,279 | $19,964 |
| Net educational and general | $ 608 | $ 497 | $ 299 |
| Auxiliary enterprises: | | | |
| Revenue | $ 5,038 | $ 5,515 | $ 5,540 |
| Expenditures | 5,253 | 5,654 | 5,751 |
| Auxiliary, net | $ (215) | $ (139) | $ (211) |
| Net income | $ 296 | $ 255 | $ 20 |

lieved that with its reputation and its new campus, Suard could maintain its enrollment at 2,000 high quality students despite the decrease in the total population. These people believed that less selective colleges would suffer, that some of them would be forced to close (some already had closed), and that the selective colleges could maintain their enrollment by drawing students that otherwise would have gone to these colleges. Suard had increased the size and activities of its admissions and public relations offices in recent years so as to provide greater assurance of enrolling the necessary number of high quality students. A minority thought the view of the majority was too optimistic.

## Discussion of a Five-Year Plan

From time to time, most recently in 1979, committees had made studies of long-range strategy. These long-range planning committees usually had members from the faculty, administration, trustees, and the student body. Their reports had led to some changes in the curriculum, but these were generally considered to have been minor. In particular, every study concluded that the emphasis on the liberal arts should continue, and that graduate programs or vocationally oriented programs (e.g., nursing) should not be instituted. Long-range financial projections had been made from time to time, in some cases in connection with the long-range studies and in other cases as a separate exercise.

In the May 1983 meeting of the Budget Committee, a trustee suggested that the time had come to make a five-year program and financial plan, to consider its implications thoroughly, and to revise it annually thereafter. Time did not permit discussion of this proposal then, but it was decided to discuss it at the next meeting in October 1983. In informal discussions subsequent to the May meeting, it became clear that the idea was controversial.

A programming effort obviously would be concerned with the coming decline in student age population, and might develop strategies for dealing with a possible decline in Suard enrollment. Some committee members thought that the fact that such strategies were being considered would alarm the faculty unnecessarily and therefore would hurt morale. If the plan assumed faculty reductions in specified departments, the members of those departments would be upset; if it did not specifically describe departmental manning, everyone would wonder how a reduction would affect them.

Others pointed out that previous five-year financial plans had not amounted to much. These plans were primarily mechanical extrapolations of current revenues and expenditures, with assumptions as to tuition, salary, and other cost increases as a consequence of inflation. It was pointed out that tuition and other charges for a given year could not be estimated much in advance because Suard's tuition had to remain competitive with other colleges, and the decisions of these colleges were not typically made until January. Although the rate of inflation in 1983 was much lower than in recent years, no one knew what future inflation rates would be. Thus, although the annual budget was discussed thoroughly, little attention had been given to longer projections.

As an alternative to long-range planning, some believed that the college should adopt the policy of meeting a financial stringency when the need arose. Specifically, if opening enrollment in a given year was below the budgeted amount, the college would reduce discretionary expenses by about $200,000 and absorb the remaining deficit in that year from the operating surplus of some $600,000 that had been accumulated in prior years. It would immediately plan the expenditure reductions necessary to balance the budget in the following year. An enrollment decline would affect initially only the Freshman class; thus, if the entering Freshman class was, say, 8 percent below budget, total revenues should decrease by only ¼ of this, or 2 percent below budget.

Those favoring a formal programming effort pointed out that the library renovation, the new dormitory, and other factors might have long-range expenditure implications that needed to be explicitly considered. Suard now had access to a computer service bureau that quickly and at relatively low cost would provide five-year financial projections under any specified set of assumptions.

## Questions

1. Assuming that the college decided to prepare a five-year program and financial plan, how should the assumptions incorporated in it be arrived at? Should the plan be a single "best estimate," or should several alternatives be studied?
2. Should the college prepare a formal five-year program and financial plan?

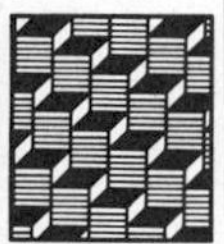

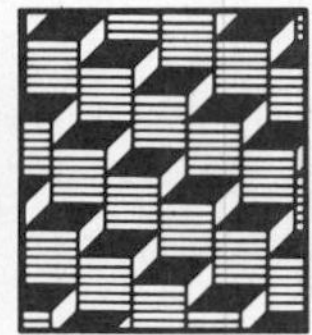

# chapter 8

# Program Analysis

Chapter 7 indicated that a key step in the programming process was analysis. This aspect of the process has both technical and political components. As the terms imply, the former is quite quantitative, while the latter is more behavioral and subjective in nature.

## TECHNICAL ANALYSIS

The technical approach to the analysis of proposed new programs is called *benefit/cost* analysis. The underlying concept is the obvious one that a program should not be undertaken unless its benefits exceed its costs, and the approach therefore involves an attempt to measure both benefits and costs. The term *cost/effectiveness* analysis is also used, sometimes as a synonym for benefit/cost analysis, and sometimes for a special version of the general approach.[1] The approach is sometimes called *systems analysis.*

### Status of Benefit/Cost Analysis

The idea of comparing the benefits of a proposed course of action with its costs is not new. Techniques for analyzing the profitability of proposed busi-

[1] If two proposals have approximately the same benefits, but one has lower costs, that one is said to be more cost-effective than the other.

ness investments involve essentially the same approach, and certain government agencies, such as the Bureau of Reclamation, have made such analyses for decades. Proposals to build new dams, for example, frequently were justified on the grounds that their benefits exceeded their costs.

Interest in benefit/cost analysis grew rapidly in the 1960s when the Department of Defense applied it to problems for which no formal analysis previously had been attempted, and suddenly it became fashionable to apply benefit/cost analysis to all sorts of proposed programs in nonprofit organizations. The results of these efforts were mixed, and considerable controversy about the merits of the whole approach developed.

At one extreme are indictments, such as that in Ida Hoos's *Systems Analysis in Public Policy.* The following quotation illustrates her attitude:

> The mythology of systems analysis accompanies its forward march into the future. Presented as though it had accomplished wonders and taken the guesswork out of planning, the technique is represented as the key and clue to the salvation of mankind on this planet. Those who sell this notion believe their own sales story and they are finding buyers among decision makers in the far flung corners of the earth. What is new and portentous here is that invocation of "scientific" tools and techniques, which provide a dutiful and convenient rationale for whatever course of action seems politically expedient, may stifle thoughtful research and experimentation. Heady with heterogeneous facts and shy of theory, the futurists may be directly or indirectly abetting the anti-intellectualism that has already gained considerable momentum in this country and abroad.[2]

At the other extreme are promotional brochures, journal articles, and proposals by certain individuals and organizations that imply that benefit/cost analysis does everything: "it takes the guesswork out of management." For example, a proposal for a $275,000 research project submitted to the National Institute of Education promised to "address the Cost-Effectiveness Benefit questions by making a Macro Management and Policy analysis of alternate Cost opportunities in Elementary-Secondary and Post-Secondary Education" and to provide the results in nine months. Translated, this means that the proposer promised to find the optimum amount and character of educational programs from kindergarten through college, in nine months, and all for $275,000!

## Role of Benefit/Cost Analysis

Although overexuberant persons and outright charlatans do exist, and their works are properly criticized, there is no doubt that benefit/cost analysis has produced useful results. There are two essential points:

1. Benefit/cost analysis focuses on those consequences of a proposal which can be estimated in quantitative terms. Since there is no important prob-

---

[2] Ida R. Hoos, *Systems Analysis in Public Policy* (Berkeley: University of California Press, 1972), p. 240.

lem in which *all* the relevant factors can be reduced to numbers, benefit/cost analysis will never provide the complete answer to any important problem. Since not everything can be quantified, no one should expect any benefit/cost analysis to do so. An analysis that claims to have quantified everything is of dubious merit.

***Example:*** The National Academy of Sciences reviewed the evidence of the effect of saccharin, based on results of experiments on rats. It reported that if all Americans consumed one bottle of diet soft drink per day for the remainder of their lives, the number of cases of bladder cancer resulting from persons currently alive would be somewhere between 0.22 and 1,144,000, depending on the mathematical model used. (National Academy of Sciences, *Saccharin: Technical Assessment of Risks and Benefits,* Report No. 1, November 1978.)

2. However, if *some* of the important factors can be reduced to quantitative terms, it is often better to do so than not. The resulting analysis narrows the area within which management judgment is required, even though it does not eliminate the need for judgment.

Charles Schultze, at the time Director of the Bureau of the Budget, summarized the middle ground in a statement which has become a classic:[3]

> Much has been published on PPB.[4] Learned articles have treated it sometimes as the greatest thing since the invention of the wheel. Other articles attack it, either as a naive attempt to quantify and computerize the imponderable, or as an arrogant effort on the part of latter-day technocrats to usurp the decision-making function in a political democracy.
>
> PPB is neither. It *is* a means of *helping* responsible officials make decisions. It is *not* a mechanical substitute for the good judgment, political wisdom, and leadership of those officials. . . .
>
> PPB *does* call for systematic analysis of program proposals and decisions, concentrating upon those decisions which have budgetary consequences. But systematic analysis does not have to be and is not coextensive with quantitative analysis. The word "analyze" does not, in any man's dictionary, have the same meaning as the words "quantify" or "measure," although analysis often includes measurement.
>
> Systematic analysis is an aid to policy debate. Too often these debates revolve around a simple list of pros and cons. There are no means of making progress in the debate, since participants simply repeat, in different words, their original positions. . . .
>
> Now such analysis often does, and must, involve quantitative estimates. Most of our decisions—in fact, all of our budgetary decisions—willy-nilly involve quantitative consideration. For example, take the question of how many doctors to train and how much aid to give to medical schools. We can debate this simply in

[3] From his Statement to the Subcommittee on National Security and International Operations of the Committee on Government Operations, U.S. Senate, 90th Cong., 1st sess., August 23, 1967.

[4] PPB stands for Planning, Programming, Budgeting, which was the name given to the overall approach of which benefit/cost analysis was one part.

terms of arguing more or fewer budget dollars for the program. Alternatively, we can calculate the current and projected ratio of doctors to population, examine the relationship between the doctor/population ratio and various indices of health, review the distribution of doctors throughout various areas in the nation, estimate the costs of training doctors, and a host of similar factors. We cannot, of course, measure precisely, or even close to precisely, the national advantages to be gained from a program of aid to medical schools, nor can we account for all of the costs. But we can isolate, in a quantitative form, a number of the key elements involved in the program. The debate then can proceed in terms of weighing fairly specifically the advantages the nation gains from alternative increases in the supply of doctors against the costs of achieving each alternative.

In short, the issue is not whether benefit/cost analysis is a panacea or whether it is a fraud, for in general it is neither. The issue rather is to define the circumstances under which benefit/cost analysis is likely to be useful. Some aspects of this question are discussed below.

### Clarifying Goals

Since the "benefit" in a benefit/cost analysis is related to an organization's goals, there is no point in making a benefit/cost analysis unless there is some measure of agreement on what the goals are. Hoos summarizes a report made by the General Accounting Office of three successive study contracts made by the same consulting firm on the "problem" of civil defense.[5] The studies cost $600,000; and in the opinion of the General Accounting Office, they were worthless. The reason was that no one, either prior to the study or in the course of the study, had defined what the goals of a civil defense program should be.

The basic purpose of a benefit/cost analysis is not to formulate goals but rather to suggest the best alternative way of reaching a goal. The formulation of goals is largely a judgmental process. Various members of management and various staff people may have different ideas of what the goals are. These ideas should be reconciled as much as possible. Failure to clarify goals, or failure to agree as to what they are, obviously makes it difficult to formulate programs to achieve them.

### Proposals Susceptible to Technical Analysis

In benefit/cost analysis the general principles are that (1) a program should not be adopted unless its benefits exceed its costs; and (2) as between two competing proposals, the one with the greater excess of benefits over costs, or the one with the lower costs if benefits are equal, is preferable. In order to apply these principles there must be some way of relating benefits and costs.

[5] Hoos, *Systems Analysis*, p. 117.

***"Economic" Proposals.*** For many proposals in nonprofit organizations, it is possible to estimate both costs and benefits in monetary terms. These "economic" proposals are similar to capital budgeting proposals in profit-oriented companies. A proposal to convert the heating plant of a hospital from oil to coal involves the same type of analysis as would be used for the same problem in an industrial company. Problems of this type are numerous in nonprofit organizations, and while important administratively, frequently have little programmatic impact. Conversely, for problems which do have programmatic effects, reliable monetary estimates of benefits are difficult, and frequently cannot be made.

***Alternative Ways of Reaching the Same Objective.*** Even if the benefits cannot be quantified, a benefit/cost analysis is useful in situations in which there are two or more ways of achieving a given objective. If there is a reasonable presumption that each of the alternatives will achieve the objective, then the alternative with the lowest cost is preferred.

This approach has many applications, simply because it does not require that the objective be stated in monetary terms, or even that it be quantified. We need not measure the *degree* to which a given alternative meets the objective; we need only make the "go/no-go" judgment that any of the proposed alternatives will achieve the objective, and then seek the least costly option.

*Example:* The output of an educational program is difficult to measure, and it is especially difficult to find a causal relationship between a certain teaching technique and the resulting quality of education. Nevertheless, it is possible to compare alternative teaching techniques, such as team teaching, computer assisted instruction, and conventional tests and workbooks, in terms of cost. In the absence of a judgment that one method provides better education than another, the technique with the lowest cost would be preferred.

*Example:* A calculable number of passengers arrive and depart Washington, D.C., by air. The objective of a certain analysis was to provide the optimum ground transportation and airport facilities for these passengers in the Washington area. The costs of various airport locations and associated ground transport services were estimated. The proposal that provided adequate service with the lowest cost was preferred. There was no need to measure the benefits of "adequate service" in monetary terms.

*Example:* An objective of the U.S. Air Force is to produce a specified number of qualified pilots. This objective can be attained through various means at the U.S. Air Force Academy, or through the Reserve Officers Training Corps and Officer Training School. In analyzing these alternatives, the desired number of qualified pilots is taken as given, and the analyst seeks to identify the alternative with the lowest cost (taking account of nonquantitative considerations also):[6]

---

[6] Edward B. Opperman, Donald R. Plane, and James D. Suver, "Applications of Incremental Economic Analysis for Public Sector Decisions," *Interfaces,* May 1978, pp. 13–21.

***Equal Cost Programs.*** If two competing proposals have the same cost but one produces more benefits than the other, it ordinarily is the preferred alternative. This conclusion can be reached without a measurement of the absolute levels of benefits. Such an approach is often used in deciding on the best mix of resources to be used in a program. This question is raised, for example: Will $100,000 spent to hire more teachers produce more educational benefits than $100,000 spent on a combination of teachers and teaching machines, or $100,000 spent on team teaching rather than individual teaching? The analysis involves an estimate of the amount of resources that the stated amount of money will buy and a judgment of the results that will be achieved by using this amount and mix of resources, but it does not require that the benefits be expressed numerically, only comparatively.

***Different Objectives.*** A benefit/cost comparison of proposals intended to accomplish different objectives is likely to be worthless. An analysis that attempts to compare funds to be spent for primary school education with funds to be spent for retraining of unemployed adults would not be worthwhile because such an analysis requires that monetary values be assigned to the benefits of these two programs, which is an impossible task.

***Causal Connection between Cost and Benefits.*** Many benefit/cost analyses implicitly assume that there is a causal relationship between the benefits and the costs, that is, spending $X produces Y amount of benefit. If this causal connection does not exist, such an analysis is fallacious.

*Example:* An agency defended its personnel training program with an analysis which indicated that the program would lead its participants to get new jobs which would increase their lifetime earnings by $25,000 per person. Thus, the average cost per person trained of $5,000 seemed to be well justified. However, the assertion that the proposed program would indeed generate these benefits was completely unsupported; it was strictly a guess. Without some plausible link between the amount spent and the results obtained, such an analysis is worthless.

***Benefit/Cost as a Way of Thinking.*** Benefit/cost *analysis* is feasible in only a small proportion of the problems that arise in nonprofit organizations, and these tend to be the well-structured administrative-type problems. By contrast, a benefit/cost *way of thinking* is a useful way of approaching a great many problems. One of the characteristics of competent managers is that they look at proposals, at least in a general way, in terms of whether the benefits are probably worth more than the costs. They may not be able to quantify the relationship, nor do they need to do so in many cases. This way of looking at problems tends to distinguish the factors that are relevant from those that are not relevant.

*Example:* The president of a liberal arts college was considering a proposal that the college join a consortium of three other colleges in the general area.

Those advocating the proposal argued that the consortium movement originated in Oxford in the 15th century, and the idea was therefore good because it had a long and noble history; that there were 67 American consortia in 1970 compared with only 7 in 1967, and that the idea was therefore good because it was growing rapidly; that it was good for college faculties to cooperate with one another; that central purchasing is more efficient than having each college do its own purchasing; and so on. The president said that although these statements were interesting, none of them directly addressed the questions that were on his mind. These questions were: How many students were likely to be benefited by the activities of the consortium? Was the benefit likely to be worth the cost per student benefited (the annual fee was $15,000)? What would a central purchasing office cost? Would it be likely to reduce costs sufficiently to pay for itself plus the cost of the consortium? Could a central purchasing office be created without having a formal consortium?

***Overreliance on Benefit/Cost Approach.*** The benefit/cost way of thinking can be carried to extremes. If the decision maker rejects all proposals in which no causal connection between costs and benefits have been demonstrated, the programs are unlikely to be innovative. This is because a primary characteristic of many new, experimental, promising schemes is that there is no way of estimating benefit/cost relationships in advance. Undue insistence on benefit/cost analyses can therefore result in overly conservative programs. Although the risk of failure of an innovative proposal may be higher, it may be a risk worth running.

## SOME ANALYTICAL TECHNIQUES

The literature on benefit/cost analysis is voluminous, and we do not attempt to summarize here the various techniques that are described in it. In an Appendix at the end of the text portion of this chapter the essentials of this approach are given, and also a list of selected references. In this section, we limit ourselves to a few of the particularly difficult problems that arise in making a benefit/cost analysis for a nonprofit organization.

### Use of Models

All benefit/cost analyses at least imply that there is an underlying model that describes both the essential variables in the situation being studied and the relationships among them. Many studies explicitly attempt to construct such a model as an aid to estimating the benefits and costs of each alternative. A model need not be complicated.

*Example:* Exhibit 8–1 shows a simple financial model which focuses on the relationships of important variables for the instructional program of a college. The "initial values" represent an equilibrium relationship among the variables under one set of conditions, presumably the current situation; it is an equilibrium in the sense that the revenues available for instruction equal the costs of instruction.

**Exhibit 8–1**
College Financial Model

**Variables**

| *Abbreviation* | *Name* | *Initial Value* |
|---|---|---|
| TUITN | Tuition and fees, per student | $ 4,020 |
| STUDS | Number of students | 1,572 |
| OTREV | Other revenue available for instruction (e.g., endowment) (000) | $ 200 |
| OTCOS | Instruction cost other than faculty compensation (000) | $ 3,165 |
| COURSE | Number of courses per student, per semester | 5.0 |
| SECSI | Average number of students per section | 24.3 |
| SECTS | Number of sections offered | 323 |
| TEFAC | Number of FTE teaching faculty | 107.7 |
| NOFAC | Number of FTE nonteaching faculty (sabbaticals, department head, slippage) | 12.3 |
| SALRY | Average compensation per faculty | $27,954 |
| LOAD | Number of sections per teaching faculty | 3.0 |

**Initial Equations**

$$(\text{TUITN} \times \text{STUDS}) + \text{OTREV} = \text{SALRY (TEFAC} + \text{NOFAC}) + \text{OTCOS}$$
$$(\$4{,}020 \times 1{,}572) + \$200{,}000 = \$27{,}954\ (107.7 + 12.3) + \$3{,}165{,}000$$
$$\text{SECTS} \div \text{LOAD} = \text{TEFAC}$$
$$323 \div 3.0 = 107.7$$
$$(\text{STUDS} \times \text{COURSE}) + \text{SEC SIZE} = \text{SECTS}$$
$$(1572 \times 5.0) \div 24.3 = 323$$

This model can be used to answer such questions as: How much could we increase average faculty compensation if we reduced the number of sections by *X*, or if we reduced the number of nonteaching faculty by *Y*, or if we reduced the nonfaculty instruction costs by *Z?* If we increase the course offerings, by how much would tuition have to be increased? What would happen if we increased the number of students? Beginning with this simple model, the analysis could be refined by substituting a frequency distribution of section sizes for the average section size, or by substituting a distribution of faculty compensation by rank for the overall average, by bringing in noninstruction costs, and so on.

Computer models are available for many types of nonprofit organizations. For hospitals HOFPLAN is a model that computes fees by class of patient, direct costs, and charges by cost center, reimbursement by financial class, as well as the usual financial statements, based on assumptions entered by the user. These assumptions include: the type of patient, the length of stay, unit variable costs, total fixed cost, and units of service for each cost center, allocation method preferred, growth rates, seasonal patterns, endowment revenue, depreciation, bad debts, and similar financial data. The user can quickly see the effect of varying any of these assumptions. The National Center for Higher Education Management has a system that provides for the collection of costs, their allocation to final cost objects, and comparisons of actual costs with budgets. it is called CADMS for Costing and Data Management System.

In many situations, attempts to construct models have turned out to be fruitless. Persons contemplating model building for public-oriented problems should read Brewer's *Politicians, Bureaucrats, and the Consultant*[7] to be forewarned about what can go wrong. Brewer describes several attempts to build models of the demand for housing in San Francisco and Pittsburgh. Over $1,000,000 was spent on each of these models, but no useful results were forthcoming. Some of the reasons for the failure were (1) the goals were not clearly set forth at the beginning of the study (essentially, they consisted of the vague statement: "Provide the best housing at the lowest cost for all our citizens"; (2) the consultants did not understand the housing problem; (3) the historical data used in the model were so voluminous and detailed that a single run of the model required many hours of computer time; (4) by contrast, the assumptions about population growth patterns were naive and simplistic; and (5) the output of each computer run was several inches thick, and decision makers could not comprehend it.

In order to develop useful models, one needs reliable data, and such data are often not available. Califano, with only slight exaggeration, described the situation as follows: "The disturbing truth is that the basis of recommendations by an American Cabinet officer on whether to begin, eliminate, or expand vast social programs more nearly resembles the intuitive judgment of a benevolent tribal chief in remote Africa than the elaborate, sophisticated data with which the Secretary of Defense supports a major new weapons system."[8]

## Quantifying the Value of a Human Being

In the analysis of proposed programs in nonprofit organizations, a factor is frequently encountered that rarely is relevant in proposals originating in profit-oriented organizations, namely, the value of human beings. Some programs are designed to save or prolong human lives. They include automobile safety programs, accident prevention programs, drug control programs, and medical research programs. In these programs, the value of a human life, or of a workday lost to accident or illness, is a relevant consideration in measuring benefits. Analysts are often squeamish about attaching a monetary value to a human life since there is a general belief in our culture that life is priceless, but such a monetary amount often facilitates the analysis of certain proposals. In a world of scarce resources, it is not possible to spend unlimited amounts to save lives in general (although there are circumstances in which society is willing to devote unlimited resources to saving a specific life; for example, hundreds of people may hunt for a child who is lost in the woods).

---

[7] Gary D. Brewer, *Politicians, Bureaucrats and the Consultant: A Critique of Urban Problem Solving* (New York: Basic Books, Inc., Publishers, 1973).

[8] Presidential Assistant Joseph A. Califano, Jr., in testimony before the Senate Labor Subcommittee, 1969, as quoted in Paul Dickson, *Think Tanks* (New York: Ballantine Books, Inc., 1971), p. 226.

*Example:* In an interesting article, Sagan shows how relating costs to lives can be applied fruitfully to many problems involving nuclear energy. For example, he estimates that a reduction in the permitted radiation levels in uranium mines increased operating costs by $7 million per year in order to save 1.54 cases of lung cancer among miners.[9]

There are two general approaches to the process of valuing human lives. One proposal suggests that human life is worth whatever people are willing to pay for it. Another suggests that human life should be valued at the present value of future earnings.

The amount a person is willing to pay for preservation of his or her life could be measured indirectly by examining wage increments for workers in risky occupations such as coal mining. The application of this approach has yielded a value of life between $200,000 and over $1 million in 1975 dollars.

The approach to valuing life at the discounted value of earning power tends to discriminate against programs aimed at persons with relatively low expected lifetime earnings: elderly people, members of minority groups, ministers, college professors, artists. In order to overcome such discrimination, it has been suggested that programs which involve saving or prolonging human lives be evaluated by favoring the alternative which saves the most lives per dollar spent, independent of the economic characteristics of the target group. The Federal Highway Administration has used this approach in evaluating various safety devices. Such an analysis is limited to judging whether a particular program saves more lives per dollar spent than other lifesaving or life-prolonging programs; it does not compare costs with monetary benefits.

*Example:* The General Accounting Office made a benefit/cost analysis of safety devices (e.g., seat belts, stronger windshield, crush-resistant roof) installed in automobiles in the period 1966–73. Costs of these improvements were obtained from automobile manufacturers. Benefits were taken as the decline in fatalities and injuries based on data from two states, North Carolina and New York, adjusted for such variables as gender, weather, and time of day. The results were converted to monetary terms by using estimates from three sources for the value of a human life and the savings from an injury prevented. The lowest estimates were those of the National Safety Council, $52,000 per death and $3,100 per injury. Even with these low amounts, the benefit/cost ratio was at least 1.5/1; for the highest estimate, the ratio was at least 4.0/1.[10]

Because the "lives per dollar" approach has somewhat limited application, discounting continues to be used in many situations, particularly in the case of litigation to measure the damages that should be paid to kin of persons

---

[9] L. A. Sagan, "Human Costs of Nuclear Power," *Science,* 11 (August 1972), pp. 487–93.

[10] U.S. General Accounting Office, "Effectiveness, Benefits, and Costs of Federal Safety Standards for Protection of Passenger Car Occupants," July 7, 1976. Summarized in *GAO Review,* Fall 1976, pp. 36–42.

killed in accidents, so there is much literature on it. A particularly important aspect of this process is the choice of a discount rate.

## Discount Rates

When the benefits of a proposed program occur in different time periods than those in which the costs are incurred, the proposal cannot be evaluated unless this difference in timing patterns is taken into account. This requires the use of a discount rate. Thus, a proposal to acquire an expensive piece of equipment that requires little annual maintenance can be compared with a proposal to acquire a less expensive piece of equipment that requires higher annual maintenance only if the two streams of annual maintenance costs have been made comparable by the application of discount rates to the costs of each year. The concept and the procedure are the same in nonprofit organizations as in profit-oriented companies. The special problem in nonprofit organizations is the choice of a discount rate. In profit-oriented companies the selection of the proper discount rate is also a difficult problem, but it is one that has been analyzed extensively, whereas until recently most nonprofit organizations have given little attention to it.

This problem is particularly important with respect to government proposals for public works and other capital expenditures whose benefits will accrue over a long period of time. Until fairly recently, most government agencies either did not discount the streams of costs and benefits at all, or they used the interest rate on government bonds as the discount rate. It is now generally recognized that a government bond rate is too low and that its use results in the approval of projects that actually should not be undertaken.

In the 1960s there was considerable discussion of what the appropriate discount rate should be, and there emerged a consensus that the rate should approximate the average rate of return on private sector investments. There is room for disagreement as to just what this rate is, but the controversy was effectively ended by the revision of Office of Management and Budget Circular No. A-94 in March 1972, which specified that in most circumstances a rate of 10 percent should be used.[11] Circular A-94 also gives concise, useful guidance on applying the discounting principle.

Exhibit 8–2 illustrates the nature of the errors that result from failure to discount at all and from the use of a discount rate that is too low. The essential characteristics of three projects are listed, together with the present value of the benefits under three assumptions: *(a)* undiscounted, *(b)* at a discount rate of 5 percent and *(c)* at a discount rate of 10 percent. Several conclusions can be drawn:

1. If the benefits are not discounted, Project C, with savings worth $20,000, appears to be the best project. Actually, the present value of Project

[11] The 10 percent rate does not apply to the U.S. Postal Service, to water resource projects, to buy-or-lease decisions, or to certain make-or-buy decisions.

**Exhibit 8–2**
Effect of Discount Rates

| | Project | | |
|---|---|---|---|
| | *A* | *B* | *C* |
| Investment | $10,000 | $10,000 | $10,000 |
| Annual benefits | 3,000 | 1,800 | 1,000 |
| Life (years) | 5 | 10 | 20 |
| Present value of benefits: | | | |
| At 0% | 15,000 | 18,000 | 20,000 |
| At 5% | 12,900 | 13,900 | 12,500 |
| At 10% (proper rate) | 11,400 | 11,000 | 8,500 |

C's benefits is only $8,500 which is less than its cost, so the project should not be undertaken. Prior to 1940 the Soviet Union did not use discount rates, and consequently invested erroneously in projects similar to Project C, that is, in capital-intensive, long-lived projects such as hydroelectric power facilities.

2. If the government is deciding how best to spend a fixed sum of money, and therefore must rank projects in order of desirability, it will favor Project B over Project A if it uses a discount rate of 5 percent. At this rate, the present value of Project B's benefits ($13,900) exceeds that of Project A's ($12,900). Actually, Project A is better than Project B ($11,400 compared with $11,000). In general, with a low rate, projects which are capital-intensive and long-lived appear to be more attractive than they actually are. In India the use of a low rate has led to the construction of large cement plants built at infrequent intervals, rather than to smaller plants built more frequently. This mistake resulted from the use of a discount rate that was too low.
3. If agencies are permitted to use different rates, an agency that uses a low rate can justify a larger capital budget than an agency that uses a high rate. An agency that uses 5 percent can justify Projects A, B, and C, since in each case the benefits exceed the cost; an agency that uses 10 percent can justify only Projects A and B.

The desirability of long-lived projects is extremely sensitive to the discount rate that is used in the analysis of them. For example, a survey made by the Water Resources Council of 245 authorized Corps of Engineers projects showed that for about one third of them, the costs would exceed the benefits if the discount rate were raised from the 5⅜ percent actually used in the analyses to 7 percent.[12]

The problem of considering differences in the timing of benefits and costs arises in nonprofit organizations of all types. A *de novo* analysis of the appro-

[12] Luther J. Carter, "Water Projects: How to Erase the 'Pork Barrel' Image?" *Science,* October 19, 1973, p. 268.

priate discount rate in a given organization can be complex and controversial. For example, some argue that resources obtained from contributions have no cost; others say that fund-raising costs associated with these contributions are analogous to interest costs (although actually the cost of obtaining a given contribution is a one-time cost, not an annual cost), and still others say that since such funds could earn a return if they were invested, the return earned on the endowment fund is the appropriate discount rate.

### Risk and Inflation

In addition to the time value of money as measured by the discount rate, the analysis should allow for the effects of risk and inflation. If risk of failure is not considered explicitly, then a very risky proposal might be evaluated in the same way as one which has a low probability of failure. Statistical techniques are available for incorporating the relative riskiness of a project. However, they require that the probabilities of possible outcomes be estimated, and good estimates of these probabilities usually cannot be made. Therefore, risk is usually taken into account when judgment is applied to the quantitative analysis.

An estimate of future inflation rates is anybody's guess. The important point is that history shows that inflation is likely to occur, and that allowance for it should somehow be made. One approach is to apply assumed inflation rates to the amounts of costs and benefits. Another is to omit inflation from the calculations, and consider the likelihood of inflation in judging the results. The former approach is usually preferable. When it is used, the assumptions about inflation should be clearly set forth, so that the decision maker can question them if alternative assumptions seem more realistic.

### Taxes

Some analyses involve the problem of whether a given activity should be performed by the government or by private enterprise. This is a version of the make-or-buy problem that is common in profit-oriented companies, and the analytical approach is the same. In a government analysis, there is the special problem of how to treat income taxes, property taxes, and other taxes that are paid by a profit-oriented company, but not by a government organization. The amounts involved can be substantial. A good approach to incorporating these costs is set forth in Office of Management and Budget Circular A-76.

### Content of Proposals

A program proposal can vary in format from a one-page memorandum to a several-hundred-page statement. If the proposal itself is long, it should of course be accompanied by a summary for the use of senior management.

Some managers require that such a summary be limited to one page; others permit more.

The proposal should describe *what* is to be done, but ordinarily it does not contain the details of *how* it is to be done. These details are the responsibility of operating management, to be worked out after the proposal has been approved. For each alternative considered, program proposals should include:

1. A description of the proposed program, and evidence that it will accomplish the organization's objectives.
2. An estimate of the resources to be devoted to the program over the next several years, divided between investment costs and operating costs. Since the principal purpose of this estimate is to show the approximate magnitude of the effort, the costs are "ballpark" amounts. A detailed analysis of the costs usually is deferred until after the program has been approved in principle.
3. The benefits expected from the program over the same time period, expressed quantitatively if feasible. One purpose of quantifying the benefits is to permit the subsequent comparison of actual results with planned results.
4. A discussion of the risks and uncertainties associated with the program.

The purpose of these analyses is to aid the decision maker. The analyses should be contrasted with those program proposals which are primarily prepared after a decision has been made to approve a project and which are primarily sales documents. Most Environmental Impact Statements and Economic Impact Statements, for example, are in the latter category.[13]

## POLITICAL ANALYSIS

The final decision on a proposed program involves political considerations (such as the predisposition of a member of Congress toward a certain policy, or the desirability of favoring a certain congressional district), as well as economic and social considerations. Ordinarily political considerations should be excluded from the analysis itself. The decision maker takes them into account separately when making a final judgment. The analysis is likely to be less lucid if political considerations are included in it.

Political considerations properly are a part of some analyses, however. If, for example, several political solutions are proposed to a problem, an analysis might be able to show the lowest cost solution and the incremental cost of other solutions. The decision maker can use such an analysis as an aid in deciding whether the political benefits of a higher cost solution outweigh the cost.

[13] See James C. Miller III, "Lessons of the Economic Impact Statement Program," *AEI Journal on Government and Society,* July/August 1977, p. 14.

*Example:* The Agricultural Stabilization and Conservation Service Peanut Program accomplishes important economic objectives with respect to the supply and price of peanuts, and the economic effect of various program proposals can be estimated with a fair degree of reliability. At the same time, the particular program selected must take into account the desires of peanut growers and of legislators in peanut growing states. This program is likely not to be optimum in an economic sense, but it may be desirable to estimate the economic consequences of proposals that are favored for political reasons, so as to judge whether the economic sacrifice is worth the political gain.

Regardless of its technical merits, it is fruitless to develop a proposal that cannot be sold to those who must provide the funds. Senior management of course may have to make an extremely difficult judgment call as to the salability of the proposal and may make many soundings before the proposal is formally surfaced. Much of the relationship between the President and the Congress reflects such judgment.

*Example:* The Family Assistance Plan was a proposal to guarantee each family of four an income of $1,600 per year and consequently to do away with many separate welfare programs. It was originally proposed in 1969, and under various names, such as "negative income tax," and is still advocated by some. It has not been acceptable to the Congress.[14]

## Advocacy Proposals

The decision maker should consider whether or not a proposal is prepared by, or influenced by, the person who advocates it. An advocacy proposal is essentially a document that is designed to sell the proposal to the decision maker. Most proposals initiated by operating managers are advocacy proposals; indeed, if the manager is not an enthusiastic supporter of the proposal, there is probably something wrong with it. Proposals initiated by a top-level planning staff presumably are more neutral, but even staff-generated proposals can incorporate an element of advocacy under certain circumstances. In general, therefore, it is safe to assume that most proposals reflect someone's advocacy. A proposal may be biased in any of the following ways:

1. Consequences are asserted without adequate substantiation. (In a benefit/cost analysis, the process may be, first, to estimate the cost and then to plug in a benefit "number" such that the resulting benefit/cost ratio looks good.)
2. Technical matters beyond the comprehension of the decision maker are discussed at length. (This is one of several possible varieties of "snow jobs" that are attempted in proposals.)
3. Opposing views are omitted or not fully and accurately reported.
4. Costs and the time required to implement the proposal are underestimated.

[14] See Daniel P. Moynihan, *The Politics of a Guaranteed Income* (New York: Random House, 1973).

Decision makers attempt to allow for these biases and to minimize them by discouraging deliberate omissions or distortions, but they usually do not have either the knowledge or the time to detect all the elements of bias that are embedded in a proposal. In reviewing proposals, therefore, they need ways of compensating for the biases. The planning staff provides one important resource for this purpose. Subject to the qualification that a planning staff can develop its own biases, the staff exists to help the decision maker, and it can do this by making a thorough analysis of advocacy proposals. In many circumstances, the staff works with the initiator of the proposal to remove unwarranted assumptions, errors of calculations, or other weaknesses before the proposal is submitted to the decision maker. The staff also may list questions for the decision maker to raise with the advocate, the answers to which will shed light on the real merits of the proposal.

An outside consultant may be hired to make the same type of review. If the consulting firm has special expertise in the topic, its appraisal is especially useful, but in many situations the internal planning staff has built up a background that permits it to do the same job more effectively. A consulting firm is also useful for another purpose: to associate its prestige either for or against a proposal, and thus either aid or hurt the chances of its adoption.

Another approach to the advocacy proposal is to establish an adversary relationship. For every important proposal, there is some group that opposes it, if only because it diverts resources that the group would like to have for its own programs. If arrangements are made to identify such an adversary party and provide for a debate between it and the program advocate, the merits and weaknesses of the proposal often can be illuminated. A danger exists, however, that the adversaries will develop a "back-scratching" relationship. The presumed adversary may not argue forcefully against the proposal with the understanding, or at least the hope, that when the roles are reversed in connection with some other proposal, the other party will act with equal charity.

In short, for a variety of reasons, there is no such thing as a decision on an important proposal being based entirely on a "rational" analysis. If proposals are arrayed along a continuum, with purely economic proposals at one extreme and purely social or political proposals at the other, the amount of rationality inevitably decreases as one moves along that continuum. Nevertheless, a decision must be made. Because resources are limited, not all worthwhile proposals can be accepted, and the decision maker must decide which of the worthwhile projects are the best.[15]

[15] In 1942, Dr. James Conant, the decision maker with respect to the atomic bomb, was presented with five possible methods of producing fissionable material, each of which required enormous expenditures. He decided to proceed with all five. Two were abandoned a few months later, but the remaining three were activly pursued. There are few problems in which this luxury of adopting several competing alternatives is possible. See Stephane Groveff, *Manhattan Project* (Boston: Little, Brown, 1967).

# APPENDIX

## TECHNICAL ASPECTS OF CAPITAL BUDGETING

A typical capital investment proposal is one that involves an outlay of money at the present time in order to realize a stream of benefits some time in the future. For example, a proposal might be to install storm windows at a cost of $10,000, with an estimated savings in heating bills of $3,000 per year. In evaluating this proposal one asks: Is it worth spending $10,000 to obtain benefits of $3,000 per year? There are several approaches to answering this question.

### Payback Period

One approach finds the number of years that the benefits will have to be obtained in order to recover the investment of $10,000. This is the payback period, calculated as:

$$\text{Payback period} = \frac{\text{Initial investment}}{\text{Annual benefits}} = \frac{\$10{,}000}{\$3{,}000} = 3.3 \text{ years}$$

If the storm windows are expected to last less than 3.3 years, the investment is not worthwhile. If more than 3.3 years, the storm windows will have "paid for themselves," and the benefits thereafter will be profit.

### Net Present Value

The payback analysis assumes that savings in the second and third years are as valuable as savings in the first year, however, and this is not realistic. No rational person would give up the right to receive $3,000 now for the promise to receive $3,000 two years from now. If a person loans $3,000 now, he or she expects to get back more than $3,000 at some time in the future. The promise of an amount to be received in the future has a lower *present value* than the same amount received today.

What is the present value to us of a specified amount of money to be received two years from now? One way of thinking about that question is to estimate how much money we would have to set aside, right now, in order to have $3,000 two years from now. In order to answer the question we have to know how much interest we could earn on the money set aside. Suppose we found a bank that will give us 8 percent interest. What we want is to calculate the amount of money which, when deposited now at 8 percent interest will yield us $3,000 in two years.

If we put $\$X$ in the bank, it will earn 8 percent interest during the course of the year and at the end of the first year will grow to be $\$X + 0.08(\$X)$, or $\$X(1 + 0.08)$, or $\$1.08X$. During the second year, the amount of money we have will grow by another 8 percent, or 0.08 ($\$1.08X$), and when added to the balance at the end of the first year the balance at the end of the second year will be $\$1.08X + 0.08\ (\$1.08X)$ or $\$1.08X\ (1 + 0.08)$ or $(\$X)(1.08)^2$. We can now solve for $X$, the amount of money we have to set aside now in order to have $3,000 two years from now.

$$(\$X)(1.08)^2 = \$3{,}000$$

$$\$X = \frac{3{,}000}{(1.08)^2} = \frac{3{,}000}{1.166} = (3{,}000)(0.857) = \$2{,}571$$

We need to put $2,571 in an 8 percent account if we wish to have $3,000 two years from now. Alternatively, the *present value* of $3,000 two years from now at an 8 percent rate is $2,571.

Suppose we estimate the useful life of the storm windows as five years. With this estimate we can calculate the net present value of the above investment proposal. Under that proposal, we assume the machine is purchased in "year 0" and begins its benefits in year 1.

If we can earn 8 percent on our money, we can calculate the present value of each year's benefits as being:

$$\text{Present value in } n\text{th year} = \frac{\$3{,}000}{(1.08)^n}$$

where $n$ = the year in which the benefits occur.

This calculation is cumbersome, but fortunately there are tables which give us the relevant data. The table below, for example, gives us the present value of $1 at 8 percent for each of 12 years:

| *Year* | *Present Value Factor* | *Year* | *Present Value Factor* |
|---|---|---|---|
| 1 | 0.926 | 7 | 0.583 |
| 2 | 0.857 | 8 | 0.540 |
| 3 | 0.794 | 9 | 0.500 |
| 4 | 0.735 | 10 | 0.463 |
| 5 | 0.681 | 11 | 0.429 |
| 6 | 0.630 | 12 | 0.397 |

To calculate the present value of $3,000 to be received one year from now we would multiply $3,000 by 0.926; the present value of $3,000 to be received two years from now can be obtained by multiplying $3,000 by 0.857; and so on for each of the five years.

Although these calculations are easier than figuring out what $(1.08)^n$ is for every year, they are still tedious. We can shortcut them even more. Notice that we multiply the present value factor of every year by $3,000. It is easier to add up the present value factors for all the five years and multiply that sum by $3,000. To do so would give us $.926 + .857 + .794 + .735 + .681 = 3.993$.

*Annuity* tables contain the results of this and similar calculations for several interest rates over a variety of different time periods.[16] They show the sum of the present value factors for each of the years they contain; thus, a two-year 8 percent annuity has a present value of 1.783 which is equal to the first year's present value factor of 0.926 plus the second year's present value factor of 0.857. A five-year 8 percent annuity is equal to 3.993. Therefore, the present value of a $3,000 annual cash flow for five years is as follows:

$$(\$3{,}000)\ (3.993) = \$11{,}979$$

This sum represents the amount of money we would have to invest right now at 8 percent in order to have yearly payments of $3,000 for five years. Thus, the stream of five $3,000 cash flows has a present value of $11,979. Yet, in order to obtain this present value of $11,979, we need only give up $10,000. Thus, on a net present value basis, the proposal is acceptable. It has a net present value of $11,979 − $10,000 = $1,979.

### Benefit/Cost Criterion

If we have a number of proposals, and we wish to rank them in order of financial desirability, we could calculate their benefit/cost ratio or:

$$\text{Benefit/cost ratio} = \frac{\text{Net present value of inflows} - \text{Outflows}}{\text{Initial investment}}$$

Suppose we hvae two $2,000 proposals: one yielding a cash inflow of $2,400 one year from now and the other yielding a cash inflow of $600 a year for five years. If we estimate that we can earn 10 percent on the average investment, the benefit/cost ratio indicates that the second proposal is preferable, as indicated below:

| Proposal | Investment | Cash Inflow | Present Value Factors at 10% | Present Value | Benefit/ Cost Ratio |
|---|---|---|---|---|---|
| One ............ | $2,000 | $2,400 Year 1 | 0.909 | $2,182 | 1.09 |
| Two ............ | 2,000 | $600 Years 1–5 | 3.791 | 2,274 | 1.14 |

In this instance Proposal Two is more valuable on a net present value basis than Proposal One. However with these proposals, as with almost all capital budgeting proposals, a wide variety of nonquantitative considerations, including political realities, will influence the final decision.

---

[16] An annuity literally means an annually repeated event. Here the event is the receipt of $3,000 in cash flows. Tables A and B at the end of the appendix give us respectively, the present value of a one-time $1 cash flow n years hence, and the present value of an annuity of $1 for n years. Some hand-held calculators calculate present values automatically.

**Table A**
Present Value of $1

| Years Hence | 1% | 2% | 4% | 6% | 8% | 10% | 12% | 14% | 15% | 16% | 18% | 20% | 22% | 24% | 25% | 26% | 28% | 30% | 35% | 40% | 45% | 50% |
|---|---|---|---|---|---|---|---|---|---|---|---|---|---|---|---|---|---|---|---|---|---|---|
| 1 | 0.990 | 0.980 | 0.962 | 0.943 | 0.926 | 0.909 | 0.893 | 0.877 | 0.870 | 0.862 | 0.847 | 0.833 | 0.820 | 0.806 | 0.800 | 0.794 | 0.781 | 0.769 | 0.741 | 0.714 | 0.690 | 0.667 |
| 2 | 0.980 | 0.961 | 0.925 | 0.890 | 0.857 | 0.826 | 0.797 | 0.769 | 0.756 | 0.743 | 0.718 | 0.694 | 0.672 | 0.650 | 0.640 | 0.630 | 0.610 | 0.592 | 0.549 | 0.510 | 0.476 | 0.444 |
| 3 | 0.971 | 0.942 | 0.889 | 0.840 | 0.794 | 0.751 | 0.712 | 0.675 | 0.658 | 0.641 | 0.609 | 0.579 | 0.551 | 0.524 | 0.512 | 0.500 | 0.477 | 0.455 | 0.406 | 0.364 | 0.328 | 0.296 |
| 4 | 0.961 | 0.924 | 0.855 | 0.792 | 0.735 | 0.683 | 0.636 | 0.592 | 0.572 | 0.552 | 0.516 | 0.482 | 0.451 | 0.423 | 0.410 | 0.397 | 0.373 | 0.350 | 0.301 | 0.260 | 0.226 | 0.198 |
| 5 | 0.951 | 0.906 | 0.822 | 0.747 | 0.681 | 0.621 | 0.567 | 0.519 | 0.497 | 0.476 | 0.437 | 0.402 | 0.370 | 0.341 | 0.328 | 0.315 | 0.291 | 0.269 | 0.223 | 0.186 | 0.156 | 0.132 |
| 6 | 0.942 | 0.888 | 0.790 | 0.705 | 0.630 | 0.564 | 0.507 | 0.456 | 0.432 | 0.410 | 0.370 | 0.335 | 0.303 | 0.275 | 0.262 | 0.250 | 0.227 | 0.207 | 0.165 | 0.133 | 0.108 | 0.088 |
| 7 | 0.933 | 0.871 | 0.760 | 0.665 | 0.583 | 0.513 | 0.452 | 0.400 | 0.376 | 0.354 | 0.314 | 0.279 | 0.249 | 0.222 | 0.210 | 0.198 | 0.178 | 0.159 | 0.122 | 0.095 | 0.074 | 0.059 |
| 8 | 0.923 | 0.853 | 0.731 | 0.627 | 0.540 | 0.467 | 0.404 | 0.351 | 0.327 | 0.305 | 0.266 | 0.233 | 0.204 | 0.179 | 0.168 | 0.157 | 0.139 | 0.123 | 0.091 | 0.068 | 0.051 | 0.039 |
| 9 | 0.914 | 0.837 | 0.703 | 0.592 | 0.500 | 0.424 | 0.361 | 0.308 | 0.284 | 0.263 | 0.225 | 0.194 | 0.167 | 0.144 | 0.134 | 0.125 | 0.108 | 0.094 | 0.067 | 0.048 | 0.035 | 0.026 |
| 10 | 0.905 | 0.820 | 0.676 | 0.558 | 0.463 | 0.386 | 0.322 | 0.270 | 0.247 | 0.227 | 0.191 | 0.162 | 0.137 | 0.116 | 0.107 | 0.099 | 0.085 | 0.073 | 0.050 | 0.035 | 0.024 | 0.017 |
| 11 | 0.896 | 0.804 | 0.650 | 0.527 | 0.429 | 0.350 | 0.287 | 0.237 | 0.215 | 0.195 | 0.162 | 0.135 | 0.112 | 0.094 | 0.086 | 0.079 | 0.066 | 0.056 | 0.037 | 0.025 | 0.017 | 0.012 |
| 12 | 0.887 | 0.788 | 0.625 | 0.497 | 0.397 | 0.319 | 0.257 | 0.208 | 0.187 | 0.168 | 0.137 | 0.112 | 0.092 | 0.076 | 0.069 | 0.062 | 0.052 | 0.043 | 0.027 | 0.018 | 0.012 | 0.008 |
| 13 | 0.879 | 0.773 | 0.601 | 0.469 | 0.368 | C.290 | 0.229 | 0.182 | 0.163 | 0.145 | 0.116 | 0.093 | 0.075 | 0.061 | 0.055 | 0.050 | 0.040 | 0.033 | 0.020 | 0.013 | 0.008 | 0.005 |
| 14 | 0.870 | 0.758 | 0.577 | 0.442 | 0.340 | 0.263 | 0.205 | 0.160 | 0.141 | 0.125 | 0.099 | 0.078 | 0.062 | 0.049 | 0.044 | 0.039 | 0.032 | 0.025 | 0.015 | 0.009 | 0.006 | 0.003 |
| 15 | 0.861 | 0.743 | 0.555 | 0.417 | 0.315 | 0.239 | 0.183 | 0.140 | 0.123 | 0.108 | 0.084 | 0.065 | 0.051 | 0.040 | 0.035 | 0.031 | 0.025 | 0.020 | 0.011 | 0.006 | 0.004 | 0.002 |
| 16 | 0.853 | 0.728 | 0.534 | 0.394 | 0.292 | 0.218 | 0.163 | 0.123 | 0.107 | 0.093 | 0.071 | 0.054 | 0.042 | 0.032 | 0.028 | 0.025 | 0.019 | 0.015 | 0.008 | 0.005 | 0.003 | 0.002 |
| 17 | 0.844 | 0.714 | 0.513 | 0.371 | 0.270 | 0.198 | 0.146 | 0.108 | 0.093 | 0.080 | 0.060 | 0.045 | 0.034 | 0.026 | 0.023 | 0.020 | 0.015 | 0.012 | 0.006 | 0.003 | 0.002 | 0.001 |
| 18 | 0.836 | 0.700 | 0.494 | 0.350 | 0.250 | 0.180 | 0.130 | 0.095 | 0.081 | 0.069 | 0.051 | 0.038 | 0.028 | 0.021 | 0.018 | 0.016 | 0.012 | 0.009 | 0.005 | 0.002 | 0.001 | 0.001 |
| 19 | 0.828 | 0.686 | 0.475 | 0.331 | 0.232 | 0.164 | 0.116 | 0.083 | 0.070 | 0.060 | 0.043 | 0.031 | 0.023 | 0.017 | 0.014 | 0.012 | 0.009 | 0.007 | 0.003 | 0.002 | 0.001 | |
| 20 | 0.820 | 0.673 | 0.456 | 0.312 | 0.215 | 0.149 | 0.104 | 0.073 | 0.061 | 0.051 | 0.037 | 0.026 | 0.019 | 0.014 | 0.012 | 0.010 | 0.007 | 0.005 | 0.002 | 0.001 | 0.001 | |
| 21 | 0.811 | 0.660 | 0.439 | 0.294 | 0.199 | 0.135 | 0.093 | 0.064 | 0.053 | 0.044 | 0.031 | 0.022 | 0.015 | 0.011 | 0.009 | 0.008 | 0.006 | 0.004 | 0.002 | 0.001 | | |
| 22 | 0.803 | 0.647 | 0.422 | 0.278 | 0.184 | 0.123 | 0.083 | 0.056 | 0.046 | 0.038 | 0.026 | 0.018 | 0.013 | 0.009 | 0.007 | 0.006 | 0.004 | 0.003 | 0.001 | 0.001 | | |
| 23 | 0.795 | 0.634 | 0.406 | 0.262 | 0.170 | 0.112 | 0.074 | 0.049 | 0.040 | 0.033 | 0.022 | 0.015 | 0.010 | 0.007 | 0.006 | 0.005 | 0.003 | 0.002 | 0.001 | | | |
| 24 | 0.788 | 0.622 | 0.390 | 0.247 | 0.158 | 0.102 | 0.066 | 0.043 | 0.035 | 0.028 | 0.019 | 0.013 | 0.008 | 0.006 | 0.005 | 0.004 | 0.003 | 0.002 | 0.001 | | | |
| 25 | 0.780 | 0.610 | 0.375 | 0.233 | 0.146 | 0.092 | 0.059 | 0.038 | 0.030 | 0.024 | 0.016 | 0.010 | 0.007 | 0.005 | 0.004 | 0.003 | 0.002 | 0.001 | 0.001 | | | |
| 26 | 0.772 | 0.598 | 0.361 | 0.220 | 0.135 | 0.084 | 0.053 | 0.033 | 0.026 | 0.021 | 0.014 | 0.009 | 0.006 | 0.004 | 0.003 | 0.002 | 0.002 | 0.001 | | | | |
| 27 | 0.764 | 0.586 | 0.347 | 0.207 | 0.125 | 0.076 | 0.047 | 0.029 | 0.023 | 0.018 | 0.011 | 0.007 | 0.005 | 0.003 | 0.002 | 0.002 | 0.001 | 0.001 | | | | |
| 28 | 0.757 | 0.574 | 0.333 | 0.196 | 0.116 | 0.069 | 0.042 | 0.026 | 0.020 | 0.016 | 0.010 | 0.006 | 0.004 | 0.002 | 0.002 | 0.002 | 0.001 | 0.001 | | | | |
| 29 | 0.749 | 0.563 | 0.321 | 0.185 | 0.107 | 0.063 | 0.037 | 0.022 | 0.017 | 0.014 | 0.008 | 0.005 | 0.003 | 0.002 | 0.002 | 0.001 | 0.001 | 0.001 | | | | |
| 30 | 0.742 | 0.552 | 0.308 | 0.174 | 0.099 | 0.057 | 0.033 | 0.020 | 0.015 | 0.012 | 0.007 | 0.004 | 0.003 | 0.002 | 0.001 | 0.001 | 0.001 | | | | | |
| 40 | 0.672 | 0.453 | 0.208 | 0.097 | 0.046 | 0.022 | 0.011 | 0.005 | 0.004 | 0.003 | 0.001 | 0.001 | | | | | | | | | | |
| 50 | 0.608 | 0.372 | 0.141 | 0.054 | 0.021 | 0.009 | 0.003 | 0.001 | 0.001 | 0.001 | | | | | | | | | | | | |

**Table B**

Present Value of $1 Received Annually for *N* Years

| Years (*N*) | 1% | 2% | 4% | 6% | 8% | 10% | 12% | 14% | 15% | 16% | 18% | 20% | 22% | 24% | 25% | 26% | 28% | 30% | 35% | 40% | 45% | 50% |
|---|---|---|---|---|---|---|---|---|---|---|---|---|---|---|---|---|---|---|---|---|---|---|
| 1 | 0.990 | 0.980 | 0.962 | 0.943 | 0.926 | 0.909 | 0.893 | 0.877 | 0.870 | 0.862 | 0.847 | 0.833 | 0.820 | 0.806 | 0.800 | 0.794 | 0.781 | 0.769 | 0.741 | 0.714 | 0.690 | 0.667 |
| 2 | 1.970 | 1.942 | 1.886 | 1.833 | 1.783 | 1.736 | 1.690 | 1.647 | 1.626 | 1.605 | 1.566 | 1.528 | 1.492 | 1.457 | 1.440 | 1.424 | 1.392 | 1.361 | 1.289 | 1.224 | 1.165 | 1.111 |
| 3 | 2.941 | 2.884 | 2.775 | 2.673 | 2.577 | 2.487 | 2.402 | 2.322 | 2.283 | 2.246 | 2.174 | 2.106 | 2.042 | 1.981 | 1.952 | 1.923 | 1.868 | 1.816 | 1.696 | 1.589 | 1.493 | 1.407 |
| 4 | 3.902 | 3.808 | 3.630 | 3.465 | 3.312 | 3.170 | 3.037 | 2.914 | 2.855 | 2.798 | 2.690 | 2.589 | 2.494 | 2.404 | 2.362 | 2.320 | 2.241 | 2.166 | 1.997 | 1.849 | 1.720 | 1.605 |
| 5 | 4.853 | 4.713 | 4.452 | 4.212 | 3.993 | 3.791 | 3.605 | 3.433 | 3.352 | 3.274 | 3.127 | 2.991 | 2.864 | 2.745 | 2.689 | 2.635 | 2.532 | 2.436 | 2.220 | 2.035 | 1.876 | 1.737 |
| 6 | 5.795 | 5.601 | 5.242 | 4.917 | 4.623 | 4.355 | 4.111 | 3.889 | 3.784 | 3.685 | 3.498 | 3.326 | 3.167 | 3.020 | 2.951 | 2.885 | 2.759 | 2.643 | 2.385 | 2.168 | 1.983 | 1.824 |
| 7 | 6.728 | 6.472 | 6.002 | 5.582 | 5.206 | 4.868 | 4.564 | 4.288 | 4.160 | 4.039 | 3.812 | 3.605 | 3.416 | 3.242 | 3.161 | 3.083 | 2.937 | 2.802 | 2.508 | 2.263 | 2.057 | 1.883 |
| 8 | 7.652 | 7.325 | 6.733 | 6.210 | 5.747 | 5.335 | 4.968 | 4.639 | 4.487 | 4.344 | 4.078 | 3.837 | 3.619 | 3.421 | 3.329 | 3.241 | 3.076 | 2.925 | 2.598 | 2.331 | 2.108 | 1.922 |
| 9 | 8.566 | 8.162 | 7.435 | 6.802 | 6.247 | 5.759 | 5.328 | 4.946 | 4.772 | 4.607 | 4.303 | 4.031 | 3.786 | 3.566 | 3.463 | 3.366 | 3.184 | 3.019 | 2.665 | 2.379 | 2.144 | 1.948 |
| 10 | 9.471 | 8.983 | 8.111 | 7.360 | 6.710 | 6.145 | 5.650 | 5.216 | 5.019 | 4.833 | 4.494 | 4.192 | 3.923 | 3.682 | 3.571 | 3.465 | 3.269 | 3.092 | 2.715 | 2.414 | 2.168 | 1.965 |
| 11 | 10.368 | 9.787 | 8.760 | 7.887 | 7.139 | 6.495 | 5.937 | 5.453 | 5.234 | 5.029 | 4.656 | 4.327 | 4.035 | 3.776 | 3.656 | 3.544 | 3.335 | 3.147 | 2.752 | 2.438 | 2.185 | 1.977 |
| 12 | 11.255 | 10.575 | 9.385 | 8.384 | 7.536 | 6.814 | 6.194 | 5.660 | 5.421 | 5.197 | 4.793 | 4.439 | 4.127 | 3.851 | 3.725 | 3.606 | 3.387 | 3.190 | 2.779 | 2.456 | 2.196 | 1.985 |
| 13 | 12.134 | 11.343 | 9.986 | 8.853 | 7.904 | 7.103 | 6.424 | 5.842 | 5.583 | 5.342 | 4.910 | 4.533 | 4.203 | 3.912 | 3.780 | 3.656 | 3.427 | 3.223 | 2.799 | 2.468 | 2.204 | 1.990 |
| 14 | 13.004 | 12.106 | 10.563 | 9.295 | 8.244 | 7.367 | 6.628 | 6.002 | 5.724 | 5.468 | 5.008 | 4.611 | 4.265 | 3.962 | 3.824 | 3.695 | 3.459 | 3.249 | 2.814 | 2.477 | 2.210 | 1.993 |
| 15 | 13.865 | 12.849 | 11.118 | 9.712 | 8.559 | 7.606 | 6.811 | 6.142 | 5.847 | 5.575 | 5.092 | 4.675 | 4.315 | 4.001 | 3.859 | 3.726 | 3.483 | 3.268 | 2.825 | 2.484 | 2.214 | 1.995 |
| 16 | 14.718 | 13.578 | 11.652 | 10.106 | 8.851 | 7.824 | 6.974 | 6.265 | 5.954 | 5.669 | 5.162 | 4.730 | 4.357 | 4.033 | 3.887 | 3.751 | 3.503 | 3.283 | 2.834 | 2.489 | 2.216 | 1.997 |
| 17 | 15.562 | 14.292 | 12.166 | 10.477 | 9.122 | 8.022 | 7.120 | 6.373 | 6.047 | 5.749 | 5.222 | 4.775 | 4.391 | 4.059 | 3.910 | 3.771 | 3.518 | 3.295 | 2.840 | 2.492 | 2.218 | 1.998 |
| 18 | 16.398 | 14.992 | 12.659 | 10.828 | 9.372 | 8.201 | 7.250 | 6.467 | 6.128 | 5.818 | 5.273 | 4.812 | 4.419 | 4.080 | 3.928 | 3.786 | 3.529 | 3.304 | 2.844 | 2.494 | 2.219 | 1.999 |
| 19 | 17.226 | 15.678 | 13.134 | 11.158 | 9.604 | 8.365 | 7.366 | 6.550 | 6.198 | 5.877 | 5.316 | 4.844 | 4.442 | 4.097 | 3.942 | 3.799 | 3.539 | 3.311 | 2.848 | 2.496 | 2.220 | 1.999 |
| 20 | 18.046 | 16.351 | 13.590 | 11.470 | 9.818 | 8.514 | 7.469 | 6.623 | 6.259 | 5.929 | 5.353 | 4.870 | 4.460 | 4.110 | 3.954 | 3.808 | 3.546 | 3.316 | 2.850 | 2.497 | 2.221 | 1.999 |
| 21 | 18.857 | 17.011 | 14.029 | 11.764 | 10.017 | 8.649 | 7.562 | 6.687 | 6.312 | 5.973 | 5.384 | 4.891 | 4.476 | 4.121 | 3.963 | 3.816 | 3.551 | 3.320 | 2.852 | 2.498 | 2.221 | 2.000 |
| 22 | 19.660 | 17.658 | 14.451 | 12.042 | 10.201 | 8.772 | 7.645 | 6.743 | 6.359 | 6.011 | 5.410 | 4.909 | 4.488 | 4.130 | 3.970 | 3.822 | 3.556 | 3.323 | 2.853 | 2.498 | 2.222 | 2.000 |
| 23 | 20.456 | 18.292 | 14.857 | 12.303 | 10.371 | 8.883 | 7.718 | 6.792 | 6.399 | 6.044 | 5.432 | 4.925 | 4.499 | 4.137 | 3.976 | 3.827 | 3.559 | 3.325 | 2.854 | 2.499 | 2.222 | 2.000 |
| 24 | 21.243 | 18.914 | 15.247 | 12.550 | 10.529 | 8.985 | 7.784 | 6.835 | 6.434 | 6.073 | 5.451 | 4.937 | 4.507 | 4.143 | 3.981 | 3.831 | 3.562 | 3.327 | 2.855 | 2.499 | 2.222 | 2.000 |
| 25 | 22.023 | 19.523 | 15.622 | 12.783 | 10.675 | 9.077 | 7.843 | 6.873 | 6.464 | 6.097 | 5.467 | 4.948 | 4.514 | 4.147 | 3.985 | 3.834 | 3.564 | 3.329 | 2.856 | 2.499 | 2.222 | 2.000 |
| 26 | 22.795 | 20.121 | 15.983 | 13.003 | 10.810 | 9.161 | 7.896 | 6.906 | 6.491 | 6.118 | 5.480 | 4.956 | 4.520 | 4.151 | 3.988 | 3.837 | 3.566 | 3.330 | 2.856 | 2.500 | 2.222 | 2.000 |
| 27 | 23.560 | 20.707 | 16.330 | 13.211 | 10.935 | 9.237 | 7.943 | 6.935 | 6.514 | 6.136 | 5.492 | 4.964 | 4.524 | 4.154 | 3.990 | 3.839 | 3.567 | 3.331 | 2.856 | 2.500 | 2.222 | 2.000 |
| 28 | 24.316 | 21.281 | 16.663 | 13.406 | 11.051 | 9.307 | 7.984 | 6.961 | 6.534 | 6.152 | 5.502 | 4.970 | 4.528 | 4.157 | 3.992 | 3.840 | 3.568 | 3.331 | 2.857 | 2.500 | 2.222 | 2.000 |
| 29 | 25.066 | 21.844 | 16.984 | 13.591 | 11.158 | 9.370 | 8.022 | 6.983 | 6.551 | 6.166 | 5.510 | 4.975 | 4.531 | 4.159 | 3.994 | 3.841 | 3.569 | 3.332 | 2.857 | 2.500 | 2.222 | 2.000 |
| 30 | 25.808 | 22.396 | 17.292 | 13.765 | 11.258 | 9.427 | 8.055 | 7.003 | 6.566 | 6.177 | 5.517 | 4.979 | 4.534 | 4.160 | 3.995 | 3.842 | 3.569 | 3.332 | 2.857 | 2.500 | 2.222 | 2.000 |
| 40 | 32.835 | 27.355 | 19.793 | 15.046 | 11.925 | 9.779 | 8.244 | 7.105 | 6.642 | 6.234 | 5.548 | 4.997 | 4.544 | 4.166 | 3.999 | 3.846 | 3.571 | 3.333 | 2.857 | 2.500 | 2.222 | 2.000 |
| 50 | 39.196 | 31.424 | 21.482 | 15.762 | 12.234 | 9.915 | 8.304 | 7.133 | 6.661 | 6.246 | 5.554 | 4.999 | 4.545 | 4.167 | 4.000 | 3.846 | 3.571 | 3.333 | 2.857 | 2.500 | 2.222 | 2.000 |

## SUGGESTED ADDITIONAL READINGS

Allison, Graham T. *Essence of Decision: Explaining the Cuban Missile Crisis.* Boston: Little, Brown., 1971.

Brewer, Gary D. *Politicians, Bureaucrats and the Consultant: A Critique of Urban Problem Solving.* New York: Basic Books, 1973.

Drake, Alvin U., Ralph L. Keeney, and Philip M. Morse, eds. *Analysis of Public Systems.* Cambridge, Mass.: MIT Press, 1972.

Emshoff, J.R., and R. L. Sisson. *Design and Use of Computer Simulation Models.* New York: Macmillan, 1970.

Enthoven, Alain C., and K. Wayne Smith. *How Much Is Enough: Shaping the Defense Program, 1961–1969.* New York: Harper & Row, 1971.

Jones, Charles O. *An Introduction to the Study of Public Policy.* Belmont, Calif.: Wadsworth, 1970.

Levey, Samuel, and N. Paul Loomba. *Health Care Administration: A Managerial Perspective.* Philadelphia: J. B. Lippincott, 1973.

Levin, R. I., and C. A. Kirkpatrick. *Quantitative Approaches to Management.* New York: McGraw-Hill, 1971.

Lindblom, Charles H. *The Policy-Making Process.* Englewood CLiffs, N.J.: Prentice-Hall, 1968.

Livingstone, J. Leslie, and Sanford C. Gunn. *Accounting for Social Goals: Budgeting and Analysis of Nonmarket Projects.* New York: Harper & Row, 1974.

Lyden, Fremont J., and Ernest C. Miller, eds. *Public Budgeting: Program Planning and Implementation,* 4th ed. (Englewood Cliffs, N.J.: Prentice-Hall, 1982).

Meltsner, Arnold J. *Policy Analysts in the Bureaucracy.* Berkeley: University of California Press, 1976.

Mowitz, Robert J. *The Design of Public Decision Systems,* Baltimore, Md.: University Park Press, 1980.

Rivlin, Alice M. *Systematic Thinking for Social Action.* Washington, D.C.: Brookings Institution, 1971.

Rumowicz, Madelyn. "In New Jersey: Capital Budgeting and Planning Process," *State Government,* Spring 1980, pp. 99–102.

Schultze, Charles L. *The Politics and Economics of Public Spending.* Washington, D.C.: Brookings Institution, 1968.

Zeckhauser, R. J. "Procedures for Valuing Lives," *Public Policy,* Fall 1975, pp. 419–64.

## Case 8–1

# YOLAND RESEARCH INSTITUTE*

Ms. Brooke Russell, Executive Director of the Yoland Research Institute was contemplating the proposal recently submitted to her by Dr. Russ Roberts, the head of the Nutrition Studies Department. Dr. Roberts' request was for the purchase of new equipment to perform operations currently being performed on different, less efficient equipment. The purchase price was $150,000 delivered and installed.

### Background

Yoland Research Institute was a nonprofit, university-affiliated organization, specializing in research in a wide variety of fields. In large part, its activities were determined by a combination of the faculty affiliated with it and their research interests, although most of its projects tended to be of a basic, rather than applied, nature. As such, it was constantly involved in projects which were attempting to advance the state of the art in the particular field of investigation. One such area was that of nutrition, where much of the work required sophisticated equipment. Sometimes the purchase of this equipment was funded by a particular research grant or contract.

### The Request

In the case of Dr. Roberts' request, no grant or contract funds were available, and hence Yoland would need to finance the cost of the new equipment itself. Dr. Roberts had worked closely with the equipment manufacturer to determine the potential benefits of the new equipment, however, and estimated that it would result in annual savings of $30,000 in labor and other direct costs, as compared with the present equipment. He also estimated that the proposed equipment's economic life was 10 years, with zero salvage value. The complication, though, was that the present equipment was in good working order, and would probably last, physically, for at least 20 more years.

The Institute had recently borrowed long-term to finance another project, and Ms. Russell was certain that it could obtain additional funds at 12 percent, although she would not plan to negotiate a loan specifically for the purchase of this equipment. She did feel, however, that an investment of this type should have a return of at least 20 percent, even though the Institute paid no taxes.

---

* This case was prepared by David W. Young, Harvard School of Public Health.

## Complicating Factors

Ms. Russell had one other concern about Dr. Roberts' proposal. Two years ago, a proposal involving the same economic life and dollar amounts had been submitted by Dr. Sharon Kim in the Sanitary Engineering Department; it had been approved. Just this week Dr. Kim had submitted another proposal for what she termed "even better equipment," informing Ms. Russell that this new equipment rendered the other equipment completely obsolete with no resale value. The new equipment would cost $300,000 delivered and installed, but was expected to result in annual savings of $75,000 above the cost of operating the other equipment. The economic life of this new equipment is estimated to be 10 years.

Although funds could be obtained to finance the purchase of Dr. Kim's proposed new equipment, Ms. Russell was concerned about the mistake that had been made two years ago with Dr. Kim's request, and wanted to be sure that a similar mistake not be made this year with Dr. Roberts' request. She also was not certain that Dr. Kim's request was justifiable.

## Questions

1. Assuming the present equipment in the Nutrition Department has zero book value and zero salvage value, should the Institute buy the equipment proposed by Dr. Roberts?
2. Assuming the present equipment is being depreciated at a straight-line rate of 10 percent, that it has a book value of $72,000 (cost $120,000; accumulated depreciation, $48,000), and has zero net salvage value today, should the Institute buy the proposed equipment?
3. Assuming this present equipment has a book value of $72,000 and a salvage value today of $45,000, and that if retained for 10 more years its salvage value will be zero, should the Institute buy the proposed equipment?
4. Assume Dr. Roberts' proposed equipment will save only $15,000 a year, but that its economic life is expected to be 20 years. If other conditions are as described in (1) above, should the Institute buy the proposed equipment?
5. What action should the Institute take with Dr. Kim's request?
6. If the Institute decides to purchase the new equipment for Dr. Kim, a mistake has been made somewhere, because good equipment, bought only two years previously, is being scrapped. How did this mistake come about?
7. A board member has pointed out that the Institute has a debt/equity structure as follows:

| | *Percent of Total* | *Average Interest Rate* | *Weighted Interest Rate* |
|---|---|---|---|
| Debt ......... | 40 | 12% | 4.8% |
| Equity ....... | 60 | 0 | — |
| Total ......... | 100 | | 4.8% |

This situation has come about because the Institute's equity consists of donations and other gifts which are essentially free, i.e., there is no interest charge. Thus, the proper discount rate to use is not 20 percent, as suggested by Ms. Russell, but only about 5 percent. What is your response to this argument? If not 5 percent, what figure would you use?

## Case 8–2

## FEDERAL AVIATION AGENCY*

In the early 1960s, the Federal Aviation Agency, anticipating a shortage of radio frequencies, decided to standardize its VHF communications system for air traffic control on 50 kc/s (kilocycles per second) channel spacing. The narrow channel spacing would permit a larger number of assigned frequencies within a given section of the radio spectrum.

At that time, many of the FAA's VHF tube-type radio receivers had 50 kc/s channel spacing, but some of the older sets used 100 kc/s and 200 kc/s spacing. In 1963 a contract was let for 3,210 50 kc/s tube-type receivers to replace the older sets, at a cost of $319.70 per receiver.

In 1964 the agency's Systems Research and Development Service (SRDS) completed specifications for 50 kc/s solid-state receivers to replace the tube-type receivers. In April 1965 the FAA's review board met to decide whether to approve the solid-state proposal for the agency's five-year plan then under discussion.

### Mission of the Federal Aviation Agency

The Federal Airway System was established to increase the safety of air travel over the United States. In 1965 it was the most extensive network of air-navigation aids in the world, ranging from small location markers to complex radar systems. Most operated 24 hours a day; a large percentage of them were unattended but were routinely checked by technicians.

In 1965 there were two FAA-approved methods of flying: (1) visual flight rules (VFR) and (2) instrument flight rules (IFR). An aircraft flying IFR would be in VHR radio contact with two types of FAA facilities: (1) airport towers and (2) air traffic control centers with their attendant RCAGs (remote communications air/ground). In addition, flight service stations (FSS) would provide weather and other general information.

Pilots wishing to take off from, for example, the Washington National

* This case was prepared by Graeme Taylor, Management Analysis Center.

Airport received taxiing instructions from ground control over one VHF frequency. When ready for takeoff, the pilots switched to clearance delivery on a second frequency to check their flight plan. Tower control then took over on a third frequency and gave final takeoff authorization. As soon as the plane was airborne, the pilot switched to a fourth frequency to communicate with departure control. Once takeoff procedures were completed, the Washington center (Leesburg, Virginia) took over on yet another frequency. As the plane traveled, for example, from Washington to Boston, the pilot would be able to communicate with the Washington, New York, and Boston centers directly via RCAGs or indirectly through FSSs located along the route.

Each VHF frequency used by the pilot required a separate FAA receiver on the ground because most of the tube-type receivers in use, as well as all the proposed solid-state receivers, were fixed-tuned.

## The Replacement Proposal

There were approximately 380 RCAGs and control centers, 350 FSSs, and 300 towers in the FAA system. Many of the tube-type receivers in each of these facilities had backup receivers available in case of failure. If a receiver without a backup failed, the pilot might be instructed to switch to another frequency.

The number and distribution of the tube-type receivers, as of December 31, 1964, was as follows:

| | *Number of VHF Receivers (tube type)* | | |
|---|---|---|---|
| *Type of Facility* | *Primary* | *Backup* | *Total* |
| RCAG and control center | 1,165 | 1,165 | 2,330 |
| FSS | 955 | — | 955 |
| Tower | 3,220 | 510 | 3,730 |
| Total | 5,340 | 1,675 | 7,015 |

***Reliability.*** One of the questions to be resolved if the tube-type receivers were replaced was whether or not solid-state receivers, with their greater reliability, would require backup receivers. In preparing its specifications, SRDS estimated the following "availability for use" of the equipment:

*a.* Solid state with no backup—99.93%
*b.* Solid state with backup—100.00 (virtually)
*c.* Tube type with backup—99.85

However, availability was also affected by control equipment and line and power failures.[1] Estimates adjusted for these factors were as follows: *(a)* 99.43 percent *(b)* 99.49 percent, and *(c)* 99.35 percent.

***Estimated Cost.*** Since SRDS's specifications for the solid-state receivers involved new technology, the staff could only estimate their actual cost. They prepared two estimates, one for replacing all 7,015 tube-type receivers and one for replacing only the 5,340 primary receivers. A contract to purchase 7,015 solid-state receivers was expected to result in a unit cost of $340 per receiver; the cost would be increased to $385 per receiver if only 5,340 were ordered. In both cases, the installation cost was estimated at $75 per receiver. If a policy of piecemeal replacement were adopted, the smaller contracts would result in a unit cost of approximately $480. Delivery was estimated to begin 12 months after the contract was let and to proceed at the rate of 325 receivers per month.

***Operating Savings.*** The use of solid-state parts would lower FAA's annual power, maintenance, and tube-replacement costs. Solid-state receivers were also more compact and thus would occupy less space in the facilities than the tube-type receivers. In addition, the longer life expectancy and greatly reduced size of the parts would significantly reduce the quantity of spare parts stocked and the storage space that they required. Additional information about each of these potential savings is given below.

1. *Maintenance labor.* Of the total of 7,015 tube-type receivers in use, 620 were multichannel receivers, involving different maintenance and utility costs from those for the 6,395 fixed-tuned receivers. The budgeted annual maintenance time for tube-type receivers was 39.6 man-hours per fixed-tuned receiver and 55.4 man-hours per multichannel receiver. The estimated annual maintenance time per solid-state receiver was 19.9 man-hours. This estimated time for the solid-state receivers represented a 50 percent reduction from the fixed-tuned tube-type receivers; however, some FAA engineers felt that the potential reduction would possibly be closer to 75 percent. Maintenance time, including travel, cost $9,602 per man-year of 2,080 man-hours.

   The FAA's maintenance staff in FY 1965 spent $135 million, of which 70 percent was for personnel ($94 million), 10 percent for material ($13 million), and 20 percent for other ($28 million). Of the $94 million for "personnel" expenses, 45 percent was direct labor, 16 percent was indirect, and 39 percent was for administrative leave.

   The maintenance staff divided the country into 550 sectors, each containing from 5 to 30 "facilities," or functional groups of equipment requir-

[1] That is, the microwave or leased telephone company cables connecting an RCAG with its control center.

ing servicing. A typical sector might spend $160,000 per year on "personnel" expenses, employing 16 maintenance personnel of whom 14 might be electronic technicians.

Workload for a sector was determined by adding together the "point counts" or man-hours per year estimated to maintain each individual component within the sector, including actual repair time, plus allowances for travel, training, leave, relief, and so forth.

For an average RCAG, total corrective maintenance time might be divided as follows:

| | |
|---|---|
| Receivers ...... | 36% |
| Antennas ...... | 2 |
| Amplifiers ...... | 2 |
| Controls ....... | 11 |
| Transmitters .... | 49 |

2. *Replacement parts.* Annual cost of replacement parts per receiver was calculated at $17.95 for the fixed-tuned tube type, $73 for the multichannel tube type, and an estimated $1.95 for the solid state.

   Procurement of spare parts was handled centrally in Oklahoma City; delivery time averaged two months. When new equipment was to be installed, estimated spares for one year were obtained. Thereafter, standard methods were used for determining minimum inventory levels of spares required. Tubes were expected to fail at the rate of four or five per tube-type receiver per year, while solid-state receivers were estimated at one failure per 10,000 hours.
3. *Power costs.* The fixed-tuned tube-type receiver was rated at 100 watts, the multichannel tube-type receiver at 265 watts, and the solid-state type at 40 watts. All receivers, whether primary or backup, tube type or solid state, were operated continuously. The cost of electric power was 1 cent per kilowatt-hour.
4. *Space utilization.* Receivers were mounted in standard racks 83 inches high; each rack cost $100. The tube-type receivers occupied 8.75 inches of vertical rack space, while the solid-state receivers would require only 3.5 inches.

***The Replacement Cycle.*** The oldest tube-type receivers still in use in 1965 were approximately 15 years old, while the average age was from 6 to 8 years. The useful life of the tube-type receivers was estimated at from 15 to 20 years. The life of the solid-state receivers would be at least 20 years.

As noted earlier, the agency had already contracted for delivery of 3,210 tube-type receivers; 605 receivers had been delivered by early 1965, and an additional 1,083 were regarded as top priority and were being shipped directly to the regions to replace older receivers. Cancellation of this contract would be considered if the solid-state proposal were approved; however, little, if any, rebate could be expected.

The maximum "salvage value" for the tube-type receivers already in service was estimated at an average of 5 percent of their original average purchase price of approximately $350 per receiver. It was anticipated, however, that these receivers would probably be turned over to AID or HEW, with no net return to the government.

A future alternative would be to employ solid-state multichannel combination transmitter/receiver units, which would require even less maintenance than separate transmitters and solid-state receivers, would use common components, and would save considerably on space. With these devices, known as "transceivers," one compact "package" unit could suffice for each facility. In addition, unlike the present multichannel receivers, they would permit almost instantaneous switching from one frequency to another. If the transceivers were installed, the solid-state receivers requested by IMS would have only limited use, primarily as backups. However, transceivers were not expected to be available before 1973.

## Questions

1. Calculate the estimated annual operating savings that would result from replacing tube-type receivers with solid-state receivers.
2. Make recommendations regarding replacement in 1965.

## Case 8–3
## DOWNTOWN PARKING AUTHORITY*

In January a meeting was held in the office of the mayor of Oakmont to discuss a proposed municipal parking facility. The participants included the mayor, the traffic commissioner, the administrator of Oakmont's Downtown Parking Authority, the city planner, and the finance director. The purpose of the meeting was to consider a report by Richard Stockton, executive assistant to the Parking Authority's administrator, concerning estimated costs and revenues for the proposed facility.

Mr. Stockton's opening statement was as follows:

> As you know, the mayor proposed two months ago that we construct a multilevel parking garage on the Elm Street site. At that time, he asked the Parking Authority to assemble all pertinent information for consideration at our meeting today. I would like to summarize our findings briefly for you.

---

* This case was prepared by Graeme Taylor, Management Analysis Center.

The Elm Street site is owned by the city. All that stands on it now are the remains of the old Embassy Cinema, which we estimate would cost approximately $40,000 to demolish. A building contractor has estimated that a multilevel structure, with space for 800 cars, could be built on the site at a cost of about $2 million. The useful life of the garage would probably be around 40 years.

The city could finance construction of the garage through the sale of bonds. The finance director has informed me that we could probably float an issue of 20-year tax-exempts at 5 percent interest. Redemption would commence after three years, with one seventeenth of the original number of bonds being recalled in each succeeding year.

A parking management firm has already contacted us with a proposal to operate the garage for the city. They estimate that their costs, exclusive of the fee, would amount to $240,000 per year. Of this amount, $175,000 would be personnel costs; the remainder would include utilities, mechanical maintenance, insurance, and so forth. In addition, they would require a management fee of $30,000 per year. Any gross revenues in excess of $270,000 per year would be shared 90 percent by the city and 10 percent by the management firm. If total annual revenues are *less* than $270,000, the city would have to pay the difference.

I suggest we offer a management contract for bid, with renegotiations every three years.

The city would derive additional income of around $50,000 per year by renting the ground floor of the structure as retail space.

We conducted a survey at a private parking garage only three blocks from the Elm Street site to help estimate revenues from the prospective garage.

The garage, which is open every day from 7:00 A.M., until midnight, charges: 75 cents for the first hour; 50 cents for the second hour; and 25 cents for each subsequent hour, with a maximum rate of $2. Their capacity is 400 spaces. Our survey indicated that during business hours, 75 percent of their spaces were occupied by "all-day parkers"—cars whose drivers and passengers work downtown. In addition, roughly 400 cars use the garage each weekday with an average stay of three hours. We did not take a survey on Saturday or Sunday, but the proprietor indicated that the garage is usually about 75 percent utilized by short-term parkers on Saturdays until 6:00 P.M., when the department stores close; the average stay is about two hours. There's a lull until about 7:00 P.M., when the moviegoers start coming in; he says the garage is almost full from 8:00 P.M., until closing time at midnight. Sundays are usually very quiet until the evening, when he estimates that his garage is 60 percent utilized from 6:00 P.M. until midnight.

In addition, we studied a report issued by the City College Economics Department last year, which estimated that we now have approximately 50,000 cars entering the central business district (CBD) every day from Monday through Saturday. Based on correlations with other cities of comparable size, the economists calculated that we need 30,000 parking spaces in the CBD. This agrees quite well with a block-by-block estimate made by the traffic commissioner's office last year, which indicated a total parking need in the CBD of 29,000 spaces. Right now we have 22,000 spaces in the CBD. Of these, 5 percent are curb spaces (half of which are metered, with a two-hour maximum limit for 20 cents), and all the rest are in privately owned garages and open lots.

Another study indicated that 60 percent of all auto passengers entering the CBD on a weekday were on their way to work, 20 percent were shoppers, and

20 percent were business executives making calls. The average number of people per car was 1.75.

Unfortunately, we have not yet had time to use the data mentioned thus far to work up estimates of the revenues to be expected from the proposed garage.

The Elm Street site is strategically located in the heart of the CBD, near the major department stores and office buildings. It is five blocks from one of the access ramps to the new crosstown freeway, which we expect will be open to traffic next year, and only three blocks from the Music Center, which the mayor dedicated last week.

As we all know, the parking situation in that section of town has steadily worsened over the last few years, with no immediate prospect of improvement. The demand for parking is clearly there, and the Parking Authority therefore recommends that we build the garage.

The mayor thanked Mr. Stockton for his report and asked for comments. The following discussion took place:

*Finance Director:* I'm all in favor of relieving parking congestion downtown, but I think we have to consider alternative uses of the Elm Street site. For example, the city could sell that site to a private developer for at least $1 million. The site could support an office building from which the city would derive property taxes of around $200,000 per year at present rates. The office building would almost certainly incorporate an underground parking garage for the use of the tenants, and therefore we would not only improve our tax base and increase revenues but also increase the availability of parking at no cost to the city. Besides, an office building on that site would improve the amenity of downtown; a multilevel garage built above ground, on the other hand, would not.

*Planning Director:* I'm not sure I agree completely with the finance director. Within a certain range we can increase the value of downtown land by judicious provision of parking. Adequate, efficient parking facilities will encourage more intensive use of downtown traffic generators such as shops, offices, and places of entertainment, thus enhancing land values. A garage contained within an office building might, as the finance director suggests, provide more spaces, but I suspect these would be occupied almost exclusively by workers in the building and thus would not increase the total available supply.

I think long-term parking downtown should be discouraged by the city. We should attempt to encourage short-term parking—particularly among shoppers—in an effort to counteract the growth of business in the suburbs and the consequent stagnation of retail outlets downtown. The rate structure in effect at the privately operated garage quoted by Mr. Stockton clearly favors the long-term parker. I believe that if the city constructs a garage on the Elm Street site, we should devise a rate structure that favors the short-term parker. People who work downtown should be encouraged to use our mass transit system.

*Finance Director:* I'm glad you mentioned mass transit because this raises another issue. As you know, our subways are not now used to capacity and are running at a substantial annual deficit borne by the city. We have just spent millions of dollars on the new subway station under the Music Center. Why build a city garage only three blocks away that will still further increase the subway system's deficit? Each person who drives downtown instead of taking the subway represents a loss of 50 cents (the average round trip fare) to the subway system. I have read a report stating that approximately two thirds of all persons entering the CBD by car would still have made the trip by *subway* if they had *not* been able to use their cars.

*Mayor:* On the other hand, I think shoppers prefer to drive rather than take the subway, particularly if they intend to make substantial purchases. No one likes to take the subway burdened down by packages and shopping bags. You know, the Downtown Merchants Association has informed me that they estimate that each new parking space in the CBD generates on average an additional $10,000 in annual retail sales. That represents substantial extra profit to retailers; I think retailing aftertax profits average about 3 percent of gross sales. Besides, the city treasury benefits directly from our 3 percent sales tax.

*Traffic Commissioner:* But what about some of the other costs of increasing parking downtown and therefore, presumably, the number of cars entering the CBD? I'm thinking of such costs as the increased wear and tear on city streets, the additional congestion produced with consequent delays and frustration for the drivers, the impeding of the movement of city vehicles, noise, air pollution, and so on. How do we weigh these costs in coming to a decision?

*Parking Administrator:* I don't think we can make a decision at this meeting. I suggest that Dick Stockton be asked to prepare an analysis of the proposed garage that will answer the following questions:

1. Using the information presented at this discussion, should the city of Oakmont construct the proposed garage?
2. What rates should be charged?
3. What additional information, if any, should be obtained before making a final decision?

---

Note: Several ideas for this case were suggested by a study titled *Municipal Garages in Boston: A Cost-Benefit Analysis,* by George Berkley, which appeared in the April 1965 issue of *Traffic Quarterly.* The interested reader may wish to refer to this study, and also to *Downtown Parking Report 1966* prepared by the Division of Economic Development, City of Milwaukee, for further reading.

## Case 8–4

## DISEASE CONTROL PROGRAMS*

In February 1967, Mr. Harley Davidson, an analyst in the office of the Injury Control Program, Public Health Service (Department of Health, Education and Welfare) was reviewing DHEW's recently published Program Analysis 1966–1 titled *Disease Control Programs—Motor Vehicle Injury Prevention*

---

* This case was prepared by Charles J. Christenson, Harvard Business School.

*Program.* Included therein were nine program units. Mr. Davidson was a member of a task force established within DHEW to evaluate a series of benefit/cost analyses of various proposed disease control programs. In addition to motor vehicle injury prevention, benefit/cost studies had been made of programs dealing with control of arthritis, cancer, tuberculosis, and syphilis. Mr. Davidson's specific responsibility was to review Program Unit No. 8 of the motor vehicle injury prevention program (Increase Use of Improved Safety Devices by Motorcyclists) in order to (a) evaluate the methodology and results of the benefit/cost analysis of Program Unit No. 8, and (b) recommend whether or not the analysis justified the level of funding contemplated in the program unit.

## THE MOTORCYCLE PROGRAM

The following is the description of Program Unit No. 8, which appeared in Program Analysis 1966–1:

### Increase Use of Improved Safety Devices by Motorcyclists

To prevent accidental deaths due to head injuries of motorcycle riders through appropriate health activity at the national, state, and local levels.

*Approach.* The Public Health Service approach to solving the motorcycle injury problem will involve four phases. Although each of the four phases of activity is identified separately, all will be closely coordinated and carried out simultaneously. The four phases of activity are:

1. A national education program on use of protective head gear aimed primarily at motorcycle users. It will also include efforts to prepare operators of other motor vehicles to share the road with motorcycles.
2. A cooperative program with other national organizations and the motorcycle industry to improve protective and safety devices.
3. Involvement of state and local health departments and medical organizations in programs and activities designed to minimize accidental injury in motorcycle accidents.
4. Conduct surveillance activity on appropriate aspects of the motorcycle accident and injury problem.

The program unit was estimated to require the following level of new funding during the five-year planning period 1968–72:

| | *Estimated Program Level (millions of dollars)* |
|---|---|
| 1968 | $1.679 |
| 1969 | 1.609 |
| 1970 | 1.574 |
| 1971 | 1.569 |
| 1972 | 1.569 |

**Exhibit 1**
Proposed Budget for Program to Increase Use of Protective Devices by Motorcyclists (1968–1972; $000)

| | *1968* | *1969* | *1970* | *1971* | *1972* |
|---|---|---|---|---|---|
| Total number of persons | 42 | 42 | 42 | 42 | 42 |
| Total costs | $1,679 | $1,609 | $1,574 | $1,569 | $1,569 |
| Personnel | 504 | 504 | 504 | 504 | 504 |
| Program | 1,175 | 1,105 | 1,070 | 1,065 | 1,065 |
| Staff: | | | | | |
| Central office | 13 | 13 | 13 | 13 | 13 |
| Regional office | 9 | 9 | 9 | 9 | 9 |
| State assignees | 20 | 20 | 20 | 20 | 20 |
| Personnel | $ 504 | $ 504 | $ 504 | $ 504 | $ 504 |
| Evaluation and surveillance | 300 | 300 | 300 | 300 | 300 |
| State projects* | 500* | 500 | 500 | 500 | 500 |
| National TV spots | 60 | 60 | 60 | 60 | 60 |
| Educational TV series | 100 | 100 | 100 | 100 | 100 |
| Safety films | 40 | 40 | 20 | 20 | 20 |
| Publications | 100 | 30 | 30 | 30 | 30 |
| Exhibits | 30 | 30 | 15 | 15 | 15 |
| Community projects | 25 | 25 | 25 | 25 | 25 |
| Campus projects | 20 | 20 | 20 | 15 | 15 |

* Ten projects at $50,000 per project.

**Exhibit 2**
Costs per Death Averted and Benefit-Cost Ratios for All Program Units Studied

| *Program Unit* | *Program Cost per Death Averted* | *Benefit/Cost Ratio* |
|---|---|---|
| Motor vehicle injury prevention programs: | | |
| Increase seat belt use | $ 87 | 1,351.4:1 |
| Use of improved restraint devices | 100 | 1,117.1:1 |
| Reduce pedestrian injury | 600 | 144.3:1 |
| Increase use of protective devices by motorcyclists | 1,860 | 55.6:1 |
| Improve driving environment | 2,330 | 49.4:1 |
| Reduce driver drinking | 5,330 | 21.5:1 |
| Improve driver licensing | 13,800 | 3.8:1 |
| Improve emergency medical services | 45,000 | 2.4:1 |
| Improve driver training | 88,000 | 1.7:1 |
| Other disease control programs studied: | | |
| Arthritis | n.a. | 42.5:1 |
| Syphilis | 22,252 | 16.7:1 |
| Uterine cervix cancer | 3,470 | 9.0:1 |
| Lung cancer | 6,400 | 5.7:1 |
| Breast cancer | 7,663 | 4.5:1 |
| Tuberculosis | 22,807 | 4.4:1 |
| Head and neck cancer | 29,100 | 1.1:1 |
| Colon-rectum cancer | 42,944 | 0.5:1 |

n.a. = Not available.

Exhibit 1 gives a summary of the way in which the proposed funds would be spent.

The benefit/cost study estimated that the above program would result in the saving of 4,006 lives over the five-year period 1968–72 (no reduction in injuries was considered). The cost of the program discounted at 4 percent was $7,419,000; the benefits of the program, based on the lifetime earnings discounted at 3 percent of those whose deaths would be averted, were estimated at $412,754,000. Hence, the benefit/cost ratio equaled 55.6:1. Another measure of program effectiveness was the cost per death averted, $1,860. Exhibit 2 summarizes the benefit/cost ratios and the costs per death averted for all nine motor vehicle injury prevention program units and for the arthritis, cancer, tuberculosis, and syphilis programs. Exhibit 3 presents, for all programs, the estimated five-year reduction in numbers of injuries and deaths and the estimated discounted five-year program dollar costs and benefits.

**Exhibit 3**
Reduction in Injuries and Deaths and Total Discounted Program Costs and Savings for All Program Units Studied (1968–1972)

| *Program Unit* | *Discounted Program Costs ($000)* | *Discounted Program Savings ($000)* | *Reduction in Injuries* | *Reduction in Deaths* |
|---|---|---|---|---|
| Motor vehicle injury prevention programs: | | | | |
| Seat belts | 2,019 | 2,728,374 | 1,904,000 | 22,930 |
| Restraint devices | 610 | 681,452 | 471,600 | 5,811 |
| Pedestrian injury | 1,061 | 153,110 | 142,700 | 1,650 |
| Motorcyclists | 7,419 | 412,754 | — | 4,006 |
| Driving environment | 28,545 | 1,409,891 | 1,015,500 | 12,250 |
| Driver drinking | 28,545 | 612,970 | 440,630 | 5,340 |
| Driver licensing | 6,113 | 22,938 | 23,200 | 442 |
| Emergency medical services | 721,478* | 1,726,000 | † | 16,000 |
| Driver training | 750,550 | 1,287,022 | 665,300 | 8,515 |
| Other disease control programs studied: | | | | |
| Arthritis | 35,000 | 1,489,000 | n.a. | n.a. |
| Syphilis | 179,300‡ | 2,993,000 | n.a. | 11,590 |
| Uterine cervix cancer | 118,100‡ | 1,071,000 | n.a. | 34,200 |
| Lung cancer | 47,000‡ | 268,000 | n.a. | 7,000 |
| Breast cancer | 22,400 | 101,000 | n.a. | 2,396 |
| Tuberculosis | 130,000 | 573,000 | n.a. | 5,700 |
| Head and neck cancer | 7,800 | 9,000 | n.a. | 268 |
| Colon-rectum cancer | 7,300 | 4,000 | n.a. | 170 |

n.a. = Not available.
* Includes $300 million state matching funds.
† This program does not reduce injury; however, it is estimated to reduce hospital bed days by 2,401,000 and work loss days by 8,180.00
‡ Funding shown used as basis for analysis—includes funds estimated to come from sources other than DHEW.

## OVERALL METHODOLOGY

In this effort to apply benefit/cost analysis to the domain of vehicular accidents, three major constraints were laid down:

1. The problem of motor vehicle accidents is examined exclusively in terms of public health concerns. This mandate focused on the role of human factors in vehicular accidents and the amelioration of injury caused by vehicular accidents. In adopting this posture, three major factors in vehicular accident complex—law enforcement, road design, and traffic engineering—were, for the most part, excluded. This constraint had the effect of limiting the problem to considerations traditionally within the purview of DHEW, while excluding those elements which are traditionally handled by the Department of Commerce and other government agencies.
2. The problem of motor vehicle accidents is handled by nine programs which, in the opinion of committee members, were feasible and realistic. Criteria for determining "feasible and realistic" were not made explicit. However, program proposals which were rejected, such as no person under 21 being allowed to drive, reduction of maximum speeds on all roads by 20 percent, the federal government paying for the installation of $100 worth of safety devices on all automobiles, indicate the cultural values and assumed cost factors which were two issues involved in judging "feasible and realistic."
3. The problem of motor vehicle accidents is handled by programs based on what is known today. This constraint ruled out dependence on new findings based on future research. Unlike the other constraints, this ruling, in the minds of the committee members, constituted a basic condition for undertaking a benefit/cost analysis of alternative program strategies. Unless the analysis was restricted to "what is known," the "need for more research" would allow one partner in the dialogue to withdraw from the struggle without even having been engaged.

The report then went on to describe the rationale behind benefit/cost analysis:

> The reasoning behind the benefit/cost ananlysis is quite straightforward. The idea is to allow for a meaningful comparison of the change which results in a given situation as a result of applying alternative programs. In order to bring about this state of affairs, a measurable common denominator is useful for rating program outcome and program costs. This common denominator is dollars. Granting the existence of the common denominator, there must, in addition, be a point on which to take a "fix" in order to support the contention that change has, in fact, taken place. This point for fixing position and shifts in relation to change wrought by program is the baseline.
>
> In this exercise the baseline was created by assessing past rates for motor vehicle and pedestrian deaths and injuries. The assumption was made that the current level of program effort in DHEW would remain constant through 1972 with the

exception of increases for obligated administrative costs. The observed trend was then projected and applied to the anticipated population distribution for the years 1967–72. Program costs and savings due to the introduction of the program were limited to the five-year period 1968–72, although certain programs were just gathering momentum by the end of this period. . . . The required common denominator was incorporated into the baseline by converting fatalities into lost earnings and by translating lost work days, bed disability days, length of hospitalization, physician visits, and other medical services resulting from injuries into the direct and indirect costs represented by these statistical measures. . . . Throughout this analysis, the total dollar costs and benefit for the five-year period are discounted to 1968, the base year, to convert the stream of costs and benefits into its worth in the base year. . . .

With the baseline and common denominator established, the Committee was able to examine the potential payoff for a variety of program units even though these units differed with respect to such factors as cost of implementation, target group to be reached, method to be employed, and facet of the total program addressed by the proposed program.

With the establishment of the baseline and the development of techniques to convert all elements of the equation to a common denominator, the energies of the Committee were given over to the creation of program units. There are a number of variables which may contribute to the occurrence of a vehicular accident and its resultant injury or death. The skill of the driver, the condition of the road, the speed of the vehicle, the condition of the car, the failure to have or to use safety devices incorporated in the car are just a few of many that are mentioned in the literature. What we know about vehicular accidents is expressed in terms of these variables and, as a consequence, program formulations are generally placed in the context of managing these variables, either singly or in combination. A program unit, as developed by the Committee, usually addressed a single variable.

There are two links needed to effect the benefit/cost analysis in vehicular accidents. The first link is associated with the estimate of reduction that could be realized if a given variable were addressed by a program of some sort. This link is supplied in vehicular accidents by the expertise of the Committee members and recourse to studies on the particular variable in question. The Second link is associated with the effectiveness of the program proposed to bring about the estimated reduction. In vehicular accidents this is supplied by the experience with programs of the Committee members and the success in the past of programs, similar in content, devoted to public health problems.

## ESTIMATE OF BENEFITS

The benefit/cost studies of the motor vehicle injury prevention programs began with a stipulation of a "base line," or the number of deaths and injuries to be expected if the level of DHEW effort remained constant. Next an estimate was made of the number of deaths and injuries which would be avoided if the proposed program unit were adopted. Finally, the reduction in deaths and injuries was translated into dollar terms. These three steps will now be described as they applied to Program Unit No. 8.

## The Baseline

The team working on the motorcycle unit had available the information given in Table 1.

**Table 1**
Historical Data on Motorcycle Registrations and Fatalities

| *Year* | *Total Number of Registered Motorcycles in the U.S.* | *Number of Deaths from Motorcycle Accidents* | *Rate of Deaths per 100,000 Motorcycles* |
|---|---|---|---|
| 1959 .......... | 565,352 | 752 | 133.0 |
| 1960 .......... | 569,691 | 730 | 128.1 |
| 1961 .......... | 595,669 | 697 | 117.0 |
| 1962 .......... | 660,400 | 759 | 114.9 |
| 1963 .......... | 786,318 | 882 | 112.2 |
| 1964 .......... | 984,760 | 1,118 | 113.5 |

The team estimated that (1) the number of registered motorcycles would continue to increase at an increasing rate, and (2) the death rate would decline, in the absence of new safety programs, to a level of 110 deaths per 100,000 registered motorcycles. Accordingly, the number of motorcycle accident deaths to be expected without the safety program was projected as shown in Table 2.

**Table 2**
Projected Baseline Case

| *Year* | *Projected Total Number of Registered Motorcycles in the U.S.* | *Projected Number of Deaths from Motorcycle Accidents without Program (based on 110 deaths per 100,000 registered motorcycles)* |
|---|---|---|
| 1968 ............... | 2,900,000 | 3,190 |
| 1969 ............... | 3,500,000 | 3,850 |
| 1970 ............... | 4,200,000 | 4,620 |
| 1971 ............... | 5,000,000 | 5,500 |
| 1972 ............... | 6,000,000 | 6,600 |

## Effectiveness of the Program Unit

Calculation of the anticipated reduction in the number of deaths resulting from the proposed program unit involved two separate estimates: (1) the effectiveness of the program in persuading motorcyclists to wear helmets and protective eyeshields; and (2) the effectiveness of these devices in reducing deaths (injuries were not considered in the analysis of this program unit). The team's judgment was that the program would result in use of helmets and eyeshields to the degree shown in Table 3:

**Table 3**
Estimated Effectiveness of Program in Encouraging Protective Devices

| *Year* | *Estimated Percentage of Motorcyclists Using Helmets and Eyeshields* |
|---|---|
| 1968 | 20 |
| 1969 | 30 |
| 1970 | 40 |
| 1971 | 50 |
| 1972 | 55 |

Regarding the second factor, the effectiveness of protective devices in reducing deaths, the team relied on a study entitled "Effect of Compulsory Safety Helmets on Motorcycle Accident Fatalities" which appeared in *Australian Road Research,* vol. 2, no. 1, September 1964. This study reported that the number of motorcycle fatalities occurring in the Australian state of Victoria in the two years following the effective date of a law requiring the wearing of helmets was only 31 while the number of fatalities projected on the basis of the experience of the two preceding years was 62.5, for a reduction of about 50 percent. Other states, which did not have such a law, had shown a reduction of about 12 percent in the same period, a difference of 38 percent. The committee concluded that 100 percent usage of helmets and eyeshields by American motorcyclists would reduce the number of deaths by about 40 percent.

Multiplication of the figures for projected usage of protective devices given in Table 3 by 40 percent gave the estimated percentage reduction in deaths, and application of these percentages to the baseline data of Table 2 gave the estimated reduction in number of deaths. The results are summarized in Table 4.

## Conversion to Economic Benefits

For the purpose of calculating the lifetime earnings lost in the event of a motorcycle fatality, it was necessary to estimate the distribution of fatalities

**Table 4**
Estimated Reduction in Deaths from Proposed Program

| *Year* | *Projected Number of Deaths from Motorcycle Accidents without Program* | *Estimated Percentage Reduction in Deaths with Program* | *Estimated Reduction in Number of Deaths with Program* |
|---|---|---|---|
| 1968 | 3,190 | 8 | 255 |
| 1969 | 3,850 | 12 | 462 |
| 1970 | 4,620 | 16 | 739 |
| 1971 | 5,500 | 20 | 1,100 |
| 1972 | 6,600 | 22 | 1,450 |
| 5-year total | 23,760 | — | 4,006 |

**Table 5**
Estimated Reduction in Deaths by Age and Sex

| | *Age 15–24* | | *Age 25–34* | | |
|---|---|---|---|---|---|
| *Year* | *Males* | *Females* | *Males* | *Females* | *Total* |
| 1968 ...... | 207 | 23 | 22 | 3 | 255 |
| 1969 ...... | 374 | 42 | 41 | 5 | 462 |
| 1970 ...... | 598 | 67 | 67 | 7 | 739 |
| 1971 ...... | 891 | 99 | 99 | 11 | 1,100 |
| 1972 ...... | 1,174 | 131 | 130 | 15 | 1,450 |
| Total ...... | 3,244 | 362 | 359 | 41 | 4,006 |

by age and sex. In 1964, approximately 90 percent of the victims of motorcycle accidents had been male and 10 percent female; similarly, about 90 percent had been in the age group 15–24 and 10 percent in the age group 25–34. The data were not cross-classified, so it was considered necessary to assume that the sex distribution of fatalities in each age group was the same as the overall distribution, i.e., 90:10. Projecting these percentages into the future, it was calculated that, of the 255 fatalities which the proposed program was expected to avoid in 1968, 207 would be males between 15 and 24 inclusive (i.e., .9 × .9 × 255). Combining this procedure for all categories and years resulted in the estimates of the distribution of death reductions over the five-year period shown in Table 5.

The final step in calculating the expected benefits of the proposed program was to assign the appropriate dollar benefits to the above estimates of decreases in deaths by age group and sex. This was done by multiplying the decrease in deaths in each sex-age group "cell" in the above table by the applicable discounted lifetime earnings figure for that particular cell.

Table 6 shows lifetime earnings by age and sex, discounted at 3 percent used in computing the dollar benefits of reducing motorcycle accident fatalities. (The report contained a detailed description of the methodology used in deriving these amounts.)

The number of deaths saved in each cell of Table 5 was multiplied by the appropriate earnings figure from Table 6, and discounted at 3 percent

**Table 6**
Discounted Lifetime Earnings by Age and Sex

| *Age* | *Males* | *Females* |
|---|---|---|
| Under 1 ............ | $ 84,371 | $50,842 |
| 1–4 ................ | 98,986 | 54,636 |
| 5–9 ................ | 105,836 | 63,494 |
| 10–14 .............. | 122,933 | 73,719 |
| 15–19 .............. | 139,729 | 81,929 |
| 20–24 .............. | 150,536 | 84,152 |
| 25–29 .............. | 150,512 | 81,702 |
| 30–34 .............. | 141,356 | 77,888 |

**Table 7**
Discounted Savings Resulting from Program to Promote Use of Protective Devices by Motorcyclists (000s)

| | | Age 15–24 | | Age 25–34 | |
|---|---|---|---|---|---|
| *Year* | *Total* | *Males* | *Females* | *Males* | *Females* |
| Total | $412,754 | $344,002 | $27,164 | $48,714 | $2,874 |
| 1968 | 36,140 | 30,347 | 1,976 | 3,578 | 239 |
| 1969 | 61,972 | 52,423 | 3,282 | 5,895 | 372 |
| 1970 | 97,152 | 82,363 | 5,059 | 9,248 | 482 |
| 1971 | 39,547 | 117,928 | 7,408 | 13,393 | 818 |
| 1972 | 177,943 | 150,941 | 9,439 | 16,600 | 963 |

to the base year, 1968. For example, Table 5 indicates that it was estimated that, in 1968, the lives of three females between the ages of 25 and 34 would be saved. The discounted lifetime earnings of females in this age group was found from Table 6 by averaging the discounted lifetime earnings for females 25–29 and 30–34, the average of $81,702 and $77,888 being $79,795. This was multiplied by 3 to give $239,385; using a present value factor of 1 (since 1968 was the base year), the figure derived was $239,385. Similarly, discounted figures were obtained for each year by age group and sex; the results are shown below in Table 7.

Thus, over the five-year program period, 1968–72, it was estimated that 4,006 deaths could be averted (Table 5), at a present-value cost of $7,419,000. The present value of the lifetime earnings of the 4,006 persons whose lives would be saved during this period was shown in Table 7 to be $412,754,000.

These data were summarized in the form of two measures of program effectiveness:

$$\text{Program cost per death averted} = \frac{\$7{,}419{,}000}{4{,}006} = \underline{\underline{\$1{,}860}}$$

$$\text{Benefit/cost ratio} = \frac{\$412{,}754{,}000}{\$7{,}419{,}000} = \underline{\underline{55.6}}$$

## Questions

1. As Mr. Davidson, prepare a critique of the methodology and findings of the benefit/cost analysis of Program Unit No. 8.
2. Based on your evaluation of the analysis, would you recommend the level of funding proposed?

# chapter 9

# Budget Formulation

The general character of the budgeting process in a nonprofit organization is similar to that in a profit-oriented one, but there are significant differences in emphasis. This chapter focuses on both the similarities and the differences.

## NATURE OF THE BUDGETING PROCESS

A budget is a plan expressed in monetary terms. There are several types of budgets, including the *capital budget,* which lists and describes planned capital acquisitions; the *cash budget,* which summarizes planned cash receipts and disbursements; and the *operating budget,* which describes planned operating activities for a specified period of time, usually one year.[1] The discussion in this chapter relates primarily to the operating budget because the capital budget is derived more or less automatically from decisions made during the programming process, and the cash budget is derived from the operating budget.

[1] Some states prepare a biennial (once every two years) budget. Budget (or fiscal) years end in different months of the calendar year. In colleges and universities, for example, the fiscal year ends on June 30, July 31, or August 31. In nongovernment organizations, the budget year is usually the calendar year. In the federal government, the fiscal year ends on September 30. In many state and local governments the fiscal year ends on June 30.

## Relation to Programming

In concept, the budgeting process follows, but is separate from, the programming process discussed in Chapters 7 and 8. The budget is supposed to be a "fine tuning" of the program for a given year, incorporating the final decisions on the amounts to be spent for each program, and making clear who is responsible for carrying out each part of the program. These decisions are supposed to be made within the context of the basic decisions that were made during the programming process. In practice, however, no such clean separation between programming and budgeting exists, nor can it exist. Even in organizations that have a well-developed programming system, circumstances may be discovered during the budgeting process that require revision of program decisions. In organizations that have no recognizable, separate programming process, program decisions are made as part of the budgeting process.

Despite this overlap, it is useful to think about the two processes separately because they have different characteristics. The purpose of the programming process is to make decisions about programs. The purpose of the budgeting process is to decide on the actual operating plan for a year. The budgeting process requires careful estimates of expenses and revenues, using the most current information on prices; and the budget must be formulated within a ceiling that represents estimated available resources.

In some organizations, programmatic objectives also are incorporated into the operating budget. Since the budget will be used during the year as a plan against which actual performance will be checked, it is essential that the budget be related to individual responsibility centers. Thus, the budget provides a basis for control of responsibility center managers; the program is not a basis for control, unless a program is also a responsibility center.

## Two-Stage Budgets

Although this chapter will generally refer to "the" budget as if there were only one, in government organizations and in some other nonprofit organizations, there actually are two budgets. One, which may be referred to as the *legislative budget,* is essentially a request for funds. It does not correspond to the budget that is prepared in a profit-oriented company. Its closest counterpart is the prospectus that a company prepares when it seeks to raise money. Most of the media reports about government budgets relate to the legislative budget, and many textbook descriptions of government budgeting focus on this budget.

The second budget, which may be called the *management budget,* is prepared after the legislature has decided on the amount of funds that is to be provided (or, if the legislature is dilatory, it is prepared as soon as the executive branch can make a good estimate of what the legislature eventually will approve). This budget corresponds to the budget prepared in a profit-oriented company; that is, it is a plan showing the amount of spending that each responsibility center is authorized to undertake. If the amount of revenue is known within reasonable limits, the management budget can be an accurate reflection of the organization's plans for the year.

## APPROACH TO BUDGETING

### Contrast with Profit-Oriented Companies

Budgeting is an important part of the management control process in any organization, but it is even more important in a nonprofit organization than in a profit-oriented company. There are several reasons for this.

In a profit-oriented company, particularly a manufacturing company, a large fraction of the costs are *engineered costs.* The amount of labor and the quantity of material required to manufacture products are determined within rather close limits by the specifications of the products and of the manufacturing process. Consequently, little can be done to affect these costs during the budgeting process. By contrast, in most nonprofit organizations a large fraction of the costs are *discretionary;* that is, the amount that is to be spent can be varied within wide limits according to decisions made by management. The most important of these decisions are made during the budget formulation process.

In a profit-oriented company, a budget is a fairly tentative statement of plans. It is subject to change as conditions change, and such changes, particularly in the level and mix of sales, can occur frequently during the year. Furthermore, there is general agreement on the way in which managers should react to such changes; they should make revised plans that are consistent with the overall objective of profitability. In most nonprofit organizations, conditions are more stable and predictable. In a university, the number of students enrolled in September governs the pattern of spending for the whole year. A hospital gears up for a certain number of beds, and although there may be temporary fluctuations in demand, these ordinarily do not cause major changes in spending patterns. A government agency has a certain authorized program for the year; it operates so as to execute that program. Under these circumstances, the budget can be, and should be, a fairly accurate statement of what is to be done during the year and of the resources that are to be used. It is therefore important that it be prepared carefully. Much time, including much top-management time, should be devoted to it.

### Budget Philosophy

As pointed out in Chapter 2, the general purpose of a nonprofit organization is to provide as much service as it can with available resources. This suggests that the basic approach to budgeting should be first to estimate the available resources and second, to plan spending to match the available resources, neither more nor less.

In a federal or state government organization, application of this principle requires that a careful estimate be made of funds that are likely to be provided by the legislature. In municipal governments it requires a judgment as to feasible taxation revenues. In other organizations it requires an estimate of revenues to be derived from fees charged to clients, from gifts and grants, from endowment earnings, and from other sources.

In many of these organizations, the total amount of such revenue in the budget year is, for all practical purposes, fixed within quite narrow limits. In these "fixed revenue" organizations, the approach to budgeting is therefore to decide how best to spend the available revenue.

In any organization, subject to the qualifications stated in Chapter 2, if current expenses are substantially less than current revenues, current clients are not receiving the services to which they are entitled. They are entitled to these services partly by virtue of the fees paid (tuition, church pledges, hospital charges) and partly by the intention of donors of endowment funds or other givers. On the other hand, if current costs exceed current revenues, some of the endowment principal is consumed, or a deficit is incurred which must be made up out of future revenues; in either case the effect is to favor current clients at the expense of future clients.[2]

The management of fixed-revenue institutions should be proud of a balanced budget; they should not be proud of *either* a larger-than-necessary surplus or a deficit. The treasurer of Yale University wrote: "An Operating Surplus evidences lack of achievement rather than good management."[3]

Sometimes churches budget their expenses without regard to anticipated revenue. They justify the deficit with the argument, "God will provide." Such a policy can lead to disaster. Although somewhat different words are used, a similar approach is sometimes followed by organizations other than churches. The results can be equally disastrous.

> ***Example:*** In 1962, New York University embarked on a major expansion program. Substantial amounts of additional revenue were obtained from additional enrollments, fund-raising campaigns, and government grants. Beginning in 1968, funds from all these sources began to shrink. Instead of cutting costs to meet the lower level of revenues, however, deficits were permitted. They reached a peak of $14 million in 1973. In 1972 drastic steps were finally taken to bring costs in line with revenue, but by then a considerable fraction of the university's capital had been dissipated.[4]

---

[2] Some nonprofit organizations adopt a "countercyclical" fiscal policy as a conscious strategy, reasoning that when the economy is in a downswing, more clients who cannot pay will need their services, with the opposite effect taking place during economic expansion. They thus plan to incur deficits in bad times and surpluses during good times.

[3] *Report of the Treasurer of Yale University,* 1967, p. 2.

[4] Condensed from a report in *Science,* December 8, 1972, p. 1072–75.

One great advantage of the policy of anticipating revenue first and then budgeting expenses to equal revenue is that this approach provides a bulwark against the arguments, often made by highly articulate and persuasive people, for programs that the institution cannot in fact afford. (Especially pernicious is the argument: "We can't afford *not* to do this.")

If the first approximation to the budget indicates a deficit, the least painful course of action is to anticipate additional sources of revenue that will eliminate this deficit. This is, however, a highly dangerous course of action. Presumably, all feasible sources of revenue were thought of when the revenue estimate was initially made. New ideas that arise subsequently *may* produce the additional revenue, but the evidence that they will do so is usually not strong. If they do *not* produce the revenue, then operations may proceed without taking the steps that are necessary to provide a balance between revenues and expenses.

The safer course of action is to take the steps that are necessary to bring expenses into balance with revenues.

## Exceptions to the General Rule

The policy that budgeted revenue sets the limit on expenses is not applicable under certain conditions. Some of these are discussed below.

***The Federal Budget.*** The considerations mentioned above do not apply to the federal budget. This budget may be either a surplus or a deficit, the amount of either being determined by the administration's conclusion (with the concurrence of the Congress) as to the proper fiscal policy in a given year. The federal government rarely plans for a balanced budget.

***Discretionary Revenue.*** In some organizations management can increase revenues by appropriate tactics. For example, it may be possible to increase the revenues from current gifts by an intensified fund-raising effort. This is "spending money to make money" in the same sense that a profit-oriented company considers its marketing budget. To the extent that this argument is valid, it is appropriate to speak of "discretionary revenue" as well as "discretionary costs." Such opportunities are ordinarily not of major significance, however. In most situations, the organization has already used all the fund-raising devices that it can think of, and it must take the probable revenues from such efforts as a given, not subject to major alteration.

***Hard Money and Soft Money.*** A college with a reasonable expectation of meeting its enrollment quota can count on a certain amount of tuition revenue; this is *hard money.* Income from endowment is also hard money. It is prudent to make long-term commitments, such as tenured faculty appointments, when they will be financed by hard money. By contrast, revenue from annual gifts or from short-lived grants for research projects is *soft* *money*. In a recession, gifts may drop drastically; and grantors may decide not to renew their grants. The institution must be careful about making long-term commitments that are financed with *soft money*.

Some organizations budget costs in anticipation of receiving grants to cover them. Universities, research organizations, some social service agencies, and others may apply for grants, but not learn whether the funds will be approved until well into the fiscal year. If personnel and other costs were budgeted only on the basis of known revenues, key professional staff might be laid off and obtain employment elsewhere. Thus, some organizations decide to incur deficits in anticipation of receiving grant awards. Such a strategy is risky and can be sustained only if grants of sufficient magnitude are received.

***Short-Run Fluctuations.*** When it is expected that there will be short-term fluctuations around an average, it is appropriate to budget for the average revenue, rather than for the level of revenue in a specific year; that is, in some years expenses may exceed revenue if in other years revenues exceed expenses by a corresponding amount. Reserves are provided for equalization. This averaging process is difficult. If the policy is overly conservative, the effect is to deprive current clients of services that are rightfully theirs. Conversely, as is the case with uncertain revenue, if it is assumed that next year will be better, and when this doesn't happen it is assumed that the following year *surely* will be better, the institution may be headed for disaster.

***The Promoter.*** Occasionally, the amount of resources available can be increased by a dynamic individual. The governing board thereupon authorizes a budget in excess of current revenues in anticipation of the new resources that the promoter will provide. Such a decision is obviously a gamble. If it works, the institution may be elevated to a permanently higher plateau. If it doesn't work, painful cutbacks may soon be necessary to bring expenses back in line with revenues.

***Deliberate Capital Erosion.*** There are situations where the current revenue is deliberately not regarded as a ceiling, and part of the permanent capital is used for current operations. This may represent a gamble in anticipation of new resources as described above, or it may reflect a conscious policy to go out of existence after the capital has been consumed. In effect, though, any budget which incurs a deficit is one in which permanent capital is being consumed. Thus, decisions to use permanent capital for current operations should be made with great care because no organization can live beyond its means indefinitely.

## COMPONENTS OF THE OPERATING BUDGET

The numerical part of the operating budget (which is often supplemented by explanatory text) consist of three components; (1) revenues, (2) expenses or expenditures, and (3) output measures. The nature of the revenue component is straightforward; some general comments about the other two components are given below.

## Program and Line-Item Budgets

There are two general formats for the spending portion of the budget. The traditional format is called the *line-item budget,* although this term is not descriptive because every budget has items arranged in lines. A line-item budget focuses on *expense elements,* that is, wages, fringe benefits, supplies,

**Exhibit 9–1**
Examples of Types of Budgets—Municipal Public Safety Activities ($000)

A. Line-Item Budget

| | *Estimated Actual 19x1* | *Budget 19x2* |
|---|---|---|
| Wages and salaries | $4,232 | $4,655 |
| Overtime | 217 | 72 |
| Fringe benefits | 783 | 861 |
| Retirement plan | 720 | 792 |
| Operating supplies | 216 | 220 |
| Fuel | 337 | 410 |
| Uniforms | 68 | 70 |
| Repairs and maintenance | 340 | 392 |
| Professional services | 71 | 0 |
| Communications | 226 | 236 |
| Vehicles | 482 | 450 |
| Printing and publications | 61 | 65 |
| Building rental | 447 | 450 |
| Other | 396 | 478 |
| Total | $8,597 | $9,151 |

B. Program Budget

| | *Estimated Actual 19x1* | *Budget 19x2* |
|---|---|---|
| Crime control and investigation | $2,677 | $2,845 |
| Traffic control | 1,610 | 1,771 |
| Correctional institutions | 470 | 482 |
| Inspections and licenses | 320 | 347 |
| Police training | 182 | 180 |
| Police administration | 640 | 704 |
| Fire fighting | 1,427 | 1,530 |
| Fire prevention | 86 | 92 |
| Fire training | 64 | 70 |
| Fire administration | 236 | 260 |
| Other protection | 563 | 560 |
| General administration | 282 | 310 |
| Total | $8,597 | $9,151 |

and other types of resources. In *program budget* formats the focus is on programs and program elements which represent the activities for which the funds are to be spent. Examples for each type for the public safety department of a municipality are shown in Exhibit 9–1. Although the focus of a program element is on programs, condensed element information—such as the amount of personnel costs, supplies, and other operating costs—are usually shown for each program element as well.

The program budget permits the decision maker to judge the appropriate amount of resources that should be devoted to each activity, and hence the emphasis to be given to that activity. It also permits spending to be matched with measures of the planned output of each activity. These are important advantages of the program budget format, and its use is growing rapidly.

## Output Measures

The third component of a budget is information about planned outputs. As described in Chapter 11, these can be either process measures or results measures. In budgeting parlance, the former type is usually called a workload measure and the latter a measure of objectives.

***Management by Objectives.*** The use of quantified measures of the planned objectives during the budget period is relatively new. It is often described as a "Management by Objectives" system, and under this label is being increasingly emphasized in the federal government,[5] and is spreading to other types of nonprofit organizations. An example is given in Exhibit 9–2.

If at all possible, as discussed in Chapter 7, the objectives should be quantified so that actual performance can be compared with them. These statements of objectives take the place of the profitability objective which is a key part of the budgeting process in a profit-oriented company. In a nonprofit organization, such an overall yardstick for judging the adequacy of the budget does not exist, and a comparison of expenses with the anticipated results may be the best substitute.

Some organizations use a "management by objectives" procedure that is quite separate from the budgeting process. Generally, this separation came about because the technique happened to be sponsored by persons who were outside the controller organization, since the controller is usually responsible for the budgeting process. Such a separation is undesirable. In discussing plans for next year, both the expenses and the results expected from incurring these expenses should be considered together.

---

[5] For a description of the federal program, see Rodney Brady, "MBO Goes to Work in the Public Sector," *Harvard Business Review,* 51 (March/April 1973), pp. 65–74.

**Exhibit 9–2**
Sample Statement of Objectives

THE OBJECTIVES OF REGITITLE DIVISION

In seeking to fulfill its mission—

1. To collect revenue as a condition of titling and registration for all vehicles other than those for which the Commercial and Farm Truck Division has specific responsibility.
2. To provide acceptable unique instruments as evidence of ownership and vehicle registration.
3. To assure proper titling and registering of vehicles.
4. To serve the users of information regarding ownership and registration of vehicles.

the following objectives have been set for the remainder of fiscal year 1975:

*Objectives to Maintain Operations*

By June 30, 1975, the direct salary cost per letter produced by the Correspondence Unit will be maintained at the current level of $__ (year to date).

*Objectives to Strengthen Operations*

By June 30, 1975, the process time, from mail receipt at work processing center to receipt by Data Processing, will be decreased from current level of __ days to __ days.

By June 30, 1975, the processing time, from Data Processing release to internal files, will be decreased from current level of __ weeks to __ weeks.

By June 30, 1975, the methods of handling current categories of "Go-back" letters will be altered, resulting in a 10 percent reduction in mailed correspondence—a reduction of 2,000 letters per month from the current level of 20,000 at an estimated cost savings of $__ per month (i.e., $__ per letter).

By June 30, 1975, the distribution of forms to the public will be tightened in such a way that the total purchase quantity for the year will be reduced from __ million to __ million (a reduction of approximately 50 percent).

*Objectives to Improve Operations*

By June 30, 1975, the time taken for release of an I.D. card from the work processing center to issuance of a plate to the public will be reduced from __ days to __ days.

By June 30, 1975, the time for release of the application from the work processing center to the issuance of a title will be reduced from __ days to __ days.

By June 30, 1975, the average processing time for routine title applications will be reduced from the current __ week average to __ working days.

Source: Michael J. Howlett, "Strategic Planning in State Government," *Managerial Planning,* November/December 1975. Reprinted in *Managing Nonprofit Organizations,* ed. (New York: AMACOM, 1977), p. 133.

## STEPS IN THE BUDGETING PROCESS

In the federal government, the budgeting process starts about six months before the budget is submitted to the Congress (see Appendix B). In less complex organizations, the period is shorter, about one to three months. The problem of timing is a delicate one. If the budget is prepared too far in advance, it will not be based on the most current information. If, on the other hand, not enough time is allowed, the process may be rushed and hence superficial.

The principal steps involved in the process are (1) dissemination of guidelines, (2) preparation of the budget estimates, and (3) review and approval of these estimates. The review process may lead to a redoing of the original estimates, so the proposed budget may be recycled one or more times before being approved.

### Preparation of Guidelines

The process begins with the formulation of guidelines and the communication of these guidelines to operating managers. If a formal program exists, one guideline is that the budget should be consistent with the approved program. This does not necessarily mean that the budget should consist only of approved programs. Frustrations of operating managers may be minimized, and desirable innovations may occasionally (although not frequently) come to light if managers are permitted to propose activities that are not part of the approved program. These unapproved activities should be clearly distinguished from those in the approved program, however, and operating managers should understand that the chances that new programs will be approved during the budget formulation process are slight. Any other impression downgrades the importance of the programming process.

Even if there is no formal program, operating managers should be made aware of the constraints within which the budget should be prepared. These constraints can be expressed in an overall statement such as "budget for not more than 105 percent of the amount spent this year," or they can be stated in much more detail. These might include planned changes in the activities of the organization, assumptions to be made about wage rates and other prices, conditions under which additional personnel can be requested, number of personnel who may be promoted, services to be provided by support responsibility centers, planned productivity gains, and so on. In the absence of guidance to the contrary, the usual assumption is that next year's activities will be similar to this year's.

The guidelines should be approved by senior management. Considerable senior management attention to them is warranted since if the budget is formulated on the basis of unrealistic assumptions, it may have to be redone with consequent wasted effort.

In addition to the substantive guidelines, there are also guidelines about the format and content of the proposed budget. These are intended to ensure that the budget estimates are submitted in a fashion that both facilitates analysis and also that permits their subsequent use in the comparison of actual performance against planned performance.

## Budget Preparation

Managers at the lowest level in the organization are responsible for preparing the budget for their activities. This *participatory budgeting* approach is the common practice currently, as contrasted with the former practice of *imposed budgeting* in which the budgets were prepared by top-level staffs and then imposed on the operating organization. Staff assistants may help managers by making calculations and filling out the forms, but the basic decisions that are reflected in the proposed budget are made by the line managers, not by the staff.

***Relation to Program.*** If an approval program exists, the expense budget is constructed essentially by fine tuning the estimated program costs. For new programs, this involves assigning program responsibility to responsibility centers and constructing careful cost estimates in each responsibility center. For example, a research/development *program* may be costed at $400,000 simply by estimating that it will require four professional work years at $100,000 a work year. In constructing the *budget,* the salaries of professionals and the other support costs that make up the overall estimate of $100,000 per work year will each be stated. The total amount will usually approximate $400,000 but will vary somewhat from this estimate as the costs are examined in more detail.

***Arriving at Budget Amounts.*** Assuming the current level of spending is used as a starting point, the budget is constructed by adjusting these amounts for changes in wage rates and prices, for the elimination of unusual factors that may have affected current spending, for changes in programs, and possibly for adjustments in certain discretionary items (such as expenses for attendance at conventions) that may have been mandated in the guidelines.[6]

Some have the impression that the budget process consists of adding a certain percentage onto the previous year's spending. This is by no means the case. Exhibit 9–3 is an analysis of budget actions in the Department of Agriculture over the period 1946–71. Note the wide dispersion in the size

[6] In the 1970s considerable publicity was given to a system called zero-base budgeting, and the system was tried out in many organizations. Experience demonstrated that time did not permit the use of this technique during the budget formulation process, and zero-base budgeting, as originally described, has pretty much disappeared. However, a process called zero-base *review* is used frequently as part of the evaluation process, as described in Chapter 13.

**Exhibit 9–3**

Changes in Agency Requests Made by Reviewing Bodies

*Relative Assertiveness*

| *Change in Agency Request from Previous Budget* | *Number of Cases* | *Average Percent Change by Department* | *Average Percent Change by OMB* | *Average Percent Change by Congress* | *Budget Results: Average Percent Change in Agency Appropriation* |
|---|---|---|---|---|---|
| Request decrease | 60 | +25.5% | − 6.5% | + 2.4% | − 21.0% |
| Request increase: | | | | | |
| 0–9.9% | 99 | − 2.0% | − 3.0% | − 0.3% | 0% |
| 10–24.9% | 121 | + 1.3% | − 8.0% | − 0.5% | + 1.3% |
| 25–49.9% | 103 | −13.0% | −11.0% | − 0.7% | + 4.6% |
| 50–99.9% | 79 | −16.5% | −14.4% | − 1.3% | + 17.0% |
| Greater than 100% | 36 | −20.2% | −16.2% | −10.5% | +130.0% |
| Average for all agencies | 498 | − 4.4% | − 9.0% | − 2.0% | + 11.0% |

Source: Leland T. LeLoup and William B. Moreland, "Agency Strategies and Executive Review," *Public Administration Review,* May/June 1978, pp. 232–39.

of the requests compared with the previous year in the actions of the various review agencies.

***Variable Budgets.*** If the workload for the budget year can be estimated and if unit costs are available, the budget can be constructed so as to take changes in workload into account. In a welfare office, for example, if the number of cases can be predicted, the number of budgeted social workers can be found by using a standard allowance of number of cases per social worker. Other elements of cost can be estimated as a function of the number of social workers. An example of such data for a school district is given in Exhibit 9–4.

If costs vary with volume, as is the case with food service costs in a hospital, the budget may be stated in terms of a fixed amount plus a variable

**Exhibit 9–4**
Budget and Planning Factors for a School District ($000)

| | | *1976–77 Structure* | | | |
|---|---|---|---|---|---|
| *Cost Determinants* | *Total Cost* | *Students* | *Teachers* | *Buildings* | *Basic Ratio Formula* |
| Elementary—1 teacher/27 students | $ 5,600 | 6,400 | 238 | | $23.5/27 students |
| —building staff | 2,500 | | | 13 | $192.3/building |
| Junior High—1 teacher/19 students | 2,600 | 2,100 | 111 | | $23.4/19 students |
| —building staff | 600 | | | 3 | $200.0/building |
| Senior High—1 teacher/19 students | 5,400 | 4,300 | 227 | | $23.8/19 students |
| —building staff | 1,500 | | | 3 | $500.0/building |
| Guidance—1 counselor/350 students | 500 | 6,400 | 18 | | $27.8/350 students |
| Transportation | 1,200 | 13,200 | | | $9.1/100 students |
| Facilities | 3,000 | | | 20 | $150.0/facility |
| Educational operations | 2,100 | | | | $2,100/year |
| District operations | 4,700 | | | | $4,700/year |
| Totals | $29,700 | 13,200 | 594 | | |
| Self-funding, other programs | $ 1,300 | | | | |
| Total budget | $31,000 | | | | |

*Decision/Planning Guides derived from the basic ratio formula:*

re: Student/Teacher ratio:

1. Each change of +1 in the elementary ratio will reduce costs by $211.5 (9 teachers).
2. Each change of +1 in the junior high ratio will reduce costs by $140.6 (6 teachers).
3. Each change of +1 in the senior high ratio will reduce costs by $261.8 (11 teachers).

re: Building closings

4. Closing an elementary school will reduce costs by $340.3 ($192.3 staff, $150.0 facility).
5. Closing a junior high school will reduce costs by $350.0 ($200.0 staff, $150.0 facility).
6. Closing a senior high school will reduce costs by $650.0 ($500.0 staff, $150.0 facility).

re: District staff

7. A reduction of 10% in educational operations will reduce costs by $210.0.
8. A reduction of 10% in district operations will reduce costs by $470.0.

re: Student enrollment 4

9. Declining enrollment will reduce costs in 1977–78 by $213.0 (−200 students).
   Declining enrollment will reduce costs in 1978–79 by $238.0 (−300 students).
   Declining enrollment will reduce costs in 1979–80 by $234.0 (−200 students).

Source: A. F. Brueningsen, "SCATT II-A Process for Planning," *Management Accounting*, December 1977, p. 58.

rate per unit of volume (e.g., $100,000 + $3 per patient day). It is appropriate to budget food service in a hospital or a school in this fashion because the *revenue* from patient care or student board varies with volume. In other circumstances, however, it is doubtful that a variable budget allowance should be stated. For example, the snow removal budget in a municipality may be arrived at by estimating costs at $10,000 per inch of snow, which would be $300,000 if 30 inches of snow is estimated. Since the actual amount of snow probably will be more or less than 30 inches, actual snow removal costs are likely to be more or less than $300,000. Nevertheless, it usually is desirable to set the snow removal budget at the fixed amount of $300,000 and to require a budget revision when the snowfall exceeds or falls short of the budget amount. If the budget were permitted to vary automatically with the amount of snowfall, there would be no way of assuring that the total amount of funds appropriated were not exceeded. With budget revision, an offsetting change can be made in some other item or, if necessary, supplemental funds can be sought.

Despite the logic of developing the budget from workload estimates and unit costs, the budget guidelines may prohibit increases above a certain amount, regardless of the workload. This requirement overrides the workload calculations. The manager may point out, however, that the budgeted amounts are inadequate to carry out the planned workload so that trade-off decisions must be made.

***Advanced Techniques.*** Various analytical techniques, such as the use of subjective probabilities, preference theory, multiple regression analysis, and models, have been advocated as an aid to budget formulation, but few of these are used in practice. One experiment is Roche's use of preference theory in the preparation of a budget for a public school.[7] In this experiment, the heads of the language arts, science, mathematics, and social studies program in an elementary school system were asked to estimate what the effect on student learning would be if the budgets for each of their programs were increased by stated amounts. Safeguards were set up to minimize the biases in these estimates. Decision makers (the superintendent and the school committee) were asked to state their preferences as to the relative importance of increased learning in each of the four programs. Preference theory was then used to arrive at the optimum way of spreading an increment of funds among programs. Although this method has actually been used in the preparation of a budget, and although those involved in the process found it to be helpful, it is complicated, and for this reason probably will not become popular in the near future.

---

[7] James G. Roche, *Preference Tradeoffs among Instructional Programs; An Investigation of Cost-Benefit and Decision Analysis Techniques in Local Education Decision-Making* (Boston: Graduate School of Business Administration, Harvard University, 1971, ICH #9–175–079).

***Budget Detail.*** Many dollar amounts in the budget are the product of a physical quantity times a cost per unit; for example, personnel costs are a product of number of persons times average salary. These amounts should be shown separately because a breakdown of quantities and unit costs both facilitates review of the budget and also is useful in subsequently analyzing the differences between budgeted and actual expenses.

In addition to the numbers, the proposed budget usually includes explanatory material. In particular, if additional personnel are requested, a complete justification for their need is usually required.[8]

## Budget Review, Technical Aspects

***Time Constraints.*** An important, but sometimes overlooked, fact about the review process is that not much time is available for it. The proposed budgets for every responsibility center must be examined in the space of, at most, a few weeks. This is in contrast with the programming process in which one program, covering only a small fraction of the organization's activities, can be examined in depth. Because there is not enough time to do otherwise, the level of current spending is typically taken as the starting point in examining the proposed budget. Although the burden of proof to justify amounts above that level is on the budgetee, there is an implication that budgetees are "entitled to" the current level. This practice is widely criticized (it is called the "blight of incrementalism"), but there is little that can be done about it as a practical matter, simply because of the time pressure. The place for a more thorough analysis of spending needs is the programming process.

***Methods of Analysis.*** Proposed budgets are first reviewed by the budget staff, which makes recommendations to line managers. This review has two aspects: (1) that relating to programs, and (2) that relating to ongoing support activities.

If the program is new, little can be done to change the program estimates during the budget review process. If the program is ongoing, the appropriateness of proposed budget amounts can be analyzed from time to time by a zero-base review.

The budget analyst therefore focuses primarily on the support activities, that is, the administrative organization and service organizations that are not directly involved in program work. If the entity's size will change because of program decisions, corresponding adjustments are made in the current

---

[8] Undoubtedly, the most complicated budget is that of the U.S. government, and its complexities are increasing. For the fiscal year 1979 budget, the U.S. Air Force submitted to the Congress 2,580 pages of justification material; for 1981, the submission consisted of 3,748 pages, an increase of 47 percent.

level of spending for these activities. After making approximate adjustments for changes in size, the budget reviewer makes a careful review of the details of support activities, using the adjusted current levels of spending as a starting point. If comparable data are available on similar activities in other organizations, these can be used for comparisons. Comparisons are also made among the unit costs of similar activities within the organization. The budget is checked for consistency with the guidelines; wage rates and costs of significant materials are checked for reasonableness; and other checks—including the simple but essential check of arithmetic accuracy—are made.

There is a tendency for support costs to creep upward, and this is especially the case in affluent organizations.[9] Special efforts are made to detect and eliminate this fat. If unit costs or ratios can be calculated, a comparison of these with similar numbers in other responsibility centers, or with published data for other organizations, may be helpful. In the absence of such a basis for comparison, reviewers rely on their feel for the appropriateness of the requested amounts. These two fairly different approaches to budget review should be kept in mind: for programs, a general approach, except to incorporate the results of zero-base reviews; for support activities, a careful analysis.

The nature of the activities described above suggests an important distinction between the ideal budget analyst and the ideal program analyst. The former must work under great time pressure, possess a "feel" for what is the right amount of cost, and be able and willing to get to the essence of the calculations quickly. The latter is less interested in accuracy and more interested in judging, even in a rough way, the relation between costs and benefits of the proposed program.

***Budget Review, Behavioral Aspects.*** In estimating the labor cost of making shoes, there is little ground for disagreement on the part of well-informed people because the cost of each operation can be estimated within close limits, and the total labor cost can be found by adding the costs of each operation and multiplying by the number of pairs of shoes. As noted above, such engineered costs constitute a relatively large fraction of the costs of an industrial company. By contrast, discretionary costs—costs for which the optimum amount is not known, and often not knowable—constitute a relatively large fraction of the budget of a nonprofit organization. Since there is no "scientific" way of estimating the amount of discretionary costs, the budget amounts must be determined through negotiation. Negotiation is also required because there is no objective way of deciding which requests for funds have the highest priority.

This process of negotiation has been described as a two-person nonzero

[9] In a survey of 91 public high school districts, it was found that budgets of schools in affluent communities had a significantly higher proportion of administrative costs than budgets of schools in poorer communities. Richard L. Daft, "System Influence on Organizational Decision-Making: The Case of Resource Allocation," *Academy of Management Journal,* March 1978, p. 6.

sum game.[10] The players are the budgetee, who is advocating a proposed budget, and the supervisor, who must approve, modify, or deny the request. Except for the lowest echelon, all managers are supervisors at one stage in the budget process, and they become budgetees in the next stage. Even senior management becomes a budgetee in presenting the budget to the outside agency or board that is responsible for providing the funds. Although in one sense a new game is played each year, there are important carryover consequences from one year to the next. The judgment that each party develops in one year, about the ability, integrity, and forthrightness of the other party affects attitudes in subsequent years.

As in any negotiation, the two parties have a common interest in reaching a satisfactory outcome, but they have antagonistic interests in what that outcome should be. The essence of this antagonism is that budgetees want as large a budget as possible, and supervisors want to cut the proposed budget as much as they safely can.

The attitude of professionals is also an important factor. For example, in a hospital, the budgetee may be a physician and the supervisor a hospital administrator. Physicians are primarily interested in improving the quality of patient care, improving the status of the hospital as perceived by their peers, and increasing their own prestige; their interest in the amount of costs involved generally is secondary. By contrast, hospital administrators are primarily interested in costs, although they realize that costs must not be so low that the quality of care or the status of the hospital is impaired. Thus, the two parties weight the relevant factors considerably differently.

The budget process is most effective when the supervisor and the budgetee behave in a certain manner. In general, effective behavior by supervisors is as follows: They trust their subordinates. They assume that subordinates are competent and that they have goodwill and honesty. They feel secure enough, have enough self-esteem, so that they do not frequently impose their own solutions. They do not feel overly threatened if the budgetee does not always agree with them. They repress in themselves, and in their subordinates, signs of what could be interpreted as disrespect or rebellion against authority. They do not hide information in order to get leverage on subordinates. They do not force goals onto subordinates.

Effective budgetees also trust their superiors. A plan is necessarily based on certain assumptions about the external world, assumptions which often prove to be wrong. If budgetees do not trust supervisors to recognize this fact, they will be reluctant to make realistic estimates. They may be so afraid of their bosses that they cannot negotiate, that is, enter a give-and-take collaboration with them.

In general, both senior management and lower-level line managers must trust the budget analysts' recommendations as to the details of the budget.

---

[10] See G. H. Hofstede, *The Game of Budget Control* (Assen, The Netherlands: Van Gorcum & Co., N.V., 1967).

If the analysts believe that four, not five, new employees are needed for a new function, then ordinarily this must be accepted (subject to "reclama" or dispute). If each of these detailed decisions is challenged, then the whole process will bog down. This means that as the budget goes up the chain of command, key issues must be identified, and the decision maker should concentrate on these. Obviously, such an approach will work only if line management has confidence in the judgment of the budget analysts. The solution, if such confidence is lacking, is to reeducate, or in the extreme, replace them.

***Rules of the Game.*** It is usually considered improper to refer to the budget process as a game; therefore, many of its rules are unwritten. Nevertheless, as in any game, rules do exist. They vary considerably from organization to organization. They depend in large part upon the size of the organization and on the relationship between the two participants, the supervisor and the budgetee. In a small organization, the chances are good that the two persons can establish a close relationship, with considerable understanding and trust. As a result they can be more frank with each other. In larger organizations, with attendant greater separation between budgetee and supervisor, and a larger number of distinct sources of demands for resources, the relationship between parties is likely to be more formal and the rules of the game therefore become more complex and more important.

***Budget Ploys.*** In order to play the budget game well, each party should be familiar with its ploys and the appropriate responses to these ploys. Ploys can be divided into two main categories: (1) those used primarily within an organization and (2) those used primarily externally, that is, between the head of the organization and the legislative body or governing board that authorizes funds for the organization. External ploys are so well described in Wildavsky's *The Politics of the Budgeting Process* that it would be redundant to repeat them.[11] Some internal ploys are given in Appendix A.

***Hunger.*** The attitude of managers of responsibility centers whose output cannot be reliably measured has been characterized as one of "hunger"; that is, they are motivated to acquire as many resources as they can. This phenomenon is thoroughly analyzed by economists in socialist countries because it is crucial to understanding the budget preparation process in those countries. Kornai lists the following factors as causing this "hunger": a good manager wants to do his job properly and therefore wants all the resources that may be needed to do the job; the manager wants the operation to run smoothly and for this purpose needs "slack" in order to meet peaks in demand; the manager wants the unit to be viewed favorably in comparison with other units and therefore wants the resources to be up to date; the manager's

[11] Aaron Wildavsky, *The Politics of the Budgetary Process,* 2d ed. (Boston: Little, Brown, 1974).

power and prestige is perceived as being related to the size of the responsibility center, and, in contrast with profit centers, there is no penalty in having too many resources.

For these reasons, the manager's hunger is "insatiable"; no amount of resources is too much. If the hunger is appeased this year by granting all the budget requests, the requests next year will be even larger.[12]

***The Commitment.*** The end product of the negotiation process is an agreed budget which represents a commitment by each party, the budgetee and the supervisor. By the act of agreeing to the budget estimates, the budgetee says, in effect: "I can and will operate my responsibility center in accordance with the plan described in this budget." By approving the budget estimates, the superior in effect says: "If you operate your responsibility center in accordance with this plan, you will be doing what we consider to be a good job." Both of these statements contain the implicit qualification, "subject to adjustment for unanticipated changes in circumstances."

Some organizations go so far as to state this commitment in the form of a formal contract, in which the budgetee agrees to "deliver" specified services for a specified sum of money, which is the amount in the approved budget.

### Budget Approval

The final set of discussions is held between senior management and whatever body has ultimate authority for approving the organization's plans—the trustees or a similar group for private, nonprofit organizations, or the legislature for a public organization. (As noted above, this is the case with respect to the "legislative" budget, but the process of formulating the "management" budget takes place separately and subsequently.) After being approved, the budget is disseminated down through the organization and becomes the authorized plan to which the organization is expected to adhere unless compelling circumstances warrant a change.[13]

## THE CAPITAL BUDGET

In addition to the operating budget, most nonprofit organizations prepare a capital budget. The capital budget contains a list of the capital projects that are proposed for financing during the coming year. If the operating

[12] For a development of this analysis in Hungary, see Janos Kornai, *Economics of Shortage,* Amsterdam: North-Holland Publishing Co., 1980, especially pp. 62–64 and 191–95.

[13] Some people refer to actual operations as "executing the budget." This is an unfortunate term because it implies that the operating manager's job is to spend whatever the budget says can be spent. A better term is "executing the *program.*" This implies that the primary job is to accomplish the program objectives; the budget shows the resources that are available for this purpose.

budget is prepared on an expense basis, the capital budget will include all acquisitions of long-lived assets planned for the year.

If the operating budget is prepared on an expenditure basis, it may include a considerable amount for equipment and similar long-lived assets, and only buildings and major capital acquisitions will be included in the capital budget. It is important that a clear-cut distinction be made between the types of items included in these two budgets. Otherwise, there is a temptation to balance the operating budget by moving some items from it to the capital budget.

> *Example:* Officials in New York City made many maneuvers in the early 1970s to hide the true operating deficit. One was to shift operating items to the capital budget where they presumably would be financed by bonds rather than by current revenues. An extreme example was vocational education expenses, which were shifted to the capital budget on the grounds that students would enjoy the benefits for many years to come and that vocational education was therefore a long-lived asset!

The items to be included in the capital budget emerge from decisions made during the programming process. In the budget review, there is the same scrutiny of the amounts as was described above for operating items. Moreover, it may turn out that the total of approved capital expenditures is larger than can be financed, and this requires cutting back the capital budget. Since these capital projects affect program execution for years to come, such cutbacks are made only after great soul searching.

# APPENDIX A

## SOME BUDGET PLOYS

Internal ploys used in the budget game can be divided into roughly four categories:

1. Ploys for new programs.
2. Ploys for maintaining or increasing ongoing programs.
3. Ploys to resist cuts.
4. Ploys primarily for supervisors.

There is some overlap among the categories. Some ploys relate to programming as well as to budgeting. Each ploy is described briefly, and an appropriate response is given.

## PLOYS FOR NEW PROGRAMS

### 1. Foot in the Door

*Description:* Sell a modest program initially; conceal its real magnitude until after it has gotten under way and has built a constituency.

*Illustration:* In a certain state, the legislature was sold on a program to educate handicapped children in regular schools rather than in the special schools then used. The costs were said to be transportation costs and a few additional teachers. Within five years, the definition of "handicapped" had been greatly broadened, and the resources devoted to the program were four times the amount originally estimated.

*Response:* This ploy can elicit either of two responses: *(a)* detect the ploy when it is proposed, consider that it is merely a foot in the door and that actual eventual costs will exceed estimates by a wide margin, and therefore disapprove the project (but this is difficult to do); or *(b)* hold to the original decision, limiting spending to the original cost estimate, despite pleas for enlarging it. (The latter is effective only if the ploy is detected in time.)

*Variations:* One variation on this ploy is *buying in,* that is underestimating the real cost of a program. An example is the B-1 bomber program. In 1981, this program was estimated to cost $11.9 billion. The Air Force submission for the B-1 bomber for FY 1983 "certified" that the cost of the program was $20.5 billion. However, two independent audit groups within the Pentagon estimated its cost as $23.6 billion and $26.7 billion, respectively. The Congressional Budget Office estimated the cost at $40 billion.

Another variation is *bait and switch;* that is, initially requesting an inexpensive program but increasing its scope (and cost) after initial approval has been obtained.

### 2. Hidden Ball

*Description:* Conceal the nature of a politically unattractive program by hiding it within an attractive program.

*Illustration:* Some years ago the Air Force had difficulty in obtaining funds for general-purpose buildings but found it easy to get funds for intercontinental missiles, so there was included in the budget for the missile program an amount to provide for construction of a new office building. Initially this building was used by a contractor in the missile program, but eventually it became a general-purpose Air Force office building.

*Response:* Break down programs so that such items become visible. Discourage recurrence by special punishment.

### 3. Divide and Conquer

*Description:* Seek approval of a budget request from more than one supervisor.

*Illustration:* The City Planning Commission in New York City was so organized that each member was supposed to be responsible for certain specified areas. The distinctions were not clear, however, so budgetees would deal with more than one supervisor, hoping that one of them would react favorably.

*Response:* Responsibilities should be clearly defined, but this is easier said than done.

*Caution:* In some situations, especially in research, it is dangerous to have a single decision point. It is often desirable to have two places in which a person with a new idea for research may obtain a hearing. New ideas are extremely difficult to evaluate, and a divided authority, even though superficially inefficient, lessens the chance that a good idea will be rejected.

## 4. Distraction

*Description:* Base a specific request on the premise that an overall program has been approved when this is not in fact the case. (Difficult, but not impossible, to use successfully.)

*Illustration:* At a legislative committee, a university presented arguments as to why some buildings should be replaced with a new set of buildings in order to implement an "approved plan" for doubling the capacity of a certain professional school. The argument was that newer buildings would be more useful and efficient than the existing buildings. The merits were discussed in terms of the return on investment arising from the greater efficiency of the new buildings. This discussion went on for some time until a committee member asked who had approved the plan for expansion of the school in the first place. It turned out that the expansion had never been approved; approval of the new buildings would have de facto approved the expansion.

*Response:* Expose the hidden aims, but this is very difficult.

## 5. Shell Game

*Description:* Use statistics to mislead supervisors as to the true state of affairs.

*Illustration:* The budgetee was head of the Model Cities program for a certain city. He wanted available funds to be used primarily for health and education programs but knew that his superiors were more interested in "economic" programs (new businesses and housing). He drew up the following chart:

| | *Source* | | |
|---|---|---|---|
| *Purpose* | *Federal* | *Other* | *Total* |
| Health and education ....... | $2,000,000 | $ 15,000 | $2,015,000 |
| Economic ................. | 50,000 | 2,300,000 | 2,350,000 |

The budgetee emphasized to the mayor and interested groups that over half the funds were intended for economic purposes. The catch was that the source of "other" funds was not known, and there were no firm plans for obtaining such funds. This was not discovered by the supervisor until just prior to the deadline for submitting the request for federal Model Cities funding, at which time the budgetee successfully used the delayed buck ploy (No. 17).

*Response:* Careful analysis.

### 6. It's Free

*Description:* Argue that someone else will pay for the project so the organization might as well approve it.

*Illustrations: (a)* A state decided to build a highway, reckoning the cost as low since the federal government would reimburse it for 95 percent of the cost. The state overlooked the fact that maintenance of the highway would be 100 percent a state cost.

*(b)* Title III of the Elementary and Secondary Education Act of 1965 provided for grants of money to school districts for a variety of experimental programs. Many districts rapidly expanded or began instructional and special service programs that would fit under this Title. As funds have become less readily available in later years, school boards have had to decide whether to discontinue programs or pay the bill from their own pockets. In the instance of special service programs, the choice has been expensive, and experimental grants are now being explored carefully to determine their long-run financial implications.

*Response:* Require an analysis of the long-run costs, not merely the costs for next year.

### 7. Implied Top-Level Support

*Description:* The budgetee says that although the request is not something that he personnaly is enthusiastic about, it is for a program that someone higher up in the organization asked to be included in the budget. Preferably this person is not well known to, and is more prestigious than, the budgetee's superior. The budgetee hopes that the supervisor will not take the time to bring this third party into the discussion.

*Response:* Examine the documentation. If it is vague, not well justified, or nonexistent, check with the alleged sponsor.

*Note:* In a related ploy, the *end run,* the budgetee actually goes to the supervisor's boss without discussing the matter with the supervisor first. This tactic should not be tolerated.

### 8. You're to Blame

*Description:* Imply that the supervisor is at fault and that defects in the budget submission therefore should be overlooked.

*Illustration:* It is alleged that the supervisor was late in transmitting budget instructions, or that the instructions were not clear, and that this accounts for inadequacies in the justifications furnished.

*Response:* If the assertion is valid, this is a difficult ploy to counter. It may be necessary to be contrite, but arbitrary, in order to hold the budget within the guidelines.

## 9. Nothing Too Good for Our People

*Description:* Used, whether warranted or not, to justify items for the personal comfort and safety of military personnel, for new cemeteries, for new hospital equipment, for research laboratory equipment (especially computers), and for various facilities in public schools and colleges.

*Response:* Attempt to shift the discussion from emotional grounds to logical grounds by analyzing the request to see if the benefits are even remotely related to the cost. Emphasize that in a world of scarce resources, not everyone can get all that is deserved.

## 10. Keeping Up with the Joneses

*Illustration:* Minneapolis must have new street lights because St. Paul has them.

*Response:* Analyze the proposal on its own merits.

## 11. We Must Be Up to Date

*Description:* This differs from Ploy No. 10 in that it does not require that a "Jones" be found and cited. The argument is that the organization must be a leader and must therefore adopt the newest technology. Currently, this is a fashionable ploy for computers and related equipment, for hospital equipment, and for laboratory equipment.

*Response:* Require that a benefit be shown that exceeds the cost of adopting the new technology.

*Caution:* Sometimes the state of the art is such that benefits cannot be conclusively demonstrated. If this leads to a deferral of proposals year after year, opportunities may be missed.

## 12. If We Don't, Someone Else Will

*Description:* Appeal to people's innate desire to be at least as good as the competition.

*Illustration:* A university budgetee argued that a proposed new program was breaking new ground, was important to the national interest, and that if her university didn't initiate it, some other university would start it, obtain funds from the appropriate government agency, and thus make it more difficult for her university to start the program later on.

*Response:* Point out that a long list of possible programs have this characteristic, and the university must select those few which are within its capabilities.

### 13. Call It a Rose

*Description:* Use misleading, but appealing, labels.

*Illustration:* In the early 1960s the National Institutes of Health were unable to obtain approval for the construction of new buildings but were able to build "annexes." It is said that Building 12A (the annex) is at least double the size of Building 12.

*Response:* Look behind the euphemism to the real function. If the disguise is intentional, deny the request, and if feasible, discourage recurrence by special punishment.

### 14. Outside Experts

*Description:* The agency hires outside experts to support its request, either formally in hearings, or informally in the press.

*Response:* Show that these experts are biased, either because of a present connection with the agency or because they are likely to benefit if the request is approved.

## PLOYS FOR MAINTAINING OR INCREASING ONGOING PROGRAMS

### 15. Show of Strength

*Description:* Arrange demonstrations in support of the request; occasionally, threaten violence, work stoppages, or other unpleasant consequences if the request is not approved.

*Illustration:* In the summer of 1966 when the Community Development Agency of New York City was trying to decide which 50 of the 500 summer programs would be funded for the full year, a director of one of these programs got the entire staff of about 150 people to come down to the central office to sit in. The director had told the staff that for no apparent reason the city had not forwarded the last reimbursement, and therefore the payroll could not be met. On leaving the central office, the director dropped the hint that the sit-in might recur if his program was not extended.[14]

*Response:* Have fair criteria for selecting programs and have the conviction to stand by your decision.

---

[14] This ploy is developed in depth in Tom Wolfe, *Radical Chic and Mau-Mauing the Flak Catchers* (New York: Farrar, Straus, and Giroux, 1970).

### 16. Razzle-Dazzle

*Description:* Support the request with voluminous data, but arranged in such a way that their significance is not clear. The data need not be valid.

*Illustration:* A public works department submitted a 20-page list of repairs to municipal buildings that were said to be vitally needed, couched in highly technical language. This was actually a "wish list," prepared without a detailed analysis.

*Response: (a)* Ask why the repair budget should be greater next year than in the current year. *(b)* Find a single soft spot in the original request and use it to discredit the whole analysis.

### 17. Delayed Buck

*Description:* Submit the data late, arguing that the budget guidelines required so much detailed calculation that the job could not be done on time.

*Illustration:* The budget guidelines requested a "complete justification" of requested additions to inventory. The motor vehicle repair shop of a state did not submit its budget on time. At the last minute, it submitted an itemized list of parts to be ordered, based on a newly installed system of calculating economic order quantities. It argued that its tardiness was a consequence of getting the bugs out of the new system (which was installed at the controller's instigation), but that it was generally agreed that the economic order quantity formula was the best way of justifying the amount of parts to be purchased.

*Response:* This is a difficult ploy to counter. Complaining about the delay may make the supervisor feel better but will not produce the data. One possible response, designed to prevent recurrence, is to penalize the delay by making an entirely arbitrary cut in the amount requested, although this runs the risk that needed funds will be denied.

### 18. Reverence for the Past

*Description:* Whatever was spent last year must have been necessary in order to carry out last year's program; therefore, the only matters to be negotiated are the proposed increments above this sacred base.

*Response:* As a practical matter, this attitude must be accepted for a great many programs because there is not time to challenge this statement. For selected programs, there can be a zero-base review (see Chapter 13).

### 19. Sprinkling

*Description:* "Watering" was a device used in the early 20th century to make assets and profits in prospectuses for new stock offerings look substantially higher than they really were. "Sprinkling" is a more subtle ploy, which increases budget estimates by only a few percent, either across-the-board or in hard-to-detect areas. Often it is done in anticipation that the supervisor will make arbitrary reductions, so that the final budget will be what it would have been if neither the sprinkling nor the arbitrary cuts had been made.

*Response:* Since this ploy, when done by an expert, is extremely difficult to detect, the best response is to remove the need for doing it; that is, create an atmosphere in which the budgetees trust the supervisor not to make arbitrary cuts.

## PLOYS TO RESIST CUTS

### 20. Make a Study

*Description:* The budget guidelines contain a statement that a certain program is to be curtailed or discontinued. The budgetee responds that the proposed action should not be taken until its consequences have been studied thoroughly.

*Illustration:* In 1967 the General Services Administration proposed that the government replace automobiles every year. It cited five studies conducted over 15 years in support of this proposal. The Bureau of the Budget (predecessor of the Office of Management and Budget) responded by asking for a study. Such a study was submitted in 1967. Another study was requested and submitted in 1968, and still another in 1969. The policy was not adopted, but neither was it rejected outright.[15]

*Response:* Make the study; be persistent; supplement with other ploys.

### 21. Gold Watch

*Description:* When asked in general terms to cut the budget, propose specific actions that do more harm than good.

*Illustration:* This well-known ploy derives its name from an incident in which Robert McNamara was involved when he was with the Ford Motor Company. In a period of stringency, all division heads were asked to make a special effort to cut costs. Most responded with genuine belt tightening; however, one division manager, with $100 million sales, reported that the only cost reduction opportunity he had found was to eliminate the gold watches that were customarily given to employees upon their retirement with 30 or more years of satisfactory service.

*Response:* Reject the proposal. (In the illustration, disciplinary action was also taken with respect to the division manager.)

---

[15] Arnold J. Meltsner, *Policy Analysts in the Bureaucracy* (Berkeley: University of California Press, 1976), pp. 246–50.

## 22. Arouse Client Antagonism

*Description:* When a budget cut is ordered, cut a popular program, hoping to divert attention away from lower priority areas where cuts are indeed feasible. (This is a variation of the gold watch ploy.)

*Illustration:* When Mayor Abraham Beame was asked in 1975 by the federal government to reduce spending in New York City in order to avoid bankruptcy, he responded by dismissing 7,000 police officers and firefighters and closing 26 firehouses. Many people believe he did this to inflame public opinion against budget cuts. It did have this effect, and the order was reversed.

*Response:* Try to redirect client attention by publicizing areas where cuts are feasible.

## 23. Witches and Goblins

*Description:* The budgetee asserts that if the request is not approved, dire consequences will occur. It is used often by the House Armed Services Committee in its reports to Congress. For example, in 1968 an antiballistic missile system was recommended as a counterdefense to the "Talinin System" that the Soviets were alleged to be building. In fact, the Soviets were not building such a system.

*Response:* Analysis based on evidence rather than on emotion.

## 24. We Are the Experts

*Description:* The budgetee asserts that the proposal must be accepted because he has expert knowledge which the supervisor cannot possibly match. This ploy is used by professionals of all types: military officers, scientists, professors, physicians, and clergy.

*Response:* If the basic premise is accepted, the budget process cannot proceed rationally, for the supervisor tends to be a generalist and the budgetee a specialist. The supervisor should insist that the expert express the basis for his judgment in terms that are comprehensible to the generalist.

## 25. End Run

*Description:* Go outside normal channels to obtain reversal of a decision.

*Illustration:* In Massachusetts in the early 1980s, many hospitals that had been denied a certificate of need (CON) to engage in capital building projects, asked their state legislature to introduce a bill overriding the decision by the public health council (an executive branch agency) and permitting the project to proceed. Other legislators, knowing that the next CON denial might be in their district, supported their colleague, and the entire CON process was weakened.

*Response:* If the end run is made to the legislature or an equivalently powerful body, the executive probably has no choice except to grin and bear it (pressures for a veto frequently are hard to muster). In other cases, anyone who attempts an end run should be reprimanded and the request denied because attempts to go outside of proper channels upset the authority of the whole budgetary process.

## PLOYS PRIMARILY FOR SUPERVISORS

### 26. Keep Them Lean and Hungry

*Description:* The supervisor tells the budgetee that the latter's organization will work harder, and possibly more effectively, if it doesn't have to carry so much fat.

*Response:* Show that the analogy with human biology is false, or go along with the analogy, and show that the cuts represent muscle rather than fat.

### 27. Productivity Cuts

*Description:* It is assumed that many capital expenditures are made with the intention of cutting operating costs. Although few systems permit individual cost reductions to be identified, it is reasonable to assume that they, together with continuing management improvements, should lead to lower operating costs in the aggregate. Some organizations therefore reduce personnel-related costs by about 1½ percent from the previous year's level. In the entire economy, productivity increases by about 3 percent annually; the lower percentage assumes that nonprofit organizations are only half as susceptible to productivity gains as the economy as a whole.

In some organizations the cost reductions can be specifically traced. When an organization makes a large capital expenditure to convert its recordkeeping to computers, this presumably results in lower operating costs, and the planned savings should be specifically identified. When a program in 1984 reflects a decision to convert to a computer operation by 1986, the programmed clerical costs for 1986 should reflect a cost reduction.

*Response:* Point out that dismissals are politically inexpedient, and retirements and resignations may not be rapid enough to permit costs to be reduced to the desired level.

### 28. Arbitrary Cuts

*Illustration:* The supervisor, who was director of research of a large company, followed the practice of reducing the budget for certain discretionary items (travel, publications, professional dues) in certain departments by approximately 10 percent. Although the supervisor did this on a purely random basis, he achieved a reputation for astute analysis.

*Response:* Challenge the reason for the cuts (but the items tend to be so unimportant and difficult to defend that such challenges may consume more time than they are worth).

### 29. I Only Work Here

*Description:* The supervisor says she cannot grant the budgetee's request because it is not within the scope of ground rules that her superiors have laid down.

*Response:* Carry the issue to higher authority (although never by an *end run;* see No. 25).

### 30. Closing Gambits

*Description:* The supervisor uses various tactics to bring the negotiation to a close. A simple one is simply to glance at his or her watch, indicating that time is valuable. Another is to "split the difference" between the amount requested and the amount the supervisor initially wanted to approve. Still another is the proposal to settle on a small amount now, with an indication that a larger amount will be considered later on.

# APPENDIX B*

## DEPARTMENT OF JUSTICE: THE BUDGET AND AUTHORIZATION PROCESS

The process of obtaining and controlling the Department's resources consists of four major components: executive budget formulation, the authorization process, the appropriations process, and budget execution. *Executive budget formulation* is the function whereby the President and the Department mutually determine the level of resources necessary to carry out the Department's policies and programs for a given fiscal year. *Authorization* is a mechanism established by law whereby the Congress annually approves the Department's programs and activities and sets target funding levels for these programs and activities. By law, authorization is to precede appropriation. *Appropriation* is the final congressional act that provides the actual amount of resources which are considered necessary to carry out the Department's mandate. *Budget execution* is the function of controlling funds and monitoring resource consumption to ensure compliance with legal and administrative limitations imposed by Congress and the Office of Management and Budget (OMB) as well as Departmental policies.

It is essential to recognize that the components of the above process are

* Prepared by the Office of the Controller, Justice Management Division, U.S. Department of Justice.

interdependent. Actions taken within the context of one of the components has considerable impact on the others. The budget and authorization process may be the single most important device for controlling the direction and activities of the Department and its subordinate organizations. Recent congressional actions within the authorization and appropriation process are indicative of the Congress' increased use of the budget as a major policy and control mechanism for the federal, civil, and criminal justice system.

## EXECUTIVE BUDGET FORMULATION

The executive budget formulation process begins in the Department of Justice some 18 to 21 months prior to the start of the fiscal year involved (i.e., February 1980 for fiscal year 1982, which begins on October 1, 1981). The process is started by the issuance of a Spring Planning "Call for Estimates" and the Attorney General's annual Policy and Program Guidelines. The call for estimates provides detailed instructions relative to format and presentation of the budget estimate. It does not include program policy or financial guidelines. The Attorney General's policy and program guidelines provide a framework for most of the Department organizations to formulate their program plans and supporting budget estimates required by the call for estimates. These guidelines describe general policy and program activities the Attorney General believes should be given priority and incorporates any guidance that has been received from OMB.

Resulting from the call for estimates and Attorney General's policy and program guidelines are the organizations' Spring Planning Submissions which contain estimates of resource levels necessary to carry out their assigned functions and justification for the levels requested. These estimates also provide a comprehensive picture of each organization's programs, objectives, and accomplishments to be used by senior Department officials in determining resource levels to be requested. This process has been refined and improved in numerous ways, the most significant of which has been the prioritization of programs. The challenge and importance of assigning a priority ranking of all Department programs for use of officials at the Department, the OMB, and the Congress who review and make decisions relative to resource requests for those programs cannot be overstated.

The initial review of organizations' resource requests is accomplished during June and July by the Department's Budget Review Committee (BRC) which consists of the Deputy Attorney General, Associate Attorney General, and Assistant Attorney General for Administration. The Budget Staff of the Justice Management Division (Office of the Controller) plays a major role in the review process by doing an in-depth programmatic analysis of the organizations' submission. These analyses are formalized in documents provided to the BRC and the organizations and are used for "hearings" where the Budget Staff presents its analysis to the BRC and the organization involved. Major issues are raised and recommended resource levels are provided by the Budget Staff for discussion at the hearings. The BRC must then make recommendations on resource levels and priority ranking of programs for the Attorney General's final approval.

Following decisions by the Attorney General, organizations are provided with an opportunity to make an appeal to the Attorney General on items that have not been approved. Final decisions are then made through a routine similar to the one followed during initial review. Organizations are then advised to modify their original submissions to incorporate changes approved by the Attorney General and also prepare the necessary technical exhibits which together become the OMB submission which is due on September 15 of each year.

At OMB, the Department's budget estimate follows a pattern similar to the internal Department one, including hearings where Department officials provide responses to questions and issues raised by the OMB examiners. Following the OMB review, the Department receives a "pass-back" which includes resource levels that OMB is recommending as the amounts to be included in the congressional budget estimate. The Department may then appeal these resource levels if they are considered to be inadequate. If OMB does not approve the items being appealed, the Attorney General may make a final appeal to the President for consideration of items he considers to be vital to the Department's operation. Once final decisions have been made by the President, the Department then incorporates changes resulting from the decisions into its budget which becomes the congressional submission.

As indicated earlier, the Department's programs must be authorized by Congress prior to the appropriation of any funds for the Department's activities and programs. In the past, the authorization process and appropriations process have required separate submissions; however, we are working with congressional staff to develop one submission that will satisfy the requirements of both authorizations and appropriations.

## AUTHORIZATION PROCESS

Title II Section 204 of PL 94–503 requires an annual authorization prior to an appropriation of any funds for the Department's activities and programs. The section reads:

> No sums shall be deemed to be authorized to be appropriated for any fiscal year beginning on or after October 1, 1978, for the Department of Justice (including any bureau, agency, or other similar subdivision thereof), except as specifically authorized by Act of Congress with respect to such fiscal year. Neither the creation of a sub-division in the Department of Justice nor the authorization of an activity of the Department, any subdivision or officer thereof, shall be deemed in itself to be an authorization of appropriation for the Department of Justice, such subdivision or activity with respect to any fiscal year beginning on or after October 1, 1978.

The authorization process is principally administered by the House and Senate Judiciary Committees with certain exceptions. In the case of the Department's intelligence programs, jurisdiction is shared by the Judiciary Committees with the House and Senate Intelligence Committees. In the case of the Drug Enforcement Administration, the House Judiciary Committee shares jurisdiction with the Health and Environment Subcommittee of the House Interstate and Foreign Commerce Committee, as well as the House Intelligence Committee. These Committees, as well as the Congress, view the authorization process as an integral part of the Congress' oversight role. The FY 1980 and FY 1981 congressional authorization hearings demonstrated that Congress uses the authorization process both to review the Department's activities and programs, and to indicate Congress' own policy and funding priorities for the Department. It is important to note that the authorization process is designed to provide congressional guidance not only for the executive branch but also to Congress, especially the Budget and Appropriations Committees.

To support the process, the Department must prepare and formally submit to the Congress an *annual* Authorization bill. This legislation is coordinated with the Office of Management and Budget and submitted shortly after the President submits his annual budget.

The Authorization bill requests target funding levels. These target levels, once set by congressional action, are funding ceilings up to which the Congress can then appropriate funds. In setting these funding levels, the Congress creates the crucial link between resource allocation and the program activities of the Department. Through the setting of funding levels, the Congress either concurs with the program priorities suggested by the President and the Department, or indicates its own program priorities by providing additional resources for programs it believes essential or reducing the funding ceiling for programs it wishes to minimize or eliminate. The legislation also provides general program-related authority. Such items as the expenditure of funds for certain emergency situations by the Attorney General, the conduct by the Federal Bureau of Investigation (FBI) of certain undercover activities, the payment of rewards to informants by the FBI, Drug Enforcement Administration (DEA), Immigration and Naturalization Service (I&NS), and Bureau of Prisons (BOP), the protection of the President and the Attorney General by the FBI, the supervision of U.S. prisoners by the U.S. marshals in nonfederal instutitions and numerous other vital activities are included.

In addition to the legislation, the Department must prepare supporting material to justify its request. This material is submitted on an organization and program level and is used by the Congress, after its review, as the basis for formulating the Department's final authorization legislation. Primarily, the Authorization Committees require that the justification material provide a clear definition of the Department's (and the individual organization's) major policy thrusts, especially policy changes or changes in the methods of financing that are necessary to carry out legislative intent, fair appraisals of current programs and past program performance, assessments of the anticipated benefit of the Department's programs to the general public, the economy or the environment and appraisals of the program funding required to carry out the programs. Priority rankings for each program by organization is also required.

The Department's senior policy staff have a significant role in the authorization process. This role begins with the internal funding and resource decisions they make on the proposed fiscal year budget and extends to the role of principal witnesses before the Judiciary or other committees justifying Department's program and resource requirements. As in the case of the appropriation process, senior Department policy staff are not expected to completely know or defend each agency program within their jurisdiction; rather senior staff are usually asked to discuss major program and policy thrusts and indicate how the individual organization efforts proposed for the fiscal year will assist the nation's overall civil and criminal justice efforts. The head of each organization is the principal witness supporting the program and resource request of the organizations.

## APPROPRIATION PROCESS

The request for appropriations for a fiscal year begins when the President transmits his budget message to the Congress about January 20. Although the message is very general, the supporting estimates contained in the President's Budget Appendix and the accompanying special analysis are quite specific. The estimates transmitted by the Administration commit the Department to support them both in program content and resource requirements until formally amended. After the election of a new President, there may be a considerable number of amendments proposed to accommodate changes in policy thrusts.

All budget estimates for the Department of Justice fall under the jurisdiction of the Subcommittee for the Departments of State, Justice, and Commerce, the Judiciary and Related Agencies. This is one of 13 subcommittees in both the House and Senate that review appropriation requests.

Because the enactment of appropriations requires considerable time, the Appropriations Committees expect executive agencies to submit detailed justification material in support of the President's budget shortly after the President transmits his budget estimates. The format of the estimates is worked out between the Department and the subcommittees several months in advance.

By tradition, the House always acts first on appropriation requests. The House Subcommittee holds hearings with Departmental witnesses sometime between February and April. Hearings for the Department of Justice usually take a little more than a week and are almost always held on a schedule that enables the subcommittee to hear the entire Department without interruption. When the House Subcommittee meets to "mark-up" the bill in April or May, it also considers any budget amendments and supplemental estimates that may have been transmitted by the President. Action by the full House Appropriations Committee is delayed until the end of May so that the committee can take into account the impact of the Budget Resolution and the various authorization acts. Appropriation bills are scheduled for floor debate so that the Senate will have enough time to act before the beginning of the new fiscal year. In recent years, appropriation bills have been the subject of a number of floor amendments that have significantly delayed their passage.

Senate review of appropriation requests has been increasing in breadth and scope for several years. Because of its increasing involvement, the Senate may begin its hearings with Department officials before the House. The Senate schedule is subject to more changes and the hearings tend to be shorter and require fewer witnesses. The Senate Subcommittee is usually ready to "mark-up" the bill shortly after it receives its appeal letter from the Department and the House completes floor action. Enactment of a Senate version of an appropriation bill is often delayed, however, because supplemental appropriations usually take precedence over regular appropriation bills and because the necessary actions have not been taken on the Budget Resolution or appropriation authorizations. The Senate will also consider any late budget estimates transmitted by the President that were not considered by the House.

Because the Senate version of the appropriations bill always differs from the bill enacted by the House, each chamber appoints conferees to resolve the differences. The conferees then report a single version of the bill back to each house for ratification. If approved, the bill is sent to the President for signature.

In addition to the regular appropriation bill, the Congress each year enacts one or more supplemental appropriations. The process is essentially identical to that used for regular appropriations but occurs earlier. The major supplemental bill contains sections to fund pay increases, additional programs requirements, and rescissions. Occasionally, the Congress will entertain an emergency supplemental, but late supplemental requirements are increasingly appended to the regular appropriation act.

## BUDGET EXECUTION

Following completion of the appropriation and authorization process, Congress enacts appropriations (or a Continuing Resolution) for the new fiscal year which begins on October 1 of each year. It is at this point that the budget execution process starts. In order to accomplish this part of the process the Department has established the necessary funds control procedures and a reporting system that provides information necessary to monitor the use of funds. Based on the congressional appropriation, each Department organization has a resource level established against which its spending must be monitored during the operating fiscal year. In addition to the spending levels that must be monitored at the total appropriation level, Congress has over the past several years established reprogramming criteria that require congressional notification prior to realigning funds between programs or activities. These criteria, $150,000 or less in some cases, are such that spending trends must be analyzed very closely in order to ensure that the congressional notification requirements are satisfied prior to realignment of funds for new programs or even normal spending increases that would break the threshold (i.e., payment of increased gasoline costs due to cost escalation).

The Budget Staff prepares monthly financial status reports which show the spending trends and provide narrative analysis on projected surplus or deficits in various funding areas. These reports and narrative provide the necessary management tools to be used in assessing needs for supplemental funding or reprogramming of existing funds which would require congressional notification in advance.

## SUGGESTED ADDITIONAL READINGS

Anthony, Robert N. "Zero-Base Budgeting: A Useful Fraud?" *The Government Accountant,* Summer 1977, p. 7.

Harmer, W. Gary. "Bridging the GAAP Between Budgeting and Accounting," *Governmental Finance,* March 1981, pp. 19–24.

Hofstede, G. H. *The Game of Budget Control.* Assen, The Netherlands: Van Gorcum & Co., NV., 1967.

Lynn, Laurence E., Jr., and John M. Seidel. "Bottom Line Management for Public Agencies," *Harvard Business Review,* January 1977, pp. 13–23.

McLeod, R. K., "Program Budgeting Works in Nonprofit Organizations," *Harvard Business Review,* September–October, 1971.

Wildavsky, Aaron. *The Politics of the Budgetary Process,* 2d ed. Boston: Little, Brown, 1974.

## Case 9–1

## SOMERSTOWN PUBLIC SCHOOLS*

"Although we have been developing our program budgeting system for almost a year and a half," said Dr. John Nelson, superintendent of the Somerstown, New Jersey, public schools, "we have a long way to go before we will be satisfied. Program budgeting has yet to reach the point of being in the 'mainstream' of our operations. For example, our budget was approved by the school board by 'line item,' although we prepared it in both program and line-item format; our accounting will continue to be line item; and both budgeting and accounting continue to be central office activities, with limited teaching staff involvement. Most important, program budgeting has yet to result in any major changes in our total educational program."

### Background

Somerstown, New Jersey, located within easy commuting distance of downtown Philadelphia, like many suburban communities, was a town in the midst of rapid change. Until the mid-1950s it was a small farming community, raising tomatoes for the nearby Camden, New Jersey, Campbell Soup Company plant, and raising apples. Then the combination of the sprawling metropolitan area and the sale of several large farms for both industrial and residential developments began to take effect. Population increased from less than 5,000 to nearly 15,000 during the 1960s. The predominate characteristics of the new families were that they were young, well educated, with children. Soon, Somerstown had a higher percentage of its population in its local school system than any of its neighboring towns.

The combination of the large number of school-age children, resulting in school budgets representing approximately 75 percent of the town's budget, and the diverse educational philosophies espoused by the older, conservative farmers on the one hand, and the younger and more liberal professionals on the other, tended to keep the school continually in the center of controversy.

Somerstown had two, or more accurately, one and a third, school systems. First, there was the Somerstown Public School System, consisting of Grades 1 through 8. Second, there was the Wampanoag Regional High School, Grades 9 through 12, for the three communities of Carleton, Somerstown, and Winsor. Each was independent in that it had its own staff, administration, and school board. There were, however, frequent attempts by both staffs, administrations, and school boards to coordinate educational programs.

### The Program Budgeting System

"We began our program budgeting efforts two years ago," Dr. Nelson continued. "One of the school board members is a business school professor, and

* This case was prepared by Robert Howell, Harvard Business School.

**Exhibit 1**
This Year's Budget (actual and given)

| *Code* | *Description* | *Current Budget* | *Last Year's Budget* |
|---|---|---|---|
| 1100 | School committee | $ 2,190 | $ 2,063 |
| 1200 | Superintendent's office | 83,322 | 78,540 |
| | Total administration | $ 85,512 | $ 80,603 |
| 2100 | Supervision | $ 9,420 | $ 15,930 |
| 2200 | Principals | 177,350 | 155,197 |
| 2300 | Teachers | 1,756,058 | 1,579,922 |
| 2400 | Texts | 38,126 | 37,025 |
| 2500 | Library | 20,693 | 19,745 |
| 2600 | Audiovisual | 23,331 | 19,664 |
| 2700 | Guidance | 83,526 | 62,350 |
| 2800 | Pupil personnel | 17,130 | 15,235 |
| | Total instruction | $2,125,634 | $1,905,068 |
| 3100 | Attendance | $ 200 | $ 200 |
| 3200 | Health services | 41,482 | 35,023 |
| 3300 | Transportation | 165,703 | 166,753 |
| 3400 | Food services | 11,116 | 10,079 |
| 3500 | Student activities | 2,512 | 2,246 |
| | Total other services | $ 221,013 | $ 214,301 |
| 4100 | Operation | $ 194,618 | $ 171,685 |
| 4200 | Maintenance | 57,959 | 61,518 |
| | Total operation and maintenance | $ 252,577 | $ 233,203 |
| 7200 | Improvement | $ 0 | $ 0 |
| 7300 | Acquisition | 14,469 | 10,355 |
| 7400 | Replacement | 2,552 | 3,870 |
| | Total improvement, acquisition, replacement | $ 17,021 | $ 14,225 |
| 9100 | Tuition | $ 8,234 | $ 2,600 |
| | Total budget | $2,710,000 | $2,450,000 |
| | Current: (92 + 46.5) | | |
| | New: (1.5) | | |
| | Sabbatical: (2.0) | | |
| 2300–11–1.1 | Classroom | $1,395,027 | $1,255,541 |
| 1.2 | Specialists | 147,579 | 133,175 |
| 1.4 | Substitutes | 20,000 | 18,000 |
| 1.5 | Tutors, physical handicap | 1,500 | 1,500 |
| 1.6a | Curriculum workshops | 15,000 | 10,000 |
| 1.6b | Professional advancement | 5,000 | 4,000 |
| 2.a | Aides, academic | 10,942 | 7,680 |
| 2.b | Aides, noon | 18,400 | 18,400 |
| 4 | Contracted services | 1,950 | 9,137 |
| 5.1 | Supplies, routine | 12,800 | 14,000 |
| 5.2 | Elementary | 46,504 | 40,403 |
| 5.3 | Junior high | 21,256 | 18,440 |
| 6.1a | Travel in-state | 2,245 | 2,215 |
| 6.2a | Travel out-of-state | 1,715 | 1,460 |
| 2300–11 | Total basic education teachers | $1,699,918 | $1,533,951 |
| 2300–12 | Total special education teachers | 56,140 | 45,971 |
| 2300 | Total teachers | $1,756,058 | $1,579,922 |
| 2400–11–5.2 | Elementary text | $ 26,347 | $ 24,925 |
| 5.3 | Junior high text | 11,429 | 11,850 |
| 2400–11 | Total | $ 37,776 | $ 36,775 |
| 2400–12–5.1 | Special class text | 350 | 250 |
| 2400 | Total text | $ 38,126 | $ 37,025 |

at his urging and with his help, he and I developed a very detailed program structure and recast our budget into program format. Then my staff and I prepared the next year's budget in both program and line-item format. That version provided costs by level (elementary and junior high), building (we have seven), and program. At the elementary level our program was a grade; at the junior high, it was a subject.

"Our current budget has omitted the individual building as a primary dimension. More important, we have shifted to a subject orientation at the elementary level. And we have put much more emphasis on our planning at the individual program level.

"Let me show you the line-item budget, then the program budget we now have. You can draw your own conclusions regarding the relative usefulness of each." With that, Dr. Nelson described both the line-item and program budget schedules attached to this case. The following paragraphs summarize his remarks:

> Exhibit 1 is the current Somerstown Public Schools Budget in line-item format. In addition to the summary page, the details for two line items, 2,300 teachers and 2,400 texts, are shown. As one can see, teachers' salaries, representing more than 50 percent of the total budget, are presented as a single "line." Teachers and texts applied to the same educational program are included in different line items.
>
> Exhibit 2 is the current Somerstown Public Schools Budget in program format. Exhibit 3, columns A, B, and C, provide more detail along program, organizational, and expenditure dimensions, respectively.

**Exhibit 2**
Budget by Program: Summary of Expenditures by Program Level

| | *Budget* | *Percent of Total* |
|---|---|---|
| Instructional programs: | | |
| Basic education | $1,748,665 | 64.53 |
| Special education | 56,490 | 2.08 |
| Tuition pupils | 8,043 | 0.30 |
| Adult education | 200 | 0.01 |
| Total instructional programs | $1,813,398 | 66.92 |
| Instructional support programs: | | |
| District management | $ 276,802 | 10.21 |
| Learning resources | 20,693 | 0.76 |
| Pupil personnel services | 125,008 | 4.61 |
| Facilities | 273,918 | 10.11 |
| Transportation | 165,703 | 6.11 |
| Food service | 11,116 | 0.41 |
| Nonprogram | 19,150 | 0.71 |
| Total instructional support programs | $ 892,390 | 32.92 |
| Community services programs: | | |
| Community groups | $ 4,212 | 0.16 |
| Total community services programs | $ 4,212 | 0.16 |
| Grand total | $2,710,000 | 100.00 |

**Exhibit 3**
Current Budget by Program: Summary of Selected Expenditures

| Code | Program Title | Total Budget | A (by program) Percent Total | $ per Student | B (by organization) Elem. (1–5) | Hoyes (6) | Jr. High (7–8) | District-wide | C (by expenditures) Certified Salaries | Noncert. Salaries | Other Expenses |
|---|---|---|---|---|---|---|---|---|---|---|---|
| | Instructional programs: | | | | | | | | | | |
| 60 | English, language arts 1–8 | $ 306,713 | 11.32 | $ 96 | $182,310 | $ 32,328 | $ 92,075 | $ — | $ 285,456 | $ — | $ 21,257 |
| 61 | Reading 1–8 | 292,619 | 10.80 | 122 | 249,609 | 37,725 | 5,285 | — | 260,435 | 3,300 | 28,884 |
| 62 | Science 1–8 | 168,967 | 6.23 | 53 | 54,398 | 33,584 | 80,985 | — | 142,172 | 5,555 | 21,240 |
| 63 | Health 1–8 | 39,501 | 1.46 | 13 | 31,303 | 4,995 | 3,203 | — | 35,006 | — | 4,495 |
| 64 | Mathematics 1–8 | 228,675 | 8.44 | 72 | 130,708 | 21,684 | 76,283 | — | 215,889 | — | 12,786 |
| 65 | Social studies 1–8 | 169,803 | 6.27 | 53 | 69,412 | 25,310 | 75,081 | — | 145,448 | — | 24,355 |
| 59 | Physical education 1–8 | 122,011 | 4.50 | 59 | 77,395 | 13,808 | 30,808 | — | 111,376 | 2,090 | 8,545 |
| 66 | Typing 7–8 | 23,790 | 0.88 | 33 | — | — | 23,790 | — | 19,824 | — | 3,966 |
| 67 | Foreign language 7–8 | 21,645 | 0.80 | 43 | — | — | 21,645 | — | 20,229 | — | 1,416 |
| 68 | Home economics 7–8 | 26,914 | 0.99 | 68 | — | — | 26,914 | — | 25,458 | — | 1,456 |
| 69 | Industrial arts | 37,277 | 1.38 | 86 | — | — | 37,277 | — | 32,031 | — | 5,246 |
| 57 | Art 1–8 | 119,220 | 4.40 | 37 | 79,410 | — | 24,020 | — | 109,342 | — | 9,878 |
| 58 | Music 1–8 | 126,143 | 4.65 | 44 | 84,980 | — | 26,117 | — | 114,106 | — | 12,037 |
| 00 | Nonprogram | 65,387 | 2.41 | 21 | — | — | — | 65,387 | 47,000 | — | 18,387 |
| | Total basic education | $1,748,665 | 64.53 | $ — | $959,525 | $200,270 | $523,483 | $ 65,387 | $1,563,772 | $10,945 | $173,948 |
| 76 | Special education | 56,490 | 2.08 | 1,027 | — | — | — | 56,490 | 52,485 | 2,430 | 1,575 |
| 77 | Tuition pupils | 8,043 | 0.30 | 731 | — | — | — | 8,043 | — | — | 8,043 |
| 74 | Adult education | 200 | 0.01 | 29 | — | — | — | 200 | | — | 200 |
| | Total instructional programs | $1,813,398 | 66.92 | $ — | $959,525 | $200,270 | $523,483 | $130,120 | $1,616,257 | $13,375 | $183,766 |
| | Instructional support programs: | | | | | | | | | | |
| 85 | School management | $ 175,350 | 6.47 | $ 55 | $108,342 | $ 22,903 | $ 44,105 | $ — | $ 136,285 | $34,336 | $ 4,729 |
| 86 | Central office management | 101,452 | 3.74 | 32 | — | — | — | 101,452 | 57,600 | 33,442 | 10,410 |
| | Total district management | $ 276,802 | 10.21 | $ — | $108,342 | $ 22,903 | $ 44,105 | $101,452 | $ 193,885 | $67,778 | $ 15,139 |

Exhibit 4 provides further explanation and cost information for the reading program, elementary level. The program approach consolidates all expenditures that can be clearly identified, such as teachers and texts, with a given program.

**Exhibit 4**

1971 Education Program: Summary Description of Existing Elementary-Grade Reading Program

1. *Brief summary of program:* Multibasal program augmented by teacher-chosen materials designed to help children grow in five stages of reading: (1) readiness, (2) beginning reading, (3) stimulating rapid growth, (4) establishing power, and (5) refining tastes. One reading director, two reading consultants, and one reading aide assist teachers in choosing appropriate materials and executing effective reading programs.
2. *Student text materials:* (list follows)
3. *Teachers' resource guides:* (list follows)
4. *Certified staff:* 21.7
5. *Noncertified staff:* 1
6. *Instructional time provided,* based on 180 days per year:

| | *Hours per Day* | *Total Hours per Year* |
|---|---|---|
| Grades 1–3 ....... | 2.0 | 360 |
| Grades 4–5 ....... | 1.5 | 270 |

7. *Number of teaching stations required:* 47
8. *Methods of evaluation—students:* Use of tests, designed (1) by teachers, (2) by consultants, (3) system-wide, and (4) by textbook publishing companies, with results evaluated by reading consultants, principals, and teacher/observers.
9. *Methods of evaluation—staff:* Use of various levels of committee assessment, including reading department, principals, reading consultants, grade-level committees, primary and intermediate subgroups.

10 *Methods of evaluation—program:* Use of committees of teachers and reading consultants together.

Current Education Program: Multiyear Financial and Statistical Plan

| | *Budget Year* | *Next Year* | *Year after Next* |
|---|---|---|---|
| I. *Multiyear Financial Plan (whole dollars)* | | | |
| 1. Salaries—certified ........ | $219,609 | $236,245 | $255,904 |
| 2. Salaries—noncertified ........ | 3,300 | 3,600 | 3,950 |
| 3. Extra-duty compensation ........ | — | — | — |
| 4. Equipment ........ | 1,200 | 3,000 | 4,000 |
| 5. Supplies ........ | 2,500 | 4,000 | 5,000 |
| 6. Workbooks ........ | 9,000 | 13,000 | 14,000 |
| 7. Textbooks ........ | 13,000 | 13,000 | 14,000 |
| 8. Other expense ........ | 1,000 | 1,500 | 1,500 |
| 9. Total ........ | 249,609 | 274,345 | 298,354 |
| 10. Offsetting revenues | | | |
| II. *Multiyear Statistical Plan* | | | |
| 11. Total number of classes or sections ........ | 73 | 71 | 69 |
| 12. Number certified staff (FTE) ........ | 21.7 | 22.5 | 21.8 |

**Exhibit 4 *(concluded)***

| | | | |
|---|---|---|---|
| 13. Number noncertified staff (FTE) .... | 1 | 1 | 1 |
| 14. Number of teaching stations ....... | 47 | 47 | 47 |
| 15. Total hours of instruction time | 1–3: 360 | K–3: 360 | K–3: 360 |
| given to student .................. | 4–5: 270 | 4: 270 | 4: 270 |
| 16. Total teacher hours of | 1–3: 15,120 | K–3: 20,520 | K–3: 19,800 |
| instruction ...................... | 4–5: 8,370 | 4: 3,780 | 4: 3,780 |
| | 23,490 | 24,300 | 23,580 |
| 17. Student enrollment (list each grade or course separately) | | | |
| Kindergarten ........................... | | 260 | 260 |
| Grade 1 ............................... | 369 | 328 | 267 |
| Grade 2 ............................... | 374 | 376 | 335 |
| Grade 3 ............................... | 373 | 377 | 379 |
| Grade 4 ............................... | 370 | 376 | 380 |
| Grade 5 ............................... | 423 | | |

Prepared by John Greene.

## Questions

1. The two systems depicted in this case should be totally congruent; that is, if the line-item system accounts for $2,710,000, then the program system should account for exactly the same amount. On Exhibit 1 of the case, the total teachers' expenses are given as $1,699,918. Where, if anywhere, does this amount appear in the program system?
2. The program budget indicates that the reading program in Grades 1 to 5 will cost $249,609. How was this number obtained? What is the cost per child for reading in Grades 1 to 5? Is this too much, just right, not enough? What additional data might you need to answer that question?
3. Is the programmatic method of collecting expenses any better than the line-item method? Would a different program structure be more useful?

## Case 9–2

## ORION COLLEGE*

Orion College was a small, private, liberal arts college located in Fleming, Ohio. It granted a bachelor of arts degree. Originally founded as a men's college, it had remained as such until 4 years ago when, after several heated trustee meetings, it had opened its doors to women.

The admissions office felt that the decision to go coed had significantly

* This case was prepared by Claudine B. Malone, Harvard Business School.

offset the negative reaction to the small, rural Ohio town in which the college was located. Over the past four years, its applications from both men and women had increased, and projected enrollment for next year was 3,000 students (all residents). Despite the strong enrollment figures and a large endowment, a deficit of $530,000 was projected (see Exhibit 1).

**Exhibit 1**
Operating Budget

| | *Preliminary Budget Next Year* | *Actual Last Year ($ in 000)* |
|---|---|---|
| Revenues: | | |
| Student tuition and fees | $ 7,800,000 | $ 7,280 |
| Dining | 2,700,000 | 2,520 |
| Housing | 3,300,000 | 3,080 |
| Auxiliary enterprises | 1,400,000 | 1,270 |
| Gifts for current use | 700,000 | 630 |
| Endowment income | 950,000 | 718 |
| Reimbursement of direct and indirect expenses related to research grants | 80,000 | 72 |
| Total revenue | $16,930,000 | $15,570 |
| Expenses | | |
| Salaries | | |
| Faculty (teaching and research) | $ 6,856,000 | $ 5,962 |
| Administration | 1,210,000 | 1,052 |
| Staff | 2,800,000 | 2,435 |
| | $10,866,000 | $ 9,449 |
| Student support: | | |
| Library and audiovisual | $ 433,000 | $ 363 |
| Equipment and supplies | 105,540 | 91 |
| Food | 2,086,240 | 1,812 |
| Student activities and athletics | 340,000 | 296 |
| Scholarships | 350,000 | 320 |
| | $ 3,314,780 | $ 2,882 |
| Plant: | | |
| Maintenance (salaries, supplies, and minor parts) | $ 353,800 | $ 307 |
| Utilities | 400,500 | 320 |
| Equipment | 300,000 | 378 |
| Interest | 46,000 | 38 |
| | $ 1,100,300 | $ 1,043 |
| General and administration: | | |
| Employee benefits | $ 866,880 | $ 754 |
| Insurance | 62,000 | 54 |
| Professional fees | 40,000 | 35 |
| Communications and data processing | 430,030 | 398 |
| Travel | 84,000 | 73 |
| Services purchases | 45,000 | 39 |
| Security | 68,000 | 32 |
| Health services | 272,950 | 237 |
| Miscellaneous | 12,000 | 14 |
| | $ 1,880,920 | $ 1,636 |
| Research costs (excluding faculty salaries) | $ 300,000 | $ 261 |
| Total expenses | $17,460,000 | $15,271 |
| Surplus (deficit) | $ (530,000) | $ 299 |

In its recent meeting, the trustee finance committee had not approved the proposed budget. Instead, it asked President Haas to review the budget with the business officer, academic department heads, and other department heads in order to reduce costs. The finance committee was unwilling to consider even an increase in tuition and fees until it was convinced that adequate measures had been taken to control expenses. In addition, they felt that the budget, as submitted, gave them no indication of where the college's resources were being consumed. Any cost reductions, they felt, should be considered in the light of explicit educational objectives. They requested that President Haas and his business officer prepare a budget format that would be more informative in this regard.

## Questions

1. Restructure the preliminary budget in "program format" using the worksheet and data provided in the Appendix below. All administrative expenses and plant expenses should be allocated to one of the programs.
2. Recommend actions that President Haas should take.

## APPENDIX

In trying to understand how the college's resources were being consumed, President Haas studied the data presented below. To this he added some notes to expedite the business office's first cut at a new budget format using the form they recently worked out.

1. Revenue from auxiliary enterprises represents the surplus of income over expenses for the bookstore, faculty club, and college printing office. It does not include any revenue from the college infirmary (health services). A health service fee of $75 is included in the total tuition charge of $2,600 per student.
2. The health services expenses includes expenses for medicine and drugs dispensed in the infirmary but not special prescriptions which students pay for themselves. The health services expense also includes salaries for nurses and doctors but does not include any costs for plant, housekeeping, food, or utilities.
3. For next year, there are 10 full-time equivalent (FTE) faculty assigned to research. Average faculty salaries are budgeted for $26,000 per year. Salaries for faculty secretaries are included in the budget line for staff salaries. For budgeting purposes, each member of the faculty (whether a department head, teaching faculty, or assigned to research) is considered to have 0.3 FTE secretaries at an average salary of $8,400 for an FTE. The budget line for salaries does not include fringes. Next year's teaching faculty (including department heads) number 290 FTEs.

4. For budgeting purposes, administrators are assumed to have 0.2 FTE secretaries. The one exception is the development office. The director of development (salary $24,500) has a full-time secretary, and the office staff comprises an additional six FTE secretary/clerks as well as three administrators (average administrative salaries are $18,500).
5. Salaries for librarians, library clericals, and the audiovisual staff are included in the budget line for library and audiovisual. However, the chief librarian's salary of $18,600 is included in the budget line for administrative salaries.
6. The budget line for student activities and athletics includes all the expenses for the varsity sports program, as well as intramural athletic activities, the student association, required physical education classes, athletic equipment, travel for athletic activities, and other student organization expenses. Revenues from athletic fees and game receipts have been credited to these expenses. Salaries totaling $66,000 for the athletic director, assistant athletic director, and the director of student services have been included in the budget line for administrative salaries.
7. There is very little information readily available on the breakdown of plant expenses. The business office records indicate that utilities for the dormitories have been budgeted for $100,000. The utility budget for all the athletic buildings is $60,000. The dining center utility budget is $40,000. And the infirmary utility expense is planned for $18,000. It was not possible to separate administrative and classroom building utilities since administrators and student activities personnel share space in the classroom complex of buildings. Nor was it possible to isolate housekeeping salaries and expenses from other maintenance salaries and expenses. The salary for the director of the physical plant ($23,200) is in the budget line for administrative salaries.

   It was possible to allocate building space among the different users, as indicated below:

| *Program* | *Percent of Building Square Feet Used* |
|---|---|
| Administration | 5 |
| Instruction | 40 |
| Research | 10 |
| Plant | 1 |
| Housing | 40 |
| Dining center | 1 |
| Health services | 1 |
| Student activities | 1 |
| Development | 1 |

8. Professional fees cannot be immediately identified by program. Nor have travel expenses ever been broken down by department. Travel

## ORION COLLEGE WORKSHEET ($000)
### Programs

| Line Items | | Admin-istration | Instruc-tion | Re-search | Plant | Housing |
|---|---|---|---|---|---|---|
| Salaries: Faculty | (1) | | | | | |
| Administrative | (2) | | | | | |
| Staff | (3) | | | | | |
| Student support: Library and audiovisual | (4) | | | | | |
| Equipment and supplies | (5) | | | | | |
| Food | (6) | | | | | |
| Student activities and athletics | (7) | | | | | |
| Scholarships | (8) | | | | | |
| Plant: Maintenance | (9) | | | | | |
| Utilities | (10) | | | | | |
| Equipment | (11) | | | | | |
| Interest | (12) | | | | | |
| General and administrative: Employee benefits | (13) | | | | | |
| Insurance | (14) | | | | | |
| Professional fees | (15) | | | | | |
| Communication and data process | (16) | | | | | |
| Travel | (17) | | | | | |
| Services purchases | (18) | | | | | |
| Security | (19) | | | | | |
| Health services | (20) | | | | | |
| Miscellaneous | (21) | | | | | |
| Research | (22) | | | | | |
| Subtotal | (23) | | | | | |
| Allocation in (out) | (24) | | | | | |
| | (25) | | | | | |
| | (26) | | | | | |
| Total | (27) | | | | | |

Programs

| *Dining Center* | *Health Services* | *Student Activities and Athletics* | *Devel-opment* | *Total* | *Adjust-ments* | *Adjusted Total* |
|---|---|---|---|---|---|---|
| | | | | 6,856 | | |
| | | | | 1,210 | | |
| | | | | 2,800 | | |
| | | | | 433 | | |
| | | | | 105<br>2,086 | | |
| | | | | 340 | | |
| | | | | 350 | | |
| | | | | 353 | | |
| | | | | 400 | | |
| | | | | 300 | | |
| | | | | 46 | | |
| | | | | 867 | | |
| | | | | 62 | | |
| | | | | 40 | | |
| | | | | 430 | | |
| | | | | 84 | | |
| | | | | 45 | | |
| | | | | 68 | | |
| | | | | 273 | | |
| | | | | 12 | | |
| | | | | 300 | | |
| | | | | 17,460 | | |
| | | | | | | |
| | | | | | | |
| | | | | | | |
| | | | | | | |

requests have to be approved in advance by the business office except for the $2,000 in travel expenses included in the development office budget and the $4,500 in travel expenses designated for the recruiting office.

9. The $430,000 budgeted for communications and data processing includes $128,000 for the college switchboard, telephones, and operator's salaries. The remainder covers computer rental and data processing personnel salaries except for the $24,000 salary for the director of computer services included in the budget line for administrative salaries.
10. Professional services purchased include legal fees, consulting fees, and auditing fees. Historically, legal fees have been very low because of the long-standing relationship between the college and the firm. Likewise, the fee for the annual audit was well below market.
11. Maintenance of the athletic fields costs about $15,000 a year.

---

Notes: For this first budget review, no attempt will be made to examine the individual faculty department salaries and expenses.

Where data are not immediately available on a direct-expense basis, make reasonable assumptions, using average salaries and average expenses.

## Case 9–3

## METROPOLITAN MUSEUM OF ART*

The "first cut" at the operating budget of the Metropolitan Museum of Art for fiscal year 1973 (i.e., the year ended June 30, 1973) indicated a substantial deficit. Management was considering what steps, if any, should be taken to reduce or eliminate this deficit.

The Metropolitan Museum was organized in New York City in 1870. In 1972 it had over 1 million works of art, the largest collection of its kind in the Western Hemisphere. It had an endowment fund of $150 million.

### Governance and Management

***The Board.*** Fiscal authority for direction of the Metropolitan Museum of Art was vested in the Board of Trustees. The board was responsible for the broad direction and control of the Museum and for the establishment and approval of basic policies and plans. Meeting quarterly, it also considered important operational matters.

---

* This case was prepared by Fred K. Foulkes, Harvard Business School.

**The Director.** The director was the museum's chief executive officer. He was responsible for formulating policies and programs for the board's consideration and for implementing decisions made by the board. In addition to being responsible for overall planning and administration of the Museum's affairs, he was also involved in fund-raising and negotiating major art acquisitions. He presided at rehearsals of presentations by the curators and was present at actual presentations made to the Board of Trustees Acquisition Committee. Since 1966, the director was Thomas P. F. Hoving. Dr. Hoving had achieved national recognition as the commissioner of parks of New York City, particularly for his campaign to make New York a "fun city." He earned a Ph.D. in Art History at Princeton in 1959, and was hired as curatorial assistant at the Cloisters, the medieval art department of the Metropolitan. In 1965 he became curator of the Cloisters.

**Curatorial.** The vice director, curator-in-chief, was responsible for 17 curatorial departments and the Conservation Laboratory, with a curatorial staff of nearly 200 persons.

The 17 curatorial departments varied considerably in the size of their staffs and collections, and in the range of their activities. While all departments collected art objects, some were more active than others. In general the more active departments were those that collected works of art currently available in the open market.

In addition to collection and display, curatorial departments were responsible for maintaining relations with collectors and art dealers, for developing scholarly and general literature on the collection, and for answering inquiries from the public. Some members of the curatorial staff also taught courses and lectured at the Museum or at other institutions.

**Education.** The vice director of education had general responsibility for developing educational programs for students and for the general public. Included in his domain were five departments: the Library, the Junior Museum, Secondary and Higher Education, Community Programs, and the Photograph and Slide Library.

**Finance and Treasurer.** The vice director for finance and treasurer was the chief financial officer of the Museum. Reporting to him were four financial administrators, each with his own staff and task assignment. The assistant treasurer was responsible for the physical receipt and payment of funds, accounts receivable, the payroll, and general accounting. The controller prepared the annual budget and was responsible for accounts payable. The registrar maintained catalog descriptions of all objects belonging to the Museum, recorded the physical movement of these objects in and out of the Museum, and obtained insurance and custom handling for art shipments. The city liaison officer was responsible for developing and maintaining good relations with the New York City administration, in particular those officials with whom the Museum had financial transactions.

***Public Affairs.*** The vice director of public affairs, a position that was at the time vacant, had overall responsibility for eight departments, each of which had direct contact with the public. These departments were as follows: public information, information desk, bookshop and reproduction, development and promotion (fund-raising), membership office, publications, exhibition design, and the auditorium.

***Operations.*** The operating administrator had general responsibility for the provision of the Museum's many service functions. These included: guardianship, maintenance, cleaning, purchasing stockroom supplies, telephone and office services, photograph studio, and the several restaurant facilities. This large department employed approximately 400 of the Museum's 800 employees.

Staffing levels for these activities are given in Exhibit 1.

In the late 1960s there was increasing interest among professional staff employees in establishing a union to represent them. Apparently this interest had been increasing despite efforts by the Museum's administration to be responsive to the needs of the professional staff. The administration had a publicly announced goal of bringing curatorial salaries up to the level received by professors in leading colleges and universities. From 1967 to 1971 there was a 30 percent increase in curatorial salaries. The 1972 budget, prepared in the spring of 1971, called for additional salary increases of between 11.6 percent and 17.9 percent depending on the level of curatorial rank.

The administration had also attempted to increase the extent of participation by professional employees. In 1970 the curators, acting with the backing of the administration, established a Curatorial Forum, which comprised the entire curatorial staff, and had a representative on the Staff Policy Committee, the executive team which made recommendations to the director and conducted routine business operations.

**Exhibit 1**
Staffing Levels: 1967–1971 (excluding auxiliary activities)

| | *1971* | *1970* | *1969* | *1968* | *1967* |
|---|---|---|---|---|---|
| Director and several offices | 27 | 23 | 22 | 21 | 20 |
| Vice director—curator-in-chief | 199 | 185 | 170 | 172 | 167 |
| Vice director for finance and treasurer | 51 | 48 | 46 | 42 | 42 |
| Vice director for education | 63 | 55 | 53 | 52 | 52 |
| Vice director for public affairs | 31 | 28 | 28 | 28 | 25 |
| Vice director for operations | 412 | 407 | 370 | 365 | 361 |
| Subtotal | 783 | 746 | 689 | 680 | 667 |
| 100th Anniversary | 19 | 21 | — | — | — |
| Total | 802 | 767 | 689 | 680 | 667 |

By April 1972, it appeared to management that the unionization issue was no longer alive and that many of the specific changes that had been introduced had been well received.

## FINANCIAL BACKGROUND

The Museum began to suffer operating losses in the late 1960s. Historical financial data are shown in Exhibits 2 and 3.

The emergence of financial problems was not a condition unique to the Metropolitan Museum of Art; many museums were faced with similar situations. The Museum of Modern Art, for example, reported a record deficit of $1.2 million in 1970. Also in 1970, a study conducted by the American Association of Museums found that 44 percent of its members were operating at a loss. Furthermore, at the time of the study the AAM spokesman said that the dismal trend was expected to continue.

Two broad explanations were advanced for the growing disparity between revenues and expenses. First, museums, like other entities which relied on a relatively fixed income, suffered from the effects of inflation. Second, in order to adapt to a changing environment, museums had incurred new types of expenses.

One cause of the difficulty was the rapid increase in museum attendance. It was noted that the 1971 exhibit entitled the "Drug Scene" at the Museum of the City of New York drew more people in three months of 1971 than the entire museum did in all of 1970. However, the cost of contemporary exhibits was high. The American Museum of Natural History, for example, spent $526,000 for its centennial exhibit "Can Man Survive?"

Another relatively new cost was the emergence of vigorous demands by

**Exhibit 2**
Financial Record: 1960–1972

| *Fiscal year** | *Operating income* | *Operating expenses* | *Surplus (loss)†* |
|---|---|---|---|
| 1960 | $ 4,006,943 | $ 3,618,197 | $388,746 |
| 1961 | 4,328,603 | 4,042,561 | 286,042 |
| 1962 | 5,181,647 | 4,433,087 | 748,560 |
| 1963 | 5,066,399 | 4,605,688 | 460,711 |
| 1964 | 5,280,503 | 4,802,832 | 477,671 |
| 1965 | 5,807,116 | 5,278,279 | 528,837 |
| 1966 | 6,128,155 | 5,698,411 | 429,714 |
| 1967 | 6,496,767 | 6,236,532 | 260,235 |
| 1968 | 7,054,341 | 7,461,354 | (407,013) |
| 1969 | 8,393,332 | 8,531,833 | (138,501) |
| 1970 | 8,405,569 | 9,226,513 | (820,944) |
| 1971 | 11,363,519 | 11,773,117 | (409,598)‡ |
| 1972 (budget) | 12,415,600 | 13,128,793 | (713,193) |

* Fiscal year ends June 30.

† For fiscal years prior to 1970 Surplus (loss) is before extraordinary charges.

‡ Plus an accumulated Centennial deficit of $1,121,697.

**Exhibit 3**
Sources of Income 1960–1971

| *Sources* | *1960* | *1961* | *1962* | *1963* | *1964* | *1965* | *1966* | *1967* | *1968* | *1969* | *1970* | *1971* |
|---|---|---|---|---|---|---|---|---|---|---|---|---|
| Unrestricted investment income | $2,737 | $2,890 | $3,591 | $3,474 | $3,621 | $4,051 | $4,174 | $4,380 | $4,461 | $4,658 | $4,670 | $ 4,722 |
| Transfer of unrestricted endowment funds* | 0 | 0 | 0 | 0 | 0 | 0 | 0 | 0 | 0 | 0 | 0 | 844 |
| Appropriation from City of New York | 974 | 1,038 | 1,191 | 1,259 | 1,293 | 1,385 | 1,528 | 1,554 | 1,678 | 1,853 | 1,947 | 2,323 |
| Grants | 0 | 0 | 0 | 0 | 0 | 0 | 0 | 53 | 160 | 577 | 126 | 683 |
| Memberships | 180 | 205 | 234 | 252 | 267 | 289 | 314 | 399 | 415 | 453 | 419 | 1,057 |
| Admission fees | 0 | 65 | 72 | 0 | 0 | 80 | 15 | 0 | 45 | 353 | 390 | 821 |
| Contributions for general purposes | 62 | 66 | 20 | 16 | 18 | 17 | 18 | 19 | 181 | 151 | 191 | 204 |
| Other† | 64 | 65 | 73 | 66 | 81 | 71 | 81 | 91 | 113 | 137 | 278 | 260 |
| Subtotal | 4,007 | 4,329 | 5,181 | 5,066 | 5,281 | 5,807 | 6,128 | 6,497 | 7,054 | 8,183 | 8,021 | 10,914 |
| Plus: Net income for auxiliary activities | 0 | 0 | 0 | 0 | 0 | 0 | 0 | 0 | 0 | 210 | 385 | 449 |
| Total | $4,007 | $4,329 | $5,181 | $5,066 | $5,281 | $5,807 | $6,128 | $6,497 | $7,054 | $8,393 | $8,406 | $11,364 |

* In 1971 a fixed rate of return (5 percent) was used for the first time to determine endowment income.

† Includes income from slide and photograph sales, guide service, course fees and special seminars.

professional employees for higher pay and more job security. According to Ann R. Leven, assistant treasurer of the Metropolitan, this new demand reflected the fact that curators no longer came predominantly from the ranks of the wealthy. Many curators had to live off salaries which were traditionally quite low.

The Metropolitan took action in 1971 to combat the trend of increasing deficits. The actions taken can be grouped into two categories, those which reduced costs, and those which generated additional revenues.

One cost cutting action was a curtailment in the hiring of new personnel. Mr. Daniel Herrick, vice director for finance and treasurer, instituted the policy of not filling a vacancy unless the position was deemed essential.

A second austerity measure was the decision to close the Museum one day a week (Monday) beginning in July 1971. Prior to this decision the Museum had remained open to the public seven days a week, 365 days a year. Consequently, many maintenance activities had to be performed at odd hours: before the Museum opened and after it closed. These scheduling demands, coupled with ordinary absences, resulted in (1) having to pay guards and maintenance personnel overtime pay, and (2) having to hire temporary personnel on a per diem basis. The budget for 1971–72 estimated that Monday closings would save the Metropolitan nearly $200,000 in annual labor cost. Ten New York City art museums, including the Guggenheim and the Whitney, adopted this policy before the Metropolitan did.

Another cutback was the elimination from the operating budget of various projects which the Museum had planned to carry out. Among the postponed items were the following: (1) the publication of a catalog of the Museum's programs of research and education; (2) hiring of a specialist for foundation and government fund-raising; (3) installation of a public education gallery dealing with current events in the art world; (4) free acoustiguide equipment; (5) redecoration of the restaurant; (6) development of a computer program for an art catalog. Perhaps the biggest disappointment to many people was the curtailment of the final Centennial exhibition, "Masterpieces of Fifty Centuries." In the words of Mr. Hoving, "Our budget could no longer afford the expenses involved in the foreign loans that we planned for the last great Centennial show, especially the cost of insurance, which has skyrocketed in the last few years."

At the same time that these cost reduction activities were undertaken the Museum also initiated steps to increase its revenues. One approach was the introduction in 1970 of discretionary admission charges at the main building and at the Cloisters. Mr. Hoving commented that "after investigating different ways of charging admission to the Museum, the pay-as-you-wish plan emerged as the most satisfactory for two reasons. It created no economic barriers for the public and it proved that income was higher than with a set admission fee." (*New York Times,* October 9, 1970.) After a five-month trial period the average contribution per visitor was 64 cents. One reason for the high average was that the Museum "strongly hinted" that $1 would be a "very nice" contribution for adults, 50 cents for youngsters. The 1971–72 budget estimated that total receipts from the voluntary admission contributions would approximate $1 million. (The Museum found out in 1971 after it purchased electronic counting equipment that the earlier handcounted records of attendance were about four times too high.)

The introduction of a discretionary admission fee provoked sharp criticism from several sources. Among them was Mr. Carter Burden, a New York City councilman, who noted that "of the 15 institutions which receive city funds, with the exception of the Bronx Zoo, the Metropolitan was the only one with a general admission fee." He added, "Our society should be going in the opposite direction."

Another step taken to enhance revenues was the adoption of the fixed-rate-of-return concept for endowment funds. Whereas in past years endowment income was limited to interest and dividends, beginning in 1971 the Museum recorded as income 5 percent of the average market value of unrestricted endowment funds for the three previous years. It was anticipated that over the long run actual capital appreciation combined with dividends and interest would result in an annual yield at least equal to the fixed rate. This approach had the added advantage of making endowment income a constant amount during the course of the fiscal year. (See Exhibit 3).

Also beginning in 1970 the Museum undertook an energetic campaign to enroll new members. As a result of this campaign 8,667 new memberships were sold by April 1971, bringing in added receipts of $360,000. One incentive to join by this time was that beginning in April 1971, the prices of individual and family memberships were raised from $15 to $25 and $40, respectively. Because of the price increase the Museum expected only a small increase in memberships for 1972.

The recent history of membership growth was marred by only one major downturn. This occurred in 1967 when prices were raised. However, there was a short downturn for a few months in the fall of 1968 as a result of the contemporary exhibition. "Harlem on My Mind." One hundred and sixty-five members canceled their memberships and many others failed to renew. The two major criticisms were an anti-Semitic comment in the catalog, and the view that this exhibit was not "real" art.

Another approach to enhancing revenues were efforts to make the Museum's auxiliary activities more profitable. Additional merchandising operations were opened and prices on prints, books, and other items were set at levels to bring an optimum return. As a result of these changes the 1971–72 budget anticipated an increase in contribution on these activities from $415,000 to $615,000.

Still another revenue-producing activity was the search for nontraditional sources of funds. In 1970 the state of New York broke new ground when it appropriated $18 million for support of the arts. The Metropolitan received a total of $418,500 of the appropriation in 1971, and expected continued support from the state. Another new source of funds was the federal government which under the National Endowment for the Arts was expected to make an initial contribution to the Metropolitan of $110,000 in 1972.

Yet by far the largest public contribution came from the City of New York which gave $2.3 million in 1971 to cover the costs of guardianship and maintenance. While the city's contribution to the operating income had declined from 27 percent in 1959–60 to 21 percent in 1970–71, the amount contributed had increased. It was estimated, furthermore, that by 1976 the city would increase its annual commitment by an additional $585,000. (*The Wall Street Journal,* July 27, 1971.) Consequently, some administrators at the Metropolitan felt uneasy when elected city officials began to urge the city to reduce or even eliminate its contributions to the Museum.

## CURRENT FINANCIAL SITUATION

During the 1971–72 fiscal year it became increasingly evident that the financial plans for the year were not going to be met. A deficit of $713,000 was originally budgeted compared to the preceding year's deficit of $1,531,000. The reduction had been planned to be accomplished by keeping 1972 expenditures near the 1971 level ($13.1 million in 1972 versus $12.9 million in the prior year), while revenue was to be increased by $1 million. However, by April 1972 it appeared that the actual deficit for the fiscal year ending June 30 would approximate $1.4 million. The chief reason for this turn of events was that revenue had not increased as planned.

Attendance in the Main Building was down approximately 25 percent from the year before, and admission income was one third below the budgeted figure of $930,000. Mr. Daniel Herrick, the vice director of finance and treasurer, attributed the falloff to several factors: a post-Centennial slump in public interest, reduced hotel occupancies in New York, and a growing reluctance of New York City residents to go out at night. As a direct result of decreased attendance, the contribution to expenses provided by the restaurant and bookstores was reduced by $130,000.

Two additional factors contributed to lower than planned revenues. In fiscal 1970–71 the Museum undertook a special membership campaign whereby new individual and family members were encouraged to join at the old rates (before new, increased rates went into effect), and existing members were allowed to extend their memberships for an additional year at the old rates. The effect of this campaign was an extraordinary increase in memberships. From 1963 through 1968 membership fluctuated between 20,000 and 23,000 each year. In 1969 it rose to over 24,000, in 1970 to 27,000, and in 1971 to 37,760. However, in early 1972 as memberships began to expire, the renewal rates were lower than anticipated, mostly among the lower membership categories. In the single month of February, for example, 937 individual and family memberships were not renewed. As a result of this higher than anticipated lapse rate, membership income was about $90,000 below the budget. A final financial disappointment was the reduction in grants received by the Museum. New York State reduced its grant to $221,000 from $418,000 the year before, and the National Endowment for the Arts contributed $60,000 less than budgeted. Total grant income was $280,000 short of the budgeted level.

## THE BUDGET FOR 1972–1973

The preliminary budget for the forthcoming year indicated that total revenue would decline slightly to $11.7 million, principally reflecting a further reduction in grants to the Museum. The budget report suggested that there were three principal options to be considered:

*Option 1.* Deficit $1,000,000. Across-the-board cut in expenditures of 10.3 percent. Staff cut of 36 (excluding auxiliary activities). Requires effecting efficiencies in all departments and certain cutbacks most notably in the Curatorial and Operations area. Reduce advertising. Reduce number of activities for members. Close Monday holidays, 11 A.M. to 1 P.M. Sundays, Friday evenings. Cancel employees' Christmas party.

*Option 2.* Deficit $500,000. Across-the-board cut in expenditures of 16.4 percent. Staff cut of 60. The effect falls heaviest on those departments with limited program money, cutting deeply into the Curatorial and Operating staffs. Allows for basic maintenance of collections; study rooms would close; conservation and research would stop; exhibitions would be severely limited. Reduce community education activities unless outside funding obtained. Close 83rd Street entrance.

*Option 3.* No deficit. Across-the-board cut in expenditures of 22.5 percent. Staff cut of 91. Merely maintains the Museum as a repository for works of art. Requires a major functional reorganization of the staff. All cataloging ceases. Closes libraries during the summer, eliminates weekend and summer education programs. Consolidates Development and Membership offices.

When Mr. Herrick was asked whether the administration had considered the possibility of passing the hat among the trustees in order to make up operating deficits, he said:

> The days when a few wealthy contributors would ante up the money to cover a deficit are over. Even the richest person in the world doesn't have an inclination to keep giving money if you have continuing deficits of over $1 million a year. Furthermore, anteing up to fill a deficit is the least attractive type of donation from the viewpoint of most contributors. Philanthropists far prefer to donate money for works of art, buildings, or even endowed chairs before giving to cover operating losses.

Mr. Herrick continued discussing the financial problems of the Museum:

> We are reluctant to cut back expenses especially since the staff takes intense pride in what has been accomplished at the Metropolitan Museum. At a time when other aspects of New York City life are deteriorating, the Museum has been on

a planned and vigorous course of greater service to the community in maintaining and communicating the meaning of its collection of works of art to the public.

We have considered numerous alternative forms of retrenchment but because salaries comprise roughly 70 percent of our total costs (see Exhibits 4 and 5), there is virtually no way to avoid laying off people. Furthermore, this raises the difficult problem of deciding which people to release and how to handle the dismissals. We are even exploring the possibility of converting to a four-day week, perhaps in lieu of salary increases.

The fact of the matter is that even if the Museum were to cut its expenditures to create a balanced budget in the forthcoming year, the same problem would recur again next year. As long as the Museum exists in an inflationary economy, where there is an inevitable upward push in terms of wages, fringe benefits, and opening costs, the Museum must seek some means of achieving an adequate and dependable source of funding to maintain the status quo at least.

**Exhibit 4**
Administration Expenses (as budgeted for the year ended June 30, 1972)*

| | *Personal service* | *Other expense* | *Total* |
|---|---|---|---|
| Director and several offices | $ 404,095 | $ 173,085 | $ 577,180 |
| Vice director, curator-in-chief | 2,455,227 | 695,316 | 3,150,543 |
| Vice director for finance and treasurer | 555,561 | 355,910 | 911,471 |
| Vice director for education | 783,708 | 812,586 | 1,596,294 |
| Vice director for public affairs | 467,725 | 701,815 | 1,169,540 |
| Vice director for operations | 3,625,199 | 1,435,570 | 5,060,769 |
| Benefits and allowances | 1,764,170 | — | 1,764,170 |
| Adjustments† | (566,295) | (156,478) | (722,773) |
| Total estimated operating expenses | $9,489,390 | $4,017,804 | $13,507,194 |

* As revised 3/31/72.

† Accounting deductions distributed among capital budget, auxiliary activities, the Cloisters.

**Exhibit 5**
Actual Administration Expenses

| | *1971* | *1970* | *1969* | *1968* | *1967* |
|---|---|---|---|---|---|
| Personal service (including benefits and allowances) | $ 8,287,400 | $ 6,909,700 | $6,151,300 | $5,422,000 | $5,181,400 |
| Other than personal service | 3,138,000 | 2,086,500 | 1,971,300 | 1,398,600 | 1,119,300 |
| Subtotal | $11,425,400 | $ 8,996,200 | $8,122,600 | $6,820,600 | $6,300,700 |
| 100th Anniversary personal service | 96,100 | 210,100 | | | |
| Other than personal service | 1,454,00 | 1,595,900 | | | |
| Total | $12,975,900 | $10,802,200 | $8,122,600 | $6,820,600 | $6,300,700 |

## POSSIBLE REPERCUSSIONS OF CUTBACKS

The administration was well aware of the possibility that cutbacks might lead to renewed interest in unionization among the professional staff. John Conger, the personnel manager, identified the immediate costs to the Museum of collective bargaining. First, more time would be spent in negotiating contracts. Second, there was a high probability that the final contract agreement would be more costly to the Museum.

Mr. Hoving stated that the union would have little overall impact on the Museum. "There are very few things they could bargain for. Salaries of curators are at the level of university professors, working conditions are excellent, as is the grievance procedure. A union would actually make management's position stronger. It would absolutely define the areas of bargaining as stipulated by the NLRB. The staff would have much less say on policy matters."

Mr. Herrick noted that "the chances are pretty good that if we decide to have layoffs there may be a professional union. But if there is, that wouldn't be the end of the world."

### Question

What actions, if any, would you tentatively recommend as a means of reducing the budgeted deficit?

## Case 9–4

## MASSACHUSETTS EYE AND EAR INFIRMARY (B)*

In addition to stressing the cost accounting advantages possessed by the split cost accounting system at Massachusetts Eye and Ear Infirmary (see Case 5–3), Mr. Charles Wood believed the system possessed some important attributes for the Infirmary's management control process: He commented:

> The split cost accounting system is a significant tool for stabilizing hospital budget forecasts. Presently, hospital administrators have a single figure with which to work: the so-called "per diem all-inclusive room rate." In this per diem system, unexpected declines in patient days can lead to serious "block" revenue losses. With the split cost accounting system at MEEI, there are three cost categories with a potential for adjustment: per patient revenue from the one-time hospitaliza-

---

* This case was prepared by Patricia O'Brien under the direction of David W. Young, Harvard School of Public Health.

tion charge (related to number of admissions), revenue from the daily room rate charge (related to length of stay), and revenue from the clinical care units charge (related to the intensity of clinical care given).

With the per diem system, it is extremely difficult to put one's finger on where problems are, and therefore, when adjustments are indicated there is a danger that they will be made in the wrong areas. With the split cost accounting system, however, with its separate areas clearly identified, we can easily see which areas are affected by changes in volume, and adjustments can be made accordingly.

Because each of these categories has a unit measurement which is rather closely aligned to what actually goes on in the hospital, I can more accurately measure the degree to which we are meeting our budget, and when we are over or under budget, we can take appropriate action in the area where the variance occurs. The result is that, despite inflation and the uncertainties of running a health care organization, we are able to operate very close to budget.

Ms. Margarete Arndt, Director of Patient Services at MEEI, highlighted the management control differences between the split cost accounting system and the traditional per diem system:

I think one can appreciate the advantages of our cost accounting system by looking at some hypothetical hospital activities for one year. For example, suppose a given hospital had 1,000 admissions during a year, 10,000 patient days, and 100,000 CCUs. Suppose now, that patient days decreased to, say, 9,000, while admissions remained the same, or admissions decreased to, say, 900, while length of stay remained the same; or suppose there was an increase or decrease in the intensity of care such that more or fewer CCUs were rendered. You could then make comparisons between the hospital using a split cost accounting system and one using a per diem rate to see the differences. What happens, of course, is that hospitals using a per diem system lose revenue as soon as patient days fall, while at the same time they may be delivering more intensive care on the existing patient days.

She pointed out that the system also had a major impact on the hospital's nursing department:

One of the real advantages of the split cost accounting system is that it has eliminated some unnecessary conflict in our decision making. Barbara Corey (Director of Nursing) no longer has to defend the amount of care she has to deliver. Once we have projected CCUs for the year, the nursing staff requirements are all but self-determined. The nursing department can be in a precarious position in hospitals that operate under per diem systems. It is probably the largest department and would be an easy target when cutting expenses becomes necessary. The average hours per care for nursing day statistics means nothing retrospectively because it reflects the census more than anything else. Further, as the length of stay gets shorter and shorter, all you leave for the acute care institution is the very sick-stay period for each patient. If nursing has to budget on a per diem basis, they lose, because they have no statistics to show how much care they delivered. But the CCUs deal with that problem by separating intensity of care from number of patient days.

Ms. Corey agreed, pointing out the impact of the system on her staffing decisions:

> Before the split cost accounting system, we really never had anything concrete to hang our hat on when it came to asking for additions to staff. While the system can, of course, backfire on you, it does give us a handle on how much time is being spent. The CCUs are based on an eight-hour shift, and we estimate that one nurse can handle about 12,900 CCUs a year. Margarete Arndt can predict pretty closely what our CCU needs are going to be for each fiscal year, and then it is a relatively simple matter for me to determine my staffing needs for the nursing department. Our curve of estimated CCUs is updated periodically. Once a year we study our patients for three months, but that's really the only additional effort involved. We didn't want to get into a process where we concurrently clock every service performed on each patient. Rather, while every patient gets the individual attention he or she may require, patients are *billed* according to the curve that goes with their procedure.

Mr. Anthony Reis supported these views, adding still another dimension.

> The split cost accounting system has allowed us to be more accurate in our budgetary process. Nursing is about 20 percent of our total payroll dollars, which makes it very significant and which in turn makes CCUs very important. Thus, by building CCUs into the budget process, we are able to have better control over the nursing portion of our budget.
>
> It is important to emphasize, though, that the use of CCUs does not automatically trigger decisions; rather, it helps us ask the right question. If CCUs are down, we first try to find out why they are down, then we can make decisions. So we have a better tool than the old patient day thing to try to make better management decisions.
>
> Thus, because the split cost accounting system isolates cost centers and presents a more accurate financial picture of the institution than the accounting system in general use today, it lends itself to more effective budget forecasting. Cost centers can be isolated for the predicted number of patient discharges for the coming year, and the accurate figures can be extrapolated for budgeting purposes. Taking this one logical step further, if we can prepare accurate budget forecasts based on this split cost accounting system, we then have the credibility and confidence to enter into prospective reimbursement programs with third-party payors.

## Questions

1. Using Ms. Arndt's hypothetical data, describe in detail the differences between the system in use at MEEI and one relying on a per diem system. How might MEEI lose under its system?
2. Enumerate the steps which MEEI might take in preparing its budget for a year. Is this process better or worse than one relying on a traditional per diem system?
3. What changes, if any, would you recommend be made in the system?

## Case 9–5

# FERNWOOD COLLEGE*

The nose of the United 727 aircraft sliced through the crisp, cool October morning sky. Jason Bourne like to fly, especially in the morning. Even airline coffee tasted good.

But the coffee was only a diversion. Bourne's mind shifted to his purpose. The D.C. to Columbus flight would take 45 minutes, and he needed the time to think. As his left hand mechanically pressed the plastic coffee cup to his lips, Bourne's right hand dug through the deep, Italian-leather attaché case. There he found the president's letter. With his forefinger and thumb, Bourne pinched the six frayed white pages, and his eyes, like waterbugs on a pond, raced through the letter for the umpteenth time.

The letter contained a recommendation from Thomas Hartman, President of Fernwood College, to the finance committee of the Board of Trustees, suggesting a $550,000 supplemental allocation to the 1979–80 budget. Late that same Friday afternoon, the finance committee, of which Bourne was the youngest member, was to discuss this subject. Jason was unsure whether he could go along with the president's recommendations. He was especially concerned with the president's proposal that $207,000 of the allocation be used for an increase in compensation for faculty and administration.

Bourne knew that the nine members of the finance committee were split into two camps: four who sided with the president on all compensation issues and four who, for various reasons, did not always follow the president's recommendations. Bourne wasn't sure which camp he fell into, but he was sure of one thing: the meeting that afternoon would be long and heated.

## Background

Fernwood College was located in Fernwood, Ohio, a city of about 5,000 people located 20 miles south of Columbus. It was founded in 1866 as an academy under the patronage of the Episcopal Church. Fernwood had an average enrollment of 2,200 students, a faculty of about 160 full-time persons (175 Full-Time Equivalents) and a roster of more than 15,000 living alumni. It was coeducational, undergraduate, and primarily a liberal arts college. In recent years, several types of vocational programs had been added that emphasized the importance of preparation for a career.

Fernwood's financial affairs were regarded by the administration as "excellent." Revenues regularly exceeded expectations, private donors contributed

---

* This case was written by Richard J. Parsons and Robert E. Harvey, MBA 1980, Colgate Darden Graduate School of Business Administration, under the supervision of Professor John L. Snook.  Distributed by HBS Case Services, Harvard Business School, Boston, Mass. 02163.

record amounts, and the value of endowment assets increased significantly. Exhibit 1 shows sources and uses of College funds for 1977–79.

## Governance

The college was governed by a Board of Trustees of 45 members (42 elected, 3 ex-officio). They were elected, respectively, by the Alumni Association (15),

**Exhibit 1**

Fernwood College
Comparison of Educational and General
Expenditures and Mandatory Transfers
For the Years Ended June 30, 1979, 1978, and 1977

| | *Dollars Amounts* | | | *Percent* | | |
|---|---|---|---|---|---|---|
| | *1979* | *1978* | *1977* | *1979* | *1978* | *1977* |
| Unrestricted sources: | | | | | | |
| Tuition | $ 8,926,283 | $ 8,293,989 | $ 7,574,181 | 72.3 | 72.7 | 72.7 |
| Summer term fees | 134,197 | 56,021 | 65,627 | 1.1 | .5 | .6 |
| English language program fees | 391,789 | 283,993 | 314,104 | 3.2 | 2.5 | 3.0 |
| Other student fees | 183,463 | 180,618 | 170,788 | 1.5 | 1.6 | 1.6 |
| Total student fees | 9,635,732 | 8,814,621 | 8,124,700 | 78.1 | 77.3 | 77.9 |
| Gifts | 715,293 | 655,778 | 632,861 | 5.8 | 5.8 | 6.1 |
| Endowment income distributed | 453,212 | 412,631 | 349,918 | 3.7 | 3.6 | 3.4 |
| Other general sources | 160,889 | 100,426 | 86,275 | 1.3 | .9 | .8 |
| Auxiliary enterprises contribution margin | 97,834 | 164,124 | 93,626 | .7 | 1.4 | .9 |
| Total unrestricted sources | 11,062,960 | 10,147,580 | 9,287,380 | 89.6 | 89.0 | 89.1 |
| Restricted current funds used | 1,281,410 | 1,249,510 | 1,137,066 | 10.4 | 11.0 | 10.9 |
| Total provided | 12,344,370 | 11,397,090 | 10,424,446 | 100.0 | 100.0 | 100.0 |
| Deduct amounts used for: | | | | | | |
| Additions to current funds | 118,070 | 121,886 | 34,814 | | | |
| | $12,226,300 | $11,275,224 | $10,389,632 | | | |
| Instruction and research: | | | | | | |
| General | $ 4,546,648 | $ 4,265,100 | $ 3,945,946 | 37.2 | 37.8 | 38.0 |
| Summer term | 84,514 | 43,984 | 44,568 | .7 | .4 | .4 |
| English language program | 338,999 | 188,568 | 217,338 | 2.8 | 1.7 | 2.1 |
| Institutes | 139,998 | 132,636 | 112,708 | 1.1 | 1.2 | 1.1 |
| Academic development | 11,060 | 20,562 | 68,845 | .1 | .2 | .7 |
| Research | 75,187 | 69,054 | 37,170 | .6 | .6 | .3 |
| Total instruction and research | 5,196,406 | 4,719,904 | 4,426,575 | 42.5 | 41.9 | 42.6 |
| Library and audiovisual | 412,808 | 385,284 | 356,893 | 3.4 | 3.4 | 3.4 |
| Academic administration | 278,671 | 153,957 | 145,269 | 2.3 | 1.4 | 1.4 |
| Student services | 884,480 | 814,091 | 705,611 | 7.2 | 7.2 | 6.8 |
| Athletic equipment and game costs | 243,975 | 211,790 | 169,792 | 2.0 | 1.9 | 1.6 |
| Institutional support | 1,481,787 | 1,450,996 | 1,366,446 | 12.1 | 12.9 | 13.1 |
| Educational plant operation | 1,549,236 | 1,489,781 | 1,335,817 | 12.7 | 13.2 | 12.9 |
| Unfunded pension payments | 300,912 | 297,691 | 286,722 | 2.5 | 2.6 | 2.9 |
| Student financial aid grants | 1,876,469 | 1,746,905 | 1,594,219 | 15.3 | 15.5 | 15.3 |
| Mandatory transfers, net | 1,556 | 4,825 | 2,288 | | | |
| | $12,226,300 | $11,275,224 | $10,389,632 | 100.0 | 100.0 | 100.0 |

the Ohio East Area Conference of the Episcopal Church (6), and the Ohio West Area Conference of the Episcopal Church (6); the remainder were elected as trustees-at-large (15). Each trustee was elected for a three-year term; after three consecutive three-year terms, rotation was mandatory.

The trustees constituted a working board, were generally kept well informed by the president, and took an active and strong interest in policy determination for the institution. Much of the work of the board was conducted by the various committees (Executive, Organization, Finance, Endowments, Student Affairs, Academic Affairs, University Facilities, and University Relations). The Board of Trustees met three times during the school year (October, February, and May). Committee meetings took place on Fridays, with the full Board meeting on the following Saturday.

## The $550,000 Allocation

Fernwood College's annual budget for 1979–80 had been approved by the Board of Trustees at their February 1979 meeting. The February budget was based on an enrollment of 2,220 students. The actual enrollment for 1979–80 was considerably higher (2,290 actual in the Fall Quarter, 2,250 estimated in the Winter Quarter, and 2,210 estimated in the Spring Quarter). The higher enrollment made necessary a revision of the school's budget in order to accommodate the resulting increase in tuition income of approximately $550,000. The finance committee had been asked to consider the president's proposed use of the unallocated funds. He suggested the sum be divided among the following areas: (1) accumulated unrestricted reserve for operations; (2) salaries and compensation; (3) accumulated plant deficits; (4) deferred maintenance and special project needs; and (5) academic projects.

## The Finance Committee Meeting

The October Finance Committee meeting began promptly at 2 P.M. In attendance were: James Matlock, Chairman (attorney); Bernard Osterman (chairman of board, engineering firm); Peter Chancellor (vice president, IBM); Victor Fontine (investment banker); David Spaulding (professor, Ohio college); Gretchen Beaumont (publisher); Jason Bourne (graduate student); Noel Holcroft (bank president); Brandon Scofield (attorney); Munro St. Clair, Chairman, Board of Trustees (attorney); Thomas Hartman, President, Fernwood; and Merle Smit, Vice President for Business Affairs, Fernwood. The major item of business was the $550,000 allocation. Chairman Matlock opened the meeting by referring to the five recommendations made by President Hartman in the letter he had sent to the committee members 10 days earlier. The recommendations from the president's letter were as follows:

**I. Accumulated, Unrestricted Reserve for Operations**

*Summary Statement*

1. Neither the Board nor the Committee on Finance has established a target for the contingency reserve. The Committee has given the administration

**Exhibit 2**
Accumulated Unrestricted Reserve for Operations

| *End of* | *Total* | *Enrollment Coverage** |
|---|---|---|
| 1973–74 .................. | $250,000 | 89 |
| 1974–75 .................. | 28,000 | 9 |
| 1975–76 .................. | 43,000 | 13 |
| 1976–77 .................. | 78,000 | 22 |
| 1977–78 .................. | 199,000 | 50 |
| 1978–79 .................. | 318,000 | 74 |
| 1979–80 (projected) ........ | 475,000 | 100 |

* Accumulated reserve as related to tuition per student.

a guideline that the annual contingency in the February budget should be not less than 1 percent of the total budget ($165,000 for 1979–80 February budget). A reserve which allows for a 5 percent decrease in enrollment in one year should be more than adequate to deal with a random fluctuation. The reserve will need to increase in size at least as rapidly as tuition rises merely to provide the same enrollment coverage. The 1 percent guideline will provide sufficient reserve funds to increase the enrollment coverage by 20 students per year (see Exhibit 2).

*Recommendation*

We should continue to add to that reserve until we have a coverage of 100 students (Exhibit 2). When that is achieved, we can evaluate our position. We would need to set aside about *$157,000* of the expected current supplemental allocation for that purpose in 1979–80.

## II. Salaries and Compensation

*Summary Statements*

1. Since 1971–72 real salary for a representative faculty member has dropped almost 15 percent; total compensation has dropped about 6 percent. (See Exhibit 3 for a table showing Consumer Price Index changes and salaries and compensation for continuing faculty.)

**Exhibit 3**
Consumer Price Index Change and Salaries and Compensation for Continuing Faculty

| | *Prices Percent Change* | | *Tuition Percent Change* | | *Salaries Percent Change* | | *Compensation Percent Change* | |
|---|---|---|---|---|---|---|---|---|
| *Year* | *Annual* | *Cum. 1971–72* | *Annual* | *Cum. 1971–72* | *Annual* | *Cum. 1971–72* | *Annual* | *Cum. 1971–72* |
| 1972–73 ....... | 4.6 | 4.6 | 3.1 | 3.1 | 4.0 | 4.0 | 6.6 | 6.6 |
| 1972–74 ....... | 9.8 | 14.9 | 5.0 | 8.2 | 3.9 | 8.0 | 5.2 | 12.1 |
| 1974–75 ....... | 10.6 | 27.1 | 5.7 | 14.3 | 7.6 | 16.3 | 6.5 | 19.4 |
| 1975–76 ....... | 6.5 | 35.3 | 9.8 | 25.5 | 7.7 | 25.2 | 7.6 | 28.5 |
| 1976–77 ....... | 6.0 | 43.4 | 9.8 | 37.8 | 7.1 | 34.1 | 8.3 | 39.2 |
| 1977–78 ....... | 6.9 | 53.3 | 7.4 | 48.0 | 7.5 | 44.2 | 8.2 | 50.6 |
| 1978–79 ....... | 10.0 | 68.6 | 9.0 | 61.2 | 6.9 | 54.1 | 7.9 | 62.5 |
| Projected 1979–80 ..... | 12.5 | 89.7 | 10.2 | 76.1 | 10.0 | 69.5 | 10.5 | 79.4 |

2. We had made steady progress from 1975 through 1978; real salaries increased 4 percent and total compensation 6 percent during that three-year period.
3. Our budget and salary decisions for 1978–79 were intended to continue that upward trend. Rapid inflation (10%), however, caused a decrease in real salaries of 3.1 percent and a decrease in total compensation of 2.1 percent last year.
4. Our budget and salary decisions for 1979–80 also were intended to increase real salaries and compensation. However, if the present 13 percent inflation rate continued for the entire academic year (through August 1980), real salaries will fall another 3 percent, total compensation another 2.5 percent.
5. The estimated salary and compensation for 1978–79 are as follows:

| | |
|---|---|
| Wages and salaries | $6,000,000 |
| Fringe benefits | 1,455,000 |
| Total compensation | $7,455,000 |

Because not all fringe benefits are wage-related, we estimate that a 1 percent increase in wages and salaries would cost about $69,000 if discretionary fringe benefits are included as well.

| | | Costs ($000) | |
|---|---|---|---|
| | *Type of Adjustment* | *1979–80* | *1980–81* |
| *A.* | 3%—full year, eff. Sept. 1 | $207 | $207 |
| | 5/6 year, eff. Nov. 1 | 173 | 207 |
| | 2/3 year, eff. Jan. 1 | 138 | 207 |
| *B.* | 2%—full year, eff. Sept. 1 | 138 | 138 |
| | 5/6 year, eff. Nov. 1 | 115 | 138 |
| | 2/3 year, eff. Jan. 1 | 52 | 138 |
| *C.* | 1%—full year, eff. Sept. 1 | 69 | 69 |
| | 5/6 year, eff. Nov. 1 | 58 | 69 |
| | 2/3 year, eff. Jan. 1 | 46 | 69 |

*Recommendation*

We recommend a *3 percent* adjustment including all fringe benefits effective retroactively to September 1, 1979. This move will cost approximately *$207,000* in both 1979–80 and 1980–81, which represents just over one half of the funds available from the supplemental allocation after setting aside $157,000 for the unrestricted contingency reserve.

## III. Accumulated Plant Deficits

*Summary Statements*

1. Over the last decade we have accumulated substantial deficits in the plant accounts. These deficits are of three types:
   *a.* *Land*—a result of outlays for land acquisition in excess of inflow of funds from the sale of excess property.
   *b.* *Plant Projects*—the result of accumulated interest charges arising because available plant funds have not been sufficient to meet project costs. The balance has been borrowed against pledges. The interest

deficit continues to grow as long as total plant fund balances are negative.

2. These deficits have been financed by borrowing from current funds. At the end of 1976–1977, our auditors, Ernst & Whinney, urged (but did not order) us to develop a mechanism to reduce and eventually to eliminate such deficits. Our response was to adopt a policy that designated annually $25,000 or 20 percent of the undesignated plant gifts, whichever is larger, to reduce these deficit balances. In 1977–78, $51,000 was allocated to these deficits; in 1978–79, $26,000, for a total of $77,000 over the two-year period. The table below shows the balances in these three types of plant deficit amounts over the recent years:

| | *Plant Deficits End of Year ($000)* | | | |
|---|---|---|---|---|
| | *1975–76* | *1976–77* | *1977–78* | *1978–79* |
| 1. Land | $129 | $137 | $159 | $ 41 |
| 2. Total plant projects | 309 | 288 | 275 | 328 |
| 3. Interest accumulated | 56 | 133 | 176 | 189 |
| 4. Total | 494 | 542 | 611 | 558 |
| 5. Less cumulative reduction | — | — | 51 | 77 |
| 6. Balances | $494 | $542 | $560 | $481 |

*Recommendation*

Since these facilities are in use and no depreciation expense is charged against current operations, it is appropriate that the current interest being accumulated on these plant debts be carried as an expense in the budget. We recommend that *$40,000* of the projected contingency be applied to meet the interest costs on the plant deficit accounts for 1979–80.

**IV. Deferred Maintenance and Special Projects Needs**

*Summary Statements*

1. In the 1979–80 budget we budgeted $165,000 to fund special projects and deferred maintenance. The particular projects to be undertaken in any year are determined by the administration.
2. Several such projects (see below) have a high priority with the administration but could not be funded in the present budget.

*Recommendations*

The following allocations should be made for maintenance and special projects.

1. Conversion of the Student Union area formerly occupied by the bowling alleys to an area to be used by students as a coffee house and pub. *($35,000).*
2. Conversion of the public safety and buildings and grounds communication system from VHF to UHF *($25,000).*
3. Additional hookup of electrical power users (motors, lights) to the Buildings and Grounds mini-computer to control energy usage *($25,000).*
4. Acceleration of the conversion and upgrading of administrative computer operations *($36,000).*

**V. Academic Projects**

*Recommendations*

1. We would like to recommend that *$25,000* be designated for academic projects such as the following: books for the library, expansion of the Learning Resources Center; and modest funding for student research projects.

Discussion centered first on the compensation increases. Chairman Matlock first explained to new committee members the actions taken regarding compensation at the February meeting. The committee had then approved an average 10 percent increase which was intended to cover inflation plus some real economic increase. Projected inflation at that time was 9 percent. The rate at the time of October meeting was 13 percent.

Mr. Spalding moved adoption of all of President Hartman's proposals. Extensive discussion, particularly of the compensation increase, followed:

*Mr. Osterman:* I second. We all know that the faculty is the life-blood of Fernwood. Despite the Board's sincere efforts in the past to improve the faculty's real purchasing power, the faculty has fallen behind. [Osterman referred to the figures shown in Exhibit 3.] If President Hartman says that faculty morale is hurting due to inadequate compensation levels, I believe him. We pay him to understand the day-to-day operations of the school. If the president says a salary adjustment is needed, then I back him on it.

*Mr. Holcroft:* I'm opposed to any increases in compensation *at this time.* This committee sets a dangerous precedent in reopening the issue of salaries. Last February we adopted, after much discussion, a budget which we honestly believed would provide adequate measures for keeping faculty and staff compensation ahead in real terms. At some point in time, and I think this is that time, this Board must stand firm. We've done the best we can, and we'll continue to try, but not mid-year in the budget!

*Mr. Scofield:* I really wonder if we have any choice but to approve the 3 percent compensation package recommended by President Hartman. Hasn't the Faculty Governance Committee already learned that there is a "windfall" $550,000? I understand from what I read in the student newspaper that a representative for the faculty stated that he expected that the lion's share of the $550,000 would be used to improve compensation for faculty and staff.

*Mr. Holcroft:* Since the $550,000 "windfall" resulted from an unexpected increase in enrollment, does that mean that, if we approved a compensation increase now, we could cut back compensation in the future if enrollment unexpectedly fell? Something tells me that the faculty will not view this issue as a two-way street.

*Mr. Spaulding:* As Mr. Osterman said, the faculty of Fernwood is the school's greatest asset. Fernwood's salaries must remain competitive.

*Mr. Fontine:* [interrupting] First, who says that we need to be "competitive"—the market is glutted with talented Ph.D.s. President Hartman has told us himself that every time the school has an open faculty position, nearly 100 applicants vie for the position. Maybe our faculty is paid too much? Which brings me to my second point: My understanding is that our faculty is well paid relative to their colleagues throughout the country. I recently read in the August 1979 issue of the *Chronicle of Higher Education* that the average compensation for Fernwood faculty in all three categories (i.e., professor, associate, and assistant) is in the highest quintile distribution among four-year colleges.

*Mr. Osterman:* I have a question for President Hartman: the survey referred to by Mr. Fontine includes all four-year colleges throughout the country. I'm particularly interested in how Fernwood compares with colleges like itself in the Midwest. Have you any data on this?

*President Hartman:* According to a recent survey among 24 colleges in the Associated Colleges of the Midwest, Fernwood's average compensation ranks fourth. [President Hartman distributed the list of colleges. The top four colleges were Kalamazoo with average compensation of $27,096; Carleton, $26,913; Oberlin, $26,230; and Fernwood $25,517. The median was $24,300, the lower quartile was $23,500, and the lowest was $20,674.]

*Ms. Beaumont:* We must remember that this committee and the full Board made a commitment four years ago to maintain and improve the real income level of staff and faculty. During the past eight months, inflation heated up and ate into what we thought last February was an improvement in real income. We must not forget our commitment.

*Chairman Matlock:* I agree with Ms. Beaumont, our Board cannot forget our commitment made four years ago. I am concerned, however, that the comparative measuring stick that we have used in the past to gauge real income against inflation is adequate. I am referring to the Consumer Price Index. Although I'm not an economist, I understand that the CPI can overstate real inflation. My understanding is that the CPI includes the effect of rising mortgage rates, which is a factor that does not affect people who already own a house. In addition, we all know that the cost of living in Fernwood, Ohio, is lower than most places in the country.

*Mr. Fontine:* "I want the committee members to remember that last February I voted in favor of the 10 percent compensation increase for 1979–80. At that time, the committee agreed to my proposal that future compensation for faculty and administration would be contingent on improvements in efficiency. The Faculty Governance Committee was told this back in February. Why haven't I heard during this meeting anything about improvements in efficiency? I ask you, President Hartman, what improvements have taken place?"

*President Hartman:* I think this group will recall that in February there was considerable debate as to what exactly "efficiency" meant for an academic institution. I don't believe we adequately defined efficiency. I will report that the Faculty Governance Committee and my staff are committed to increasing the student/faculty ratio from the present 14.5/1 ratio to 15/1. Also, many faculty members have become involved in special tutorial programs for students of exceptional ability.

*Mr. Chancellor:* I, too, am concerned with the efficiency issue. Perhaps we should set aside some time later to adequately define the term. The point I wish to make at this time has to do with the accumulated plant deficits. I believe that President Hartman's figure of $40,000 is horrendously too low. There should be more attention given to this. Our auditors have strongly recommended that we develop definitive plans for funding these deficits. I don't believe that our current plan will accomplish this. We must be more fiscally responsible here. I recommend we use President Hartman's original $40,000 together with the $207,000 originally earmarked for compensation increases to extinguish part of the accumulated plant deficit.

*Chairman Matlock:* Before our committee considers another recommendation, we first must vote on Mr. Spaulding's motion that we accept all of President Hartman's proposals. Are there any last questions or comments relevant to Mr. Spaulding's motion?

*Mr. Bourne:* I have a question for President Hartman. In your table showing a comparison of the CPI to salaries and compensation (Exhibit 3), you used 1971–72 as your base year. Why?

*President Hartman:* It was in 1971–72 that faculty compensation was considered to be at its peak level of real purchasing power.

*Chairman Matlock:* Any other questions or comments? If not, let's vote.

## Question

How should Mr. Bourne vote?

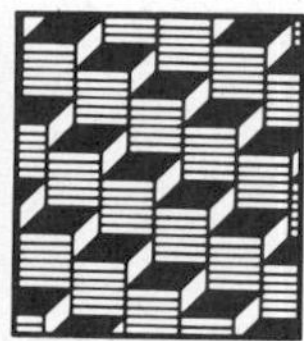

# chapter 10

# Control of Operations

The third phase in the management control cycle is that of operations and measurement. Although described as a single phase, it actually consists of two separate but related activities: control of operations and measurement of output. This chapter describes the tools and techniques that are useful in the control of operations. The next chapter examines the question of output measurement.

## ENCUMBRANCE ACCOUNTING

For reasons discussed earlier, the budget is a more important control device in a nonprofit organization than in a profit-oriented company. In government organizations, amounts appropriated in accordance with the budget cannot legally be exceeded, and violators are subject to criminal penalties under the federal Anti-Deficiency Act (R.S. Sec. 3679) and corresponding legislation in most states.[1] Furthermore appropriations for operating purposes usually cannot be encumbered after the end of the fiscal year; that is, they *lapse.*

[1] As a practical matter, punishment under these acts is rare. In the Department of Defense there have been 245 violations in the past 15 years. In 1977, because of a breakdown in its control system, the Army spent $225 million more than was appropriated, but no one went to jail, much less paid back the $225 million. Nevertheless, the possibility of criminal action is always present.

There is therefore a natural tendency not to permit appropriated funds to go unused. The encumbrance accounting system is designed to avoid spending more than the amount appropriated; in practice, it also discourages spending *less* than the amount appropriated.

## The Accounting Process

An appropriation by a state or local government is an authority to *encumber* (a federal appropriation is an authority to *obligate,* which means the same thing). An encumbrance arises when the organization becomes obligated to pay for goods or services. Usually, this occurs when a contract is entered into, or when personnel work; at the time they work they become entitled to salaries and related benefits.

The first step in an encumbrance accounting system is to record the amount appropriated for each fund. The next step is to charge the appropriated amount for encumbrances. If the legislature appropriates $1,000,000 for operations in 1983, this amount is set up in the accounts, and this amount is reduced as contracts are entered into, so the accounts show at all times how much of the $1,000,000 has not yet been encumbered. The organization has complied with the law if, by the end of 1983, it has not encumbered more than $1,000,000, whether or not the goods or services contracted for have been received, and whether or not cash disbursements to vendors or employees have been made.

When goods or services are received, the accounting system records this fact. A similar record is made in a business accounting system, the entry being a credit to accounts payable or cash and a debit to an asset or expense account. From this point on, the accounting process can be the same in a nonprofit organization as in a business.

In a business, however, resources are held in asset accounts until the period in which they are used, at which time they are charged as expenses to responsibility centers and programs. By contrast, some nonprofit organizations charge responsibility centers and programs as soon as the amounts are encumbered, and others make these charges when the goods or services are acquired, rather than when they are consumed. The latter is called the *expenditure* basis of accounting. Furthermore, the charge may be made to the responsibility center that incurs the encumbrance or the expenditure, which is not necessarily the same as the responsibility center that uses the resources.

> ***Example:*** Consider $1,000 of supplies to be used by an operating agency but purchased by a central supply office. The supplies are purchased in March and consumed in April. Under encumbrance accounting, the $1,000 is recorded as a charge to the central supply office in the month of March; it is never recorded as an expense of the operating agency. Under accrual accounting, it is recorded as an expense of the operating agency in the month of April.

As explained in Chapter 3, these differences can have a tremendous effect on the amount of resources reported by a given responsibility center.

## Reconciling Encumbrance and Expense Accounting

It is perfectly feasible to design an accounting system that keeps track of encumbrances, expenditures, and expenses. This is accomplished by the use of working capital accounts that hold costs in suspense until the resources are consumed. The inventory accounts in a business accounting system serve this purpose, and inventory accounts can be used for the same purpose in organizations that record encumbrances. In addition, such organizations need an account called *Undelivered Orders* that holds items in suspense between the time the contract is placed and the time the goods are received.

The procedure is illustrated in Exhibit 10–1. In the month of April, labor services of $100,000 were used, and orders were placed for $80,000 of material and $60,000 of other services (e.g., a contract was let for painting buildings). Total encumbrances for the agency in April were therefore $240,000.

Labor is accounted for essentially the same on an encumbrance basis as on an expense basis, so labor expense is here assumed to be $100,000. In order to record material expense and services expense, however, two types of working capital accounts are necessary. One is *Undelivered Orders.* As orders are placed, they are debited to this account, and as the services are rendered or material received, the account is credited. Thus, for $70,000 of services performed in April (e.g., the buildings were painted and $10,000

**Exhibit 10–1**
Reconciliation of Encumbrance and Expense Accounting Transactions for April ($000)

| *Encumbrance Basis* | |
|---|---|
| Labor | 100 |
| Material ordered | 80 → |
| Services ordered | 60 → |
| Obligations | 240 |

*Undelivered Orders*

| Debit | | Credit | |
|---|---|---|---|
| Balance | 200 | Services | 70 → |
| Material | 80 | Material | 50 → Inventory Received |
| Services | 60 | | |
| Balance | 220 | | |

*Inventory*

| Debit | | Credit | |
|---|---|---|---|
| Balance | 90 | Used | 40 → |
| Received | 50 | | |
| Balance | 100 | | |

| *Expense Basis* | |
|---|---|
| Labor | 100 |
| Services | 70 |
| Material | 40 |
| Total expenses | 210 |

To reconcile: Change in Working Capital + Expenses = Encumbrance

| | |
|---|---|
| Undelivered orders (220 − 200) | 20 |
| Inventory (100 − 90) | 10 |
| Total | 30 + 210 = 240 |

of work was done under contracts let in earlier months), a credit is made to Undelivered Orders, with a corresponding debit to an expense account. The undelivered orders account has no counterpart in a profit-oriented company.

The other working capital account is *Inventory,* and it has the same nature in a nonprofit organization as in a profit-oriented business; namely, it records the amount of material that is on hand at any time, which, by definition, is an asset at that time. In other words, it holds the cost of material between the time of acquisition and the time of consumption. In the above example, $50,000 of material was received in April, reducing Undelivered Orders by $50,000 and increasing Inventory by the same amount. In April, $40,000 of material was issued from inventory for use in current operations, so Inventory was credited $40,000, with a corresponding debit to an expense account.

As Exhibit 10–1 shows, total expenses for April can be reconciled to total encumbrances for April by measuring the changes in the two working capital accounts.

A program budget can reflect these working capital accounts. It can show the amount of expense authorized for each program, and also the amounts authorized for changes in working capital (which may be either positive or negative). The amount appropriated is the algebraic sum of these amounts.

### Other Working Capital Accounts

The mechanism described above provides a way of holding charges in suspense between the *time* of acquisition and the time of consumption. Working capital accounts can also hold items in suspense so as to differentiate between the *place* of acquisition and of consumption. Again, this is a function that inventory accounts serve in a business. All the costs of manufacturing goods are accumulated in Goods in Process Inventory accounts until the manufacturing process is completed, at which time the responsibility for them is shifted from the manufacturing department to the marketing department. Similarly, the costs incurred by service centers in nonprofit organizations can be held in suspense in inventory accounts until the goods or services are furnished to the responsibility centers that benefit from them.

## FINANCIAL CONTROL OVER SPENDING

The approved operating budget, consisting both of planned expenses and expected outputs, is the principal financial guideline for operations. Presumably, management wants the organization to operate in a way that is consistent with this plan, *unless* there is a good reason to depart from it. This qualification is important, for it means that the control process is necessarily more complicated than simply insisting that the organization do what the budget prescribes. The purpose of the management control process is to assure that objectives are accomplished effectively and efficiently. If, because of changed conditions, a different course of action than is specified in the budget will do a better job of attaining objectives, that course of action should be followed. Thus, the control mechanism should have two aspects: (1) it should assure that in the absence of reasons to do otherwise the plan set forth in the budget is adhered to, and (2) it should provide a way of changing the plan if conditions warrant.

## Types of Control

The total amount in the approved budget is ordinaily a ceiling that is not supposed to be exceeded; indeed, as discussed in the previous section, if there is an appropriation mechanism, it is a ceiling that legally cannot be exceeded. Within this total, more detailed controls are sometimes desirable. These usually take the form of detailed ceilings, but in some cases they are floors.

> ***Example:*** In a recent year the Congress required the National Science Foundation to spend *not more than* $5 million for construction of a very large array telescope, and *not less than* $25 million on energy research.

Although the budget may contain a detailed listing of amounts for expense elements, these amounts are normally guides, rather than ceilings which cannot be exceeded. The primary focus should be on the program and on the responsibility center that is charged with executing the program, rather than on what specific resources are to be used. Some years ago, control systems focused instead on individual line items of expense, that is, so much for personnel, so much for supplies, so much for travel, and so forth. The shift from this "line-item control" to program control is one of the most significant developments in recent years. Nevertheless, many nonprofit organizations persist in using line-item controls.

***Object Restrictions.*** The shift, however, should be one of emphasis, for it is desirable that control be exercised over spending for certain line items, even though the primary focus is on programs. A line-item restriction means that operating managers are not given complete freedom to decide the best way to use resources in executing their program, but instead must obtain top management approval for expenditures which exceed the line item amount by more than a given percentage. The item "Travel for professional meetings" is a common example. There is a delicate balance between the restrictions that are desirable in order to curb imprudent spending and the restrictions that are undesirable because they unduly limit the manager's ability to make decisions on how best to use available resources.

***Personnel Restrictions.*** One common restriction is on the number of personnel. In most nonprofit organizations, personnel not only constitute by far the largest item of expense but also indirectly cause many of the other items of expense. (One additional person requires an additional desk, telephone, supplies, travel, and so on.) Further, if a person is added to the organization, there tends to be a permanent increase in its costs, for it is much easier to increase the size of an organization than to shrink it. Personnel additions therefore need to be carefully monitored. In some situations, the most effective way to do this is with a personnel ceiling; in others a ceiling may unduly restrict management flexibility, and lead to the wrong mix between personnel costs and costs for contractual services, for example. In any event, if a person is to be added to an existing program, approval of higher authority usually is required.

***Other Restrictions.*** Responsibility center managers also may be required to obtain approval before making commitments for supplies, outside contracts, and items of equipment above a certain dollar amount. This approval may require the consent of several higher levels of authority depending on the size of the organization and the dollar amount involved in the proposed purchase.

## Flow of Spending Authority

The flow of spending authority within an organization should generally follow the lines of operating management responsibility; that is, spending should be authorized from higher levels to lower levels according to the formal organizational hierarchy. Difficulties arise when funds are received directly by organizational units, rather than through the organizational hierarchy. If it does not control the distribution of spending authority, senior management often cannot exercise appropriate control over its subordinate elements because it does not have "the power of the purse."

*Examples:* 1. In some universities, each school is an independent "profit center," with complete autonomy in the use of its tuition, research, and other funds. While such a system presumably gives the individual schools an incentive to be efficient, it also limits the ability of the university's central administration to exercise control over them. The result can be a situation in which the university's larger educational goals are compromised because of an inability to cross-subsidize among its schools.

2. In New York City, mental health services are provided to the public on a contractual basis by private institutions. These institutions are supposed to be accountable to the city's Department of Mental Health; however, funds for the operation of these institutions are provided directly by the state, and the institutions therefore tend to disregard the city agency.

***Funds from Several Sources.*** If funds are received from several outside sources, the head of an operating organization is inhibited from making good decisions on the best use of operating resources because the separate funds are compartmentalized. In the Navy, ships have been known to steam on unneeded missions, even though they lacked vital parts for radar, because they had ample funds for fuel, but no funds for radar parts. The overall effectiveness of the ship would have been enhanced if less money had been spent on steaming and an equivalent amount had been spent on radar repair.

Also, if there are several funding sources, an operating organization can play one funding source against another. For example, although top management may desire that the overall level of spending be reduced, the operating manager can sometimes defeat this desire by finding one source, among the several available, which provides additional funds.

Finally, if funds are received from several sources, measurement of performance is difficult because each funding source tends to focus on the aspect of operations in which it is interested, but no one may focus on the operation as a whole.

## The Accounting System

The central part of the system for reporting internal operating information is the accounting system. It is central because accounting deals with monetary amounts, and money provides the best way of aggregating and summarizing information about the heterogeneous elements of input. (It does not follow that the most *important* information is accounting information.) A few comments about the accounting system are appropriate here.

***Double Entry.*** In the first place, the accounting system should be a double-entry system, that is, a system in which debits equal credits. A sentence like the preceding would never appear in a description of the accounting system of a profit-oriented company because double-entry accounting is taken for granted in these companies. Some nonprofit organizations, however, including some very large government organizations, collect important types of information in single-entry systems. Information collected in a single-entry system is not likely to be reliable. Technically, it is a simple matter to convert such systems to double entry.

***Consistent with the Budget.*** A second important point to make about an accounting system is that it should be consistent with the budget. The budget states the approved plan for spending and the accounting system reports actual spending. Unless the two are consistent, there is no reliable way of finding out whether actual spending occurred according to plan. This does not mean that the accounting system should contain only the accounts that appear in the budget, however. Management usually needs more accounting detail than is suggested by the budget items, and it needs rearrangements of the basic data for various purposes. Nevertheless, there should be, as a part of the accounting system, accounts that match each item on the budget.

The usual reason an accounting system does not match the budget is that the budgeting system has been revised but the accounting system has not been revised to match it. This is often the case in organizations which have recently adopted program budgets. The task of designing a program budgeting system is difficult by itself, but the task of revising an accounting system is much more difficult—perhaps by a factor of 10 or even 100. It is not surprising, therefore, that the revision of the accounting system has not kept pace with the revision of the budget formulation process.

If accounts do not match the budget, it generally is possible to develop a mechanism for reconciling the two. This mechanism, called a *crosswalk*, is a rearrangement of the accounts so that they match the budget categories. The crosswalk is often not done on a careful basis, and in any event does not provide an assurance of accuracy that is associated with entries made in the debit-and-credit system.

***Integrated Systems.*** Not only should the budget and accounting data be consistent but it is desirable that the accounting system be an integral part of a total information system which reports on both outputs and inputs. Achievement of such integration is a difficult task, but some organizations are succeeding in it. The federal government, through its Federal Urban Information Systems Interagency Committee Program, has been encouraging municipalities to develop such integrated systems, and has provided substantial sums for this purpose. Such an integrated system includes budget and accounting information and also information on demography, physical and economic development programs, and public safety. Accounting data on costs are integrated with output data throughout the system.

## Budget Adjustments

In many nonprofit organizations, the total of the budget for a year constitutes an absolute ceiling which cannot be exceeded except under highly unusual circumstances. Nevertheless, changed circumstances will usually require changes in detailed spending requirements. There is therefore the problem of accommodating these detailed changes within the prescribed ceiling. There are two general techniques for solving this problem: contingency allowances and revisions. The choice between them is a matter of personal preference.

***Contingency Allowances.*** In this approach, amounts are set aside at various levels in the organization for unforeseen contingencies. Ordinarily, such amounts are not more than 5 percent of the budget for that level, but if these allowances exist at a number of levels, they can cumulate to considerably more than 5 percent of the total budget for the organization. Under this plan, the budgeted expenses for each responsibility center and program are targets which can be exceeded, if necessary, with the excess being absorbed by the contingency allowance.

An advantage of this approach is that increases in spending can be accommodated without the painful task of finding an offsetting decrease. A risk is that if there is a 5 percent contingency allowance, there may be a tendency to regard the actual ceiling as 105 percent of the target in all responsibility centers, thus defeating the purpose of the contingency allowances.

A variation of the contingency allowance is the practice of releasing somewhat less than the proportionate amount of funds in the early part of the year. For example, in an agency whose spending is expected to be spread evenly throughout the year, only 22 percent of the funds, rather than 25 percent, might be released in the first quarter. As the year progresses and spending needs become clearer, the contingency allowance thus created is allocated in subsequent releases to those responsibility centers that appear to need it the most.

***Revision Procedure.*** In the second approach, 100 percent of the authorized amount is divided among responsibility centers. Changed circumstances are accommodated by increasing the budget of one responsibility center and making a corresponding reduction in the budget of some other responsibility center(s). Under this plan the budget for each responsibility center is a ceiling; it cannot be exceeded without specific approval.

Although not an authorized practice in the second approach, operating managers frequently will tend to create an informal contingency allowance so as to avoid the necessity of seeking formal approval for changed spending needs. Thus, allowances exist in both approaches, even though they are not visible in the second type.

Whichever approach is used, it is important to recognize the likelihood that changes will be necessary, and the mechanism for making these changes should be well understood. Otherwise, the budget may not conform to the realities of the situation, and it will then not serve as a reliable plan against which actual performance can be measured.

## OTHER CONTROLS

In addition to the financial controls described above, people in an organization are guided or constrained by rules and procedures that state how specific matters are to be handled, what practices are encouraged and discouraged, and what activities are forbidden. The larger and more complex the organization, the larger the number of these rules. Also, a mature organization tends to have more formal rules and procedures than a young organization.

Many of these rules are necessary since similar situations arising in various places throughout the organization should be handled in a similar manner, and the rules help to ensure that this is done. Some rules, however, may have been devised to deal with situations that no longer exist, or they may unduly restrict the ability of managers to use good judgment. From time to time, an organization is well advised to review its rules and to prune out those that no longer serve a useful purpose. Otherwise, frustrations such as those implicit in the following apocryphal description of procurement procedures may impede the functioning of the organization:

> . . . If you want to buy a short length of coaxial cable, please fill out a requisition sheet, university budget form 16-j. (Use the orange form if the money is to come from operating funds, and blue if the money is to come from capital funds.) Never indent on any line more than five spaces or the form will be returned. Submit in triplicate to the Office of Budget Approval, Administration Building, Room 1619, attention Mrs. Bagley. After Mrs. Bagley initials the form signifying that you have the $38 in your budget, the form is sent to the Technical Buyer, located in Room 1823. There Mr. Ted Rosler puts out a request for bids. If there is only one coaxial cable distributor in the region, it presents difficulties, but they can be surmounted with a special Sole Source form, which should be approved by the Comptroller's Council of Purchases and Services. The Council meets bimonthly. To get on their agenda, you must submit, in duplicate. . . .[2]

## Project Control

The foregoing description has focused on the control of individual responsibility centers. Somewhat different techniques are appropriate for the control of projects, such as individual research projects or the building of a major capital asset. The differences arise principally because in responsibility center control the focus is on the work done in a specified period of time, such as a month, a quarter, or a year, whereas in project control, the focus is on the accomplishment of the project, which in many cases extends over a period of years. Space limitations preclude more than a brief description of project control.[3]

A project control system must take account of three aspects of the project, and of the interrelationships among them: (1) the cost of the work, (2) the quality of the work, and (3) the time required. The essentials of the system for doing this are as follows:

1. As near to the inception of the project as possible, the work to be done, the resources planned to do the work, and the anticipated time required are estimated. This estimate is made in terms of "work packages," which are relatively small units of work.[4] The responsibility centers responsible for doing the work are specified.

---

[2] By Frederick Brietenfeld, Jr., executive director, the Maryland Center for Public Broadcasting.

[3] For a more complete description, see Robert N. Anthony, John Dearden, and Norton M. Bedford, *Management Control Systems,* 5th ed. (Homewood, Ill.: Richard D. Irwin, 1984), chap. 20; David I. Cleland and William R. King, *Systems Analysis and Project Management* (New York: McGraw-Hill, 1968); for an excellent description of the management and behavioral aspects of project control, see Eileen Morley and Andrew Silver, "A Film Director's Approach to Managing Creativity," *Harvard Business Review,* March/April 1977, pp. 59–70.

[4] A "work package" is a measurable increment of work that can be related to a physical product, milestone, or other measurable indicator of progress. It should be of short duration with a discrete start and completion point, and the responsibility of a single organizational unit. Once the work package is begun, its budget and schedule must not change or the performance baseline will be lost.

2. Based on these statements, a work schedule and related budget are prepared. These show *(a)* the physical products, milestones, technical performance goals, or other indicators that will be used to measure output; *(b)* budgets for the cost expected to be incurred on each work package and for overhead costs; (c) the starting and completion time for each work package; and *(d)* the unit responsible for the work; and *(e)* the interdependencies among the work packages.
3. Records are kept of actual outputs and of actual costs incurred. These records should be entirely consistent with the definitions and accounting principles used in the work plans and budgets. Cost data are collected in a disciplined accounting system.
4. Reports are prepared from these records at frequent intervals, showing, both for the interval and cumulatively, significant differences between:
   *a.* Costs incurred for direct work performed and the budgeted costs of such work.
   *b.* Overhead costs incurred and budgeted overhead costs.
   *c.* Budgeted costs for work actually performed and budgeted costs for work scheduled.
   *d.* Actual and planned schedule.
   *e.* Actual and planned technical performance.
5. Based on these reports, revisions in the plans and budgets are made as necessary so that the revised budget shows the current estimate of schedule, technical performance, and cost. The records should be such that the reasons for significant revisions can be readily identified.
6. Once plans and budgets have been revised, subsequent management reports should show comparisons *both* with the original (i.e., baseline) budget and with the current budget.

## AUDITING

### Internal Auditing

The management control system should contain its own controls, and in large organizations there should be an internal audit staff to ensure that these controls are effective. These controls have three general purposes: (1) to minimize the possibility of loss by theft, fraud, or defalcation; (2) to ensure that rules governing the receipt and spending of money and the use of other resources are adhered to; and (3) to ensure that the information flowing through the system is accurate. Some organizations, including many state and municipal governments, do not have even minimal controls, as indicated by the fairly frequent newspaper exposés of contracts being let in an unauthorized manner, persons who are on the payroll but who do not actually work, or welfare payments being made to persons not entitled to receive them. Situations such as these are unacceptable.

Internal controls are not perfect, nor can they be. Their limitations are well described in these standard paragraphs which appear in reports prepared by independent auditors who have been engaged to examine the adequacy of an agency's internal control system, a process called *compliance auditing:*

> The objective of internal accounting control is to provide reasonable, but not absolute, assurance as to the safeguarding of assets against loss from unauthorized use or disposition, and the reliability of financial records for preparing financial statements and maintaining accountability for assets. The concept of reasonable assurance recognizes that the cost of a system of internal control should not exceed the benefits derived and also recognizes that the evaluation of these factors necessarily requires estimates and judgments by management.
>
> There are inherent limitations that should be recognized in considering the potential effectiveness of any system of internal control. In the performance of most control procedures, errors can result from misunderstanding of instructions, mistakes of judgment, carelessness, or other personal factors. Control procedures whose effectiveness depends upon segregation of duties can be circumvented by collusion. Similarly, control procedures can be circumvented intentionally or with respect to the estimates and judgments required in the preparation of financial statements. Further, projection of any evaluation of internal control to future periods is subject to the risk that the procedures may become inadequate because of changes in conditions, and that the degree of compliance with the procedures may deteriorate.[5]

In recent years there has been a shift in the focus of internal auditing away from the practice of having the auditor check individual transactions and toward a system that is designed to be largely self-checking. For example, the U.S. General Accounting Office at one time examined each voucher generated in the federal government; today it examines only a few highly unusual transactions. The function of the modern auditor is to see that the system is well designed and to test that it is functioning properly. In a small organization, this function can be performed by an outside accounting firm; a larger organization has its own specialists for this purpose.

Resources devoted to internal auditing have increased greatly in recent years. In most agencies, the additional emphasis has resulted in the detection of fraud and waste many times larger than the additional cost, but there is a long way to go. Thomas Morris, at the time Inspector General of the Department of Health Education and Welfare, estimated that of the $136 billion spent by that agency in 1977, $5.5 billion was for fraud, abuse, or waste.[6]

## Incorrect Charges

The focus of internal auditing is extremely important. Many nonprofit organizations, for example, spend considerable effort in assuring that the rules

[5] Committee on Auditing Procedures of the American Institute of Certified Public Accountants, 1973.

[6] *The Wall Street Journal,* December 18, 1978, p. 32.

are obeyed precisely (for example, they check each travel voucher to ensure that per diem calculations are accurate and that mileages between points are correctly stated), and they also have voucher systems, locked petty cash boxes, and other devices that inhibit the obvious possibilities for theft. By contrast, they may pay little attention to procedures for assuring the accuracy of information. Clearly, this latter activity has the potential to detect larger dollar errors, but fewer individual errors.

Some systems which are adequate in other respects do not have safeguards against charging costs to the wrong accounts, that is, to projects or other items that do not correspond to those for which the costs were actually incurred. If the amounts charged to accounts are used as a basis for reimbursement by a client, as is often the case, deliberate mischarging can amount to culpable dishonesty. The situation is even more flagrant when the persons responsible sign their names to a certificate that states that the costs are correctly recorded, knowing full well that they are not. In addition to the illegality of this practice, one obvious consequence is that the recorded data are inaccurate; reports derived from such data may give management an incorrect impression about current performance and provide a misleading basis for making future plans. Internal auditors generally should pay more attention to the prevention and detection of this type of inaccuracy than they typically do.

> ***Example.*** Auditors at one university found that 7 percent of faculty members charged more of their time to research projects than they actually spent. Over a 2½-year period, this amounted to $100,000 of excess charges.[7]

An interesting ethical question arises when the rules under which an agency is forced to operate are such that effective and efficient operations are inhibited. Should managers get the job done and cover up the fact that in order to do the job they had to break rules, or should they use the existence of the rule as an excuse for not getting the job done? Managers with different temperaments answer this question in different ways.

> ***Example:*** In a certain state the legislature has set maximum rates at which part-time psychiatrists can be employed by state mental health institutions. These rates are about one half the going rate for psychiatrists, so at these rates, few psychiatrists would work for the state. Consequently, administrators hire psychiatrists for half a day and pay them for a full day; this is the only way they can hire a sufficient number of psychiatrists. On balance, have they done wrong? Whether or not they have done wrong, it is a fact that the records show that twice as many psychiatrist work-hours were provided as actually was the case.

## External Auditing

An increasing number of nonprofit organizations have their accounts audited by external parties. In part, this results from an increasing insistence by

[7] *Chronicle of Higher Education,* April 19, 1976, p. 1.

the federal government on such audits. Any state or local government unit receiving more than $25,000 annually in revenue sharing funds is subject to audit. There are 11,000 such units, which must be audited at least once every three years. Many of these audits are conducted by state auditors, although an increasing number are made by outside independent public accountants. Organizations which receive grants from government agencies are also subject to audit.[8]

Even though not required by law or by grantors, there is coming to be a general recognition of the principle that a nonprofit organization has a responsibility to account to the public, and that, for purposes of reliability and continuity, such reports should be audited by an outside auditor. These audits determine: *(a)* Whether financial operations are properly conducted, *(b)* Whether the financial reports of an audited entity are presented fairly, and *(c)* Whether the entity has complied with applicable laws and regulations.[9] Two other types of audits, *(a)* economy and efficiency and *(b)* program results, are described in Chapters 12 and 13.

## APPENDIX

### Federal Government Terminology and Entries

The terminology used in federal government budgeting and accounting has a highly specialized meaning. The principal terms are here stated in chronological order, that is, in the order in which the events take place. The relationship among them is also indicated in Exhibit 10–2, using data from the 1983 budget.

The first legislative step in the process is the enactment of *authorization* legislation, which authorizes the executive branch to carry out specified programs. Authorization legislation is not permission to spend money, however. Such permission comes only from an *appropriation* act, which is ordinarily enacted after the passage of the authorization act.

An appropriation authorizes an agency to incur *obligations* (also called *budget authorities*). An obligation arises when the agency takes action that legally requires the payment of money either immediately or in the future.

Appropriations are either current or permanent. A *current* appropriation is one that is enacted each year. Most of them state a dollar amount, but in a few cases, the appropriation act states only a formula from which the amount appropriated subsequently is calculated. A *permanent* appropriation

[8] See Office of Management and Budget Circular A-102 (for state and local governments), OMB Circular A-110 (for other nonprofit organizations), and U.S. Office of Revenue Sharing, *Audit Guide and Standards for Revenue Sharing and Antirecession Fiscal Assistance Receipts.*

[9] U.S. General Accounting Office, *Standards for Audit of Governmental Organizations, Programs, Activities and Functions,* p. 2.

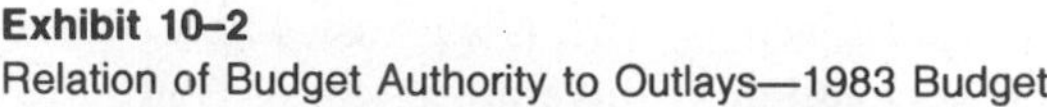

**Exhibit 10–2**
Relation of Budget Authority to Outlays—1983 Budget

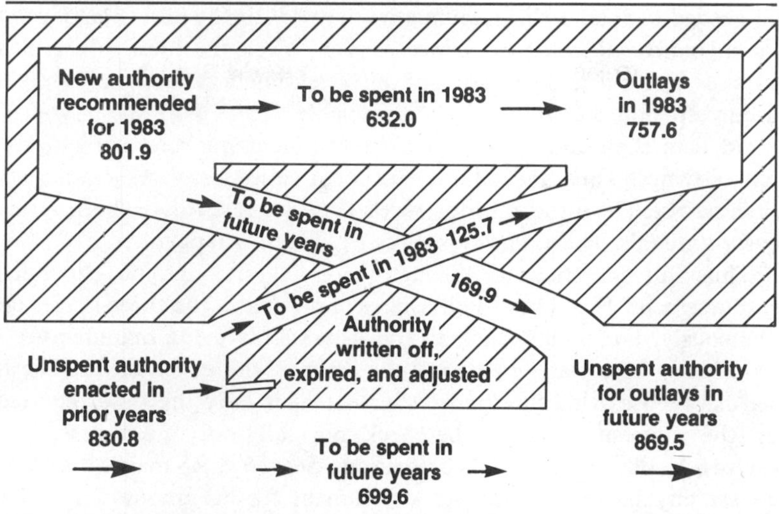


Source: *The Budget of the United States Government, Fiscal Year 1983.*

provides for funds to become available each year, without the enactment of a new appropriation act.

An appropriation also may be either annual, multiple year, or no year. In an *annual* appropriation, the authority to obligate expires at the end of the fiscal year. Annual appropriations are used for most operating programs. A *multiple-year* appropriation is available for obligation for a specified period of time longer than one year, and is relatively uncommon. A *no-year* appropriation is available for obligation until the project's purpose has been achieved. It is used for programs involving the construction or acquisition of capital assets, which may require several years to carry out, for certain research and development programs, and for other programs in which the focus is on the end result to be achieved, rather than on the authorized level of activity for a given year.

The Congress may also enact *contract authorization,* which is authority to enter into a contract in advance of the appropriation of funds. The Congress guarantees that amounts will subsequently be appropriated to liquidate the contract authorization. Contract authorization tends to provide loose control and therefore is used only rarely now; it was used in a major way during World War II.

The appropriation act normally is stated in terms of *New Obligational Authority* (NOA). The *total obligational authority* (TOA) for a program is the sum of NOA plus any unused obligation balances carried forward from prior years.

Many agencies also have working capital funds. The size of each agency's fund (called the corpus) is determined by the Congress. These funds are designed to provide for the acquisition of inventory *(stock funds)* or for capital needed to finance the manufacture of goods or the provision of services to others (*industrial funds* or *service funds*). When the fund sells goods or provides services, the appropriation of the benefiting organization is obligated, and a corresponding amount is made available to the working capital fund. The fund uses these amounts as a basis for incurring new obligations for its own activities. Thus, these funds are often called *revolving funds.*

When payment is authorized for goods or services that have been received, an *expenditure* (also called *outlay*) is created. The actual payment is a *disbursement.* Thus all transactions go through three stages: obligation, expenditure, and disbursement. For some, such as a cash purchase, the three stages occur simultaneously. For others, such as transactions involving manufacture, the obligation may take place many months prior to the expenditure. The time interval between expenditure and disbursement is only the time required to process the payment and issue the check, normally only a few days.

Congress focuses its control on obligations. Sec. 3679 RS makes it a criminal offense for anyone to obligate the government for an amount in excess of that appropriated. Every fiscal officer is so well indoctrinated in the importance of Sec. 3679 that overobligations occur only rarely, and then almost entirely because of a bookkeeping error. There is no need to exercise a separate control over expenditures because no expenditure can be made in excess of the amount obligated. If actual contract costs appear to be exceeding the amount obligated—the phenomenon called *cost overrun*—additional amounts must be obligated for the contract. They are funded usually by transferring unneeded obligating authority from some other program; occasionally, a supplemental appropriation is required. If additional obligations were not made, the contractor would not get paid.

## Accounting Entries

Accounting entries associated with the various stages of the process described above are given below.

1. *Authorization.* Since authorizing legislation does not provide funds, no accounting entry is made.

2. *Appropriation.* Assume the Congress appropriates $10,000,000 to an agency for the fiscal year beginning October 1. The effect on the agency's account would be:

| | | |
|---|---|---|
| Fund Balances with U.S. Treasury .................... | 10,000,000 | |
| Unapportioned Appropriation .................... | | 10,000,000 |

3. *Apportionment.* Assume the Office of Management and Budget releases appropriations in quarterly installments, and if it releases one fourth of the amount in the first quarter, the effect on the agency's account would be:

| | | |
|---|---|---|
| Unapportioned Appropriation | 2,500,000 | |
| Unallotted Apportionment | | 2,500,000 |

4. *Allotment.* Although the agency has been apportioned $2,500,000, the agency head need not allot the entire amount. Assuming the full amount is allotted, the entry would be:

| | | |
|---|---|---|
| Unallotted Apportionment | 2,500,000 | |
| Unobligated Allotments | | 2,500,000 |

5. *Obligation.* During the first quarter the agency entered into obligations for $2,000,000, representing $500,000 of salaries earned and $1,500,000 of materials and services ordered. The entry would be:

| | | |
|---|---|---|
| Unobligated Allotments | 2,000,000 | |
| Unliquidated Obligations | | 2,000,000 |

This entry has no counterpart in business accounting.

6. *Expenditure.* During the first quarter, $500,000 of salaries were recorded as due employees and $400,000 of materials and services were received. Two entries are required: the first adjusts the status of the appropriation:

| | | |
|---|---|---|
| Unliquidated Obligations | 900,000 | |
| Expended Appropriation | | 900,000 |

The second entry corresponds to the entry in business accounting that records expenses and the related accounts payable:

| | | |
|---|---|---|
| Various Expenditure Accounts | 900,000 | |
| Accounts Payable | | 900,000 |

7. *Disbursement.* The agency draws checks on the U.S. Treasury totaling $800,000. The entry, which corresponds to the disbursement of cash by a business, would be:

| | | |
|---|---|---|
| Accounts Payable | 800,000 | |
| Fund Balances with U.S. Treasury | | 800,000 |

At the end of the quarter the fund accounts would show the following balances:

| | |
|---|---|
| Unapportioned appropriation | $ 7,500,000 |
| Unallotted apportionments | 0 |
| Unobligated allotments | 500,000 |
| Unliquidated obligations (awaiting receipt of materials and services) | 1,100,000 |
| Expended appropriation | 900,000 |
| | $10,000,000 |

The accounts would also show that $900,000 of expenditures were incurred during the quarter, and that $100,000 of accounts payable had not yet been paid.

Case 10–1

# COMPETITIVE BARRIERS COMMISSION*

Ms. Lucinda Brown, the Deputy Director of the Competitive Barriers Commission (CBC), was examining the agency's books for the first month of fiscal year 1984. Ms. Brown had arrived at the agency earlier that month, and although she had a reputation as a skilled public sector manager, this was her first position with the federal government. She found the accounting terminology and procedures somewhat confusing. She decided to contact the agency's controller for an explanation of the various events which had transpired during the month.

## Background

CBC was the agency of the federal government charged with designing, implementing, and evaluating a variety of programs aimed at assisting low-income farmers to compete with large agricultural complexes. CBC's programs included Plowshares for Progress, a well-known agricultural assistance program conceived under the administration of President Eisenhower in the late 1950s.

Because of severe budget cutbacks, many of CBC's programs were being sharply curtailed, and Ms. Brown wanted to assure herself that the programs were being implemented as planned. Her first step had been to turn to the agency's accounting data.

## Data

The following events had taken place during the month:

| *Event* | *Date* | *Action* |
|---|---|---|
| 1 | March 2 ..... | Congress appropriated $6,000,000 for the agency. |
| 2 | March 5 ..... | The Office of Management and Budget apportioned $5,000,000 to the agency. |
| 3 | March 7 ..... | Allotments of $3,000,000 took place. |
| 4 | March 10 .... | Fertilizer and seeds were ordered, amounting to $300,000. |
| 5 | March 15 .... | The agency had a payroll of $900,000. |
| 6 | March 20 .... | The agency placed an order to purchase some tractors, costing $1,200,000. |
| 7 | March 21 .... | The agency received $180,000 worth of fertilizer and seeds. |
| 8 | March 22 .... | The Controller asked the United States Treasury to issue checks totaling $1,000,000 to pay for some of the items the agency had received. |

* This case was prepared by David W. Young, Harvard School of Public Health.

9 March 31 .... The agency took title to the tractors (although no payment had yet been made).

The Controller informed Ms. Brown that the tractors which had been purchased had an expected life of 5 years, at the end of which they would have no salvage value. Also, since the agency had taken title to the tractors during the month, it should record a full month's depreciation for them, even though they had not been in use for the full month. Finally, he informed her that there was a fertilizer and seed inventory of $50,000 on hand as of March 31.

## Questions

1. How would these transactions be accounted for in the federal government?
2. Prepare a balance sheet for the CBC as of March 31. What does it tell you about the agency's operations?

## Case 10–2

## NORTHEAST RESEARCH LABORATORY (A)*

In the fall of 1974, the problem of assuring that the time of professionals was recorded properly (which is a chronic problem in research and development organizations) seemed to Andrew Carter, president of Northeast Research Laboratory, to be becoming acute. Carter wondered what, if any, additional steps should be taken to mitigate this problem.

Northeast Research Laboratory (NRL) was a large, multidisciplinary research and development organization, employing approximately 1,000 professionals. Approximately half its revenue came from contracts for research projects that were undertaken for various government agencies, particularly agencies of the Department of Defense, and the other half came from industrial companies and from nonfederal government agencies.

The typical research contract specified that the client would reimburse NRL for direct costs involved in the project, plus an allowance for overhead, plus a small fee, with total reimbursement being limited to a specified ceiling. For this amount, NRL agreed to deliver reports or other completed work. The overhead allowance was determined on the basis of an overhead rate which was expressed as a percentage of direct labor costs. For defense con-

---

* This case was prepared by Robert N. Anthony, Harvard Business School.

**Exhibit 1**
Overhead Costs

| | First Ten Months ($000) | |
|---|---|---|
| | *1974* | *1973* |
| Administration and planning | 6,490 | 6,644 |
| Information dissemination | 2,500 | 1,958 |
| Division research and development | 845 | 824 |
| General research and development | 189 | 165 |
| Staff development | 623 | 371 |
| Staffing | 673 | 465 |
| Facility expense | 6,506 | 5,298 |
| Interim technical studies | 389 | 278 |
| Proposal liaison | 243 | 238 |
| Concept formulation | 551 | 515 |
| Proposal preparation | 1,475 | 1,155 |
| Total overhead | 20,484 | 17,911 |

tracts, the overhead rate was negotiated annually with the Department of Defense. Some nondefense agencies negotiated a separate rate because they did not allow the same overhead components as were allowed by the Department of Defense. For example, the Department of Defense permitted the cost of preparing bids and proposals for contracts to be included as an item of overhead cost, but the Atomic Energy Commission excluded this cost. Exhibit 1 shows the principal components of overhead and their magnitude. The type of work that was to be charged to the various overhead accounts was spelled out in a five-page section of the NRL procedures manual. Exhibit 2 summarizes this material.

Employees were supposed to fill out weekly timecards on which they recorded how they spent their time to the nearest 0.1 hour. The time was charged either as a direct cost of a research project or to one of the overhead activity codes listed on Exhibit 2. The timecard was also signed by the employee's supervisor.

## Problems with Time Reporting

As was the case with all defense contractors, NRL was subject to audit by representatives of the Defense Contract Audit Agency (DCAA). In 1964, DCAA had made a spot check of the timecards, had uncovered several errors, and consequently had disallowed $150,000 of overhead costs; that is, NRL's revenue from defense was $150,000 less than it would have been if this disallowance had not been made. This was about 25 percent of NRL's profit for 1964. As a consequence of this experience, NRL management had placed increased emphasis on accurate time recording, by means of talks at management meetings and memoranda to the staff.

In the period 1965–72, DCAA did not check on time recording, but begin-

**Exhibit 2**
NRL Activity Codes

Administration and planning:
511 Administrative duties (such as handling personnel actions, timecards, requisitions, financial reports, etc.); costs of nonproject office supplies, stationery, etc. (see also 561).

Information dissemination:
521 Formal NRL publications; work order required (see also 525).
522 Technical articles and papers (writing, editing, and publishing charges); reprints.
523 Symposia or seminars, nonproject; work order required.
525 Client liaison and tours, nonproject (use 581 for proposal followup); preparation and publication of division/department brochures or program descriptions.

NRL research and development:
532 Division IR&D task; subnumber required (use NRL form 4823).
535 General IR&D task; subnumber required (use NRL form 4823).

Staff development:
541 Formal education and training courses.
542 Orientation and staff training.
543 Professional society participation.
544 Overseas travel, nonproject.

Staffing:
551 Recruiting, review of applications, and interviews.
552 Relocation and transfer, nonproject; new hire moving costs.

Facility expense:
561 Support services by Central Staff, nonproject translations, periodicals, books, small hand tools, tool boxes, and small parts cabinets—division personnel time charges only for work on security and property.
562 Nonproject laboratory equipment maintenance, calibration, and repair.
563 Minor laboratory and office moving costs; work order required if cost is to exceed $250.
564 Minor construction including leasehold or building improvements less than $250; work order required.

Interim technical study:
571 Informal study and assigned reading of journals, technical articles, or other library materials.

Bid and proposal expense:
581 Proposal liaison; work order required.
582 Concept formulation; work order required.
583 Proposal preparation; work order required.

ning in 1973, DCAA auditors showed renewed interest in the topic. On three occasions in 1973, auditors made a "gate check"; that is, they stood at the NRL entrance, took the names of employees who arrived after the official starting time, and then checked to see whether these employees had recorded their correct starting time on their timecards. Although no action was taken as a result of these gate checks, they led to resentment on the part of employees who learned of them. It was felt that professionals should be trusted to do a good day's work and that if a person started late, he usually quit late; on balance, most employees put in more than the 40 hours a week that their employment contract called for, it was felt.

The controller of NRL reported to Mr. Carter that in the spring of 1974 DCAA auditors had conducted at least three "floor checks" (a type of audit that is described in the following section). The auditors had made no comments to him, nor to anyone else so far as he knew, as to what the results of these floor checks were. The controller suspected that the auditors were gathering ammunition that would be used in connection with the next overhead rate negotiation, which took place in November.

## Internal Audits

In 1974 NRL's Internal Audit Department conducted a series of floor checks to validate time recording practices. The first of these, on March 6, involved 15 professionals assigned to one of the engineering departments. Of these 15 persons, 7 were away from the department premises for one reason or another, so only 8 were interviewed. These 8 were asked to describe the nature of the work they were doing. Subsequently, their time cards were examined, and in each case the work was correctly reported on the timecard.

The next floor check was on June 12 in another engineering department. Eight employees were selected who in the preceding week had charged three or more hours to overhead accounts. Each of these persons was asked to describe the nature of the work for which an overhead account was charged. In all cases, the work described was clearly of an overhead nature, as contrasted with work on research projects, but in three of the cases, there was some question to whether the correct overhead account had been charged. There was room for difference of opinion as to this, however, so the auditors did not take a formal "Exception," which was the standard practice when an improper procedure was observed.

On June 25, 1974, a similar floor check of seven employees in still another department produced similar results for six of them; that is, although there were some differences of opinion as to the proper overhead account to be charged, there was no doubt that the work was of an overhead nature. For the seventh employee, 27.5 hours were erroneously charged to overhead. The report stated that the person "had been told to charge work on Project 8366 the previous week to Interim Technical Study, an overhead account. Project 8366 is in an overrun condition, and management felt that since it would eventually have to be charged to overhead the charge may as well go there now."

In a study of five employees on July 25, one person was found to have charged time to the wrong overhead account. For another employee, the report read:

> When we checked the timecard of one of the employees who was working at home, we noted he had charged five hours on that day to Interim Technical Study. We had discussed the matter of working at home with the director of his organization on the day of the test. The director stated it was sometimes necessary for employees who are trying to meet deadlines to stay home to prevent unimportant

interruptions from personnel and telephones. He further stated that he practiced this policy himself occasionally.

It does not seem necessary, however, to stay at home for the sake of privacy to study because of the lack of other work or to keep up with professional journals, technical articles, and so forth, either on an assigned or unassigned basis.

We recommend using NRL facilities, rather than working in the home.

A floor check of six employees on August 12, 1974, revealed several errors in the proper overhead account to be charged, but no project work charged to overhead.

On September 19, a follow-up audit was made on eight of the employees who had made incorrect or questionable charges as reported in earlier audits. In this follow-up, two exceptions were noted:

*a.* A biologist had charged four hours to grounds maintenance and described his work to the auditor as "fertilizing and watering the plants landscaping our building." The auditor recommended that when the biologist noted the need for maintenance, he should notify the grounds maintenance department rather than doing the work himself.

*b.* The other employee said he could not remember the nature of the work for which he had charged time to overhead, in the preceding week. It turned out that the timecard had been made out by his supervisor, and the supervisor had made an erroneous entry.

On September 20, an incident was reported to the controller that was relevant to the floor check program. On September 10, an internal auditor telephoned the Chicago office, asked for K. Smithson, and was told that he was not available. In a subsequent conversation with Smithson, the auditor was told that he had been participating in a TV program on September 10. Smithson's timecard for the week showed that he worked 40 hours on Project 8122, however. Further investigation showed that Smithson participated in a TV program, unrelated to NRL work, approximately two days a month, but that all of his time, except vacation and illness, was charged to some project. It turned out that timecards in the Chicago office were made out by an administrative assistant, based on her general knowledge of the activities there, but without checking with the employees involved.

The foregoing is a summary of all internal audit floor checks for the first nine months of 1974. The internal audit staff consisted of two professionals and an assistant.

The persons involved and their supervisors were informed of the results of these audits, but no formal disciplinary action was taken.

## The McCabe Memorandum

On May 3, 1974, partly motivated by the reports of DCAA and internal audit floor checks, Robert McCabe, vice president for research operations, circulated the following memorandum to all professionals in the organization:

Many members of the staff may not be aware of the reasoning behind the structure of NRL overhead charge numbers. As a consequence, they are sometimes not as careful as they should be when filling out their weekly timecards, with resulting erroneous apportioning of time charges between accounts.

Under our pricing system, we agree to charge each customer the direct costs of performing his project, plus an allocated share of the indirect costs necessary to the general operations of NRL. Our federal government customers have the right (and obligation) to audit not only the direct charges but the pool of expenses upon which the indirect allocation is based. In order to furnish the detail upon which they can base an audit, our accounting system provides a series of descriptive activity codes. Errors in proper accounting result in a cost disallowance and the reduction of net earnings available for capital purchases.

As a part of their audit function the government auditors make periodic floor checks to determine the relationship between the time charges and the work actually performed. These checks take two forms. In one case, they ask selected personnel what accounts they are charging on a particular day, and later check the timecards to make sure that the time charges correspond. In the other case, they select a number of people who have charges against a particular charge number and ask them what they were doing on the day they charged that number. Recent floor checks have revealed a serious number of discrepancies between time charges and activities. It is absolutely essential that we charge time to the project account or to the overhead activity code directly related to the work being performed. Errors in this area raise questions concerning the validity of our entire system and could have serious consequences.

The attached abbreviated schedule of activity codes has been prepared for your use. [This is reproduced as Exhibit 2.] I suggest that you keep this in a handy place for ready reference when you are filling out your timecards. If there are any questions, consult your supervisor or business office; they can furnish a schedule with more complete activity code definitions if you need them.

I would expect most overhead charges for project professionals to be recorded against Codes 525, 532, 535, 581, 582, and 583. Code 511 will more frequently be used by directors, managers, and their administrative staff.

It is absolutely essential that each of you take the care necessary to assure that your time is accurately charged.

## Views of the Financial Vice President

Carter discussed the time charging problem on several occasions with Spencer Bean, financial vice president. Bean said that professionals did not appear to realize that deliberate falsification of timecards was as much a crime as submitting a fraudulent invoice. In both cases, a client was billed for work that actually had not been done. The situation in NRL was probably no different from that in similar organizations. For example, Bean knew of a case in a large, highly regarded university in which the salary of a professor had been charged to a research project for a whole year, even though the professor did no work on the project. Instances of this type had been uncovered and publicized from time to time by the U.S. General Accounting Office, but the publicized examples were "only the tip of the iceberg."

Bean thought that in NRL, the principal reasons for erroneous charging were as follows:

1. On the one hand, an important measure of employee performance was the percentage of "billed time"; that is, the percentage of his total time that was recorded as a direct charge to some research project. Staff members were motivated to keep this percentage high, since it was invariably taken into account in their semiannual performance review. They therefore were tempted to charge time to projects even when their activities were temporarily of an overhead nature.
2. On the other hand, professionals were also judged on the basis of whether they were able to complete projects within the stated ceiling. A project overrun was considered by some managers to be as bad a sin as a low billed time percentage, and by other managers it was considered to be a worse sin. This was particularly the case with the "old-timers" because some years ago the evils of overrunning a project had been much more strongly stressed than they were currently. An overrun could occur simply because the project turned out to be more time-consuming than originally anticipated. It could also occur because project leaders made overly optimistic estimates of time requirements when the project proposal was being prepared. In some cases there was a deliberate underestimate of requirements so that a low price could be quoted in order to help get the contract, with the hope that additional funds could be negotiated when the original amount was used up. In particular, in the 1970s, government research/development funds were "tight," and some agencies insisted on an unreasonably low contract ceiling because they did not have adequate available funds. Project leaders accepted these contracts because they wanted to continue on work for such agencies, particularly when they considered the work as being exciting, important to the national interest, and leading to scientific advances.
3. Some professionals didn't see any substantial difference between a direct project charge and overhead. Either way, the client pays—in the one case as a direct charge, in the other case via the overhead rate. Getting the work done somehow was more important than who paid for it.
4. Professionals tend to be idealists. They spend their time in ways that they judge to be best, and they sincerely believe that their work benefits society. They don't want a superior, and especially they don't want an auditor, to second-guess them. They regard timekeeping in general as unnecessary paperwork.
5. Some types of overhead activity were regarded as being less desirable than others, and this tended to affect how time was charged. For example, bid and proposal costs were regarded as being high. Within this general

category, "concept formulation" was regarded as being less defensible than "proposal preparation," although the line between these two activities was not sharp.

Bean had the following suggestions as possible ways to mitigate the problem:

1. There should be more training of lower level supervisors so that they would learn to act as managers, rather than as researchers. It was their responsibility, in Bean's view, to see to it that the staff charged time correctly.
2. Top management should do more to get across the message that the government has rules and NRL personnel must abide by these rules no matter how much it may hurt to do so, and also the message that without reliable data on project and overhead costs, management would be likely to make erroneous decisions.
3. In performance reviews, there should be less criticism of project overruns and less emphasis on the billed time percentage.

Bean cautioned against overreacting to the problem. Scientists and engineers, he said, had strong opinions. Their loyalty is primarily to their profession and only secondarily to the organization in which they happen to work. If they feel that their professional activities are being affected adversely by the organization's policies, they will as a minimum resent these policies, and they may well leave the organization.

## Conclusion

Carter thought that there was a good chance that alleged erroneous charges would be an important factor in the next overhead negotiation with the Department of Defense, and he wanted to have a course of action in mind if this occurred. Even if NRL got through these negotiations unscathed, the danger of trouble at some future time was present so long as erroneous charges continued to be made.

## Question

What course of action should Mr. Carter pursue?

## Case 10–3

## NORTHEAST RESEARCH LABORATORY (B)*

On a Friday morning in late December 1973, Sam Lacy, head of the Physical Sciences Division of Northeast Research Laboratory (NRL) thought about two letters which lay on his desk. One, which he had received a few weeks before, was a progress report from Robert Kirk, recently assigned project leader of the Exco Project, who reported that earlier frictions between the NRL team and the client had lessened considerably, that high-quality research was under way, and that the prospects for retaining the Exco project on a long-term basis appeared fairly good. The other letter, which had just arrived in the morning's mail, came from Gray Kenney, a vice president of Exco, and stated that the company wished to terminate the Exco contract effective immediately.

Lacy was puzzled. He remembered how pleased Gray Kenney had been only a few months before when the Exco project produced its second patentable process. On the other hand, he also recalled some of the difficulties the project had encountered within NRL which had ultimately led to the replacement of project leader Alan North in order to avoid losing the contract. Lacy decided to call in the participants in an effort to piece together an understanding of what had happened. Some of what he learned is described below. But the problem remained for him to decide what he should report to senior management. What should he recommend to avoid the recurrence of such a situation in the future?

### Company Background

Northeast Research Laboratory was a multidisciplinary research and development organization employing approximately 1,000 professionals. It was organized into two main sectors, one for economics and business administration and the other for the physical and natural sciences. Within the pysical and natural sciences sector, the organization was essentially by branches of science. The main units were called divisions and the subunits were called laboratories. A partial organization chart is shown in Exhibit 1.

Most of the company's work was done on the basis of contracts with clients. Each contract was a project. Responsibility for the project was vested in a project leader, and through him up the organizational structure in which his laboratory was located. Typically, some members of the project team were drawn from laboratories other than that in which the project leader worked; it was the ability to put together a team with a variety of technical talents that was one of the principal strengths of a multidisciplinary laboratory. Team members worked under the direction of the project leader during

* This case was prepared by Robert N. Anthony, Harvard Business School.

**Exhibit 1**
Organization Chart (simplified)

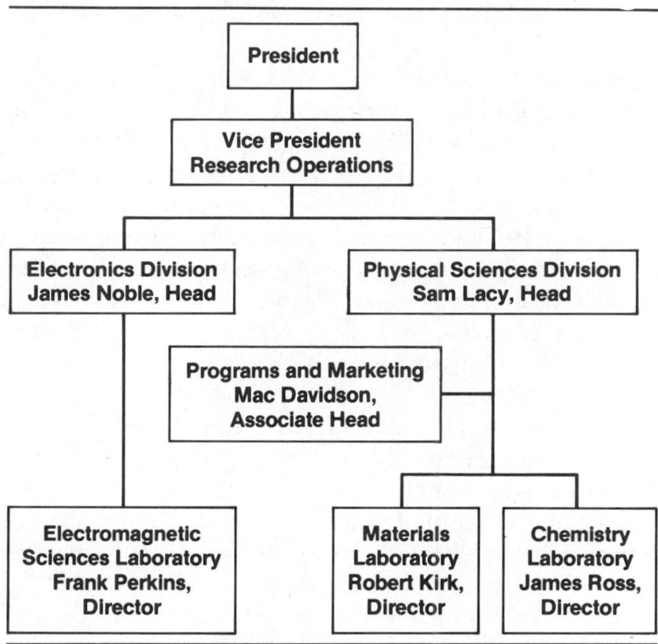


the period in which they were assigned to the project. An individual might be working on more than one project concurrently. The project leader could also draw on the resources of central service organizations, such as model shops, computer services, editorial, and drafting. The project was billed for the services of these units at rates which were intended to cover their full costs.

## Inception of the Exco Project

In October 1972, Gray Kenney, vice president of Exco, had telephoned Mac Davidson of NRL to outline a research project which would examine the effect of microwaves on various ores and minerals. Davidson was associate head of the Physical Sciences Division and had known Kenney for several years. During the conversation Kenney asserted that NRL ought to be particularly intrigued by the research aspects of the project, and Davidson readily agreed. Davidson was also pleased because the Physical Sciences Division was under pressure to generate more revenue, and this potentially long-term project from Exco would make good use of the available work force. In addition, top management of NRL had recently circulated several memos indicating that more emphasis should be put on commercial rather than government work. Davidson was, however, a little concerned that the project did not fall neatly into one laboratory or even one division, but in fact required assistance from the Electronics Division to complement work that would be done in two different Physical Sciences Laboratories (the Chemistry Laboratory and the Materials Laboratory).

A few days later Davidson organized a joint client-NRL conference to determine what Exco wanted and to plan the proposal. Kenney sent his assistant, Tod Denby, who was to serve as the Exco liaison officer for the project. Representing NRL were Davidson; Sam Lacey; Dr. Robert Kirk, director of the Materials Laboratory (one of the two Physical Sciences laboratories involved in the project); Dr. Alan North, manager of Chemical Development and Engineering (and associate director of the Chemistry Laboratory); Dr. James Noble, executive director of the Electronics Division; and a few researchers chosen by Kirk and North. Davidson also would have liked to invite Dr. James Ross, director of the Chemistry Laboratory, but Ross was out of town and couldn't attend the pre-proposal meeting.

Denby described the project as a study of the use of microwaves for the conversion of basic ores and minerals to more valuable commercial products. The study was to consist of two parts:

Task A—An experimental program to examine the effect of mircowaves on 50 ores and minerals, and to select those processes appearing to have the most promise.

Task B—A basic study to obtain an understanding of how and why microwaves interact with certain minerals.

It was agreed that the project would be a joint effort of three laboratories: (1) Materials, (2) Chemistry, and (3) Electromagnetic. The first two laboratories were in the Physical Sciences Division, and the last was in the Electronics Division.

Denby proposed that the contract be open-ended, with a level of effort of around $10,000–$12,000 per month. Agreement was quickly reached on the content of the proposal. Denby emphasized to the group that an early start was essential if Exco were to remain ahead of its competition.

After the meeting Lacy, who was to have overall responsibility for the project, discussed the choice of project leader with Davidson. Davidson proposed Alan North, a 37-year-old chemist who had had experience as a project leader on several projects. North had impressed Davidson at the pre-proposal meeting and seemed well suited to head the interdisciplinary team. Lacy agreed. Lacy regretted that Dr. Ross (head of the laboratory in which North worked) was unable to participate in the decision of who should head the joint project. In fact, because he was out of town, Ross was neither aware of the Exco project nor of his laboratory's involvement in it.

The following day, Alan North was told of his appointment as project leader. During the next few days, he conferred with Robert Kirk, head of the other Physical Sciences laboratory involved in the project. Toward the end of October Denby began to exert pressure on North to finalize the proposal, stating that the substance had been agreed upon at the pre-proposal conference. North thereupon drafted a five-page letter as a substitute for a formal proposal, describing the nature of the project and outlining the procedures and equipment necessary. At Denby's request, North included a paragraph which authorized members of the client's staff to visit NRL frequently and observe progress of the research program. The proposal's cover sheet contained approval signatures from the laboratories and divisions involved. North signed for his own area and for laboratory director Ross. He telephoned Dr. Noble of the Electronics Division, relayed the client's sense of urgency, and Noble authorized North to sign for him. Davidson signed for the Physical Sciences Division as a whole.

At this stage, North relied principally on the advice of colleagues within his own division. As he did not know personally the individuals in the Electronics Division, they were not called upon at this point. Since North understood informally that the director of the Electromagnetic Sciences Laboratory, Dr. Perkins, was quite busy and often out of town, North did not attempt to discuss the project with Perkins.

After the proposal had been signed and mailed, Dr. Perkins was sent a copy. It listed the engineering equipment which the client wanted purchased for the project and described how it was to be used. Perkins worried that performance characteristics of the power supply (necessary for quantitative measurement) specified in the proposal were inadequate for the task. He asked North about it and North said that the client had made up his mind as to the microwave equipment he wanted and how it was to be used. Denby had said he was paying for that equipment and intended to move it to Exco's laboratories after the completion of the NRL contract.

All these events had transpired rather quickly. By the time Dr. Ross, director of the Chemistry Laboratory, returned, the proposal for the Exco project had been signed and accepted. Ross went to see Lacy and said that he had dealt with Denby on a previous project and had serious misgivings about working with him. Lacy assuaged some of Ross's fears by observing that if anyone could succeed in working with Denby it would be North—a flexible man, professionally competent, who could move with the tide and get along with clients of all types.

## Conduct of the Project

Thus the project began. Periodically, when decisions arose, North would seek opinions from division management. However, he was somewhat unclear about whom he should talk to. Davidson had been the person who had actually appointed him project leader. Normally, however, North worked for Ross. Although Kirk's laboratory was heavily involved in the project, Kirk was very busy with other Materials Laboratory work. Adding to his uncertainty, North periodically received telepone calls from Perkins of the

Electronics Division, whom he didn't know well. Perkins expected to be heavily involved in the project.

Difficulties and delays began to plague the project. The microwave equipment specified by the client was not delivered by the manufacturer on schedule, and there were problems in filtering the power supply of the radio frequency source. Over the objection of NRL Electromagnetic Sciences engineers, but at the insistence of the client, one of the chemical engineers tried to improve the power supply filter. Eventually the equipment had to be sent back to the manufacturer for modification. This required several months

In the spring of 1973, Denby, who had made his presence felt from the outset, began to apply strong pressure. "Listen," he said to North, "top management of Exco is starting to get on my back and we need results. Besides, I'm up for review in four months and I can't afford to let this project affect my promotion." Denby was constantly at NRL during the next few months. He was often in the labs conferring individually with members of the NRL teams. Denby also visited North's office frequently.

A number of related problems began to surface. North had agreed to do both experimental and theoretical work for this project, but Denby's constant pushing for experimental results began to tilt the emphasis. Theoretical studies began to lapse, and experimental work became the focus of the Exco project. From time to time North argued that the theoretical work should precede or at least accompany the experimental program, but Denby's insistence on concrete results led North to temporarily deemphasize the theoretical work. Symptoms of this shifting emphasis were evident. One day a senior researcher from Kirk's laboratory came to North to complain that people were being "stolen" from his team. "How can we do a balanced project if the theoretical studies are not given enough work force?" he asked. North explained the client's position and asked the researcher to bear with this temporary realignment of the project's resources.

As the six-month milestone approached, Denby expressed increasing dissatisfaction with the project's progress. In order to have concrete results to report to Exco management, he directed North a number of times to change the direction of the research. On several occasions various members of the project team had vigorous discussions with Denby about the risks of changing results without laying a careful foundation. North himself spent a good deal of time talking with Denby on this subject, but Denby seemed to discount its importance. Denby began to avoid North and to spend most of his time with the other team members. Eventually the experimental program, initially dedicated to a careful screening of some 50 materials, deteriorated to a somewhat frantic and erratic pursuit of what appeared to be "promising leads." Lacy and Noble played little or no role in this shift of emphasis.

On June 21, 1973, Denby visited North in his office and severely criticized him for proposing a process (hydrochloric acid pickling) that was economically infeasible. In defense, North asked an NRL economist to check his figures. The economist reported back that North's numbers were sound and that, in fact, a source at U.S. Steel indicated that hydrochloric acid pickling was "generally more economic than the traditional process and was increasingly being adopted." Through this and subsequent encounters, the relationship between Denby and North became increasingly strained.

Denby continued to express concern about the Exco project's payoff. In an effort to save time, he discouraged the NRL team from repeating experiments, a practice that was designed to ensure accuracy. Data received from initial experiments were frequently taken as sufficiently accurate, and after hasty analysis were adopted for the purposes of the moment. Not surprisingly, Denby periodically discovered errors in these data. He informed NRL of them.

Denby's visits to NRL became more frequent as the summer progressed. Some days he would visit all three laboratories, talking to the researchers involved and asking them about encouraging leads. North occasionally cautioned Denby against too much optimism. Nonetheless, North continued to oblige the client by restructuring the Exco project to allow for more "production line" scheduling of experiments and for less systematic research.

In August, North discovered that vertile could be obtained from iron ore. This discovery was a significant one, and the client applied for a patent. If the reaction could be proved commercially, its potential would be measured in millions of dollars. Soon thereafter, the NRL team discovered that the operation could, in fact, be handled commercially in a rotary kiln. The client was notified and soon began planning a pilot plant that would use the rotary kiln process.

Exco's engineering department, after reviewing the plans for the pilot plant, rejected them. It was argued that the rotary process was infeasible and that a fluid bed process would have to be used instead. Denby returned to NRL and insisted on an experiment to test the fluid bed process. North warned Denby that agglomeration (a sticking together of the material) would probably take place. It did. Denby was highly upset, reported to Gray Kenney that he had not received "timely" warning of the probability of agglomeration taking place, and indicated that he had been misled as to the feasibility of the rotary kiln process.[1]

Work continued, and two other "disclosures of invention" were turned over to the client by the end of September.

## Personnel Changes

On September 30, Denby came to North's office to request that Charles Fenton be removed from the Exco project. Denby reported he had been watching Fenton in the Electromagnetic Laboratory, which he visited often,

---

[1] Ten months later the client was experimenting with the rotary kiln process for producing vertile from iron ore in his own laboratory.

and had observed that Fenton spent relatively little time on the Exco project. North, who did not know Fenton well, agreed to look into it. But Denby insisted that Fenton be removed immediately and threatened to terminate the contract if he were allowed to remain.

North was unable to talk to Fenton before taking action because Fenton was on vacation. He did talk to Fenton as soon as he returned, and the researcher admitted that due to the pressure of other work he had not devoted as much time or effort to the Exco work as perhaps he should have.

Three weeks later, Denby called a meeting with Mac Davidson and Sam Lacy. It was their first meeting since the pre-proposal conference for the Exco project. Denby was brief and to the point:

*Denby:* I'm here because we have to replace North. He's become increasingly difficult to work with and is obstructing the progress of the project.

*Lacy:* but North is an awfully good man . . .

*Davidson:* Look, he's come up with some good solid work thus far. What about the process of extracting vertile from iron ore he came up with. And . . .

*Denby:* I'm sorry, but we have to have a new project leader. I don't mean to be abrupt, but it's either replace North or forget the contract.

Davidson reluctantly appointed Robert Kirk project leader and informed North of the decision. North went to see Davidson a few days later. Davidson told him that although management did not agree with the client, North had been replaced in order to save the contract. Later Dr. Lacy told North the same thing. Neither Lacy nor Davidson made an effort to contact Exco senior management on the matter.

Following the change of project leadership, the record became more difficult to reconstruct. It appeared that Kirk made many efforts to get the team together, but morale remained low. Denby continued to make periodic visits to NRL but found that the NRL researchers were not talking as freely with him as they had in the past. Denby became skeptical about the project's value. Weeks slipped by. No further breakthroughs emerged.

## Lacy's Problem

Doctor Lacy had received weekly status reports on the project, the latest of which is shown in Exhibit 2. He had had a few informal conversations about the project, principally with North and Kirk. He had not read the reports submitted to Exco. If the project had been placed on NRL's "problem list," which comprised about 10 percent of the projects which seemed to be experiencing the most difficulty, Lacy would have received a written report on its status weekly, but the Exco project was not on that list.

With the background given above, Lacy reread Kenney's letter terminating the Exco contract. It seemed likely that Kenney, too, had not had full knowledge of what went on during the project's existence. In his letter, Kenney

**Exhibit 2**
Weekly Project Status Report

PROJECT/ACCOUNT STATUS REPORT

| ORG | PROJ/ACCT | SUB | W/O | WEEK ENDING DATE | TYPE | REV TYPE | PRICE | CLIENT | | INT/DOM | NOTICES | PAGE |
|---|---|---|---|---|---|---|---|---|---|---|---|---|
| 325 | 3273 | 000 | 000 | 12-22-73 | PROJ | INDUS | SCA | YD | | DOMESTIC | | 1 |

| DIVISION | DEPARTMENT | SUPERVISOR | LEADER |
|---|---|---|---|
| PHYSICAL SCI | CHEMISTRY LAB | ROBERT KIRK | ROBERT KIRK |

PROJECT TITLE: MICROWAVES IN CONVERSION OF BASIC ORES AND MINERALS

| INST | READY DATE | STOP WORK DATE | TERM DATE | BURDEN % | OVERHEAD % | FEE % |
|---|---|---|---|---|---|---|
| EXCO | 11-06-72 | - - | 11-06-74 | 28.00 | 105.00 | 15.00 |

| COST CATEGORIES | (OBJECT CODE) | DOLLARS PTD13WK1 | DOLLARS TO DATE | LABOR HOURS ESTIMATE | LABOR HOURS TO DATE | LABOR HOURS BALANCE |
|---|---|---|---|---|---|---|
| SUPERVISOR | (11, 12) | | 560 | | 36 | |
| SENIOR | (13) | 192 | 17986 | | 1348 | |
| PROFESSIONAL | (14) | 150 | 16787 | | 1678 | |
| TECHNICAL | (15) | 529 | 5299 | | 1037 | |
| CLER/SUPP | (16, 17, 18) | | 301 | | 84 | |
| OTHER | (10) (19) | 72 | 72 | | 12 | |
| LABOR (S. T.) | | 943 | 41005 | | 1644 | |
| BURDEN | | 248 | 11481 | | | |
| OVERHEAD | | 1227 | 55110 | | | |
| OVERTIME PREM | (21) | 160 | 1540 | | | |
| OVS./OTH. PREM | (22-29) | 242 | 476 | | | |
| TOTAL PERSONNEL COSTS | | 2820 | 109612 | | | |
| TRAVEL | (56-59) | | 776 | | | |
| SUBCONTRACT | (36) | | | | | |
| MATERIAL | (41, 42) | | 3726 | | | |
| EQUIPMENT | (43) | | | | | |
| COMPUTER | (37, 45) | | | | | |
| COMMUN | (62, 63, 70, 71) | 2 | 507 | | | |
| CONSULTANT | (74, 75) | | | | | |
| REPORT COST | (44, 47) | | | | | |
| OTHER M&S | | 54 | 99 | | | |
| TOTAL M&S COST | | 56 | 5098 | | | |
| COMMITMENTS | | | 26847 | | | |
| TOTAL LESS FEE | | 2876 | 141557 | | | |
| FEE (15.00) | | 158 | 24376 | | | |
| TOTAL | | 3031 | 165933 | | | |

| LAST BILLING: | |
|---|---|
| DATE | 11-30-73 |
| AMOUNT | 11350 |
| ACCOUNT STATUS TO DATE: | |
| BILLED | 154583 |
| PAID | 154583 |

| | |
|---|---|
| TIME BALANCE % | 39.4 |
| COST BALANCE % | 43.5 |
| TIME BALANCE WKS. | 41 |

| ESTIMATED | BALANCE |
|---|---|
| 250435 | 108878 |
| 37565 | 13189 |
| 288000 | 122067 |

COMMITMENT STATUS TO DATE

| PO NO | | OBJ | VENDOR/DESCRIPTION | TOTAL | CHARGES | BALANCE |
|---|---|---|---|---|---|---|
| A61289 | 11-21-73 | 41 | MINNESOTA MINING | 111 | 61 | 50 |
| A61313 | 11-23-73 | 41 | ALDRICH CHEMICAL | 348 | | 348 |
| A95209 | 11-28-73 | 43 | TENNECO CHEMICAL CO | 5 | | 5 |
| A95093 | 11-15-73 | 41 | UNION CARBIDE CORP | 23194 | | 23194 |
| B 95104 | 11-19-73 | 37 | SCIENTIFIC PRODUCTS | 600 | | 600 |
| B 95232 | 11-25-73 | 41 | VAN WATERS & ROGERS | 2500 | | 2500 |
| 018046 | 12-15-73 | 5/ | ROGER MD | 300 | 150 | 150 |
| | | | | | | T 26847 |

TRANSACTIONS RECORDED 12-15-73 - 12-22-73

LABOR

| ORG | ID | W/E DATE | T/S NO | OBJ | NAME | HOURS WEEK | HOURS TO DATE |
|---|---|---|---|---|---|---|---|
| 322 | 02345 | 12-22-73 | 363073 | 13 | KIRK | 6.0 | 150 |
| 322 | 02345 | 12-22-73 | 363073 | 22 | KIRK | 6.0 | |
| 322 | 03212 | 12-22-73 | 363082 | 13 | DENSMORE | 8.0 | 25 |
| 322 | 03260 | 12-22-73 | 236544 | 14 | COOK | 15.0 | 30 |
| 325 | 12110 | 12-08-73 | C30093 | 15 | HOWARD | 15.0 | 82 |
| 325 | 12110 | 12-15-73 | 236548 | 15 | HOWARD | 36.0 | |
| 325 | 12110 | 12-22-73 | 376147 | 15 | HOWARD | 8.0 | |
| 325 | 12357 | 12-22-73 | 376149 | 15 | SPELTZ | 15.0 | 68 |
| 325 | 12369 | 12-22-73 | 376150 | 15 | GYUIRE | 15.0 | 17 |
| 325 | 12384 | 12-22-73 | R08416 | 15 | DILLON | 40.0- | 44 |
| 325 | 12397 | 12-22-73 | 336527 | 15 | NAGY | 31.0 | 31 |
| 325 | 12397 | 12-22-73 | 336527 | 21 | NAGY | 15.0 | |
| 652 | 12475 | 12-22-73 | 236548 | 15 | KAIN | 8.0 | 20 |
| 652 | 12475 | 12-22-73 | 236548 | 21 | KAIN | 15.0 | |

| | HOURS | DOLLARS |
|---|---|---|
| LABOR (STRAIGHT TIME) | 117.0 | 943 |
| PAYROLL BURDEN | | 248 |
| OVERHEAD RECOVERY | | 1227 |
| OVERTIME PREMIUM LABOR | 30.0 | 160 |
| OTHER PREMIUM LABOR | 6.0 | 242 |
| TOTAL PERSONNEL COSTS | | 2820 S |

MATERIALS & SERVICES

| PO NO | REF NO | OBJ | | DESCRIPTION | REQUESTOR | |
|---|---|---|---|---|---|---|
| 61289 | 54065 | 48 | 438 | REA EXPRESS | KIRK | 42 |
| 17234 | 87413 | 48 | 456 | GED SUPPLY CO | COOK | 10 |
| | 04461 | 71 | 448 | P.T.&T. 326-6200 | NAGY | 2 |
| | | | | TOTAL M&S COSTS | | 56 S |
| | | | | FEE | | 158 |
| | | | | TRANSACTION TOTAL | | 3034 T |

mentioned the "glowing reports" which reached his ears in the early stages of the work. These reports, which came to him only from Denby, were later significantly modified, and Denby apparently implied that NRL had been "leading him on." Kenney pointed to the complete lack of economic evaluation of alternative processes in the experimentation. He seemed unaware of the fact that at Denby's insistence all economic analysis was supposed to be done by the client. Kenney was most dissatisfied that NRL had not complied with all the provisions of the proposal, particularly those that re-

**Exhibit 3**
Technical Evaluation

By Ronald M. Benton
*Director, Process Economics Program*

*Principal Conclusions*

1. The original approach to the investigation as presented in the proposal is technically sound. The accomplishments could have been greater had this been followed throughout the course of the project, but the altered character of the investigation did not prevent accomplishment of fruitful research.

**Exhibit 3** ***(continued)***

2. The technical conduct of this project on NRL's part was good despite the handicaps under which the work was carried out. Fundamental and theoretical considerations were employed in suggesting the course of research and in interpreting the data. There is no evidence to indicate that the experimental work itself was badly executed.
3. Significant accomplishments of this project were as follows:

   *a.* *Extraction of vertile from iron ore by several alternative processes.* Conception of these processes was based on fundamental considerations and demonstrated considerable imagination. As far as the work was carried out at NRL, one or more of these processes offers promise of commercial feasibility.
   *b.* *Nitrogen fixation.* This development resulted from a laboratory observation. The work was not carried far enough to ascertain whether or not the process offers any commercial significance. It was, however, shown that the yield of nitrogen oxides was substantially greater than has previously been achieved by either thermal or plasma processes.
   *c.* *Reduction of nickel oxide and probably also garnerite to nickel.* These findings were never carried beyond very preliminary stages and the ultimate commercial significance cannot be assessed at this time.
   *d.* *Discovery that microwave plasmas can be generated at atmospheric pressure.* Again the commercial significance of this finding cannot be appraised at present. However, it opens the possibility that many processes can be conducted economically that would be too costly at the reduced pressures previously thought to be necessary.

4. The proposal specifically stated that the selection of processes for scale-up and economic studies would be the responsibility of the client. I interpret this to mean that NRL was not excluded from making recommendations based on economic considerations. Throughout the course of the investigation, NRL did take economic factors into account in its recommendations.
5. Actual and effective decisions of significance were not documented by NRL and only to a limited extent by the client. There was no attempt on NRL's part to convey the nature or consequences of such decisions to the client's management.
6. The NRL reports were not well prepared even considering the circumstances under which they were written.
7. It is possible that maximum advantage was not taken of the technical capabilities of personnel in the Electromagnetic Sciences Laboratory. Furthermore, they appeared to have been incompletely informed as to the overall approach to the investigation.
8. There was excessive involvement of the client in the details of experimental work. Moreover, there were frequent changes of direction dictated by the client. Undoubtedly these conditions hampered progress and adequate consideration of major objectives and accomplishments.
9. In the later stages of the project, the client rejected a number of processes and equipment types proposed by NRL for investigation of their commercial feasibility. From the information available to me, I believe that these judgments were based on arbitrary opinions as to technical feasibility and superficial extrapolations from other experience as to economic feasibiity that are probably not valid.

**Exhibit 3 *(continued)***

*Evaluation of Client's Complaints*

Following are the comments responding to the points raised by the client management during your conversation:

1. *Client anticipated a "full research capability." He had hoped for participation by engineers, chemists, economists and particularly counted on the provision of an "analytical capability." It was this combination of talents that brought him to NRL rather than* [*a competitor*]. *He feels that the project was dominated almost exclusively by chemists.*

   This complaint is completely unfounded. All the disciplines appropriate to the investigation (as called for in the proposal) were engaged on the project to some degree. In addition, men of exceptional capabilities devoted an unusually large amount of time to the project. The client never officially altered the conditions of the proposal stating that no economic studies should be performed by NRL and there was no explicit expression of this desire on the part of the client until near the project termination.

2. *The analytical services were poor. They were sometimes erroneous and there were frequent "deviations." Data was given to the client too hastily, without further experiment and careful analysis, and as a result a significant amount of the data was not reproducible, NRL was inclined to be overly optimistic. "Glowing reports" would be made only to be cancelled or seriously modified later.*

   There is no way of determining whether the analytical services were good or bad, but one can never expect all analytical work to be correct or accurate. Because the client insisted on obtaining raw data, they would certainly receive some analyses that were erroneous. With respect to the allegation that NRL was overly optimistic, there were no recommendations or opinions expressed in the NRL reports or included in the client's notes that can be placed in this category. Whether or not there were verbal statements of this kind cannot of course be ascertained.

3. *There were "errors in the equations and the client was not informed of the changes." This refers to the case of a computer program that had not been "de-bugged." It was the client who discovered the errors and informed NRL of the discrepancies. (The program was eventually straightened out by the Math Sciences Department.)*

   The client's complaint that they were given a computer program which had not been "de-bugged" is valid, but it is not certain that the project leadership gave them the program without exercising normal precautions for its accuracy. The program was developed by a person not presently with NRL and for another project. He transmitted it without any warning that "de-bugging" had not been conducted. It is even possible that the existence and source of error could not have been determined in his usage and would only appear in a different application.

4. *NRL told the client that the "vertile from iron ore" process could be handled commercially in a rotary kiln process and then was informed by his Engineering Division that this was completely infeasible. Plans were then shifted to a fluid bed process and much time and money had been wasted. Client claims that he was not warned that in the fluid bed agglomeration would probably take place.*

**Exhibit 3** ***(continued)***

*Agglomeration did take place the first time this process was tried ("open boats") and the client was greatly upset.*

It is unclear whether the original suggestion that a rotary kiln be used in the vertile process came from the client or NRL. In any event, it is a logical choice of equipment and is used for the production of such low cost items as cement. Without the benefit of at least pilot plant experience that revealed highly abnormal and unfavorable conditions leading to excessive costs, no one would be in a position to state that such equipment would be uneconomic. It is true that a completely standard rotary kiln probably could not be employed, if for no other reason than to prevent the escape of toxic hydrogen sulfide gas from the equipment. At least special design would be needed and probably some mechanical development. However, it is rare that any new process can be installed without special design and development and it is naive to expect otherwise.

I do not know, of course, how much time was actually spent on the "elaborate plans" for the vertile process using a rotary kiln. I can, however, compare it with generally similar types of studies that we carry out in the Process Economics Program. For this kind of process we would expend about 45 engineering man-hours, and the design calculations would be more detailed than the client's engineer made (his cost estimates incidentally reflected inexperience in this field). I doubt, therefore, that this effort represented a serious expenditure of money and would not have been a complete waste even if the process had been based on a partially false premise. The contention that the client was not informed of the agglomeration properties of the vertile while the reaction was taking place seems unlikely. The client's representatives were so intimately concerned with the experimental work that it would be unusual if the subject had not been raised. Moreover, it is doubtful that the client would have been deterred by NRL's warning, in view of their subsequent insistence that considerable effort be devoted to finding means by which a fluid bed could be operated.

5. *The meetings were poorly planned by NRL.*
   There is no way of evaluating this complaint, but certainly the extreme frequency of the meetings would not be conducive to a well-organized meeting.

6. *Experimental procedures were not well planned.*
   Apparently this refers to the client's desire that experiments be planned in detail as much as three months in advance. Such an approach might conceivably be useful merely for purposes of gathering routine data. It is naive to think that research can or should be planned to this degree and certainly if NRL had acceded to the request it would have been a fruitless time-consuming exercise.

7. *Economic support was not given by NRL.*
   As mentioned above, the proposed specifically excluded NRL from economic evaluations, but NRL did make use of economic considerations in its suggestions and recommendations.

8. *NRL promised to obtain some manganese nodules but never produced them.*
   Manganese nodules were obtained by NRL but no experiments were ever run with them. Many other screening experiments originally planned were never

**Exhibit 3 *(continued)***

carried out because of the changed direction of the project. It seems likely, therefore, that the failure to conduct an experiment with manganese nodules was not NRL's responsibility.

9. *The client claims that he does not criticize NRL for failing "to produce a process." He says that he never expected one, that he wanted a good screening of ores and reactions as called for in the proposal, and that he had hoped for results from the theoretical studies—Task B. This he feels he did not get. We did not do what the proposal called for.*

   The statement that a process was not expected seems entirely contrary to the course of the project. There was universal agreement among NRL personnel involved that almost immediately after the project was initiated it was converted into a crash program to find a commercial process. In fact, the whole tenor of the project suggests a degree of urgency incompatible with a systematic research program. It is quite true that the theoretical studies as a part of Task B were never carried out. According to the project leader this part of the proposal was never formally abandoned, it was merely postponed. Unfortunately, this situation was never documented by NRL, as was the case with other significant effective decisions.

*Additional Comments*

1. It appears that the first indication that the client expected economic studies or evaluations of commercial feasibility occurred during the summer of 1973. At this time the project leader was severely criticized by the client's representatives for having proposed a process (hydrochloric acid pickling) that was economically infeasible. The basis for this criticism was that hydrochloric acid pickling of steel had not proved to be economically feasible. It is totally unreasonable to expect that NRL would have access to information of this kind, and such a reaction would certainly have the effect of discouraging any further contributions of an economic or commercial nature by NRL rather than encouraging them. Actually it is patently ridiculous to directly translate economic experience of the steel industry with steel pickling to leaching a sulfided titanium ore. Nevertheless, I directed an inquiry to a responsible person in U.S. Steel as to the status of hydrochloric acid pickling. His response (based on the consensus of their experts) was diametrically opposite to the client's information. While there are situations that are more favorable to sulfuric acid pickling, hydrochloric acid pickling is generally more economic and is becoming increasingly adopted.
2. The reports written by NRL were requested by the client, but on an urgent and "not fancy" basis. If such were the case, it is understandable that the project leader would be reluctant to expend enough time and money on the report to make it representative of NRL's normal reports. However, the nature of the reports seems to indicate that they are directed toward the same individuals with whom NRL was in frequent contact, or persons with a strong interest in the purely scientific aspects. The actual accomplishments of the project were not brought out in a manner that would have been readily understandable to client's management.

*Recommendations*

It is recommended that consideration be given to the establishment of a simple formal procedure by which high risk projects could be identified at the proposal

**Exhibit 3** ***(concluded)***

stage and brought to the attention of the division vice president. There should also be a formal procedure, operative after project acceptance, in which specific responsiblities are assigned for averting or correcting subsequent developments that would be adverse to NRL's and the client's interests.

Some of the factors that would contribute to a high risk condition are insufficient funding, insufficient time, low chance of successfully attaining objectives, an unsophisticated client, public or private political conditions, and so forth. The characteristics that made this a high risk project were certainly apparent at the time the proposal was prepared.

---

**Exhibit 4**

---

MEMORANDUM

January 8, 1974

To: Sam Lacy
From: Mac Davidson
Re: The Exco Project—Conclusions

The decision to undertake this project was made without sufficient consideration of the fact that this was a "high risk" project.

The proposal was technically sound and within the capabilities of the groups assigned to work on the project.

There was virtually no coordination between the working elements of Physical Sciences and Electronics in the preparation of the proposal.

The technical conduct of this project, with few exceptions, was, considering the handicaps under which the work was carried out, good and at times outstanding. The exceptions were primarily due to lack of attention to detail.

The NRL reports were not well prepared, even considering the circumstances under which they were written.

The client, acting under pressure from his own management, involved himself excessively in the details of experimental work and dictated frequent changes of direction and emphasis. The proposal opened the door to this kind of interference.

There was no documentation by NRL of the decisions made by the client which altered the character, direction, and emphasis of the work.

There was no serious attempt on the part of NRL to convey the nature or consequence of the above actions to the client.

Less than half of the major complaints made by the client concerning NRL's performance are valid.

The project team acquiesced too readily in the client's interference and management acquiesced too easily to the client's demands.

Management exercised insufficient supervision and gave inadequate support to the project leader in his relations with the client.

There were no "overruns" either in time or funds.

---

quired full screening of all materials and the completion of the theoretical work.

Lacy wondered why Denby's changes of the proposal had not been documented by the NRL team. Why hadn't he heard more of the problems of the Exco project before? Lacy requested a technical evaluation of the project from the economics process director, and asked Davidson for *his* evaluation of the project. These reports are given in Exhibits 3 and 4. When he reviewed these reports, Lacy wondered what, if any, additional information he should submit to NRL senior management.

## Questions

1. What additional information should Dr. Lacy submit to NRL senior management?
2. What should Dr. Lacy recommend be done to avoid similar problems with other contracts?

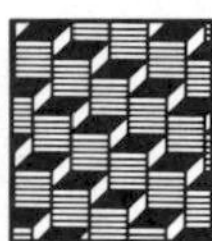

# chapter 11

# Measurement of Output

Output information is needed for two purposes: (1) to measure efficiency, which is the ratio of outputs to inputs (i.e., expenses); and (2) to measure effectiveness, which is the extent to which actual output corresponds to the organization's goals and objectives. In a profit-oriented organization, gross margin or net income are measures that are useful for both these purposes. In a nonprofit organization, no such monetary measure exists because, as explained in Chapter 2, revenues do not reflect true output in the same sense as in a profit-oriented company. This chapter discusses alternative ways of measuring outputs in nonprofit organizations.

In the absence of a profit measure, neither efficiency nor effectiveness can be analyzed unless an adequate substitute can be found. Despite the importance of devising good measures of output, current management control systems tend to be deficient in this respect. For example, until 1970 the New York City Sanitation Department, with 15,000 employees, did not have a single person engaged in the analysis of output. A profit-oriented company of comparable size would probably have a sizable group making such analyses.

The problem of measuring output in nonrevenue terms is not unique to nonprofit organizations. The same problem exists in those responsibility centers in profit-oriented organizations in which discretionary costs predominate (e.g., research, law, personnel). Conversely, output of many individual activities in nonprofit organizations can be measured as readily as corresponding activities in profit-oriented organizations (e.g., food service, vehicle maintenance, clerical activities).

## BASIC MEASUREMENT CATEGORIES

Many different terms are used to classify output measures according to what it is that they purport to measure. For our purposes, three terms will suffice: (1) results measures, (2) process measures, and (3) social indicators.

### Results Measures

A results measure is a measure of output expressed in terms that are supposedly related to an organization's objectives. In the ideal situation, the objective is stated in measurable terms, and the output measure is stated in these same terms. When this relationship is not feasible, as is often the case, the output measure represents the closest feasible way of measuring the accomplishment of an objective that cannot itself be expressed quantitatively. Such a measure is called a *surrogate* or a *proxy.*

*Example:* A goal of the Department of Defense (see Chapter 7) was to procure and support forces as economically as possible. An objective associated with this goal was to buy at the lowest sound price. Surrogates used to measure this objective are the following:

1. Percent of contracts let after competition.
2. Percent of incentive-type contracts.

A results measure relates to the impact that the organization has on the outside world. If the organization is client-oriented, a results measure relates to what the organization did for the client. Organizations that render service to a class of clients, such as alcoholics or unemployed persons, may measure output in terms of the results for the whole class, or *target group.*

### Process Measures

A process measure relates to an activity carried on by the organization. Examples are the number of livestock inspected in a week, the number of lines types in an hour, the number of requisitions filled in a month, or the number of purchase orders written. The essential difference between a results measure and a process measure is that the former is "ends oriented," while the latter is "means oriented." An ends-oriented indicator is a direct measure of success in achieving an objective. A means-oriented indicator is a measure of what a responsibility center or an individual does. There is an implicit assumption that what the responsibility center does helps to achieve the organization's objectives, but this is not always a valid assumption. For example, in an air pollution program, the change in the amount of $SO_2$ in the atmosphere is an ends-oriented results measure, while the number of inspections made of possible violators is a means-oriented process measure. The implication of a causal relationship between the number of inspections made and the amount of air pollution may or may not be valid. The terms "performance oriented" and "work oriented" are other names for the same distinction between ends-oriented and means-oriented indicators.

Process measures are most useful in the measurement of current, short-run performance. They are the easiest type of output measure to interpret because there presumably is a close causal relationship between inputs and process measures. They measure efficiency, but not effectiveness. Being only remotely related to goals, they are of little use in strategic planning. They are useful in constructing relevant parts of a budget, but only for those activities for which it is feasible to obtain process measures. They are useful in the control of lower-level responsibility centers.

Process measures can lead to ineffective performance if they are unrelated to results measures. For example, the U.S. Air Force measured performance of certain squadrons by the number of hours flown, which is a process measure. Sometimes squadrons would build up a record of performance based on this measure simply by flying for many hours in large circles around a base, without any real accomplishments.

***Productivity Measures.*** Process measures are often called productivity measures. In order to develop a productivity measurement system, the outputs of a person or a responsibility center must be identified, and a unit standard time must be established for each type of output. Total output is calculated by multiplying the quantity of output by these unit standard times. This total is then compared with the actual time.

There are three types of approaches to arriving at unit standards for "office-type" activities:

1. Organizations have developed time standards for individual office operations. One is called MODAPTS (Modular Arrangement of Predetermined Time Standards) developed by the Australian Association for Predetermined Time Standards and Research.
2. Employees keep detailed records of the time taken to perform specific activities, and averages of these records are used to set standards.
3. Observers record the time required to perform activities and the amount of idle time, according to a random plan of observations, and averages of these times are used to set standards. (This procedure is called *work sampling.*)

*Example:* The National Institutes of Health has established productivity measurement systems for many of its support activities. One is the Accounts Payable section, whose function is to examine about 30,000 vouchers monthly to determine whether they are a proper basis for payment.

Various types of vouchers require different amounts of examination time, and standard times have been established by engineering studies. For convenience in calculating, these unit standards were expressed as "equivalent units." The simplest voucher, a transportation request, had a standard time of 7.37 minutes, and this was designated as one equivalent unit. Equivalent units for the other 14 types of documents were determined as the ratio of their standard time to 7.37. For example, a purchase order accompanied by a record of the call had a standard time of 16.68 minutes, which was 2.3 standard units (16.68 ÷ 7.37).

Exhibit 11–1 shows how these measures were used to calculate one person's productivity for a four-week period. Employee F worked 125 productive hours during this period and produced 2,163 equivalent units or 17.31 per productive hour. The standard per productive hour is 8.14 units (60 minutes ÷ 7.37). Employee F therefore performed at 213 percent of standard.[1]

**Exhibit 11–1**
Productivity Calculation

Name: Team 02 Employee: F
Workstation: 15
Period Reported: June 2 to June 28

| *Type of vouchers processed* | *Equiv. Units* | *Invoices Quantity* | *Processed Equiv. Units* |
|---|---|---|---|
| Telephone charge order | 1.20 | 170 | 204.00 |
| Purchase order—No ROC | 2.10 | 197 | 413.70 |
| Purchase Order—ROC | 2.30 | 237 | 545.10 |
| Research contract | 2.80 | 2 | 5.60 |
| Contract—ROC | 2.30 | 341 | 784.30 |
| Contract—No ROC | 2.20 | 51 | 112.20 |
| Library MOD | 2.10 | 47 | 98.70 |
| Total invoices processed | | 1,045 | 2,163.60 |

| | *Hours* |
|---|---|
| Total available hours | 160 |
| Less annual leave | |
| Less sick leave | 8 |
| Less others | |
| Total regular hours | 152 |
| Plus overtime hours | 40 |
| Total hours worked | 192 |
| Less nonproductive hours | 67* |
| Total productive hours | 125 |
| Equivalent units produced per productive hour | 17.31 |
| Performance rating (17.31 ÷ 8.14) | 213% |
| Total treasury rejections charged to the individual | 2 |

* This is a senior level employee who spends quite a bit of time training others, which is reported as nonproductive hours.

[1] From *Measuring Productivity in Accounting and Finance Offices,* Washington, D.C.: Joint Financial Management Improvement Program, September 1981, pp. 4–12.

Productivity *should* mean output per unit of input, and the inputs in this ratio should include labor, energy, equipment, and all the other resources used to achieve the output. In practice, however, productivity usually has a much narrower definition. The term usually means output per person-hour or person-year. Such a measure assumes that labor is the critical resource. An increase in output per person-hour is equivalent to an increase in efficiency if, but only if, input factors other than personnel remain constant.

## Social Indicators

A social indicator is a broad measure of output which is significantly the result of the work of the organization. Unfortunately, few social indicators can be related to the work of a single organization because in almost all cases they are affected by exogenous forces, that is, forces other than those of the organization being measured. The crime rate in a city may reflect the activities of the police department and the court system, but it is also affected by unemployment, housing conditions, and other factors unrelated to the effectiveness of these organizations. Life expectancy (or its converse, morbidity and mortality) is partly influenced by the quality of health care, but it is also affected by nutrition, environmental influences, and other factors. Thus, at best, social indicators are a rough indication of what an organization has accomplished.

Social indicators are so nebulous, so difficult to obtain on a current basis, so little affected by current program effort, and so much affected by external influences that they are of limited usefulness in day-to-day management. They are, however, useful in strategic planning.

Valid social indicators are difficult to collect. They are also difficult to use properly because there is no demonstrable cause-effect relationship. Social indicators that can be collected fairly easily are likely to be of dubious validity. The proportion of youth from a certain school district who fail to pass the armed forces qualifying test may indicate the quality of the educational program in that school district, but only in a tenuous way. Likewise, proxy indicators for intangible factors, such as percentage of registered citizens voting as an indicator of citizenship, or crime and disturbance statistics as an indicator of social unrest, may be collected fairly easily, but are of limited reliability.

Social indicators are often stated in broad terms (e.g., "the expectation of healthy life free of serious disability and institutionalization"). Such statements are generally not so useful as those expressed in more specific, preferably measurable, terms (e.g., infant mortality rates, life expectancy).

## Output Vectors

It is rarely possible to find a single overall measure of the performance of a nonprofit organization that is analogous to the profit measure in a profit-oriented company. The goals of nonprofit organizations are usually complex and often intangible. The outputs of such organizations are accordingly complex, and many separate devices are used to measure them. It is sometimes feasible to combine a multidimensional array of indicators into an aggregate which provides patterns, trends, and indicators of output quality and organizational performance. This may be called an *output vector.*

The weights placed on each component of this output vector should reflect the values of the policymakers, not of the systems analysts or the accountants. The outputs of many programs conceivably could be described by such an output vector if enough work were devoted to constructing it; the question is whether the effort is worthwhile. The Strategic Air Command, for example, for many years measured the performance of each of its wings by an output vector computed by weighting scores for each of several dozen measures of performance. Some observers judged this system to be highly valuable; others were dubious as to whether it was worth its cost.

Dennis Gillings describes an elaborate way of measuring performance in terms of objectives which he (with the assistance of Priscilla Gould) devised for the Lincoln Community Health Center.[2] The nature of this measurement plan is suggested by Exhibits 11–2 and 11–3. Exhibit 11–2 shows the eight goals that were established for this organization. Under each goal, specific activities were identified, and a measure of accomplishment, or target, was agreed to by the center's management for each activity. Some of the activities for one goal are listed in Exhibit 11–3. The outcome measures were set so that an outcome of 0.6 was rated as satisfactory performance, and the relative effectiveness of activities for the whole goal was determined by weighting each of the separate outcomes and adding them. Note that some of the activities were measured on a "yes-no" basis, and others were rated along a scale such that accomplishment of the designated target resulted in an achievement of 0.6.

Many managers decide that such a plan of measuring outputs is more time-consuming than the results justify, but simplified versions of this general approach may be eminently worthwhile.

## OTHER CHARACTERISTICS OF OUTPUT MEASURES

### Subjective or Objective

An output measure may result from the subjective judgment of a person or a group of persons, or it may be derived from data that (unless consciously manipulated) are not dependent on human judgment. A judgment made by a qualified person is usually a better measure of the *quality* of performance

[2] Dennis Gillings, "Evaluation: A Methodology for Determining the Effectiveness of a Social Program in Terms of Goal Fulfillment" (Chapel Hill, N.C.: Department of Biostatistics, School of Public Health, University of North Carolina, October 1972).

**Exhibit 11–2**
Goals and Activities in a Primary Care Organization

**Program level 1:** Program

**Goals level 2** and **Activities level 3:**

- **Target population**
  - Define
  - Check target population being served
- **Operation of center**
  - Building
  - Staff
  - Facilities
  - Courtesy
  - Pleasant decorations
  - Appointment system
  - Walk-ins
  - Patients encouraged to make appointments
  - Reimbursement
  - Registration and encounter forms
  - Reporting system
  - Evaluation
- **Accessibility of health care**
  - Registration
  - Family care
  - Encourage enrollment
  - Transportation of patients
  - Opening hours
  - Keep appointments
  - Transport for CHWs
  - Map
- **Improvement of health**
  - Adult health assessments
  - Child health assessments
  - Immunization
  - Sickle cell
  - EKG
  - Chest X-ray
  - GYN exam
  - Prenatal screening
  - Hypertension follow-up
  - Follow up external referrals
  - Ensure patients keep appointments
  - Health education
  - General improvement of health
- **Quality of care**
  - Review health assessments
  - Encourage patients to keep appointments
  - Follow up external referrals
  - Patients have no difficulty making appointments
  - Waiting time
  - Opening hours
  - Patients comfortable expressing health needs
  - Understand doctors
- **Contribution to quality of life**
  - Employment
  - Training
  - Youth employment
  - Services helpful
  - Other centers
  - Arrange compensation for specialty care
- **Relation to other programs**
  - Liaison with voluntary primary health care facilities
  - Liaison with FOOD project
  - Liaison with local health agencies
- **Catalyst for social reform**
  - Liaison with agencies and corporations for training
  - Other health centers

**Exhibit 11–3**

Activities, Targets, Measures, and Weights—Goal V: Deliver High Quality Health Care; Goal Weight = 5

| *Activity* | *Assessment Regime* | | | *Outcome* | *Achievement* | *Effectiveness* |
|---|---|---|---|---|---|---|
| | *Target* | *Outcome Measure* | *Weight* | | | |
| Establish a routine series of tests and examinations for a complete health assessment. | September 1971. | $x = \begin{cases} 0.4 \text{ if no} \\ 0.6 \text{ if yes} \end{cases}$ Achievement $= x$ | 4 | Yes | 0.60 | 1.00 |
| Encourage patients to keep appointments. | 65 percent of appointments should be kept. | $\left[\text{Proportion of appointments that are kept January–June 1972}\right] \times \frac{12}{13}$ | 2 | 61 percent | 0.56 | 0.93 |
| Establish mechanisms to facilitate follow-up of patients referred to other institutions. | Mechanisms established by March 1972. | $x = \begin{cases} 0.4 \text{ if no} \\ 0.6 \text{ if yes} \end{cases}$ Achievement $= x$ | 3 | Yes | 0.60 | 1.00 |
| Ensure that patients referred to other institutions appear for a consultation. | 50 percent of externally referred patients appear for a consultation at the institution to which they are referred and notification of results sent to center. | $\left[\text{Proportion of externally referred appointments kept about which center notified}\right] \times \frac{6}{5}$ | 3 | 161 appointments. Notification received for 60 i.e., 37.3 percent | 0.45 | 0.75 |
| Ensure that patients have no difficulty making an appointment at the center. | 85 percent of a sample of patients answer negatively to the question: "Have you ever had any difficulty making an appointment at this center." | $\left[\text{Proportion of a sample of patients who answer negatively}\right] \times \frac{12}{17}$ | 2 | 97 percent | 0.68 | 1.14 |

than any objective measure because humans incorporate in their judgment the effect of circumstances and nuances of performance that no set of objective measures can take into account. (Numerical ways of measuring beauty, for example, are far inferior to a visual judgment.) Hospitals are usually reluctant to measure the performance of physicians by any means other than peer review. Professors also prefer peer review judgments but will increasingly accept ratings made by students; many will not accept number of students electing a course, or number of articles published, as valid measures of performance, however.

Subjective judgments are, however, subjective; that is, they depend on the person making the judgment and may be affected by the prejudices, attitudes, and even the person's emotional and physical state at the time the judgment is formed. Objective measures, if properly obtained, do not have these defects.

### Quantitative or Nonquantitative

Strictly speaking, a measure is, by definition, quantitative; nevertheless, much information about output is nonquantitative, that is, it is expressed in words. Information in control systems is usually quantitative so that it can be summarized or compared. Subjective judgments also can be expressed in quantitative terms, however. Grades in schools, even though numerical, are an expression of the instructor's judgment as to where the student's performance is located along some scale. Performance in figure skating contests, ski jumping, and certain other athletic events is measured by the subjective judgments of the judges; the performer is ranked along a numerical scale by each judge, and these ranks are then averaged.

### Discrete or Scalar

A measure of performance may be either a dichotomy ("satisfactory/unsatisfactory" or "go/no-go"), or it may be measured along a scale. For example, in measuring performance of a reading program in a school, a target could be established, such as "80 percent of students should read at or above grade level on a standardized test." If the measure were discrete, any performance of 80 percent or higher would be counted as success, and any performance below 80 percent would be counted as failure. If the measure were scalar, the percentage of students reading at grade level on a standardized test would be used as the measure of output. Each of these types of output measures has its place.

### Quantity or Quality

Performance has both a quantity and a quality dimension. Usually it is more feasible to measure quantity (e.g., number of students graduated) than to measure quality (e.g., how well the students were educated). Despite this difficulty, the quality dimension should not be overlooked. Indeed, the indicator that is chosen to measure quantity usually implies some standard of quality. "Number of lines typed per hour" usually carries with it the implication that the lines were typed satisfactorily in order to be counted, and there may even be an explicit statement of what constitutes a satisfactory line of typing, such as the requirement that it be free of errors. Similarly, the measure "number of students graduated" implies that the students have met the standards of quality that are prescribed for graduation.

In some situations, judgments about quality are limited to such "go/no-go" statements as those given above; either a line of typing was error-free or it was not; either students met the requirements for graduation or they did not. In these situations, it is not feasible to measure quality along a scale; for example, to determine if this year's graduates received a better education than last year's.

***Importance of Quality.*** In a nonprofit organization, measures of quality tend to be more important than in a profit-oriented company because in a profit-oriented company the market mechanism provides an automatic check on quality. If the perceived design and construction of a pair of shoes is shoddy, people will not buy them. The factory will then have to raise quality in order to stay in business. If it doesn't do so, other factories will take its customers away. There is no such mechanism for consumer reaction to the output of many nonprofit organizations. Hospital patients may not be competent to judge the quality of patient care; even if they are dissatisfied, there is little they can do, except in extreme cases. Clients of welfare departments, courts, public safety departments, license bureaus, and other government offices cannot "vote with their feet" as customers of commercial businesses can; they have nowhere else to go. Because of the absence of client checks on quality, it is usually worthwhile to devote considerable effort to developing other measures.

Further, in most public programs, the private motive for the program and the social motive for sponsoring it may diverge so that private and social measure of quality differ. Thus, even if a preschool program produces indifferent results or neurotic children, mothers may still send their children to the program just to get them out of the home. Similarly, if a personnel program neither trains nor places its clients properly, unemployed people may still participate in it out of boredom, or because they *hope* it will assist them, or because they receive a stipend for participation. In such circumstances, unless there are adequate measures of quality in the program's management control system, the program will continue to operate without challenge.

***Surrogates for Quality.*** The absence of quality measures in management control systems may lead to a detrimental emphasis on quantity, for example, people being rapidly pushed through an education program; a large number of quick and careless pollution inspections; quick, shoddy construction jobs. Thus, every effort should be made to find some acceptable quality measure, even though it is crude. Such quality measures are usually available, even in the short run, For example;

In preschool programs one can measure a child's degree of literacy, social acclimation, and so forth before and after the program.

In personnel training, one can ask employers to rate the graduates.

In construction, one can test fulfillment of construction standards.

Even though these measures are crude, and even though they may not even contain the "proper" attribute of quality, they may, if nothing else, serve as good motivators for the program's management.

If, however, there is no demonstrable relationship between inputs and the quality of outputs, it may not be worthwhile to attempt scalar measurements of quality for either planning or for control purposes.

*Example:* The Peace Corps sponsored an attempt at a scalar measurement of the qualitative effectiveness of its program in Peru, using measures that purported to show the change in the well-being of Peruvians during a two-year period. Since there was no plausible way of relating the measures of well-being to the efforts of Peace Corps workers, this effort to measure outputs was probably a waste of time and money.

In the absence of objective data, judgmental estimates of quality may be useful. For example, in a university, subjective comparisons can be made between the standing of a college or department within its professional discipline, or its position currently with its position in the past.

Measurements of quality may require so much elapsed time and be so expensive that they are unwarranted for management control. The same measures may nevertheless be warranted, at least on a sampling basis, as an aid in strategic planning.

*Example:* In 1976 the Rand Corporation reported on an intensive evaluation of the educational voucher program at Alum Rock, California. The technique used was to measure the performance of pupils after the program. This measurement, at best, reflected the performance of the schools at least a year previously, and therefore was of no use in making decisions about the current performance in such schools. Nevertheless, it was undoubtedly useful to those responsible for making strategic decisions about continuing, dropping, or redirecting the educational voucher program.[3]

***Service Measures.*** In some organizations, aspects of the quality of services provided, such as accuracy and response time, are important indica-

---

[3] Margaret A. Thomas, "Multiple Options in Education," *A Working Note* (Santa Monica, Calif.: Rand Corporation, 1976).

tors of quality. Often, objective measures of such aspects may be readily obtainable. Examples are the backlog of requests, the number of checks returned because of error, average time taken to process an application, and the number of applications completed within seven days after their receipt.

## SELECTION OF OUTPUT MEASURES

This section describes considerations that are relevant in selecting the output measures that are to be part of the management control system. Eight general propositions are stated first, and some of these are amplified in the subsections that follow.

### General Propositions

1. *Some measure of output is usually better than none.* Valid criticisms can be made about almost every output measure. Few, if any, of them measure output perfectly. There is a tendency on the part of some managers to magnify the imperfections and thus downgrade the attempt to collect and use output information. In most situations a sounder approach is to take account of the imperfections and to qualify the results accordingly, but nevertheless to recognize that some output data, however crude, is of more use to management than no data at all. The whole idea of "benefit/cost analysis" which was discussed in Chapter 8 rests on the foundation of some measure of "benefits," which means output. For control, measurement of both effectiveness and efficiency depends on some measure of output. It follows that a considerable expenditure of effort in finding and developing output measures is worthwhile.

> ***Example:*** The Income Maintenance Program of Canada administers many social programs. Its ultimate output is the well-being it provides to the families it serves. Its management believes that the following are satisfactory proxies to this output:
>
> Number of accounts administered per man-year.
>
> Units of service performed for clients per man-year.
>
> Processing error rates.
>
> Average waiting time for client interviews.
>
> Percentage of checks returned.

2. *If feasible, relate output measures to measures available from outside sources.* Several professional associations, including those for hospitals, schools, colleges and universities, and welfare organizations, collect information from their members and compile averages and other statistics. These statistics may provide a valuable starting point in analyzing the performance of an organization. Similar data are available from government sources, such as the Office of Productivity and Technology of the Bureau of Labor Statistics

(although not much for nonprofit organizations), the U.S. Department of Health and Human Services, and various state agencies. In some cases the measures reported are too detailed, or not well suited to management needs, but some of the available statistics may nevertheless be useful. In using these published statistics, the organization must be sure that its data are prepared according to the same definitions and ground rules as those used by the compiling organization.

3. *Use measures that can be reported in a timely manner.* There is no point in furnishing information after the need for it has passed. If management needs information quickly in order to act on it, some way of compiling the information quickly must be developed. Timeliness requirements are different for different types of information, however.

4. *Develop different measures for different purposes.* There is no such thing as a general-purpose report on output that is analogous to a general-purpose financial statement. Just as internal accounting statements must be tailor-made to the needs of individual managers, so reports of output must be prepared to meet the needs of the various persons who use them.

5. *Focus on important measures.* For most responsibility centers, and for an organization as a whole, there are usually a relatively few *key result measures* that are the important indicators of the quality and quantity of performance. In a given situation, opinions may differ as to what these are, but it is usually worthwhile to give careful thought to identifying them.[4]

6. *Don't report more information than is likely to be used.* This is related to the preceding point. In developing a new system, there is a tendency to collect a great mass of data so as to be certain that somewhere within the mass are data that will meet everyone's desires. Too much data may swamp the system, increase its "noise level," draw attention away from important information, and lessen the credibility of the system as a whole. In a report on an output measurement effort for the government of Canada, one of the major criticisms was "some early projects focused too much on detail and the systems which emerged were too complex and cumbersome to administer."[5]

7. *If feasible, tie output measures to expense measures.* For several purposes, it is useful to develop a cost per unit of output, and this ratio obviously can be calculated only if the definition of output corresponds to the definition of the cost object involved.

8. *Don't give more credence to surrogates than is warranted.* A surrogate can be a useful approximation of actual output, but it never should be interpreted as representing actual output. Its limitations must be kept in mind when using the information.

---

[4] For an excellent discussion of this point, see David V. Mollenhoff, "How to Measure the Work of Professionals," *Management Review,* November 1977, p. 39.

[5] Hon. Robert Andras, "Progress Report on the Measurement of Performance in the Public Service of Canada," Report to the House of Commons, November 1977, p. 4.

## Comparability

When one organization's output information is being compared with averages of other organizations, it is important that the data be comparable. This requires that the detailed definitions used in compiling the averages be studied carefully; the user should not rely on the brief titles given in the tables themselves.

> ***Example:*** The reporting system of the Department of Health of the State of New York defines "hospital bed" three different ways: "certified beds," "bed complement," and "total beds." Unless users know which of these definitions corresponds to the meaning of "beds" that they are accustomed to (e.g., which of them include bassinets?), they may make invalid comparisons.

Comparability is especially important when the reported data are for costs per unit of output. If the organization's definitions do not correspond to those used for both the numerator and the denominator of this ratio, the comparison is invalid. "Cost per FTE student" can be a valuable statistic, but there are several different ways of defining the denominator of this ratio, "Full-time equivalent student," and innumerable ways of defining the elements of cost that make up the numerator.

One should also ensure that the underlying data from which the statistics were derived were reliable. Many people believe that certain statistics on education published by the Department of Education were compiled from data of dubious validity submitted by respondents. Obviously, one can't expect to obtain valid averages from poor raw data.

> ***Example:*** An urban manager started monitoring the amount of waste collected per day, as measured by the sanitation workers in his department. He was surprised to find that it was remarkably consistent from one day to the next. The manager called in some sanitation workers to try to understand these results, but to no avail. Finally the manager said to one worker, "Just how do you measure those cubic yards of garbage?" Shamefacedly, the worker replied, "To tell the truth, I can't tell a cubic yard from a front yard."

Within an organization, the output measures must be compatible with the expense measures if costs per unit of output are to be obtained. It sometimes happens that the output measurement system is developed by one group and the expense reporting system by another group, and under these circumstances incompatability is likely. If the ratio is for responsibility centers, the responsibility center must be defined in the same way in measuring outputs and in measuring expenses; this is also the case for program elements or for other cost objects.

## Timeliness

For management control purposes a timely, but less accurate, output measure is usually preferable for an accurate, but less timely, measure. Timeliness is not equivalent to speed in this context, but rather is related to the time span of the task.

> *Example:* Mortality from emphysema, which can be measured only years after the occurrence of the cause of the disease, is less useful for control of air pollution programs than less accurate but more timely meaures, such as the number of persons with eye/ear/nose/throat irritations, or the number who are advised by physicians to move to another locality, or the amount of effluent in the air.

The problem of timeliness is different in nonprofit organizations (especially government) than it is in profit-oriented organizations, for several reasons. The first is that output often cannot be measured immediately after the effort has been applied. The results of funds invested in a school program in September may not be measurable until the following June. The effect of interest rate subsidies on the stock of low-income housing may not be measurable for two or three years after the program was initiated because of the time necessary to design and construct buildings.

Second, reports on a program may work their way through several organizational layers. Thus Title I, an educational program, provides grants through a state educational agency, then through a local educational agency, and ultimately to the local Title I administrator. The data which work their way back through this chain could well be several months old by the time they reach program analysts in Washington.

Third, some data, although not timely, may indicate a situation which is not likely to have changed since the time of measurement. Thus, the data are as important as if they were current. School segregation data is an example of data that need not be collected frequently.

## Different Measures for Different Purposes

The types of output measures that are appropriate for use in a given organization tend to be arranged along a continuum. At one end are rough social indicators that are closely related to the goals of the organization, and at the other end are precisely stated process measures that are only remotely related to the goals of the organization.

> *Example:* For the U.S. Information Agency, one extreme is the degree to which the agency influences international behavior through its activities. A second level indicates the extent to which specific attitudes and opinions of the governing members of other nations have been changed by the agency's work. A third level represents a measurement of the increase of understanding of people overseas in regard to specific issues. A fourth level is a count of the number of times people have been reached by media of different kinds. A fifth and lowest level is a count of the number of "media products" produced by the agency.

It is useful to think of output measures in terms of this continuum for two reasons. First, higher-level output measures are better indicators of program effectiveness than are lower-level measures. The latter often are not closely related to program goals. Second, lower-level indicators are easier to specify and quantify than are higher-level indicators. This fact explains the prevalence of measures of project efficency or effectiveness which are irrelevant to overall program goals.

The continuum also corresponds to the relative usefulness of types of output indicators at various levels in the organization hierarchy. Social indicators and results measures are most useful to top management, whereas process measures are most useful to first-line supervisors.

> ***Example:*** A regional Air Pollution Control Administration headquarters has a broad variety of measures. It is concerned with its own efficient functioning; that is, it has its own process measures (how fast a request is considered, how quickly budget and project requests can be handled, etc.). At the other end of the spectrum, it has objectives for air quality in each region. The progress toward these objectives can be measured by the appropriate instrumentation.
>
> In between these process measures and results measures there is a variety of measures related to the functioning of the regional administrator and the state programs within a region. For example, the agency may establish as an objective the improvement of air quality in the New England region by more vigorous antipollution efforts on the part of the Commonwealth of Massachusetts.

In comparing the output measurement problem of various agencies, it is useful to think of another continuum, one that is expressed in terms of the degree to which the goals and the means of reaching those goals are understood. At one extreme are agencies in which there is disagreement among policymakers as to what the goals should be and as to the relative importance of various goals, and in which the effectiveness of various techniques is not well understood (e.g., little is known about the relative effectiveness of various methods of teaching preschool children). At the other extreme are agencies where goals and the optimum means of reaching them are reasonably clear-cut (e.g., U.S. Postal Service). In agencies of the former type, determination of what the program should be trying to accomplish is itself one of the objectives of the program, and the management control system should facilitate this process of discovery.

## Variety of Measures

In a single organization, there can be a variety of measures, each used for a different purpose. For example, with respect to health care in a community:

1. There can be a measure of the total cost of the health care system as a basis for comparison with the cost of other community services; this measures the relative emphasis given to each service. Expressed as a cost per person in the community, this can be compared with costs per person in other communities as another expression of relative emphasis.
2. There can be an overall cost per patient day in each hospital as a basis

for detecting gross differences in the operating characteristics of each hospital. Per-patient costs for each service (medicine, surgery, pediatrics, psychiatric, etc.) are useful for similar reasons.

3. At a lower level, information can be collected on the cost per episode of care, or cost per admission.
4. At a still lower level, costs per unit of service rendered, such as cost per meal served, can be collected.

## Strategic Planning and Management Control

The control system should provide output information that is useful both for strategic planning and for management control. The criteria governing output measures that are useful for making strategic plans tend to differ from those that are useful for management control in the following ways:

***Precision.*** For strategic planning, rough estimates of output generally are satisfactory. For management control, the measure must be more precise in order to be credible, although, as indicated above, timeliness considerations sometimes outweigh precision ones.

***Causality.*** For management control, there should be a quite plausible link between the efffort (i.e., inputs) of the organization and the output measure. For strategic planning, the connection can be more tenuous, although there should be *some* connection between inputs and outputs if output measures are to be used in analyzing a proposal for a specific program. To include correlating but noncausal output numbers in an analysis is not only a waste of time, but may do more harm than good if it leads people to believe that there is a causal connection when none in fact exists.

The fact that a causal connection cannot be demonstrated is no reason to avoid analyzing plausible connections in order to assess a certain program, however. It simply means that decisions must be based on judgments unaided by this kind of quantitative information. For example, it seems obviously desirable to spend money on a judiciary system even though no good measurement of output is available. Conversely, a statistical correlation is not necessarily evidence of a causal connection.

> *Example:* One of the dietary goals cited in an example in Chapter 7 was to reduce cholesterol consumption. Since the mid-1960s there has been a sharp decrease in cardiovascular death rates in the United States, and there has also been a sharp decrease in the average person's daily intake of cholesterol. Some people use this statistical association as evidence of a causal connection between cholesterol and heart disease. Others point out that the 25 percent decrease in smoking by adult males, the more effective treatment of high blood pressure, and better coronary surgery may account for the decline in cardiovascular death rates. Nevertheless, many physicians believe that a decline in cholesterol consumption reduces the risk of heart disease.

***Responsibility.*** For management control, the output measure must be related to the responsibility of a specific person or organization unit. For strategic planning, this is unnecessary. It follows that strategic considerations may require that operating personnel collect data for which they themselves have no use.

*Example:* In connection with Title I education programs which are intended to provide funds for improvement of education of low-income and disadvantaged children, planners in Washington require the collection of data (e.g., test scores) that will be of no use to operating managers. They are nevertheless necessary for reformulating program goals and strategies.

***Timeliness.*** For management control, data on output must be available shortly after the event. For strategic planning, this is less important.

*Example:* Measures of the subsequent performance of elementary students in school are useful for strategic planning, but they cannot be part of a management control system.

***Cost.*** For both strategic planning and management control, the benefits of obtaining information about inputs and outputs must exceed the costs of obtaining such information. For strategic planning purposes, it may be possible to obtain certain data on an *ad hoc* or sampling basis, whereas the continuous collection of these data for management control may be prohibitively expensive.

### Relation to Program Elements

Output measures are desirably, but not necessarily, related to individual program elements. They may also be related to program categories, or even to overall goals or objectives.

*Example:* In education, an output measure may be the number of students with a specified reading skill level. This probably cannot be related to costs or to program elements, except possibly in the primary grades where the development of reading skills may constitute an important specific objective. In other grades and classes, teachers may spend only a fraction of their time on improving reading skills. Nevertheless, the reading skill level attained, along with a number of similar measures, may be a good way of measuring the overall performance of a school.

Although teacher salaries and other costs could be allocated to reading, for example, it would be *(a)* an expensive job to do so, and more importantly, *(b)* students learn reading indirectly as well as directly from reading instruction.

Just as the economy has many indicators of "healthiness" which various people interpret differently, nonprofit organizations have numerous ways of looking at their complex outputs. The results in the social field are often indirect and unexpected. To peg indicators directly to programs may totally overlook some of the lasting results of a program. Thus, a variety of output measures, including a number of surrogates, are often necessary in order to obtain a valid impression of the effectiveness of a program. A series of indirect output measures may make it difficult for top management to measure the effectiveness of a responsibility center, but it is unfair and depressing to morale when "output" is defined in terms that are too narrow.

## Inputs as a Measure of Outputs

Although generally less desirable than a true output measure, inputs are often a better measure of output than no measure at all. For example, it may not be feasible to construct output measures for research projects. In the absence of such measures, the amount spent on a research project may provide a useful clue to output. In the extreme, if no money was spent, it is apparent that nothing was accomplished. (This assumes that the accounting records show what actually was spent, which sometimes is not the case.)

> *Example:* The New Communities Program offers assistance to private and public developers of new communities. Although funds are available, no new projects have been financed since 1974. This is conclusive evidence that the program is not generating outputs.

When inputs are used as proxy output measures, care must be exercised to avoid undue reliance on them, and the organization should try to develop usable measures of output.

## Caution on Use of Surrogates

A surrogate should be closely related to an objective. By definition, however, a surrogate does not correspond exactly to an objective, and it should be used with this limitation in mind. If the lack of correspondence is not recognized, the organization may focus too much attention on the surrogate, and this may be dysfunctional. Achieving the *surrogate* should not be permitted to become more important than achieving the *objective.* The following examples illustrate the principle that caution must be exercised in the selection and use of surrogates.

> ***Example—Small Business Administration:***[6] Consider some of the loan programs of the federal government. Many of these programs, rightly or wrongly, have supposedly the objective of providing loan capital to small enterprises which are too risky for investment by commercial lenders. The Small Business Administration is a case in point. Measures have not been developed, however, which can be used to judge the performance of various regional loan offices in terms of overall program objectives. Defaulted loans, on the other hand, are easily identified;

[6] Charles L. Schultz, Brookings Institution, in testimony before the Joint Economic Committee, October 6, 1969.

and a significant default rate is sure to invite congressional questions. Therefore, loan officials tend to avoid risky loans. As a consequence, far from meeting their original objectives, the programs end up (in many cases) simply in making loans of commercial quality at less than commercial rates. It is difficult to expect public officials to pursue the basic objectives of a program unless they are judged on the basis of performance measures which have some relevance to those objectives.

***Example—Number of Complaints:*** A city used "number of complaints" as a surrogate measure for the performance of the agency that managed low-cost rental housing units. It was later discovered that after this measure was introduced, the agency put considerable pressure on tenants not to make complaints. This made performance as measured by the surrogate appear to improve, whereas service to tenants had actually deteriorated.

***Example—Job Training and Employment:*** When "effectiveness" of a Job Corps training program was being calculated by the contractor, "completions" were the mark of success; "dropouts" were the failures. When the latter appeared to be on the increase, "certificates of completion" were issued every other Saturday instead of the diploma originally given at the end of some previously designated period, such as six months. Immediately, the number of "completions" rose, "dropouts" declined, the "effectiveness" of the enterprise was assured, and so was its continued funding.[7]

Similarly, the success of other U.S. Department of Labor employment was measured by the proportion of people placed in jobs. This led to the practice known as "creaming," accepting as job applicants the "cream" of the unemployed, that is, persons temporarily unemployed and with a high probability of being placed.

***Example—Veterans Administration Hospitals:*** Performance of these hospitals is measured in part by the percentage of beds occupied. Moreover, because many hospital costs are fixed, a high occupancy rate results in a low cost per patient day. Studies have shown that some veterans hospitals tend to keep patients, particularly mental patients, longer than their legitimate need for hospitalization.

The inappropriateness of an output measure may cause the discontinuance of a useful program, but more likely it will support the continuance of a useless one with a corresponding waste of resources. Inappropriate measures also cause agencies to be self-satisfied even though they are not reaching their objectives.

## Reactions to Output Measurement

Attempts to measure output in nonprofit organizations are relatively new, especially attempts to measure the output of professionals. They tend to be resisted by those whose output is to be measured.

---

[7] Ida R. Hoos, *Retraining the Workforce; Analysis of Current Experience* (Berkeley and Los Angeles: University of California Press, 1967), p. 173.

*Example:* Following is a summary of a paper prepared by the Academic Council of the University of California objecting to a proposal to measure and control faculty workload:

A standard workload for the system, the professors said, would encourage large lectures, discourage individual tutorials, demean the status of the faculty, undercut its morale, and inhibit the recruitment of outstanding scholars.

Trying to measure faculty output is an extremely complicated matter, they said, because of the variety of campuses, departments, disciplines, and teaching methods. Simple formulas would be meaningless and misleading, they maintained.

The professors did not address the auditors' specific suggestions that a formula be developed to measure faculty effort in terms of classroom contact hours, type of course, number of tutorial students, number of student credit hours generated, and the participation of teaching assistants. However, they did analyze and reject two of the most important elements in the proposed formula—contact hours and credit hours produced.

Their biggest objection was that the measures did not take into account the growing number of hours spent on field trips and tutorials as well as time spent on class preparation, grading exams, reading terms papers, keeping up with the literature, and supervising teaching assistants.

Further, the council's paper said, neither of those measures gives any clue to the quality of teaching.

All such complexities make generalizations about faculty workloads suspect, the professors said.[8]

This problem will be discussed in more detail in Chapter 14 on implementation.

## SUGGESTED ADDITIONAL READINGS

Association of Government Accountants. *Executive Reporting on Internal Controls in Government.* U.S. General Accounting Office, 1980.

Comptroller General of the United States. *Standards for Audit of Governmental Operations, Programs, Activities, and Functions.* Washington, D.C.: General Accounting Office, 1981.

U.S. General Accounting Office. *Evaluating a Performance Measurement System,* FGMSD 80–57, May 12, 1980.

U.S. Office of Personnel Mangement. *Increasing Federal Work Force Productivity,* January 1980.

U.S. Joint Financial Management Improvement Program. *Implementing a Productivity Program: Points to Consider, 1977* (with minor updates in reprinted versions).

——— *Measuring Productivity in Accounting and Finance Offices,* September 1981.

[8] *The Chronicle of Higher Education,* April 24, 1972, p. 1.

## Case 11–1

# U.S. NAVAL SUPPLY CENTER, NEWPORT, R.I.*

The Naval Supply Center at Newport, Rhode Island, serviced the almost 300 fleet and shore units of the U.S. Navy based throughout New England, New York, and New Jersey. From its 85 buildings and 5 fuel tank farms stretched along five miles of the Narragansett Bay shoreline, the Naval Center received, stored, and issued materials for its customers, whether at home base or deployed on the other side of the globe.

Although handling supplies was the Center's principal mission, it also provided a variety of services for other Navy operations, including purchasing, accounting, data processing, disposal, and household goods shipment.

The Center's 547 civilian employees at Newport were managed by 19 military officers who occupy the key positions, including commanding officer and all department heads. All but one of the officers were members of the Supply Corps, and many held graduate degrees in business administration. In addition to its Newport facilities, the Center had an annex at Bayonne, New Jersey, which employed another 85 civilians to supply ships operating from New York, and to make many of the Center's overseas shipments. The Center was also assigned 10 enlisted men for special functions giving a grand total of 661 employees.

The annual operating budgets for 1974–77 are shown in Exhibit 1.

**Exhibit 1**

| | *Fiscal Year* | | | |
|---|---|---|---|---|
| *Net Funds Authorized** | *1974* | *1975* | *1976* | *Estimated 1977* |
| Operations | $6,177,000 | $5,881,000 | $6,259,000 | $6,408,500 |
| Facilities maintenance | 601,000 | 545,000 | 395,000 | 435,000 |
| Disposal | 191,000 | 170,000 | 214,000 | 232,000 |
| Data processing | 388,000 | 419,000 | 395,000 | 395,000 |
| Total | $7,357,000 | $7,015,000 | $7,263,000 | $7,470,000 |
| * Does not include reimbursables of | $1,098,000 | $1,120,000 | $ 846,000 | $ 528,000 |

Although the budget had increased each year, the increases had not kept pace with inflation. Approximately 70 percent of the budget was for labor, and substantial pay increases were granted to federal employees annually. The 661 employees on March 31, 1977, was a reduction of 16 percent, or 127 people, from the fiscal year 1975 average employment of 788. About half of this reduction was due to a drop in work done by the data processing

* This case was prepared by Joseph E. Kasputys, Harvard Business School. Amounts have been updated subsequently.

and comptroller departments on a reimbursable basis for other Navy operations.

The Center's annual operating budget did not finance the inventory. The customers "bought" items using funds from their own annual operating budgets, which money was then used to replenish the inventory.

## Inventory

The material supplied by the Center covered a spectrum from fuel to electronic repair parts to frozen meats. Some 48,100 different items were carried in inventory, excluding fuel oil.

| *Principal Categories* | *Number of Items* | *Value (millions)* |
|---|---|---|
| Personnel support (food, clothing, medical supplies) | 3,550 | $ 2.2 |
| Technical items (repair parts) | 37,050 | 15.5 |
| Other material (forms, office supplies, housekeeping items, etc.) | 7,500 | 7.4 |
| Total | 48,100 | $25.1 |

For management purposes, the inventory was divided into two major categories:

*"Push" material.* Material automatically sent to the Center for stock. Decisions on items and quantities to be carried were made by central offices that control Navy-wide inventory levels for technical supplies, and were based on material usage rates and the anticipated requirements for new equipment being introduced into the fleet. "Push" material, which included all the 37,050 line items of technical supplies, accounted for approximately 90 percent of the dollar value of the inventory.

*"Pull" material.* Material, including most personnel, general, and industrial supplies, that was ordered by the Center for stock from wholesalers such as the Defense Supply Agency and the General Services Administration. The demands placed upon the Center by customers are used to determine the range (number of different items) and depth (quantity of each item) that are carried.

Prior to 1961, all customers had to submit requisitions to the Center and wait, often for several days, for processing and delivery of the material. Although high-priority requisitions did move through the system rapidly, customers often experienced costly delays when ordering material for lower priority work. The Servmart, a self-service "supermarket" of high-usage items, was developed at Newport to reduce this problem. The customers merely selected what they needed and "checked out" at a checkout counter, which saved the Center handling and delivery costs and put the material in the customers' hands when they needed it. The Servmart accounted for 50 percent of the Center's issues. Due to budgetary restrictions, changing support patterns, and management improvements, the range of the Center's inventory had been steadily shrinking. As a result, an increasingly greater percentage of issues would be made through the Servmart.

## Output Measurement

Outputs for the Center's primary mission, its supply operation, were measured at three different levels—performance of the total Center, of each cost account, and of each different task.

***Overall Performance of the Center.*** The speed of delivery and the success of the inventory in satisfying customer demands were watched carefully by the Center's top management and Washington headquarters. The principal indicators used to measure these outputs were *receipts* of wholesale supplies, *demands* for supplies, *issues* of invoices for shipment, and *shipment.* Receipts, issues, and shipment were measured in both line items and measurement tons, since they involved the actual movement of material. Customer demands were measured only in line items, since they may have to be referred elsewhere for issues.

Washington headquarters gave the Center an objective for each of the four areas. Exhibit 2 summarizes these objectives and shows the Center's performance against them for 1974–77. For receipts, the objective was to process 85 percent within seven days so that they were taken up on the stock records and are in the proper storage location, ready for issue. It was felt that the amount of receipts in process should be kept at a minimum, since they represented unusable stock that tied up inventory dollars.

The objective for issues was a warehouse refusal rate of less than 1 percent. Warehouse refusals occur when the computer indicates material is on hand and issues an invoice, but the material department cannot locate the material in the warehouse. The more common reasons for warehouse refusals are improper recordkeeping or storing the material in the wrong location.

The "shipped on time" objective affected both issues and shipments. Each customer demand carried a priority assigned by the customer, which indicated the maximum time allowed for delivery, varying from 1 day for issue Group 1 to 12 days for issue Group 4. The Center's objective was to ship 95 percent of all issues within these times. Although the assignment of higher priorities did not cost the customer anything extra, there were clear rules governing their use that were policed by both the Center and operational commanders.

Finally, gross and net material availability measured how well the Center's inventory was meeting customer demands. Gross availability was measured against *all* demands received from customers and was a measure of (1) how well the items for the inventory were selected and (2) how well the selected items were managed. From the customer's point of view, gross availability represented the probability that a demand will be filled by the Center in a

**Exhibit 2**
Objectives and Performance Measures for Supply Operations

| | Monthly Average by Fiscal Year (to 3/31/77) | | | | |
|---|---|---|---|---|---|
| | *Obj.* | *1974* | *1975* | *1976* | *1977* |
| Receipts: | | | | | |
| Receipts (M/T) | | 9,800 | 9,520 | 10,935 | 9,577 |
| Receipts (L/I)* | | 16,480 | 17,750 | 16,989 | 10,187 |
| Receipt processing time (85% of all receipts processed through storage within 7 days): | | | | | |
| Regular receipts | 85% | n.a. | 65.7 | 75.6 | 91.0 |
| Material returned by customers | 85 | n.a. | 25.7 | 57.8 | 76.0 |
| Issues: | | | | | |
| Issues (M/T) | | 9,820 | 10,203 | 10,587 | 9,355 |
| Issues (L/I)* | | 57,870 | 57,600 | 57,903 | 53,122 |
| Warehouse refusal rate—less than | 1 | 0.40 | 0.32 | 0.45 | 0.60 |
| Shipped: | | | | | |
| Shipped (M/T) (includes Center issues and transshipments) | | 11,254 | 11,700 | 12,347 | 11,844 |
| Shipped (L/I) (transshipments only) | | 3,650 | 2,865 | 4,187 | 4,888 |
| Shipped on time (95% of all items shipped on time) | 95 | 98.8 | 93.4 | 96.9 | 96.0 |
| Demands: | | | | | |
| Demands (L/I) | | 108,426 | 89,568 | 87,780 | 77,211 |
| Material availability: | | | | | |
| Gross: | | | | | |
| "Pull" material | None | n.a. | 61.9 | 61.2 | 64.2 |
| "Push" material | None | n.a. | 54.9 | 37.1 | 39.9 |
| Net: | | | | | |
| "Pull" material | 94 | 93.5 | 91.6 | 92.2 | 92.2 |
| "Push" material | 75 | 73.1 | 73.6 | 75.2 | 74.7 |

* The discrepancy in receipts and issues line items reflects the fact that the Center received in bulk and issued in smaller quantities.
n.a. = Not available.

timely fashion. Given a particular set of items for the inventory, net availability shows whether these items were in stock when demanded.

Because of the differences in management, separate measurements were made for "Push" and "Pull" material. Although no specific goals were established for gross availability, the "Push" inventory always achieved poorer results than the "Pull" inventory, since only a fraction of all possible technical repair parts were carried in the Center's stocks. Although additional repair parts were carried at the largest Naval Centers, such as the one at Norfolk, many parts were not carried by the supply system at all, and were purchased or fabricated when needed. The goals for net availability were 75 percent for the "Push" inventory and 94 percent for the "Pull" inventory. Since the Center determined neither the range nor depth of the "Push" inventory, meeting the goals for its gross and net availability was the responsibility, not of the Center, but the Navy's central inventory control offices.

All of the output measures in Exhibit 2 were reported on the Weekly Operations Report Measurement Summary (WORMS). Exhibit 3 is a copy of this report, referred to as **WORMS** not only because of its acronym but also because of the problems it could reveal. The only parts of Exhibit 2 filled in are those that have been discussed or are self-explanatory. The report was used by Center management to evaluate the past week's performance and to anticipate problems due to backlogs for the coming week. Since the

**Exhibit 3**
Weekly Operations Report Measurement Summary

NSCNPT 4400/6 (REV 12-69)

PART I - CENTER BUSINESS

| | PRIORITY / CATEGORY | CURRENT WEEK TOTAL | CURRENT WEEK % | PREVIOUS WEEK TOTAL | PREVIOUS WEEK % |
|---|---|---|---|---|---|
| REQUISITION INPUT | GROUP I | 151 | 1.9 | 195 | 2.2 |
| | GROUP II | 2290 | 29.0 | 2388 | 26.8 |
| | GROUP III | 3184 | 40.3 | 4311 | 48.3 |
| | GROUP IV | 2272 | 28.8 | 2024 | 22.7 |
| | TOTAL | 7897 | 100 | 8918 | 100.0 |
| | NSC BEARERS | | | | |
| | ALLOW LISTS | | | | |
| ISSUES | SERVMART | 4495 | 52.4 | 5120 | 50.0 |
| | MAIN SUPPLY | 4086 | 47.6 | 5045 | 50.0 |
| | W'HSE REFUSALS | 34 | 0.4 | 57 | 1.0 |
| | SHIPS PRESENT | PIERS 19 | OTHER 6 | PIERS 16 | OTHER 6 |

PART II PROCESSING TIME

| PRIORITY / CATEGORY % SHIPPED ON TIME | CURRENT WEEK | PREVIOUS WEEK | MONTH TO DATE |
|---|---|---|---|
| GROUP I | 100.0 | 96.0 | 100.0 |
| GROUP II | 97.0 | 95.0 | 97.0 |
| GROUP III | 99.0 | 95.0 | 99.0 |
| GROUP IV | 100.0 | 100.0 | 100.0 |
| OVERALL | 98.0 | 97.0 | 98.0 |
| REC. PROC. WITHIN 0-7 DAYS | | | |
| REG REC THRU STK RECORDS | | | |
| REG REC THRU STORAGE | 97.0 | 90.0 | 97.0 |
| MTIS THRU STK RECORDS | | | |
| MTIS THRU STORAGE | 98.0 | 92.0 | 98.0 |

PART III - SERVMART INFORMATION

| ISSUES (L/I) | REPLENTISHMENT (L/I) | NOT IN STOCK (L/I) |
|---|---|---|
| 4495 | 337 | 80 |

| INVENTORY VALUE ($) | VALUE OF ISSUES ($) |
|---|---|
| | |

PART IV - PURCHASE MEAN LEAD TIME ISSUES

| PRIORITY | OBJ DAYS | OVERALL | IN-DEPT | %PROC ON TIME | DOCS |
|---|---|---|---|---|---|
| GROUP I | 2 | | | 100.0 | 4 |
| GROUP II | 8 | | | 52.0 | 152 |
| GROUP III & IV | 16 | | | 35.0 | 149 |

PART V - MATERIAL AVAILABILITY

POINT OF ENTRY

| WEEKLY | TOTAL | PUSH | PULL |
|---|---|---|---|
| W/SERVMART | 79.0 | | |
| W/O SERVMART | 62.0 | 37.4 | 68.1 |
| MONTH TO DATE | TOTAL | PUSH | PULL |
| W/ SERVMART | 79.0 | | |
| W/O SERVMART | 62.0 | 37.4 | 68.1 |

NET EFFECTIVENESS

| WEEKLY | TOTAL | PUSH | PULL |
|---|---|---|---|
| W/ SERVMART | 93.6 | | |
| W/O SERVMART | 87.5 | 74.6 | 91.2 |
| MONTH TO DATE | TOTAL | PUSH | PULL |
| W/ SERVMART | 93.6 | | |
| W/O SERVMART | 87.5 | 74.6 | 91.2 |

| WEEKLY | CURRENT WEEK | PREVIOUS WEEK |
|---|---|---|
| TECHNICAL COGS | | |
| PERSONNEL COGS | | |
| MONTH TO DATE | CURRENT WEEK | PREVIOUS WEEK |
| TECHNICAL COGS | | |
| PERSONNEL COGS | | |

PART VI - MISCELLANEOUS

| ITEM | INPUT | PRODUCTION | BACKLOG |
|---|---|---|---|
| STORAGE ISSUE L/I | 4982 | 5434 | 953 |
| STORAGE ISSUE M/T | | 514 | |
| STORAGE RECPT L/I | 1409 | 1609 | 69 |
| STORAGE RECPT M/T | | 709 | |
| SHIPPING L/I | 1101 | 1632 | 335 |
| SHIPPING M/T | 211 | 211 | 59 |
| DELIVERY - PALLETS | | | |
| PACKING L/I | | | |
| SCREENING L/I | | | |

| ITEM | INPUT | PRODUCTION | BACKLOG |
|---|---|---|---|
| RECEIVING | | | |
| HHG CONTRACT JOBS | | | |
| HHG CLAIMS | | | |
| DEMAND PROCESSING | | | |
| KEYPUNCH (DOCS) | | | |
| PURCHASE L/I | | | BUYER |
| PURCHASE DOCUMENTS | | | TYPE |
| DISPOSAL | | | |

**Exhibit 3** ***(concluded)***

NSCNPT 4400/6 (BACK)

PART VIII - BAYONNE ANNEX WORKLOAD

| CATEGORY | CURRENT WEEK | PREVIOUS WEEK | MONTH TO DATE | |
|---|---|---|---|---|
| REQUISITION INPUT | | | | |
| MAT AVAIL - POINT OF ENTRY | | | | |
| MAT AVAIL - NET | | | | |

| CATEGORY | RECEIPTS | | ISSUES | |
|---|---|---|---|---|
| | CURRENT WEEK | PREVIOUS WEEK | CURRENT WEEK | PREVIOUS WEEK |
| STORAGE L/I | | | | |
| STORAGE M/T | | | | |
| COLD STORAGE L/I | | | | |
| COLD STORAGE M/T | | | | |
| PURCHASE (DOCS) | | | | |

PART VIII - STAFFING

| DEPARTMENT | CEILING | ON BOARD | | |
|---|---|---|---|---|
| | | GRADED | UNGRADED | TOTAL |
| COMMAND | 5 | 5 | - | 5 |
| 10 | 19 | 15 | 2 | 17 |
| 50 | 121 | 120 | - | 120 |
| 60 | 66 | 58 | - | 58 |
| 100 | 41 | 42 | - | 42 |
| 200 | 19 | 20 | - | 20 |
| 300 | 245 | 73 | 181 | 254 |
| 700 | 30 | 3 | 26 | 29 |
| BX | 85 | 24 | 60 | 84 |
| TOTALS•• | 631 | 360 | 269 | 629 |

REMARKS:

••FUNDED CEILING -

AVERAGE GRADE ______ (NPT ______, BX ______

•CODE 60 CEILING ON BOARD

PART IX - OVERTIME - FISCAL YEAR

| | | |
|---|---|---|
| FUNDS AUTHORIZED (FY 71) | | $75,000 (100%) |
| EXPENDED TO DATE: (FROM 1 JULY) | | |
| NEWPORT | $36,472 (63.5%) | |
| BAYONNE | 20,924 (36.5%) | |
| TOTAL | 57,396 (100.0%) | |
| BALANCE OF FUNDS REMAINING THIS FISCAL YEAR | | 17,604 (23.5%) |
| CALENDAR DAYS REMAINING THIS FISCAL YEAR | | 54 (14.8%) |

REMARKS:

use of overtime was a principal means of reducing backlog, the status of overtime funds was also shown. The only material availability figures that were reported to Washington were those without the Servmart activity, since headquarters believes that the high volume but low dollar value Servmart business would mask main supply performance.

## The Resource Management System

Outputs were also measured by cost account, as part of the Resource Management System (RMS) implemented throughout the Department of Defense in 1968. Under RMS, budgets were on an accrual basis and reflect expenses (the use of resources) rather than obligations (a government accounting concept reflecting essentially the purchase of resources) as in the past. As a result, responsibility centers were charged with all measurable expenses, as opposed to as little as 40 percent under former systems. This new system permitted managers to determine the true costs of specific missions, compare actual progress with planned progress, and, with accurate output measurement, relate resources consumed to work done. The RMS accounting techniques provided vastly improved data on inputs, which need to be compared to equally reliable data on outputs.

Following RMS procedures, the Center collected all costs by job order, which uniquely identified both a responsibility center and a cost account. The cost account covered a function such as incoming storage operations, key punch operations, or bulk fuel distribution. Within the cost account, costs were segregated by type, such as military and civilian salaries, overtime, material, and so forth. Each month, costs were summarized by cost account within responsibility center to get total expenses, which were then compared to the responsibility center's budget. The Center was divided into some 50 responsibility centers and 115 cost accounts, 60 of which had an associated output measure. Each cost account and its related output measure, which was called a work unit, had been carefully defined.

Below is a sample definition for the "Bulk Issue" cost account, which was charged chiefly by the material department:

*Cost Account 21B2, Bulk Issue*

a. *Scope.* The cost account includes all physical handling (including the operation of materials handling equipment) incident to the breaking out of material for issue from large- and medium-lot bulk stores and the loading of the material for movement to packing, preservation, bin location, shop stores, Servmarts, advance base assembly areas when no intermediate operations are necessary prior to consolidation of material being issued, and for delivery to central or marine terminals; and direct supervision of the foregoing operations. This cost account *excludes* physical movement of material from one bulk storage location to another; physical handling, selection or off-loading of material to and from preservation, packaging and packing areas or repair shops for minor repairs when such operations are incident to care of material in storage; physical handling of bulk stock from permanent storage location directly into transportation carrier; and physical movement of bulk stock to other work areas when the movement exceeds normal forklift truck travel distances.

b. *Work Unit.* Measurement tons.

   1. *Definition.* Measurement tons (1 M/T = 40 cubic feet) of material physically handled incident to the issue of material from storage for shipment or delivery including issues to Servmarts.

2. *Point of Count.* In the land–air freight and water freight operations upon completion of the final loading of material onto carriers for final shipment or delivery and in bulk issue for tonnage moved to shop stores and Serv-marts.
3. *Backlog.* Will not be reported.

Several departments could charge the same cost account. For example, cost account 21AK, Incoming Storage Operations, was charged by the material department for all physical handling of material upon receipt. These costs, together with the output measure which is measurement tons, were shown on the material department's monthly reports. At the same time, the data processing department charged this cost account for the operation of a remote computer terminal serving the incoming storage operation. These latter costs appeared on the data processing department's monthly reports with no related output measure. Thus, although 60 of the cost accounts did have related output measures, each measure was used for only one of the several responsibility centers that could charge the account.

At the end of the month, a report was prepared that gave budgeted and actual expenses and work units. To eliminate the effects of volume fluctuations, unit costs were calculated on an actual and budgeted basis and a standard unit cost was shown, if available. Backlogs were also reported, if required. This report, called Local Performance Statement, was prepared monthly and cumulatively each fiscal year for each responsibility center. Exhibit 4 is a monthly report for responsibility center 310, the storage division of the material department. The Bulk Issue cost account described above appears on this report.

For further analysis, expenses were segregated by type for each cost account within a responsibility center, also on a monthly and cumulative basis.

***The Manpower Utilization and Control System.*** At the third and final level, output was measured by task for each worker and compared to a standard, using the Manpower Utilization and Control System (MUACS). The standards, which have been set through time studies, were used for workload planning and budgeting, while the actual output was used to evaluate and control performance. The following sample monthly figures for the material department illustrate the four basic types of standards and man-hours earned against each one.

| *Type of Standard* | *Man-Hours Earned* |
|---|---|
| 1. Engineered Standard (ES) | 17,764 |
| 2. Statistical Standard (SS) | 230 |
| 3. Engineered Fixed Allowance (EFA) | 20,138 |
| 4. Statistical Fixed Allowance (SFA) | 8,329 |
| Total | 46,461 |

**Exhibit 4**

Local Performance Statement, Monthly—For Period Ending April 30, 1977

| | | | | Expenses | | Work Units | | Unit Cost | | |
|---|---|---|---|---|---|---|---|---|---|---|
| *LMC* | *FC* | *CA* | *Title* | *Actual* | *Budget* | *Actual* | *Budget* | *Actual* | *Budget* | *Standard Backlog WU* |
| 310 | | | | | | | | | | |
| | A5 | 21AJ | Receiving operations | 1,384 | 757 | | | | | |
| | A5 | 21AK | Incoming storage | 2,822 | 3,331 | 3,943 | | 0.72 | | 0.87 |
| | A5 | 21BA | Light packing | 895 | 625 | | | | | |
| | A5 | 21B2 | Bulk issue | 7,801 | 7,686 | 3,762 | 4,020 | 2.07 | 1.91 | 1.91 |
| | A5 | 21B3 | Bin issue | 5,476 | 4,595 | 14,971 | 15,755 | 0.37 | 0.29 | 0.29 |
| | A5 | 21B4 | Shipping | 866 | 1,109 | | | | | |
| | A5 | 21B9 | Package issue support | 9,397 | 8,087 | | | | | |
| | A5 | 21C1 | Care material in store | 6,415 | 4,050 | | 53 | | 76.42 | 76.17 |
| | A5 | 21C2 | Rewarehousing | 3,617 | 2,680 | | 87 | | 30.80 | 30.80 |
| | A5 | 21C6 | Inventory | 377 | 444 | 990 | 596 | 0.38 | 0.74 | 0.74 |
| | A5 | 21D5 | Material screen identification | 84 | 399 | | | | | |
| | A5 | 21H1 | Storage and warehouse support | 1,698 | 951 | | | | | |
| | A5 | 21H3 | | 221 | | | | | | |
| | A5 | 21 | Storage warehouse operations | 41,053 | 34,714 | | | | | |
| | A5 | 22BA | SC require division | 314 | 124 | | | | | |
| | A5 | 22 | | 314 | 124 | | | | | |
| | A5 | 2330 | Household goods | 165 | | | | | | |
| | A5 | 23 | Traffic management | 165 | | | | | | |
| | A5 | | Direct product expense | 41,532 | 34,838 | | | | | |
| 310 | | | | 41,532 | 34,838 | | | | | |

Abbreviations:
CA Cost Account.
FC Fund Code.
LMC Local Management Code.
WU Work Units.
N Number.

Within each cost account, different standards were set for each type of material being handled. The reason for this can be found by examining the Bulk Issue (21B2) cost account, which is described above. While the RMS can ascertain the average cost of bulk issue per measurement ton, it does not account for the fact that issues of different materials require different amounts of time. Some of the standards MUACS uses to make this discrimination were as follows:

| *Type of Material* | *Hours per Line Item* |
|---|---|
| Gas cylinders | 0.0177 |
| Electronic parts | 0.0832 |
| General material | 0.0832 |
| Paints | 0.0990 |
| Clothing | 0.1242 |
| Medical supplies | 0.1544 |
| Metals, pipes, and cables | 0.4226 |

Supervisors recorded both man-hours and output for each worker and turned in reports biweekly, at the end of each pay period. To aid supervisors in using the system, the various tasks and associated standards were grouped together for each responsibility center and published in a manual, containing 97 closely printed pages.

Data furnished by the supervisors were used to produce a monthly production report showing performance against each standard, which was used to judge the efficiency of labor. A page from this report is shown in Exhibit 5. The LMC code 3100 identifies the storage division in the material department. The second code, headed "MS," identifies the work area. Codes E, F, and G are unique to Building 12. Only some of the E codes are shown at the bottom of the page, with the remainder of the Building 12 information continued on additional pages. The sixth line from the bottom is job order 3105, which is bulk issue. Since 444 work units were completed and the standard was 0.4226 hours per work unit, Building 12 earned 188 man-hours. However, this work was accomplished with 157.50 man-hours, giving production efficiency of 119.4 percent. This means that 2.8 line items were issued for each man-hour in lieu of the 2.4 line items per man-hour anticipated by the standard. The report also shows that there was a backlog of 97 line items to be issued from Building 12, which, according to the standard, should require 41 man-hours.

## Reports for Headquarters

Washington headquarters were periodically furnished reports on costs and outputs for all three levels—Center, cost account, and task. These reports,

**Exhibit 5**

MUACS Production Report, Month—April 30, 1977

| LMC | M S | Job Order | Type Std. | EARNED/ AUTH MH | Actual MH | PRD EFF/ VAR MH | Planned Rate | Actual Rate | WU Com-pleted | WU Back-log | MH Back-log | Planned Workload | Std. |
|---|---|---|---|---|---|---|---|---|---|---|---|---|---|
| 3100 | A | 3102 | SFA | 148 | 126.00 | 22 | | | | | | | 6.73 |
| 3100 | A | 3103 | SFA | 148 | 146.00 | 2 | | | | | | | 6.73 |
| 3100 | A | 3105 | ES | 209 | 197.00 | 106.1 | 8.1 | 8.5 | 1,684 | | | 1,210 | 0.1242 |
| 3100 | A | 3106 | ES | 17 | 18.00 | 94.4 | 20.5 | 19.4 | 349 | | | 559 | 0.0476 |
| 3100 | A | 3107 | ES | 22 | 16.00 | 137.5 | 14.0 | 19.2 | 307 | | | 220 | 0.0702 |
| 3100 | A | 3111 | ES | 96 | 67.00 | 143.3 | 2.9 | 4.1 | 274 | | | 220 | 0.3518 |
| 3100 | B | 3108 | EFA | 55 | 93.00 | 38 – | | | | | | | 2.50 |
| 3100 | C | 3103 | EFA | 308 | 90.00 | 218 | | | | | | | 14.00 |
| 3100 | C | 3104 | ES | 5 | 6.50 | 76.9 | 22.6 | 17.4 | 113 | | | 8,646 | 0.0476 |
| 3100 | C | 3105 | ES | 72 | 86.00 | 83.7 | 12.1 | 10.1 | 869 | | | 880 | 0.0832 |
| 3100 | C | 3106 | ES | 4 | 4.00 | 100.0 | 15.0 | 15.0 | 60 | | | 154 | 0.0627 |
| 3100 | C | 3107 | ES | 2 | 4.00 | 50.0 | 26.0 | 13.0 | 52 | | | 132 | 0.0314 |
| 3100 | C | 3108 | ES | 1 | 2.00 | 50.0 | 20.0 | 10.0 | 20 | | | 704 | 0.0563 |
| 3100 | C | 3109 | EFA | 9 | 17.00 | 8 – | | | | | | | 0.40 |
| 3100 | C | 3111 | ES | 23 | 33.00 | 69.7 | 7.3 | 5.1 | 169 | | | 154 | 0.1342 |
| 3100 | C | 3112 | ES | 14 | 15.00 | 93.3 | 12.6 | 11.8 | 177 | | | 1,188 | 0.0780 |
| 3100 | D | 3108 | EFA | 90 | 31.50 | 58 | | | | | | | 4.10 |
| 3100 | E | 3103 | EFA | 308 | 274.50 | 33. | | | | | | | 14.00 |
| 3100 | E | 3105 | ES | 188 | 157.50 | 119.4 | 2.4 | 2.8 | 444 | 97 | 41 | 653 | 0.4226 |
| 3100 | E | 3106 | ES | 16 | 7.50 | 213.3 | 8.1 | 17.3 | 130 | | | 427 | 0.1218 |
| 3100 | E | 3107 | ES | 16 | 5.00 | 320.0 | 6.3 | 20.0 | 100 | | | 150 | 0.1639 |
| 3100 | E | 3108 | ES | 11 | 9.00 | 122.2 | 2.2 | 2.7 | 24 | | | 132 | 0.4509 |
| 3100 | E | 3109 | EFA | 4 | 3.00 | 1 | | | | | | | 0.20 |
| 3100 | E | 3110 | SFA | | 9.00 | 9 – | | | | | | | 0.01 |

Abbreviations:

LMC—Local Management Code.
EARNED/AUTH MH—Earned or Authorized Man-Hours.
PRD EFF/VAR MH—Production Efficiency or Man-Hour Variance.
WU—Work Units.
N—Number.

which were summaries of those used by the Center's management, were used to evaluate the Center and compare its performance to that of other supply centers.

## Questions

1. Based upon the outputs and costs shown, how would you evaluate the Center's recent performance?
2. Were the output measurements taken at the Center adequate to assess effectiveness? Efficiency?
3. Were three separate levels of output measurement necessary? What advantages and disadvantages were there to this structure?
4. How did the externally imposed objectives affect the structure and operation of the Center? What is your opinion of this "management by objectives"?
5. Were the reports shown in Exhibits 4 and 5 useful management tools? What problems, if any, are evident in these reports?

## Case 11–2

## MORAZAN AND IZALTENANGO*

In late 1967, the government of the Latin American republic of Soledad agreed to assign a share of the national budget for public health to family planning. Soon afterward, a Family Planning Office was established as a dependency of the Maternal-Child and Nutrition Division of the Ministry of Public Health. By the end of 1972, family planning services were being offered at over 80 health facilities throughout the republic.

Dr. Arturo Vivas, head of the Family Planning Office since late 1972, had just completed the annual evaluation of the performance of each clinic. The evaluation was based upon the percentage of "target population," or women of fertile age (generally considered to be 20 percent of the total population), that each clinic had been able to attract as new users of family planning services. He believed that this was the most appropriate standard of evaluation, since national program goals were defined in terms of coverage, by percent, of Soledad's target population.

At a meeting of the Division's central office staff held on a warm afternoon in February 1973, Dr. Vivas circulated a list of the family planning clinics,

---

* This case was prepared by John C. Ickis. © Copyright 1973 by INCAE, Managua, Nicaragua. It is based on a real situation in which only the names have been changed to preserve the anonymity of the individuals involved.

ordered by percentage of target population covered. "As you can see from these statistics," he said, "performance among the clinics varied widely during 1972."

Dr. Luis Delgado, Director of the Division and Vivas' immediate superior, ran his finger down the list and said, "I notice that the Morazan clinic is near the top of the list, but that Izaltenango is down toward the bottom."

"That's right," Dr. Vivas responded. "Morazan did a tremendous job and attracted 5.4 percent of the target population in the area that it serves as new users during 1972. But Izaltenango turned in a poor performance, attracting only about 1.6 percent."

"Do you have the monthly statistics on those two clinics, Dr. Vivas?" he asked. Vivas nervously dug through the papers in his briefcase and produced the reports shown in Exhibits 1 and 2.

"Morazan may attract a lot of new users," Dr. Delgado continued, "but I think it is inefficient. In fact, I would bet that a consultation there costs double what it does at Izaltenango. When you evaluate your family planning clinics, don't you take cost efficiency into account?"

Dr. Vivas was momentarily silent. He knew why Dr. Delgado had chosen to comment on these particular clinics. Several months earlier Dr. Delgado had been asked by the Minister to serve on a special commission charged with analyzing costs within the health facilities. They had chosen four facilities—two urban clinics and two outlying health centers—for comparative analysis, including Morazan and Izaltenango. The final report was not yet complete, but now Dr. Delgado was passing Vivas a summary of the analysis (Exhibit 3). "Does this change your evaluation of those two clinics?" Delgado asked.

"But these costs are for the health services in general," Dr. Vivas protested. "Not just family planning."

"Maybe we can't attribute all the high costs to family planning," conceded Dr. Delgado. "Still, it is an important part of the health services at Morazan and it has to share the blame."

Dr. Roberto Fernandez, head of the National Nutrition Program, interrupted: "I know the family planning doctor out at Izaltenango personally. He is also the director of the health center. He is a dedicated man and I'm sure he's doing the best he can. But he has to face attitudes and beliefs that have been formed over centuries. It is not fair to compare his situation with Morazan, where the women eagerly line up at the doctor's door."

"It is true that there is a lot of activity in the Morazan clinic and they work very hard there," said Dr. de Reyes, head of the Division's Education Department. "But it is my impression that the rotation of users there is quite high. A lot of women drop out after only a short time in the program. Don't you take that into account?"

"This brings up another point," interjected Dr. Fernandez before Dr. Vivas could respond. "Just because a clinic looks active doesn't really mean that they are seeing a lot of people. I know of one clinic where the doctor

**Exhibit 1**

Morazan: Family Planning Statistics, 1972

| *Medical Consultations* | *Jan.* | *Feb.* | *Mar.* | *Apr.* | *May* | *June* | *July* | *Aug.* | *Sept.* | *Oct.* | *Nov.* | *Dec.* | *Total* |
|---|---|---|---|---|---|---|---|---|---|---|---|---|---|
| IUD | | | | | | | | | | | | | |
| First visit | 0 | 10 | 31 | 16 | 16 | 10 | 15 | 5 | 12 | 9 | 9 | 7 | 140 |
| Subsequent | 0 | 0 | 1 | 8 | 8 | 14 | 13 | 18 | 17 | 44 | 20 | 9 | 152 |
| Oral contraceptive | | | | | | | | | | | | | |
| First visit | 0 | 96 | 140 | 84 | 80 | 71 | 59 | 79 | 64 | 43 | 66 | 26 | 808 |
| Subsequent | 0 | 0 | 28 | 78 | 78 | 92 | 94 | 77 | 59 | 83 | 47 | 36 | 672 |
| Other | | | | | | | | | | | | | |
| First visit | 0 | 1 | 8 | 1 | 1 | 1 | 3 | 3 | 4 | 4 | 1 | 1 | 28 |
| Subsequent | 0 | 0 | 0 | 0 | 0 | 0 | 0 | 0 | 0 | 1 | 4 | 0 | 5 |
| Total | | | | | | | | | | | | | |
| First visit | 0 | 107 | 179 | 101 | 97 | 82 | 77 | 87 | 80 | 56 | 76 | 34 | 976 |
| Subsequent | 0 | 0 | 29 | 86 | 86 | 106 | 107 | 95 | 76 | 128 | 71 | 45 | 829 |
| Total visits | 0 | 107 | 208 | 187 | 183 | 188 | 184 | 182 | 156 | 184 | 147 | 79 | 1,805 |
| Deserters | 0 | 0 | 0 | 31 | 31 | 30 | 27 | 27 | 56 | 0* | 36 | 21 | 259 |
| Cycles of oral contraceptives distributed* | 0 | 106 | 294 | 453 | 449 | 472 | 532 | 453 | 493 | 0† | 459 | 396 | 4,107 |

* May be distributed without medical consultation.

† No data available.

**Exhibit 2**

Izaltenango: Family Planning Statistics, 1972

| *Medical Consultations* | *Jan.* | *Feb.* | *Mar.* | *Apr.* | *May* | *June* | *July* | *Aug.* | *Sept.* | *Oct.* | *Nov.* | *Dec.* | *Total* |
|---|---|---|---|---|---|---|---|---|---|---|---|---|---|
| IUD | | | | | | | | | | | | | |
| First visit | 0 | 2 | 2 | 0 | 0 | 4 | 0 | 0 | 6 | 9 | 3 | 3 | 29 |
| Subsequent | 3 | 1 | 0 | 5 | 1 | 3 | 6 | 3 | 9 | 10 | 3 | 7 | 51 |
| Oral contraceptive | | | | | | | | | | | | | |
| First visit | 11 | 2 | 5 | 9 | 12 | 8 | 11 | 7 | 7 | 7 | 5 | 10 | 94 |
| Subsequent | 12 | 17 | 25 | 19 | 20 | 24 | 25 | 8 | 22 | 22 | 20 | 10 | 224 |
| Other | | | | | | | | | | | | | |
| First visit | 0 | | | | | | | | | | | | 0 |
| Subsequent | 0 | | | | | | | | | | | | 0 |
| Total | | | | | | | | | | | | | |
| First visit | 11 | 4 | 7 | 9 | 12 | 12 | 11 | 7 | 13 | 16 | 8 | 13 | 123 |
| Subsequent | 15 | 18 | 25 | 24 | 21 | 27 | 31 | 11 | 31 | 32 | 23 | 17 | 275 |
| Total visits | 26 | 22 | 32 | 33 | 33 | 39 | 42 | 18 | 44 | 48 | 31 | 30 | 398 |
| Deserters | 3 | 1 | 2 | 2 | 3 | 2 | 2 | 1 | 3 | 2 | 1 | 0 | 22 |
| Cycles of oral contraceptives distributed* | 154 | 141 | 151 | 154 | 116 | 157 | 179 | 70† | 176 | 155 | 140 | 122 | 1,750 |

* May be distributed without medical consultation.

† Stockout of oral contraceptives recorded during this month.

**Exhibit 3**
Selected Statistics from Results of an Analysis of Four Health Facilities, Ministry of Public Health, Soledad

| | (A) Rural Health Center | (B) Izalte-nango | (C) Mora-zan | (D) Urban Clinic |
|---|---|---|---|---|
| 1. Cost per outpatient medical consultation (does not include hospitalization) | | | | |
| *a.* Direct costs (P/*) | 5.80 | 5.48 | 8.54 | 9.10 |
| *b.* Indirect costs† | 3.66 | 2.36 | 4.86 | 2.76 |
| *c.* Total | 9.46 | 7.84 | 13.40 | 11.86 |
| 2. Cost of personnel per medical hour (outpatient only) | | | | |
| *a.* Doctors | 10.00 | 8.00 | 20.00 | 24.00 |
| *b.* Nurses | 7.00 | 6.00 | 10.00 | 6.50 |
| *c.* Auxiliaries | 4.00 | 6.00 | 6.00 | 6.00 |
| *d.* Filing secretaries | 1.50 | 1.50 | 5.00 | 0.75 |
| *e.* Total | 22.50 | 21.50 | 41.00 | 38.00 |
| 3. Cost of medicines and surgical articles per medical hour (outpatient only) | 2.40 | 2.26 | 2.00 | 2.88 |
| 4. Number of consultations per medical hour (outpatient only) | 6.1 | 7.3 | 5.9 | 5.5 |
| 5. Number of laboratory examinations per outpatient consultation | 0.37 | 0.40 | 1.47 | 0.95 |

* The currency of Soledad, the peso (P/), is equal to U.S. $0.20.

† Indirect costs include administration, laboratory costs, and pharmacy costs.

just sees the same women over and over again. In order to do any kind of evaluation it seems to me you need to know the total number of women being served by a clinic."

"It seems to me that we have to do a lot more thinking about the evaluation of our family planning clinics," said Dr. Delgado, directing his words at Dr. Vivas. "If we expect to increase the effectiveness of the program we have simply got to know which clinics are using their resources well or poorly in providing services to those who desire them. At next week's meeting I would like you to recommend a system that will give us this information."

The session came to a close and Dr. Vivas soon found himself sitting alone at the long conference table. He continued to puzzle over the many factors that would have to be taken into account in the design of an evaluation system. He decided to begin by reviewing his experiences during visits that he had made to the clinics back in November of 1972, when he was first getting acquainted with his new job. Among his recollections of these visits he hoped to find some clues as to which factors might or might not be important in evaluating clinic performance.

### Visit to Morazan

Until the end of 1971, family planning services in the Morazan clinic had been provided by the Association for Family Orientation, a private organization of citizens concerned with problems arising from unwanted pregnancies. The Association had been assigned certain hours when their own staff offered family planning services in a designated area of the clinic. When it was announced that the Ministry of Public Health would offer family planning services, the Association's doctor resigned and family planning services were not offered until the Ministry program was begun in February 1972. The new doctor, Dr. de Mendoza, gave family planning consultations five days a week from 5 to 7 in the evening.

Morazan was a lower-middle-class neighborhood in the capital of Soledad, only a five-minute drive from the buildings that housed the Ministry. The neighborhood was composed of over 90,000 people. Many of them were employed as workers in industry, and many others had small shops and garages or were otherwise self-employed. Nearly half of Morazan's population was covered by the national social security system and used its health facilities. The remainder, most of whom could not afford private medical services, used the facilities of the Ministry of Public Health.

Finding doctors to staff the Morazan clinic had never been a problem, as it had been in some outlying health facilities. The clinic's convenience to the center of the capital made it much sought after by the most senior and best-paid doctors employed by the Ministry.

The Morazan clinic was located in a large, two-story wooden structure, built in Spanish style, with an interior courtyard. During the early 1900's it had been the fashionable residence of one of Soledad's wealthy families, but like the structures that surrounded it the house had been left to deteriorate over the years. The wood was warped with age and the paint was old and chipped.

There were 54 personnel employed at the Morazan clinic. It had no hospitalization facilities and normal working hours were from 7 to 12 and 3 to 5. Those who worked beyond 5 P.M., including the family planning doctor and the nurse and auxiliary who assisted her, received additional pay for the extra hours.

Dr. Vivas arrived at the Morazan clinic on a late afternoon in November. It was his first visit to a clinic since he had been named head of the Family Planning Office, and he was still not completely familiar with all the standards and procedures. He decided that, rather than pretending that he "knew it all," he would momentarily forget what he had read in the documents his predecessor had left behind, assume he knew nothing at all about the operations of the family planning clinics, and ask some very basic questions in each location he visited.

Family planning medical consultations were given in a room on the first floor, to the left of the main entrance. The door of the room faced on a corridor along which fifteen or twenty women were seated on a wooden bench. Several wore colorful dresses and high-heeled shoes. Just outside the door was a desk, cluttered with papers. From behind it, the auxiliary nurse, Mrs. Gonzalez, stood up to greet Dr. Vivas as he entered. He introduced himself and asked her to explain the operation of the clinic.

*Auxiliary:* Dr. de Mendoza should be here any minute. She will see up to 12 women between 5 and 7 P.M., after the rest of the clinic is closed. In that room over there the graduate nurse is just finishing up her interviews with women who have come for the first time. These women will have to return in another month to see the doctor again, but those without any side effects or problems will not have to return for a third time for another year. Of course, if a woman is using the oral contraceptive, she will have to make monthly return visits to pick up cycles of pills. But she does not have to see the doctor for that.

*Dr. Vivas:* What are your tasks?

*Auxiliary:* Taking care of the paperwork. Also, I have to prepare the women for the medical consultation. I arrive about 3 P.M., two hours before the doctor does. Women with medical appointments are expected to be here at that time. If there are more than 12 waiting I select the most important cases and make another appointment for the others. Then I take each woman's weight, temperature, and blood pressure, ask her the date of her last menstrual cycle, and record this information in the medical history forms. Then I send her to see the nurse.

*Dr. Vivas:* What problems do you have?

*Auxiliary:* Trying to keep up with my work is the biggest problem. You see, in addition to my other tasks I have to give out cycles of pills to women who return for them each month. That's what these women here are waiting for. But this is nothing . . . you should see this place on a *busy* afternoon!

*Dr. Vivas:* How long do you work in family planning?

*Auxiliary:* For four hours, from 3 P.M. to 7 P.M. Sometimes I have to stay longer to hand out pills. The nurse arrives a bit later, around 4 or 4:30 P.M.

*Dr. Vivas:* How long must the women wait for cycles of pills?

*Auxiliary:* That depends. If there are women waiting for pills when the clinic opens at 3, I try to see that they get them immediately. But I also have to make sure that all the women with medical appointments are ready for the nurse when she arrives. On some afternoons we may get 40 or 50 women in here wanting cycles of pills. So I have to tell them to wait until I have finished with the women who have medical appointments. Also, I must take the weight and blood pressure of each woman returning for pills and ask her whether she has experienced any side effects. Sometimes the doctor finishes before I do.

*Dr. Vivas:* Do these women sometimes get upset about having to wait?

*Auxiliary:* Do they! They get very angry sometimes . . . some women march out of here and we never see them again.

*Dr. Vivas:* How do you determine when a patient is inactive?

*Auxiliary:* Cards are kept on all patients in this file box. If an appointment is missed, a woman is put into a category known as *"faltista."* If in the case of IUD users three months pass or in the case of OC users two months pass, the woman is classified inactive. If, after that time, she chooses to re-enter the program, she is recorded as a new user.

*Dr. Vivas:* How many "actives" does the Morazan clinic have at the present time?

*Auxiliary:* It would be quite a job to go through these hundreds of cards and figure that out. Some of the cards may be in the wrong categories. I try to keep this card file up to date but with all my other tasks here there is just no time. Last month I got so far behind that I could not turn in a report on the number of women who left the program.

*Dr. Vivas:* Have you always worked in family planning?

*Auxiliary:* No, we rotate from one job to another. There are some problems, but we all enjoy working in family planning, and we are eager for our turn to come around. Especially the nurses. But I think their job is easier.

*Dr. Vivas:* Do you find much resistance to family planning here?

*Auxiliary:* Here? No . . . women here are experienced in family planning. They accept it.

## Journey to Izaltenango

A week after his visit to Morazan, Dr. Vivas went on a trip with several other Ministry personnel to see the health facilities in the northern, mountainous provinces of Soledad. After an exhausting drive along winding and dusty roads, they arrived at the village of Izaltenango. Its rough cobbled streets, lined with white adobe walls and red-tiled roofs, were practically deserted in the mid-morning heat.

The health center at Izaltenango was a large, two-story concrete structure located on the extreme north end of town. The original structure had been built in the 1940s, but some additions had been made over the years to accommodate the growing medical demands of the area. Even the expansion of the hospital wing to 80 beds in 1970 had not been sufficient and it was sometimes necessary to place two patients in one bed.

The health center served a population of 38,000 including the 6,000 inhabitants of the village of Izaltenango. The remainder came from small settlements scattered widely among the mountains, some as far as 30 kilometers from the village. The only form of transportation from these settlements was by muleback or on foot, and they remained isolated by swollen rivers during the rainy season.

Family planning services were held for two hours per day, from 11 to 12 in the morning and from 2 to 3 in the afternoon. This schedule allowed most of the rural women ample time to travel to the clinic and to return to their communities before nightfall.

Izaltenango had been one of the first clinics in which the Ministry of Public Health had begun offering family planning services, and the director of the health center, Dr. Sandino, had served as its family planning doctor since the program's inception in 1968. Two additional doctors who were recent graduates from medical school and were serving their required one year of government social service, worked in the center. During this period they received a salary of about 8 pesos (5 pesos = U.S.$1) per medical hour or 1,600 pesos per month for an eight-hour day. Regular doctors were generally paid a minimum of twice that amount. These "social-service" doctors were assigned to facilities in remote parts of the country and seldom if ever worked in urban clinics like Morazan.

After they had introduced themselves, Dr. Sandino began to describe for Dr. Vivas the history of family planning in Izaltenango.

*Dr. Sandino:* When family planning was introduced here by the Ministry, we were sent educational materials and we were told to go out and motivate the members of the community. There was a strong reaction to our educational campaign by religious groups. This is a very conservative area and there are many religious societies and leagues. People were warned to stay away from the family planning clinic. There was also some opposition from the clinic personnel. The decision to introduce the program was taken very rapidly and it was done without consulting them. The social-service doctors, just out of the University, thought that it was part of a foreign-inspired plan to limit our population. Many of the nurses and auxiliaries had religious reservations.

*Dr. Vivas:* How do people feel about family planning now? Do these attitudes persist?

*Dr. Sandino:* There is now less vocal opposition by the community, but perhaps this is because we discontinued our publicity campaigns. The social-service doctors who are with us now do not object. They understand that it is a voluntary program which contributes to maternal health and to the improvement of living conditions.

*Dr. Vivas:* How about the nursing personnel?

*Dr. Sandino:* We have nine nurses here, and several of them are really motivated toward family planning. The problem is that they rotate jobs every couple of weeks, so that when you do get a nurse who is really interested she doesn't stay very long.

*Dr. Vivas:* If some nurses really want to work on family planning, why not let them do it full time?

*Dr. Sandino:* It's not that simple. Because of the hospital wing this health center operates during 3 shifts, 24 hours a day. No nurse wants to be stuck with the night shift all the time. So we have to rotate.

*Dr. Vivas:* What are some of your other problems?

*Dr. Sandino:* Because we are located so far from the warehouse in the capital we sometimes have difficulty getting the supplies we need. But the real problem is with the laboratory results. This is true for all medical consultations, not just family planning. We have sent in many laboratory samples by public transportation and never heard about them again. We have decided it's just not worth the trouble, and we only take tests when it's absolutely necessary.

On his way out of Dr. Sandino's office, Dr. Vivas stopped to talk to the nurse in charge of family planning.

*Dr. Vivas:* What are your duties?

*Nurse:* I give the educational talks to women who come to the clinic for the first time and I hold an interview with each woman before she sees the doctor. After the medical appointment I make any necessary explanations. If she is using oral contraceptives, I give her one cycle.

*Dr. Vivas:* Do you ever give her more than just one?

*Nurse:* No, almost never. We like the women to return to the clinic once each month so that we can make sure that they are using the pills correctly and see whether they are having any reaction to them.

*Dr. Vivas:* How many family planning users see the doctor each day?

*Nurse:* Possibly three or four.

*Dr. Vivas:* Do you have any idea why more do not come?

*Nurse:* I think there are many reasons. Some of the women must walk for hours to get here. Many feel ashamed to sit in the waiting room among their neighbors who come in for health problems. These women do not want more children, but they do not want anyone to know that they are using family planning services. There are many religious and social taboos in this area.

*Dr. Vivas:* How many active patients does the clinic have?

*Nurse:* That is difficult to say . . . we would have to go through the card file. Over one hundred women joined the clinic last year, but many of them have not come back for cycles of pills. They are probably pregnant now.

As he left the Izaltenango health center, Dr. Vivas looked around the waiting room. Most of the people seated on the wooden benches were women, several of them breast-feeding babies. He noticed their calloused bare feet and the hard lines of hunger on their faces and thought to himself how sharply they contrasted in appearance to the well-dressed women he had seen in the Morazan clinic.

## Questions

1. What issues does Dr. Vivas need to consider in measuring the performance of the clinics?
2. What changes, if any, should Dr. Vivas make to the management control system?

## Case 11–3

## LINCOLN COMMUNITY HEALTH CENTER*

Exhibits 11–2 and 11–3 of the text describe the performance measurement system used in Lincoln Community Health Center. In order to evaluate the Center's overall performance, a standard numerical measure of achievement had been developed. It was decided to let the real line [0,1] represent a failure/success continuum, where 0 = complete failure and 1 = complete success. The point 0.6 was designated the minimum desirable level of achievement, that is, the target that the staff had chosen for a particular activity; any score in excess of 0.6 would show the degree to which a target had been surpassed. A score of 0.4 was taken to indicate that the Center had failed to achieve an objective; any score below 0.4 would show a proportionally greater degree of failure. The interval (0.4, 0.5) represented a "blurred region" suggestive of failure and (0.5, 0.6) a "blurred region" indicative of success.

In some cases it was necessary to transform the target level to 0.6 by using a suitable multiplying factor. For example, for the activity, "Encourage patients to keep appointments," the target was "65 percent of appointments should be kept." A naturally occuring outcome measure is the proportion *(p)* of kept appointments. This must be multiplied by 12/13 so that the target level of 0.65 corresponds to an achievement of 0.6, that is, 0.65 × 12/13 = 0.60.

### Questions

1. Is this a conceptually sound approach to performance measurement?
2. What problems do you think would arise in practice in applying this approach?
3. Would you recommend this approach, or some modification of it, to other community health centers?

* This case was prepared by Robert N. Anthony, Harvard Business School.

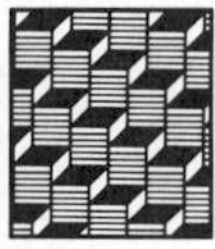

# chapter 12

# Reporting on Performance

Management generally reviews an organization's performance in two somewhat different ways. First, it monitors the results of current operations on a regular, recurring basis, using a set of reports designed for this purpose, together with other information. This type of review is discussed in this chapter. Second, management conducts reviews of programs and activities at infrequent intervals, using information that is developed specifically for each program and activity. These reviews are discussed in Chapter 13.

## FLOW OF INFORMATION

Reports of performance are customarily called control reports since their purpose is to aid the management control process. The dissemination of such reports, coupled with an analysis of the information they contain is only one facet of this process, however. The whole process consists of several phases as well as a variety of formal and informal devices. The place of reports in this latter aspect of the process is indicated by Exhibit 12–1.[1]

In monitoring current performance, management relies on three main types of information, two of which are quantitative and one which may be either quantitative or nonquantitative.

[1] Reproduced by permission from Gene W. Dalton and Paul R. Lawrence, eds., *Motivation and Control in Organizations* (Homewood, Ill.: Richard D. Irwin, 1971).

**Exhibit 12–1**
Types of Control in Organizations

| *Controls Administered by—* | *Direction for Controls Deriving from—* | *Behavioral and Performance Measures* | *Signal for Corrective Action* | *Reinforcements or Rewards for Compliance* | *Sanctions or Punishments for Noncompliance* |
|---|---|---|---|---|---|
| Organization | Organizational plans, strategies, responses to competitive demands | Budgets, standard costs, sales targets | Variance | Management commendation ↓ Monetary incentives, promotions | Requests for explanation ↓ Dismissal |
| Informal group | Mutual commitments, group ideals | Group norms | Deviance | Peer approval, membership, leadership | Kidding ↓ Ostracism, hostility |
| Individual | Individual goals, aspirations | Self-expectations, intermediate targets | Perceived impending failure, missed targets | Satisfaction of "being in control" ↓ Elation | Sense of disappointment ↓ Feeling of failure |

Source: Gene W. Dalton and Paul R. Lawrence, eds., *Motivation and Control in Organizations* (Homewood, Ill.: Richard D. Irwin, 1971).

## Quantitative Information

The first type of quantitative information is financial. Basically it consists of reports that show actual revenues and expenses compared with budgeted revenues and expenses. The information is identified with responsibility centers because senior management usually acts by communicating with heads of responsibility centers. These reports are summaries, showing only significant items of spending. The same format is usually used for all responsibility centers, but there is some device (such as an *) for calling attention to significant differences between actual and budgeted amounts.

The other type of quantitative information is output information. Depending on the nature of the responsibility center, the output measures may be either process information or results information, as described in Chapter 11. If feasible, the output information is shown on the same page as the financial information, and the two types are related by reporting costs per unit of output.

## Other Information

In addition to these routine reports, which tend to have the same format and content month after month, a wide variety of nonroutine, unsystematic, and generally nonquantitative information comes to management's attention. Some of it comes from trade publications, newspapers, and other outside sources. Some of it comes from conversations within the organization, from memoranda, or from the manager's personal observations as he or she visits the responsibility centers and talks with people there. Although the regular reports serve as a useful starting point in monitoring performance, the additional information picked up from these other sources is essential to an understanding of what has happened and often is more important than that contained in the routine reports.

## Report Characteristics

***Information Overload.*** The recurring reports should be carefully designed so that they show all the information that is needed, but not more. With the widespread use of computers, there is a temptation to provide more information than management can digest. Experiments have shown that if information overload exists, that is, if too much information flows through the reporting system, there is a tendency to disregard the whole reporting mechanism. Management should intervene where necessary to assure itself that it is receiving only the information that it needs.

*Examples:* 1. A high school in Sacramento, California, had a computerized attendance system installed at a cost of $100,000. It electronically transmitted to the accounting office the attendance of each pupil in each class period. One full-time person was required to operate the system. It provided instantaneous data, but data that no one needed instantaneously.[2]

2. A reporting system installed in Naval Shipyards in the early 1970s produced 5,000 pages of computer printout per month in each shipyard. This was far more than managers could use.

The types of data, the levels of aggregation, the reporting period, confidentiality, and other matters about reports are all worthy of careful consideration. Top management needs highly aggregated output data which shows the total results of programs or program categories. Operating personnel, or those responsible for program elements, need a different type of output. They need data more frequently. Their level of management sophistication may be low; consequently data for their use should be expressed in simple terms. The display format should be easily understood.

***Unknown Information.*** Less well publicized than information overload is the opposite problem, that of the need to provide enough information. In many organizations, particularly large ones, relevant information exists, but is not provided to managers to whom it would be helpful.

*Example:* In 1972 the United States government negotiated the sale of a large quantity of wheat to the Soviet Union. In retrospect, it appears that the quantity sold was too high and the price was too low because the negotiators in the Department of Agriculture were not aware that there was going to be a shortage of wheat, both in the United States and worldwide. The Department of Agriculture has a large staff of professional economists, and this staff had full knowledge of the impending shortage. The simple, but difficult to explain, fact is that this information did not flow from the economists to the negotiators.

In a large organization there is no perfect solution to the problem of making everyone aware of all the information that is available because the quantity is so vast that no person and no computer program can identify all of it. If one unit, such as the controller's office, is given the responsibility for the collection and dissemination of all information, the problem is mitigated, however.

The flow of information may be impeded by the reluctance of some managers to disclose freely or clearly all the information they have. They operate on the premise that "knowledge is power," and believe that sharing knowledge may dilute power. One author puts it this way:

> A major reason that local governments have not developed adequate financial systems is that city employees often find it in their interest to retain the obfuscation inherent in outmoded systems. Information is power, and if no one but the bureau-

[2] Ida Hoos, *Systems Analysis in Public Policy* (Berkeley: University of California Press, 1972), p. 153.

> cracy can understand what is happening, bureaucrats retain effective control over operations.[3]

A competent top management will not tolerate such a situation.

***Timeliness.*** In controlling operating activities, certain information may need to be reported daily or even hourly. For management purposes, though, the usual reporting period is the month. In all instances, it is important that the reports be made available in a timely fashion, i.e., soon enough to facilitate whatever action might be called for. Generally, this means that the reports should arrive as soon as possible, even at the risk of some loss of accuracy. Most large multinational corporations prepare reports on their worldwide activities, with reasonable accuracy, by the eighth working day after the end of the month, and many companies have monthly reports available even more quickly. Indeed, one large multinational profit-oriented company invested several hundred thousand dollars in a computerized reporting system that would shorten the waiting period for monthly financial statements by only one day!

Given the importance of good management control information for timely decision making, a large, geographically dispersed nonprofit organization should have a waiting period of not much longer than one week for its monthly reports, and an organization that has a single location should have management reports available within a few days after the end of the month. Approximately accurate reports that are available soon enough to provide a basis for action are far preferable to precisely accurate reports that are available so long after the event that nothing can be done about the problems they reveal.

## ANALYSIS OF BUSINESSLIKE ORGANIZATIONS

Some nonprofit organizations, or parts of such organizations, have activities that are essentially similar to those in a profit-oriented business. Analysis of management performance in such organizations is discussed in this section. In a later section, the special problems of monitoring performance in other types of nonprofit organizations are discussed.

We use the term *businesslike organization* for a nonprofit organization that obtains a substantial fraction of its revenues from fees charged to clients, either directly or through third parties, such as Medicare, Medicaid, or Blue Cross. In its operations, such an organization can influence either the amount of revenues earned, the amount of expenses incurred, or both. The analysis of its operating performance thus is similar to that used by a business company.

[3] Jan M. Lodal, "Improving Local Government Financial Information Systems," *Duke Law Journal,* 1976, p. 1133.

*Example:* While a hospital cannot influence the number of individuals in its community who need hospital care, it can—through a variety of techniques—influence the number of those individuals who are admitted to its facility. Moreover, while management cannot directly influence physician-ordering patterns, it can have a direct effect on unit costs in terms of efficiency of personnel, wage rates, and unit prices for supplies and materials.

*Example:* A museum or symphony orchestra can engage in a wide array of marketing activities in an attempt to increase the number of clients using its services. Choice of programming, prices charged, promotional activities, and the like are all comparable in nature to those of a profit-oriented company. Furthermore, cost analysis and control are of equally great significance.

## Variances

The difference, or *variance,* between planned performance and actual performance can be explained by four principal factors: volume, mix, price, and efficiency. These variances need to be considered separately because they have different causes, usually involve different responsibility center managers, and require different types of corrective action. Basic techniques for calculating these variances are given below; more complex techniques are described in cost accounting textbooks. Generally, computer programs can be prepared quite easily to perform the actual calculations. While many situations are such that approximations of variances can be made mentally, others are sufficiently complex that a complete variance analysis is necessary to determine the nature and financial impact of what transpired.

## Volume Variance

***Revenue Volume Variance.*** If the actual quantity of services rendered differs from the quantity assumed in the budget, both revenue and certain expense items will be different from the budgeted amounts. The revenue volume variance is simply the difference between the planned volume and the actual volume multiplied by the budgeted unit price.

*Example:* If a hospital budgets 10,000 patient days per month at $200 per day, its budgeted monthly revenue is $2,000,000. If in April it had 11,000 patient days at $200 per day, its revenue volume variance would be $200,000. This amount can also be found by multiplying the difference between actual and budgeted volume, 1,000 patient days, by the budgeted price per unit of $200.

***Expense Volume Variance.*** The calculation of the expense volume variance is more complicated. It requires that expense items be classified as either fixed, variable, or semivariable. Fixed expenses do not vary at all with volume, variable items vary directly with volume, and semivariable items vary with volume but less than proportionately. In an organization whose budget is a specified amount of expenses per month, which is called a fixed budget, the expense volume variance is associated only with the variable expenses and the variable portion of the semivariable expenses.

> ***Example:*** Assume that the budget for the dietary department of a hospital is \$130,000 per month. Of this amount, \$60,000 represents salaries and benefits, occupancy costs, and other costs that are unaffected by the number of meals served. The other \$70,000 results from an estimate that raw food costs, supplies, utilities, and other costs that vary with the number of patient days is \$7 per day and that there will be 10,000 patient days in a month. The expense volume variance is associated exclusively with this \$70,000 of variable costs.

The expense volume variance is found by multiplying the difference between actual and budgeted volume by the *variable* budgeted expense per unit of volume.

> ***Example:*** If in April the hospital had 1,000 patient days more than budgeted, the expense volume variance for the dietary department would be 1,000 times \$7, or \$7,000.

***Contribution Margin.*** Differences in volume affect the operating margin by the difference between revenue per unit of volume and *variable expenses* per unit of volume. This difference is called the *contribution margin.* The smaller the proportion of variable expenses to total expenses, the larger is the contribution margin. Because of its existence, changes in volume have a greater than proportional effect on the operating margin.

> ***Example:*** If the \$200 per day fee includes \$13 for dietary costs, and assuming \$7 variable dietary costs per day, each additional patient day generates \$6 of additional income (disregarding an adjustment of fees that subsequently may be required by third-party payors). By contrast, if the \$200-per-day fee included \$12 for the plant operation and maintenance department, all of whose expenses were essentially fixed, each additional patient day adds \$12 to operating income with respect to that department because additional patient days do not require additional expenses.

## Mix Variance

The volume variance computed above implicitly assumes that every patient day is similar. If there is a difference in the proportion of services either billed for or provided per patient day, a mix variance develops. A mix variance can result either from a change in the hospital's *case types* (e.g., more coronary artery bypass surgery than planned), from a change in the *mix of services* used to treat a given case type (e.g., more or different radiological procedures ordered for each patient undergoing coronary artery bypass surgery), or from some combination of the two. Techniques are available for calculating the amount of this variance, but they are not widely used in practice.[4]

## Price Variance

The price variance is the difference between the budgeted prices per unit and the actual price per unit. Like the volume variance, a price variance can be developed both for revenues and for expenses. If daily patient fees are changed during the year, there is a revenue price variance. If salaries, raw food prices, utilities, or other items of expense change, there is an expense price variance. This variance affects both fixed costs and variable costs. In order to compute it, one must know the unit prices that were assumed in computing the budget, and this is the reason that in Chapter 9 we suggested that the budget show both quantity and unit price components. In the absence of such a breakdown, an approximation of the price variance can be obtained by using percentages. If a salary increase of 8 percent is granted in July, from then on the actual salary components will contain an 8 percent price variance.

> *Example:* If the number of patient days for the month was budgeted at 10,000 and the actual figure was 10,000 there would be no volume variance. If, however, the actual revenue per day was $5 more than budgeted, and the variable portion of the dietary department was $0.20 less than budgeted, there would be both a revenue and an expense price variance. The revenue price variance would be $5 times 10,000, or $50,000. The expense price variance would be a negative amount of $0.20 times 10,000, or $2,000. Income would thus increase by $52,000.

## Efficiency Variance

The efficiency variance is the difference between actual expenses and budgeted expenses that is not explained by the volume, mix, and price variances. A principal reason for identifying the volume and price variances is to eliminate their influence so that attention can be focused on efficiency variances and on the managers responsible for these variances. Volume and mix of services supplied is usually not controllable by operating managers, and the unit prices for salaries and other items often are also beyond their control. They are therefore basically responsible for variances that are not explained by these factors. (This is not precisely the case because they may be able to exert some influence over these other factors, and this possibility should not be overlooked.)

In any event, management needs to have an adequate explanation of signifi-

[4] See, for example, Robert N. Anthony and James S. Reece, *Accounting Principles* (Homewood, Ill.: Richard D. Irwin, 1983), chaps. 20 and 26. See also David W. Young and Richard B. Saltman, "Preventive Medicine for Hospital Costs," *Harvard Business Review*, January–February, 1983.

cant amounts of efficiency variances and especially needs to know whether unfavorable variances are likely to persist or whether steps are under way to correct them. By distinguishing between efficiency variances and all other variances, top management is in a better position to discuss these steps with operating managers.

## Effectiveness Measures

Effectiveness is the degree to which an organization attains its objectives. In a nonprofit organization, by definition, effectiveness cannot be measured by financial data. If reliable measures of the organization's accomplishments can be found, a comparison of planned and actual output provides a numerical measure of effectiveness. In many situations, however, the most that quantitative measures can do is give clues to the organization's effectiveness. As discussed in Chapter 11, efforts to provide quantitative reports on effectiveness in nonprofit organizations are relatively new, and great opportunities for improvement exist. Good output measures can lead to a completely different attitude toward the management of such organizations, as is indicated in the following observation:

> The major implication of the development of effectiveness measures for the field of welfare is that "welfare management style" can change. This change in management style can take place because effectiveness measures concentrate on the results of a program, rather than on the operation of a program. Thus, they can alter the traditional focus of welfare managers from emphasis on process to concern with the product turned out by the process. This new welfare orientation can establish a new framework in which goals and objectives buttress a program's intent.
>
> Effectiveness measures can pinpoint program areas where objectives are not achieved. They can cast a spotlight on areas where additional study is needed. The end product will provide an improved basis for decisions on which welfare programs should be maintained, which should be modified, which should be deleted so that a greater impact may be made on defined problems.
>
> The conceptual system undergirding the development of effectiveness measures (and measures of efficiency as well) also provides the welfare administrator with a basis for assessing the work performance of personnel. The administrator will be in a more knowledgeable position to know whether to modify staff delivery of a program service. He may use agency objectives to establish more specific objectives for units of work or for individual workers. He will also have better information for determining whether he needs more or less staff, or more or less funds to operate programs from year to year.[5]

***Process Measures.*** In some situations, it is feasible to report at least the process type of output measurement, even though all parties recognize

[5] John J. Foran and Robert Elkin, "A New Approach to Measuring the Effectiveness of Welfare Programs." Paper presented to National Conference on Social Welfare, Chicago: June 1, 1970.

that process measures do not reflect the quality of the work done nor are they necessarily congruent with the actual objectives of the organization. Usually such reports are most useful when outputs are related to costs. This is the central idea behind the "Management by Objectives" program described in Chapter 9. In such a program reports of output may be useful even though they are separate from cost information:

*Example:* A typical monthly report to hospital top management and governing boards includes morbidity and mortality rates, consultation rate, percent of caesarian sections, sterilization rate, post-operative infection rate, infant mortality rate, maternal death rate, anesthesia death rate, autopsy rate, number of patients discharged, number of patient days, average length of stay, births, deaths, operations, anesthesias, emergency room visits, clinic visits, X-ray and laboratory procedures, and hours of nursing care.

*Example:* The New York City school system measures output at each school by a combination of (1) attendance figures, (2) extracurricular activity participation, (3) number of diplomas, (4) number of scholarships, (5) percent of pupils with five or more major subjects, (6) percent of pupils with an 85 percent grade average or above, (7) standard test results, and (8) number of students discharged.[6] None of these measures reflects true output, which is the amount of education, but they are nevertheless useful as indicators of what is happening in a school.

## Other Controls on Effectiveness

Because everyone knows that effectiveness is important, control systems are criticized on the gounds that they omit this important element. Indeed, the absence of information on effectiveness is used as a reason for not giving appropriate attention to the information that *is* provided by the system. For example, in a hospital there may be no adequate formal mechanism for measuring the quality of care, and this fact leads some people to argue that little attention should be given to the control of costs because of the danger that an emphasis on cost control might lead to a lowering of quality.

Actually, notwithstanding the absence of good data, there are powerful forces at work to ensure that the quality of service is adequate, or, if it becomes inadequate, to ensure that this fact is brought to management's attention. Physicians, who dominate nonprofessionals and who are vitally interested in patient welfare, will not tolerate reductions in quality. Patients may complain, and when these complaints are about poor food, dirty floors, or other matters within the patient's competence, they are relevant; they may even come to the attention of the general public, which management wants to avoid at all costs. The trustees, as representatives of the public, are interested in the maintenance of quality. In recognition of this fact, some

[6] Harry J. Hartley, "Program Budgeting and Cost-Effectiveness in Local Schools," *Budgeting, Programme Analysis, and Cost-Effectiveness in Educational Planning* (Paris: Organization for Economic Cooperation and Development, 1968).

hospitals use volunteers or paid patient care representatives to question patients about the quality of care they receive, and to bring patient complaints to the attention of management.

> *Example:* In Mid Maine Medical Center, volunteers interview eight patients each in the course of a month, following a printed interview guide. Serious problems, if any, are brought to the attention of management immediately. A summary report is discussed monthly at a meeting between management and the volunteer team.

The presence of competing hospitals may also affect quality, for if quality levels deteriorate in one hospital, physicians may threaten to use, or actually use, another. Accrediting and licensing agencies make periodic inspections and check actual conditions against prescribed standards. Thus, physicians, patients, trustees, competition, and outside agencies are all of some help in assuring adequate quality levels, even in the absence of a formal method of measurement.

***Peer Review.*** Currently, there is a widespread feeling that the devices to control quality, as listed above, are inadequate. Consequently, major efforts are under way in several professions to devise new methods of ensuring that the quality of service provided is adequate. Although the movements have different labels, they share in common the concept that the work of one professional should be subject to review by his or her peers.

Of these efforts, the most important, and also the most controversial, was the establishment of Professional Standards Review Organizations (PSROs) in the medical profession. PSROs began to function in 1976 to review the service provided by hospitals to Medicare patients, including answers to the following questions:

1. Is the service medically necessary?
2. Is the treatment up to recognized standards?
3. Are the services delivered in the most economical fashion?

PSROs were separate organizations established solely to provide this function and were staffed by practicing physicians. At the peak of the program's activity, there was at least one PSRO in each state, and many states had several. The PSRO Program was all but eliminated in the early 1980s because of massive budget cuts at the federal level.

Although PSROs as such have been effectively dismantled, versions of peer review have existed for a long time, and continue to exist in many hospitals. Hospitals have medical records committees, tissue committees, and utilization review committees that review the accuracy and completeness of records, the accuracy of surgical diagnoses, and length of patient stay, respectively.

Peer review also exists in other organizations in which professional decision making is a critical activity. Colleges and universities have mechanisms for reviewing the performance of faculty members, and the schools are themselves subject to review by accrediting agencies. In research organizations, the work done by one research group is reviewed by other groups. In general, when the principal output of an organization is the work of professionals, the quality of that output is best judged by other professionals. Professionals tend to resist peer review activities, however, and there is a strong possibility of backscratching, so the mechanism needs senior management attention if it is to be effective.

### Danger Signals

An analysis of performance that compares actual performance with budgeted performance implicitly assumes that if operations proceed as planned, matters are satisfactory. Ordinarily, this is a reasonable assumption. However, conditions in the environment may have changed in such a way that the plan itself needs changing, and management must be alert constantly to signals that indicate that trouble may be brewing; such signals may come from various sources. The important fact is that a formal set of reports cannot be counted on to reveal these danger signals since these reports accept the budgeted amounts as standards of satisfactory performance. The idea of key results measures, discussed in Chapter 11, is the closest that the process can come to being formalized.

> *Example:* In a college, management needs to be alert to such danger signals as the following: a decrease in the number of inquiries, a decrease in the number of applications, a decrease in the quality of applicants, a decrease in yield (i.e., percentage of admitted applicants who register), a shift in enrollment among majors, an increase in student aid needs, an unplanned change in sections per faculty member, an increase in student attrition rates, an increase in administrative and support personnel, and a decrease in gifts.

### Comparative Information

For organizations that are members of industry associations, such as hospitals, universities, and welfare organizations, the association furnishes useful information both about changes in the general environment, and current average data on costs and other statistics of member institutions that provide helpful indicators of whether an organization is drifting out of line.

> *Example:* The Healthcare Financial Management Association publishes detailed data on hospitals in its *Hospital Industry Analysis Report.* Its 1981 report contained 29 financial ratios based on information supplied by 675 hospitals, with hospitals classified by type and bed size. Medians, upper quartiles, and lower quartiles are published.

As pointed out in Chapter 11, however, such data are of little use unless they are prepared in accordance with carefully worked out and well-understood definitions.

*Example:* State governments publish data on cost per mile of highway maintained, but some states define this amount as trunkline miles, others use miles adjusted for number of lanes, others "equivalent" trunkline miles, and so forth. In the absence of an agreed-upon definition of "mile of highway," these data are useless for comparison purposes.[7]

Comparative measures are especially useful in situations where there are a large number of moderately small, discrete, and independent entities with similar clientele, operations, and cost structure (e.g., day-care centers, urban schools, suburban schools, community hospitals, inner-city job placement programs). In these cases the indicators measuring similar aspects of performance (such as pupil-teacher ratio, cost of instruction, cost of supervisory personnel, cost of maintenance and construction, etc.) may be valid indicators of relative performance even though there is no way of expressing what performance should be in absolute terms.

## ANALYSIS OF OTHER ORGANIZATIONS

Some nonprofit organizations are unlike a business in that they are not "self-financing." Instead the amount of resources that are available for operation in a given year is essentially fixed in advance. In other organizations, the job that they are required to do is relatively fixed, regardless of the amount of resources planned. Both of these types of organizations can use some of the techniques described above to monitor performance, but they have special characteristics that are described in this section.

### Fixed Resource Organizations

In many nonprofit organizations, the amount of resources available for operations in a given year is essentially fixed. This is the case with many religious organizations and other membership organizations whose resources are fixed by the amount of pledges or dues. Colleges with a fixed enrollment know their available resources, within narrow limits, as soon as the students enter. Health maintenance organizations (HMOs) know their resources based on annual enrollments. These organizations must carefully monitor their spending to assure that they spend no more than the amount of available resources. Moreover, their success is measured by how much service they provide with these resources. In these organizations, an "unfavorable" budget variance could portend financial disaster, and too large a "favorable" budget variance may be the first sign of impending client dissatisfaction.

Furthermore, since the amount of service provided is a subjective judgment rather than a measured quantity, the output for the whole organization cannot be expressed in quantitative terms, and measures of efficiency therefore cannot

[7] The Urban Institute, *The Status of Productivity Measurement in State Government: An Initial Examination* (Washington, D.C., September 1975), p. 221.

**Exhibit 12–2**

ILLUSTRATIVE COLLEGE
Statement of Operations
Six Months Ended December 31, 1983
($000)

| | *July 1–Dec. 21* | | *Year 1983–84* | | |
|---|---|---|---|---|---|
| | *Budget* | *Actual* | *Budget* | *Projection* | *Variance* |
| Revenue: | | | | | |
| Tuition and fees | $1,375 | $1,395 | $2,800 | $2,838 | $ 38 |
| Federal appropriations | 260 | 245 | 525 | 525 | — |
| State appropriations | 405 | 405 | 805 | 805 | — |
| Federal grants and contracts | 190 | 200 | 380 | 380 | — |
| State grants and contracts | 20 | 20 | 35 | 35 | — |
| Private gifts, grants, and contracts | 800 | 1,000 | 1,150 | 1,300 | 150 |
| Endowment earnings | 360 | 340 | 725 | 692 | (33) |
| Sales of educational services | 100 | 100 | 200 | 200 | — |
| Subtotal | $3,510 | $3,705 | $6,620 | $6,775 | $155 |
| Educational and general: | | | | | |
| Expenses: | | | | | |
| Instruction | $1,825 | $1,865 | $3,670 | $3,690 | $(20) |
| Research | 245 | 255 | 485 | 485 | — |
| Public service | 85 | 87 | 168 | 168 | — |
| Academic support | 130 | 128 | 260 | 260 | — |
| Student services | 105 | 110 | 210 | 210 | — |
| Institutional support | 235 | 245 | 470 | 490 | (20) |
| Operation and maintenance of plant | 110 | 130 | 215 | 255 | (40) |
| Scholarships and fellowships | 100 | 80 | 200 | 180 | 20 |
| Other | 100 | 100 | 192 | 192 | — |
| Subtotal | $2,935 | $3,000 | $5,870 | $5,930 | $(60) |
| Excess (deficit) | $ 575 | $ 705 | $ 750 | $ 845 | $ 95 |
| Auxiliary revenues | $1,110 | $1,160 | $2,225 | $2,300 | $ 75 |
| Auxiliary expenses | 1,075 | 1,100 | 2,150 | 2,200 | (50) |
| Excess (deficit) | $ 35 | $ 60 | $ 75 | $ 100 | $ 25 |
| Transfers | $ (400) | $ (400) | $ (800) | $ (800) | — |
| Surplus (deficit) | $ 210 | $ 365 | $ 25 | $ 145 | $120 |

( )Unfavorable.

| | *Fall Term* | | |
|---|---|---|---|
| | *1983* | *1982* | *1981* |
| Admission data: | | | |
| Average SAT scores | 945 | 952 | 958 |
| Percent requesting financial aid | 25% | 22% | 21% |
| Percent minority applications | 18% | 16% | 15% |
| Percent applicants below 20 years old | 96% | 97% | 97% |
| Full-time students to part-time | 17:1 | 15:1 | 14:1 |
| Applicants admitted | 87% | 82% | 64% |
| Admits enrolled | 54% | 55% | 59% |

Source: Adapted from a report suggested by the National Association of College and University Business Officers.

be developed. Nevertheless, within such an organization there may well be service units whose output can be measured, and efficiency measures can be developed for these units. It also may be possible to calculate volume, mix, price, and efficiency variances to assist management in determining appropriate kinds of corrective action.

***Illustrative Analysis.*** Exhibit 12–2 shows the operating statement for a college. It provides a basis for commenting both on the format of such reports and on methods of analyzing the data.[8] A quarterly meeting of the board of trustees is held in January, so this report summarizes results for the fiscal year to date, that is, from July through December. Some comments about it follow.

## Format

1. For the year to date, the report compares actual amounts with budgeted amounts. Budgeted amounts are *not* obtained by taking one-half of the annual budget but rather are constructed by estimating the correct proportion of the annual budget that is applicable to the current period. This is extremely important. Some organizations compare actual spending for, say, a quarter with one fourth of the annual budget. Others compare actual for the quarter with the total annual budget. Neither comparison is of much use to management.
2. The report also compares the budget for the year with management's current estimate of revenues and expenses for the year. This is the most important part of the report. Management should be prepared to explain each of the significant differences and to seek board approval of controllable differences before the expenses are incurred.
3. The report is structured so that revenues and expenses of auxiliary enterprises are shown separately from educational revenues and expenses and the net excess of these activities is shown. (It may be desirable to show separately the revenues and expenses of each important auxiliary activity, such as dormitory, food service, bookstore, varsity athletics.) In some reports all the revenues are presented first, and then all the expenses, so that such relationships are difficult to determine. This report is structured so that attention is focused on the revenues of the primary program, education, and the expenses of that program.
4. The report is short, and the numbers are rounded so that a maximum of four digits is shown. It nevertheless conveys the significant information

[8] Many examples are shown in Leon E. Hay, *Accounting for Governmental and Nonprofit Entities* (Homewood, Ill.: Richard D. Irwin, 1980); Malvern J. Gross, Jr., *Financial and Accounting Guide for Nonprofit Organizations* (New York: Ronald Press, 1983); and Edward S. Lynn and Robert J. Freeman, *Fund Accounting: Theory and Practice* (Englewood Cliffs, N.J.: Prentice-Hall, 1983).

that the board needs in order to understand what has happened and what is likely to happen. No manager needs more than four digits of information, and three digits frequently are enough.

5. No mention is made of funds or fund accounting. This is a report of operations, and to structure it according to funds would be an unnecessary complication.

6. "Unfavorable" variances, i.e., those that reduce income, are enclosed in parentheses. These are revenue items for which the estimated actual is *less* than budget, and expense items for which the estimated actual is *more* than budget.

7. Comparisons are made with the budget, not with the corresponding period last year. An historical comparison represents a holdover from the days when budgets were generally nonexistent or unreliable. A good budget provides a much better basis for comparison than last year's performance because the budget presumably incorporates the significant changes that have occurred since last year.

***Questions about the Report.*** In examining this report, management and the board probably will ask questions such as the following:

1. If revenue items are lower than estimated, is the shortfall likely to be made up? If not, should expenses be cut correspondingly? (This question should be asked about endowment earnings in Exhibit 12–2.)
2. Has an unexpected gift obscured a shortfall in revenue planned from other sources? (The surplus in Exhibit 12–2 is less than the $150,000 in additional revenue from private gifts, grants, and contracts.)
3. If expense items currently are different than budgeted amounts, but the difference is expected to be eliminated by the end of the year, is this a reasonable explanation?
4. For expenses that are expected to exceed budget, is there a reasonable explanation? (In Exhibit 12–2, tuition revenue shows a positive variance, and it is possible that certain expenses increased as a result of higher-than-budgeted enrollment.)
5. For expenses that are expected to be lower than budget, is there an indication that services are inadequate? (In Exhibit 12–2, the $20,000 "favorable" variance for scholarships and fellowships may indicate a failure to provide needed financial aid, particularly since admissions data show an increase in the percent of applicants requesting financial aid and a decrease in the percent of "admits enrolled.")

## Fixed Job Organization

A fire department has a specified job to do; it must be ready to fight all the fires that occur in its service area. Variances from planned amounts of spending may exist in either direction because of the nature of the job that had to be done. Similarly, if there are many snowstorms, the budget for snowplowing has to be exceeded. Judgments about the performance of such organizations must therefore be in terms of how well they did, whatever they were supposed to do, and whether a minimum amount of resources was used in doing whatever they did. It is more important, for example, to consider the cost of snow removal per snowstorm or per inch of snow than the total snow removal cost of the year.

In these organizations, there is a tendency to ascribe differences between actual and budgeted amounts in a general way to the requirements of the job, whereas a detailed analysis may reveal inefficiencies. It is not sufficient to explain away a budget overrun in the highway maintenance department on the grounds that the winter was severe. Analysis of the variable costs that are caused by snowstorm of varying depths may indicate that the overrun was greater than it should have been. Thus, in almost all of these situations, a variance analysis which distinguishes, as a minimum, among expense volume, expense price, and efficiency is an essential management tool.

## OPERATIONAL AUDITING

In Chapter 10 we described an internal auditing process called *compliance auditing* that was intended to determine whether the financial data were being properly recorded, and whether rules were being complied with. In recent years, another type of auditing, called *operational auditing* has become increasingly important. Its development was fostered by the publication in 1973 by the U.S. Comptroller General of *Standards for Audit of Governmental Organizations, Programs, Activities and Functions.* This booklet defines the new type of auditing in the following way: "[it] determines whether the entity is managing or utilizing its resources (personnel, property, space, and so forth) in an economical and efficient manner and the causes of any inefficiencies or uneconomical practices, including inadequacies in management information systems, administrative procedures, or organizational structure."[9]

The movement was given further impetus by the enactment in 1978 of federal legislation setting up the office of Inspector General in the principal federal agencies with specific responsibility for uncovering fraud and abuse.[10]

The Comptroller General has recognized that operational auditing requires a quite different approach and a quite different type of auditor from that

---

[9] Comptroller General of the United States, *Standards for Audit of Governmental Organizations, Programs, Activities and Functions* (Washington, D.C.: Government Printing Office, 1973), pp. 1–2.

[10] In the military and in some civilian organizations, there has been an inspector general function for many years. Typically, the inspector general was responsible for "trouble shooting" on behalf of the chief executive, following up reports of serious inefficiency, incompetence, or malfeasance that came to the chief's attention. In these organizations there was a separate internal auditing unit that was responsible for compliance auditing, and, in some cases, operational auditing. The 1978 legislation combines all these functions into a single office, reporting to the agency head.

appropriate for compliance auditing. This is evidenced by the fact that in its current recruiting program, the General Accounting Office hires operations analysts, economists, and social psychologists, as well as accountants. In fact, it currently recruits an approximately equal number of nonaccountants and accountants. Many other agencies do not yet appear to be aware of the different requirements of operational auditing and use persons with an accounting background for this work, simply because their current auditing organization consists exclusively of such persons. When accountants imply that they know how to run a school, a hospital, or any other organization better than the professionals who have spent their careers working in and managing such organizations, their work is resented and, if possible, disregarded.

Operational auditing, if properly conducted, can be a valuable tool in the management of a nonprofit organization. If not properly conducted, however, it can be a source of friction and frustration, with no constructive results. The operational auditor must recognize that all managers make mistakes and that it is easy in any organization to identify, by hindsight, decisions that should have been made differently. There is no point, however, in publicizing such decisions if they were judgments made in good faith, based on the information available at the time. Operational auditing serves a useful purpose if, but only if, it shows how *future* decisions can be made in a better way, that is, if it demonstrates that changes in policies or procedures are necessary.

The Comptroller General's *Standards* booklet is sensitive to these problems of operational auditing. For example, it states:

> **Efficiency and economy** are both relative terms and it is virtually impossible to give an opinion as to whether an organization has reached the maximum practicable level of either. Therefore it is not contemplated in these standards that the auditor will be called upon to give such an opinion.[11]

## BEHAVIORAL CONSIDERATIONS

Thus far, we have described largely the technical aspects of the system for monitoring performances. These matters are important, but they are far less important than the attitudes of those who use the information that the system produces and those who are affected by this information.

### Senior Management Involvement

A management control system is likely to be ineffective unless members of the organization's units perceive that it is considered important by their superiors. This requires that the top manager use the system in decision making, in appraising the results of performance, and as a basis for salary

[11] Comptroller General, *Standards,* p. 12.

adjustments, promotions, and other personnel actions. In particular, it requires that superiors at all levels discuss the results of operations with their subordinates.

Some managers convene regular meetings at which the reports for the whole organization are discussed. Others prefer individual discussions with responsibility center heads. Still others prefer to make their comments in writing, holding only infrequent meetings.

In discussing performance, subordinates are given an opportunity to explain happenings not revealed in the reports. If corrective action seems called for, constructive suggestions for such action can be put forth, and subordinates can commit themselves to a course of action. If the performance is good, appropriate recognition of this should be conveyed.

It sometimes is difficult for management to convey the correct impression about the importance of quantitative information, especially the comparison of budget and actual revenues and expenses. Inadequate attention leads to a disregard of these numbers. On the other hand, if senior management places too much emphasis on numerical measures of performance, operating managers may act in such a way that their performance looks good according to the measures that are emphasized, but to the detriment of the real objectives of the organization. These actions are called "playing the numbers game." They can be avoided only by convincing operating managers that they should concentrate on accomplishing the real objectives of the organization and that they will not be penalized if such efforts do not show up in numerical measures of performance.

## Importance of Adequate Staffs

Variance analysis and other devices for appraising performance cannot be used unless qualified people are available to make the calculations. Except in very small organizations, managers do not have time to make these calculations themselves. Unfortunately, a great many nonprofit organizations, including some very large ones, do not have staffs that are large enough to make such analyses in a thorough and systematic way. For example, one state government agency, with a multibillion dollar budget, has only six professionals who are engaged in the regular analysis of operating reports. Some states have none at all.

## Balance between Freedom and Restraint

In any organization, profit or nonprofit, the right balance has to be struck between *(a)* the need for *freedom* in order to take advantage of the ability and knowledge of the person on the firing line, to motivate that person, and to reduce paperwork; and *(b)* the need for *restraint,* in order to ensure that management policies are followed, and to reduce the effect of poor judgments or self-interest decisions by lower-level managers. In nonprofit organizations, because of the absence of profit as an overall basis for measuring performance, there probably should be somewhat less freedom and somewhat more restraint than in a profit-oriented organization.

This is, however, a matter of degree. Many nonprofit organizations, particularly government organizations, impose far too many and too detailed restraints on first-line managers. Sometimes this is caused by the *goldfish bowl* problem. Errors are likely to be played up in the newspapers, and as a protective device top managers prescribe rules, which they can point to when errors come to light: "I am not to blame; he (the sinner) broke my rule." The detailed restraints also result from *encrustation:* a sin is committed, and a rule is promulgated to avoid that sin in the future; but the rule continues even after the need for it has disappeared. No one considers whether the likelihood and seriousness of error is great enough to warrant continuation of the rule.

## Motivation

A central purpose of any control system is to motivate operating managers to take actions that help accomplish the organization's objectives efficiently and effectively. The problem of inducing the desired degree and direction of motivation is a difficult one in any organization, but it is particularly difficult in a nonprofit organization.

In any organization, individuals have a set of goals. Some of these goals relate to the overall goals of the organization, but others relate to the career goals of the individuals and the groups that they compose. In a school system, for example, all groups are interested in better education, but teachers as individuals also are concerned with salary, educational advancement, and professional status. To make an organization effective and efficient, managers must create the highest possible correspondence between the interests of the individuals and those of the organization. Divergent goals and objectives of individuals should be considered, and to the extent possible reconciled with the goals of the organization. Many organizations do not succeed in attaining this congruence. For example, a survey of 126 administrators in a state social service agency found that 70 percent perceived no strong relationship between attaining their objectives and future compensation or future promotion.[12]

***The Problem of Budget Conformance.*** The fact that performance in a nonprofit organization is measured in part by how well managers conform to their budget can have dysfunctional consequences. Suppose a manager has a $1,000,000 budget and by careful, hard work performs the required job and does it by spending only $990,000. In many organizations, the budget for the following year, other things equal, will be $990,000. The manager

[12] Stuart Murray and Tom Kuffel, "MBO and Performance Linked Compensation in the Public Sector," *Public Personnel Management,* May 1978, p. 175.

is punished, rather than rewarded, for reducing costs, for now there is less money to work with than would have been the case if the entire $1,000,000 had been spent.

The typical attitude toward budgets is that it is almost sinful not to spend the full amount that is available, as indicated in the following:

Beetle Bailey

It is a difficult matter to create the right attitude in these circumstances. On the one hand if a program can be run more efficiently or if the demand for it has fallen, its budget *should* be reduced. On the other hand, it is important to give managers incentives to be efficient *this year* which do not penalize them in future years. One possibility is to guarantee the manager that if the job can be done at less than the amount budgeted, the budget will not be reduced for the current year and the succeeding year. In order to make this policy work, the definition of operating expenses may be expanded to include minor capital expenditures, for it is on items of this type that the manager will wish to spend the "extra" money. (In government, however, the person who makes such a promise may not be in the same job long enough to make good on it.)

An alternative course of action is to convince operating managers that a budget reduction, per se, should not be viewed as a punishment and that there is top management emphasis on recognizing and rewarding cost reduction. A manager is rewarded by a combination of promotion, salary, and the respect of peers, superiors, and subordinates. If top management stresses the importance of cost reduction and rewards, there need not be a negative reaction to reducing the budget.

Another alternative is to release to managers substantially less (say 20 percent less) funds than they probably need. They know that additional funds are available, but they can never be sure of getting them. This may make them more than ordinarily careful in spending available funds. However, this practice may risk stifling their initiative and may result in a reluctance to introduce new programs or in an undermaintenance of existing facilities.

> ***Example:*** The State of Tennessee permits a college or university to earn a bonus of up to 2 percent of its budget based on its performance of five variables:
>
> Number of academic programs accredited.

Performance of graduates on outcomes related to general education, as measured by tests administered to alumni.

Performance of graduates on tests in their major fields.

Evaluation of programs by students, alumni, and community representatives, by questionnaires.

Evaluation by peers at other institutions.[13]

***Monetary Incentives.*** Profit-oriented organizations often pay cash bonuses when savings are realized or profits are high, but a nonprofit organization is not able to do this to the same extent. It can nevertheless take steps in this direction. For example some federal government organizations pay incentive awards for cost-saving ideas that can amount to as much as $25,000 to one person. However, when the manager of direct mission departments (e.g., deans of faculty, chiefs of hospital services) do not have opportunities to receive incentive compensation, it is dangerous to provide a significant amount of incentive compensation to the heads of support services. A bonus based on cost performance in the support service may create animosity in the mission departments.

In recent years, some nonprofit organizations have become increasingly creative in designing monetary incentives for improved financial performance. The accumulation of extra vacation days is one feasible approach, with the possibility of an extended "sabbatical" leave at some point in the future. (If the system is designed in such a way that these days are not paid if the employee leaves the organization voluntarily, there is a supplemental incentive for the employee to remain with the organization). A system of merit increases in salary based on financial performance is another possibility, although unless there are "demerit decreases" the increase is locked in regardless of the employee's performance in the future.

> *Example.* One nonprofit organization has designed a particularly creative incentive plan in which a portion of each manager's "salary" is withheld monthly with the understanding that it may not be paid at all. Depending on the extent to which the organization *as a whole* achieves its financial objectives for the year, all or a portion of this salary is then paid out as a "bonus." Since all managers receive the same proportion of the amount withheld, and since the proportion is based on the performance of the entire organization, managers have a major incentive to collaborate, which is an essential activity for the success of this particular organization.

***Cost-Reduction Programs.*** Another motivating device is a cost-reduction program. If properly designed, such a program takes advantage of the knowledge of possible improvements that usually exist in the lower levels of an organization. Possible difficulties should be foreseen. For instance, a suggestion by an employee that a colleague's job should be abolished can

---

[13] E. Grady Bogue and Wayne Brown, "Performance Incentives for State Colleges," *Harvard Business Review* November–December 1981, pp. 123–28.

be regarded by the supervisor as a personal criticism; it implies that the supervisor should have foreseen this possibility. Also, in a cost-reduction program there is a tendency to hold back some ideas for next year so that there will be constant evidence of effort.

In any event, without some financial incentive, managers may not be motivated to reduce costs. Indeed, managers who can successfully negotiate a larger budget frequently are able to expand the scope of their efforts; this may be viewed favorably and even rewarded by promotion.

***Incentives Related to Output.*** An alternative to reducing a budget is to hold the budget constant and to expect managers to accomplish more work than last year with the same amount of resources. This increases efficiency just as much as a policy of expecting the same amount of work to be done with fewer resources. This approach assumes that there is a genuine need for the organizational unit to accomplish more work; otherwise, the creation of additional tasks for the same amount of resources is a wasteful way of achieving a higher output/input ratio.

## The Bureaucracy

There are many comments to the effect that in government organizations and in certain other large nonprofit organizations effective management control is inhibited by the existence of the bureaucracy. "Bureaucracy" is often used as a label for any organization that operates by complicated rules and routines, or that is characterized by delays and buck passing or that treats its clients impolitely. In particular, government organizations are labeled bureaucracies, with the implication that nongovernmental organizations are *not* bureaucracies.

The fact is that any large and complex organization is necessarily a bureaucracy. The classic analysis of bureaucracy is that of Max Weber.[14] Weber describes a bureaucratic organization as one in which the chief executive derives his authority by law or by election by an authorized body, rather than by tradition or charisma; subordinates are responsible to the chief executive through a clearly defined hierarchy; they are selected on the basis of their technical competence, rather than by election; they are promoted according to seniority or achievement, or both; and they are subject to systematic discipline and control.

In the bureaucratic form of organization, complex problems are solved by segmenting them into a series of simpler ones and delegating authority for solving each of the segments to specialized subunits, consisting of experts who are equipped to solve problems in their area of expertise. Such technical superiority based on increased specialization is supposed to lead to objective and impersonal decision making at the subunit level. Weber noted that an

---

[14] Max Weber, *The Theory of Social and Economic Organization,* 1922. See the English translation by A. M. Henderson and Talcott Parsons (New York: Oxford University Press, 1947).

individual who applied personal subjective values to policy or decision making could seriously lessen the effectiveness of the organization, and that a bureaucracy avoided this possibility by replacing the subjective judgment of individuals with routinized work tasks and by a set of rules, values and attitudes, or goals, which are approved by the individual's superior.[15]

## ASSET MANAGEMENT

The foregoing sections have focused on operating activities, which in financial terms means revenues and expenses. In addition, management needs to watch the progress of capital acquisition programs, the management of cash, the level of inventories and accounts receivables, the amount of encumbrances, and other aspects of the control of assets and related liabilities. In general, techniques used for this purpose are beyond the scope of this book.

***Endowment Earnings.*** One aspect of asset management in many nonprofit organizations is the performance of those responsible for the investment of endowment and similar funds. The performance of the investment manager or investment committee should be considered by itself; their performance in generating earnings on endowment is an entirely separate matter from the use made of endowment earnings. The governing body presumably adopted a policy with respect to the relative balance between risk and return that it regarded as optimal, and there are well-established (albeit complicated) methods of judging how well the investment manager has implemented this policy. These techniques compare the return on a given endowment with that of other funds with similar objectives, or with overall market averages. The important point is, as a Twentieth Century Fund report states, "spending need should not dictate investment policy nor investment policy dictate conditions of spending."[16]

## SUGGESTED ADDITIONAL READINGS

Anthony, Robert N. and James S. Reece, *Accounting Principles* (Homewood, Ill., Richard D. Irwin, Inc., 1983), Chapters 20 and 26.

Sorensen, James E., and Hugh Grove. "Cost-Outcome and Cost-Effectiveness Analysis: Emerging Nonprofit Performance Evaluation Techniques." *The Accounting Review,* July 1977, pp. 658–75.

Usher, Charles L., and Gary C. Cornia. "Goal Setting and Performance Assessment in Municipal Budgeting. *Public Administration Review,* March–April 1981, pp. 229–35.

---

[15] For an argument that just the opposite takes place see Michel Crozier, *The Bureaucratic Phenomenon* (Chicago, The University of Chicago Press, 1964).

[16] Funds for the Future, *Report of the Twentieth Century Fund Task Force on College and University Endowment Policy* (New York: McGraw-Hill, 1975), p. 17. For techniques of appraisal, see J. Peter Williamson, *Background Paper* in this publication.

## Case 12–1

# ARNICA MISSION*

Arnica Mission was located in the heart of a large metropolitan area in the north-central United States. Founded in the late 1800s, it had been serving the homeless ever since, providing hot meals, shelter, and companionship. Situated on a busy urban thoroughfare, it was a haven of last resort for many of the city's indigent, and "home" for many others. As might be expected, the demand for its services was especially high in the winter, when temperatures frequently dropped to below zero, and life "on the street" became unbearable.

The Mission provided three types of services. By far, its most significant activity was the Hot Meal Program, in which it served hundreds of meals a day. A meal of hot soup and a sandwich was available to anyone who arrived between the hours of 12:00 and 2:00 in the afternoon and 5:00 and 7:00 in the evening. Its second program was its Overnight Hostel, in which it made available 150 beds on a first-come, first-served basis. The linen was changed daily, so that its clients could look forward to "clean sheets and a hot shower." Finally, it had a counseling program, in which a staff of three full-time social workers assisted the Mission's clients in coping with the difficulties which had brought them to the Mission, and in establishing themselves in a more self-sufficient lifestyle.

In March 1983, Arnica Mission had hired a new administrator to improve its business activities. A business school graduate with prior experience in manufacturing and service companies in the private sector, one of his first steps had been to introduce responsibility accounting. The new budget reporting system had been announced along with the provision of quarterly cost reports to the Mission's department heads. (Previously, cost data had been presented to department heads only infrequently.) The following is an excerpt from the memorandum and report received by the laundry supervisor in mid-January, 1984.

> The Mission has adopted a responsibility accounting system. From now on you will receive quarterly reports comparing the costs of operating your department with budgeted costs. The reports will highlight the differences (variations) so you can zero in on the departure from budgeted costs (This is called *management by exception*.) Responsibility accounting means you are accountable for keeping the costs in your department within the budget. The variations from the budget will help you identify what costs are out of line and the size of the variation will indicate which ones are the most important. Your first such report accompanies this announcement.

---

* This case was prepared by David W. Young, Harvard School of Public Health.

ARNICA MISSION
Performance Report—Laundry Department
October–December, 1983

| | Budget | Actual | (Over) Under Budget | Percentage (Over) Under Budget |
|---|---|---|---|---|
| Bed days | 9,500 | 11,900 | ( 2,400) | (25) |
| Pounds of laundry processed | 125,000 | 156,000 | (31,000) | (25) |
| Costs | | | | |
| Laundry labor | $ 9,000 | $ 12,500 | $( 3,500) | (39) |
| Supplies | 1,100 | 1,875 | (775) | (70) |
| Water and water heating and softening | 1,700 | 2,500 | (800) | (47) |
| Maintenance | 1,400 | 2,200 | (800) | (57) |
| Supervisor's salary | 3,150 | 3,750 | (600) | (19) |
| Allocated administration costs | 4,000 | 5,000 | ( 1,000) | (25) |
| Equipment depreciation | 1,200 | 1,250 | (50) | ( 4) |
| | $ 21,550 | $ 29,075 | $( 7,525) | (35) |

Administrator's comments: Costs are significantly above budget for the quarter. Particular attention needs to be paid to labor, supplies, and maintenance.

The annual budget for fiscal year 1984 (July 1983–June 1984) had been constructed by the new administrator. Quarterly budgets were computed as one fourth of the annual budget. The administrator compiled the budget from an analysis of the prior three years' costs. The analysis showed that all costs increased each year, with more rapid increases between the second and third year. He considered establishing the budget at an average of the prior three years' costs hoping that the installation of the system would reduce costs to this level. However, in view of the rapidly increasing prices, he finally chose FY 1983 costs less 3 percent for the FY 1984 budget. The activity level measured by patient days and pounds of laundry processed was set at FY 1983 volume, which was approximately equal to the volume of each of the past three years.

## Questions

1. What is your assessment of the method used to construct the budget?
2. Recast the budget and performance report assuming the following:
   *a.* Laundry labor, supplies, water and water heating and softening, and maintenance are variable costs. The remaining costs are fixed.
   *b.* Actual prices are expected to be approximately 20 percent above the levels in the budget prepared by the hospital administrator.
3. What does this new information tell you about the activities of the Laundry Department?
4. What should be done about the variations from the budget?

## Case 12–2

# MOUNTAINVIEW PSRO*

Ms. Claudia Nugent, Executive Director of the Mountainview Professional Standards Review Organization (PSRO), was reviewing her most recent set of budget reports. The variance analysis report (Exhibit 1) indicated that the PSRO had overspent its budget by approximately $4,000 during the first half of the year. Inasmuch as the organization was under constant pressure to keep its costs down, Ms. Nugent was most interested in determining the reasons for the variance and taking steps to correct the situation.

**Exhibit 1**

Mountainview PSRO
Variance Analysis Report—First Six Months

| | *Budget* | *Actual* | *Variance* |
|---|---|---|---|
| Abstracting personnel | $ 48,000 | $ 54,000 | $(6,000) |
| Non–MD, MCE personnel | 320 | 420 | (100) |
| Review coordinators | 32,784 | 29,376 | 3,408 |
| MDs | 4,116 | 5,040 | (924) |
| Subtotals | $ 85,220 | $ 88,836 | $(3,616) |
| Administration and general | 16,000 | 16,450 | (450) |
| Totals | $101,220 | $105,286 | (4,066) |

## Background

The PSRO program was established in 1972, and was administered by the Health Care Financing Administration of the Department of Health and Human Services, which was also responsible for administering the Medicare program. The law establishing PSROs (PL 92–603) stipulated that payment for Medicare and Medicaid services was contingent upon both medical necessity and the provision of services in an appropriate health care facility. In particular, the law stipulated that hospital care would not be reimbursed if the patient could have received the necessary services in a less costly mode, such as on an outpatient basis or in a nursing home.

At the peak of its activity, the PSRO program included 195 state or area-wide organizations. Established by physicians, a PSRO could either delegate the review of cases to hospitals or perform all review activities itself. These activities included utilization review and quality assurance, with criteria for both types of reviews established by each PSRO within certain general guidelines. Each PSRO had a physician board which held final responsibility for the organization's activities.

Because of severe reductions in funding in the early 1980s, many PSROs went out of existence. Some, such as Mountainview, remained, funded by a

* This case was prepared by David W. Young, Harvard School of Public Health.

combination of both federal and state monies. In all instances, however, there was intense pressure to keep review costs down.

Mountainview PSRO had been in operation for approximately five years. It carried out both medical audits (called medical care evaluation studies, or MCE Studies) and utilization review activities (called concurrent reviews). These activities required four kinds of personnel: abstracting personnel, who were high-level clerical personnel used exclusively for the concurrent reviews; nonphysician, research assistant personnel used for the MCE studies; review coordinators, used for both types of activities; and physicians, also used for both types of activities.

The budget for the first half of the year had been based on rough estimates of the number of reviews or studies expected, an estimate of the amount of time necessary to conduct each review or study by each type of personnel, and an estimate of the hourly rate paid to the four categories of personnel. A summary of the budget data (excluding administration and general) for the first six months is contained in Exhibit 2. As this exhibit indicates, the organization planned to do a total of four MCE studies and 12,000 concurrent reviews. Although nonphysician MCE personnel, review coordinators, and physicians were to work on all four MCE studies, cost considerations prevented the organization from engaging in such a comprehensive effort for concurrent reviews. Accordingly, abstracting personnel worked on the full 12,000 concurrent reviews, but review coordinators then worked on only

**Exhibit 2**
Budget Data for First Six Months

| | *Type of Activity* | | *Cost* |
|---|---|---|---|
| | *MCE Study* | *Concurrent Review* | *Totals* |
| Number of studies/reviews | 4 | 12,000 | — |
| *Abstracting Personnel:* | | | |
| Rate/hour | | $ 8 | |
| Hours per review | | .5 | |
| Budget total | | $48,000 | $48,000 |
| *Non–MD MCE Personnel:* | | | |
| Rate/hour | $ 10 | | |
| Hours per study | 8 | | |
| Budget total | $320 | | $ 320 |
| *Review Coordinators:* | | | |
| Number of reviews | 4 | 3,600 | |
| Rate/hour | $ 12 | $ 12 | |
| Hours per study/review | 8 | .75 | |
| Budget total | $384 | $32,400 | $32,784 |
| *MDs:* | | | |
| Number of reviews | 4 | 900 | |
| Rate/hour | $ 42 | $ 42 | |
| Hours per study/review | 2 | .1 | |
| Budget total | $336 | $ 3,780 | $ 4,116 |
| Total budget | | | $85,220 |

30 percent of those reviews, and physicians looked at only 900 of the reviews, or less than 10 percent of the total. It was felt that this process assured quality control without excessive costs.

In attempting to discern the reasons for the budget variation, Ms. Nugent gathered the data shown in Exhibit 3. From these data, she learned that the nonphysician MCE personnel had used only seven hours per study rather than the eight which had been budgeted. Their hourly rate was $10. Review coordinators used the full eight hours budgeted and were paid $12/hour. Physicians, on the other hand, while needing only the budgeted two hours per study, cost $45/hour, rather than the budgeted $42. Rather than the four MCE studies planned, however, the organization actually completed six such studies.

With respect to the concurrent reviews, the abstracting personnel completed only 10,000 rather than the 12,000 budgeted, but required 0.6 rather than 0.5 hours per review; their hourly rate was $9 rather than the $8 which had been budgeted. The review coordinators worked on only 3,000 reviews rather than the 3,600 anticipated, but took 0.8 hours per review; their hourly rate was $12. Finally, physicians worked on 1,000 rather than 900 reviews, needing only the budgeted 0.1 hour per review, but costing $45 rather than $42 per hour.

Ms. Nugent realized that in some instances the personnel had been more

**Exhibit 3**
Actual Data for First Six Months

| | *Type of Activity* | | |
|---|---|---|---|
| | *MCE Study* | *Concurrent Review* | *Cost* |
| Number of studies/reviews | 6 | 10,000 | — |
| *Abstracting Personnel:* | | | |
| Rate/hour | | $ 9 | |
| Hours per review | | .6 | |
| Total | | $54,000 | $54,000 |
| *Non–MD MCE Personnel:* | | | |
| Rate/hour | $ 10 | | |
| Hours per study | 7 | | |
| Total | $420 | | $ 420 |
| *Review Coordinators:* | | | |
| Number of reviews | 6 | 3,000 | |
| Rate/hour | $ 12 | $ 12 | |
| Hours per study/review | 8 | .8 | |
| Actual total | $576 | $28,800 | $29,376 |
| *MDs:* | | | |
| Number of reviews | 6 | 1,000 | |
| Rate/hour | $ 45 | $ 45 | |
| Hours per study/review | 2 | 1 | |
| Budget total | $540 | $ 4,500 | $ 5,040 |
| Total actual | | | $88,836 |

efficient than anticipated, and in others they had been less efficient. She wondered how she might best structure the information so as to determine the reasons for the $3,616 negative variance in such a way that she could work more closely with the PSRO's personnel to bring the budget back in line for the second six months of the fiscal year.

## Questions

1. What are the specific reasons for the $3,616 negative variance shown in Exhibit 1?
2. How much of the total variance resulted from the changes in numbers of studies or reviews?
3. What does the information tell you about Ms. Nugent's management decisions during the first six months of the year?
4. What should Ms. Nugent do?

## Case 12–3

## RURAL HEALTH ASSOCIATES*

In July 1981, Margaret Reber, Research Assistant at the Harvard School of Public Health, interviewed Jack Bourbeau, manager of Rural Group Practice (RGP), for the purpose of writing a case on the management control system at RGP. RGP was a division of Rural Health Associates, a large health care organization located in the rural community of Farmington, Maine. At the time of the interview Mr. Bourbeau had worked at RGP for eight months, and had already instituted some changes in the group practice, which he described in the following interview.

*Bourbeau:* When I first came here in November 1980, I looked at the physicians' generation of revenue and the corresponding expenses, and I knew something was wrong. Here, look at the Statement of Operations and Comparisons for that month (Exhibit 1). You can see how the generation figures in all categories were less than budgeted, but the expenses were not proportionally less, so we ended up with a big deficit.

*Reber:* Was meeting budgeted figures a matter of high priority to RGP providers when you came?

*Bourbeau:* No. At that time, the physicians didn't care whether or not they met budgeted amounts. They had no incentives to do so, as they were paid prospectively based on anticipated revenue for the budget year.

* This case was prepared by Margaret B. Reber, under the direction of David W. Young, Harvard School of Public Health.

**Exhibit 1**

RURAL HEALTH ASSOCIATES (B)
Rural Group Practice
Statement of Operations and Comparisons*

| | *1979 Month November* | *1980 Month November* | *1979–80 YTD 11/30/79* | *1980–81 YTD 11/30/80* | *1980–81 Prorated Budget* |
|---|---|---|---|---|---|
| Generation: | | | | | |
| Medical | $ 81,349 | $ 81,073 | $454,111 | $486,622 | $574,319 |
| Dental | 13,658 | 13,023 | 60,104 | 66,603 | 77,621 |
| Optometry | 10,788 | 11,030 | 56,587 | 55,955 | 69,807 |
| Pharmacy | 3,076 | 2,799 | 14,155 | 15,160 | 17,269 |
| Laboratory | 8,634 | 8,165 | 43,953 | 46,948 | 53,623 |
| X-ray | 7,253 | 5,296 | 34,338 | 32,187 | 41,892 |
| Total | 124,758 | 121,386 | 663,248 | 703,475 | 834,531 |
| Grants | 3,054 | 2,039 | 15,269 | 12,696 | 12,500 |
| Other income | 504 | (9) | 4,746 | 989 | — |
| Total operating support | 128,316 | 123,416 | 683,263 | 717,160 | 847,031 |
| Less uncollectibles: | | | | | |
| Provision for bad debts | 3,569 | 3,455 | 19,022 | 20,014 | |
| Cash discount | 1,173 | 1,066 | 5,685 | 6,791 | |
| Courtesy and employee discount | 1,635 | 189 | 9,936 | 1,152 | |
| Disallowed charges | 12,108 | 11,960 | 38,454 | 42,171 | |
| Total uncollectibles | 18,485 | 16,670 | 73,097 | 70,128 | 84,703 |
| Total operating revenue | 109,831 | 106,746 | 610,166 | 647,032 | 762,328 |
| Operating expenses: | | | | | |
| Medical | 62,933 | 65,453 | 326,936 | 386,170 | 398,383 |
| Dental | 7,844 | 8,701 | 45,501 | 51,170 | 55,277 |
| Optometry | 8,868 | 9,582 | 45,093 | 50,726 | 50,015 |
| Pharmacy | 3,738 | 2,933 | 14,024 | 15,475 | 15,834 |
| Laboratory | 4,785 | 4,518 | 20,819 | 21,996 | 25,252 |
| X-Ray | 5,058 | 4,075 | 23,086 | 23,485 | 25,753 |
| Medical records | 1,606 | 3,056 | 8,706 | 9,948 | 9,042 |
| Facilities | 12,197 | 11,571 | 60,100 | 56,329 | 65,239 |
| Administration | 19,022 | 18,269 | 88,290 | 96,303 | 114,614 |
| Total operating expense | 126,051 | 128,158 | 632,555 | 711,602 | 759,409 |
| Interest | 300 | 244 | 3,749 | 2,215 | 1,667 |
| Total operating expense including interest | 126,351 | 128,402 | 636,304 | 713,817 | 761,076 |
| Excess of revenue over expenses (expenses over revenue) | $(16,520) | $(21,656) | $(26,138) | $(66,785) | $ 1,252 |

* The fiscal year was from July–June. FY 1981 began on July 1, 1980.

*Reber:* How did you interest the providers in the problem?

*Bourbeau:* The providers eventually became concerned when they realized the group practice would go under if we didn't reverse the deficit trend. Then I had their support.

*Reber:* How did you approach the problem?

*Bourbeau:* I decided to do an analysis to find out why our actual revenue was lower than budgeted. I focused on each individual provider. Although the year's budgeted values for physician generation were derived somewhat subjectively from discussions with individual physicians and examination of past trends, there were some standards I thought I could use to find the revenue we could expect from each physician. First, I identified each physician's specialty area and used the fee guidelines to determine the typical fee per visit for each provider (Exhibit 2). Next, I talked to the physicians to determine how many hours per week they were scheduled to be in the office (Exhibit 2). Although all of our providers are full time, some of them spend a greater percentage of their working time at RGP. For example, Dr. Sewall, one of our dentists, is available for office visits 40 hours/week, whereas Dr. Dixon, our general surgeon, spends a good deal of time at the hospital.

*Reber:* What happened next?

*Bourbeau:* Using some general guidelines, each provider determined how many patients she or he could see in an hour's time based on the length of an average office visit (Exhibit 2). Then I multiplied the expected number of hours worked per week by the expected number of patients in a week. In order to give the physician some leeway for telephone calls and paperwork, we use a 4.5 day workweek. This amount was multiplied by the expected number of provider days in the month, which I determined by subtracting all legitimate sick and vacation days for the particular month (Exhibit 2). This gave me the expected number of patients per month. Finally, I multiplied this number by 0.80 to get a more realistic number of patients the physician was expected to see for a month.

*Reber:* Why did you provide the physicians with this additional leeway?

*Bourbeau:* The physicians engage in many nonincome generating activities and they thought some allowance should be incorporated to account for the time they spend in the reexamination of patients, delivery of medication and shots, and public relations activities for which there is a minimal charge or perhaps no charge at all.

*Reber:* I see. Anything else?

*Bourbeau:* Well, my final step was to take this adjusted figure and multiply it by the average fee per visit to get the revenue which I could expect each provider to generate.

*Reber:* Then you compared this expected revenue with actual?

*Bourbeau:* Yes. Using the physicians' schedule books, my secretary tallied up office visit, office surgery, and injection charges for the month for each physician to get the actual office visit generation. She also computed the number of patients seen, the total hours worked, the number of appointments rescheduled or canceled and the number of no shows. My secretary spent about six hours each month tabulating this information. She gave this information to me (Exhibit 3) and then I subtracted the actual from the expected and prepared a report for each physician contrasting expected and actual values. I have been doing this since November. Here is a sample of a recent report showing performance for Dr. Bitterauf for the month of May (Exhibit 4), as well as the totals for all departments for May (Exhibit 5).

*Reber:* What have you learned from the reports?

*Bourbeau:* Well, as might be expected, the revenue of some providers was way below expected. In certain cases, it was due to low productivity; in others, it was

**Exhibit 2**

Expected Provider Charges, Office Hours, Visits, and Workdays

| *Provider* | *Specialty* | (a) *Average Fee per Visit* | (b) *Expected Number of Office Hours/Week* | (c) *Expected Number of Office Visits/Hour* | (d) *Expected Number of Workdays in May* |
|---|---|---|---|---|---|
| Bitterauf | Orthopedic surgery | $20 | 16 | 4 | 16 |
| Condit | Family practice | $17 | 32 | 4 | 20 |
| Dixon | General surgery | $18 | 16 | 4 | 15 |
| Fuson | Family practice | $17 | 32 | 4 | 15 |
| Haeger | Dentistry | $30 | 40 | 2 | 20 |
| Hurst | Otorhinolaryngology (ENT) | $20 | 16 | 4 | 16 |
| MacMahon | Pediatrics/family practice | $17 | 32 | 6 | 10 |
| Prior | Internal medicine | $17 | 23 | 4 | 18 |
| Record | Internal medicine | $17 | 23 | 4 | 16 |
| Sewall | Dentistry | $30 | 40 | 2 | 20 |

**Exhibit 3**
Actual Provider Visits, Hours Worked, and Generation

| *Provider* | *Actual Number of Visits in May* | *Actual Number of Hours Worked in May* | *Actual Generation in May* |
|---|---|---|---|
| Bitterauf | 208 | 44 | $ 3,816 |
| Condit | 413 | 107 | 6,890 |
| Dixon | 88 | 30 | 2,398 |
| Fuson | 242 | 87 | 4,271 |
| Haeger | 218 | 130 | 7,493 |
| Hurst | 203 | 61 | 6,704 |
| MacMahon | 191 | 43 | 3,758 |
| Prior | 207 | 70 | 3,860 |
| Record | 182 | 56 | 3,717 |
| Sewall | 211 | 133 | 10,100 |
| Totals | 2,163 | 761 | $53,007 |

because the physicians weren't charging enough or they weren't spending enough time in the office. So I decided to talk to the providers.

*Reber:* How did the physicians respond?

*Bourbeau:* Pretty well. The first time I produced the report, I sat down with each physician individually and explained the figures. I had to convince them that I was right. I had to be able to back up my words with figures. For every hour I spent with a physician, I spent 12 to 15 hours in hard work documenting what I was talking about. When I showed them all the data, they accepted it. Let me give you an example of a conversation I had with one of our physicians who was undercharging patients. I said, "Roger, I've been studying the way you've been practicing, and I'd like to talk to you about it. Although you see a lot of patients, your total generation is under what we expected." Then Roger said, "How do you know?" After I showed him the numbers, we progressed

**Exhibit 4**
Sample Physician's Report

Dr. Bitterauf — May, 1981

16 hrs/wk × 4 pts/hr = 64 pts/wk

| #pts | #hrs | Generation |
|---|---|---|
| 208 | 44 | $3,816 |
| $18.35 | $86.73 | 4.7pt/hr |

64 pt/wk ÷ 4.5 days/wk = 14.2 pt/day

14.2 pt/day × #provider days (16) = 227 pt/mo (max)

227 pt/mo × .80 = 182 × $20.00 = $3,640

$3,816 − $3,640 = $176

**Exhibit 5**

RURAL HEALTH ASSOCIATES (B)
Rural Group Practice
Statement of Operations and Comparisons

| | *1980 Month May* | *1981 Month May* | *1979–80 YTD 5/31/80* | *1980–81 YTD 5/31/81* | *1980–81 Budget* |
|---|---|---|---|---|---|
| Generation: | | | | | |
| Medical | $109,941 | $100,794 | $1,057,539 | $1,157,234 | $1,443,817 |
| Dental | 14,511 | 18,685 | 140,431 | 163,694 | 195,136 |
| Optometry | 10,185 | 14,984 | 122,943 | 142,061 | 175,492 |
| Pharmacy | 3,218 | 2,778 | 33,007 | 35,949 | 43,414 |
| Laboratory | 11,431 | 12,042 | 102,508 | 117,396 | 134,806 |
| X-ray | 8,332 | 7,044 | 85,109 | 80,646 | 105,315 |
| Total | 157,618 | 156,327 | 1,541,537 | 1,696,980 | $2,097,980 |
| Grants | 2,823 | 2,039 | 34,299 | 24,931 | 30,000 |
| Other income | (29) | (8) | 13,603 | 1,064 | |
| Total operating support | 160,412 | 158,358 | 1,589,439 | 1,722,975 | 2,127,980 |
| Less uncollectibles: | | | | | |
| Provision for bad debts | 4,431 | 4,402 | 43,663 | 47,964 | |
| Cash discount | 1,473 | 1,367 | 13,133 | 15,502 | |
| Courtesy and employee discount | 195 | 214 | 13,001 | 2,546 | |
| Disallowed charges | 9,885 | 12,878 | 104,125 | 131,486 | |
| Total uncollectibles | 15,984 | 18,861 | 173,922 | 197,498 | 212,798 |
| Total operating revenue | 144,428 | 139,497 | 1,415,517 | 1,525,477 | 1,915,182 |
| Operating expenses: | | | | | |
| Medical | 75,224 | 66,966 | 758,746 | 837,488 | 1,022,252 |
| Dental | 8,751 | 9,686 | 101,844 | 117,134 | 133,759 |
| Optometry | 11,853 | 15,341 | 105,491 | 124,971 | 121,761 |
| Pharmacy | 2,734 | 3,055 | 30,706 | 36,858 | 38,000 |
| Laboratory | 4,510 | 4,297 | 49,916 | 56,504 | 60,600 |
| X-ray | 3,874 | 5,353 | 53,993 | 56,082 | 64,800 |
| Medical records | 1,556 | 1,735 | 18,892 | 19,049 | 21,700 |
| Facilities | 11,887 | 11,350 | 132,823 | 131,512 | 156,560 |
| Administration | 17,900 | 21,584 | 198,905 | 235,251 | 290,250 |
| Total operating expense | 138,289 | 139,367 | 1,451,316 | 1,614,849 | 1,909,682 |
| Interest | 1,000 | 746 | 7,593 | 5,573 | 4,000 |
| Total operating expense including interest | 139,289 | 140,113 | 1,458,909 | 1,620,422 | 1,913,682 |
| Excess of revenue over expenses (expenses over revenue) | $ 5,139 | $ (616) | $ (43,392) | $ (94,945) | $ 1,500 |

to a discussion of his pattern of undercharging. Roger told me that some people didn't have much money, so he didn't charge as much. Then I told him, "You can't do that. You can't charge one patient less than another for the same service. That's discrimination." Now, we're gradually getting Roger's fees up to what they should be. But I couldn't do it without this report.

*Reber:* So you feel that the physician's report has been a useful tool for controlling revenue?

*Bourbeau:* Yes indeed. This report has enabled me to pinpoint the sources of our low revenue generation problem and it has provided me with the necessary back-up to discuss problems with the providers. We have seen some dramatic increases in certain physician's office visit revenue since we instituted the report. We have a ways to go, but this report is helping us get our feet back on the ground.

*Reber:* What additional activities do you plan?

*Bourbeau:* The most important thing to do now is to be able to give the providers a breakdown of why they are not achieving their budgeted levels of performance. This is going to require designing a somewhat more sophisticated report than we have right now.

## Case 12–4

## COOK COUNTY HOSPITAL (B)*

Cook County Hospital A (Case 7–1), describes the programming and budgeting system that was introduced in 1971. This case describes how information from this system, together with other information, was used in the management of the radiology department. It is based on interviews with Lou Pinckney, administrative assistant. Mr. Pinckney had extensive experience in the radiology department. A fully trained technician, he had taken courses in business administration. He described his job as follows:

> I think we have come a long way. The concept of management of a department, as extensive and complex as this [radiology] is being appreciated. People recognize it as a key function, not paper shuffling. We need managerial skills. I am called an Administrative Assistant but my job is that of a Business Manager.

Exhibit 1 is an illustration of Mr. Pinckney's conception of his job and the nature of the relationships that were involved.

*Q:* How would you characterize the nature of changes that have taken place in the radiology department in the last three years?

*Pinckney:* I would say we have built up a whole new concept of patient care and have acquired the capability to deliver it, almost from scratch. It has been a very challenging and rewarding experience.

*Q:* What has been the role of the budgeting system?

*Pinckney:* Substantial. The budget has provided us the impetus. It is no more whom you know in downtown that matters but what is the merit of your programs. We have a better managed operation now.

*Q:* As an administrative assistant in the division, what sources of data do you use to develop your budget and evaluate your performance?

---

* This case was prepared by C. K. Prahalad, under the direction of J. B. Silvers, Harvard Business School.

**Exhibit 1**
Administrative Assistant—Radiology Division: A Conception of the Job

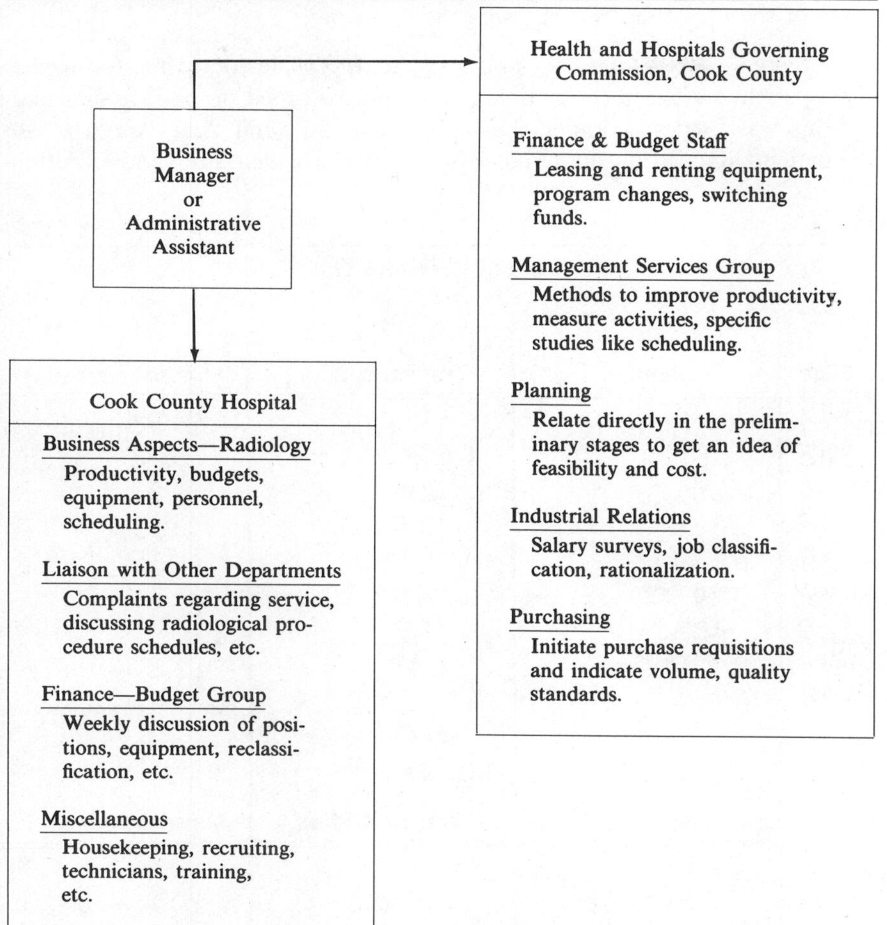


*Pinckney:* As you know we work on the basis of programs. Development of programs is based on our judgment and understanding of the demand for a specific service or procedures. We make the equipment decisions as well as personnel decisions on that basis. We do not use management techniques like discounted cash flows or return on investment but I am confident that we can satisfy any accountant of the reasonableness of our decision.

We do not have data on cost per procedure by the type of procedures, but we use extensive checks on technician productivity to measure efficiency. Basically, the controls that I exercise here are based on controlling output in physical terms, not in financial terms. Financial data can mask a lot of trends and shifts that are taking place. Moreover, we are at present concerned about increasing the quality of patient care and we do not want to get caught in a numbers game.

Mr. Pinckney received a variety of reports from his supervisors and maintained a series of charts showing trends in a variety of performance indices. Some of the important reports were the following:

1. *Average waiting time per patient* (Exhibit 2). The total time for which a patient waited in the radiology unit was recorded on patient slips and this was used to compile the report. The "in" and "out" times of all patients divided by the number of patients provided an average waiting

**Exhibit 2**

**Patient's Waiting Time**

April 14-20-73

| Date | Minutes | Transport-Slips | Minutes (per slip) |
|---|---|---|---|
| April 14 | 624 minutes | 15 slips | 0:52 minutes/slip |
| 15 | 585 | 14 | 0:42 |
| 16 | 2384 | 29 | 1:22 |
| 17 | 2828 | 37 | 1:16 |
| 18 | 5284 | 62 | 1:25 |
| 19 | 5791 | 47 | 1:31 |
| 20 | 923 | 19 | :45 |
| 7 days total | 18,419 | 223 | 1 : 23 average for week for regular cases |

**Specials**

| Date | Minutes | Transport-Slips | Minutes (per slip) |
|---|---|---|---|
| April 14 | — | — | — |
| 15 | 171 minutes | 1 slip | 2:51 minutes/slip |
| 16 | 4680 | 29 | 2:41 |
| 17 | 3261 | 19 | 2:51 |
| 18 | 4270 | 40 | 1:47 |
| 19 | 3690 | 27 | 2:17 |
| 20 | — | — | — |
| 7 days total | 16,072 | 116 | 2:18 average for week for special cases |

**Combined-Cases**

| | Minutes | Transport-Slips | Minutes |
|---|---|---|---|
| 7 days total (April 14-20) | 34,491 | 339 | 1:42 average wait for week for all cases |

**Exhibit 3**
Technician Worksheet

**8am—4pm** ✓
**4pm—12mid.**
**12mid.—8am**

**Signature** Cotton, M.R.T.

**Date** May 5, 1973
**Room No.** 10

| Name | X-Ray No. | Examination | No. of Films | Time In | Time Out | Ward | Comments |
|---|---|---|---|---|---|---|---|
| 1. BROWN, CHARLIE | 1866 | Rt. Ankle Chest | $14^1$-$8^3$ | 9:15 | 9:30 | 33 | w/c |
| 2. WASHINGTON, ANNA | 1886 | Lt. Hip L.S. Spine | $10^2$-$11^2$8 | 10:40 | 11:10 | TR | w/c |
| 3. WILDER, TYRONE | 1890 | Chest Lt. Ribs | $14^2$ | 11:30 | 12:50 | TR | Str |
| 4. McNEASE, NATHANIEL | 1902 | Rt. Forearm Skull | $10^4$-$11^1$ | 1:05 | 1:30 | TR | w. |
| 5. FLOWERS, ANNIE | 1912 | Chest Skull, Cerv. | $8^3 10^4 14^2$ | 2:00 | 2:35 | 10 | str. |
| 6. SMITH, JAMES | 1927 | Cer. Sp. Skull | 8-10 | 3:40 | 4:00 | TR | str |
| | | | | | | | |
| | | | | | | | |

time. The waiting time for regular and special cases was separately computed. The segment of the total waiting time that was measured is shown below:

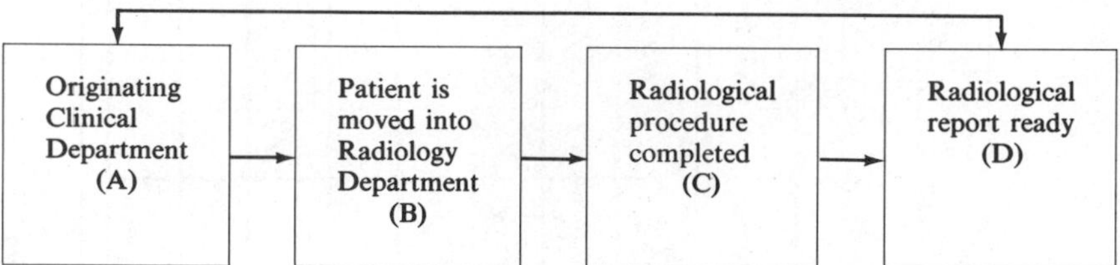


1. The segment that was measured was the time it took to go through Steps (B) and (C). Mr. Pinckney was initiating steps to measure and report the total time delay—i.e., for segments (A) through (D).
2. *Number of procedures performed* on a daily basis classified by *wards* which initiated the request as well as by *type of procedures.*
3. *A Technician Worksheet* (Exhibit 3), which shows the utilization of time of the technician. All log sheets which show a slack, like the one in Exhibit 3, are referred to Mr. Pinckney.
4. *Procedures per inpatient day* (Exhibit 4) as an index of the quality of service. The log sheet for the pediatrics department is shown in Exhibit 4.

**Exhibit 4**
Procedures per Inpatient Day—Pediatrics

| Mo | Yr | Inpatient Procedures | Days in Month | Average Procedures per Day | Average Daily Census | Procedures per Inpatient Day |
|---|---|---|---|---|---|---|
| Dec. | 70 | 1012 | 31 | 33 | 281 | .117 |
| Jan. | 71 | 1351 | 31 | 44 | 299 | .147 |
| Feb. | | 1291 | 28 | 46 | 296 | .155 |
| Mar. | | 1235 | 31 | 40 | 273 | .147 |
| Apr. | | 1198 | 30 | 40 | 239 | .167 |
| May | | 1174 | 31 | 38 | 227 | .167 |
| June | | 1096 | 30 | 37 | 296 | .123 |
| July | | 1004 | 31 | 32 | 313 | .102 |
| Aug. | | 1107 | 31 | 35 | 316 | .113 |
| Sept. | | 829 | 30 | 27 | 344 | .078 |
| Oct. | | 880 | 31 | 28 | 314 | .089 |
| Nov. | | 922 | 30 | 31 | 300 | .109 |
| Dec. | | 867 | 31 | 28 | 308 | .091 |
| Jan. | 72 | 1030 | 31 | 33 | 312 | .106 |
| Feb. | | 1142 | 29 | 35 | 326 | .107 |

**Exhibit 5**
Procedures per Employee—Total Diagnostic Department

| Mo | Yr | Procedures | Days in Month | Average Daily Procedures | Payroll Employees | Procedures per Employee |
|---|---|---|---|---|---|---|
| Dec. | | 24372 | 31 | 786 | 140 | 4.11 |
| Jan. | 71 | 25937 | 31 | 836 | 140 | 5.97 |
| Feb. | | 26037 | 28 | 992 | 135 | 7.34 |
| Mar. | | 27297 | 31 | 880 | 140 | 6.29 |
| Apr. | | 20700 | 30 | 693 | 144 | 4.81 |
| May | | 19770 | 31 | 637 | 156 | 4.08 |
| June | | 24014 | 30 | 827 | 168 | 4.76 |
| July | | 32908 | 31 | 1061 | 177 | 5.94 |
| Aug. | | 28519 | 31 | 933 | 207 | 4.50 |
| Sept. | | 29566 | 30 | 985 | 227 | 4.03 |
| Oct. | | 26267 | 31 | 847 | 222 | 3.06 |
| Nov. | | 27559 | 30 | 918 | 224 | 4.05 |
| Dec. | | 27934 | 31 | 901 | 221 | 4.07 |
| Jan. | 72 | 28699 | 31 | 732 | 227 | 3.22 |
| Feb. | | 28589 | 29 | 986 | 221 | 4.46 |

5. *Procedures per employee* (Exhibit 5) as an index of productivity is measured on a monthly basis.

Mr. Pickney relied heavily on the scheduling system for optimum utilization of his machines. This system worked as follows. The clerk in each clinic contacted the master scheduler at the radiology department and gave information on patients in his ward and the procedures called for. The master scheduler split the requests into routine, specials, and G.I.s (Gastro-intestinal) and passed it on to schedulers assigned to these groups. A log sheet was prepared by each group and, based on the loading chart, a transportation slip was prepared. Transportation personnel brought in patients to appropriate machine locations based on the transportation slips.

Mr. Pinckney reflected on the reports and the scheduling system and remarked:

> We still do not have a comprehensive measure of activity. Our patient mix is changing, the nature of procedures are changing. So is the number of procedures per patient. We need to develop, in-house, a measure of activity which combines all these variations. This is the objective I have set for myself. In the meanwhile I will have to do with cruder measures of performance. I do not think financial measures and variance reports tell me what I want to know. I am confident that

we can develop adequate systems. Some complain that we are slowly becoming a super-bureaucracy. Maybe. That doesn't bother me. What excites me here is that things are happening.

## Questions

1. Evaluate the performance reporting system contained in Exhibits 2–5. What changes, if any, would you recommend?
2. What additional reports would you recommend be designed to meet Mr. Pinckney's needs? The needs of the Chief of Radiology?
3. How might these reports be modified for other departments in the hospital?

# chapter 13

# Evaluation

In Chapter 12 we described the regular, recurring process of monitoring the current activities of the organization. In this chapter we describe two other techniques that are used to evaluate what the organization has done. Although there is no consensus on the names of these techniques, we shall refer to them as operations analysis and program evaluation.

## BASIC DISTINCTIONS

The evaluation processes described in this chapter differ from the monitoring process described in Chapter 12 in the following principal respects: (1) the evaluation process occurs at irregular, infrequent intervals, usually once every five years or so, rather than at monthly or quarterly intervals; (2) the evaluation of a given activity or program is much more thorough and more time-consuming than routine performance monitoring; (3) the evaluation is usually conducted by someone other than the operating manager's line superior; and (4) the techniques of analysis are different.

The essential difference between operations analysis and program evaluation is that the former focuses on an organization's efficiency and the latter on its effectiveness. Using terms developed in earlier chapters, the former may be called an evaluation of *process* and the latter an evaluation of *results.*[1]

An operations analysis accepts the objectives of the responsibility center as a given. Although there may be problems in finding out what these objectives are, once they have been identified, they are not challenged. The operations analysis assumes that the unit will continue its activities in achieving the overall goals of the organization (although occasionally the analysis may lead to the conclusion that an activity should be discontinued). The purpose of the analysis is to find ways of carrying out these activities, whatever they are, more efficiently.

A program evaluation, by contrast, asks whether the objectives of the program are appropriate and whether the organization is attaining these objectives in the most effective way. The purpose of a program evaluation is to make a judgment about whether the program should be continued, redirected, or discontinued.

Taking a job training program as an example, an operations analysis would accept the fact that the responsibility center is supposed to train a certain target group for certain types of jobs and examines ways of improving the efficiency of the training process. A program evaluation would attempt to find out whether the training in fact results in personnel who have acquired the desired skills, and perhaps also whether society needs persons with these skills.

## OPERATIONS ANALYSIS

An operations analysis is called by some a "management audit." Although the techniques can be applied to any type of ongoing activity, they are especially applicable to service, support, and administration activities and to such ongoing mission activities as police and fire protection, and the regular activities of a hospital or educational institution. The need for continuing these activities in some form is usually not debatable. With respect to mission activities—those directly related to carrying out programs—an operations analysis is sometimes combined with a program evaluation; that is, the examination involves both efficiency and effectiveness.

### Need for Operations Analysis

In many organization units, as is the case with many people and other mammals, fat tends to accumulate with the passage of time. Senior management

[1] The U.S. General Accounting Office uses the term "economy and efficiency audit" for what is labeled here "operations analysis" and the term "program results audit" for what is labeled "program evaluation." (Comptroller General of the United States, *Standards for Audit of Governmental Organizations, Programs, Activities, and Functions,* 1981 Rev. p. 3.) However, policy and procedures for the latter type of audits are developed by a GAO office called the Institute for Program Evaluation. To some people, the word "audit" implies that the evaluation is made by auditors, i.e., accountants, and this is incorrect. According to its 1982 Annual Report, out of the total GAO professional staff of 4,088, there were 3,141 "evaluators," and these included attorneys, actuaries, engineers, computer specialists, economists, management analysts, and personnel specialists, as well as accountants.

attempts to slow this accumulation by careful examination of budgets and by monitoring current performance; however, adequate time usually is not available to make a thorough analysis. Furthermore, new technology and new methods develop, and they tend to make obsolete current ways of doing things; however, management, because of the time limitations, cannot ordinarily be expected to take the effect of these developments into account in reviewing the budget. Management must rely basically on the current performance of the unit as a guide to what future performance will be.

Proposed programs have advocates, and these advocates work hard to ensure that proposals get favorable consideration by senior management and funds providers. By contrast, once a program is under way, it is less likely that operating managers will take the initiative in advocating improvements, especially improvements that have the effect of reducing costs. Exhortation alone is unlikely to produce such improvements. For example, the federal government has had a Joint Financial Management Improvement Program since 1948, and it has issued statements on at least an annual basis about the need for increased productivity. Although these statements were signed by cabinet level officials, their impact has not been great. (In the 1980s, however, there are indications that the Joint Financial Management Improvement Program has become more effective.)

There is therefore a need for an occasional, basic review of activities. Such a review is often called a *zero-base review,* the term indicating that the analysis does not assume that any of the current ways of doing things are accepted as given; all are open to scrutiny. When people use the term *zero-base budgeting,* they usually mean zero-base review because there simply is not enough time in the annual budgeting process to conduct the thorough analysis that is implied by the term "zero base."

## Impetus for Operations Analysis

In some large organizations, the operations analysis is conducted on a more-or-less regular cycle that is scheduled so as to cover all responsibility centers once every five to eight years. The results of this audit are used to establish a new benchmark for the responsibility center, and in the subsequent budget reviews top management attempts to hold to this benchmark, recognizing that it is likely to become gradually eroded over time until the next evaluation takes place.

An operations analysis may be initiated because of a financial crisis. The situation in New York City in the early 1970s is perhaps the most publicized example, but there are many others. The "citizen's revolt" against increased property taxation in the late 1970s touched off operations analyses in many municipalities. A decrease in the inflow of financial resources, indeed any situation in which expenses seem to be permanently in excess of revenues, constitutes such a crisis. Allegations, or even rumors, of fraud or gross inefficiency emanating from either inside or outside the organization also may touch off an analysis.

## Who Conducts the Operations Analysis?

Human nature is such that it is unreasonable to expect an operating manager to conduct a review of his or her own activities. Presumably the manager is satisfied with the way these activities currently are carried out and defends present practices in discussions with superiors. (Occasionally, a cost reduction program with adequate incentives can result in such self-appraisals, but this is an exception to the general rule.) In most cases the analysis must be conducted by a person or group not associated with the responsibility center being studied.

In those organizations that have a systematic review process, the analysis may be conducted by a staff unit whose full-time responsibility is to conduct such reviews. This unit may be designated as internal audit, industrial engineering, or, more recently, inspector general.

Outside consultants are often used for operations analyses. Although their hourly fees tend to be higher than the costs of internal personnel, they may complete the analysis in fewer hours because of the expertise and the knowledge they have accumulated about how other organizations carry on the activities being reviewed.

Occasionally, a government agency may create a "blue ribbon commission" of qualified citizens to conduct an operations analysis. The largest such undertaking was the President's Private Sector Cost Survey, under the leadership of J. Peter Grace, in 1982–83. This survey covered most activities of the federal government, and its volunteer staff, recruited mostly from private business, numbered approximately 1,500.

> *Example:* By 1975, Niagara Falls, New York, had a seven-year history of increasing budget deficits, accumulating to $5.8 million. Under the leadership of William H. Wendel, president of the largest company headquartered in the city, a City Management Advisory Board was organized. Local companies contributed services of their experts. Within a year, working closely with a cooperative city manager, the group had discovered and implemented opportunities for improvement that resulted in a budget surplus of $700,000 in 1976, and an anticipated surplus of $3 million in 1977.

Unless properly led, however, an evaluation by business executives can be unproductive, or even counterproductive. The group must understand the differences between the management of a government entity and the management of a profit-oriented business. As one city manager said: "All the Commission did was to describe the problems that we already knew about; they didn't help us implement solutions to them."

## The Operations Analysis Process

Depending on the size and complexity of the activity, an operations analysis may require anywhere from a few days to a year, or even longer. The following are the principal steps in the process, arranged approximately, but not necessarily exactly, in the order in which they are carried out:

1. Obtain a mandate.
2. Identify objectives of the activity.
3. Identify fruitful areas of investigation.
4. Judge the appropriate level of service.
5. Analyze operations.
6. Make and sell recommendations for change.

***Obtaining a Mandate.*** Before the work begins, the audit team should obtain a clear mandate from top management, the governing board, or whatever body has the power to ensure that recommendations are implemented. There must be a mutual understanding of the boundaries of the activities to be encompassed by the analysis, assurance of complete freedom to investigate within these boundaries, and a likelihood that the body that sponsors the analysis will provide the necessary support during its conduct and will be prepared to see that the recommendations are implemented. In some cases, the analysis is instituted as a delaying action in response to public criticism, in the expectation that the furor will fade away without the necessity for making substantial changes. Although identifying such a motive may be difficult, the analysis team is wasting its time if it undertakes work that is sponsored for this purpose.

An operations analysis can be painful to the operating managers of the unit being examined. As a minimum, the analysts' interviews take time that the manager could be using in day-to-day activities. And the possibility exists that the recommendations may lead to criticism or, in the extreme, dismissal. Consequently, the mandate from top management or the outside body that sponsors the audit must be strong enough to assure that noncooperation by operating managers is not tolerated.

***Identifying Objectives.*** At the outset, the analysis team identifies the objectives of the activity. What is it supposed to be doing? Typically, the objectives are fairly clear-cut, but in some cases misunderstandings or perhaps duplication of functions have developed over the years. As mentioned earlier, the purpose of the analysis is not to challenge the appropriateness of these objectives but rather to find more efficient ways of achieving them.

***Identifying Fruitful Areas.*** Operations analysis teams and consulting firms often have a checklist of possible topics that might be investigated, a list that includes every conceivable aspect of activities, organizational relationships, systems, personnel and other policies, communication devices, and the like. It is not worthwhile to analyze every topic on this list. Rather, the team uses it as a basis for identifying those areas where the opportunities for a significant payoff seem to exist. Experienced reviewers often can spot such opportunities simply by a visual inspection and by asking appropriate questions.

*Example:* The following is the reminiscence of a member of the team from Ernst & Whinney, a consulting firm, that examined the operations of the Louisville, Kentucky, Police Court:

"You remember one clerk, in particular, who was industriously banging away at a typewriter. You asked her what she was doing. She looked up briefly from her keyboard to explain that she was typing case dispositions. What happens to them when they're typed? you asked. Why, she answered, they go into the judge's order book. What's the book used for? you asked. She didn't know. So you went to her superior. Why is this done? you asked. You learned why. It's done because a city ordinance says it must be done. But nobody ever uses the book. The same information is available in other records that are easier to use."

Another approach is to compare unit costs for similar operations. Such comparisons may identify activities that appear to be out of line, and thus lead to a more thorough examination of these activities. These comparisons can be useful even though there are problems in achieving comparability and finding a "correct" relationship between cost and output. They often lead to the following interesting question: If other organizations get the job done for $X, why can't this one? Good cost data for such comparisons exist on a national basis for only a few types of nonprofit organizations, principally hospitals and certain municipal functions. Nevertheless, it may be possible to find data for activities within a state, or it may be feasible to compare units performing similar functions within a single organization, as in the case of local housing offices.

*Example:* A study of the costs of processing payroll in eight county governments showed results that ranged from one payroll employee for every 641 other employees down to one payroll employee for every 166 other employees, with an average of one per 424 others. If the two counties with the worst record improved to the average, they would need 38 fewer employees for their payroll functions.[2]

The comparisons in most cases are simple, such as the cost per student in one school compared with an average cost per student in similar schools. In some circumstances, more sophisticated approaches are illuminating. For example, algorithms incorporating a number of interrelated variables have been developed for hospital costs.

***Judging the Appropriate Level of Activity.*** At some stage, possibly in the preliminary investigation, thought should be given to the appropriate amount of service that the unit being evaluated should be furnishing. Although the overall objectives are accepted as given, the level of activity in attaining these objectives is a proper subject for analysis. In some situations, the services

[2] R. A. Smardon, "Cutting the Cost of Local Government," *Harvard Business Review,* March 1977, p. 25.

provided may be inadequate. More commonly, the question is: Is the unit doing more than really needs to be done for the overall good of the organization? The addition of functions of questionable value is often found in administrative units.

*Example:* Over a period of five years, the budget of a certain personnel department tripled, although the number of employees in the whole organization increased only slightly. The personnel department had instituted two house organs (one for professionals, the other for the entire staff), it had set up an elaborate computerized system of personnel records; it had started a clipping service which found and circulated published information about people in the organization; it conducted management training programs, clerical training programs, and interpersonal relations training programs; it had instituted psychological testing and counseling; its members went to and delivered papers at many professional meetings. There was general agreement that people in the personnel department worked diligently. The question was whether all this work was necessary.

***Making the Detailed Analysis.*** The tentative list of areas to be investigated is discussed with the operating manager and often with top management. After their concurrence, a detailed analysis is made of these areas. These may involve analysis of work flows, methods, organizational relationships and the like, using formal techniques developed for this purpose. Occasionally, they may involve sophisticated operations research techniques. Often, the principal tools are an inquiring mind and common sense.

*Example:* In 1968, 38 percent of the garbage trucks in New York City were off the streets on the average. The city bought new trucks, but this "downtime" didn't change. So the city asked Andrew P. Kerr, a management consultant, to look into the problem.

The maintenance system, it seems, had a central repair shop for major overhauls, plus 76 local garages. "But because of union seniority," Mr. Kerr says, "the best mechanics wound up in the local garages doing simple jobs because they were near their homes." The solution: The central shop was replaced with district garages where the senior mechanics could work and still be close to home. Downtime dropped to 18 percent.[3]

One possible approach to the improvement of efficiency in a nonprofit organization is to have certain activities performed by the private sector where the spur of competition may result in lower costs. Some organizations explore such possibilities systematically as a part of their operations analyses. Opportunities range from such specialized activities as building cleaning and maintenance to activities that are usually thought of as belonging exclusively to the public sector.

*Example:* In Arizona, fire protection for an area that includes 18 percent of the state's population is furnished to municipalities by a profit-oriented company.

[3] "The Vise Squad," *The Wall Street Journal,* April 12, 1973, p. 1.

The city manager of Scottsdale, Arizona, says that the city received comparable fire protection from the private company for about half the cost of fire protection in comparable cities with municipal fire departments.[4]

Managers of organization units whose functions might be taken over by the private sector naturally resist such threats to their continued existence, and studies of these possibilities must therefore be conducted as a part of operations analyses, rather than as part of the budget process.

It should not be assumed that a profit-oriented company will perform a function more efficiently than a nonprofit organization, although there are those who act as if this were the case. The proper approach is, of course, to make a careful analysis of the cost of the alternative ways of performing the function. Circular No. A-76 of the U.S. Office of Management and Budget, "Policies for Acquiring Commercial or Industrial Type Products and Services Needed by the Government," provides excellent guidelines for making such comparisons. Even if such an analysis leads to the conclusion that the function should continue to be performed by the nonprofit organization, the fact that such comparisons are being made tends to keep the organization on its toes.

***Making and Selling Recommendations.*** In some cases, recommendations for improvements can be made, accepted and implemented while the operations analysis is in process. To the extent that this can be done on a cooperative basis with the operating manager, the changes are likely to have longer-lasting effects than those that are imposed by higher authority. The team may even be well advised to forego public recognition of its own role in obtaining such changes and give credit to the operating manager.

The team cannot count on such a favorable reaction to its suggestions, however. Challenges to the established way of doing things are often not well received. Recommendations are subject to all the ploys used in the annual budget review, described in Chapter 9, but the game is usually played with much more gusto because more is at stake. Managers under scrutiny will not only do their best to justify their current level of spending but they will also do their best to torpedo the entire effort. They consider the annual budget review as a necessary evil, but an operations analysis as something to be put off indefinitely in favor of "more pressing business." If all else fails, they attempt to create enough doubts about the competence of the audit team that the findings are inconclusive and the status quo prevails.[5]

A team that writes a report and then leaves is therefore not likely to accomplish much, if anything, of enduring value. In most cases, the team

---

[4] *Newsweek,* January 1, 1973, p. 37.

[5] The General Accounting Office, although conducting operations analyses with statutory authority and with the full backing of the Congress, has difficulty in getting agencies to implement its recommendations, even those recommendations that the agency explicitly agreed were sound. See the GAO Report, *Disappointing Progress in Improving Systems for Resolving Billions in Audit Findings,* January 23, 1981.

must devote a considerable amount of its time in planning how its recommendations are to be sold to those who are in a position to act, and laying out a program of implementation and of follow up. If it turns out that the commitment to action obtained in the first stage of the process has, for some reason, disapppeared, the team may decide to attempt a new approach to action, perhaps through publicity. This step is sometimes necessary with the "blue-ribbon commission" type of effort mentioned earlier.

## PROGRAM EVALUATION

### Need for Program Evaluation

Programs tend to go on forever unless they are subject to periodic, hard-headed reexamination.[6] There is a need to look at operations in program terms to ascertain whether the benefits of each program continue to exceed its cost, and whether there are ways to improve its effectiveness. Although opportunities for improvement exist in every organization, there is a general feeling that these opportunities are especially significant in nonprofit organizations, primarily because the semiautomatic measure of efficiency that is provided by the "bottom line" on a business income statement does not exist in nonprofit organizations. Moreover, those who initially authorized a program did so with the belief that it would accomplish some worthwhile purpose. After the program has been in existence for a reasonable length of time, they naturally want to know how well it has achieved this purpose. They presumably will use this information as a basis for decisions on the future conduct of the program.

### Impetus for Program Evaluation

Evaluations of some type have been going on ever since there have been programs. It has been estimated that a moderately large metropolitan hospital is periodically evaluated by 100 or more agencies, ranging from fire inspection to the Joint Commission on Hospital Accreditation, without whose certificate the hospital cannot continue to operate. We are here concerned not with evaluations of specific aspects of a program, but rather with the broad evaluation of a program as a whole, particularly of those programs whose continued existence is optional. If these programs are not effective, they should be discontinued, or at least redirected.

At the federal level, legislation requiring oversight of programs has been in effect since 1946. The scope of formal evaluation efforts was greatly enlarged

[6] A Brookings study showed that of 175 federal government organizations that existed in 1923, 148 were in existence 50 years later; 246 more were created in the same period. Herbert Kaufman, *Are Government Organizations Immortal?* (Washington, D.C.: Brookings Institution, 1976), p. 35.

in the early 1970s when the federal government delegated to the states the task of providing many social services and required as a condition of funding these programs that a formal means of evaluating them be established. At about the same time, there was widespread interest in "sunset legislation"—laws that provided for the automatic discontinuance of a program unless it was evaluated every six to eight years and found to be effective. As of 1982, about 35 states have sunset laws, usually providing for evaluations of selected programs on a five-year cycle. Some other states have legislative bodies that perform similar work.

Program evaluation has become a growth industry. A GAO survey showed that 164 federal evaluation units conducted a total of 2,362 evaluations in fiscal year 1980. Rutgers University accumulates abstracts of evaluation reports prepared by state legislative units; the number increased from 130 in the five years 1970–74 to 805 in the five years 1975–79, an increase of 520 percent.[7] A GAO publication has 460 pages of listings of research at the state and local government level.[8] Professional journals, such as *Evaluation Quarterly, Evaluation, Evaluation and Program Planning,* and *Journal of Evaluation Research,* have come into being. There is a professional organization, the Evaluation Research Society.

## Problems in Program Evaluation

In Utopia the process of evaluating a program would be as follows: (1) at the time a program was approved, its objectives would be clearly stated; (2) as a part of the plan for implementation, quantitative ways of measuring the attainment of these objectives, that is, criteria or results measures, would be set forth; (3) at a specified time after the program had been in operation, an evaluation team would collect data on actual attainment and compare these with the stated criteria, allowing for the influence of extraneous factors; and (4) based on this comparison, a judgment would be made as to the program's success or failure, and appropriate action would be taken to continue, modify, or stop the program. Unfortunately, in the real world, things don't work out that way.

***Problems of Discerning Objectives.*** Those who approve a program have in mind one or more objectives that they hope will be accomplished.

---

[7] Data in this paragraph are from James T. Campbell and Frank K. Gibson, "Program Evaluation by States and Localities," *GAO Review,* Spring 1982, pp. 10–14. For an analysis of the work of state legislative oversight bodies, see Richard E. Brown, ed., *The Effectiveness of Legislative Program Review,* New Brunswick, N.J.: Transaction Books, 1979; and Ralph Craft, *Legislative Follow-Through: Profiles of Oversight in Five States,* New Brunswick N.J.: Eagleton Institute of Politics, 1979.

[8] Government Finance Research Center, *State and Local Government Finance and Financial Management: A Compendium of Current Research* (Washington, D.C.: 1978).

If the program is enacted by legislation, these objectives are supposed to be stated in the authorizing act. The fact is, however, that various supporters of a program may differ in their ideas about what it is supposed to accomplish, the stated objectives may be fuzzily worded in order to accommodate various points of view, and the objectives, either stated or unstated, may be numerous and possibly contradictory.

*Example:* Some people viewed the purpose of the Comprehensive Employment and Training Act (CETA) as primarily to remove people from the unemployment rolls, others as a way of training unskilled persons so that they would qualify for better jobs, others as a device for channeling federal funds to reduce the tax burden of hard-pressed municipalities, others as a way of providing welfare payments, and still others as a device for reducing crime by taking youths off the street. Most advocates had more than one of these objectives in mind, but they differed as to the relative importance of each.

The evaluators must make their best guess as to what the objectives really are and what the relative importance of each objective is. If they guess wrong, the whole evaluation may be discredited on the grounds that it is based on a false premise.

***Problems of Results Measures.*** In Chapter 11 we discussed problems of measuring a program's output and the limitations on various output measures. For many programs there are no valid techniques for measuring what actually happened as a consequence of undertaking the program. In educational programs, for example, there are no reliable ways of measuring how much, if any, additional education a given program produces, except in the case of certain basic skills such as reading and arithmetic. Therefore, a comparison of some new educational effort, such as computer-assisted instruction, team teaching, or programmed learning, is unlikely to reveal any significant difference between those who learned in the new way and those who learned by conventional methods. (It is said, with considerable truth, that the best way to kill an educational experiment is to evaluate it. One can be almost certain in advance that the measurable results will not show a significant improvement.)

*Example:* The Manpower Development and Training Act of 1962 established an institutional program whose objective was to provide training that would increase the future earnings of workers whose jobs had been eliminated for technological reasons and for other groups of disadvantaged persons. It would appear that "earnings" is a quantity that could be measured fairly readily. O'Neill summarized 11 attempts to make such measurements. Only three of the studies were well designed, and none of these showed that the program had a significant effect on the earnings of the participants. Of the other eight, six showed an improvement in earnings and two did not. However, O'Neill demonstrates that each of these eight studies had such serious methodological weaknesses that no valid conclusion could be drawn from them.[9] From 1962, $179.4 million was spent on these evaluation efforts.

Although comparable cost data may be obtainable, data for comparing effectiveness do not exist in many types of nonprofit organizations. In education, reference is often made to the "Coleman effect," a term derived from a report by James S. Coleman and his colleagues,[10] which gave an impressive body of evidence to support the conclusion that no important quantifiable correlation exists between the cost of education and its quality, and specifically between pupil learning and class size, teachers' salary, teachers' experience, age of plant, or type of plant. The effects of these variables were swamped by the influence of the pupil's family environment. Although not everyone agrees with Coleman's conclusions, most people agree that it is extremely difficult to devise experiments that demonstrate quantitatively that one teaching tool or technique is more effective than another.

The use of any quantitative basis or comparison causes concern to some people. For example, Sol M. Linowitz, a highly respected business leader and university trustee, wrote:

> As to a numerical ratio of students per teacher, I am deeply disquieted—not because I am nurturing a romantic kind of Mark Hopkins hangover, but simply because I think this is the result of regarding a college as first a business operation and only secondarily as an educational institution trying to turn out the right kind of men and women.[11]

Although the faculty-student ratio can be misused, its proper use does not imply that a college is primarily a business operation and only secondarily an educational institution. A college is, in fact, both; neither aspect can be slighted.

An especially difficult problem is that of measuring the *impact* of the program, as contrasted with its *output.* For example, the Clean Air Act limits the amount of pollutants that industrial plants may release into the air, and the results of the Environmental Protection Agency's programs can be assessed by measuring the pollutants in the atmosphere. However, if the objective of these limitations is to reduce to tolerable limits the amount of "acid rain" that is damaging forests and water supplies, it is much more difficult to determine whether this objective has been achieved. In particular, the impact of such programs may not be measurable for many years after the presumed corrective action has occurred.

---

[9] Dave M. O'Neill, *The Federal Government and Manpower* (Washington, D.C.: American Enterprise Institute for Public Policy Research, 1973).

[10] James S. Coleman et al., *Equality of Educational Opportunity* (Washington, D.C.: U.S. Department of HEW, OE-38001, 1966).

[11] Sol M. Linowitz, "A Liberal Arts College Isn't a Railroad," *The Chronicle of Higher Education,* February 26, 1973, p. 12.

***Problems of Allowing for Extraneous Influences.*** Although the measurements may show that the target group has improved, as measured in terms of the specified criteria, the improvement may have been caused by factors other than the program. The evaluators may not even know of the existence of these extraneous variables. Even if the team does know of their existence, their importance in explaining the results may not be measurable.

> *Example:* Under the Law Enforcement Assistance Act (LEAA), the federal government spent hundreds of millions of dollars for programs to reduce crime. It is a demonstrable fact that crime rates, or at least the rate of increase in crime rates, in certain cities were reduced. It is by no means certain, however, that this improvement was attributable to the LEAA programs. It may have been caused by general economic conditions, a change in social mores, population shifts, or any of a number of other factors.

***Problems of Obtaining Action.*** Some groups who evaluate programs view the evaluation as a challenging research effort, and lose interest when the research has been completed. They do not plan, or care about, how the results can be sold to those who should use them as a basis for action on the program. In other cases, the evaluation effort is undertaken by the program manager in order to prove that the program is beneficial; if the evaluation comes to a contrary conclusion, it is buried. An unused program evaluation is just as wasteful as a useless program.

Furthermore, the conclusion that a program is worthwhile is a necessary, but not sufficient, reason for continuing it. In a world of finite resources, worthwhile programs must compete with other programs that may be even more worthwhile. The legislative body, or other group that must decide how best to use limited resources, has a more complicated task than that of the team that evaluates a single program, namely, to decide which of the worthwhile programs should continue to be supported and at what level.

## Judging Validity

The validity of a program evaluation can be judged along several dimensions. The principal ones are: construct validity, statistical validity, results validity, and external validity. Each is described below, using an evaluation of the "Follow Through" educational program as an example.[12] The Follow Through program was designed to provide special education to low-income children in kindergarten through third grade.

The "constructs" are the elements of the process that is being evaluated. In the Follow Through evaluation, these were the learning models, educational

---

[12] The example is based on Carl E. Wisler, "Trends in Evaluation," *GAO Review*, Spring 1982, pp. 5–7. For an excellent discussion of this topic, see Eleanor Chelimsky, "The Nature, Definition, and Measurement of Quality in Program Evaluation," *GAO Review*, Fall 1982, pp. 41–47.

attainment, and poor children. *Construct validity* relates to how well the information collected in the evaluation relates to the construct itself. In the Follow Through evaluation, standardized achievement tests were used to measure the educational attainment construct, these were judged by some people to be satisfactory and by others to be too narrow a measure.

*Statistical validity* relates to the techniques used to analyze the data and the significance of the results. Evaluations usually involve samples, and the statistical significance of the results depends on the sample size, the representativeness of the sample, and the arithmetic accuracy of the analysis. (This is often called "conclusion validity.")

*Results validity* depends on whether there is a cause-and-effect relationship, that is, whether the observed results probably were caused by the process being studied. In the Follow Through evaluation, it is possible that the students' better performance in certain schools was because students in these schools were inherently superior, or because of other unknown factors. (This is often called "internal validity.")

*External validity* relates to the applicability of the experimental situation to other environments. If the Follow Through program was successful in the schools being evaluated, can we conclude that it would be successful if applied to other schools?

## Types of Program Evaluations

Each nonprofit organization has at least one program. In the federal government, 6,000 separate programs have been identified. Each of these programs needs to be evaluated in some manner every five years or so. Such an evaluation is essentially a form of benefit/cost analysis. For many programs, the costs incurred in carrying on the program can be measured within acceptable limits of accuracy. The more difficult problem is to measure the benefits.

There are three broad types of program evaluation: (1) subjective, (2) statistical, and (3) experimental. The type appropriate for a given program depends on the nature of the problems described above. Before a full-scale evaluation is undertaken, the team presumably will make a preliminary reconnaissance to settle on one of these types and to work out a plan for the evaluation effort.

***Subjective Evaluations.*** In a subjective evaluation, the evaluation team relies primarily on its "feel" for how well the program is going. It does collect and use such output data as are available, but it does not base its conclusion primarily on these data. Rather, it compares the program in question with other programs with which team members are familiar. The evaluation is therefore heavily dependent on the expertise of the team members in the area being examined. One of the disadvantages of the subjective evaluation is that the support for the recommendations is primarily the unsubstantiated opinions of the experts, and many decision makers are unconvinced by recommendations that are not supported by hard evidence. For this reason, even though the team reaches a conclusion based primarily on its own expertise, it may develop statistical data of the type described in the next section simply as a device for adding credence to its recommendations.

In some situations, a subjective evaluation is used simply because no more elaborate investigation is warranted. If by visiting a vocational education school and examining readily available data, the team observes that only half the students regularly attend class, and that those who do attend are taught by incompetent teachers using ineffective methods, there is no need to collect much data on the effectiveness of the school (except as may be necessary to add conviction to the obvious conclusion that the program is not worthwhile).

In other circumstances, a subjective evaluation is used because the problems with the other types of evaluation are judged to be too great to warrant using one of these types. Accreditation committees evaluate colleges and universities primarily on a subjective basis. They do look at statistics, such as the student/faculty ratio and the number of books in the library, but they know that these statistics are less important than impressions gained by their eyes and ears. The situation is similar to that involved in judging the performance of an individual professor: although data on research output and student ratings are of some help, the conclusion primarily depends on the subjective opinions of those making the judgment.

***Statistical Evaluations.*** In a statistical evaluation, the team collects data that presumably measure the results of the program in terms of stated criteria and compares these results with something. Four general bases of comparison are described in the literature: (1) current results are compared with results at some time prior to the initiation of the program; (2) the trend of performance is measured, so as to ascertain whether performance tends to have improved after the program was initiated; (3) current results are compared with current results of other, presumably similar programs; and (4) current results are compared with the results anticipated when the program was initiated.

In general, the first three methods are arranged in increasing order of validity; that is, the first is likely to be the least valid and the third, the most valid. The validity of the fourth method obviously depends on the validity of the originally anticipated results.

> *Example:* In 1955, Connecticut initiated a crackdown on speeding. A before-and-after comparison (Method 1) showed that motor vehicle fatalities decreased in 1956 as compared with 1955; however, 1955 fatalities were much higher than those in any previous year, so this comparison is highly suspect. A trend comparison (Method 2) showed a decline for several years after 1955, but this comparison is suspect because the opening of superhighways, the greater use of seat belts, and other extraneous factors may have caused a general decline of fatalities. A program-to-program comparison (Method 3) showed that Connecticut's fatalities declined

more than did those in neighboring states; since these states were affected by the same extraneous factors as Connecticut, this is the most convincing evidence of the success of the program.[13]

Many problems are involved in these statistical evaluations: in defining the measures to be used, in collecting valid data, in allowing for extraneous factors, and in determining when a difference is statistically significant. The team needs to decide in advance whether these problems are sufficiently manageable to make the statistical approach worthwhile.

In general, many believe that all of the following conditions should exist:

1. The objectives of the program, or at least some of them, should be well defined and agreed to, both by the program manager and by those who will act on the results of the evaluation.
2. Measures of results, in terms of these objectives, can be defined, and the parties involved agree in advance that these measures are valid.
3. A sufficiently large quantity of reasonably accurate data of these results measures can be collected at a reasonable cost.
4. The program has been in existence long enough so that it is reasonable to expect that its intended results should have been achieved.
5. Comparable data for one of the types of comparison listed above are available or can be assembled at reasonable cost.
6. The comparison is unlikely to be swamped by other extraneous factors ("exogenous variables") whose influence cannot be allowed for.
7. There is a reasonable chance that differences between the two sets of data will be statistically significant (which depends in part on the size of the sample).
8. There is reason to believe that decision makers will act on the results (e.g., they do not have an aversion toward all statistics).

In order to assess the feasibility of making a statistical evaluation, the team should make a preliminary reconnaissance of the situation to assure itself that *all* of the above characteristics are present. If they are not, the evaluation should be subjective. In many cases, a pilot study is a useful way of exploring the situation.

> ***Example:*** An evaluation was made of three educational institutions with similar missions. As a basis of measuring the quality of education, the team developed an extensive questionnaire which was sent to a large sample of alumni, asking for their opinion on the quality of their education. The process required a year. Analysis of the responses to this questionnaire did not reveal any significant difference in perceived educational quality. A pilot questionnaire, or even the judgment of educational experts, probably would have led to the conclusion that comparative educational quality cannot be assessed by questionnaires addressed to alumni.

---

[13] D. T. Campbell and H. L. Ross, "The Connecticut Crackdown on Speeding," *Law and Society Review,* 1968, p. 33.

***Evaluation Experiments.*** In evaluating the efficacy of a new drug or a new medical or surgical procedure, medical researchers have a well-developed protocol. Two groups of subjects (animals or humans) are created, an experimental group and a control group. Individual subjects are assigned to one of these groups either randomly or in such a way that the factors that may affect the outcome of the experiment (e.g., age, sex, weight, health) are similar for each group. The experimental treatment is administered to the experimental group. (In a "double-blind" experiment, the experimenter does not know to which group an individual subject belongs nor whether the chemical administered is the test drug or a placebo.) Factors other than the experimental treatment that might affect the outcome are either insulated from the experiment or are observed and allowed for when analyzing the results. Results are measured, and statistical tests are applied to determine if there is a significant difference, associated with the treatment, between the experimental group and the control group. If there is, the treatment is judged to be successful.

Much of the rapidly growing literature on program evaluation discusses ways of applying analogous experimental methods to social programs. Successes have been minimal however. In many cases, no significant differences between the two groups emerged from the analysis. In most of the cases with a statistically significant difference, critics maintain that the experiment did not satisfactorily answer the key question: Were the results caused by the treatment, or were they caused by something else?

> ***Example:*** By far the largest social experiment is that relating to proposals for income maintenance. It was designed to find out whether cash payments to low-income people (the "negative income tax") are preferable to current welfare programs. The first effort was in New Jersey, begun in the late 1960s, and there have been experiments in six other states, with those in Denver and Seattle being the most comprehensive. These experiments involved 8,500 families at a cost of $112 million. Despite the wealth of data, no legislation for income maintenance has been enacted.

***Problems with Social Experiments.*** With social experiments there are special problems that do not exist for medical experiments. For one thing, most people do not like to be subjects. Guinea pigs can't object, and medical patients usually do not object because they see the possible benefits to themselves, but subjects of social experiments often see no benefit in being treated like guinea pigs. In particular, the control group knows from the beginning that it is not going to benefit, and dropout rates of this group are high, thus upsetting the statistical data base. Furthermore, in order to measure results, the experimenters usually must ask personal questions of the subjects, and despite pledges of confidentiality these are often regarded as an invasion of privacy. It is difficult to determine whether the answers are honest. Even if they are honest, many answers depend on fallible memory. Furthermore, the process of answering questions is time-consuming.

In addition to these special problems of a social experiment, all the problems of program evaluation listed in the preceding section apply.

Principles for conducting social experiments are set forth in Henry W. Riecken and Robert F. Boruch, eds., *Social Experimentation.* The book shows that (1) the number of social experiments that were designed in such a way that they could lead to statistically significant results is small, and (2) the number of such experiments that actually did produce useful results is even smaller. The editors conclude:

> The national capacity for conducting social experiments is, at present, severely limited . . . There is a shortage of capable people and well-managed institutions that can wisely use the resources available for experimentation . . . agencies seem frequently to be unsure of the purpose their research is intended to fulfill . . . or what the audience is. . . . Partly as a result of the uncertainty, experiments are proposed but never carried out or begun but not finished. Information is generated that is irrelevant to decisions. Issues of prime importance to human welfare are not investigated. Hopes for change are raised, then dashed. Attention wanders to new topics.[14]

In a 1978 update,[15] Riecken and Boruch conclude that recent technical developments have advanced the state of the art considerably, but that the problems continue to be formidable. They cite only a few examples of successful experiments. (This book and article are required reading for anyone interested in doing a social experiment or in using its results.)

### Secondary Evaluations

Techniques for program evaluation are relatively new, with most developments occurring since 1960. Even newer are techniques for evaluating the evaluations. There are probably at least as many articles in the literature that analyze program evaluations as there are published reports of such evaluations. A particular problem arises when the reevaluators attempt to re-interview the original subjects. In a 1978 report to the Comptroller General, a committee of the Social Science Research Council cautioned about problems inherent in such re-interviews, particularly the likelihood that pledges of confidentiality would be broken.

### Contrast of Operations Analysis and Program Evaluation

For the same reasons given above with respect to an operations analysis, a program evaluation usually is conducted by an outside organization. Government agencies tend to hire independent firms for this purpose, although some

---

[14] Henry W. Riecken and Robert F. Boruch, *Social Experimentation* (New York: Academic Press, 1974), p. 271.

[15] Henry W. Riecken and Robert F. Boruch, "Social Experiments," *Annual Review of Sociology,* 1978, p. 511.

of them are developing internal evaluation staffs. With the rapid growth of evaluation, it is inevitable that some of the new organizations are not well qualified.

Also, for the same reasons that are relevant for an operations analysis, program managers resist the evaluation effort. They often try to kill it, or at least to make life so difficult for the evaluators by withholding information and in other ways that the final results are open to justifiable criticism.

In other respects, a program evaluation is quite different from an operations analysis. A statistical or experimental evaluation is extraordinarily time-consuming. The Comptroller General estimates that at least a year should be allowed; as noted above, the income maintenance experiment continued for more than eight years.[16] The skills desirable in the evaluation team also differ from those desirable for an operations analysis. An operations analysis requires a knowledge of the management process, of principles of human behavior, of efficient work methods, and of other techniques. These principles and techniques are similar for most types of organizations. By contrast, the program evaluator should be knowledgeable about the specific type of program being evaluated. An expert in education, for example, is not likely to make a sound assessment of a health care program. Moreover, at least one member of the evaluation team must be an expert in sophisticated statistical and experimental methods if the evaluation involves them, whereas an operations analysis usually requires only rudimentary statistics.

Finally, the objective of an operations analysis is reasonably clear-cut; it is to improve efficiency. For reasons given above, the nature of a program evaluation is much more vague. The vagueness starts with the objectives of the program and continues through each step in the process. It is for this reason that program evaluators should lay a careful plan, and obtain assent of the parties to this plan, before they undertake the evaluation. Operations analysts can proceed with much less debate about what they are trying to do.

## SUGGESTED ADDITIONAL READINGS

Brown, Richard E., Meredith C. Williams, and Thomas P. Gallagher. *Auditing Performance in Government.* New York: John Wiley & Sons, 1982.

Chelimsky, Eleanor. "The Definition and Measurement of Evaluation Quality as a Management Tool" in *New Directions for Program Evaluation: Management and Organization of Program Evaluation,* ed., R. G. St. Pierre. San Francisco: Jossey Bass, issue 18 (1983), pp. 113–36.

Hatry, Harry P., et al. *Practical Program Evaluation for State and Local Government Officials.* Washington, D.C.: The Urban Institute, 1973.

Judd, C. M., and D. A. Kenny. *Estimating the Effects of Social Intervention.* Cambridge, Mass.: Cambridge University Press, 1981.

[16] Report by the Comptroller General, *Congressional Oversight Reform Proposals,* June 8, 1978, p. 37.

National Academy of Sciences. *Risk Assessment in the Federal Government: Managing the Process.* Washington, D.C.: National Academy Press, 1983.

Poister, Theodore H. *Public Program Analysis: Applied Research Methods.* Baltimore, Md.: University Park Press, 1978.

Riecken, Henry W., and Robert F. Boruch, eds. *Social Experimentation.* New York: Academic Press, 1974.

Struening, Elmer L., and Marcia Guttenberg, eds. *Handbook of Evaluation Research.* 2 vol., Beverly Hills, Calif.: Sage Publications, 1975.

## Case 13–1

## BUREAU OF CHILD WELFARE*

Mr. Henry Brown, Special Assistant to the Director of the Bureau of Child Welfare, was evaluating the results of the Bureau's activities in its Adoption Program. Of concern to him was the fact that the number of adoptions had been declining over the past two years, and represented an increasingly smaller percentage of children in foster care (Exhibit 1). The Bureau had been emphasizing the importance of placing children in adoptive homes, when the situation warranted such a move. Mr. Brown was uncertain as to why the private agencies, with which the Bureau contracted for the delivery of social services, were not making a greater effort to place children in adoptive homes.

**Exhibit 1**
Number of Legal Adoptions, 1969–1973

| | *1969* | *1970* | *1971* | *1972* | *1973* |
|---|---|---|---|---|---|
| Legal adoptions ............... | 1,000* | 993 | 1,166 | 1,032 | 807 |
| Children in foster care ......... | 24,973 | 25,934 | 27,115 | 27,900 | 28,625 |
| Percent adopted .............. | 4.0 | 3.8 | 4.3 | 3.7 | 2.8 |

* Estimate by Bureau of Child Welfare; all figures except percentages are from the same source.

### Background

As indicated in Exhibit 1, the city's child-welfare system provides care and delivers services to some 29,000 children at any given time. Approximately 8,000–10,000 children enter the child-care system during the course of a year and slightly fewer are discharged, so that the total population increases gradually from year to year.

Although the city is legally responsible for all children in its care, it has few programs and facilities of its own. Thus, the vast majority of children actually are under the direct supervision of some 80 private (or "voluntary," as they are sometimes called) child-care agencies. The great majority of these children in placement reside with individual families in foster homes; the remaining children are distributed among facilities such as institutions, group homes, maternity shelters, and so forth.

The private agencies are funded by the city according to a reimbursement formula which is designed to cover approximately 85 to 90 percent of their reimbursable costs. The reimbursement for ongoing programs, such as foster care, is on a per diem basis; that is, the agency receives a predetermined

* This case was prepared by David W. Young, Harvard School of Public Health. It is based on David W. Young and Brandt Allen, "Benefit-Cost Analysis in the Social Services: The Example of Adoption Reimbursement," *Social Service Review,* July 1977. 

amount per day for each child in care. The amount of payment varies according to the type of program (foster home, group home, institution, etc.). A variety of costs either are not reimbursable or—as is the case with adoption—are reimbursed by means of a one-time fee. Payments made to agencies, regardless of whether they are per diem or a one-time fee, come from the Charitable Institutions Budget and total some $200 million per year.

Children may enter the child-care system for a variety of reasons. In some instances the child's parents make a request to the city because they are unable to provide adequate care in the home; in others the child enters by means of a court mandate for reasons such as neglect, abuse, delinquency, or potential delinquency. Although some children remain in care for only a few months, others remain in the system for several years, often until they reach the age of twenty-one and are no longer eligible for child-welfare services.

A variety of changes had taken place over the past 5 to 10 years which affected not only the relationship between the city and the agencies, but the whole pattern of child care. One such change was in the characteristics of the children in care. Between 1970 and 1975 the mix of children in the child-care system shifted rather dramatically, such that there are now proportionately more older children and more children who are in care because of their own emotional and behavioral problems. As a result of this change, many agencies—and the city as well—had been left with inappropriate programs and service-delivery capabilities; consequently many children were residing in programs which were not appropriate to their needs.

## Data

Mr. Brown realized that several complications existed which impinged on his evaluation. First, foster home care cost the city $12 a day, with payments made 365 days a year; this rate had remained unchanged for the full five years. The one-time adoption fee, by contrast, had risen from $400 in 1969 to $1,400 in 1973.

Second, over 40 percent of all adoptions in 1973 were "subsidized," that is the adoptive parents received payments from the city of about $1,440 per year. This percentage was up from only 1.1 percent in 1969 (see Exhibit 2).

Third, Mr. Brown had recently obtained some data on the cost to a volun-

**Exhibit 2**
Number of Subsidized Adoptions, 1969–1973

| | *1969* | *1970* | *1971* | *1972* | *1973* |
|---|---|---|---|---|---|
| Subsidized adoptions | 11 | 96 | 218 | 326 | 328 |
| Percent of total adoptions | 1.1 | 9.7 | 18.7 | 31.6 | 40.6 |

Source: All figures except percentages from the Bureau of Child Welfare.

tary agency of an adoptive effort. As he had learned, agencies incur three types of costs in placing a child in an adoptive home. First, there are the rather standard direct costs for the adoption itself. These expenditures include legal fees, casework time, administrative time, testing, and the like. Second, there is a loss of per diem payments. That is, when a child is adopted, the agency's population level falls; since reimbursement is based on a per-child per-day payment, the agency loses this payment until a replacement child is admitted. The per diem payment is designed to cover both fixed and variable child-care costs, but when a child is adopted only the variable costs stop—the fixed costs continue. Thus, until the agency can replace the adopted child it loses reimbursement for the fixed-cost portion of the per diem rate. Third, the child who replaces the one who was adopted is likely to have higher variable costs. Since children who are adopted usually require few special agency services, their variable costs are relatively low. On the other hand, new children entering the child-care system frequently have a need for one or more specialized services, so that when a replacement child is found he/she is likely to have higher variable costs, on the average, than the one who was adopted. As a result, the agency suffers a loss in the surplus of reimbursement over variable costs and consequently has fewer dollars available to cover its fixed costs.

As an example, if the fixed portion of the $12 per-child per-day reimbursement amount is $5.00, and if a month elapses before a replacement child is admitted (which frequently can be the case), the agency has lost approximately $150 ($5.00 per day ×30 days) of funds which it had previously planned to use for the payment of rent, salaries, and other expenses to which it has committed itself for the budget year. If the variable costs for the replacement child are $1.00 more per day than for the one who was adopted, the agency's annual fixed-cost reimbursement is depleted still further. Assuming children are adopted fairly consistently throughout the budget year, the $1.00 per day loss is in effect for an average of six months for each child adopted; the annual loss in reimbursement for fixed costs is thus about $180 ($1.00 per day × 180 days) per adopted child. Consequently, using thse assumptions of a $5.00 fixed-cost portion, a one-month lapse before a replacement child is admitted, and $1.00 per day more in variable costs for the replacement child, an agency's direct adoption costs increase by some $300 per placement.

Of further significance is the fact that the direct cost of adoption itself is frequently understated. While the adoption fee may adquately account for the adoption-related costs of any given child, there are many children for whom adoption is attempted unsuccessfully. An agency incurs adoption-related costs for these children as well and yet receives no reimbursement for them. The schematic diagram in Exhibit 3 illustrates the potential significance of unsuccessful attempts in the computation of adoption costs. In this example 100 children begin the adoption process, but only 45 are successfully adopted. Exhibit 4 shows the costs of this process. When only successful attempts are used and when no homefinding is necessary, the cost per adoption

**Exhibit 3**

Adoption Attempts for Children Considered Permanently Neglected (each symbol represents five children)

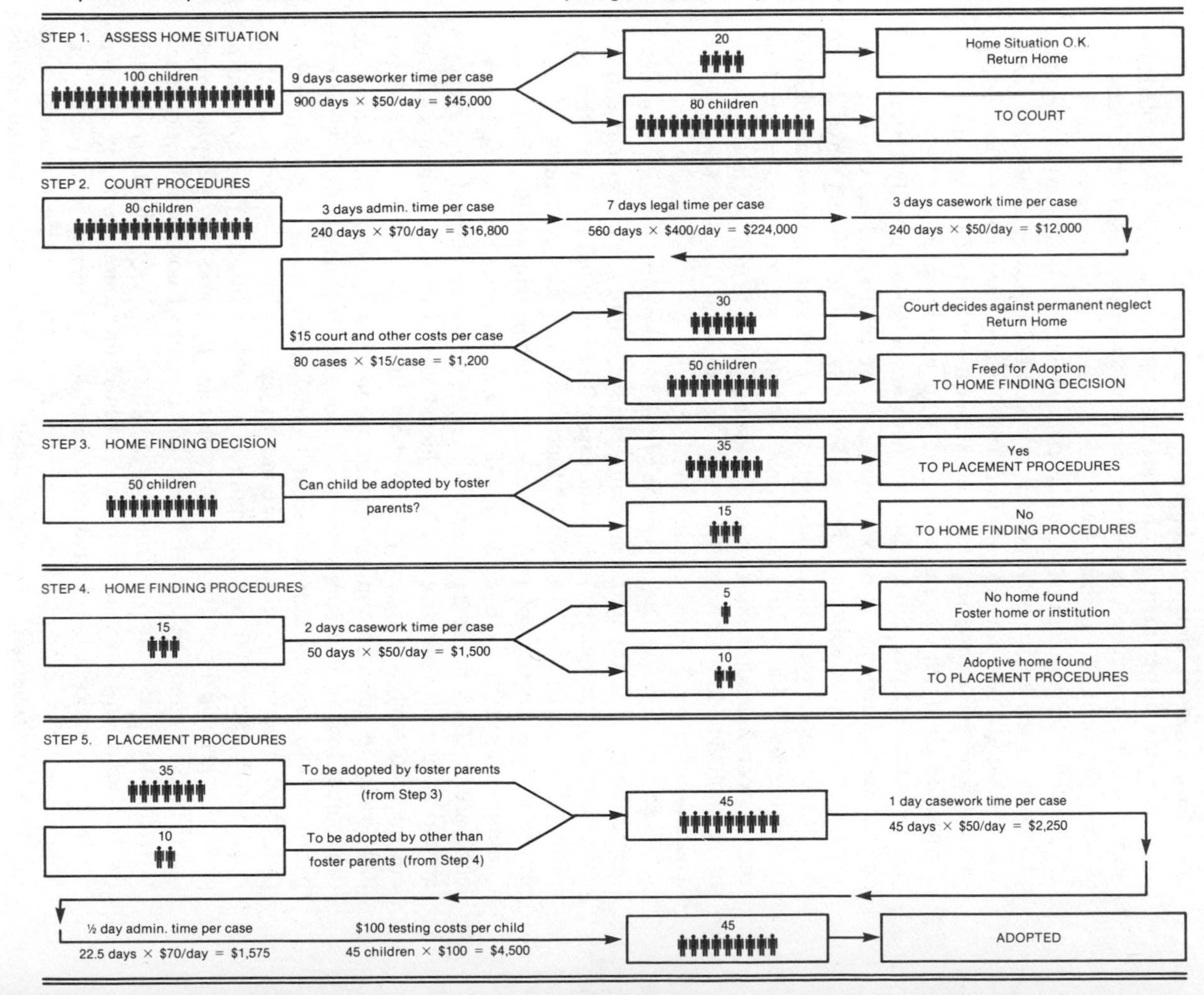

**Exhibit 4**
Adoption Costs for Permanently Neglected Children

| Activity | Cost for One Child | Using 100 Children: Number of Children Involved | Cost for Children Involved |
|---|---|---|---|
| Caseworker assessment of home situation | $ 450 | 100 | $ 45,000 |
| Court procedures: | | | |
| Administrative time | 210 | 80 | 16,800 |
| Legal time | 2,800 | 80 | 224,000 |
| Casework time | 150 | 80 | 12,000 |
| Court and other costs | 15 | 80 | 1,200 |
| Caseworker time in home-finding procedures* | — | 15 | 1,500 |
| Placement procedures: | | | |
| Casework time | 50 | 45 | 2,250 |
| Administrative time | 35 | 45 | 1,575 |
| Testing costs | 100 | 45 | 4,500 |
| Total | 3,810 | 45 | 308,825 |
| Cost per adopted child | $3,810 | | $ 6,863 |

* Not necessary for the average child. Needed for only 15 children out of the 100. Cost is $100 per child when necessary. Therefore $1,500 is included in the cost for children involved.

is $3,810. The inclusion of unsuccessful attempts and homefinding efforts brings the cost to $6,863 per completed adoption; that is, the agency has spent a total of $308,825 and has completed only 45 adoptions.

Dr. Brown noted three points with respect to this example. First, the most significant cost is that of legal fees, which are quite high when there is a charge of permanent neglect because of both the relatively large number of days necessary per case and the fact that in this example the courts decide against the agency in 30 out of 80 cases. Second, not all adoptions follow this pattern. Different legal costs would be incurred, for example, in a case where the child had been surrendered, or where the agency went to court on an abandonment petition. Third, any projected savings will depend on the length of time a child *would have* remained in foster care if he/she were not adopted. He thought 10 years was a reasonable assumption.

In sum, he realized that agencies must consider a variety of costs when deciding whether to proceed toward adoption for a given child. In order to determine more specifically the level of these costs he analyzed 144 children who were adopted through one agency during the three years from 1971 to 1973.

Because this agency had deficit funding for its adoption program, it was able to undertake an adoption whenever it felt that adoption was in the best interests of the child, regardless of the financial consequences. Because it also accepts a relatively high proportion of children classified as "hard to place," it seemed feasible to conclude that the percentage of children adopted would not be biased by the children's characteristics. He classified these children into 36 categories based on legal status, age, and level of handicaps, and found that the average adoption cost per child ranged from $2,700 in the lowest category to $4,600 in the highest.

In order to simplify his analysis, he decided to look only at 43 children whose adoptions were from this agency during 1973, and to collapse his 36 categories into 3, reflecting the most significant factor, legal status: surrendered, abandoned, or permanently neglected. Since this particular agency had had outside funding support for its adoption program, he thought that the results of its efforts might be indicative of what would happen citywide if further financial support for adoptions were made available to the agencies. The results of his analysis are contained in Exhibit 5.

**Exhibit 5**
Adoption Analysis

| | *Actual (1973)* | | | | |
|---|---|---|---|---|---|
| | Agency | | City | | |
| | *Number* | *Percent** | *Number* | *Percent** | Cost per *Adoption†* |
| Total children in care | 596 | — | 28,625 | — | — |
| Number of adoptions | 43 | 7.22 | 807 | 2.82 | — |
| Adoption breakdown: | | | | | |
| Surrendered | 27 | 4.53 | — | — | $3,000 |
| Abandoned | 10 | 1.68 | — | — | 2,700 |
| Permanently neglected | 6 | 1.01 | — | — | 4,600 |
| Subsidized/unsubsidized breakdown: | | | | | |
| Subsidized | 33 | 5.54 | 328 | 1.15 | — |
| Unsubsidized | 10 | 1.68 | 479 | 1.67 | — |

* Percent of total children in care.

† Includes "failures" and other associated costs.

With these data in hand, he began to reflect on the nature of the problem with adoptions, and what changes might be made in the Bureau's reimbursement policy in order to encourage agencies to move toward adoption when it was appropriate for the child.

## Questions

1. What is your assessment of Dr. Brown's evaluation methodology? How might it have been improved?
2. Assuming the validity of the data he has gathered, what are the next steps he should take in the evaluation? What changes, if any, would you recommend the Bureau make in its reimbursement policies? In its other policies?

## Case 13–2

## COMPREHENSIVE EMPLOYMENT AND TRAINING ACT*

The Comprehensive Employment and Training Act (CETA) was scheduled to expire in 1983. As a basis for deciding whether programs of the type financed by CETA should be continued, the House Subcommittee on Employment Opportunities requested the U.S. General Accounting Office (GAO) to assess the effectiveness of various CETA services. The 139-page GAO report was issued June 14, 1982, with the title, "CETA Programs for Disadvantaged Adults—What Do We Know about Their Enrollees, Services, and Effectiveness?" This case focuses on one section of the GAO report, that relating to the effectiveness of CETA adult programs for classroom training, on-the-job training, work experience, and public service employment, as measured by annual earnings.

### Nature of the Programs

In fiscal year 1979 about $9.4 billion was spent for programs delivered under CETA, out of about $14 billion spent for employment and training programs of all types. In 1976, about $1.7 billion was spent for classroom training, on-the-job training, and work experience programs, collectively called "comprehensive services programs," and 1.7 million persons were enrolled in these programs. In 1976, 27 percent of these persons were in the classroom training program, 11 percent in on-the-job training, and 56 percent in work experience. (Five percent, although paid for with comprehensive services program money, were in the public services program.) In 1980, 48 percent were in classroom training, 13 percent in on-the-job training, and 39 percent in work experience.

Classroom training consisted of training in occupational skills (e.g., clerical and various types of crafts) and basic educational training. On average, participants received 21 weeks of training.

On-the-job training provided specific occupational skill training, primarily in operative and craft jobs, in actual job settings, usually in a private-sector company. CETA subsidized part of the wages paid to participants, and it was expected that they would continue working for the organization that trained them after the training period. On average, participants in this program received 20 weeks of training.

The work experience program provided subsidized employment that was intended to instill basic work habits and attitudes, rather than to teach specific job skills. The average participant was enrolled in this program for 20 weeks.

The public service employment program paid wages of persons employed in newly created public sector jobs. About $2.4 billion was spent for this program in 1976 and 0.6 million persons were enrolled in it.

---

* This case was prepared by Robert N. Anthony, Harvard Business School.

These programs were managed by state and local governments through mechanisms called "prime sponsors." A prime sponsor had to represent at least 100,000 people; it could be a state, a county, a large city, or a group of smaller cities or counties. There were about 475 prime sponsors.

### Criteria for Assessment

The GAO recognized that the effectiveness of the programs should be judged in terms of a number of criteria, including economic benefits to the participants, such as increased wages and skills; noneconomic benefits to the participants, such as improved family life and social status; economic benefits to society, such as increased skills in the labor force and reduced crime; and noneconomic benefits to society, such as better race relations and more equitable income distribution. Its report considered a number of these factors, but its monetary assessment of effectiveness focused on annual earnings.

The CETA program was administered by the Department of Labor. For some years, the Department had engaged a private firm, Westat, Inc., to study the experience of a large sample of participants in the program. As of 1982, the most recent data were those for participants enrolled in 1976.[1] The lag was a function of the time required to collect data and interview participants one or two years after they left the program and to analyze these data. About 6,300 persons were in the CETA sample. Data about these persons were compared with data from a carefully matched sample of 5,200 persons whose earnings were reported in the Current Population Survey, a continuing sample survey sponsored by the Department of Labor.

### Results of the Analysis

For the entire sample, 1977 annual earnings of CETA participants averaged $300 higher than those of the comparison group. For on-the-job training, the difference was $850; for classroom training, it was $350; for public service employment, $250, and for work experience it was a negative $150. The work experience amount was not statistically significant; the other numbers were statistically significant at the 0.05 level, or higher.

Annual earnings gains for men were not statistically significant for any program. Earnings gains for white females were $550 for classroom training, $550 for on-the-job training, and $950 for public service employment. Earnings gains for minority females were $500 for classroom training, $1,200 for on-the-job training, and $650 for public service employment. (Female earnings gains for work experience were not statistically significant.)

---

[1] Westat, Inc., *Continuous Longitudinal Manpower Survey, Report No. 8* (Washington, D.C.: U.S. Department of Labor, March 1979), *Follow-Up Report No. 2* (March 1979), and *Follow-Up Report No. 3* (January 1981).

People with the lowest earnings before CETA gained the most from participation. When the sample was divided into three groups according to pre-CETA earnings, the group with the lowest pre-CETA earnings had $550 more annual earnings than the comparison group, while the middle and highest groups had no statistically significant change in earnings. For the lowest group, participants in classroom training had increased earnings (compared with the comparison group) of $600; on-the-job training, $1,300; and public service employment of $900 (work experience was not statistically significant).

Comparisons were also made by age groups, but the pattern was not clear.

The preceding numbers are averages for groups. The GAO report also reported frequency distributions. These showed that 36 percent of CETA participants had no gains or lower earnings in 1977 as compared with their pre-CETA earnings, whereas 24 percent had gains of $4,000 or more.

## Conclusion

The summary section of the GAO report contained the following paragraphs under the heading, "How effective were the services?":

> The single effectiveness study available estimates that only $300–$400 of 1977 post-program earnings can be attributed directly to CETA participation in adult-oriented services during fiscal 1976. By service type, this study estimates gains of $850 for on-the-job training, $350 for classroom training, and $250–$750 for PSE and no significant gains for work experience.
>
> White and minority women had significant net gains of $500–$600, as did participants with the poorest earnings histories. Distributions of gross earnings changes over the period 1974–1977 suggest that even though the aggregate net gain was small, some women and poor earners had fairly substantial net gains from CETA.

## Questions

1. Based on the earnings criterion, did some or all of the CETA programs probably have benefits that exceeded their costs?
2. In considering new legislation, what use could the House Committee reasonably make of the information in the GAO report?

## Case 13–3

# DIVISION OF SOCIAL SERVICES*

The State Welfare Board of a Midwestern state was created in 1937 in order to make use of the benefits of the Federal Social Security Act of 1935. As a result of the 1962 Federal Social Services Amendments, the Board's role grew to include work training projects. The State also expanded aid to dependent children, foster care children, and to children of unemployed parents. Provisions were also made that year for a medical program for public assistance recipients. The Legislature further expanded the Board's responsibilities in 1968 by transferring the vocational rehabilitation program from the Board of Vocational Rehabilitation to the State Welfare Board.

An Executive Reorganization Order abolished the State Welfare Board and replaced it with a cabinet-level Department of Social Welfare (SW) in 1973. The Secretary of the Department is appointed by the Governor and confirmed by the Senate. The Department consisted of administrative and legal support staffs and three program divisions; the Division of Social Services, the Division of Vocational Rehabilitation Services, and the Division of Mental Health and Retardation Services. In 1974, the Division of Services to Children and Youth was added as a fourth program area. The Department is currently organized as shown in Figure 1, with four program divisions, an administrative services division, and 20 area offices throughout the state.

## The Budgeting Process

Soon after the fiscal year begins on July 1, the Department prepares its budget request for the following fiscal year. This request is submitted to the Division of the Budget in the fall. This Division makes recommendations to the Governor which may be further modified through appeal by the Department. The Governor then submits his budget to the Legislature in January where it is approved, often with additional changes. The Department submits a revised budget the following fall, because after several months of operation, it is likely to be able to make a more accurate projection of its expenditures. If the Department will require additional State appropriations in order to continue its existing level of operations and services for the rest of the fiscal year, it requests a supplemental appropriation which must be approved by the Legislature. Such a request forces the Department, the Governor, and the Legislature to choose among the alternatives of shifting funds from other programs, reducing or eliminating some services for part of the year, or adding additional appropriations to the Department's budget.

The cost of medical assistance programs in the State rose approximately

---

* This case (originally titled "Legislative Post Audit") was prepared by Dr. Charles W. Boyd of Wingate College, Wingate, North Carolina.

**Figure 1**
Organization of the Department of Social Welfare

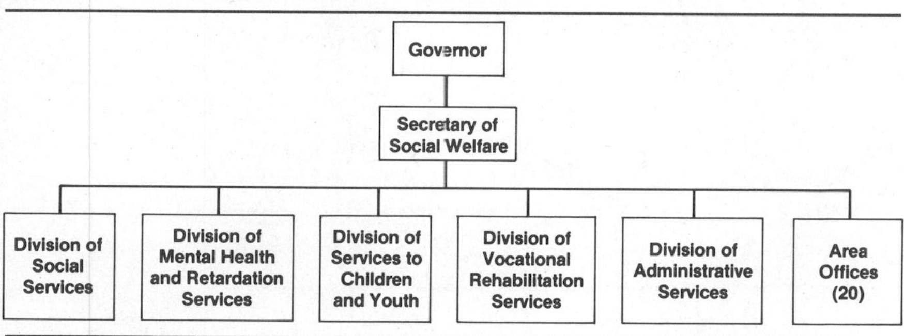


300 percent during the years 1971–77. The rise in state expenditures for these programs was 750 percent during these years, while federal expenditures rose only 150 percent. During the 1977 legislative session, the Department of Social Welfare requested a supplemental state appropriation of $20.4 million, based primarily on the grounds that rising expenditures for medical assistance had forced the Department to exceed its budget. Since there had been a pattern of similar supplemental requests during the past six fiscal years, the Legislative Post Audit Committee directed the Legislative Division of Post Audit to conduct a program audit of the state's medical assistance programs in an effort to help determine the reasons for increases in medical assistance costs.

## The Audit

The Post Audit Division submitted the first draft of its report to the Department of Social Welfare following the completion of the program audit. The draft included a review of the historical development of the Department, recent trends in medical costs and state medical assistance expenditures, and a set of conclusions and recommendations for the Department. As the first of a series of reports that were to be concerned with medical assistance, this one dealt with only two of nine such programs: General Assistance (GA) and General Assistance Related—Medical Only (GA—Medical Only). These two programs relied entirely on state funds, and together they comprised approximately 18 percent of the total expenditures for medical assistance. The Department had indicated that these two programs accounted for much of the rising medical assistance costs.

The two programs were operated within the Department's Division of Social Services. This Division contained four program sections: Income Maintenance, Social Services, Services to the Blind, and Medical Services, as depicted in Figure 2. The GA and GA—Medical Only programs were operated within the Medical Services Section.

**Figure 2**
Organization of the Division of Social Services

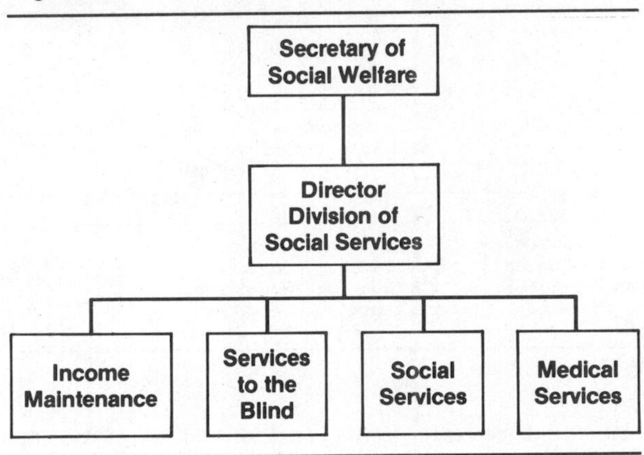


Table 1 shows the estimated expenditures for medical assistance programs for fiscal year 1977. The combined estimate for the GA and GA—Medical Only programs was $31.8 million. These two categories were established by the state for citizens who do not meet federal eligibility requirements for medical assistance but are still judged by the state to be in financial need. This group of people is divided into those needing cash assistance (GA) and those that have an adequate income to meet daily living needs but cannot afford medical care (GA—Medical Only). The seven other main program categories contain federal eligibility criteria spelled out in Title XIX of the Social Security Amendments of 1965. Federal matching funds are available for these program areas.

**Table 1**
Estimated Program Expenditures for Medical Assistance
(fiscal year 1977)

| *Program* | *Estimated Expenditures* |
|---|---|
| Old Age Assistance | $ 14,244,972 |
| Aid to the Blind | 494,446 |
| Aid to the Disabled | 22,856,252 |
| Aid to Dependent Children | 43,985,866 |
| *General assistance* | *14,408,095* |
| Aid to the Aged, Blind & Disabled Related/Medical Only | 53,885,282 |
| Aid to Dependent Children Related/ Medical Only | 7,084,940 |
| *General assistance related/medical only* | *17,387,656* |
| Child Welfare (state wards) | 271,056 |
| Other medical assistance | 64,800 |
| Total | $174,683,365 |

**Table 2**
Budget History for Title XIX Medical Assistance Programs, Fiscal Years 1971–1977 ($ millions)

| *Fiscal Year* | *Initial SW Budget Request* | *Budget Division Recommendation* | *Governor's Budget Recommendation* | *Initial Legislative Appropriations and Expenditure Limitations* | *Revised SW Budget* | *Revised Legislative Appropriations and Expenditure Limitations* | *Estimated Total Expenditures* |
|---|---|---|---|---|---|---|---|
| 1971 . . . | $ 52.8 | $ 46.1 | $ 57.6 | $ 51.6 | $ 52.2 | $ 52.2 | $ 42.7 |
| 1972 . . . | 61.8 | 53.5 | 53.5 | 53.5 | 63.6 | 63.6 | 77.3(*) |
| 1973 . . . | 76.6 | 54.7 | 54.7 | 54.7 | 86.2 | 84.6 | 84.7(*) |
| 1974 . . . | 95.9 | 88.2 | 88.2 | 88.2 | 92.8 | 90.4 | 90.0 |
| 1975 . . . | 109.6 | 93.8 | 93.7 | 103.1 | 106.9 | 106.9 | 109.6(*) |
| 1976 . . . | 127.1 | 110.4 | 128.6 | 127.2 | 138.8 | 138.1 | 136.2 |
| 1977 . . . | 168.0 | 148.6 | 147.4 | 150.1 | 173.6 | 174.7 | 174.7 |

* The difference between estimated total expenditures and revised appropriations and expenditure limitations represents funds transferred to medical assistance from other programs of the Department.

The analysts conducting the Post Audit reconstructed the Department's budgetary history for medical assistance programs during fiscal years 1971–77. These data, which are presented in Table 2, revealed a pattern of annual supplementary budget requests by the Department.

Having reviewed the extent of increased medical assistance expenditures, the Post Audit analysts attempted to determine the causes of the increases and thus the Department's need for the budget supplements. In order to accomplish this, the analysts requested program information from the Department pertaining to fiscal years 1972–77. They sought to determine the number of claims, services, recipients, and eligible persons, and the total expenditure for each major category of service (drugs, dental care, physicians' services, etc.). The analysts were unable to develop the information they desired from the reports supplied to them. They stated three major reasons for this dilemma.

The first problem they encountered was an historical inconsistency in the budget categories for GA and GA—Medical Only programs. While tracing the year-to-year budget projections, the analysts found that the names of specific program categories changed over time. As a result, they were unable to follow some of these budget trails through the entire fiscal 1972–77 period.

The second problem resulted from the fact that the Division of the Budget had made budget cuts for medical assistance programs in total rather than by program. The Department in turn had prorated past budget cuts based upon the relative size of each program's budget request. As a result, it was not possible for the analysts to understand the priorities that had governed medical assistance budgeting decisions. The analysts were pleased to note that in considering the Department's fiscal year 1978 budget, the Division of the Budget had for the first time made budget cuts by program.

Finally, Legislative Post Audit was unable to determine how the past supplemental appropriations were actually used because the appropriations for all social services were made in a lump sum. These funds could be transferred among the various programs as needs arose. This had been done in the past, and the analysts were unable to trace the movement of funds among programs over any extended period of time. Due to the past inconsistency in budget category terminology, the lump sum budget cuts, and their inability to trace the use of budget supplements, the Post Audit Analysts concluded that they were unable to accurately assess the need for the requested supplement to the fiscal year 1977 budget.

The analysts used some of the more detailed data that were available from fiscal years 1975 and 1976 to examine the Department's contention that increased costs in the GA and GA—Medical Only programs had occurred primarily due to increased enrollment or increased use of medical services. Their analysis is summarized in Table 3. These data indicate that 69 percent of GA cost increases were the result of increased use of available services and 109.9 percent of GA—Medical Only cost increases resulted from increased enrollment. While this analysis supported the Department's contention, the audit report cautioned that the data were incomplete and covered a rather short period of time.

**Table 3**
Sources of Increased Medical Cost, Fiscal Years 1975–1976

| | *Percentage of Total Cost Increase* | |
|---|---|---|
| *Source of Cost Increase* | *General Assistance Program* | *General Assistance—Medical Only Program* |
| Increased enrollment | −7.9% | 109.9% |
| Increased use of available services | 69.0 | 1.3 |
| Cost per claim | 38.9 | −11.2 |
| | 100.0% | 100.0% |

The analysts concluded their report with three major recommendations for the Department of Social Welfare:

1. The Department should develop an improved information system for its medical assistance programs that would provide for adequate collection of basic data, classification of expenditures by eligibility category, and analysis by program and service category.
2. It should develop a formal method for reconciling the existing differences in expenditure data among the reports in the Department's present information system.
3. The Department's budget should be submitted and appropriations made in enough detail that past and projected expenditures can be identified by specific program category.

## The Department's Reply

The Department of Social Welfare was provided an opportunity to respond in writing to the first draft of the program audit report. The response discussed several points, some of which attempted to explain past budgetary practices and others which took issue with some of the auditors' conclusions and recommendations.

The Department refuted what was believed to be a basic contention of the Post Audit report: that program costs could have been contained during fiscal years 1971–77 by having had a more sophisticated information system or line item appropriations. Two important factors having nothing to do with the information system were cited as contributors to the rising program costs. First, the federal match rate for program funds dropped five percent during the period. This alone accounted for an approximate $12 million decrease in federal support which had to be offset by an increase in state support. Secondly, about 5,000 persons receiving cash assistance while living in nursing homes were converted into the medical program, thus inflating medical costs. In addition, the state assumed complete financial responsibility for the nonfederal portion of the GA and GA—Medical Only programs in January 1974. Prior to that time, counties had been paying 48 percent of the nonfederal costs while the state paid 52 percent.

The Department's response also presented the following reasons for the increase in medical assistance costs:

1. The consumer price index for medical services had risen 35 percent, from 152 to 206, during the 1971–77 period.
2. The number of persons participating in the program during the period increased from 1,659,386 person-months to 2,179,282 person-months.
3. There had been an increase in the utilization of various types of medical services:
   - 3.1 Hospital inpatient service—measured by number of discharges divided by number of person-months eligible—increased from .031 in 1975 to .036 in the 1977 fiscal year.
   - 3.2 Prescription drugs—measured by number of prescriptions divided by number of person-months—increased from 1.265 in 1975 to 1.303 in fiscal year 1977.
   - 3.3 Physicians' services—measured by number of claims filed divided by number of person-months eligible—increased from .287 in 1975 to .384 in fiscal 1977.
   - 3.4 Dental services—measured by number of claims filed divided by number of person-months eligible—increased from .058 in fiscal 1975 to .077 in fiscal 1977.

The Department believed that these data concerning increasing usage rates supported their fiscal 1977 supplemental appropriation request, and that three years of data provided adequate documentation.

Although the Department did not have data concerning the number of services in each physician or dental claim, they believed that the increase in costs per claim were attributable to inflation rather than an increase in the number of services per claim. The following data were presented in support of this contention:

1975: cost/claim = $25.80
1976: cost/claim = $28.20 (increase = 11.9%)
1977: cost/claim = $29.20 (increase = 3.5%)

The Department's response went into some detail in dealing with the major issue the audit report had brought forth: the quality of the medical assistance information system. The analysts from Legislative Post Audit had developed their data from researching past issues of three routine reports prepared by the Department. Their report had stated that not only were they unable to find certain information in these reports, they also found conflicting data. They further concluded that the Department did not reconcile the differences among these three reports. In their response, the Department went to some length explaining a reconciliation process that *was* used. They concluded that by not employing the reconciliation process which the Department used, the auditors had compared data which were in fact noncomparable. To illustrate the point, one set of corrected expenditure data developed by using the Departmental reconciliation process was presented, the figures naturally differing from those in the audit report.

Each time an improvement had been made in the Department's information system, such as the manner in which a certain type of data was collected or presented, comparability with historical data was either damaged or destroyed. The Department freely admitted this; nevertheless, changes in the system had been necessitated by the growth of the medical program during the fiscal 1971–77 period. One such improvement was the adoption in fiscal 1976 of a Central Accounting System with a 3-digit activity system. This allowed much greater detail in defining expenditures than the 2-digit system it replaced.

The Department also stated that it had in the planning stage a new Medical Management Information System which, when installed, would provide more detailed data than the present system could. The estimated development cost of this system was $420,000, of which the federal government would pay 90 percent. Operational costs were not known at the time the reply was written. Net state costs were not predicted to rise since the federal matching rate was scheduled to increase by the time the system became operational.

The Department made the point that providing data is a very real cost of operating an agency. The more detailed the information became, the higher that cost would be. From the Department's viewpoint, the major issue of data availability appeared to revolve around how much data were really needed for decision making and how much the state was willing to pay for this information.

## Questions

1. Summarize and analyze the arguments on both sides. What are the strong and weak points of each set of arguments? Which agency has the stronger case?
2. What should the Department do?

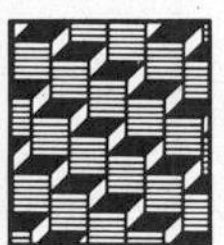

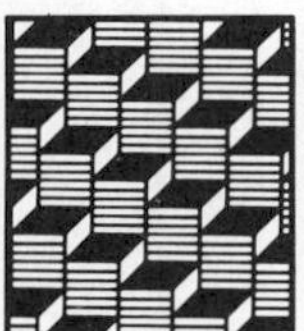

# part IV

# Implementing a Management Control System

The value of an understanding of management control principles, and the structure and process concepts which form the basis for management control systems, is in their application to real-world situations and problems. The ultimate goal is to develop management control systems which facilitate the improved operations of nonprofit organizations. This part discusses both the implementation of such systems and the characteristics of a well-managed organization.

# chapter 14

# System Design and Installation

The structure of a management control system and the uses management can make of information flowing through such a system have been described in earlier chapters. This chapter focuses on problems involved in designing and installing a new or improved system. Technical aspects of systems design such as the development of computer programs, forms, reports, and manuals are beyond the scope of this book. The emphasis here is primarily on behavioral considerations: the necessary preconditions for a successful installation, the problems that must be solved and ways of overcoming them, and the sequence of steps involved in developing and installing the system.

## NECESSARY PRECONDITIONS

Introduction of a new system is a traumatic experience for managers and others, particularly professionals, at all levels. A new system changes the way in which plans are made, it alters the way in which performance is measured and judged, and it establishes new patterns of communication and discussion among managers. The new information provided by the system is presumably better information, but it is certainly different information, and it takes some getting used to.

The problems involved in introducing a new system are generally more acute in a nonprofit organization than in a profit-oriented company because a new system is likely to represent a greater degree of change from past practice. In a profit-oriented company, many basic concepts are taken for granted: accrual accounting, the idea that results should be related to personal responsibility, the idea that it is important to control costs, and so on. In this environment, a new system essentially is a refinement within the context of existing concepts rather than the introduction of fundamentally new concepts. By contrast, many nonprofit organizations do not have even the rudiments of a satisfactory management control system, nor is there a good control "climate" that is essential for the functioning of such a system. Thus, the introduction of a new system represents a substantial change in the established way of doing things.

These problems, incidentally, are not nearly so severe in the installation of a task control system as distinguished from a management control system. A new system for processing payroll, for billing, or for keeping track of inventory may initially contain technical bugs that must be eliminated, but it is unlikely that such a system will cause serious organizational problems. If the system works technically, organizational members are unlikely to resist its introduction; indeed, they will support it as soon as they recognize that the system helps them do their jobs better. (This technical "if" is a big one, however, as we will explain later in the chapter.)

## Top Down or Bottom Up?

There is a difference of opinion as to the relative roles of senior management and operating managers in the introduction of a new system. On the one hand, there are those who believe that the impetus must come from operating managers and that a new system cannot be installed successfully unless these managers request, welcome, or at least support it. On the other hand, there are those who believe that the impetus must come from senior management, that it would be nice if operating managers also supported the idea, but that such support is not necessary. The fact that Likert labels the former approach as "participative" and the other as "authoritarian" indicates his support of the former view.[1]

The discussion in this chapter, however, is based implicitly on the latter point of view, namely, that the driving force for a new system must come from senior management, and that it is unlikely that operating managers will voluntarily embrace a new system in advance of its installation, let alone be enthusiastic advocates of it. Likert and others feel that a system development effort should not be initiated until a majority of operating managers is sold on the concept. We believe that if systems designers wait until that day arrives, they will be quite old. Some reasons why operating managers are suspicious of new management control systems are discussed in a later section of this chapter.

---

[1] Rensis Likert, *New Patterns of Management* (New York: McGraw-Hill, 1961).

## Senior-Management Support

Consistent with the point of view expressed above, we believe the prime prerequisite for the successful installation of a new management control system is the active support and involvement of senior management. Ideally, this support should come from the chief executive officer. However, if the chief executive is primarily involved in policymaking and relations with the outside world, then the necessary support can come from the principal deputy who in fact exercises most management authority. Without the support of one of these two top people, the effort is likely to be unsuccessful.

> ***Example:*** In the late 1960s an attempt was made to install a new management control system for the foreign affairs activities of the federal government. The effort was under the direction of the Deputy Undersecretary of State, who was an able person. The system designers were also able people. They were assisted by an illustrious group of advisors, including Charles Hitch, who, as controller of the Department of Defense, was responsible for the successful installation of a new system in that much larger department. The President of the United States personally endorsed the effort. Nevertheless, the effort failed.
>
> There were, in our view, two reasons for this failure, both involving senior management. First, the Deputy Undersecretary was only the Number 4 person in the Department of State. The Secretary and Undersecretaries of State gave only nominal support to the effort. Second, there was in fact no senior manager for foreign affairs. In addition to the Department of State, the Economic Cooperation Administration, Department of Defense, Agency for International Development, U.S. Information Agency, Peace Corps, and Central Intelligence Agency were all involved. A system that encompassed the activities of all these agencies could not be developed successfully unless one person were given sufficient authority over all these agencies to get the job done. The President did not assign this much authority to anyone; indeed, there is no evidence that anyone tried to convince the President that such a step was necessary.[2]

Support means more than acquiescence. Although senior management time is precious, these managers must be willing to allocate a significant amount to the systems development effort. Senior management must understand the objectives and general concepts of the proposed system well enough to see its benefits, and must explain to principal subordinates how the system will help them as individuals and help the organization as a whole. If roadblocks arise during the development and installation effort, senior management must be prepared to listen to the conflicting points of view and then make a decision which removes the roadblocks. In some situations, the senior manager must also do battle for the system with outside agencies who might otherwise prevent its adoption.

> ***Example.*** George Turcott, Associate Director of the U.S. Bureau of Land Management and responsible for the introduction of its highly regarded Management

---

[2] In his excellent paper "PPBS and Foreign Affairs," Thomas C. Schelling describes this effort in some detail. Schelling's memorandum was prepared for the Senate Subcommittee on National Security and International Operations (Senator Jackson, chairman), January 5, 1968.

by Objectives System said: "The 'top dog' has got to get involved. Don't let the assistant director for administration do it. You have to get the line director or the associate to do it. It works. You've also got to have due process. You've got to have management reasonableness the whole way through and be a gentle tyrant."[3]

If the systems designers are not convinced that this degree of senior management support will be forthcoming, they are not well advised even to begin a systems development effort for the organization as a whole. It is possible, however, that a management control system can be installed in some segment of the organization if it has the support of the management of that segment and if there is good reason to believe that the senior management of the whole organization will at least acquiesce.

## Support from Outside Agencies

A second essential precondition is that outside agencies who can influence the system either acquiesce in the development effort or are prevented by some higher authority from blocking it. Several government agencies developed program budget systems in the early 1960s, only to learn that the cognizant House Appropriations Subcommittee was unwilling to look at a budget in the program format. These efforts therefore did not lead to successful systems.

The ideal situation of course is when outside agencies are enthusiastic supporters of the effort. In the federal government effort to install program budgeting in the late 1960s, senior management and certain individuals in the Bureau of the Budget and the General Accounting Office were active supporters, but there were so many foot-draggers in both organizations that it cannot be concluded that, on balance, the effort had adequate support from these important outside agencies.

In many cases, outside agencies do not understand what a good management control system is. Furthermore, they cannot reasonably be expected to endorse the details of a new system until these details have been developed. The most that realistically can be hoped for in many situations, therefore, is that the outside agencies will maintain an open mind and will agree to support the system *if* it fulfills its promise.

In order to obtain this degree of acquiescence, all possible steps should be taken to minimize the impact of the system on outside agencies. This often requires a procedure called "crosswalking," which is discussed in a later section of this chapter.

## System Designers

A third prerequisite is the existence of an adequate staff of people to design and install the system, and a strong "charter" for this staff. System designers

[3] Paraphrased from an interview, reported in *GAO Review,* Fall 1981, p. 23–27.

of course should have the competence and the expertise that is necessary for the job (and there *is* such an expertise). They also should have a rather special set of relationships with the rest of the organization. System designers need ready access to senior management, either in person or through not more than one intermediary. The system must reflect the style of management that senior management wants, and the only way of assuring that the system does this is to discuss the proposed system design personally with senior management.

System designers also must consult with operating managers, who are busy people. Senior management must convince operating managers that the system design effort is important enough for them to take time away from their always pressing operating problems to discuss their needs for information. Few, if any, of the other staff specialists require a corresponding amount of an operating manager's time.

In order to do the job properly, the leader of the system design team ordinarily should work full time, or almost full time, at it. Since a small organization does not need a permanent full-time system designer, an outside consultant may provide the full-time attention in such an organization. Even in some large organizations, the effort is headed by a part-time person. This happens when the development and installation of the system is a temporary assignment, and qualified persons in the organization are not willing to give up their other responsibilities (and possibly their rung on the promotion ladder) to work full time on it. Under these circumstances the effort is likely to succeed only if the part-time leader is backed up by a full-time staff, by outside consultants, or both.

A systems design and installation effort requires a mix of skills that often are not found in a single person. It requires someone who can deal effectively with managers at all levels and who has a broad understanding of the management control process; but it also requires someone who will pay careful attention to detail. A large fraction of the development work-hours will be spent on tedious matters—the exact definition of accounts, the design of forms, the preparation of computer programs, and the preparation of flowcharts. Although most of this work can be delegated, the team leader must nevertheless have a sufficient knowledge of the details to be able to detect mistakes which could affect the whole system.

***Outside Consultants.*** Professional system design organizations have existed for several decades, and in the last 25 years all the large public accounting firms have created systems staffs. These firms employ many thousands of professionals.

There is a difference of opinion as to the circumstances under which an outside organization should be employed. On the one hand, outside system designers have both a general expertise and a specific knowledge that may not exist within the organization. If an outside firm has done a good job of developing a system for one hospital, it is reasonable to expect that it can install a similar system in another hospital with little waste motion, even allowing for the inevitable differences between the two hospitals. Furthermore, outsiders are often perceived by operating managers as being unbiased: they are not associated with an internal faction, they have no axe to grind, and they have a detached point of view. This, coupled with their expertise, means that they can add a degree of prestige and respectability to the effort. They also can act as a lightning rod, attracting and absorbing the hostilities that may exist about the new system and thereby shielding the members of the permanent organization from these unpleasant feelings.

On the other hand, outsiders *are* outsiders. The new system ultimately should be a vital part of the management process, and some people argue that outsiders can never obtain the essential understanding of "how things really work in our organization." Also, outsiders may be expensive. Their daily cost is higher than that of insiders who might undertake the design and development task, although the higher daily cost may be offset by the fact that outsiders should require fewer workdays to develop the system.

In many situations, the organization has no choice. A mammoth systems effort, especially if it is undertaken in order to correct grave weaknesses in the current system that suddenly have come to light, is likely to require more qualified people than are available within the organization and more than can be recruited on short notice. Even under these circumstances, however, an outside firm should have only part of the responsibility for systems development and installation; in-house personnel must also be involved. All good systems firms insist on such involvement, since at some point in the system's development outsiders will depart; there then must be insiders who will regard the system as "their" system and who will continue to work to ensure its success. This attitude can be generated only if in-house personnel are involved in the design effort in a substantial way. Such an involvement is especially important where outsiders play a major role in the design of the system and in the early phases of its installation, but where in-house personnel are responsible for later phases of the installation task.

A system that is designed by consultants, described in an impressive report, and then turned over to the organization for installation, is usually soon forgotten; competent systems firms are reluctant to accept an engagement if they believe this is likely to happen. Thus, although consultants do not want to do the whole job, neither do they want to walk away after the completion of the design phase. They prefer to participate in the installation process also, bowing out gradually and only after the system is running smoothly.

## Almost Enough Time

In a moderately large organization, at least two or three years will elapse between the time a decision is made to proceed with systems development and the date of cutover to the new system.[4] Even after the cutover date, much additional time is required in educating managers in how to obtain maximum use of the new information, and improvements in the system are never-ending. A final precondition to a successful system, therefore, is that "almost enough time" be allowed between startup and the cutover date. The time allowed is never quite enough because there are always refinements that could be added and additional educational efforts that would be worthwhile. If enough time were allowed for these worthy endeavors, however, the system never would go into operation. It seems clear in retrospect that one of the principal reasons for the failure of the PPBS effort in the federal government in the late 1960s was that not enough time was allowed. As explained in Chapter 7, the interval was only 18 months.

It does not seem feasible to be specific about the appropriate time period. In a small organization, with a fairly specific set of objectives, and especially if good systems exist in similar organizations that can be used as models (e.g., hospitals), assuming a vigorous, well-supported effort is made, a new system probably could become operational in a year, perhaps less. It should be recognized that in most circumstances, a year is quite a short period of time, however. Furthermore, it is not necessary, or even desirable, to install all parts of a system at the same time. Possibilities for breaking the total job into phases are discussed in another section of this chapter.

## PROBLEMS

The system designer must address two sets of problems. First, there are technical problems associated with designing a management control system that best meets the needs of the organization. Relevant considerations for this set of problems were discussed in earlier chapters. Second, there are the problems that arise because the system designers are "change agents." As a result of their efforts, and assuming they are successful, managers will manage in a different way than before. We are concerned here with this latter set of problems.

### Attitudes

Although life would be more pleasant if this were not the case, it is quite probable that operating managers will resist efforts to introduce a new system, or at least they will be unenthusiastic about it. The reason is *not* that people resist change. A salary increase is a change, and no one resists a salary

[4] The State of California *Programming and Budgeting* manual suggests that five years should be allowed for transition to a full PPB system.

increase. Rather, people tend to resist a change when the effect on them is uncertain.[5]

Even if operating managers perceive that the existing system is inadequate, it is nevertheless a system that they have worked with and are comfortable with. They have learned to interpret the information from the existing system, they know its virtues, and they also know and make allowances for its limitations. They must now learn how to interpret the new information, and how to recognize and allow for *its* limitations. They also are uncertain as to exactly how the new system will affect what they do. There is no way of removing this uncertainty completely because there is no way of communicating accurately to them what will happen when the new system becomes operational. Its effect must be experienced to be understood.

> ***Example:*** A management control system incorporating such conventional ideas as management participation in budgeting, variance analysis, and frequent review and revision of plans was described to 69 managers at Naval field activities, and 85 percent stated that the system would be an improvement over that used currently. However, when controllers of activities were asked to rate the acceptability of the proposed system on a scale of 1 (no) to 5 (excellent), the median rating was only 3.[6]

***Concerns of Operating Managers.*** In addition to the effects of the new system itself, it is possible that studies made in the course of developing the system may lead to changes in organizational relationships. A new system may raise questions such as the following: Who benefits from it, and who is hurt by it? How will it affect relationships between superiors and subordinates? How will it affect the informal organization structure? Is it designed to help senior management at the expense of operating managers (or vice versa)? Will it provide information to politicians or other people outside the organization that can be used to hurt people inside the organization? Is it designed to help accountants or computer specialists rather than operating managers?

A new system can change the style of management and the desired qualifications of managers. It may shift power from operating managers to senior management. It often requires professionally educated managers rather than those qualified principally by experience. These tendencies, if perceived by the members of the organization, can easily lead to resistance. This is especially the case in a mature organization whose managers are interested primarily in job security.

---

[5] This problem is not unique to the United States. In an excellent article, Chandler describes an attempt to install a huge national information system for Poland. Because of opposition from managers involved, the effort failed. The attitudes described are essentially the same as those given in this section. Margaret K. Chandler, "Project Management in the Socialist Bloc," *Columbia Journal of World Business,* Summer 1978, pp. 71–86.

[6] W. J. Donnelly, *Budget Execution at Navy Shore Activities,* Monterey, Calif.: Naval Postgraduate School, 1980.

Even if operating managers understand that the system will provide better information, their worries may not be allayed. Operating managers are part of an organizational hierarchy in which they have both subordinates and superiors. Operating managers may understand that the new system will provide them with better information about what their subordinates are doing, and therefore a better basis for controlling the efforts of their subordinates, and this they welcome. But by the same token, they may perceive that the new system provides better information to their superiors about what *they* are doing and gives superiors a better basis for controlling *their* efforts, and this they are not so happy about.

Managers who have previously collected information for their own use tend to resist a system in which information is collected, controlled, and furnished to them by an outside, impartial source. They may view their private data system as a source of power and prestige; other persons must come to them in order to obtain the information. The value of information is that it reduces uncertainty. If a proposed system provides additional information that reduces the uncertainty of superiors about the performance of a subordinate's job, then the subordinate may resist it. On the other hand, if the proposed system reduces the uncertainty about the tasks of others on the staff, the manager will support it. This leads to inevitable conflicts in proposing modifications to information systems, for the same proposal may be viewed as a threat by some people and as a valuable tool by others.

Educational efforts can reduce the force of these negative attitudes, but education probably cannot eliminate them. They disappear only after the system has been in full operation for a substantial period of time. The main point is that system designers should not minimize the importance of this resistance; they must learn to live with it as best they can. They can expect less than full cooperation in obtaining the information needed for systems design, and they can expect that efforts will be made to delay the introduction of the system in the hope that if delayed long enough, it may never materialize. They must use the good offices of the top manager who is sponsoring the system to overcome these delaying tactics. They should understand that the installation of a new system is a political process. It involves pressure, persuasion, and compromise in proper proportions as is the case with any important political action.

***Aids to Changing Attitudes.*** There are several possible ways of lessening hostility and resistance to a new system. First, to the extent that operating managers are convinced that the new system will on balance benefit them, they will support it. Educational efforts should therefore stress the benefits, some of which are (1) the system will help them to do a better job, which will be perceived as such by their superiors; (2) the system will facilitate smoother coordination with other units; (3) managers can exercise better control over their subordinates; (4) by providing an orderly, rapid flow of reliable information, the system makes life less hectic; (5) the system permits them to make better decisions about the allocation of resources (this is especially important in periods when budgets are tight); and (6) the system provides a more realistic measurement of performance.

Second, the responsibility center concept should also be stressed. If too much emphasis is placed on programs and if the relationship of programs to personal responsibility is not made clear, operating managers are unlikely to perceive the new system as being helpful. They may instead regard it solely as a mechanism for reporting performance to top management—in the extreme case, as a "spy" system.

One way of reducing hostility is to install the new system when operations are expanding. Operating managers will then associate it with increased budgets, whether or not such an association is warranted. If the system is installed in a period of contraction, it may be associated with the "screw tightening" which is characteristic of such a period, again without regard to whether such an association is warranted.

## Identifying Information Needs

Notwithstanding the possible resistance described above, the system designer must work with operating managers to find out what information they need to do their job. At one time the recommended approach was that the systems designer should ask managers what information they needed. In recent years, this approach has generally been abandoned because it was found that, in many cases, *operating managers do not know what information they need.* In particular, they cannot visualize the nature of the new information that might be made available and therefore cannot comment on its usefulness.

***Contributions from Operating Managers.*** The approach favored, therefore, is for the system designer to find out what information the operating manager needs by indirect methods. The designer does, if for no other reason than courtesy, ask managers what information they need; but in the interviews the systems designer focuses primarily on the job itself, the relationship of one responsibility center to another, the environmental influences that affect the work in the responsibility center, and so on. Based on this information, a system is designed that provides the information that the manager *should* need. This, of course, is a difficult task since systems designers are not likely to be managers themselves. Therefore, the systems designer must resist the inclination to think of information that he or she would want to manage the operation, and instead try to think of what an operating manager should want.

Operating managers can make important contributions to systems design. For one thing, they are the real experts on feasibility. Higher-level managers need, and would like to have, some information that cannot feasibly be collected, and managers on the firing line can demonstrate the impracticability of collecting such information. For example, hospital administrators would very much like to have systematic, quantitative information on the quality of patient care, but the nursing supervisor may be able to demonstrate that reliable information on quality cannot be obtained.

Discussions with operating managers are also necessary to test proposed reports, both reports intended for their use and reports containing information which they generate. An operating manager can sometimes uncover mistaken assumptions about the availability of data or the exact nature of data.

Finally, discussions with operating managers are important—second only in importance to the support of senior management—in the campaign to obtain acceptance of the proposed system. To the extent that operating managers perceive that they are genuinely involved in the construction of the new system, their willingness to accept it is increased.

***Using Existing Data.*** A study of what goes on in the bowels of the organization is also useful in uncovering operating information that provides raw material for use in a management control system. It is much less expensive to develop management summaries from data that are prepared for other purposes than to generate new data specifically for management control purposes. The system designer should be prepared to sacrifice some "ideal" type of management information if a slightly less desirable type of information can be obtained from existing data sources. For example, there are dozens of ways in which information on the status and flows of inventories can be summarized for the use of management. The system designer is well advised to use a way that can be obtained by summary of the existing inventory records, rather than insisting that the operating system for inventory control be changed to provide the information that management needs.

***Line Needs versus Staff Needs.*** Information is needed both by operating managers in carrying out their line responsibilities and also by staff people who plan and analyze proposed programs and budgets. Unfortunately, there are inherent differences between the information needed by operating managers and the information needed by program planners. Program planners need approximate costs, full costs, and opportunity costs. Operating managers need more accurate costs, direct costs, and historical costs. It may not be feasible to meet both sets of needs completely, and compromises must therefore be worked out. Since the planners may be in the same headquarters organization as the systems designers, they may be able to make their case more persuasively than the case made in the interests of the operating managers. Nevertheless, as a general guide, the needs of operating managers should take precedence. If the system collects an inordinate amount of information that is useful only to the planners, as has happened, it tends to be regarded by the operating managers as cumbersome and unnecessarily expensive.

### Requirements of Outside Agencies

As already noted, it is essential that influential outside agencies, especially those that have the power of the purse, at least acquiesce in the development of the new management control system. In an ideal world, this would not be a problem. Outside agencies should not need more information or different information than management needs; they should need the same type of information but in a more summarized form. In the real world, however, an outside agency may not appreciate this fact. It may have become accustomed to receiving information in a certain format, and it may not perceive that the new information is better. This is especially likely when the new system is only a proposal on paper. Under these circumstances, the outside agency may specify that there is to be no change in the information it receives, and the systems designer usually must accommodate this demand.

It may be feasible to design the accounting system so that it meets both internal and external needs. If these needs are incompatible, however, either of two less desirable solutions must be adopted: crosswalking or operating a dual system.

***Crosswalking.*** Crosswalking is used by federal organizations to translate management data into the format required by the Appropriation Committees of Congress; it is used by many state and municipal organizations for a similar purpose; and it is used by some organizations that are financed by grants to translate management information into the format prescribed by the grantor. The crosswalking process requires that information in the management accounts be reclassified in a manner prescribed by the outside agency. In some systems, this reclassification is exact; that is, detailed data exist in the accounts in such a form that they can be rearranged in the prescribed format. More commonly, the reclassification is only approximate; that is, some of the management accounts are subdivided and reclassified, more or less arbitrarily, to obtain the summaries required for outside agencies. Since the whole crosswalking operation is of no use to management, the organization devotes as little attention to it as possible.

***Dual Systems.*** Some outside agencies insist that the system of control that they prefer also be used as a basis for control within the organization. Since their requirements may be fundamentally incompatible with the system that is best for management purposes, the consequence is that two systems must be operated simultaneously. This can happen, for example, when the outside agency insists on the obligation basis[7] of accounting, whereas an expense basis is obviously better for management purposes, and the outside agency prohibits the use of working capital accounts that would permit the two bases to be reconciled. Some state legislative committees impose such requirements on the agencies that they deal with.

When an organization is forced to operate a dual system, there is of course

[7] It will be recalled that the obligation basis of accounting focuses on contracts placed, and thus does not provide a record of expenses incurred classified by the responsibility centers that incur them.

additional bookkeeping, but this is a relatively trivial problem. The much more important problem is behavioral. Top management wants operating managers to obtain their signals only from its management control system, but operating managers also receive signals from the system required by the outside agency. When these signals conflict, which can happen quite frequently, operating managers must decide which signal is stronger. Since they know that the outside system is associated with the agency that provides them with their funds, they are quite likely to pay more attention to the signals from that system than to the signals from the managment control system.

*Example:* Top management in the Department of Defense wants operating managers to be concerned about the costs of using military personnel, and military personnel costs are therefore a part of the management control system. Military personnel costs are excluded from the "Operations and Maintenance" appropriation that governs operations, however; and it is consequently difficult to persuade operating managers that these costs are really important. In considering trade-offs involving a choice between military personnel, civilian personnel, or contractor services, inadequate recognition of military personnel costs can lead to wrong decisions. For example, the primary reason that military personnel were used in kitchen duties was that the appropriation accounting system signalled to the installation commander that no cost was involved in using military personnel. Actually, in most installations they are more expensive than civilians who could be hired to do this work.

*Example:* In the Department of Labor, the "Cost Center Detail" report contains information on which top management presumably wishes to focus attention: outputs, and costs incurred in attaining them, with a comparison of actual performance against plan. The "Appropriation—Cost Center Report," which is specified by the Congress, however, requires that operating managers also think in terms of appropriations. The two approaches are not reconcilable, since the former report contains "unfunded" costs, i.e., costs which have been incurred but which are not included in the appropriation system.

The acquiescence of outside agencies was described earlier as a necessary precondition for a successful systems development. Some people go further and insist that a new system should not be attempted unless the outside agency is willing to accept the information that the system provides. They feel that the problems of operating a dual system are too formidable to make the attempt worthwhile. These problems are indeed serious, especially the problem of convincing operating managers that they are supposed to operate in accordance with the signals given by the management control system. Nevertheless, optimists argue that attempting to build the prestige of a sound new system is preferable to the alternative of trying to manage solely with an unsatisfactory system prescribed by an outside agency. They hope that as time goes on the outside agency will appreciate the advantages of the new system, to itself as well as to the organization, and will modify its requirements accordingly.

## Dealing with the Old System

Except in rare circumstances, a new management control system replaces an existing system. (Even in a new organization, the tendency is to install a system copied from another organization in order to get things going, even though this system may not be well suited to the new organization's needs.) The system designer has to decide what features of the existing system should be retained, and how the transition from the old to the new system should be made.

It is usually desirable to restrain the natural feeling that the old system should be completely disregarded in the design of the new system. Operating managers will have much to learn about the new system in any event, and to the extent that it incorporates familiar practices—particularly, familiar terms—it will seem less strange to them. System designers have their own preferred vocabulary; they should, however, be cautious about using these terms if those used in the old system are adequate.

Some system designers advocate that a new system should be run in parallel with the existing system until the bugs have been worked out. There are obvious advantages in doing this if it is feasible. In particular, it avoids the terrifying possibility that the new system has a bug that results in the permanent loss of vital data.

Even if the systems are run in parallel, it is important that senior management use information from the new system as soon as it becomes available and its accuracy is assured. Senior managers may be reluctant to do this because they do not feel comfortable with the new information. They should appreciate, however, that operating managers feel the same way, and that operating managers are unlikely to take the plunge until senior management breaks the ice.

Senior management's early use of the new system is especially important when a dual system is necessary. Senior management should use information from its management system exclusively; it should never use information from the system required by the outside agency, and it should insist that operating managers do the same. This is much easier said than done, for it asks managers to give up something with which they are thoroughly familiar for something which is strange.

If the old and new systems are run in parallel, the old system should be discarded as soon as the new system has been determined to be "bug-free," even if managers are not completely comfortable with the new system. This saves bookkeeping costs, but that is incidental. The principal reason is that opponents of the system may continue to seek a way of sabotaging it until such time as the old data are no longer available. After the old system has completely disappeared, they have no choice but to use the new.

## Education

All system designers are intellectually aware of the importance of a thorough educational program as a part of the system installation process. As a practical matter, however, they sometimes do not devote enough time to this effort. There are so many technical problems that must be solved by prescribed deadlines that often not enough time is left for an adequate educational campaign. In retrospect, many wish that they had devoted more time to education.

The preparation of manuals, explanations, sample reports, and other written material is a necessary part of the education process, but it is not the important part. The important part is to explain to the managers how the new system can help them do a better job. System experts, who are the only ones with detailed familiarity with the new system, necessarily play a large role in these educational programs, but management should also be involved.

Above all else, operating managers must become convinced that the new system is in fact going to be used. System designers can say this, but they are, after all, only staff people. The only message that carries conviction comes from the words and deeds of the line managers. Thus, within the limits of their knowledge about the new system, it is desirable that managers teach other managers; that is, that senior management discuss the new system with its immediate subordinates, who then convey the message to their subordinates, and so on. System designers can provide technical support at such meetings, of course, but it is preferable that the meetings be run by managers. Since teachers always also learn, this process aids in the education of those who are involved in it. Moreover, once the system goes into operation, even on a test basis, using the information that it generates is the best educational device available.

***Danger of Overselling.*** In their enthusiasm for the new system, system designers and the sponsors of the system have a natural tendency to state its advantages more strongly than is warranted and to minimize its limitations. A management control system aids management, but it does not lessen the need for management. Even with the best system, managers must analyze and interpret the data, they must allow for its inadequacies, they must take into account much information not available in the system, they must use judgment in making decisions, and they must use behavioral skills in implementing these decisions. If a contrary impression is conveyed in the educational process, hardheaded managers who know the limitations of any system will be skeptical and regard the system effort as the work of impractical theorists.

## STEPS IN SYSTEM DESIGN AND INSTALLATION

Details of the system design and installation process are set forth in many books on this subject. The main steps, assuming that the preconditions listed earlier have been met, are as follows:

1. *Diagnosis.* Analyze the objectives of the organization, the existing control system, and the existing organization structure. This analysis may reveal defects in the existing system and organization structure, in part reflect-

ing differences between the real objectives and the objectives as they are perceived by the organization.[8] It may lead to a reorganization.

2. *Planning.* Develop a plan for system design and installation, including a timetable (preferably in the form of a PERT diagram or a similar scheduling device), an estimate of financial and other resources required, a statement of what units are to be responsible for each part of the development process, and a statement of the cooperation necessary from each part of management. Obtain approval of this plan.

3. *Inventory of current information.* Examine the existing sources of information in detail. Much of the existing information must be collected for operating needs (e.g., payroll, inventory transactions), and its use in the management control system involves little incremental cost.

4. *Develop the control structure.* This involves the identification of responsibility centers, the development of a program structure, and decisions on the revenue, expense, and output elements that are to be incorporated in the system. These topics were discussed in Chapters 3 through 6, and 11. The most difficult problems are likely to be the development of a useful program structure and the choice of feasible output measures. In many cases, only crude output measures can be developed initially, and in some cases, no output measures at all are readily available. Nevertheless, the design effort should not be held up unduly because of these inadequacies.

5. *Development and Documentation.* Develop procedures and document all system flows and computer programs. Documentation is sometimes slighted, but is extremely important since it makes the system independent of the designers, programmers, and operators.

6. *Education.* Develop and implement an educational program.

7. *Test.* Test the proposed structure and procedures, preferably in one part of the organization. Not only is this desirable for debugging, but it also provides a concrete example that is helpful in educating people as to what the new system is all about.

8. *Implementation.* If feasible, run all or part of the new system concurrently with the existing system. As soon as feasible, eliminate all obsolete parts of the existing system.

One of the best descriptions of the process of designing and installing a new system is contained in the booklet, *The Design and Implementation of Pennsylvania's Planning Program, and Budgeting System.*[9] The process began in March 1968 and resulted in a completed program budgeting system in

---

[8] Not much time should be spent in defining objectives, however, for it is easy to get bogged down in semantics. For example, although the objectives of a public school system are intuitively fairly obvious, the installation of a system in the Westport, Connecticut, school system was delayed for a year or more by attempts to elucidate objectives. See John Moore, "The Development of Long Range Plans in the Kirkwood School District (R-7)" (Ph.D. diss., Harvard University).

[9] Robert J. Mowitz, *The Design and Implementation of Pennsylvania's Planning Program, and Budgeting System* (University Park: Pennsylvania State University, 1970).

December 1970. This was used to prepare the budget submitted to the legislature in May 1971. The importance of the governor's commitment to the project is demonstrated, and the methods used to educate legislative committees, individual legislatures, and managers within the executive branch are described. The work of the system design team, consisting of both state employees and outside consultants from Pennsylvania State University is described in considerable detail, and problems and their resolution are discussed with some frankness. This booklet is a useful introduction to the details of the system design and installation process.

### Phased Installation

It is often desirable to install a system in stages, allowing enough time for managers to become accustomed to using the information available at one stage before proceeding to the next. There are three possible dimensions to such a phased effort: a pilot installation, a simple beginning that is later extended, and a step-by-step approach.

***Pilot Installation.*** The system can be installed initially in one part of the organization. Information from the pilot study cannot be used to any great extent by senior management or headquarters staff for overall planning purposes because it will not mesh with the information that is provided by the system still used in other parts of the organization. Nevertheless, it can be fully used by managers within the pilot segment. When this approach is used, it is usually desirable to "build a fence" around the test site, that is, to exempt it from procedures and reports that are required of the remainder of the organization. In order to provide information about the organization as a whole, a unit may be created to "crosswalk" information from the new system to fit the requirements of the existing system. Such a unit should not be associated with the test site; all attention within the test site should be focused on the new system.

> *Example:* A particularly interesting version of the phased approach was used by the State Department in 1981. A review of the existing systems in the department showed some major deficiencies. Therefore, the department decided to design a new worldwide financial system. The department awarded two contracts, one to Price Waterhouse and another to American Management Systems, Inc., to develop a system design. Each used its own technical approach and competitively conducted a requirements study and developed alternate conceptual designs and functional requirements documents for the new system.
>
> The two contractors worked in competition during the requirements stage, conceptual design, and functional requirements definition. After this was completed, the department selected one design and contractor for subsequent implementation. The department believed that a better end product was developed because of the competition.[10]

[10] JFMIP Financial Management Conference Report, 1981.

***Simple Beginning.*** One of the principal causes of failure of a new system installation is that it is too complicated. The development of sophisticated techniques is time-consuming, design errors are likely, and the problem of educating users is made more difficult. Even though the systems designers would like to demonstrate that they are familiar with latest developments in the art, and even though they may feel open to criticism if they install a system that is less than the best, they should not bite off more than they or the organization can digest. If the elements of a sound system are installed first, the refinements can be added after users become familiar with the essentials. Two examples of difficulties with task control systems help illuminate the rationale for a simple beginning:

> *Example:* A state government installed a system for screening the validity of invoices submitted by physicians, pharmacists, and other health providers under Medicare and Medicaid programs. Development of the computer programs was such a mammoth job that it required all the available programmers in the state. The screening tests were so elaborate that even with the largest computer, invoices could not be approved in time to permit payment of invoices by their due dates. The system was scrapped.

> *Example:* In the mid-1960s, the U.S. Air Force began the development of the Advanced Logistics System. The system was to handle all aspects of inventory control, financial management related to stocks, maintenance planning, and other operations associated with receiving, storing, issuing, and transporting supplies throughout the world. By 1975, $200 million had been spent on this effort, probably the largest systems job ever undertaken. At that time it was decided that the project was unmanageable, and it was abandoned.

Horror stories of overelaborate system installations are particularly common in developing countries. Designers have been known to develop systems as if they were to be operated and used by persons with technical and managerial skills typically found in American profit-oriented companies. With a simple beginning, both system designers and managers have an opportunity to learn and grow with the system, while the cost of system development is not excessive.

***Step-by-Step Installation.*** A system may be installed in stages, permitting enough time for managers to become accustomed to using the techniques available at one stage before proceeding to the next. One feasible sequence is the following:

1. Prepare a budget by programs and responsibility centers, using out-of-pocket direct costs, with few service centers, and rough output measures. Do not change the accounting system.
2. Program in the above terms, with perhaps improved output measures.
3. Collect accounting information according to the new structure, and educate managers in the use of this information.
4. Continue development of better output measures.

5. Add sophistication by:
   *a.* Extension of the service center concept and transfer pricing.
   *b.* Collecting more detailed cost information, including cost allocations.
   *c.* Use of a capital charge.

## ENTRY STRATEGY

In a profit-oriented company, the impetus for a better management control system comes from within the organization, from senior management or from the controller. Except for consulting firms who occasionally can generate interest with management, outsiders play no part in creating the desire for a new system. By contrast, the literature contains many accounts of attempts by outsiders to stimulate interest in better management control in nonprofit organizations, especially government organizations, because every taxpayer has a valid reason for fostering improvements in the management of such organizations.

The easiest time to generate interest in systems improvement is either when there is a financial crisis or when serious scandals have been uncovered. In retrospect, it is almost inconceivable that publicly elected officials and their senior appointees in New York, Cleveland, Detroit, and certain other large cities would have tolerated woefully inadequate management control systems, but they did (and some still do).

Interested parties must move quickly to exploit such an opportunity because the public's memory tends to be short, and if the situation calms down, the need for systems improvement can be forgotten. (Those interested in management control systems tend to forget that to many people this is not a glamorous subject; promoting new programs is much more glamorous.) It is important that firm commitments to systems improvement be obtained, that they be highly publicized, that adequate resources be made available, and that some outside agency, such as the legislature or a citizen's group, accept the responsibility for seeing to it that the commitments are kept. In order to maintain interest, it may be desirable to continue to publicize horror stories, although this may antagonize the managers whose cooperation eventually is necessary.

A publicized control breakdown in some part of an organization can be used as an entering wedge. If a sound system is installed in this part, its demonstrated success can lead to general acceptance of the system throughout the organization. In recent years, municipal welfare organizations have been likely candidates for such an effort.

> ***Example:*** For years, knowledgeable people have known that the management control system in New York City was abysmally inadequate. Nevertheless, with the notable exception of the welfare department, where an effective development effort was started in 1971,[11] not much happened. In 1975 the city was on the

---

[11] For an account of this development, see Kenneth L. Harris, "Organizing to Overhaul a Mess," *California Management Review,* vol. 17, no. 3, 1975.

verge of bankruptcy; and systems inadequacies, such as the fact that management did not even know how much cash was on hand, were widely publicized. A systems development effort was started in 1976. It involved 1,000 municipal employees and 200 professionals from five public accounting and management consulting firms. Among other things, they developed 90 new procedures manuals, and trained 7,500 city employees in the operation of the system. A workable system went into operation on July 1, 1977. This, an incredibly fast job, was made possible only by the crisis situation then existing.

## Concluding Comment

We end this chapter with a comment by Aaron Wildavsky, one of the most perceptive observers of the nonprofit scene. It is the concluding section of his review of Brewer's *Politicians, Bureaucrats, and the Consultant,* a description of tremendous failures in attempts to install new systems:

> Nothing anyone says will stop people from trying an available product; so a few rough rules may be offered to guide government officials contemplating the installation of information systems.
>
> First, the rule of skepticism: no one knows how to do it. As Brewer's account suggests, the people most deceived are not necessarily the clients but may well be the consultants. Their capacity for self-deception, for becoming convinced by listening to their own testimony, should never be underestimated. Thus it may be less important to discover whether they are telling the truth than whether the truth they think they are telling is true. Unless the idea is to subsidize employment of social scientists, the burden of proof should be on the proposer.
>
> Second, the rule of delay: if it works at all, it won't work soon. Be prepared to give it years.
>
> Third, the rule of complexity: nothing complicated works. When a new information system contains more variables than, shall we say, the average age of the officials who are to use it, or more data bits than anyone can count in a year, the chances of failure are very high.
>
> Fourth, the rule of thumb: if the data are thicker than your thumb (skeptics—see rule 1—may say "pinky") they are not likely to be comprehensible to anyone.
>
> The fifth rule is to be like a child. Ask many questions; be literal in appraising answers. Unless you understand precisely who will use each data bit, how often, at what cost, relevant to which decisions they are empowered to make, don't proceed.
>
> Sixth is the rule of length and width, or how to determine whether you will be all right in the end by visualizing the sequence of steps in the beginning and middle. Potential users of information should be able to envisage the length of the data flow over time, that is, who will pass what on to whom. If there are more than three or four links in the chain it is likely to become attentuated; data will be lost, diverted, or misinterpreted. The width of the chain is also important. If the data go to more than one level in the organization, the chances that they will be equally appropriate for all are exceedingly slim. The longer the sequence of steps, the wider the band of clientele, the less likely the information is to be of use.

Seventh, the rule of anticipated anguish (sometimes known as Murphy's Law): most of the things that can go wrong, will. Prepare for the worst. If you do not have substantial reserves of money, personnel, and time to help repair breakdowns, do not start.

Eighth, the rule of the known evil. People are used to working with and getting around what they have, they can estimate the "fudge factor" in it, they know whom to trust and what to ignore. They will have to re-estimate all these relationships under a new information system, without reasonable assurance they will know more at the end than they did at the beginning.

Ninth comes the most subtle rule of all, the rule of the mounting mirage. Everybody could use better information. No one is doing as well as he could do if only he knew better. The possible benefits of better information, therefore, are readily apparent in the present. The costs lie in the future. But because the costs arrive before the benefits, the mirage mounts, as it were, to encompass an even finer future that will compensate for the increasingly miserable present. Once this relationship is understood, however, it becomes possible to discount the difficulties by stating the tenth and final rule: Hypothetical benefits should outweigh estimated costs by at least ten to one before everyone concerned starts seeing things.[12]

Sadly, these rules have been violated countless times; nevertheless they remain as valid today as they were in 1973, minicomputers and microcomputers notwithstanding.

## SUGGESTED ADDITIONAL READINGS

Austin, Charles J. *Information Systems for Hospital Administrators.* Ann Arbor, Mich.: Health Administration Press, 1979.

Herzlinger, Regina. "Why Data Systems Fail in Nonprofit Organizations," *Harvard Business Review,* January–February, 1977.

________. "Management Noninformation Systems in Health Care," *Health Care Management Review,* Volume 1, Number 2, Spring 1976.

King, John L., and Edward L. Schrems. "Cost-Benefit Analysis in Information Systems Development and Operation" in *Public Budgeting,* ed. Lyden and Miller. Chap. 7, pp. 221–42.

Mowitz, Robert J. *The Design of Public Decision Systems.* Baltimore, Md.: University Park Press, 1980.

Neuschel, Richard F. *Management Systems for Profit and Growth.* 3d ed. New York: McGraw-Hill, 1976.

[12] Aaron Wildavsky, *Science,* 28 (December 1973), pp. 1335–38.

Case 14–1

# NORTH SUFFOLK MENTAL HEALTH ASSOCIATION*

Burt Lowe wondered what action he could take to address more effectively clinicians' dissatisfaction with the management information system (MIS) at North Suffolk Mental Health Association (NSMHA). Although many of the administration's objectives for the MIS had been met and some progress had been made in addressing clinicians' dissatisfaction, it was slow and time-consuming. Burt felt that the long-range success of the MIS depended upon its ability to meet the needs of clinical personnel, as well as those of central administration.

NSMHA was a mental health service delivery network serving 146,000 people in the Boston Harbor Area. As Director of Planning and Evaluation, Burt Lowe was chiefly responsible for the development and implementation of the MIS at NSMHA. Since the inception of the MIS in 1977, he had worked with personnel at all levels of the organization in attempting to adapt it to their needs. The system had proven itself to be a useful tool for billing and government reporting purposes, but problems existed in its application to clinical work and program planning.

Some staff complained that the MIS was being used to demand unreasonable levels of productivity. Others protested that too little emphasis was placed on nonbillable activities affecting the quality of patient care. Still others objected to the use of the MIS on philosophical grounds, and questioned the reliability and usefulness of the information which it produced. Burt was aware of these complaints and wanted to remedy the problems related to clinical management and use of the MIS.

## History and Operations of NSMHA

NSMHA evolved from the North Suffolk Child Guidance Clinic, which began operations in East Boston in 1959. It operated four outpatient counseling centers and other mental health agencies serving the East Boston/Winthrop, Revere, Chelsea, and Beacon Hill/West End of Boston areas. They served populations of 13,000 to 60,000 people with clinical staffs ranging from 16 to 28 full-time equivalents (FTEs) and administrative and support staffs ranging from 3 to 5 FTEs. The populations of two of these areas were predominantly Italian and of low socioeconomic level and had recently absorbed a large influx of transients. The population served by the third clinic was characterized by a high degree of unemployment, poverty, and social distress. Fifteen to 20 percent of its residents were Puerto Rican, and the center offered special programs to them. A larger number of young transients and deinstitutional-

---

* This case was prepared by Stanley Alexander and Martin P. Charns, Boston University. Used with permission of the authors.

ized chronic mental patients inhabited the area served by the fourth clinic. Besides the four counseling centers, NSMHA also operated three day-treatment programs, an emergency services program, and several residential programs. Although the Massachusetts Department of Mental Health (MDMH) funded most of its clinical positions under a partnership agreement, NSMHA hired its own administrative and support staff. All staff were employed on a salaried basis, and no direct billing was done by clinical personnel at the centers. The Director of Clinical Services, Dr. Muriel Weckstein, supervised all clinical activities. The NSMHA central administrative office had final authority in all financial, operational, and personnel matters. In practice, however, most of this responsibility was delegated to administrative coordinators at the operating units. An organization chart is contained in Exhibit 1.

As a part of its contractual arrangements, NSMHA was obligated to report on its activities to MDMH personnel who oversaw the delivery of mental health services in the Greater Boston Area. NSMHA also was funded through federal grants and reimbursement mechanisms and had continuing reporting responsibility to federal authorities.

NSMHA could not refuse treatment to anyone requiring it. NSMHA programs, therefore, generally treated the sickest and neediest portions of the population, i.e., those rejected by private agencies because of an inability to pay or requiring too much case management to make their treatment cost-efficient. Burt Lowe felt that the organization had insufficient resources to serve all of its populations adequately, but attempted to spread its services as far as they would go.

## Development and Implementation of the MIS

The need for some sort of information gathering mechanism at NSMHA first was recognized by Eugene Thompson when he took over as business manager in 1976. At that time no budget or billing system existed. Thompson attempted to implement some rudimentary plans to organize these functions, as well as to gather statistical information regarding the delivery of services.

In 1977 Jim Cassetta had been installed as the Administrative Director for NSHMA, taking over direct responsibility for management of the firm's daily operations. Thompson had been promoted to Executive Director and his responsibilities had shifted to encompass longer-range planning and development efforts. He had explicitly incorporated responsibility for the development of a service data reporting and billing system into his role, however. His goal at that time was to develop a comprehensive system which would address all aspects of care provided by NSMHA in a useful and cost-effective manner. To this end he met with Burt Lowe, who at that time was a doctoral candidate in Clinical Psychology at Miami University of Ohio and was serving an internship in Massachusetts, split between clinical activity at a NSMHA clinic and the study of management information systems at the MDMH.

**Exhibit 1**
Organization Chart

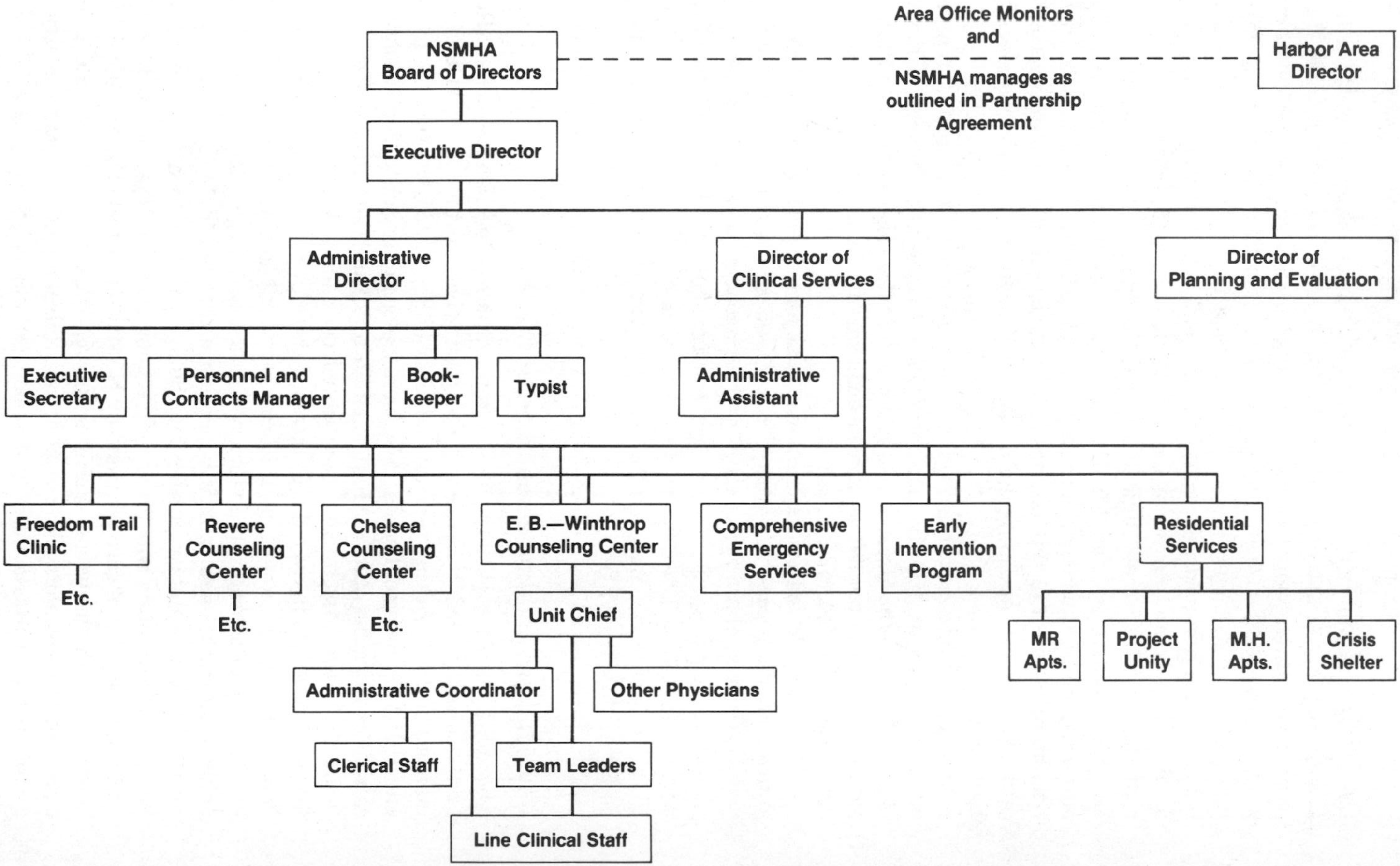

Implementation of the management information system was begun in the spring of 1977. The overall plan called for testing, debugging, and establishing the system by focusing on one unit and then successively implementing its use in other units via the same process. According to Burt Lowe, adequate planning, phased implementation, and administrative support were key elements in the implementation process.

At the beginning of 1977, the existing service data collection system consisted of monthly service logs submitted by staff. These logs recorded face-to-face direct and consultation services. There was about 40 percent compliance with the mandate to submit the logs, and of those logs received, the majority were two to six months late. Central administration also felt that much activity was going unreported, even by those staff who submitted logs. However, there was no way to determine this, since no quality control mechanisms existed.

Much of the impetus for more systematic data collection came from the need to maximize third-party reimbursements. It was estimated that up to 50 percent of potential reimbursement was not being recovered. The need for a functional MIS was also impelled by (1) data reporting requirements of the state and federal authorities, (2) grant proposal preparation needs, (3) monitoring affiliates and contracts, (4) managing existing programs, (5) inter-unit competition for resources, and (6) planning for growth and expansion.

## Phased Implementation

Implementation of the MIS was phased, with gradual introduction in all of its dimensions, rather than beginning the entire system at once. Central administration conceptualized the system as having three dimensions: (1) location, or program; (2) data collected, or input; (3) reports produced, or output. Thus, implementation was initiated utilizing one form (the service ticket), collecting limited data (direct service only), in one clinic, and producing a single report (the Unit Summary). The MIS was restricted to these parameters for three months before expansion in any dimension was begun. The initial implementation was defined as a pilot project, and it was emphasized to administrative and clinical unit staff that their suggestions and criticisms were invited.

Training sessions in data preparation were given to both clinical and clerical staff. Burt Lowe was able to be on-site during the first two weeks of implementation, dealing with any problems on the spot and pitching in to work side by side with the staff as they coped with the new procedures. An additional half-time secretary/clerk, paid for by increased third-party reimbursement, was given to each unit as it started the MIS.

As more units were brought into the MIS, a bi-weekly meeting was organized of the senior clerical person (now titled administrative coordinator) of each of those units, plus the MIS staff. The meeting served to prepare the coordinators for new MIS requirements, facilitate their sharing of procedures and techniques, and general problem solving. In the opinion of central administration, the administrative coordinators were the key people in keeping the MIS functioning. The coordinators were viewed as the best resource for training the staff of new units about to join in the MIS.

Data from the MIS were presented and discussed regularly at the Steering Committee meeting, in which policy was formulated and area-wide decisions made. This meeting was attended by unit chiefs, selected board members, and key central administrative personnel. Burt Lowe reported that one of the results of this presentation was that unit chiefs, who were psychiatrists, began requesting to become part of the MIS, whereas their initial attitude had been the opposite.

## Structure of the MIS

By spring 1981 Burt Lowe had assumed primary responsibility for the MIS. While Eugene Thompson continued to involve himself peripherally in the project, he awarded Lowe nearly complete authority for actual operation of the MIS. Lowe's qualifications for this responsibility stemmed from his involvement in the design and implementation of a number of community mental health management information systems. He was assisted in his efforts by Vic VanNeste, who performed data processing chores and aided in the continual revision and design of forms necessary to fully automate the system.

Through the implementation process various structural components were added to the system and other modifications made. Thus the structure of the system evolved by early 1981 into that presented below:

## Input Components

1. Client-tracing component: Records contact, registration and evaluation information. Records treatment plans. Keeps track of client transfers to other Harbor Area programs, referrals to outside agencies, and terminations. (Four preprinted forms were used for this purpose.)
2. Service delivery component: Records type and amount of services rendered to clients and outside agencies. (See Exhibit 2.)
3. Staffing component: Records who is working and how much. Records which programs of treatment are delivered and how often. Keeps track of how much and what type of third-party reimbursable treatment is delivered and what degree of total service delivered is direct, i.e., billable, service.

## Output Components

1. Billing component: Service ticket (Exhibit 2) produces a cash receipt and appointment slip for the client. Client monthly billing reports, unit billing summaries, and bills to third-party payors are produced.

**Exhibit 2**
Service Ticket

## SERVICE TICKET

| MON | DAY | YR |
|---|---|---|
| | | |

E 0182

| PROGRAM | | |
|---|---|---|
| | | |

| CLIENT ID | | | | | | SUFFIX | |
|---|---|---|---|---|---|---|---|
| | | | | | | | |

CLIENT'S NAME

| SERVICE CODE | |
|---|---|
| | |

| TIME (MIN) | | |
|---|---|---|
| | | |

| LOCATION | |
|---|---|
| Center—Sched. | |
| Center—Walkin | |
| Other HA | |
| Clients Home | |
| Other Agency | |
| Nursing Home | |
| School | |
| Court | |
| Telephone | |
| Other | |

| NUMBER CONTACTED OR TREATED | |
|---|---|
| Primary Client | |
| Family Collateral | |
| Other Clients | |
| Other Professionals | |

| CLINICIANS | | | |
|---|---|---|---|
| | | | |
| | | | |
| | | | |
| | | | |

| SPECIAL DATA | | | |
|---|---|---|---|
| | | | |
| | | | |

EAST BOSTON-WINTHROP
COUNSELING CENTER
10 GOVE STREET
EAST BOSTON, MA 02128

NO. E 0182

Cash Rec'd. ______

DIRECT/SUPPORTIVE

SPECIALIZED PROGRAM
01-Authorized Code

EVALUATION SERVICES
0-Psychosocial Evaluation
1-Psychiatric/Medical Evaluation
2-Psychological Testing
3-CORE (Chap. 766) Evaluation
4-Evaluation Group
5-Occupational Therapy Evaluation
9-Other Evaluation

TREATMENT SERVICES
20-Individual Medication
21-Medication Group
22-Individual Therapy
23-Group Therapy
24-Family/Couple Therapy
25-Crisis intervention
26-Combined Therapy and Medication
29-Other Treatment

REHABILITATION SERVICES
30-Counseling (vocational, etc.)
31-Education (sex, nutrition, etc.)
32-Occupational Therapy
38-Other Rehabilitation (individual)
39-Other Rehabilitation (group)

CLIENT-RELATED ACTIVITIES
40-Case Consultation
41-Case Conference
42-Supervision Provided
43-Supervision Received
44-Case Management
45-Court Appearance
46-Transportation of Client

OTHER ACTIVITIES
80-Intra-Unit Meeting
81-Inter-Unit Meeting
82-Travel
83-Administration
84-Inservice Training
97-No Show
99-Cancellation
99-Other Activity

Signature ______

CONSULTATION AND EDUCATION

FIRST CHARACTER

A—Client Centered
B—Staff Centered
C—Program Centered
D—Organization Centered
E—Community Planning
F—Outreach
G—Advocacy
H—Information & Education
J—Relationship Building
X—Other

SECOND CHARACTER

B—Planning, Preparing
C—Providing, Participating
D—Summarizing, Reporting
X—Other

YOUR NEXT APPOINTMENT

Day ______
Date ______ Time ______
To see ______

PLEASE CALL US AT 727-7720
IF YOU ARE UNABLE TO KEEP
THIS APPOINTMENT. THANK YOU.

______
Cashier Date

2. Individual staff component: Monthly activities of each therapist are reported. Details include type and amount of service delivered, productivity in terms of direct service (as a percent of available hours), etc., as well as clients not seen for some time who might be terminated.
3. Unit and subunit (i.e., child, adult, and geriatric treatment teams) component: Various operating unit and subunit reports produced for unit chief, administrative coordinators, and team leaders. Included operating unit service summary, and summary of clinician hours. (An example is shown in Exhibit 3.)
4. Area-wide component: Reports summarizing all services in all operating units (Exhibit 4).
5. External reporting component: Produced information for state and federal reporting requirements, i.e., type and amount of services, etc.
6. Fiscal component: Reports on income, expenses, and variances from budget by cost center (operating unit). Reports not tied to service components.

**Exhibit 3**

Revere Community Counseling Center Service Summary (February 1 thru 29, 1980)

| | *Children 143* | *Adult 146* | *Geriatric 148* | *DDU 145* | *All Others* | *Totals* |
|---|---|---|---|---|---|---|
| Type of direct service: | | | | | | |
| 10 Psychosocial evaluation | 17 | 28 | 5 | 4 | 0 | 54 |
| 11 Medication/medical evaluation | 3 | 17 | 0 | 0 | 0 | 20 |
| 12 Psychological testing | 1 | 0 | 0 | 0 | 0 | 1 |
| 14 Evaluation group | 2 | 0 | 0 | 0 | 0 | 2 |
| 19 Other evaluation | 10 | 0 | 0 | 0 | 0 | 10 |
| 20 Individual medication | 7 | 95 | 0 | 0 | 0 | 102 |
| 21 Medication group | 0 | 3 | 0 | 0 | 0 | 3 |
| 22 Individual therapy | 101 | 332 | 63 | 19 | 0 | 515 |
| 23 Group therapy | 18 | 58 | 1 | 0 | 0 | 77 |
| 24 Family/couple therapy | 17 | 32 | 14 | 8 | 0 | 71 |
| 25 Crisis intervention | 12 | 12 | 9 | 2 | 0 | 35 |
| 26 Medication and therapy | 0 | 53 | 0 | 0 | 0 | 53 |
| 29 Other treatment | 0 | 0 | 0 | 1 | 0 | 1 |
| 30 Counseling (voc., etc.) | 0 | 21 | 0 | 0 | 0 | 21 |
| 38 Other rehab—individual | 0 | 2 | 0 | 0 | 0 | 2 |
| 40 Case consultation | 2 | 2 | 1 | 3 | 0 | 8 |
| 41 Case conference | 2 | 2 | 0 | 0 | 0 | 4 |
| 42 Supervision provided | 8 | 0 | 1 | 0 | 0 | 9 |
| 43 Supervision received | 0 | 1 | 0 | 0 | 0 | 1 |
| 44 Case management | 9 | 3 | 2 | 0 | 0 | 14 |
| 46 Transportation of client | 1 | 0 | 0 | 0 | 0 | 1 |
| 80 Intra-unit meeting | 3 | 0 | 0 | 0 | 0 | 3 |
| 81 Inter-unit meeting | 3 | 0 | 0 | 0 | 0 | 3 |
| 82 Travel | 0 | 0 | 0 | 1 | 0 | 1 |
| 97 No show | 18 | 72 | 8 | 0 | 0 | 98 |
| 98 Cancellation | 39 | 86 | 10 | 0 | 0 | 135 |
| 99 Other activities | 1 | 0 | 0 | 0 | 0 | 1 |

... Summary (January 1 thru 31, 1980)

| | Chelsea CCC | EB/WIN CC | Freedom Trail | Revere CCC | CES | DDU | AIPU | All Others | Total |
|---|---|---|---|---|---|---|---|---|---|
| Location of direct service: | | | | | | | | | |
| At unit—scheduled appointment | 777 | 1111 | 767 | 901 | 0 | 197 | 0 | 0 | 3,753 |
| At unit—walk-in | 12 | 39 | 72 | 28 | 0 | 0 | 0 | 0 | 151 |
| Other Harbor Area facility | 1 | 99 | 6 | 14 | 0 | 1 | 0 | 0 | 121 |
| Client's home | 49 | 39 | 12 | 42 | 0 | 130 | 0 | 0 | 272 |
| Other agency | 5 | 86 | 41 | 2 | 0 | 0 | 0 | 0 | 134 |
| Nursing home | 0 | 18 | 1 | 2 | 0 | 0 | 0 | 0 | 21 |
| School | 0 | 27 | 0 | 0 | 0 | 2 | 0 | 0 | 29 |
| Court | 0 | 1 | 0 | 0 | 0 | 0 | 0 | 0 | 1 |
| Other | 3 | 15 | 0 | 2 | 0 | 0 | 0 | 0 | 20 |
| Length of direct service sessions: | | | | | | | | | |
| 1–10 minutes | 4 | 2 | 16 | 8 | 0 | 0 | 0 | 0 | 30 |
| 11–30 minutes | 145 | 316 | 259 | 271 | 0 | 33 | 0 | 0 | 1,024 |
| 31–60 minutes | 672 | 950 | 499 | 593 | 0 | 92 | 0 | 0 | 2,806 |
| 61–90 minutes | 22 | 132 | 117 | 111 | 0 | 55 | 0 | 0 | 437 |
| 91 minutes | 4 | 35 | 8 | 8 | 0 | 150 | 0 | 0 | 205 |
| No. of staff in direct sessions: | | | | | | | | | |
| 1 clinician | 648 | 1216 | 723 | 918 | 0 | 158 | 0 | 0 | 3,663 |
| 2 clinicians | 106 | 196 | 83 | 72 | 0 | 46 | 0 | 0 | 503 |
| 3 clinicians | 19 | 13 | 91 | 1 | 0 | 115 | 0 | 0 | 239 |
| 4 clinicians | 74 | 10 | 2 | 0 | 0 | 11 | 0 | 0 | 97 |
| Direct service by program: | | | | | | | | | |
| Children's program | 167 | 378 | 113 | 156 | 0 | 0 | 0 | 0 | 814 |
| Adult program | 608 | 850 | 776 | 710 | 0 | 0 | 0 | 0 | 2,944 |
| Geriatric program | 60 | 131 | 10 | 98 | 0 | 0 | 0 | 0 | 299 |
| Other | 12 | 17 | 0 | 27 | 0 | 0 | 0 | 0 | 56 |
| Type of C and E service: | | | | | | | | | |
| Client-centered consultation | 17 | 25 | 7 | 7 | 0 | 0 | 0 | 1 | 58 |
| Staff-centered consultation | 7 | 5 | 6 | 2 | 0 | 0 | 0 | 0 | 20 |
| Program-centered consultation | 4 | 25 | 3 | 0 | 0 | 0 | 0 | 0 | 32 |
| Outreach | 0 | 1 | 3 | 0 | 0 | 0 | 0 | 0 | 4 |
| Information and education | 0 | 1 | 1 | 0 | 0 | 0 | 0 | 0 | 2 |
| Other | 0 | 0 | 7 | 0 | 0 | 0 | 0 | 0 | 7 |
| C and E by organization type: | | | | | | | | | |
| Educational systems | 13 | 35 | 6 | 1 | 0 | 0 | 0 | 0 | 55 |
| Health systems | 3 | 23 | 0 | 8 | 0 | 0 | 0 | 0 | 35 |
| Criminal justice system | 2 | 0 | 0 | 0 | 0 | 0 | 0 | 0 | 2 |
| Mental health | 4 | 0 | 0 | 0 | 0 | 0 | 0 | 0 | 4 |
| Social service—welfare | 6 | 0 | 21 | 0 | 0 | 0 | 0 | 0 | 27 |

## Information Processing

Information processing varied slightly from unit to unit. There were two ways information originated: (1) from a schedule book (the service ticket was prepared in advance by clerical personnel and the therapist only filled in information regarding the type and duration of the service issued); (2) on a walk-in basis (either clerical personnel or the therapist filled in the service ticket). Service tickets were accumulated daily, and clerical staff entered the data at the operating unit terminal on the following day. Contact, registration, evaluation, transfer, termination, and staff information were entered in the same manner.

Between the second and the fifth day of each month all reports were generated and sent to the units. Central administration received reports which it utilized to review overall operating activities and fulfill funding and contract requirements. Special attention was paid to third-party billing in order to receive revenues as soon as possible.

The distribution policy of the MIS reports had both positive and negative effects. Formal policy adopted by the Board allowed information to go only one level higher in the organization than the level on which it was generated. This meant that individual information about a client only went to that client's therapist and supervisor—no higher. This policy successfully relieved clinical workers' fears regarding confidentiality. However, restrictive downward distribution policies had a detrimental effect. Workers complained that summary reports of unit activities were not available to line staff. Furthermore, clinicians generally did not know what the statistical data were used for, including their use for government reporting requirements.

## Central Administration's Approach to Use of the System

By 1981 central administration felt that the impact of the MIS on billing and funding for services delivered by NSMHA had nearly been maximized. The objective of facilitating clinical management had not been met, however. Eugene Thompson felt that the system provided some valuable information to clinicians, but knew that Burt Lowe was bothered by persistent complaints from the clinicians. According to Lowe, however, the primary function of the MIS was to assist central administration to capture funding and revenue.

> Staff expect administration to take care of money and dealing with outside agencies, so that they are able to do clinical work. If administration can't bring in enough revenue from grants and third-party payors, it affects what line staff can do, the conditions under which they work and their morale . . . When we started the automated system, the amount of services reported per unit typically jumped about 250 percent. That wasn't due to more service being delivered. It was just that more of it was being captured.

Lowe considered one of the system's real benefits to be its effect on resource management. He emphasized the role of the MIS in centralizing control of the organization. In his opinion the MIS had sped up NSHMA's evolution from a fragmented network of independent clinics to a unified system with unified policies and operating procedures. He argued that much of the resistance around the MIS was due to the centers' loss of autonomy.

On the subject of staff resistance, Lowe first focused on the initial phase of the implementation of the system. He stated that a lot less resistance than was expected had occurred.

> I think that we went overboard expecting a lot, planning for it . . . There's always resistance to change, but it was minimized here, since the system immediately replaced old forms (rather than adding new paperwork on top of old). So, it actually resulted in a reduction of paperwork . . . We were responsive. The system could be modified and was, frequently, in the early months, based on feedback from clinicians.
>
> Some resistance around the MIS is irrational. That doesn't make it less important, but no logical approach can deal with it. People just have to find out that you're not going to misuse the information . . . There's still some resistance around some areas, mostly in terms of what standards are expected of clinicians and how that information will be used.

Lowe cited tension that arose from a fiscal crisis in 1980 as a more specific cause of resistance to the MIS. He related that some clinicians blamed those problems largely on central administration. Since some workers viewed the MIS as a tool of central administration, resentment toward the system lingered among clinical staff.

In spite of the resistance, Lowe estimated that approximately 98 percent of direct service was being accounted for by early 1981. He explained that clinicians were not asked to report on all hours of their available time. Central administration asked only for recording of billable service and consultation and education activities.

## Clinician's Response to the MIS

Clinicians generally agreed that reports of their productivity in terms of direct, billable service were useful in assessing individual performances in this area. It was helpful for supervisors to see which employees were engaged in what amounts to face-to-face treatment with clients. This was the principal type of service for which the operating units and NSMHA received reimbursement from third-party payors, and both administrative and clinical supervisors at the centers stressed the importance of billable services to line staff. Reports were used to ferret out nonproductive individuals, so that supervisors might inquire about and urge them to correct their deficiencies. Such action had led to the dismissal of a number of staff who had failed to produce adequate levels of direct service despite repeated warnings.

The effectiveness of this system in getting all staff to share the load of billable service was recognized by most clinicians. However, there was opposition to the productivity levels proposed by central administration. Clinical workers felt that the emphasis placed on direct service created disincentives for other types of necessary, but nonbillable, services. Central administration was accused of fostering therapist "burn-out," i.e., workers overextending and exhausting themselves prematurely. Clinicians viewed central administration as being insensitive to the needs of line staff for supervision and consultation with other clinicians around difficult cases. They protested that case-management activities, such as advocacy appearances and interventions, assessment of client needs, development of treatment plans, and monitoring of client progress, were essential aspects of treatment.

For these reasons clinicians considered the need for increasing direct service to be a clinical rather than an administrative issue. It was felt that the service categories of the MIS excluded as nonbillable too many useful and necessary activities. Clinical staff were alarmed at what they perceived as an increasing tendency of central administration to focus on the numbers rather than on the nature of the services delivered. They feared the possibility of the numbers taking on too large a reality to the detriment of the quality of the treatment provided. This concern was shared by Vic VanNeste, who cited the "danger of the tail (the MIS) wagging the dog (clinical service)."

Broader concerns regarding the use of the MIS at NSMHA were voiced by East Boston unit personnel. One clinician stated, "Philosophically, the MIS doesn't pick up what it's like to work in East Boston with its population, as opposed to the other clinics." He noted the peculiarities of its population and the need for certain types of nonbillable services, e.g., outreach work. He felt that comparison of productivity levels across units was misleading due to difference in the populations served and the services demanded. Dr. Charles Carl, the unit chief at East Boston, felt that central administration needed to be educated regarding the relative importance of direct versus indirect services. He emphasized that his unit delivered "nonprofit, bottom-line service to the sickest people," and felt that direct service figures were not reflective of this. Dr. Carl suggested that service categories ought to be redesigned "to more accurately conceptualize activities which . . . are necessary for face-to-face service." He argued that an adequate level of understanding of clinical functioning might be hard to translate into MIS data and stated, "You can't define every minor nuance in terms of electronic data."

Dr. Carl also questioned whether the statistical data collected via the MIS was accurate enough to be used for actual planning purposes or whether it simply produced numbers in order to fulfill licensing and funding requirements. He stressed the importance of this, since taking the data seriously meant instituting change which people were not used to and often did not want.

Dr. Carl also argued that the cost of clinicians' time used in reporting to the MIS to get the most accurate data possible was an important consideration. This point was corroborated by other clinical personnel. One physician complained that the constant filling out of service tickets was a nuisance.

A clinical team leader grumbled that use of the tickets was cumbersome, requiring constant interacting around the clerical staff and the data entry terminal. She also pointed out that the tickets were often inaccurate, so that supervisors had to go over every printed report carefully with each worker.

The MIS, however, received praise in other areas. Line staff remarked that when accurately completed the service tickets did keep track of appointment information for both clients and therapists. They also appreciated lists of clients who had not been seen for some time and might merit termination. It was also felt that the system had improved the allocation of resources to specific caseloads. One supervisor stated that the MIS had "clarified the process of supervision, since supervisors now have the information as to how clinicians spend their time and with whom."

The most extreme sentiments expressed about use of the MIS, however, were that central administration attempted to compensate for its financial mistakes by suggesting arbitrarily high productivity levels. This radical view was the outgrowth of the 1980 fiscal crisis. Some acting-out against central administration via the MIS, i.e., clinicians failing to record services delivered, was noted at that time, but the level of this activity was minimal.

A host of other concerns existed around direct/support service categories and productivity data. Staff viewed some categories as too restrictive, i.e., not really descriptive of actual services. This led to a heavy use of "other" type categories in coding practice and ultimately to vague service delivery reports. Team leaders also reported that overestimates of direct service sometimes resulted from line staff coding indirect service as though it were billable. They attributed this behavior, when it was purposely deceptive, to laziness on the part of some staff but more often to frustration or disrespect for the MIS on the part of others.

Frustration arose from such incidents as no-shows (clients who do not cancel appointments beforehand but do not show up for them) not being counted into individual clinicians' direct service percentages. Clinicians considered this to be an unfair practice. They felt that no-shows should be counted into their productivity figures because workers had no control over whether or not clients showed up for scheduled appointments. If clients failed to appear under such circumstances, therapists were most often unable to schedule other direct services for the newly opened time slots on such short notice.

## Central Administration's View on Productivity

Eugene Thompson intended to address the direct service issue at an upcoming meeting where the distribution of staff activities was to be discussed.

> We've been talking about "productivity" for a long time. We want to defuse that word, try to throw it out, and really talk about where staff resources are going.

He stated that, allowing for meetings, supervision, breaks, and other activities, only about 16 hours of an average 40 hour work week was available for direct service, consultation/education, case-management, and quality assurance activities. When looked at in this light, an average of 11 or 12 hours of direct service per week did not seem so bad. That meant only four or so hours per week was being spent on the phone, recording information, etc. Based on the flexibility evident in such an analysis, it appeared that clinicians were working very hard. But Thompson felt that NSMHA had to examine its assumptions regarding the amount of staff line allotted to staff meetings, supervision, and other nonbillable activities. While he remarked that the distribution of staff time seemed to work out pretty well, he noted that there were different costs and benefits to maintaining or changing the present system.

Thompson questioned whether pushing clinicians to increase their productivity from 28 percent to 40 percent would result in any fundamental change. Such action would create further disincentives for clinicians to allot time to case-management and treatment of difficult clients. But he pointed out that the alternative to increasing revenues might turn out to be cuts in staffing and services. This was due to the political climate existing in 1981 in which government sources of funding for mental health services were being cut back both on federal and state levels. As a result, central administration was deeply concerned about the financial strength of the organization. Thompson related that some veteran staff members understood the motivation behind central administration's emphasis on productivity. However, newer clinicians objected to what they perceived to be administrative tinkering with clinical activities.

## Application of the MIS to Clinical Management

Broader issues surrounded the use of the MIS, though. One of these was the question of the appropriateness of the MIS as a clinical management tool. A number of clinicians had praised the income-producing capacities of the system, but they felt that, while it did a good job focusing on money matters, it was not very useful clinically. Thompson thought that this assessment was true in early 1981.

No external pressure had been exerted on NSMHA to produce treatment outcome information, but some clinicians had recently begun to press for such information. Thompson remarked that central administration had not pushed for this type of data in order to avoid creating further resistance to the MIS and short-circuiting those functions which it was performing well. Thompson said that central administration did consider this information to be useful though. Now that this mandate to produce clinically relevant information was coming from clinicians, it would hasten the process of gathering it. But he cited clinicians' reluctance to deal with paperwork, both of the input and output variety, as a real stumbling block in their utilizing the MIS effectively.

> The resistance, as it has presented itself to me, has just been generalized. A clinician will say, "I don't want to have to see any more paper of any kind. I don't care

whether it has to do with billing or closing out records, or anything. I don't want to read another piece. Just let me see my clients and leave me alone."

Thompson claimed that such adamance about performing clinical work before all else was a traditional stance among clinicians.

> There's nothing that a management information system is going to do for a person who basically doesn't like paperwork . . . thinks that clinical work is an organic process and it can't be managed . . . that it's mystical and it just has to flow . . . that if you have to be concerned about numbers and things that are going to be coming out on paper, it changes the clinical process.

## MIS Effect on Decision Making

In early 1981, both Burt Lowe and Eugene Thompson agreed that implementation of the MIS at NSMHA had gone pretty much according to plan. But they also concurred that management decision-making processes, which were to have been transformed by the incorporation of data generated by the system, had remained little changed. The problem, as they saw it, had more to do with internal decision-making processes at NSMHA, than with the quality of the information which the MIS provided. Regarding this issue, Burt Lowe said:

> We still try to make most decisions by consensus, since the units are semi-autonomous. But decisions by consensus aren't necessarily rational or the best decisions. Therefore, the impact of the information which the MIS provides on those decisions is less than if they were made by a single person who could use that information. It clearly influences decisions, but I don't think it has the impact that it was originally envisioned that it would. That's not because the information isn't there. It's because internal decision-making processes don't allow that data to have the weight that I think it should.

Eugene Thompson echoed Lowe's sentiments:

> The thing we're still not great in is getting the management part of the information system into place. It does influence decisions, but not in a highly structured fashion . . . and they're clinicians. The managers are clinicians at heart and by training, and they aren't comfortable with management . . . so, we really haven't taken this management information system and used it to its maximum.

With these thoughts in mind, Burt wondered what steps to take. He hoped to come up with some solutions prior to the next monthly meeting with the unit chiefs. But, presently, he was at a loss for any answers.

## Questions

1. What are the problems that Burt Lowe faces?
2. What steps should he take, and in what sequence should he take them?

## Case 14–2

# WALTON COMMUNITY HEALTH PLAN*

John Abrams, executive director of the Walton Community Health Plan (WCHP), had felt increasingly disenchanted with the computerized medical information system of the Plan since his appointment the month before, in April 1978. He knew from his contacts within WCHP that the information system had many supporters, particularly among the staff physicians, who felt that it was the only truly innovative part of the Plan.

Although Abrams had doubts about both the system's cost and its ability to produce the necessary enrollment, administrative, and medical data, he was also loath to further weaken staff morale just as WCHP was beginning to overcome critical start-up problems. He felt that he had to make a decision quickly about what action, if any, to take on the medical information system.

### Development of WCHP

The Walton Community Health Plan was a health maintenance organization (HMO) that opened in October 1977 to provide comprehensive medical care for families living in its greater metropolitan area. Although WCHP emphasized preventive care, the Plan provided for comprehensive medical services including complete hospitalization, maternity and child care, drugs and medications, 24-hour emergency service, eye care, mental health and medical-social services, laboratory and X-ray facilities, home care, and out-of-area coverage. A member of WCHP chose a particular physician from the Walton Plan medical groups to serve as his or her ongoing contact at the Plan. When this physician was unavailable, coverage was provided by other members of the physician group.

WCHP was chartered in 1973 through the efforts of the Walton Medical School, whose staff hoped it would serve as a model for programs in other communities and would enable the medical school to develop closer ties with its own community.

WCHP's designers were particularly eager to experiment with a new information system. Although they initially planned to use a manual system for maintaining records, the directors intended to computerize all medical, socioeconomic, insurance, and administrative data on each enrollee within a few years of opening. The data would be stored in one place, and, they hoped, could be analyzed in any way desired.

### Planning the Medical Information System

Paul Jacobs, associate dean for Medical Care Planning of the Walton Medical School, was in charge of planning and implementing WCHP. He had come

* This case was prepared by Ardis Burst, under the direction of Alan Sheldon, Harvard School of Public Health.

Top management broad perspective

to the school in early 1973 from St. Louis, Missouri, where he had assisted unions in developing their own health care programs.

Jacobs wanted the Plan to stress research and education in its data handling as well as in other areas:

> I was thinking in terms of a total system in which one well-designed computer system would be looking at patient care, medical records, and out of this, derive utilization and financial data. We could also compare data on our (WCHP) patient population with a like-sized population (not in the Plan) from Blue Cross and study the significant differences.

In addition, Jacobs hoped the data would provide a profile of all physicians in the Plan that could be compared to groups of physicians elsewhere.

The original planning of the information system was done by a New York consulting firm specializing in computer systems. In the summer of 1975, the consultants produced a discussion paper for Jacobs, which he felt did little more than restate the staff's original suggestions.

While the consulting firm was working on the computer system, Jacobs had begun designing a medical records system for the Plan. He was assisted by Dr. Gregory Jensen, a young physician and computer specialist who was on the Medical School faculty and was an associate director of the Tremont General Hospital Center for Computer Studies (TGHCCS), and Dr. Jensen's assistant, Larry Simpson, a TGHCCS technologist with extensive experience applying computer systems to the health field.

After witnessing the consulting firm's presentation, Simpson convinced the Plan's designers that they needed someone in the Plan who was familiar with information systems. Jacobs hired Simpson as director of information processing. With Jacobs' approval, Simpson promptly fired the consulting firm because, in his words, "They were too expensive, located in New York, and I felt they didn't understand our problems." He worked with several other sets of consultants over the next 12 months to design "a beautiful instrument" that could handle an initial patient load of 15,000 members. When the system was fully implemented in three years, it would record every transaction within the Plan, and the data would be used largely for research. Until then, the system would be used to facilitate scheduling.

The system that Simpson designed was estimated to cost over $400,000 a year (see Exhibit 1). The Plan itself was having difficulty raising the $2 million needed for basic operations (see Exhibit 2). In Simpson's words, "There was some question about how it would look if I could get money but the Plan itself couldn't." The information system was never officially submitted for funding, and Simpson resigned in June. He said:

> I don't think anybody understood what I was trying to do. I conceived a big system to fit in with the rest of the Plan. As we all started to face the realities, it was clear that the magnitude of the original idea was too large.

**Exhibit 1**
Budget Estimates for Years of Support Requested for Information System (Simpson's estimate)

| *Description* | *First Period (same as detailed budget) 7/1/76–6/30/77* | *Second Period 7/1/77–6/30/78* | *Third Period 7/1/78–6/30/79* |
|---|---|---|---|
| Personnel | $124,500 | $124,500 | $124,500 |
| Consultant services | 25,000 | 15,000 | — |
| Equipment | 100,000 | 280,000 | 280,000 |
| Supplies | 5,000 | 5,000 | 3,000 |
| Publication costs | 2,000 | 2,000 | 2,000 |
| Travel | 1,000 | 1,000 | 1,000 |
| | $257,500 | $427,500 | $410,500 |
| Total: $1,095,000 | | | |

Paul Jacobs felt that if Simpson had developed his model in concert with the rest of the Plan rather than in isolation, the resulting system might not have been too big and expensive. He commented:

> I'm not so sure we didn't make a mistake in dumping that New York consulting firm. We had a young and impetuous staff that too quickly rejected them. Larry Simpson wasn't able to do much more than the consulting firm did. He wasn't realistic enough, whereas the consulting firm might have been more realistic. In fact, it might have been preferable to have both Larry and the consulting firm, in a complementary relationship, balancing each other off. Larry needed closer supervision, not to improve the quality of his work, but as a dampening down-to-earth influence. But in an organization of the small size that we were in those early days, how could I supervise or monitor someone like Larry Simpson when I myself have very little expertise in this area? How could I control his efforts?

Because of funding difficulties throughout the entire Plan and because he was rethinking the needs for a medical information system, Jacobs chose not to replace Simpson. Instead, Jensen continued to work one day a week over the next year to design and implement a much smaller system focused primarily on medical records. Jensen decided to adapt TGHCCS's medical record system, which concentrated on medical, rather than administrative, data. Jensen felt that whatever administrative data they later decided to examine could be derived from the data base thus assembled. In addition, WCHP physicians were familiar with the TGHCCS model, and felt that its smaller size would make it more likely to be in operation by opening day and less likely to dwarf the health care delivery functions of WCHP.

In the meantime, the Plan itself continued to face serious start-up problems—depleted funds, administrative and staffing problems, and, most seriously, a failure to attract members. The WCHP designers had relied on commercial insurance carriers and Blue Cross/Blue Shield for member recruiting for several reasons: (1) to take advantage of the marketing expertise of these organizations, (2) to assure their cooperation rather than their compe-

**Exhibit 2**

Walton Medical School Prepaid Comprehensive Medical Care Plan Areas of Needed Support, Present to June 30, 1980

| Area | *Present to June 30, 1976* | | *July 1, 1976 June 30, 1978* | | *July 1, 1978 June 30, 1980* | | *Total* | |
|---|---|---|---|---|---|---|---|---|
| | *Cost* | *Request* | *Cost* | *Request* | *Cost* | *Request* | *Cost* | *Request* |
| Administration | $240,000 | $240,000 | $ 575,000 | $ 225,000 | $ 715,000 | $ 15,000 | $1,530,000 | $ 480,000 |
| Group practice development | 58,200 | 58,200 | 100,000 | 100,000 | 200,000 | 150,000 | 358,200 | 308,200 |
| Clinic and facilities planning | 58,200 | 58,200 | 60,000 | 60,000 | 120,000 | 60,000 | 238,200 | 178,200 |
| Benefit development | 124,500 | 124,500 | 214,000 | 192,000 | 214,000 | 192,000 | 552,500 | 508,500 |
| Research, statistics, and data handling | 58,200 | 58,200 | 130,000 | 65,000 | 140,000 | 70,000 | 328,200 | 193,200 |
| Manpower development | | | 200,000 | 200,000 | 200,000 | 400,000 | 400,000 | 400,000 |
| Health financing research | | | 73,000 | 73,000 | 73,000 | 73,000 | 146,000 | 146,000 |
| Epidemiology and preventive medical research | | | 100,000 | 100,000 | 100,000 | 100,000 | 200,000 | 200,000 |
| Total | $539,100 | $539,100 | $1,452,000 | $1,015,000 | $1,762,000 | $1,060,000 | $3,753,100 | $2,414,100 |

tition in recruiting members, (3) to establish a vehicle for transferring the best parts of the program to other settings, and (4) to utilize the insurer's subscribers as comparative data base for research purposes. In the spring of 1977, however, it became clear that the insurance companies that had been offering the WCHP as an alternative to their coverage had failed to attract enrollees for WCHP. Jacobs gave his interpretation of the actions of one insurance company, Blue Cross:

> When Blue Cross was asked to take a quota of new subscribers, they suggested they take 1,200. Now, if that was a realistic projection of how many they really thought they could enroll, then our Plan was headed for failure. If it was not realistic, then why so low? Something just didn't jibe! My own theory is that up to this point, Blue Cross hadn't made its mind up whether or not this Plan could go. Later on, Blue Cross did take on a larger quota, but their early reluctance was very, very damaging. What eventually saved our Plan was the insurance companies intervening to vouch for our feasibility to the money-granting foundations. We had been too optimistic. We put too much confidence in the Plan selling itself.

Jacobs described other factors contributing to recruitment problems:

> One prime difficulty was that potential members couldn't visualize what the Plan really was—not until the building itself opened and the doctors themselves actually materialized. It was necessary to break down people's ideas of a large impersonal welfare type of organization. Our assumption that the insurance companies would be good aggressive marketers of the program was incorrect. They were not familiar with our Plan, had no reason to push, had no investment in its success.

Due to low enrollment, opening of the WCHP center was pushed from July 1, 1977, to October 1, 1977.

### Administration of the Information System

Robert Price had been hired in April 1977 as clinic manager to oversee the physical plant and the Plan's "Special Services"—central appointments, reception, internal communication, and medical records (MR). Price, who had recently received an MPH in health services administration, termed himself "fairly young and inexperienced." His hiring was part of a plan to use young innovators in building WCHP. Said Jacobs:

> My original theory was to try to have the program in the hands of some pretty young "comers," with energy and a stake in the future. I hired young people who had never built such programs before. I was hoping to come up with some new ideas. I wanted to innovate.

Price, who was devoting most of his time to the massive task of preparing the physical plant itself, was anxious to turn the Special Services over to an experienced and qualified person. He first considered hiring a certified medical records librarian because he felt that the MR system being developed by Jensen was of central importance to the Plan. Price, however, did not get together with Jensen to discuss specific MR needs.

After interviewing many candidates throughout late spring to be director of Special Services, Price decided that he should hire an accredited records technician. (A records technician has less training than a MR librarian.) In May, he hired Thomas Kent, formerly a section supervisor in the MR department of a local hospital. Kent developed an operating manual for his department and determined the number of people that he would need in various positions. In August, he began recruiting and hiring his staff. The people hired as supervisors of medical records, central appointments, and reception had been his co-workers at his previous place of employment.

Price became involved with personnel policies and procedures at this time, leaving Kent mostly on his own. In October, however, Price began receiving complaints from administrative and medical staff members about the operation of the Special Services area. Jensen, who through his work with the medical information system had close contact with Kent, commented on this period of time:

> I assumed Tom Kent could do the job. He was very good about writing down things to do. I considered myself a consultant at that point and assumed I'd be working with him. I assumed all the chaos in Special Services was primarily due to the newness of the Plan and not directly Tom's fault. But toward the end of October, I began discovering that all the things I had been blithely discussing with Tom and which he was telling me were all in order were not, in fact, being done. I was finding that people were not doing their jobs. So I tried to help Tom more and more. I became more directly involved in the operation of Special Services. I began to get sucked in deeper and deeper. At some point during all this, I spoke with Bob Price and told him we needed to talk with Tom. Bob alone had a talk with him. I was not there. The next day, Tom's desk was cleaned out, and his resignation note was left on top of it.

Price interviewed a number of candidates to replace Kent and hired one, who stayed only six days. During the period when no one was in charge of Special Services, Price ran the area, but found that he had little time and few of the skills needed to handle the medical records system. He and Jensen, who had continued as a consultant for medical records, found that many of the employees that Kent had hired were not really qualified for their jobs. These people were gradually phased out, and although they were given extensive help in finding other jobs, the morale of the entire Special Services area dropped rapidly.

## Implementation Problems

As the position of director of Special Services remained open, responsibility for the medical records shifted to Jensen, who soon found that he was deluged with problems. The medical records system that he had adapted from TGHCCS required each physician to fill out a "Patient Encounter Form" after each patient visit, including diagnosis, medications, and scheduled activities. The diagnosis was to be entered in both longhand and a computer code listed in code books given to each physician. Theresa Cole, Jensen's assistant from TGHCCS, explained one problem they faced:

> It turned out that the doctors, once the Plan eventually opened, were not coding their diagnoses and medications for entry into the system. I think that it was unrealistic for us to expect that a physician would ever want to look up a code. We were asking a great deal of them when we asked them to put all their information in a prestructured format. It was more a case of unrealistic expectations than of doctors not cooperating. Originally, the physicians all thought that they were going to get such a magnificent medical record from our system and would be able to do so much with it that I think they were willing to agree to more in the planning stages than they would actually do.

Besides implementation problems, Jensen also faced administrative problems. He was responsible for the medical records system, yet he had no authority to implement changes or direct the staff and had no programming help.

> By six months into the Plan, I was at my wits' end. I was working 70–80 hours a week, processing records, getting down there working with the computer staff, just trying to keep body and soul together. It was unclear how much of what went on during those first six months reflected problems of a new organization or problems inherent in our organization and system itself.
>
> But the system was so important to me that I was willing, during those early months of the Plan's operation, to do whatever I had to do. If it failed because it was a bad system, that would have been acceptable to me. But I wasn't going to let it fail because there wasn't an operator to put in the data, or because they couldn't answer the telephone.

Jensen felt that the administrative problems of the Special Services area were compounded by the clinic manager's inexperience. As Jensen saw it:

> Bob Price was just in over his head. No one was sure what was going on with the computers and the medical information system. Other people were taking on Bob's responsibilities because they didn't think he could handle them.

Jensen realized that as long as he continued to oversee the medical records, no one else would be hired to administer them. So on February 23, 1978, he sent a memo to the Plan announcing that he would no longer be responsible for the medical records system. In their search for a replacement for Kent, the directors had to decide whether to hire: (1) an experienced and technically qualified computer expert, (2) a specialist in medical records management, or (3) a person with general managerial experience and talent.

They decided to hire a first-rate manager, regardless of his or her background in computers. Many people were interviewed and all of them spent some time with Ms. Cole, who explained the medical records system to them. Several people were hired, but no one stayed longer than three weeks.

Finally, Price asked the advice of Cole on the type of person he should hire. She suggested someone with a background similar to hers—someone with a knowledge of computers but who could supervise the whole MR system. Finally, Price decided that the person who best fit that description was Cole. He discussed offering the position of director of Special Services to her with Jensen, who agreed that it would be appropriate. But Cole was eager to return to her work with the TGHCCS. She explained:

> I really wasn't interested. It had been so difficult, and I was so tired. Mr. Price did tell me, though, that Special Services would include only medical records, appointments, and the switchboard. Reception would no longer come under Special Services. The medical staff of the Plan volunteered to bring in consultants for me to rely on, on medical records issues beyond my expertise. By now they felt that it was really important to have a person who was dedicated to the system and the organization, which I certainly was. I finally accepted. But even after I took over, things stayed chaotic. People kept leaving, the turnover was still high, procedures still hadn't been written up, and all the time the patient volume kept going up from that low opening-day figure. I really had no time to rest. I was busy hiring and training people. It was just crisis management.

Cole hired "a lot of overly qualified people" who could help her rewrite procedures, including a qualified medical records supervisor and a qualified computer supervisor. As promised, she was relieved of responsibility for appointments, reception, and the switchboard and assumed the new title, Director of Medical Information.

## A New Director Reviews the Information System

Even with all of Cole's work, the information system remained unreliable. Its problems brought it under the critical eye of John Abrams, who had succeeded Paul Jacobs when he resigned in April 1978 as executive director of the Plan.

Jacobs described some of his reasons for leaving and some of his retrospective thoughts on his management of the Plan:

> My strengths tend to be more in planning and development and idea formulation. I'm not tremendously interested in day-to-day management of such operations. The ideal scheme for me would be to offer overall guidance. But in order to do that, one must have very disciplined day-to-day operations and administration. It was difficult for me to try to serve both as planner and day-to-day executive. I would have welcomed a splitting of this role.
>
> What I regret most is that we were unable to maintain the path that I originally outlined.

Jacobs particularly regretted the decision to use young, enthusiastic managers like Simpson rather than experienced people who could have given the Plan "more stature, more security, more maturity under crisis." In addition, he pointed out:

> We were cutting edges, pushing the frontiers on many fronts—computer technology, community health care, our affiliation with a university, group practice. (Insurance companies and Blue Cross had never been involved in group practice before.) Simply pulling this off was very difficult and we were the first really to try.

William Reynolds, assistant director of the Plan, felt that additional problems with the information system had arisen because:

> In our discussion of developmental costs, we never really considered alternatives, studied their relative costs and benefits, and then made an informed decision. Instead, we slid into it, because of blurriness in our decision-making processes.

Jensen, who had continued to be involved with the computerized MR system, knew that Abrams was reassessing the system's costs and benefits and its ability to produce needed information. Jensen had worked very closely with the staff physicians and had their support for the system, both because it could meet their needs and because they considered it more innovative than any other aspect of the Plan. Jensen had not programmed the system to produce administrative data *per se* because he had felt all along that it could be culled from the medical records system. But as he and Abrams knew, the system's ability to produce that information had not yet been proved.

## Questions

1. Evaluate the content of the system and its method of implementation. What problems does the system have? What are the reasons for those problems?
2. What would you have done differently?
3. What changes do you recommend?

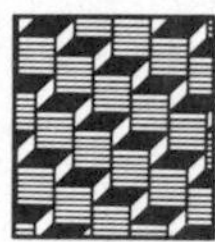

# chapter 15

# Summary: The Well-Managed Organization

By way of summary, we describe in this chapter some management control practices that we believe are characteristic of well-managed nonprofit organizations. Our opinion as to what constitutes a "well-managed organization" is of course subjective, and others may disagree with the importance, the relevance, or the validity of certain of the points made here. In this summary, we have in mind an organization of at least moderate size, say at least one hundred employees and several million dollars of annual operating expenses. Smaller organizations can operate successfully with fewer formal management control techniques than those described here, although the basic concepts underlying these techniques are applicable even in small organizations.

## THE BASIC PROBLEM

The principal characteristic that distinguishes the problem of management control in a nonprofit organization from that in a profit-oriented company is the absence of profit as an objective, as a criterion for appraising proposed alternative courses of action, and as a measure of performance. No comparable focus exists in a nonprofit organization, and the management control problem is therefore more difficult.

In a well-managed organization, this distinction is recognized. Its recognition leads not to an attitude that management control is unimportant or inappropriate, however, but rather to a commitment to devise and implement the best possible control structure and control process in these circumstances. Since profit is not an objective, management thinks carefully about what the organization's objectives are, even though they may be difficult to formulate. Since proposed courses of action cannot be judged in terms of how well they meet a profit objective, management develops other criteria for deciding on programs and budgets. Since the profit measure does not provide a semiautomatic danger signal when performance is unsatisfactory, management develops substitute performance measures and other ways of evaluating the success of the organization.

## ORGANIZATIONAL RELATIONSHIPS

The first requirement of good management control is a senior management that appreciates its importance, recognizes its feasibility, understands how to use the management control system, and is willing to devote enough time to the management control process. Such a senior management appreciates the fact that although control is not as glamorous as planning, and that although criticism is an unpleasant task, control is nevertheless essential. If, by contrast, senior management has the attitude that the effective and efficient use of resources is relatively unimportant in a nonprofit organization, or, even worse, that efforts to increase efficiency and effectiveness are beneath the dignity of the office, then management control will be ineffective, no matter how well designed the system itself may be.

A well-managed organization has a strong governing body. Some of its members spend considerable time in examining program and budget proposals before they are submitted to the full board or legislative committee, and in analyzing formal reports on performance and informal communications from clients and others as to how well the organization is performing. They are assisted in this work by a staff.[1] In a private nonprofit organization, some members of the board are professional board members who devote substantial time to board activities in this organization and in similar organizations.

In performing these functions, the governing body is careful not to infringe on the prerogatives of management. The governing body ensures that the chief executive's compensation is adequate, that the executive has full authority to execute policies, and that those decisions are backed up by the board.

Senior management is assisted by a professional staff, and it looks to this staff for innovative ideas and for the analysis of proposed programs. If the chief executive does not personally know where the levers of power exist and how to manipulate them, there is at least one staff member who has this knowledge about the organization, and who has the skill to use it.

The controller is more than a chief accountant. The controller is responsible for the operation of all aspects of the management control system. Although

[1] In particular, legislative bodies in most states need larger staffs than they now have so that they can check on the performance of the executive branch.

the controller is management's principal adviser on management control matters and the principal interpreter of information flowing from the system, the controller is nevertheless a staff person; line management makes the decisions.

Operating managers are given the authority to use their own judgment as to how results are to be accomplished, but they operate within somewhat closer budgetary and other constraints than is customary in profit-oriented organizations. Operating managers reject the stereotype of civil servants, as a group, as being lazy, incompetent, rule-bound, self-serving, and immobile. They understand that although job performance in any large organization is influenced by the inherent characteristics of bureaucracy, tolerance of laziness and incompetence is an indication of poor management, rather than an inherent characteristic of the system.

## MANAGEMENT CONTROL PRINCIPLES

### Account Classification

The control system contains two principal account classifications, one structured in terms of programs and the other structured in terms of organizational responsibility. At the lowest level are account "building blocks," each of which relates both to a single program element and to a single responsibility center. Summaries are obtained by aggregating these building blocks by program elements and program categories in the program part of the structure, and by various levels of the organizational hierarchy in the responsibility part of the structure.

The system contains both historical data and data on estimated future costs and outputs. The historical data are defined and structured in the same way as the estimated future data. Management recognizes that an accounting system that collects historical data that are inconsistent with the program budget does not provide an adequate basis for control. (Failure to provide accounting support for a program budget is the principal weakness of many of the newly installed program budget systems.)

In order to facilitate control of operating expenses, the structure provides for a clean separation between capital costs and operating costs. The definition of capital costs is unambiguous and is worded in such a way that items of minor importance are excluded, even though they are long lived. If the organization makes grants, a third category of accounts is provided for this purpose.

### External Financial Reporting

If required to do so by grantors or other external agencies, the organization prepares financial statements for external users according to principles set forth in AICPA *Audit Guides*. If it is not constrained by these forces, it departs from those aspects of the *Audit Guides* that inhibit the presentation of a clear picture of the results of operations. For example, it does not fragment the operating statement by setting up separate columns for various types of restricted funds.

The most important financial statement is the operating statement. Its central purpose is to show the extent to which the organization operated so as to maintain its operating capital, that is, so as to be viable. It was viable if its revenues for a year equalled or exceeded its expenses for that year.

In order to focus on operating results, operating revenues are reported separately from contributions of permanent capital, that is, gifts, grants, appropriations, or other resource inflows whose use is intended for the construction of plant, for endowment, or for other nonoperating purposes.

## The Accounting System

As is the case with external financial reports, management accounting reports focus on the extent to which the organization has operated so as to maintain its operating capital. In order to do this the system measures the revenues earned and the expenses incurred during an accounting period.

Revenues arise from the sale of goods and services; from membership dues; from taxes, contributions, grants, and appropriations that are used for operating purposes (as contrasted with those intended for endowment or acquisition of plant and equipment); and from endowment earnings. The governing board establishes a firm policy regarding the types of contributions and grants that are to be treated as revenues and the types that are to be capitalized. It also decides whether endowment revenues are to be measured by the spending rate approach or by the traditional method of counting dividends, interest, and possibly realized appreciation.

Expenses measure the resources used in operations during a period. They decrease the organization's equity. The accounting system in a well-managed organization measures spending for programs and by responsibility centers in terms of expenses, rather than in terms of expenditures, because expenditures measure resources acquired, which does not necessarily correspond to resources used. Expenses include the total cost of the resources used, including, for example, the present value of the pension benefits that are associated with labor costs incurred during the period. The extent to which the expenses should include depreciation of long-lived assets (or debt service on these assets in lieu of depreciation) is controversial. There is considerable doubt about the desirability of measuring depreciation on "infrastructure" assets, such as roads, dams, and public buildings.

Even if required to keep accounts on an obligation or encumbrance basis, as is the case with government agencies, a well-managed organization measures expenses on an accrual basis and uses expense data as a basis for control. It reconciles these expenses with obligations or encumbrances in a separate calculation. Expenditures, and corresponding liabilities, are also recorded and controlled.

The accounting system also reports expenditures for capital assets. In many cases, however, it is not feasible to associate these with individual program elements.

***Management Accounting.*** Most expenses recorded in management reports are measured according to the same principles that govern financial reporting, but in more detail. They are collected both by responsibility center and by program element. For responsibility center reporting, it may be necessary to measure only direct costs and to omit allocated costs. Controllable expenses are identified separately from noncontrollable expenses, but both types are reported. Some systems identify variable expenses separately from fixed expenses, but many organizations do not find such a separation useful.

## Pricing Decisions

Except in unusual circumstances, such as "public goods," a well-managed organization charges its clients for the services that they receive, although sometimes this is done through third-party payors, such as Medicare. In so doing, the organization generates a monetary measure of the quantity of its outputs, and motivates managers to be concerned about the cost and quantity of services they provide.

In general, the price charged for a service is set equal to the full cost of providing that service. A higher price would take unfair advantage of what may be the organization's monopoly position and is in any event unnecessary. A lower price would provide services for less than they are worth, and hence lead to a misallocation of resources. Although, on the average, prices of services are based on full cost, the organization may well price some services below cost in order to encourage an optimum use of resources, particularly the utilization of excess capacity in off-peak periods. As exceptions to the general rule, prices may be based on prevailing market prices when the non-profit organization competes with profit-oriented companies, particularly in providing services that are not central to its goals. Also, an organization may use a subsidy price—that is, a price that is below cost—to encourage the use of certain services, or a penalty price to discourage the use of certain other services.

The full cost of a service is its direct cost plus an equitable share of common costs. It includes depreciation if funds for the acquisition of new capital assets are to be provided from charges made to clients, rather than from gifts or grants. Cost includes a charge for the use of capital to the extent that the organization's own resources are tied up in working capital or fixed assets. Cost may include imputed costs, such as an amount in lieu of taxes, particularly when the price is used as a "yardstick" against which the prices of profit-oriented organizations are compared, as is the case with a publicly owned utility.

The unit of pricing is made as narrow as is feasible because this provides a better measure of the quantity of services rendered and a better basis for decisions on the allocation of resources. The organization does not, by contrast, have a single overall rate, such as a blanket daily charge that takes no account of the type of services rendered. An exception to this principle occurs when the pricing of very small units would lead to unwise client decisions, as would happen, for example, if the price of each college course were based on its cost.

If feasible, prices are determined prospectively rather than retrospectively; that is, they are set before the fact on the basis of anticipated costs and volume, rather than after the fact on the basis of actual costs incurred. Retrospective pricing greatly diminishes the motivation to control costs. On occasion, prices also include a fee that provides funds for expansion.

## THE CONTROL STRUCTURE

***Program Structure.*** Management has given much thought to designing a program structure that is useful in (1) making program decisions, (2) providing a basis for comparison of the costs and outputs of similar programs, and (3) providing a basis for setting selling prices for those services that are sold. If, however, the organization structure is such that each responsibility center is responsible for a single program, no separate program structure is needed, and no effort is expended in thinking up "program" labels for the work done by these responsibility centers.

The program structure consists of about 10 main programs, plus as many program categories and program elements as are needed for the purposes mentioned above. One of the program categories is administration, so that administrative costs can be collected and analyzed separately from other costs. If fund-raising costs are significant, there is a separate program element for fund raising. Program elements and, if feasible, program categories are defined in such a way that quantitative output measures can be associated with each of them.

***Responsibility Accounts.*** The responsibility account structure corresponds exactly to the organization units in the organization. Some of the responsibility centers are expense centers; that is, their expenses are measured, but not their revenues. To the extent feasible, however, responsibility centers are accounted for as profit centers; that is, their managers are held responsible for expenses and for revenues. The term "profit center" does not imply that the manager is necessarily expected to earn a profit. Rather, the objective is to achieve an agreed-upon relationship between revenues and expenses. Often, this is a break-even relationship.

The program accounts and the responsibility accounts articulate with one another, and so do the budgetary accounts (or amounts shown in the budget) and the historical accounts. Thus, the accounts collectively form a single system, in which each part can be related to the others.

## THE CONTROL PROCESS

### Programming

Unless an organization continues with the same activities, year after year, it has a procedure for generating ideas for new programs, analyzing these, reaching a decision on them, and incorporating the approved individual programs into an overall plan. This is the programming process.

Management creates an environment in which ideas for new programs are encouraged. When an idea is sufficiently attractive so that it gains the initial support of an influential advocate, it becomes a proposal. If the organization has many such proposals, it has a staff unit that analyzes each of them and submits its analysis to senior management as a basis for decision. The analysis seeks to determine how well the proposal will help the organization achieve its goals.

To the extent feasible, the analysis includes an estimate of the benefits and the costs of the proposal, both being expressed in monetary terms. A benefit/cost comparison is possible when the benefits can be measured in economic terms, such as savings in operating costs or increased output. Although many projects are of this character, unfortunately they tend to be of relatively minor importance. A benefit/cost analysis can also be made in comparing two proposals, either of which will accomplish a desired objective satisfactorily; the proposal with the lower cost is preferred. If there is no plausible causal relationship between costs and benefits, however, the organization does not waste time in attempting a benefit/cost analysis.

If the benefits cannot be valued in money, an attempt is made to estimate whether the benefits are at least as great as the costs. Management recognizes that a benefit/cost analysis does not by itself provide a basis for decision because many relevant considerations cannot be measured, so it does not give the analysis undue weight. Nevertheless, this analysis reduces the area within which judgment must be applied.

In addition to an analysis of the merits of the proposal from an economic and social viewpoint, the decision maker considers its political implications, including such matters as its salability to those who must provide resources for it and other impacts on the organization's constituencies. Usually, these political considerations are kept separate from the technical analysis.

Senior management recognizes that most proposals are advocacy proposals and that the accompanying analysis and justification is, at least to some extent, biased. It attempts to offset this bias by having its own staff make a careful review of the proposal (recognizing that the staff itself may develop biases), or by setting up an adversary relationship in which natural opponents of the proposal are encouraged to criticize it.

***Programming Systems.*** If the organization is large, if it considers a sizable number of new programs, and if its activities change substantially over time, it has a formal programming system. This system provides a mechanism for incorporating the individual programs into an overall plan, often called a five-year plan, and testing this plan for balance and feasibility.

The system used for this purpose starts with the preparation and dissemination of guidelines which specify, among other things, the constraints within which program proposals are to be prepared. Working within these constraints, operating managers prepare program memoranda that describe the activities they propose to undertake, the resources required for these activities, and the anticipated results. The memoranda cover activities for a period of several future years, often five years. These memoranda are first analyzed by a staff unit and then are the basis for a discussion between senior management and operating managers. The approved program that emerges from such a discussion constitutes approval in principle to proceed with the program, but its details are subject to refinement and modification in the budgeting process.

## Budget Formulation

Budgeting is a more important process in a nonprofit organization than in a profit-oriented one. In a profit-oriented organization, operating managers can safely be permitted to modify certain plans on their own initiative, provided that the revised plan promises to increase profits. Operating managers of nonprofit organizations, especially those whose annual revenue is essentially fixed, must adhere closely to plans as expressed in the budget. As a consequence, budgeting is perhaps the most important part of the management control process.

The annual operating budget is derived from the approved program. Essentially, it is a fine turning of the next year's slice of that program. In the course of the budgeting process, more careful estimates of costs are made than those contained in the program, and responsibility for execution of the program is assigned to individual responsibility centers. Budgeting is viewed as the most important part of the management control process because the budget specifies the way in which activities are to be conducted in the coming year. It does this much more closely than is feasible in the typical profit-oriented organization.

The budget process starts with a realistic estimate of revenues. Ordinarily, and except in the federal government, expenses are planned so that they are approximately equal to revenues. This matching of expenses to revenue differs from the approach used in profit-oriented organizations because in profit-oriented organizations the amount budgeted for marketing expenses can influence the amount of revenues.

A nonprofit organization should plan to incur expenses that are equal to its revenues. If its budgeted expenses are below revenue, it is not providing the quantity of services that those who provide the revenues have a right to expect. If its budgeted expenses exceed its revenues, the difference must be made up by the generally undesirable actions of drawing down endowment or other capital funds that are intended to provide services to future generations. If the first approximation of budgeted expenses exceeds estimated revenues, the prudent course of action usually is to reduce expenses rather than to anticipate that revenues can be increased.

The initial budget is a program budget, that is, one that focuses on the amounts to be spent on each program. Summary information on objects of expense (e.g., salaries, supplies, purchased services) may be included, but these are not the main focus. Programs are identified with the responsibility centers that are to execute them.

The first step in the budget process is the formulation of guidelines and their communication to operating managers. Operating managers prepare proposed budgets consistent with these guidelines, and negotiate these proposals with their superiors. When agreement is reached, the budget becomes a commitment between the superior and the budgetee. The budgetee commits to accomplish the planned objectives within the spending limits specified in the budget, and the superior commits to regarding such an accomplishment as representing satisfactory performance.

Although some people advocate that the analysis of a proposed budget start from a zero base, this is not feasible in the real world because of the limited amount of time available. Instead, the current level of spending is usually taken as a starting point, although some organizations do a zero-based review for one or a few programs each year.

## Control of Operations

The well-managed organization has a system to assure that actual spending is kept within limits specified in the approved budget, unless there are compelling reasons to depart from the budgeted amounts. If, as in government organizations and certain other organizations, budget limitations are stated as authority to encumber or obligate (that is, to place contracts), controls are correspondingly stated in obligation or encumbrance terms. The necessity for controlling encumbrances is not permitted to detract from a focus on the incurrence of expenses, however. Expenses measure the quantity of resources consumed, and are therefore the best financial indication of the inputs that were used to accomplish whatever the organization did. To the extent that it can do so, the system insulates operating managers from the dysfunctional messages that are often signalled by obligation or encumbrance accounting.

There is a procedure for revising the budget when circumstances require it, and the organization is required to follow this procedure, rather than to hide overruns by charging expenses to incorrect accounts.

Although conformance to the budget is emphasized, top management is aware of the natural tendency to spend 100 percent of the amount authorized, whether needed or not, and it attempts to counter this tendency by making appropriate rewards, including financial rewards if feasible, to those who are able to reduce spending and still accomplish the planned outputs.

In addition to financial controls, there are other rules and prescribed procedures. In promulgating these rules and procedures, an appropriate balance is struck between the need to assure a reasonable degree of consistency in action taken by various managers, and the need to avoid stifling initiative and sound operating decisions with rules that are too detailed.

Appropriate audit and internal control techniques are used to minimize the possibility of loss by theft, fraud, or defalcation; to ensure that both the financial and the nonfinancial rules are adhered to; and to ensure that information flowing through the system is accurate.

## Measurement of Output

A nonprofit organization does not have a way of measuring output that is comparable to the revenue, gross margin, or net income numbers that are routinely available in a business enterprise, nor can it hope to develop a nonmonetary measure that is as good as these measures. Nevertheless, it needs the best possible substitute that feasibly can be devised, because without some reasonable measure of output there is no way of assessing either the efficiency or the effectiveness of the organization's performance.

The well-managed organization therefore devotes considerable attention to developing satisfactory output measures. It recognizes that although many output measures are of limited validity, they are better than nothing. Since output should be related to an organization's goals and objectives, it is often worthwhile, as a first step, to try to state the more important objectives in quantitative terms, although this is not always feasible.

Output measures are in one of two categories: results measures, which indicate the organization's performance in accomplishing its objectives, or process measures, which indicate the quantity of work done. Reliable results measures are likely to be more difficult to devise than process measures, but they generally are of more significance to higher-level management. Process measures are relatively easy to identify and are of more use in the measurement of current, short-run performance. The management control system includes an appropriate mix of both types of measures. Some organizations combine individual measures into an overall output vector. If industry associations have developed output measures, the members of the association use these data in analyzing outputs in their own organizations.

A third type of output measure, the social indicator, is of relatively little use in management control but may be useful in strategic planning, provided that users recognize its severe limitations; at best, it is a rough measure of performance.

The notion that the search for good output measures is fruitless because output cannot be measured perfectly is rejected. There is a never ending search for new, more valid measures. At the same time, the limitations of existing output measures are recognized. In particular, managers are not permitted to emphasize the attainment of a surrogate measure when this detracts from the attainment of the organization's actual objectives. The only output measures collected are those that are actually used in the management control process. Management recognizes that many people, especially professionals, dislike the idea of "accountability," which is associated with the measurement of outputs, but it proceeds with such measurements despite resistance from these people.

A measure of the quantity of output is more reliable and easier to develop than a measure of the quality of output, but the well-managed organization does not permit this fact to lead to an overemphasis on quantity. Quality must be controlled, even though its measurement is subjective.

## Reporting on Performance

Managers are provided with all the information they need (despite occasional attempts by some to inhibit the flow of information) but not with more than they can assimilate. An important type of information is a comparison of actual expenses and results with planned expenses and results in each responsibility center. Information on actual expenses is collected in a double-entry accounting system. This system uses accounts and rules for charging accounts that are entirely consistent with those in the budget. Reports containing this information are made available quickly. They are designed so as to highlight significant information. Where appropriate, variances between planned and actual spending are isolated by cause: volume, mix, price, and efficiency.

All levels of management, including senior management, are involved in the monitoring of current performance. Considerable attention is given to a review of output information in order to judge the organization's effectiveness. Quantitative measure of both the quantity and quality of outputs are used to the extent feasible, but the limitations of these measures are recognized. Peer reviews of quality are undertaken where feasible, despite professionals' resistance to such reviews.

The organization also engages in operational auditing, recognizing that this type of auditing requires different skills from compliance auditing and that unless properly done it can lead to friction and resentment that negate its possible benefits.

## Evaluation

***Operations Evaluation.*** In many organizations, activities whose character and scope are relatively unchanged from one year to the next are not subject to much management attention. In a well-managed organization, by contrast, a systematic examination of these operations is undertaken once every five years or so. Its purpose is to ascertain whether improvements in efficiency are feasible. Such an examination is conducted by staffs that are organized for this purpose, by outside consulting organizations, or, occasionally, by a "blue-ribbon commission" of concerned citizens.

The examination can be conducted in various ways. One simple, but often effective, approach is to ask naive questions about why operations are performed in the way they are. Another is to compare costs of an activity with costs of similar activities in other organizations. Another is to apply work measurement techniques that have been developed by profit-oriented companies. Judgment is required in assessing the relationship between costs and outputs. The approach to the review is impersonal and factual.

This process is called a zero-base review. The term is derived from the fact that such a review examines each function from scratch, rather than taking the existing level of spending as a starting point, which is necessary in the budgeting process. In making such a review, the possibility that certain functions could be performed more efficiently by a profit-oriented company is carefully explored.

***Program Evaluation.*** In addition to an operations evaluation, the well-managed organization also undertakes a systematic evaluation of the effectiveness of its programs. Such an evaluation requires persons with different skills than those involved in an evaluation of operations. In particular, a program evaluation requires persons with a professional expertise in the area of the program, whereas an operations evaluation requires a knowledge of general management techniques.

A program evaluation involves, first, identification of the objectives of the program, and then a judgment as to the degree to which these objectives are being attained and whether the benefits exceed the costs. In the usual case, these judgments are based primarily on the intuition of the evaluators. The tendency to use sophisticated statistical or experimental techniques is resisted except in the relatively rare cases in which the data required for such techniques can be obtained.

Before undertaking either an operations evaluation or a program evaluation, those involved in it assure that they have adequate backing from top management or other influential people so that there is a likelihood that recommendations will be implemented.

### System Design and Installation

The preconditions for a successful system implementation effort are senior-management support, acquiescence from outside agencies, a competent system design team, and the allowance of almost enough time. Senior management is assumed to provide the first, to devote time in discussions with outside agencies so as to assure the second, to assemble the necessary staff or hire outside system designers, and to set up a timetable covering one, two, or three years, depending on the complexity of the problem.

Senior management spends adequate time on the system development effort. It satisfies itself that the system is consistent with its own management style. It seeks to convince operating managers that the new system will in fact be used and that the former system will be discarded. It holds meetings with immediate subordinates to discuss how information can be used, and expects them to hold similar meetings with their subordinates. It uses information from the new system, and only from that system, as soon as it becomes available and reliable, and discards the old system as soon as it is reasonably safe to do so.

In developing the system, the design staff relies primarily on an assessment of what information operating managers need, based on an analysis of their decision-making responsibilities. This analysis is carried out in conjunction with operating managers, but it goes beyond simply listening to what these managers say they need. Existing operating data are used to the maximum extent feasible. Crosswalks, or other techniques that permit information collected in the new system to meet the need of outside agencies, are developed. The staff spends a considerable fraction of the available time on education efforts.

If top management decides that it is not feasible to install a complete new system all at once, it approaches the task in phases. Such an approach can consist of (1) a pilot installation, (2) a simple beginning, or (3) a step-by-step installation. If the last method is followed, the first step is to have annual budgets prepared by programs and responsibility centers, but without an accounting backup.

## MAIN LINES FOR IMPROVEMENT

In conclusion, and with considerable trepidation, we venture to list what seem to use to be the principal measures that will lead to improvement in the management control process in nonprofit organizations. The items are listed roughly in the order of their importance:

1. More active interest in the effective and efficient functioning of the organization by its governing board (including legislative committees in the case of government organizations). This is listed first because it can trigger all the other improvements.
2. More top-management involvement in programming, in operations and program performance evaluation, and in systems improvement.
3. Different top-management involvement in budgeting, delegating more responsibility, where circumstances permit, to operating managers.
4. Better rewards for good management, including both better compensation for senior managers and refusal to tolerate poor management (in-

cluding refusal to accept the cliché that Civil Service protects incompetents).

5. Use of expense accounting and a corresponding downgrading of obligation or expenditure accounting. Disregarding suggestions from auditors that financial statements should show detailed transactions by funds or, if this is not feasible, disregarding such reports in the management control process.
6. Structuring reports of actual performance so that they are entirely consistent with budgets.
7. Evaluation of operations on a regular basis, including the use of performance data from comparable organizations as a benchmark, and the support of industry-wide efforts to improve such data. A search for opportunities to have functions performed by profit-oriented organizations.
8. Evaluation of program effectiveness on a regular basis, but not more sophisticated than is warranted by the nature of available data.
9. More thorough attention to programming, including the use of a carefully designed program structure. (This need is particularly significant in governmental organizations.)
10. More use of benefit/cost analysis in appropriate circumstances (but a recognition that such analyses are of little value, and can even be misleading, in other circumstances).
11. Creation of profit centers (i.e., responsibility centers that sell services to others) and a well-designed set of transfer prices.
12. More attention to the selling prices for services, including the selection of units of pricing that are as narrow as feasible. Recognition of the importance of basing prices on the full cost of services.
13. More emphasis on output measures, including more effort devoted to finding better measures, and the incorporation of output measures into both programs and budgets. The measurement of performance in terms of outputs as well as costs.

## Concluding Remarks

The early 1980s have seen sizable cutbacks in federal funding for nonprofit organizations, coupled with the dual problem of spending reductions in many states and increasing client demands for services in many sectors. If needed services are to be provided in an era of scarcity, nonprofit organizations must take seriously the challenge of management control. This challenge exists at all levels: governing boards, senior managers, operating managers, and professionals. To not undertake needed improvements is to risk both the well-being of an organization's clients and the viability of the organization itself.

Case 15–1

## THE JOHNS HOPKINS HOSPITAL*

Early in May 1977, Robert M. Heyssel, M.D., executive vice president and director of The Johns Hopkins Hospital, was reviewing the hospital's annual operating plan for 1977–78. In 1972–73 a decentralized management structure had been initiated at Hopkins. The review of the 1977–78 operating plan provided an occasion to examine and assess the decentralization move.

### Background

The Johns Hopkins Medical Institutions (JHMI) occupied a 44-acre site in the East Baltimore section of Baltimore, Maryland. A major American medical center, JHMI was made up of four components: the 1,037-bed Johns Hopkins Hospital and the Johns Hopkins University's professional health divisions—the School of Medicine; the School of Hygiene and Public Health; and the School of Health Services. The Johns Hopkins Medical Institutions described themselves as providing "a total environment in which the art of medicine and healing are carried out at a patient's bedside, in classrooms, clinics, and research laboratories, and in community outreach programs and innovative new prepaid medical plans such as those in East Baltimore and Columbia, Maryland." The John F. Kennedy Institute, located close to JHMI, was an independent institution affiliated with Hopkins; it had 40 long-term beds for mentally and physically handicapped children and was a center for training and research in mental retardation.

Johns Hopkins, in his will, provided $7 million to be divided between the university and the hospital; it was the largest single philanthropic bequest made in the United States up to that time. In an 1873 letter he stated "In all arrangements in relation to this hospital, you will bear constantly in mind that it is my wish and purpose that the institution shall ultimately form a part of the Medical School of that University . . ." The Johns Hopkins Hospital opened its doors in 1889.

The Johns Hopkins Hospital was a nonprofit corporation and was classified by the American Hospital Association in the 1970s as a "General Medical and Surgical" hospital. It treated all types of medical, surgical, and psychiatric patients in the acute stages of illness. As a teaching hospital, Johns Hopkins educated and trained over 400 residents and interns each year in multiple specialties. The JHMI also had contributed many advances in medicine: pioneering research in a host of diseases, development and improvement of surgical techniques, and the discovery of many drugs.

---

* This case was prepared by Srinivasan Umpathy, Research Assistant, under the direction of Eoin W. Trevelyan, lecturer in Management, Harvard School of Public Health.

In 1965, the Johns Hopkins Medical Institutions considered moving to the suburbs. The 1976 Annual Report commented on the decision as follows:

> It was a watershed decision . . . to remain in Baltimore City . . . [and] bespoke a responsibility to improve the health care of our largely poor, medically underserved neighborhood and also to improve the area itself.

## The Board of Trustees

The bylaws of The Johns Hopkins Hospital vested the Board of Trustees with "the control and management of the affairs, business, and properties of the Hospital." There were two board committees which helped coordinate the activities of the hospital with the rest of the Johns Hopkins Medical Institutions. The JHI Management Committee was the administrative policy-making body for the Johns Hopkins Medical Institutions; it met every Monday and focused its attention on issues which required coordination among the different divisions of JHMI. The JHMI Joint Administrative Committee met on the first and third Mondays of each month and dealt with policy and operational issues related to functions which were provided jointly to the institutions, such as library, student health services, and security.

The Board of Trustees appointed the Medical Board of the hospital. The Medical Board made recommendations to the board on matters relating to the welfare of the hospital and medical or surgical treatment of patients in the hospital. Formal appointments to the Medical Staff were made by the Board of Trustees of the hospital based on recommendations of the Medical Board, following nomination by the chief of each clinical service and review by a Quality Assurance Committee. Appointments, except for the chiefs of service, were for a period of not more than one year ending on the next June 30. The Medical Staff was divided into Active Staff, Courtesy Staff, Associate Staff, Resident Staff, and Honorary Staff categories. A chief of service was appointed by the Board of Trustees from among those recommended by the Medical Board, and served until a successor had been appointed. The chiefs of service were responsible not only for the care and treatment of patients in their respective departments, but also for the department's educational and research programs.

## The Situation in 1972

The Johns Hopkins Hospital incurred annual operating losses of between $1.2 and $1.9 million throughout the period 1967–71. In the year ended June 30, 1972, the operating loss was reduced to $437,218; after the application of current gifts and endowment income, net income was $1,029,758—the first positive net income figure in four years.

The problems faced by the hospital in October 1972 were summarized in a 1976 note by Dr. Charles Buck, the director of planning, and covered personnel, organization, and finances. The number of hospital employees had increased by more than 40 percent in one decade, there was a perception that the hospital was overstaffed and inefficient, and an aggressive union had been organized to represent the hospital's service workers. Organizationally, there was a lack of a clear definition of responsibility and accountability for operations, the central service departments seemed to be operating more in their own self-interest than in meeting the needs of the operating departments, institutional goals and objectives were either unclear or unstated, and departmental goals were either undeveloped or unrelated to institutional goals. In the face of President Nixon's wage and price control program, and impending state-based regulation, the hospital's costs were rising at a rate of 11 to 14 percent per annum. Finally, allocation of limited capital resources on an annual basis was becoming increasingly difficult, and a high demand for renewal of facilities existed in the face of what was generally considered to be inefficient use of existing resources.

### Developments during 1972–1973

Fiscal year 1972–73 saw an operating loss of $1.2 million. The Hospital's Annual Report for that year observed:

> The Johns Hopkins Hospital has contributed more than $17 million in unreimbursed services to the community through its outpatient department.
>
> The Hospital shoulders the loss by including a portion of it in its overall charges for care and by using a basic resource, the income earned by its endowment. It has not yet had to touch its endowment principal, but with hospital and medical care costs rising rapidly, an ominous threat to the lifeblood of Johns Hopkins has become very real.

Dr. Steven Muller, a specialist in comparative government and international relations, assumed office as the president of The Johns Hopkins University and president of The Johns Hopkins Hospital in 1972. He was the first person in this century to fill both the university and hospital presidencies.

In October 1972, Robert Heyssel, M.D., was appointed executive vice president and director of The Johns Hopkins Hospital. Dr. Heyssel had joined Johns Hopkins University School of Medicine in 1968 as associate dean, and at the same time was appointed director of Outpatient Services and director of the Office of Health Care Programs at The Johns Hopkins Hospital.

When Dr. Heyssel took charge, he found that there was "a strong hierarchy of central service departments; indicative of this is the fact that of the costs distributed to operating units, only 30 percent were direct costs and 70 percent were allocated or indirect costs. With control over only 30 percent of their costs, it was impossible to make any unit responsible or accountable for their total costs as related to budget or revenue." Dr. Heyssel also felt that the traditional organization structure of the hospital (Exhibit 1) was not suitable for Johns Hopkins. In addition, the budgeting process appeared to

**Exhibit 1**
Organization Chart of The Johns Hopkins Hospital (1972)

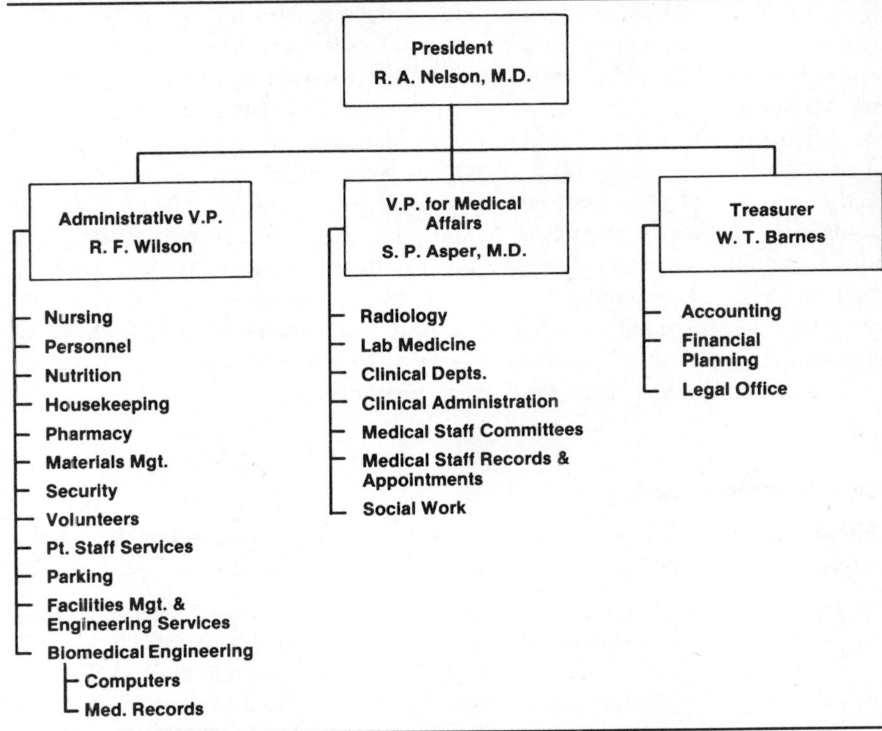


be taking place as a "top down" process with very little input from the patient care units. There were no agreed-upon targets or goals which the units were expected to achieve with regard to occupancy of beds or other resources allocated to them, or to unit costs. For these reasons, it was decided to proceed with a process of decentralization.

In Dr. Heyssel's words:

> The chiefs of service [were] responsible for the overall operational planning, management, and results. The respective departmental administrative staff were to report directly to the chiefs. . . . Furthermore, the decision was made to decentralize the Department of Nursing for operational purposes with the departmental directors of nursing also responsible to the chiefs of service for operations but to a Central Nursing Staff for professional nursing standards. . . . Any service provided centrally which could logically be provided more effectively and at the same or lesser cost by the units would be provided by the unit itself. . . .

As the Hospital's Annual Report noted:

> The objective of decentralization is to reduce operating costs by more efficient management, to improve and expedite the decision-making process, and to place budgetary responsibility at the level closest to the delivery of hospital services.

## Implementation of Decentralization

The decision to "decentralize" was announced by Dr. Heyssel at the first meeting with the board of trustees after his appointment. This decision was made with the concurrence of the chairman of the board, Mr. William E. McGuirk, Jr. A graduate of the U.S. Naval Academy at Annapolis, Mr. McGuirk was chairman of the board of the Mercantile Safe Deposit and Trust Company (a bank holding company with headquarters in Baltimore) and a strong proponent of decentralization.

A Decentralization Committee was established and consulted with individuals throughout the institution on the implementation of decentralization. The committee, which consisted entirely of nonphysicians, recommended that the directors of functional units should be lay administrators. On this point, however, Dr. Heyssel differed and decided to give this responsibility to the chiefs of the clinical services.

In February 1973 Dr. Heyssel presented to the chiefs and senior administrative officers of the hospital a written report which described in broad terms the proposed plan for decentralization. The report stated in part:

> . . . responsibility for each functional management unit will be placed in the hands of the appropriate departmental chairman who will have a functional management unit administrator reporting to him . . . There will also be a director of nursing for each of the functional management units reporting to the chairman. Decision making with regard to allocation of resources to meet patient care needs and to attain objectives within stated fiscal goals will be the responsibility of the departmental chairman, who will confer with the administrator and the director of nursing service in his area . . .
>
> The departmental chairman will prepare one- and five-year budgets for his functional management unit. Upon review by hospital general management and approval by the board, such budgets became the operating plan of the hospital.
>
> Departmental chairmen will be expected both to achieve the occupancy rates necessary to attain the total budgeted revenues for their . . . units and to control expenses . . .

During the following months progress was made in anticipating and resolving problems and potential conflicts. As Dr. Heyssel noted in a status report in May 1973, one issue raised was the reason for pursuing decentralization:

> A valid question with regard to decentralization is "Why bother?" Won't there be additional costs? Why should the departments take on additional administrative workload? What are the real benefits? Why is decentralization necessary now if it wasn't necessary in the past?
>
> There are no easy answers to these questions. The fact is, however, that the hospital has grown considerably in size and complexity over the past few years. The advent of the state of Maryland hospital rate setting commission and utilization review impose new and critical demands on our operations. Most importantly, current trends of various critical measures of the hospital's own welfare, such as declining occupancy and rising per diem costs, must be reversed. This can only be accomplished by achieving a better alignment of responsibility and authority

**Exhibit 2**
Organization Chart of The Johns Hopkins Hospital (April 1977)

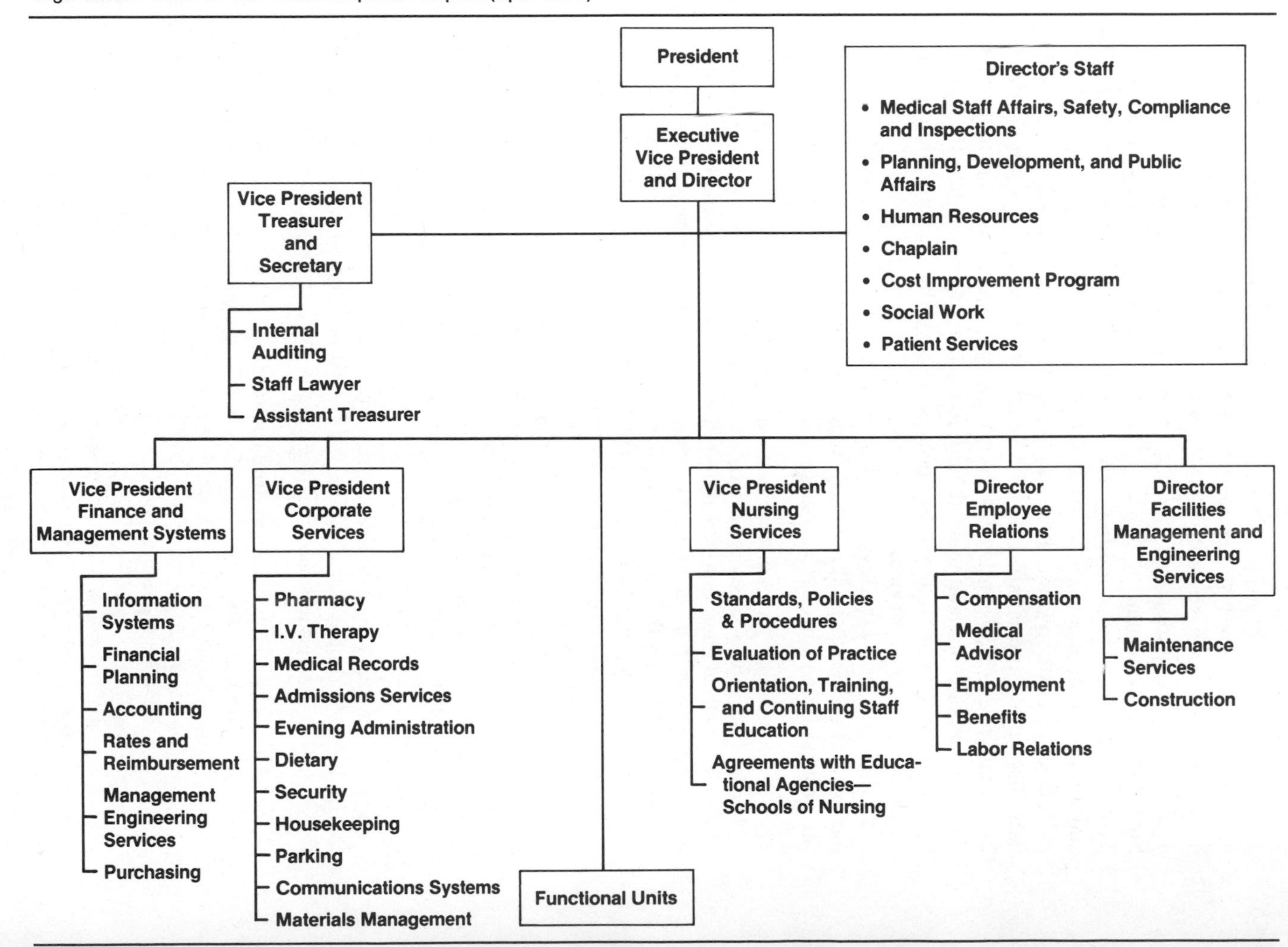

for patient care and fiscal matters, which is the primary objective of decentralization.

At this time, a schedule for decentralization had been developed. Yet, as Dr. Heyssel's report observed:

> Decentralization of management responsibility of the hospital is not going to take place overnight. The fiscal year beginning July 1, 1973, is regarded as a year of transition, but certain key changes will occur on or before July 1. Most of the organizational changes, new budgeting and reporting procedures, and new informational systems will become operational during that period . . . The objective, nonetheless, is to begin achieving the full benefits of decentralization during the next fiscal year starting July 1, 1974.

To evaluate and monitor performance under the new management plan, an outside consultant was retained early in 1973 to develop a rudimentary management information system and to advise concerning future information needs. The monthly management information report proposed by the consultant was designed to meet the informational needs of the executive vice president of the hospital. Functional units were also to receive complete copies of the report, although it was not designed to meet their information needs. Most of the raw data used in preparing the report were readily available. The report contained charts showing budgeted and actual amounts, and consisted of five sections: (1) summary reports, (2) inpatient statistics, (3) outpatient statistics, (4) patient care statistics, and (5) key operating ratios.

## Other Developments, 1973–1977

Dr. Heyssel brought a number of persons into senior administrative posts in the hospital, including a new administrator of the outpatient clinics, an assistant director for planning and program development, a director of planning, a vice president for finance and management systems, a manager of employee relations, an administrator of cost improvement programs, and a vice president of nursing. Several of these persons had no prior hospital experience, but had had considerable experience in areas such as industrial engineering, commercial credit, computer operations, human resources planning, industrial relations, and manufacturing industry. The administrative organization structure created by Dr. Heyssel by 1977 is shown in Exhibits 2 and 3.

Operational planning and budgeting processes in the hospital were changed and now included the development of planning guidelines, planning meetings, and the creation of an annual operating plan. Charles Buck, director of planning, commented:

> We began to implement three years ago. Initially, it was viewed as a joint Medical School and Hospital effort and we initially focused on the clinical departments. During the first year the clinical departments were asked to prepare statements of their internal strengths and weaknesses and external threats and opportunities,

**Exhibit 3**
Organization Chart of The Johns Hopkins Hospital (April 1977)

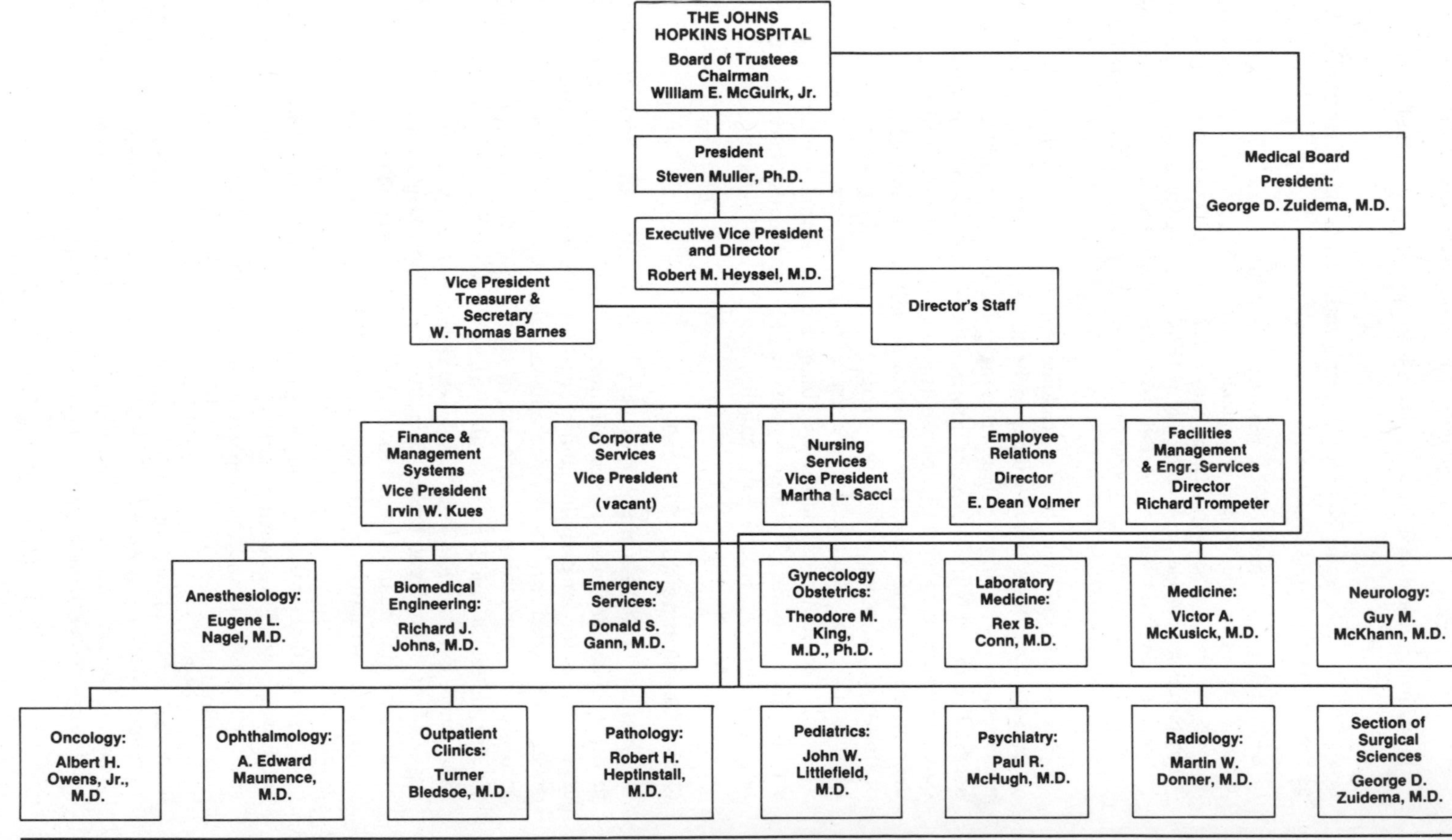

**Exhibit 4**
STATEMENT OF DIRECT INCOME & EXPENSE

706 GENERAL OPERATING ROOMS — FOR 5-31-77 — ISSUED 6-18-77 — PAGE 1

| CURRENT PERIOD | | | | YEAR TO DATE | | | |
|---|---|---|---|---|---|---|---|
| ACTUAL | BUDGET | VARIANCE | | ACTUAL | BUDGET | VARIANCE | PERCENT VARIANCE |
| | | | TOTAL OPERATING PERFORMANCE | | | | |
| 673,907 | 407,778 | 266,129 | GROSS REVENUE | 5,284,600 | 4,284,328 | 1,000,272 | 23.00 |
| | | | DIRECT EXPENSES | | | | |
| 116,382 | 113,695 | 2,687– | SALARIES | 1,201,922 | 1,213,453 | 11,531 | .00 |
| 18,621 | 18,850 | 229 | BENEFITS | 203,076 | 203,539 | 463 | .00 |
| 128,711 | 86,743 | 41,968– | SUPPLIES | 1,296,889 | 954,107 | 342,782– | 35.00– |
| 10,066 | 10,066 | | JOINT AGREEMENT | 105,967 | 110,718 | 4,751 | 4.00 |
| 1,147 | 2,043 | 896 | REPAIRS | 21,755 | 22,457 | 702 | 3.00 |
| 39,699 | 19,167 | 20,532– | TRANSFERS | 317,902 | 210,833 | 107,069– | 50.00– |
| 314,626 | 250,564 | 64,062– | TOTAL DIRECT EXPENSES | 3,147,511 | 2,715,107 | 432,404– | 15.00– |
| 359,281 | 157,214 | 202,067– | TOTAL—(SEE FOOTNOTE) | 2,137,089 | 1,569,221 | 567,868– | 36.00– |
| | | | UNITS OF SERVICE | | | | |
| | 1,930 | 1,930– | | 8,956 | 21,350 | 12,394– | 58.00– |
| | | | UNIT COST | | | | |
| .00 | 211.28 | 211.28– | GROSS REVENUE | 590.06 | 200.67 | 389.39 | 194.00 |
| | | | DIRECT EXPENSES | | | | |
| .00 | 58.90 | 58.90 | SALARIES | 134.20 | 56.83 | 77.36– | 136.00– |
| .00 | 9.76 | 9.76 | BENEFITS | 22.67 | 9.53 | 13.14– | 137.00– |
| .00 | 44.94 | 44.94 | SUPPLIES | 144.80 | 44.68 | 100.11– | 224.00– |
| .00 | 5.21 | 5.21 | JOINT AGREEMENT | 11.83 | 5.18 | 6.64– | 128.00– |
| .00 | .00 | .00 | PURCHASED SERVICES | .00 | .00 | .00 | 999.99 |
| .00 | 1.05 | 1.05 | REPAIRS | 2.42 | 1.05 | 1.37– | 130.00– |
| .00 | 9.93 | 9.93 | TRANSFERS | 35.49 | 9.87 | 25.62– | 259.00– |
| .00 | 129.82 | 129.82 | TOTAL DIRECT EXPENSES | 351.44 | 127.17 | 224.27– | 176.00– |
| .00 | 81.45 | 81.45– | INCOME CONTRIBUTION | 238.62 | 73.49 | 165.12 | 224.00 |

************************************************************
* A NEGATIVE VARIANCE IS UNFAVORABLE EXCEPT ON THE *
* "TOTAL" LINE. ON THE "TOTAL" LINE, A NEGATIVE VARIANCE IS *
* FAVORABLE IF THE COST CENTER HAS A "GROSS REVENUE" LINE. *
************************************************************

**Exhibit 5**

Departmental Expense with Budget

GENERAL FUND — PAGE 1

706 GENERAL OPERATING ROOMS — FOR 5–31–77 — ISSUED 6–18–77

| CURRENT PERIOD | | | | YEAR TO DATE | | | |
|---|---|---|---|---|---|---|---|
| ACTUAL | PLAN | VARIANCE | | ACTUAL | PLAN | VARIANCE | PLAN BALANCE |
| 6,121 | 5,393 | 728– | 140000 PROFESSIONAL & TECHNICAL | 61,308 | 57,870 | 3,438– | 5,044 |
| 101,277 | 100,180 | 1,097– | 150000 NURSING | 1,046,725 | 1,069,292 | 22,567 | 93,490 |
| 5,196 | 4,809 | 387– | 160000 CLERICAL | 51,204 | 51,164 | 40– | 4,504 |
| 3,788 | 3,313 | 475– | 170000 SERVICE | 42,685 | 35,127 | 7,558– | 3,100 |
| 116,382 | 113,695 | 2,687– | TOTAL SALARIES | 1,201,922 | 1,213,453 | 11,531 | 106,138 |
| 0 | 0 | 0 | TOTAL FRINGE BENEFITS | 0 | 0 | 0 | 0 |
| 228 | 175 | 53– | 302000 OFFICE SUPPLIES | 1,334 | 1,925 | 591 | 175 |
| 16,302 | 15,084 | 1,218– | 305000 MEDICAL & SURGICAL | 195,338 | 165,916 | 29,422– | 15,084 |
| 309 | 300 | 9– | 307000 GLASSWARE | 3,884 | 3,300 | 584– | 300 |
| 0 | 0 | 0 | 308000 BOOKS, PERIODICALS & SUBS | 0 | 0 | 0 | 0 |
| 423 | 459 | 36 | 309000 FURNITURE, NON-CAPITAL | 9,797 | 5,041 | 4,756– | 459 |
| 638 | 2,667 | 2,029 | 310000 INSTRUMENTS | 33,239 | 29,333 | 3,906– | 2,667 |
| 0 | 0 | 0 | 310001 INSTRUMENTS—REPLACE LOSS | 0 | 0 | 0 | 0 |
| 68 | 0 | 68– | 310002 INSTRUMENTS—REPLACE BREAK | 3,058 | 0 | 3,058– | 0 |
| 0 | 0 | 0 | 311000 DIETARY | 89 | 0 | 89– | 0 |
| 0 | 0 | 0 | 315000 OTHER SUPPLIES & EQUIPMENT | 0 | 0 | 0 | 0 |
| 243 | 0 | 243– | 319000 FILMS & SOLUTIONS | 2,172 | 0 | 2,172– | 0 |
| 3,136 | 1,834 | 1,302– | 319001 SOLUTIONS—I V | 37,102 | 20,166 | 16,936– | 1,834 |
| 2,447 | 1,584 | 863– | 319002 SOLUTIONS—IRRIGATING | 27,132 | 17,416 | 9,716– | 1,584 |
| 0 | 159 | 159 | 320000 GASES | 672 | 1,741 | 1,069 | 159 |
| 0 | 0 | 0 | 348000 REAGENT STRIPS & TABLETS | 9 | 0 | 9– | 0 |
| 2,921 | 0 | 2,921– | 349000 SUTURES | 45,347 | 0 | 45,347– | 0 |
| 0 | 4,167 | 4,167 | 349001 SUTURES—STANDARD | 0 | 45,833 | 45,833 | 4,167 |
| 12,057 | 6,000 | 6,057– | 349002 SUTURES—SPECIAL PURCHASES | 102,149 | 66,000 | 36,149– | 6,000 |
| 15,732 | 9,667 | 6,065– | 352000 PUMP, OXYGENATOR | 170,744 | 106,333 | 64,411– | 9,667 |
| 0 | 0 | 0 | 354000 PACEMAKERS | 2,645– | 0 | 2,645 | 0 |
| 5,362 | 4,250 | 1,112– | 373000 MATRONS | 58,787 | 46,750 | 12,037– | 4,250 |

| | | | | | | | |
|---|---|---|---|---|---|---|---|
| 0 | 21 | 21 | 376000 COPYING EXPENSE | 119 | 229 | 110 | 21 |
| 3,889 | 3,584 | 305— | 377000 STOCK DRUGS | 48,438 | 39,416 | 9,022— | 3,584 |
| 73 | 0 | 73— | 378000 STOCK DRUGS—CHG TO PATIENT | 7,384 | 0 | 7,384— | 0 |
| 57,949 | 36,792 | 21,157— | 389000 DIRECT PURCHASES, SURG SPL | 510,607 | 404,708 | 105,899— | 36,792 |
| 6,934 | 0 | 6,934— | 398000 MISCELLANEOUS | 42,133 | 0 | 42,133— | 0 |
| 128,711 | 86,743 | 41,968— | TOTAL SUPPLIES | 1,296,889 | 954,107 | 342,782— | 86,743 |
| 0 | 0 | 0 | TOTAL PURCHASED SERVICES | 0 | 0 | 0 | 0 |
| 33 | 1,209 | 1,176 | 520000 EQUIPMENT REPAIRS & MAINT | 2,472 | 13,291 | 10,819 | 1,209 |
| 1,114 | 834 | 280— | 540000 INSTRUMENT REPAIRS | 19,283 | 9,166 | 10,117— | 834 |
| 1,147 | 2,043 | 896 | TOTAL REPAIRS & MAINTENANCE | 21,755 | 22,457 | 702 | 2,043 |
| 0 | 0 | 0 | TOTAL DEPRECIATION | 0 | 0 | 0 | 0 |
| 0 | 0 | 0 | TOTAL INTEREST | 0 | 0 | 0 | 0 |
| 2,367 | 2,292 | 75— | 704000 MAINTENANCE TRANSFER | 21,587 | 25,208 | 3,421 | 2,292 |
| 22,649 | 3,125 | 19,524— | 705000 CENTRAL SUPPLY TRANSFER | 142,647 | 34,375 | 108,272— | 3,125 |
| 14,683 | 13,750 | 933— | 707000 LAUNDRY & LINEN TRANSFER | 153,668 | 151,250 | 2,418— | 13,750 |
| 39,699 | 19,167 | 20,532— | TOTAL COST TRANSFER | 317,902 | 210,833 | 107,069— | 19,167 |
| 10,066 | 10,066 | 0 | 832000 J/A—HOUSESTAFF | 110,719 | 110,718 | 1— | 10,066 |
| 0 | 0 | 0 | 899000 J/A—PRIOR YEAR SETTLEMENT | 4,752— | 0 | 4,752 | 0 |
| 10,066 | 10,066 | 0 | TOTAL JOINT AGREEMENT | 105,967 | 110,718 | 4,751 | 10,060 |
| 296,005 | 231,714 | 64,291— | TOTAL EXPENSES | 2,944,435 | 2,511,568 | 432,867— | 224,157 |

> along with their objectives for the forthcoming one or two years. This approach followed the corporate long-range planning model. In follow-up to these documents, the director of the hospital and the dean of the medical school, along with the director of planning had a one- to two-hour discussion with each of the department chairmen centered on the issues raised in the documents. These discussions were "where are you headed?" types of issues and did not deal with money or budgets. In the next year we began to focus on action plans, or programs, desired in order to meet objectives. This approach turned out to generate a rather long "wish list" of desired programs which was unwieldy to work with and too expensive to fund. We also observed that the process has more applicability to the hospital than to the medical school. The major resource requests are related to the hospital. On the university side the dean supplies only a small portion of the total budget. We produced a list of approved projects from those originally submitted. This year, the process will take the form of reviewing new requests and updating that list. An important accomplishment is that the list has been made public; it will serve as a means for placing future requests in the context of our other outstanding needs. We will probably review this list and update it three times a year.

A budget reporting system also was developed to support the new decentralized structure. The new system related expenses to the output produced by the department, both in terms of units of service and revenue (see Exhibits 4 and 5) and compared actuals with budgeted amounts for both the current month and the year to date. Supplementary reports provided detailed information on staffing patterns and salaries.

Several other changes and activities had also been initiated. For example:

In 1972 a revised University Faculty Incentive Plan for practice was introduced. Medical staff were encouraged to increase patient care income since this might be reflected in increased individual salaries or discretionary departmental surplus funds. This, and the addition of new members of the professional staff, were seen as means of increasing occupancy.

A Union Avoidance Program was initiated in 1976; a key element in this program was the establishment of nonbargaining unit grievance procedures which included an automatic review and approval mechanism by the executive vice president.

Late in 1976, a compensation study covering all employees of the hospital was initiated to ensure rationalization of pay scales.

A Performance Evaluation System was gradually developed. All salary increase requests considered in 1977 were to be decided only after considering information on the performance appraisal forms.

## The Johns Hopkins Hospital Building Program

In 1976, on the occasion of their centennial, the Johns Hopkins Institutions launched the most ambitious fund raising effort in their history. The program sought endowment of 50 named professorships at $1 million each, bringing

**Exhibit 6**

Five-Year Trend in Operating Data* ($000)

| | 1973 Actual | 1974 Actual | 1975 Actual | 1976 Actual | 1977 Budget | 1977 Est. Actual | 1978 Budget | ($000) Annual Growth Rate (Percent) |
|---|---|---|---|---|---|---|---|---|
| Gross revenue | $69,674 | $72,742 | $87,399 | $101,718 | $107,500 | $109,000 | $119,500 | 11.4 |
| Net operating revenue | 59,946 | 64,822 | 75,136 | 88,538 | 96,842 | 96,023 | 107,601 | 12.4 |
| Expenses: | | | | | | | | |
| Salaries and benefits | 37,218 | 39,681 | 44,144 | 51,656 | 56,011 | 55,950 | 61,200 | 10.6 |
| Other expenses | 23,975 | 26,589 | 31,864 | 36,626 | 40,081 | 39,964 | 45,201 | 13.6 |
| Total expenses | 61,193 | 66,270 | 76,008 | 88,282 | 96,092 | 95,914 | 106,401 | 11.7 |
| Operating profit/(loss) | $(1,247) | $(1,448) | $ (872) | $ 256 | $ 750 | $ 1,109 | $ 1,200 | — |
| Visits | 468,484 | 471,114 | 460,900 | 422,000 | 416,872 | 375,000 | 375,000 | (4.5) |
| Patients days | 299,888 | 294,386 | 295,764 | 306,152 | 305,000 | 307,000 | 312,763 | 0.8 |
| Cost per patient day | $155.20 | $171.90 | $194.70 | $218.70 | $238.90 | $236.90 | $258.24 | 10.7 |
| Full-time equivalent personnel | 3,963 | 3,921 | 4,043 | 4,080 | 4,230 | 4,090 | 4,200 | 1.2 |
| Number of beds | 1,063 | 1,077 | 1,100 | 1,058 | | 1,037 | 1,077 | 1.4 |
| % revenue from Blue Cross, Medicare, and Medicaid | 63% | 62% | 70% | 70% | n.a. | n.a. | n.a. | |

n.a. = Not available.

* Data exclude Oncology Department, which was to be fully operational by July 1st.

to 100 the number of such chairs, and $20 million to make possible a $100 million rebuilding program at the hospital.

The building program was designed in two phases. Phase I, completed in 1977, cost $49 million and was financed by a combination of federal and state funds ($10.7 million), Maryland Health and Higher Education Facilities Authority Loan ($24.7 million), university funds ($6.0 million), and hospital funds ($8.3 million). Phase II was to be completed in 1982 and was expected to involve expenditures of $40 to $60 million.

## Results

A memorandum from Dr. Heyssel to all senior members of functional units and central staff dated April 22, 1977, stated some of the advantages and benefits of decentralization:

> Our entire response to HSCRC [the state of Maryland's Health Services Cost Review Commission], as well as our ability to adapt to its methodology, was and is due to the generation of unit cost data for operating units under the decentralized mode of management.
>
> The Statements of Financial Position of the Hospital provide hard evidence of the economic success of the process (Exhibit 6).

Since 1975 The Johns Hopkins Hospital had a progressive decline in its annual rate of unit cost increase (i.e., total expenses divided by total patient days). The rate of increase fell from a high of 14.6 percent (FY 1975 over FY 1974) to 12.2 percent (FY 1976 over FY 1975). The rate of cost increase for FY 1977 over FY 1976 was projected at slightly more than 10 percent (see Exhibit 7). Several factors were seen to have contributed to these results. As noted in the 1976 Annual Report:

> The one-year-old cost improvement program is showing commendable progress. Cost savings projects initiated in such areas as energy, preventive maintenance, and materials handling will achieve annualized savings of $650,000 . . . In the Employee Relations Department, a major program was launched to train and upgrade our supervisory personnel . . . Continuing to make more effective use of existing resources, we have increased bed occupancy from 76 percent in 1972 to 82 percent in 1976.

## Comments of Senior Officials on Changes Made Since 1972

Edward Halle, administrator, Outpatient Clinics and Emergency Medical Services:

> Decentralization has been an excellent motivator for all types of individuals. The absence of the profit motive has traditionally been a disincentive for efficiency and economy in the health care industry; the very fact that our managers are being measured serves as an incentive to do things better. The information system

**Exhibit 7**
Summary of Functional Unit Performance Trends (unit cost increases*)

| | Fiscal Year Increase (Percent) | | | | | |
|---|---|---|---|---|---|---|
| | *74 over 73* | *75 over 74* | *76 over 75* | *77E over 76* | *78 Budget over 77E* | *Average* |
| Hospital Average | 10.3 | 14.6 | 12.2 | 10.0 | 8.9 | 11.4 |
| *Units* | | | | | | |
| Emergency medicine | 25.5 | 28.2 | 16.5 | 12.9 | 6.7 | 17.7 |
| OB-GYN | 15.2 | 14.5 | 25.2 | 7.2 | 12.6 | 14.7 |
| Outpatient department—adult | 13.6 | 7.4 | 11.5 | 20.2 | 16.6 | 13.8 |
| Anesthesiology/adult ICUs | 6.7 | 32.2 | 17.8 | 5.0 | 7.8 | 13.6 |
| Pediatrics | 25.5 | 10.0 | 17.5 | 7.4 | 7.4 | 13.4 |
| Pharmacy | 12.4 | 13.9 | 16.2 | 16.6 | 4.2 | 12.6 |
| Radiology | 24.3 | 11.0 | 11.0 | 6.8 | 6.3 | 11.7 |
| Medicine | 13.5 | 18.7 | 8.1 | 8.4 | 7.0 | 11.1 |
| Laboratory medicine | 19.8 | 22.3 | 10.9 | (2.6) | 3.4 | 10.4 |
| GOR | 20.0 | 6.6 | 6.9 | 1.0 | 12.0 | 9.1 |
| Surgery | 12.0 | 18.0 | 4.6 | 9.8 | 1.0 | 9.0 |
| Psychiatry | 12.0 | 5.0 | 12.6 | 4.0 | 9.5 | 8.6 |
| Pathology | 6.8 | 16.9 | 2.4 | 7.2 | 6.2 | 7.8 |
| Ophthalmology | 4.4 | 7.2 | 7.5 | 11.9 | 4.3 | 7.0 |
| Rehabilitation medicine | 1.1 | 5.5 | 9.0 | 7.2 | 11.9 | 6.9 |
| Neurosciences | n.a. | n.a. | (8.3) | 11.9 | 7.9 | n.a. |

n.a. = Not available.

* Average without malpractice, utilities, and collection fees = 10.0 percent.

developed over the past five years has provided the means to manage as well as to communicate management information to the physicians.

In earlier days there was no pressure for conservation. The attitude was "if it's reimbursable (by third-party payers) it's okay to do it." Physicians were kept in the dark about financial matters. It was assumed they were interested only in medicine, but that has proved to be untrue. With a little education and some good information they were well able to assume some management responsibilities. For example, about six years ago we discovered that for the average outpatient visit the cost was $15; we were charging $10 and were actually collecting $7. Physician resistance to increased charges and to efforts to reduce costs and improve collections all but disappeared. Including physicians in the management process has resulted in a better operation with much less frustration.

Dr. Theodore King, chief of Gynecology and Obstetrics, had a favorable view of the decentralization process:

I am a great enthusiast of decentralization. It is a genuine attempt to bring responsibility to people. I am programmed to solve clinical problems not management problems. That is where business school is involved. Mr. Burch, the department administrator, is formally trained, while I have acquired some information on the job. The director of nursing, Mr. Burch, and I come together and determine the alternatives that are available. After decentralization, individuals within the departments are much more aware of the dollar costs.

Dr. Martin Donner, chief of Radiology, also held a positive view of decentralization:

I personally like decentralization. We do not have to get permission from the administration for minor internal expenditures, such as overtime, supplies, etc. As long as I am within my unit cost of service, such decisions are made by our managers. Of course, we must manage effectively and responsibly to stay within our unit cost of service. We are very happy with the reorganization. We can now respond more quickly to the requests from other departments. Supervision with flexibility is now possible. The concept of "units of production" used by us in analyzing and controlling costs, permits us to employ some of the principles used in manufacturing organizations, except that our "product" is superior health care at a reasonable cost.

Now we have the feeling of contributing to the overall management of the hospital. The physicians now spend less time with budgeting and other administrative details. My administrator's organization has permitted me and the other physicians to devote more time to teaching and research. This year as well as last year the award for the best teacher of the year, as voted by the senior class of medical students, was given to a member of this department. We have not lost any senior departmental faculty members or managers since the reorganization of the hospital and our department.

Dr. Charles Buck, director of planning, commented:

When Bob Heyssel came here he was uncomfortable with the organization as it was defined then. He felt that the physicians were major actors in the decisions to use hospital resources and that somehow this needed to be acknowledged in the organizational structure. We have been moving in this direction ever since under the banner of "decentralization." Bob has a very good sense of timing as to how fast the organization can absorb new ways of doing things. None of this has caused much of an uproar.

As part of decentralization, we realized that better people were needed at the functional unit level. During his first 3 years, a number of managers were replaced. Now, if we look back, we see that a lot of people were replaced without any overt "head chopping." Administrators in Medicine, Pediatrics, Psychiatry, Materials Management, Data Processing, Nursing, Employee Relations, and Medical Records were replaced.

We did not have good financial information systems. This, of course, was important if we were to move toward a decentralized form of management. The units needed the information to make better decisions, and central management needed the information to monitor the progress of the units.

As an early step toward initiating the concept of the chiefs of service being accountable for departmental operations, they were invited to the trustee meetings. Each of the chiefs, in turn, was asked to present an overview of his department's performance. While this certainly was not a vigorous review, it served the purpose of acknowledging that the chiefs, in fact, were now in charge.

An example of the "decentralized" approach is the method used to provide new administrative help in the clinical departments. Usually, a committee from central administration reviews candidates for clinical administrative jobs and presents a slate of acceptable candidates to the chiefs of service for final decision.

They were grateful for this help and usually accepted our recommendations. Our clinical administrators are well paid. Some of them have been assistant directors of hospitals. This is important to the concept of decentralization.

Ms. Martha Sacci, vice president of Nursing, described her reactions:

I started here in February, 1977. Part of the lure was decentralization. Organizations are becoming more and more complex, and coordination between medicine, nursing, and administration is important. I think decentralization can help this process.

Currently I am working with head nurses from different clinics. Leadership development programs are needed. There is high turnover in some departments because of poor management.

The functional unit directors come to me if they are having trouble with their directors of Nursing. Otherwise, they don't. Selection of directors of Nursing is done jointly by me and the functional unit director. Regarding salaries for directors of Nursing, the manager for compensation calls me regularly, and some administrators have also called.

One of the administrators who had joined The Johns Hopkins Hospital about 10 years ago commented:

I feel that the job content of the administrator did not change after decentralization came in. After decentralization, doctors have become more involved, perhaps to their detriment. There has also been an infusion of administrators. Prior to decentralization there were only five or six administrators. Now there are 20 administrators, some of whom have not even had a college education. Everyone is calling himself an administrator.

The nurse-physician relationship has certainly improved, since the director of Nursing reports to the physician in her area of specialization, instead of reporting to an administrative nurse. There are no major problems in my functional unit since the director of Nursing reports to me for all administrative matters. The information system is okay, but it takes too long.

## Annual Operating Plan, 1977–1978

During 1975–76 and 1976–77 the approach had been to develop plans at the hospital level and ask the functional units to respond with objectives that helped implement these plans. A major problem was trying to press an iterative process into a "top down" mold, with the result that there was some contradiction and/or overlapping in goal setting among the units.

For 1977–78 this planning process was superceded by one that dealt with goals and objectives by department at the JHMI level, that is, both the university and hospital sections of each Clinical Department. This comprehensive process was begun in November 1976 by sending out a request to the units to do a self assessment—their strengths, weaknesses, and their needs over the next two years.

The evaluation process was conducted through December 1976 and January 1977 by staff members (in conjunction with unit personnel) of both the

University and the Hospital and ended with a tentative JHMI program plan, including a total of 214 proposed new programs which were well defined and not overlapping or in conflict with each other.

This planning process was kept current by periodic updates and adjustments of priorities. The intent was to evolve it into a process of longer-range integrated planning, with financing and implementation of assure balanced growth among all departments.

The introduction to the Annual Operating Plan, 1977–78, stated:

> As has been the case for the last few years, the functional unit has been the primary focal point for the planning process. However, several important changes were made this year. Instead of projecting the 1977–78 budget from the 1976–77 "actual" figures, the new budget was projected from the 1976–77 budget. This process adds a motivational factor to the decentralization concept in that functional units that underspent the current budget are rewarded . . . "unit costs" were separated into fixed and variable components to allow for volume change calculations. Each functional unit determined the fixed ratio for its "unit costs."

In addition to financial statements and evaluation of progress against fiscal 1977 unit objectives, the Annual Operating Plan presented budgets (by functional unit and by major expenditure category) for 1977–78 (Exhibits 8 and 9) capital equipment requests for fiscal 1978, full-time equivalent staffing levels analyzed by unit, and allocation and utilization of beds by unit. Exhibit 10 presents the availability and utilization of beds for 1976–1978. Exhibit 11 shows historical trends in staffing levels, by functional units.

The Annual Operating Plan 1977–78 gave the following breakdown for the Capital Budget for Financial Year 1978:

| | | |
|---|---|---|
| Equipment: | | |
| Under $20,000 . . . . . . . . . | $600,000 | |
| Cost improvement . . . . . . | 300,000 | |
| Replacement . . . . . . . . . . . | 560,000 | |
| Hospital equipment . . . . . | 646,000 | |
| | | $2,106,000 |
| Less leasing . . . . . . . . . . | | 1,000,000 |
| Subtotal . . . . . . . . . . . . . . . . . | | $1,106,000 |
| Renovations: | | |
| Hospital renovations . . . . . | | 3,000,000 |
| | | $4,106,000 |

Referring to the above tabulation, the Annual Operating Plan noted:

> In recent years capital investment to maintain and replace the hospital's plant and equipment has been restrained by annual operating deficits. Endowment and gift income has approximated annual losses, thus placing the capital burden upon depreciation, averaging less than $3.0 million a year.
>
> Depreciation is not an adequate source of funding, causing necessary projects to be deferred. Further, with this limitation on capital, it is obvious that there is

**Exhibit 8** SUMMARY OF HOSPITAL 1977 COSTS & 1978 BUDGETS ($000)

| | 77 Budget | Est. 77 Actual | 78 Inflation $ | 78 Inflation % | 78 Vol. | 78 Tech. & Protocol | 78 Budget w/o Onco. | Percent Increase over 77 Actual $ | Percent Increase over 77 Actual Unit Cost | Oncology 77 Budget | Oncology 77 Est. Actual | Oncology Changes | Oncology 1978 Budget | Total Hospital |
|---|---|---|---|---|---|---|---|---|---|---|---|---|---|---|
| *Direct patient care:* | | | | | | | | | | | | | | |
| Ophthalmology | $ 2,118.3 | $ 2,152.2 | $ 125.6 | 5.8 | — | $ (33.9) | $ 2,243.9 | 4.3 | 4.3 | | | | | $ 2,243.9 |
| Psychiatry | 2,126.9 | 2,080.5 | 144.4 | 6.9 | — | 18.0 | 2,242.9 | 7.8 | 7.8 | | | | | 2,242.9 |
| Surgery | 6,703.2 | 6,654.4 | 436.7 | 6.6 | 194.5 | (26.8) | 7,258.8 | 9.1 | 1.0 | | | | | 7,258.8 |
| GOR | 2,957.2 | 3,277.7 | 245.0 | 7.5 | — | 145.0 | 3,667.7 | 12.0 | 12.0 | | | | | 3,667.7 |
| Neurosciences | 1,105.9 | 1,089.0 | 77.3 | 7.1 | 1.7 | 16.9 | 1,184.9 | 8.9 | 7.9 | | | | | 1,184.9 |
| OB—GYN | 4,430.5 | 4,282.1 | 280.2 | 6.5 | (74.0) | 148.0 | 4,636.3 | 8.3 | 12.6 | | | | | 4,636.3 |
| Anesthesiology | 2,782.7 | 2,688.6 | 183.3 | 6.8 | 25.1 | 174.1 | 3,071.1 | 14.2 | 7.8 | | | | | 3,071.1 |
| Adult ICU's | 2,983.7 | 3,021.0 | 206.9 | 6.8 | — | (77.8) | 3,150.1 | 4.3 | 4.3 | | | | | 3,150.1 |
| Medicine | 6,135.4 | 6,106.5 | 429.8 | 7.0 | — | — | 6,536.3 | 7.0 | 7.0 | | | | | 6,536.3 |
| Oncology | | | | | | | | | | $5,176.1 | $2,883.0 | $3,260.4 | $6,143.4 | 6,143.4 |
| Pediatrics | 6,565.9 | 6,597.4 | 520.0 | 7.9 | — | (31.5) | 7,085.9 | 7.4 | 7.4 | | | | | 7,085.9 |
| Emergency medicine | 1,421.8 | 1,379.4 | 76.9 | 5.6 | — | 16.0 | 1,472.3 | 6.7 | 6.7 | | | | | 1,472.3 |
| Outpatient—adult gen'l. | 1,722.6 | 1,636.9 | 112.8 | 6.9 | (22.3) | 50.0 | 1,777.4 | 8.6 | 14.4 | | | | | 1,777.4 |
| Outpatient—Adult Consult. | 283.2 | 267.5 | 11.4 | 4.3 | — | 15.7 | 294.6 | 10.1 | 10.1 | | | | | 294.6 |
| Subtotal | 41,337.3 | 41,233.2 | 2,850.3 | 6.9 | 125.0 | 413.7 | 44,622.2 | 8.2 | — | 5,176.1 | 2,883.0 | 3,260.4 | 6,143.4 | 50,765.6 |
| *Patient care support:* | | | | | | | | | | | | | | |
| Pathology | 1,528.3 | 1,526.4 | 91.9 | 6.0 | — | 1.9 | 1,620.2 | 6.2 | 6.2 | | | | | 1,620.2 |
| Radiology | 6,089.4 | 6,158.2 | 452.6 | 7.3 | 293.4 | — | 6,904.2 | 12.1 | 6.3 | | | | | 6,904.2 |
| Laboratory medicine | 6,450.2 | 6,444.5 | 358.0 | 5.6 | 130.0 | — | 6,932.5 | 7.6 | 3.4 | — | — | 348.3 | 348.3 | 7,280.8 |
| Pharmacy | 3,454.7 | 3,600.0 | 193.0 | 5.4 | 107.0 | — | 3,900.0 | 8.3 | 4.2 | 1,517.0 | 311.5 | 1,511.1 | 1,822.6 | 5,722.6 |
| Social services | 650.2 | 673.3 | 68.9 | 10.2 | — | (23.1) | 719.1 | 6.8 | 6.8 | | | | | 719.1 |
| Rehabilitation medicine | 546.8 | 516.3 | 30.9 | 6.0 | — | 30.5 | 577.7 | 11.9 | 11.9 | | | | | 577.7 |
| IV therapy | 953.9 | 1,060.7 | 60.0 | 5.7 | 18.7 | (13.2) | 1,126.2 | 2.1 | 2.1 | 75.0 | 30.0 | 70.0 | 100.0 | 1,226.2 |
| Sub-total | 19,673.5 | 19,979.4 | 1,255.3 | 6.3 | 549.1 | (3.9) | 21,779.9 | 9.0 | — | 1,592.0 | 341.5 | 1,929.4 | 2,270.9 | 24,050.1 |
| *Service:* | | | | | | | | | | | | | | |
| Finance | 3,757.7 | 3,693.5 | 253.2 | 6.9 | 40.0 | 41.3 | 4,028.0 | 8.9 | — | | | | | 4,028.0 |
| Systems, planning, M.R. | 2,693.0 | 2,673.6 | 144.4 | 5.4 | — | 60.0 | 2,878.0 | 7.7 | — | | | | | 2,878.0 |
| Materials management | 1,655.2 | 1,698.1 | 85.0 | 5.0 | — | — | 1,783.1 | 5.0 | — | | | | | 1,783.1 |
| Communications | 1,042.1 | 1,085.2 | 51.2 | 4.7 | — | 71.0 | 1,207.4 | 11.3 | — | | | | | 1,207.4 |
| FMLES | 2,609.7 | 2,658.7 | 131.5 | 4.9 | 67.6 | — | 2,857.8 | 7.5 | — | 119.0 | 80.0 | 27.5 | 107.5 | 2,963.3 |
| Patient services | 1,142.5 | 1,116.7 | 79.3 | 7.1 | 11.7 | — | 1,207.7 | 8.1 | — | | | | | 1,207.7 |
| General services | 3,780.2 | 3,554.4 | 226.8 | 6.4 | 149.7 | — | 3,930.9 | 10.6 | — | 300.0 | 100.0 | 250.0 | 350.0 | 4,280.9 |
| Nutrition | 5,539.9 | 5,439.9 | 221.6 | 4.1 | 50.0 | (45.4) | 5,666.1 | 4.2 | — | 100.0 | 40.0 | 110.0 | 150.0 | 5,816.1 |
| All other | 4,831.0 | 4,802.1 | 384.2 | 8.0 | 0 | 40.0 | 5,226.3 | 8.8 | — | 14.0 | 14.0 | 50.0 | 64.0 | 5,290.3 |
| Subtotal | 27,051.3 | 26,722.2 | 1,577.2 | 5.9 | 319.0 | 166.9 | 28,785.3 | 7.7 | — | 533.0 | 234.0 | 437.5 | 671.5 | 29,456.8 |
| *Institutional:* | | | | | | | | | | | | | | |
| Malpractice insurance | 1,543.0 | 1,480.0 | — | 0 | — | (285.0) | 1,195.0 | (19.3) | — | | | | | 1,195.0 |
| Collection agency fees | 471.0 | 455.0 | — | 0 | 39.0 | — | 494.0 | 8.6 | — | | | | | 495.0 |
| Utilities | 2,261.0 | 2,350.0 | 123.7 | 5.3 | 259.5 | — | 2,733.2 | 16.3 | — | 185.0 | 120.0 | 90.3 | 210.3 | 2,943.5 |
| Blood fees | 375.0 | 550.0 | 33.0 | 6.0 | — | — | 583.0 | 6.0 | — | | | | | 583.0 |
| Depreciation (excl. P.P) | 3,288.0 | 3,118.0 | — | 0 | 54.0 | — | 3,172.0 | 1.7 | — | 100.0 | 100.0 | 349.4 | 449.4 | 3,621.4 |
| Interest | 92.0 | 126.0 | — | 0 | 910.1 | — | 1,036.1 | 722.3 | — | 100.0 | 100.0 | 133.2 | 233.2 | 1,269.3 |
| Subtotal | 8,030.0 | 8,079.0 | 156.7 | 1.9 | 1,262.6 | (285.0) | 9,213.3 | 14.0 | — | 385.0 | 320.0 | 372.9 | 892.9 | 10,106.2 |
| Total | $96,092.1 | $95,913.8 | $5,839.5 | 6.1 | 2,255.7 | $ 291.7 | $104,300.7 | 6.7 | 6.7 | $7,686.1 | $3,778.5 | $6,200.2 | $9,978.7 | $114,279.4 |
| Program Budget | | | | | | 2,100.0 | 2,100.0 | | | | | | — | 2,100.0 |
| Grand total | | | | | | | $106,400.7 | | | | | | $9,978.7 | $116,379.4 |

no provision for new high technology equipment, nor are there any funds provided for cost reduction capital investment, which ultimately is a self-supporting activity.

The financial plan for fiscal 1978 projects a profit for operations, which, if achieved, will provide more capital funds than have been available to this point . . .

**Exhibit 9**
Functional Unit Direct Revenue and Expense Statements, 1977 Budget ($000)

| | | *Costs* | | | | | | | |
|---|---|---|---|---|---|---|---|---|---|
| *Units* | *Gross Revenue* | *Labor & emp. ben.* | *Sup. & Reps.* | *Pur. Ser.* | *Other* | *Joint Agreement* | *Total* | *Gross Margin* |
| **Direct Patient Care:** | | | | | | | | |
| Ophthalmology | $ 4,800 | $ 1,517 | $ 278 | $ 278 | $ 98 | $ 323 | $ 2,244 | $ 2,556 |
| Psychiatry | 4,418 | 1,865 | 30 | 12 | 65 | 272 | 2,244 | 2,174 |
| Surgery | 13,637 | 5,830 | 273 | 19 | 719 | 418 | 7,259 | 6,378 |
| GOR | 7,800 | 1,741 | 1,525 | 4 | 256 | 142 | 3,668 | 4,132 |
| Neurosciences | 1,890 | 748 | 50 | 58 | 43 | 286 | 1,185 | 705 |
| OB-GYN | 7,600 | 3,529 | 357 | 11 | 408 | 331 | 4,636 | 2,964 |
| Anesthesiology | 5,000 | 942 | 408 | 17 | 51 | 1,653 | 3.071 | 1,929 |
| Adult ICU's | 4,950 | 2,146 | 252 | 50 | 465 | 237 | 3,150 | 1,800 |
| Medicine | 12,234 | 4,375 | 296 | 257 | 659 | 949 | 6,536 | 5,698 |
| Pediatrics | 12,500 | 5,041 | 433 | 46 | 663 | 903 | 7,086 | 5,414 |
| Emergency Medicine | 2,933 | 1,086 | 146 | 8 | (245) | 477 | 1,472 | 1,461 |
| Outpatient Adult General | 1,970 | 1,307 | 173 | 31 | (66) | 332 | 1,777 | 193 |
| Outpatient Adult Consult. | — | 231 | 30 | — | 21 | 13 | 295 | (295) |
| Subtotal | 79,732 | 30,358 | 4,251 | 541 | 3,137 | 6,336 | 44,623 | 35,109 |
| **Patient Care Support:** | | | | | | | | |
| Pathology | 1,625 | 664 | 105 | 35 | 6 | 810 | 1,620 | 5 |
| Radiology | 11,350 | 2,775 | 1,521 | 244 | 155 | 2,209 | 6,904 | 4,446 |
| Laboratory Medicine | 17,100 | 4,327 | 1,087 | 721 | 37 | 761 | 6,933 | 10,167 |
| Pharmacy | 6,420 | 1,284 | 2,363 | 90 | 163 | — | 3,900 | 2,520 |
| Social Services | — | 678 | 15 | 24 | 2 | — | 719 | (719) |
| Rehabilitation Medicine | 1,173 | 497 | 28 | 6 | 26 | 21 | 578 | 595 |
| I.V. Therapy | 1,600 | 354 | 766 | 1 | 5 | — | 1,126 | 474 |
| Subtotal | 39,268 | 10,579 | 5,885 | 1,121 | 394 | 3,801 | 21,780 | 17,488 |
| **Service:** | | | | | | | | |
| Finance | — | 2,181 | 160 | 473 | 1,214 | — | 4,028 | |
| Systems, Planning & Medical Records | — | 3,345 | 263 | 1,078 | (1,857) | 49 | 2,878 | |
| Materials Management | — | 1,655 | 1,638 | 1,268 | (2,781) | 3 | 1,783 | |
| Communications | — | 413 | 30 | 758 | 6 | — | 1,207 | |
| FM&ES | — | 2,347 | 469 | 184 | (165) | 23 | 2,858 | |
| Patient Services | — | 971 | 158 | 68 | 11 | — | 1,208 | |
| General Services | — | 2,607 | 135 | 1,166 | 23 | — | 3,931 | |
| Nutrition | — | 2,691 | 6 | 2,916 | 53 | — | 5,666 | |
| All Other | — | 3,040 | 291 | — | 357 | 1,538 | 5,226 | |
| Subtotal | — | 19,250 | 3,150 | 7,911 | (3,139) | 1,613 | 28,785 | (28,785) |
| **Institutional:** | | | | | | | | |
| Malpractice Insurance | — | — | — | 1,195 | — | — | 1,195 | |
| Collection Agency Fees | — | — | — | 494 | — | — | 494 | |
| Utilities | — | — | 2,601 | 132 | — | — | 2,733 | |
| Blood Fees | — | — | 577 | 6 | — | — | 583 | |
| Depreciation | — | — | — | — | 3,172 | — | 3,172 | |
| Interest | — | — | — | — | 1,036 | — | 1,036 | |
| Subtotal | — | — | 3,178 | 1,827 | 4,208 | — | 9,213 | (9,213) |
| Total hospital | $119,000 | $60,187 | $16,164 | $11,400 | $4,800 | $11,750 | $104,301 | 14,699 |
| **Adjustments:** | | | | | | | | |
| Other Revenue | | | | | | | | 6,000 |
| Bad Debts & Free Work | | | | | | | | (5,900) |
| Third Party Discounts | | | | | | | | (12,779) |
| Grand Total | $119,000 | | | | | | | $ 2,020 |

## Exhibit 10

Comparison of Census (1978 budget versus 1976 actual and 1977 estimate)

| | 1976 | | | 1977 Estimate | | | | 1978 Budget | | | Change | | |
|---|---|---|---|---|---|---|---|---|---|---|---|---|---|
| | | | | | | Percent of Occupancy | | | | | | | |
| Units | Beds Avail. | Days | Percent Occup. | Beds Avail. | Days | Plan | Actual | Beds Avail. | Days | Percent Occup. | Beds Avail. | Days | Percent Occup. |
| Wilmer* | 78 | 23,471 | 82.4 | 78 | 23,900 | 82.5 | 83.9 | 78 | 23,500 | 82.5 | — | (400) | (1.4) |
| Psychiatry | 75 | 26,024 | 95.0 | 75 | 26,400 | 95.0 | 96.4 | 75 | 26,000 | 95.0 | — | (400) | (1.4) |
| Surgery | 292 | 87,021 | 88.4 | 263 | 84,100 | 87.5 | 87.6 | 290 | 91,586 | 86.5 | 27 | 7,486 | (1.1) |
| Neurology | 19 | 6,040 | 87.1 | 19 | 6,300 | 89.0 | 90.8 | 19 | 6,172 | 89.0 | 0 | (128) | (1.8) |
| OB-GYN | 100 | 29,017 | 80.1 | 100 | 29,100 | 81.4 | 79.7 | 96 | 27,927 | 79.7 | (4) | (1,173) | 0 |
| Adult-ICU | 35 | 9,140 | 71.5 | 35 | 9,800 | 71.9 | 76.7 | 36 | 9,528 | 72.5 | 1 | (272) | (4.2) |
| Medicine | 230 | 73,114 | 87.1 | 225 | 73,700 | 86.9 | 89.7 | 230 | 72,815 | 86.7 | 5 | (885) | (3.0) |
| Pediatrics | 207 | 52,325 | 69.2 | 197 | 53,700 | 74.4 | 74.7 | 197 | 55,235 | 76.8 | — | 1,535 | 2.1 |
| Total | 1,036 | 306,152 | 82.0 | 992 | 307,000 | 83.3 | 84.8 | 1,021 | 312,763 | 83.9 | 29 | 5,763 | ( .9) |
| Oncology | — | — | — | 45 | 7,000 | 80.4 | 42.6 | 56 | 16,470 | 80.6 | 11 | 9,470 | 38.0 |
| Grand total | 1,036 | 306,152 | 82.0 | 1,037 | 314,000 | 82.6 | 83.0 | 1,077 | 329,233 | 83.8 | 40 | 15,233 | .8 |

* Wilmer Ophthalmological Institute for the treatment of eye diseases; includes emergency room for eye injuries.

**Exhibit 11**
Full-Time-Equivalents Summary Comparison, 1973–1978B

| | *1973* | *1974* | *1975* | *1976* | *1977E* | *1978B* | *Percent Average Yearly Change* |
|---|---|---|---|---|---|---|---|
| Ophthalmology | 86 | 97 | 97 | 103 | 101 | 104 | |
| Psychiatry | 116 | 116 | 123 | 128 | 129 | 130 | |
| Surgery | 262 | 261 | 285 | 358* | 368 | 378 | |
| GOR | 125 | 124 | 120 | 114 | 115 | 123 | |
| Neurosciences | 13 | 25 | 52 | 52 | 51 | 54 | |
| OB-GYN | 179 | 179 | 204 | 192 | 231 | 237 | |
| Anesthesiology-ICU | 189 | 203 | 199 | 178 | 182 | 195 | |
| Medicine | 301 | 321 | 328 | 250* | 297 | 299 | |
| Pediatrics | 279 | 292 | 292 | 330 | 357 | 370 | |
| Emergency medicine | 67 | 70 | 74 | 69 | 67 | 70 | |
| Outpatient-adult consult. | 30 | 31 | 30 | 28 | 18 | 20 | |
| Outpatient-adult general | 110 | 116 | 117 | 115 | 72 | 77 | |
| Subtotal | 1,757 | 1,835 | 1,921 | 1,917 | 1,988 | 2,057 | +3.2 |
| Pathology | 48 | 53 | 50 | 47 | 51 | 51 | |
| Radiology | 170 | 177 | 189 | 200 | 202 | 202 | |
| Laboratory medicine | 240 | 258 | 277 | 278 | 268 | 272 | |
| Rehabilitation medicine | 34 | 32 | 30 | 32 | 31 | 34 | |
| Pharmacy | 70 | 72 | 84 | 88 | 88 | 88 | |
| Social services | 28 | 23 | 41 | 41 | 42 | 43 | |
| IV therapy | — | — | — | 23 | 21 | 23 | |
| Subtotal | 590 | 615 | 671 | 709 | 703 | 713 | +3.8 |
| Service units | 1,616 | 1,471 | 1,451 | 1,407 | 1,399 | 1,430 | −2.5 |
| Total | 3,963 | 3,921 | 4,043 | 4,033 | 4,090 | 4,200 | +1.2 |
| Oncology: direct | | | | 29 | 180 | 293 | — |
| service | | | | — | 19 | 35 | — |
| Total w/ oncology | | | | 4,062 | 4,289 | 4,528 | +2.7 |

* Administrative transfer of Marburg 3 and 4 from Medicine to Surgery. Earlier Marburg provided private rooms for both medical and surgical patients.

Mr. Jack Murphy, Director of Operations Planning and Budgeting, explained the capital budgeting process:

> The Financial Planning Department allocates, from the total funds available, the amount available for the capital budget. To handle requests over $20,000, a Capital Resource Allocation Committee has been set up. The committee meets three times a year and consists of Dr. Heyssel, Dr. Ross (Vice President for Medicine and Dean of the Medical Faculty at the Johns Hopkins University), the heads of service, and three or four faculty members.

## Current Issues

In April 1977 Dr. Heyssel had established a Standing Committee for Policy Development Furthering Decentralization. This committee was expected to develop a policy framework to guide units and to address topics which had been raised by staff at different levels, such as:

Policies within which functional unit directors would have authority to adjust patient bills under a defined charity policy.

The degree to which functional units should have authority to let contracts to outside vendors.

The appropriate authority to grant to units to engage in capital equipment expenditures.

In discussing the decentralized management structure, Dr. Heyssel identified the major issues he faced in May 1977 as follows:

1. The division of program dollars and capital between functional units—and tying such decisions to unit plans and objectives.
2. Gaining a better understanding of the parameters within which functional units operate, development of units of measurement for assessing departments' performance, and clarification of the relationship between central staff and functional units.
3. Human development of management at the functional unit level.

Overall, Dr. Heyssel observed: "My life as director is a lot better now. I do not have to deal with trivial issues any longer. The next three to five years will be a testing period. But if we face a shortage of funds, we are now capable of taking quick action."

## Questions

1. What are the most important changes that Dr. Heyssel has introduced into the organization?
2. What are the key characteristics of the new management control system? How do they relate to the changes that have taken place in the organization?
3. What changes, if any, should be made in the management control system?

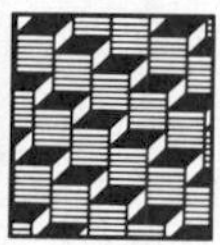

# Index

**Q–R**

*This book has been set Videocomp, in 10 and 9 point Times Roman, leaded 2 points. Part and chapter numbers are 18 point Helvetica medium. Part and chapter titles are 24 point Helvetica medium. The size of the type page is 27 by 46½ picas.*